SUSTAINING CHANGE in ORGANIZATIONS

'Julie Hodges and Roger Gill have presented a comprehensive summary of the landscape of organizational change. *Sustaining Change in Organizations* capably brings together a range of perspectives and concepts of change, using these as a foundation for bringing the subject right up to date with contemporary ideas and examples. While the book will win fans from business academia (it is very well referenced and has signposts to further reading in each chapter), its accessible style with plenty of bite-sized cases, together with regular summaries, will no doubt see it gracing the desks of those of us tasked with delivering change for a living.'

Dr Simon Haslam, Visiting Fellow at Durham University Business School and head of the Institute of Directors' strategy faculty.

SUSTAINING CHANGE in ORGANIZATIONS

Julie Hodges & Roger Gill

Los Angeles | London | New Delhi
Singapore | Washington DC

Los Angeles | London | New Delhi
Singapore | Washington DC

SAGE Publications Ltd
1 Oliver's Yard
55 City Road
London EC1Y 1SP

SAGE Publications Inc.
2455 Teller Road
Thousand Oaks, California 91320

SAGE Publications India Pvt Ltd
B 1/I 1 Mohan Cooperative Industrial Area
Mathura Road
New Delhi 110 044

SAGE Publications Asia-Pacific Pte Ltd
3 Church Street
#10-04 Samsung Hub
Singapore 049483

Editor: Kirsty Smy
Assistant editor: Nina Smith
Production editor: Tom Bedford
Copyeditor: Elaine Leek
Proofreader: Martin Noble
Indexer: David Rudeforth
Marketing manager: Alison Borg
Cover design: Francis Kenney
Typeset by: C&M Digitals (P) Ltd, Chennai, India
Printed in Great Britain by Henry Ling Limited at
The Dorset Press, Dorchester, DT1 1HD

Library of Congress Control Number: 2014940079

British Library Cataloguing in Publication data

A catalogue record for this book is available from
the British Library

ISBN 978-1-4462-0778-9
ISBN 978-1-4462-0779-6 (pbk)

At SAGE we take sustainability seriously. Most of our products are printed in the UK using FSC papers and boards.
When we print overseas we ensure sustainable papers are used as measured by the Egmont grading system.
We undertake an annual audit to monitor our sustainability.

Contents

Notes on the authors

Julie Hodges (PhD, MA, BA, PGCert) is an academic and consultant. She is currently the Director of MBA Programmes at Durham University Business School in the UK. Prior to joining academia, Julie worked for 20 years in a variety of management and leadership roles in companies across the globe, including the British Council, Vertex and PricewaterhouseCoopers (PwC). Julie has worked extensively in the academic and business world in the field of organizational change and development. She has led change and transformation initiatives across the globe, with organizations in the private and public sectors. Julie is an experienced facilitator of individuals, groups and organizations facing change. Her areas of teaching and research expertise include leading and sustaining change in organizations. Julie has co-authored a book entitled *Public and Third Sector Leadership: Experience Speaks*. She has also written articles on leadership branding, change in organizations and the changing careers of mid-life women. Julie is one of the founders of the Leading Well, a social enterprise that focuses on developing leaders in public and third sector organizations. Julie is a Senior fellow of the FME (Foundation for Management Education).

Julie is the proud mother of Elliot, and lives in Durham, UK, with her husband, Mick.

Roger Gill is Visiting Professor of Leadership Studies at Durham University Business School in the UK, and an independent consultant on leadership and leadership development. He supervises research both in DUBS and in Durham University's Department of Theology and Religion. He founded the Research Centre for Leadership Studies at the Leadership Trust in England in 1997 and he was its Director for nine years. He is also founder and former Director of the MBA in Leadership Studies run jointly by the Leadership Trust and the University of Strathclyde Business School.

Roger was formerly Professor of Business Administration and Director of Executive Development Programmes at Strathclyde. He has held full-time academic posts at the State University of New York and the University of Bradford and has also taught at business schools in the UK, Switzerland, Germany, Southeast Asia and the Gulf region. He has held management positions in HRM in the UK and has many years' experience in management consulting in the UK, France, USA, Gulf Region and Far East. He ran his own consultancy in Singapore for eight years.

Roger is a Chartered Psychologist and a graduate of the universities of Oxford (MA), Liverpool (BPhil) and Bradford (PhD). In 2010 he was honoured with a Fellowship of the Leadership Trust Foundation in recognition of his contribution to the field of leadership and leadership development. He is the author of *Theory and Practice of Leadership*, 2nd edition (SAGE Publications, 2011), which was shortlisted for the Chartered Management Institute's 'Management Book of the Year' Award, 2013. He lives with his wife, Pat, in Northumberland, UK.

Notes on case study contributors

Lindsey Agness is the Managing Director of The Change Corporation (www. thechangecorporation.com). Lindsey has studied behavioural change for more than 20 years. She began her career in local government then moved into change management consultancy with PricewaterhouseCoopers (PwC). She worked for 11 years with leaders of large global companies to define and manage transformational change programmes to achieve measurable benefits, focusing on the 'people side' of change. These programmes involved defining the change vision, strategy and plan, developing the communications and stakeholder management strategies, re-designs, behavioural and culture change and delivery of the programme. She also has experience of developing senior management teams and executive coaching. Since pursuing her own business, she continues to work with large public and private sector organizations. She is also the author of four published best-selling books on personal and organizational change.

Ritienne Bajada currently holds the position of Senior Sector Manager for the Energy Sector in the Career Services department at London Business School. Prior to this role, she has worked with alumni across all sectors, helping them with their job search and career strategy. She has also worked as an executive search consultant within the investment banking sector predominately focusing on technical roles and sales and trading roles in equity derivatives. Ritienne has also done extensive qualitative research on the key challenges faced by midlife women leaders in their career progression, as part of her MBA dissertation at Durham Business School. This research focused on the numerous changes that midlife women leaders face, as various forces come into play and they find themselves having to choose or find a balance between conflicting priorities in order to progress in their professional life.

Shontelle Bryan is a Project and Operations Consultant. Shontelle has been helping organizations from various sectors manage change for over a decade. Her varied roles included helping the NHS and commercial banks adapt to new systems and technology, working on a steering committee to embed cultural change practices within a previous organization and advising Halifax Bank of Scotland on a restructuring exercise. Helping businesses function more efficiently by adopting new processes and equipping employees with tools is also her key focus; as businesses are now expected to produce superior gains with very little.

Alison Clare is a freelance project, programme and change manager with 25 years' experience implementing business change and IT applications across both the public and private sectors. An ex-Oracle employee, she has delivered change projects in the NHS since 2006, specifically at the Royal Liverpool University Hospital and more recently at Leeds Teaching Hospital, rolling out the electronic patient record programme of work. Since completing an MBA in 2007, she has been researching change and sustaining change. Alison is currently completing her PhD from Durham University and also lectures on a part-time basis on business transformation and benefits management.

Martin Davis is the Vice President of IT for J D Irving Ltd, Saint John, New Brunswick, Canada, and also a Board Member of the New Brunswick IT Council. He is an experienced PMP (Project Management Professional) certified senior IT leader/CIO with over 25 years of IT experience, ranging from project/programme management to IT leadership roles in the UK, Canada and the USA. Martin's experience spans global corporations, privately owned companies, manufacturing, automotive, consumer goods and transportation industries.

Karen Geary has more than 20 years of international HR and business transformation experience across a variety of industries where she has managed organizations through periods of large-scale change, acquisition and integration. She is currently Chief People Officer of WANdisco plc, a software business based in San Francisco, USA. Prior to this she was Group Human Resources Director and a member of the Executive Committee at The Sage Group plc, a FTSE100 business and the world's largest provider of business software to SMEs. She also spent six years at Swedish transport and leisure operator Stena Line, ultimately as Director of Human Resources. Her early career was with global process control and electronics distribution businesses. Karen participates in the FTSE100 Cross-Company Mentoring Programme, promoting the nomination of women onto UK public and private boards. She previously served on the Advisory Board of Durham University Business School, and was also a member of the School's MBA Advisory Group. In 2012, Karen appeared at number 26 in the 'HR Most Influential' list.

Martin Gray is the Service Director – Children's Commissioning, Gateshead Council, UK. His current role involves leading on a wide range of range of activities as part of a change agenda to introduce a commissioning focus to the way services for children are planned and delivered in Gateshead. Martin has been at Gateshead since 2007, having previously worked in Leeds and London in a range of planning, regeneration and public policy roles. He is married, with no children, and enjoys reading, cooking, sport and walking.

Anthony Greenfield (PhD) is the founder and Director of 5 Forces of Change™ (www.5forcesofchange.com). He has more than 25 years' hands-on experience of leading business transformation and a deep understanding of how to help people respond constructively to change. He has brought both these strands together to write two books: *The 5 Forces of Change* and *5 Tales of Change*. His consulting clients include Royal Mail, Marks & Spencer and Northern Trust Bank, and he is a regular speaker at business schools and international conferences.

Simon Haslam (PhD) is co-owner and director of the market and social research firm FMR Research Ltd, whose work has been cited in Westminster and Scottish Parliaments. He is a Visiting Fellow with Durham University Business School and a Fellow of the Royal Society of Arts. He is a dual finalist for the Institute of Consulting's 'Consultant of the Year' award and his firm was nominated to represent the UK in the 2012 international management consultancy awards. He now sits on the UK Institute of Consulting's advisory committee. His clients include award-winning public, private and third sector organizations, notably a 2008 Queen's Award winner, for whom Simon was lead consultant on its strategic review and mentor to one of its executive directors, and a 2008 UK National Training Award winner, for whom he designed and delivered the Strategic Decision-making module for its director development programme. Simon works with a range of organizations on executive development programmes around strategy, personal performance and change, including the Institute of Directors, where he is head of the Institute of Directors' strategy faculty.

Keith Marriott is Centre Director for Chartered Management Institute Studies at Sunderland College, UK. He is a Fellow of the Chartered Management Institute and a NEESPR registered mentor to North East businesses, and having completed an MBA at Durham University Business School in 2010, where he was also a guest lecturer, he is now in the third year of his Doctorate at Sunderland University. He brings a very practical approach to leadership and management studies because he has an impressive commercial background. He has previously run his own business and also worked for several well-known consumer electronics companies such as Vax and Dirt Devil, as well as starting Power Devil, which went on to turn over more than £25m for the Alba Group. Before that he had been Sales and Marketing Director of Hinari Electronics and Morphy Richards Consumer Electronics.

Benjamin Paul is Head of Trade and Marketing, Maersk Line, Malaysia and Singapore Cluster. He joined the Danish AP Moller Group on leaving university in their graduate scheme (Maersk International Shipping Education) and has worked in various roles and countries since then in the UK, Singapore, Denmark, Cambodia and now Malaysia.

Jonathan Reeves has enjoyed a career in sales and marketing in the UK technology markets, spanning 15 years. He has witnessed many mergers and takeovers by global companies seeking to acquire innovation. His initial experience was gained in the UK ISP sector, which saw aggressive mergers. Large multinationals bought small independents to expand their networks and client base. His firm INS was acquired by Cable & Wireless in 1995. He then enjoyed tenures with a variety of global software companies where he was employed in a strategic alliances role. At the centre of the technology boom and subsequent bust, he also worked in several UK start-ups. His primary function was to create new routes to market via strategic partnerships with distributors and system integrators. Jonathan has also launched new products and services and has extensive experience of the mobile applications arena. He was employed by the American CRM company Sterling Commerce, which was acquired by IBM in 2010. Having finished his MBA at Durham University in 2011, he is currently working in Cambridge assisting small innovative pre-IPO software firms build go-to-market strategies.

Craig Smith is the Senior Consultant and Director within Flint Consulting, UK. Before founding Flint Consulting in 2007, Craig previously worked for PepsiCo for 6 years in operational and HR roles. Prior to that, Craig worked in senior operational roles within Royal Mail and Northumbrian Water. A keen runner, with 12 international marathons under his belt, Craig has also trekked to the summit of the highest mountain in Africa, Mount Kilimanjaro, in 2008. These endeavours demonstrate the mental toughness and tenacity Craig also brings to his professional career. His recent client experience includes delivering interventions with PepsiCo, Aero Engine Controls, Heinz, Rolls–Royce, Isos Housing, Newcastle University and Teesside University. Other recent client work includes the development and delivery of Leadership Development programmes within PepsiCo and Disney and the deployment of Culture and Values programmes with Business and Enterprise North East. Craig has also recently facilitated large conferences for clients. He regularly speaks to professional organizations and is a member of many networks and professional groups.

Lynne Smith was born and raised in the North East. After completing a Biochemistry degree in Manchester, she spent the next 11 years working as a scientist two years as a research and development chemist followed by nine years as a scientific officer with a water authority in Gloucestershire. Taking a career break to look after her two sons, she studied part time for a degree in Business IT. A move to Surrey was followed by a return to working in various business management roles with organizations including BAE Systems, Nestlé Purina and Hyder Consulting. A great believer in lifelong learning, Lynne followed her ambition to complete an MBA at Durham University. She has since worked as an Engagement Officer with a charity for the visually impaired and is currently a business manager for a local heritage centre in Durham City.

Fiona Sweeney is the People Director, Virgin Active South Africa. Fiona's professional career has focused on supporting strategic and operational management teams to effectively address and manage organizational change issues. Her experience spans different industry sectors and geographies, but the common thread is about engaging with people and the business in order to deliver sustainable change and improve performance. Prior to joining Virgin Active, Fiona worked as a management consultant for over 16 years, both as a freelancer and with PricewaterhouseCoopers (PwC). She also worked in the UK with BskyB.

Steve Taylor is the Director of Taylor Made Solutions. Steve grew up in the English Lake District before taking a degree in Life Sciences from Imperial College in London. He is a qualified business coach and teacher and holds an MA in People Management. Having been the Director of Training for an International Development Training Centre for 5 years, he became the CEO from 2001 to 2006. Steve now splits his work time between executive coaching, lecturing and working in corporate change. He has lectured at Lancaster University as a teacher educator and at the Management Development Centre, Durham University Business School delivering bespoke and accredited programmes up to Master's level. He was the programme leader for both the Jordanian and UK MA in Management, Leadership and Enterprise. He currently runs an MA in Managing Change. He has worked or is working with the following organizations amongst others: RWE Power, the Improvement Service, the Scottish Police College, Cumbria County Council, Global Energy Group, Skills Development Scotland, BBC, EMC2, Talk Talk, Atkins, INSEAD France: Management Acceleration programme, Barclays, RBS, Deutsche Bank and HBOS. Steve loves the outdoors and is a highly qualified outdoor professional. He also runs watercolour painting courses and loves to explore out-of-the-way places searching for weird wildlife in his spare time. He has two daughters who have taught him all he knows. They now live in Madrid, Spain, and Liverpool, England.

David Wardrop-White is an Associate at Paradigm Development, Dalkeith, Scotland. David worked in healthcare management before joining PricewaterhouseCoopers (PwC), where he consulted on change management to private and public sector clients for more than 20 years. He now focuses on bringing about sustainable change in fields as diverse as universities, family cycling, tourism and his local community near Edinburgh.

Acknowledgements

Julie is especially grateful to the many colleagues and friends who took the time to contribute to this book – the case studies they provided are invaluable. She is also indebted to the students from across the globe who have applied much of the material in this book during classes and workshops which Julie has taught (and also in their organizations) and have provided feedback on the many tools and frameworks for sustaining change.

Julie would especially like to thank Mick for his support and enduring love and patience while she wrote this book – keeping her supplied with cups of tea. Elliot for his amazing strength, resilience and empathy. And her parents for their love and support always.

Finally, she would like to thank the team at Sage publishers, especially Kirsty who provided the opportunity to make this book happen. Thanks for all your patience and guidance.

Roger would like to acknowledge the loving forbearance and support of his wife, Pat, during the writing of this book, especially the times when he disappeared into his 'shed' for hours on end.

We would both like to thank for permission to use copyright material, John Smythe of consultancy Engage for Change (http://www.engageforchange.com/make_contact. html) and the FT.com (*Financial Times*).

Guided tour

Overview

- Summarises the main issues and topics that will be covered in each chapter.

Learning objectives

- Will focus your learning on the key points to understand and remember.

Activity

Activities ask you to reflect on your own experiences or explore an idea further.

CASE STUDY

Organisational case studies will help you to relate theory to real-world practice.

Discussion Questions

1   Encourage class discussion and debate around key issues.

Further reading

Lists of useful and important readings which will enhance your understanding of the chapter.

Glossary terms are **bolded** in the text and defined in the end-of-book Glossary, allowing you to quickly reference new terms.

Companion website

Sustaining Change in Organizations by Julie Hodges and Roger Gill is supported by a companion website.

Visit https://study.sagepub.com/hodgesgill to access the following resources:

For lecturers

Instructors' manual: including, for each chapter, learning outcomes, a brief overview of the chapter, additional exercises and activities, discussion questions, exam/assignment questions, suggested teaching tips, online resources including video clips, and additional case studies with questions.

PowerPoint slides: containing the key points, and tables and figures from each chapter.

For students

Annotated web links: additional links to tools, resources and further reading.

SAGE Online Journals: free access to relevant SAGE articles, for a deeper understanding.

PART ONE
The Essence of Change and Transformation

Introduction to Organizational Change and Transformation

1

Overview

- One of the main tasks of managers and business leaders across the globe today is to implement and sustain change effectively. This book will provide guidance to help business leaders, managers and students achieve this crucial task, through theoretical and practical perspectives. In the book we synthesize what is known about change in organizations and then provide practical ways of sustaining it, using perspectives from managers and leaders based on their experience.

- In this introductory chapter we briefly review the literature on organizational change. The literature varies in format and tone, encompassing descriptive accounts of change, theoretical models for analysing change, prescriptive models that aim to guide the change process, typologies of different approaches to change in organizations and empirical studies of the success or failure of various initiatives, programmes and tools. The literature can be broadly divided into populist and academic categories.

- Three concepts appear frequently in the literature and in discussions of organizational change. They are (i) change, (ii) transition and (iii) transformation. We define each of these in this chapter.

- This chapter also provides an overview of the aim and structure of the book.

- The range of approaches to change, and the confusion over their strengths, weaknesses and suitability, is such that the field of organizational change has been described as more an overgrown weed patch than a well-tended garden (Burnes, 2003: xii). This chapter outlines how this book brings together old and new material and perspectives, and how it goes further than other books in that it covers a breadth of issues pertinent to sustaining change in organizations.

A changing world

We are living in an age of accelerating change and turbulence. The magnitude, speed, unpredictability and impact of change are greater than ever before. Even the concept of change itself has changed. According to the Centre for Creative Leadership in the USA (CCL, 2012), change today is less a sudden and dramatic disruptive event and more a fluid and constant continuous process. Hammer and Champy (1993: 23) support this, in saying that 'change has become both pervasive and persistent. It is normality'. However, despite the fact that change is constant, it seems that **organizations** are, in some cases, not getting any better at leading and managing it successfully. There is a widely held view that attempts to implement organizational change are predominantly unsuccessful (for example, Beer, 2000; Elrod and Tippett, 2002; Kotter, 1995; Pettigrew et al., 2001). As a result of this, the Number One critical issue for organizations today is, according to research by the Institute for Corporate Productivity in Seattle (2013), managing and sustaining change.

As Senior (2002) points out, no leader or manager needs convincing that improvement and change are at the top of the agenda and that the required experience and skills to do so are a necessity in order to survive in a highly competitive and continuously evolving and turbulent environment. Julie Meyer, the technology entrepreneur, puts her finger on the pulse of how the world is transforming. In her book, *Welcome to Entrepreneur Country*, Meyer (2012) compares the world's transition in the 1930s and 1940s from a largely agricultural to an industrial economy with today's shift, as the whole world moves to a networked, digital marketplace. Her contention is that in this new world, industries are being driven not by companies, monopolies and regulators but by competing ecosystems. Those who embrace this change, says Meyer, will emerge as winners. Her views are echoed by Howieson and Hodges (2014) in their book about **leadership** and change in the public and third sectors in the UK. The authors say leaders in both sectors need to recognize the **drivers** for change and develop the capability to cope with them.

Many of these drivers for change are coming from the external environment. As Fiona Graetz acknowledges:

> against a backdrop of increasing globalization, deregulation, the rapid pace of technological innovation, a growing knowledge workforce, and shifting social and demographic trends, few would dispute that the primary task for management today is the leadership of organizational change. (2000: 550)

As Graetz points out, there are forces at work that are fundamentally changing the environment and shifting much of what we take for granted about employees, work and organizations. These forces include, but are not limited to: increasing globalization; shifts in the global economy; the continuing changes in the climate; profound changes in longevity and demography; rapid advances in technology; increasing competition; and the expansion of the knowledge economy (see Chapter 5 for a discussion on each of these drivers). The combination of these five forces is fundamentally changing organizations and how we work in them.

Many of the ways of working which we have taken for granted are disappearing, such as working from '9 to 5', working with only one company in one's lifetime, taking weekends off, and working with people we have known for years in the offices we go to every day. Changes are also happening in the way organizations operate. The idea that hierarchy is the best way to manage information flows is disappearing in many companies, as are the notions that most people will work with team members in the same office and that the majority of talent will be held within the boundaries of the organization. Despite these and other changes, organizations still seem to be struggling to sustain change.

It may seem paradoxical that, on the one hand, the failure rate of change initiatives appears to be immense while, on the other hand, there is now more advice on how to lead and manage change than ever before. In opposition to this, there is a growing body of research which questions whether it is possible to meaningfully 'manage' change at all (Hughes, 2006). This school of thought questions the ability to manage and control change on the basis of the inherent complexity of organizations and the self-organizing properties of systems (Shaw, 2002; Stacey, 2001). Change is seen not as an entity to be conquered, outwitted or prevented, but as an ongoing process that is never completed (Bruhn, 2004). What is evident, as Luecke (2003) points out, is that a state of continuous change has become a constant, with change an ever-present feature of organizational life, at both an operational and a strategic level, which individuals within organizations need to cope with.

The pace of change that affects organizations today may or may not be unprecedented but it is certainly spectacular, and likely to accelerate in the future. But like most things in business, rapid change is a two-edged sword – a threat but also an opportunity. Change puts a premium on adapting; the faster the pace of change, the greater the premium. Take away change and there is no need to adapt; if it worked yesterday, there is every reason to believe it will work today. Alas, that is not remotely what organizations are now facing. Today's business conditions give new meaning to the words of the Greek philosopher Heraclitus: 'All is flux, nothing stays still – there is nothing permanent except change.'

Organizations that adapt to rapid change better than their competitors make great strides, while those that ignore rapidly changing circumstances might go the way of the dinosaur. Sixty million years ago, dinosaurs suddenly disappeared after more than 100 million years on the planet. Palaeontologists hotly debate the cause of the dinosaurs' extinction, but high on the list of hypotheses is their failure to adapt to rapidly changing climatic conditions. There is a long trail of companies who have gone the way of the dinosaurs: not adapting to change, they have either declined swiftly or agonizingly slowly over a long period of time.

An organization's ability to change is essential for its survival in a changing market environment. Companies such as ABB, AT&T, DaimlerChrysler, France Telecom, Time Warner and Vivendi Universal have all witnessed failure in recent decades. As Probst and Raisch (2005) point out, the lack of change can lead to increasingly outdated product offerings and cost structures significantly above the competitive level. A prime example of a company that failed to adapt is Eastman Kodak. To protect its core film business, the company ignored the trend to digital photography. Kodak's competition therefore profited from the growth market in digital photography. At Xerox, the American giant in the copier business, something similar occurred. Although the crucial products of the digital age had been developed in their own research laboratories, Xerox focused exclusively on the core copier business. The copier market is nevertheless decreasing constantly, and Xerox has lost market share to cheaper producers.

The challenge for leaders and managers is to understand, lead and manage change so that it is shaped and sustained in a way that benefits the organization and its **stakeholders**. How to sustain change is not, however, a new issue. As far back as the 1940s, Kurt Lewin (1947) argued that all too often change is short-lived: after a 'shot in the arm', life returns to the way it was before. Lewin noted that it was not enough to think of change in terms of simply reaching a new state, as this did not guarantee success. More recent evidence supports this argument and suggests that the majority of change projects fail to achieve what Hayes (2014) calls 'stickability' and sustain the change required. Buchanan and colleagues (2005) point out that this is because there appears to be no simple prescription for managing change, in order to achieve benefits. Or perhaps it is because practitioners are often so immersed in the everyday life of organizations, that it is often difficult for them to **recognize the need for change**.

Managers and leaders of organizations need to have an awareness of the need for change, and also the **capability** and **capacity** to be able to sustain change effectively. The aim of this book is to provide guidance to help business leaders, managers and students achieve this, through both theoretical and practical perspectives. We begin by briefly examining the literature on organizational change.

Literature on organizational change

There is a growing library of books and articles on organizational change, which appear, at first glance, to offer hope to anyone who wants to be successful with change initiatives. The literature contains contributions from several different academic disciplines, including psychology, sociology, business and **management**. It consists of evidence, examples and illustrations generated from a wide variety of organizations and from a diverse range of methodologies with varying degrees of rigour. The literature differs in format and tone, encompassing descriptive accounts of change, theoretical models for analysing change, prescriptive models that aim to guide the change process, typologies of different approaches to change in organizations, and empirical studies of the success or failure of various initiatives, programmes and tools. The literature can be broadly divided into populist and academic categories.

The populist view

There is a huge commercial market in popular management books on change, which range from hero-leader reflections and biographies to works by so-called gurus in the subject. Such books tend to be characterized by evangelical-style exhortations about change and accompanied by convincing stories and sound bites. They have been defined as 'karaoke texts', in a reference to their 'I did it my way' approach (Clegg and Palmer, 1996) and range from 'how to lead change step by step' through to quantum-change made easy. Such texts have snappy titles such as 'Onward', 'Real People, Real Change' and 'Our Iceberg is Melting'. Some of them, such as 'Who Says Elephants Can't Dance' by Louis Gerstner, are informative to read and a lot can be learnt from their honest insights into the practicalities of change.

The populist bandwagon tends to be epitomized by the use of parables about change using, in some cases, abstract stories about animals. The most popular of such books, having sold more than 22 million copies in 37 languages, is entitled *Who Moved My Cheese?* (Spencer, 1999) and describes itself as an amazing way to deal with change in work and in life. It is a tale that can be read in about 45 minutes, and which we have briefly summarized below.

> There are two 'little people' (Hem and Haw) and two mice (Sniff and Scurry). All of them live in a maze. For a time, they have an abundance of cheese to eat (whatever they want in life). Then one day, the cheese disappears. The mice instinctively understand that their world has changed and that they need to adapt and look for cheese in a different place. So they do, and they find new cheese.
>
> The humans are more resistant to change. Hem indignantly bellows 'Who moved my cheese?' and refuses to accept reality. Haw too is initially resistant but comes to understand that he has to leave his comfort zone to survive and thrive. *Voilà*! New cheese awaits him.

This book and others like it are open to criticism for attempting to convince managers of simple one-size-fits-all approaches towards managing change. The problem is that in some organizations employees have been burnt out by too much organizational change, which has failed to be sustained. For them, the cheese never stops moving.

Populist books on change provide an often longed-for level of simplicity about how to do change in organizations. In many cases they may be easy to read but do not necessarily deliver results. As Louis Lavelle, a book reviewer for *BusinessWeek* magazine, so aptly wrote:

> To hear most authors of business books tell it, there is no management conundrum so great that it can't be solved by the deft application of seven or eight basic principles. The authors are almost always wrong as big public companies have too many moving parts to conform to any set of simple precepts. (2005: 2)

This is a relevant criticism for populist books on change, which tend to be concerned with offering simple prescriptions and lists of techniques that will lead to successful change. Such books deliver reassuring rationality that change can be managed in several steps. We have all read them – even the authors of this book – and some of us have even learnt from them. However, we caution our readers to view such books from a critical perspective and not to try to implement and sustain change guided by the wisdom of mice and cheese.

The academic view

The academic literature provides some well-grounded and very well written texts on organizational change (such as Burke, 2002; Burnes, 2009a; Carnall, 2007; Cummings and Worley, 2009; Hayes, 2014) as well as critical monographs and research studies (such as Nadler and Tushman, 1995; Ogbonna and Harris, 2002; Pettigrew et al., 2001). However, the paucity of empirical studies and the dominance of US-based thinking, cases and data still characterize the academic literature. What is available is a wide range of theories and approaches with varying degrees of strengths and weaknesses. As Bernard Burnes points out in the Preface to Patrick Dawson's book *Reshaping Change: A Processual Perspective* (2003b):

> the range of approaches to change, and the confusion over their strengths, weaknesses and suitability, is such that the field of organizational change resembles more an overgrown weed patch than a well-tended garden. (Burnes, 2003: xii)

Many of the academic approaches are well thought-out and grounded in theory and practice, while others are disconnected from the reality of the business world. They tend to posit change as a complex phenomenon and critique the 'programmatic', linear approach to change often espoused in the popular literature (Pettigrew, 2000; Ruigrok et al., 1999; Stace, 1996). For many academics there is no simple prescription for change, no silver bullet and no one way to deliver change. Change is not a one-dimensional process and hardly ever characterized by a linear progression towards a final goal. Although the literature criticizes the simple process models of change as not working, what they propose does work is not always clear.

Case studies provide a useful practical perspective, but even those have come under attack since they tend to be written after the event and result in what Andrew Pettigrew and colleagues (2001) call the 'trajectories of change' (pace, sequence) being presented in a sanitized, relatively smooth, well-planned, orchestrated, cohesive narrative, with all the unsightly mess, cock-ups and boring inertia being airbrushed out.

In his book on organizational change Jim Grieves (2010) identifies two challenges that are emerging in the academic literature. First, an enduring aspect of the work on change over the years has been a strong humanistic orientation (concern for people and increasing human potential). But this strand of humanism has been subordinated in the pursuit of efficiency and profit maximization, in order to enhance organizational performance. Second, organizational change has traditionally been something that has been undertaken by managers and consultants with employees positioned as recipients of change. In effect, managers and consultants have been largely portrayed as having agency – as **change agents** and change leaders – while employees are depicted as relatively agentless (Grieves, 2010). In this regard, the change literature is perhaps guilty of conflating '**change management**' with 'change managers' and over-emphasizing actors over acts (By et al., 2011). There has been a call to reframe change management as a micro-situated, everyday, distributed practice, similar to Gronn's (2002) notion of **distributed leadership**, rather than perpetuating the dominant perspective that treats it as a strategic tool deployed by key actors in the corporate hierarchy (By et al., 2011). Such views shift change from a traditional top-down process to a more emergent concept involving employees across the organization (see the discussion of emergent change in Chapter 2).

Mike Young (2009) suggests that attempts to make sense of the plethora of literature on change in organizations has led to typologies that differentiate change rather than identifying common themes – indeed 'common sense' or basic factors – that might be useful in guiding efforts to sustain change. In a review of the change literature, Young focuses on nine areas and, through a meta-analysis, has identified the common themes within them, which are outlined in Figure 1.1.

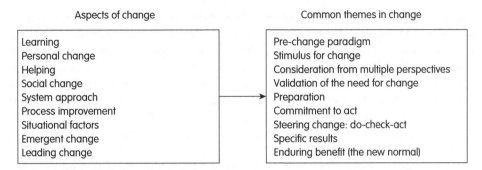

Aspects of change	Common themes in change
Learning Personal change Helping Social change System approach Process improvement Situational factors Emergent change Leading change	Pre-change paradigm Stimulus for change Consideration from multiple perspectives Validation of the need for change Preparation Commitment to act Steering change: do-check-act Specific results Enduring benefit (the new normal)

Figure 1.1   Aspects of change and common themes

Young's intention is to draw attention to the kinds of variables that need to be conceptualized, observed or enacted when change is studied or implemented. The meta-model proves a useful guide. The benefit of considering such a broad range of change-related fields is that each brings a different perspective to the stages of the common underlying journey. As a consequence, the meta-model offers both a lens, to provide focus on the stages in the common change progression, and a prism, to reveal the full spectrum of applicable concepts and activities.

Populist versus academic literature?

Leaders and managers face a challenge when attempting to choose between the practical prescriptions of the popular approach and the evidence-based criticisms of change fads and fashions offered by academics. Salaman and Asch (2003) articulate the conundrum:

> The populist material tries to sell them [managers and leaders] packages, beautifully presented, forcefully marketed, clearly stated in persuasive language, which promise radical dramatic transformation … On the other hand, the academic commentators warn against too easy acceptance, noting a number of problems with the advice and recommendations on offer, pointing out inconsistencies, contradictions and simplifications. (2003: 22)

Although it is difficult to identify any consensus on organizational change in the populist and academic literature, there does seem to be, according to Rune Todnem By and colleagues (2011), an agreement on three important issues. First, it is agreed that the pace of change has never been greater than in the current business environment (Balogun and Hope Hailey, 2004; Burnes, 2009a; Carnall, 2007). Second, change is triggered by internal or external factors and comes in all forms, shapes and sizes. Third, there is little doubt that the ability to manage and lead change successfully needs to be a core competence for organizations (Burnes, 2009a). So the pace, drivers and capability to lead and manage change are important factors affecting organizational change, which are recognized in the literature.

Although there is a need to be critical of much that is written about change, we must not lose sight of the very real practical challenge of planning, implementing and sustaining change in organizations. There is a multitude of books on how to lead and manage change. Many of these make excellent reference guides and provide valuable suggestions. Yet despite the number of books on change, the literature is still lacking. There is much more that we need to know about change and how to sustain it, as the concept itself is changing, within a transforming world. This presents a great opportunity. For the greater our understanding of change in organizations from different perspectives, the more we will know about the essence of how organizations undertake change and how change can be sustained in different contexts.

This book aims to contribute to the literature and address some of the gaps using theory and practice. We cover parts of the change process, which may have been discussed in other books and articles, but have not been pulled together into a coherent whole. We also use case studies and the experiences and reflections of people, from the coalface, who have been responsible for planning, implementing and sustaining change in different types of sectors and business environments across the globe. This book therefore adds to the literature on organizational change from a practical as well as a theoretical perspective.

Definitions of change, transition and transformation

Three concepts appear frequently in discussions of change, including, of course, **change** itself as well as **transition** and **transformation**. In this section we will clarify what these are and how they are defined, in the context of this book.

Change

Change is the introduction or experience of something that is different. When we think of organizational change, we tend to think of the fine-tuning of processes and systems such as technology, performance management, reward and recognition schemes, financial payment systems and improvements to operations. We also think of larger changes such as **mergers**, **acquisitions**, restructures, outsourcing and the launch of new products or services in the marketplace. Change comes in many guises including: modification, development, metamorphosis, transmutation, evolution, regeneration and revolution. For some, change is inherently messy, confusing and loaded with unpredictability. Andrew Pettigrew (1987) points out that change is a complex and untidy cocktail of rational decisions, mixed with competing individual perceptions, stimulated by visionary leadership, spiced with 'power plays' and attempts to recruit support and build coalitions behind a particular idea.

The various definitions of change carry the same connotation that change involves making something different, in some particular way. In its broadest sense, change is 'any alteration to the status quo' (Bartol and Martin, 1994: 199). It is an opportunity to make or become different (Oxford dictionairies.com) through new ways of organizing and working (Dawson, 2003a: 11). The difference can be small (incremental) or radical (transformational).

Moran and Brightman (2001: 111) define change as 'the process of continually renewing an organization's direction, structure and capabilities to serve the ever-changing needs of external and internal [stakeholders]'. In this sense, organizational change can be planned or emergent alterations to the whole or parts of an organization to improve the effectiveness and efficiency of the organization (see Chapter 2 for a discussion on **planned change** and **emergent change**). This can include changes to: the mission and value of the organization, the **strategy**, goals, structure, processes, systems, technology and people in the organization. However, it is not just about 'what' changes, for as Barnett and Carroll (1995) conceptualize, organizational change is about the content and process. The content is 'what' actually changes in the organization (structure, process, systems and behaviour). The process is 'how' the change occurs and draws attention to issues such as the pace of change and the sequence activities, the way decisions are made and communicated, and the ways in which people respond to change. So when discussing change in this book, we will examine what changes as well as 'how' it changes and the impact of change.

Sustainable change

The word 'sustainable' derives from the Latin *sustinere*, which literally means 'to hold up' or 'to maintain'. Something is **sustainable**, therefore, if it endures, persists or holds up over time. In the context of change in organizations there are a variety of definitions that have been put forward. Some definitions focus on the embedding of new processes, whereas others focus attention on performance improvements independent of the methods employed. Some definitions are relatively static, focusing on the maintenance of improvements within a particular setting, while others are more dynamic and concerned with translating initial gains into a process of continual improvement. Dale (1996), for example, defines sustaining change in terms of increasing the pace of improvement while holding the gains made. Another useful definition comes from the UK's National Health Service (NHS):

> [Sustainable change is] when new ways of working and improved outcomes become the norm. Not only have the process and outcome changed, but also the thinking and attitudes behind them are fundamentally altered and the systems surrounding them are transformed in support. (NHS Modernisation Agency, 2002: 12)

Change is sustained, therefore, when it becomes an integrated or mainstream way of working and behaving in an organization, rather than something added on. As a result, when we look at the process, outcome or people's behaviour one year from now, or longer ahead, we should be able to see that at a minimum it has not reverted to the old ways or previous level of performance. It should have been able to withstand challenge and disruption – and evolved alongside other changes in the organization and perhaps even actually continued to improve over time.

Although this provides the most succinct working definition, it is important to take into account contextual issues, for as Buchanan and Fitzgerald (2007) conclude, 'the definition and timing that matter are those applicable to a particular organizational setting' (2007: 22).

Transition

Transition is the process or period of adapting to the change. Transition involves shifting from the current state or phase to another, for example, an individual changing from one role to another, a group changing from one decision process to another, or an organization going from one structural arrangement to another. The impact of the transition on people needs to be understood and managed, and the emotional response to change needs to be recognized. It is often transition, not the change itself, that people react to. They resist giving up the status quo and their sense of who they are – their identity as it is expressed in their current work. For example, individuals may fear the chaos and uncertainty caused by change. They might feel threatened by the **risk** of a new beginning – of doing and being what they have never done and been before. To sustain change it is important to help people through the transition.

In his book *Managing Transitions*, William Bridges (1992) outlines his transition model. The main strength of the model is that it focuses on transition, not change. The difference between this is subtle but important. Change is something that happens *to* people, even if they do not agree with it. Transition, on the other hand, is what happens *as* people go through change. Change can happen very quickly, while transition usually occurs more slowly. Bridges' model highlights three stages of transition that people go through when they experience change. These are: (i) ending, losing and letting go; (ii) the neutral zone; and (iii) the new beginning. Bridges states that people will go through each of these stages at their own pace. For example, those who are comfortable with the change are likely to move ahead to the third stage quickly, while others will linger at the first or second stages. Each stage of the model is examined in greater detail in Chapter 11. Transition is therefore about adopting the change.

Transformation

Transformation is the marked change in nature, form or appearance of something. While change involves anything that is different from the norm, a transformation involves a 'metamorphosis' from one state to another. As a caterpillar grows, it changes. When it becomes a butterfly, however, a metamorphosis or transformation has occurred. This involves a catalysing change in belief and awareness, and a marked change in form, nature or appearance (Ackerman, 1986).

Transformational or **strategic change** and everyday incremental change can be viewed as different, not just in terms of their objectives but also in terms of their processes and size, scope and breadth, and what they demand of leadership. Transformational change is much more disruptive to what people do and the way they work. It reflects major shifts in environmental changes and demands and consequential new management, technological, organizational, cultural and social characteristics and processes within the organization.

Transformation involves massive programmes of change to turn around or renew an organization (Mintzberg et al., 1998) or an industry. For example, a significant transformation occurred in the book and the music industry in the 2000s, when both industries moved from hard copy to digital download. Transformation is typified by a radical reconceptualization of an organization's mission, **culture**, critical success factors and leadership style.

Aim of the book

This book seeks to inform the practice of the management and leadership of change in organizations. The strength of this book is that it provides a theoretical overview of the key issues followed by a focused practitioner orientation.

We aim to go beyond what is already known and to set out new frameworks, perspectives and practical approaches and recommendations for current and future managers and leaders in organizations, based on what has been learnt about change from theoretical and practical perspectives. We do this in four ways.

First, we focus on what has been learnt about change by considering existing theories and concepts, as well as occasions on which leaders and managers appear to have successfully accomplished change as well as when they appear to have failed to do so. This is important because learning is a prerequisite of change, and change is a prerequisite for learning (Hughes, 2006). The understanding of organizational change can be furthered through learning from failures as well as successes (we discuss learning from failure in Chapter 8). Ignoring failure can limit our understanding of the theory and practice of organizational change. Sorge and Van Witteloostuijn (2004) point out that there is a view in the literature that organizational change has an undeniable tendency to fail. Ghoshal and Bartlett support this view and say that for 'every successful corporate transformation, there is a least one equally prominent failure' (1977: 195). Other failure rates are cited as higher. For instance, it has been estimated, but without any valid empirical evidence to back it up, that up to 70% of change initiatives fail (Burnes and Jackson, 2011; Hughes, 2011). John Kotter (1995) has described the result of such a high level of failure as carnage, with wasted resources and burnt-out, scared, or frustrated employees.

Writers about change, if they mention failure, inevitably describe it as a lack of success. As Thorne (2000) points out, a crucial difference between writers on change and writers on organizational learning is how the latter group actively embrace failure as a valuable and positive part of learning and development. In contrast, change writers, if they mention failure, almost invariably describe it negatively as a lack of success. Sennet (2001) echoes this and says that there appears to be potential in learning from change which fails, yet talking and writing about it is seen as engaging with an organizational taboo. Carnall (2007) warns that achieving change is one thing; learning from the process of change is entirely different. In this book we make an optimistic start for such learning by considering occasions on which organizations appear to have successfully accomplished change, and occasions when they appear to have failed to achieve change. We provide examples, through case studies, of where change has been successful as well where it has failed in organizations, and, importantly, point to the lessons learnt from failure.

Second, this book, whenever possible, considers change from an individual, group/team and organizational perspective. The importance of organizational change is frequently mentioned in the literature (for example, Balogun and Hope Hailey, 2004; Carnall, 2007), while analysis of individual-level change is less prevalent and the group/team approach is the least common. This book argues for a greater understanding of individual, group/team and organization learning as a result of change initiatives. It therefore examines change at different levels in organizations.

Third, the book takes into account contextual issues, which are important in arriving at a deeper level of understanding of how change is sustained in practice. To focus on the context, content and process of the success and failure of change, we asked practising managers, leaders and individuals to provide their personal experience of change in organizations. They were each asked to reflect on the following:

- What was the type of organization in which the change took place?
- What was specifically changed?
- Why did change take place?
- Who made the decision to change?
- What has been the recent organizational history of change?
- How was the change communicated?
- What were the scale and scope of the change?
- What were the temporal aspects of the change?
- Who led the change and how was it led?
- Who managed the change and how was it managed?
- What was the outcome of the change?
- Who influenced the outcome of the change?
- What influenced the outcome?
- Was a successful outcome specified and communicated, and, if so, what were the criteria for establishing the achievement of the successful outcome?
- What have you/your team/the organization learnt from the change initiatives?
- What will you do differently with the next change initiative based on your learning?

We have included personal stories from managers and leaders of change across a diverse variety of companies in different sectors, based on their answers to these questions. This is important because the phenomenon of change requires an approach to its study that combines academic rigour and practical relevance. In this vein, an increasing number of researchers are proposing higher levels of **engagement** of practising managers and leaders in organizations with the research process and the employment of real-life experiences as empirical data (Huff, 2000; Stacey and Griffin, 2005). Although a number of studies have begun to address this issue (for example, Balogun and Johnson, 2004; Maitlis, 2005), few have provided data drawn from samples that cover a range of organizations. This book attempts to address this by including contributions from managers and leaders from a range of organizations across the globe.

Fourth, we [the authors] contribute our own experiences from the business and academic worlds. Many of the most successful books on change have been produced from the comfort of a business school campus or a consulting head office, or involved high-profile executives telling their story of trials and turnarounds. But there have been few attempts to craft a theoretical and practical book on change by people with academic and business experience. Throughout the years, we have acquired in-depth familiarity with many organizational change situations; sometimes we have learnt from our experiences working in management, leadership and consultancy roles, while other learning has come from having been the recipients of change.

Learning outcomes of the book

The intended learning outcomes of this book are to help you to do the following:

- Enhance your understanding of the theoretical concepts of change
- Develop your skills so that you are able to be more effective in managing and leading change in organizations

- Increase your ability to deal with issues arising from organizational change/s
- Improve your capability to work with and through people affected by change
- Sustain change in the organization in which you work

Overview of the book

This book aims to provide a comprehensive overview of the main perspectives on organizational change. It does this, first, by providing both a theoretical and a practical focus. Secondly, the book is meant for students, in particular those who strive to assess and understand the phenomenon of change in organizations. It is also meant for managers and leaders who are responsible for identifying the need and **readiness for change** as well as implementing, evaluating and sustaining change in organizations. It will be a helpful resource for specialists in organizational development, **project management**, human resources and other related disciplines responsible for facilitating change and transformation. Readers will find here a considerable number of frameworks, tools and different perspectives. We do, however, need to emphasize caution in that it is important to adapt the tools and techniques to the context of the organization or situation in which you are working, rather than attempting a cut-and-paste approach of 'one size fits all'. It is impossible to conceive of an approach that is suitable for all types of change, all types of situations and all types of organizations. Some may be too narrow in applicability whilst others may be too general. Some may be complementary to each other whilst others are clearly incompatible. We therefore recommend that readers adapt the frameworks, tools and different perspectives to the context of the organization in which they work.

Finally, the book synthesizes what is known about change in organizations and suggests ways of sustaining change. It brings together familiar as well as new material and perspectives. In this way, the book goes further than other texts in that it covers a breadth of issues pertinent to sustaining change in organizations.

Structure of the book

The distinctive feature of this book is that it focuses on *sustaining* change in organizations. The book is divided into five parts. In *Part One – The Essence of Change and Transformation* – there are two chapters, which provide an overview of context and theory. *Chapter 1* provides an introduction and outlines the key purpose of the book. *Chapter 2 – Theoretical Approaches to Organizational Change and Transformation* – introduces the nature of change. The aim of this chapter is to provide an overview of the theories of change and to consider the contemporary debates that populate the literature on the nature of change. We do this by examining some of the theories relating to change and exploring the different types of change. Our aim is not to provide an in-depth analysis, as this has been done elsewhere (for example Hayes, 2014). In this chapter we classify change according to how it emerges, its magnitude, focus and level in organizations. We address some key questions such as: How can change in organizations be classified? How does change come about? What should the pace of change be – will it be easier if it is introduced quickly or over a longer period of time? And should change be process-driven or people-driven? In *Chapter 3 – Leading Change* and *Chapter 4 – Managing Change* we look at how designing, implementing, evaluating and sustaining change strategies depends on the ability and motivation of leaders and managers. While it must be managed, change also requires effective leadership. Depending on the type and scale of change, different styles of leadership may be appropriate. In *Chapter 3* we explain how an integrative model of six core leadership themes and practices can help to establish sustainable change. This model comprises **vision**, **purpose** (mission), **values**, strategy, **empowerment** and engagement as themes and practices of leadership for organizational change and transformation. We address some key questions, such as the following: What is the role of leaders in the change process? What do leaders need to do to nurture the change once it is on its way? And what is the difference between leading and managing change?

Managing change is the focus of *Chapter 4*. Change must be managed – it must be planned, organized, directed and controlled. This is a necessary (but alone not sufficient) condition for successful change. Management can be thought of as a function that is part of an organization's formal structure. This is evident in Mullin's (2007) statement that he regards management as taking place within a structured organizational setting and with prescribed roles; directed towards the attainment of aims and objectives; achieved through the efforts of other people; and using systems and procedures. Other writers have concentrated more on the roles that managers play, that is, what managers do (Kotter, 1990a; Mintzberg, 1973). The chapter discusses the definitions of management in relation to change in organizations. It also reviews the role of managers during organizational transformations. The chapter addresses several questions, including: What is the role of managers in change? And what are the capabilities required to effectively manage change?

In *Part Two – Recognizing the Need for Change* we explore diagnosing the need for change and identifying the readiness for change. *Chapter 5 – The Drivers for Change and Transformation* examines the context in which change takes place. We begin by discussing the external and internal triggers for change. The chapter explores how the triggers for change can be identified through conducting an analysis of the environment in which the organization operates. The chapter also considers the concept of 'learning disabled' – what happens when organizations fail to recognize the need for change. *Chapter 6 – Diagnosing the Need and Readiness for Change* discusses whether change is always necessary. It focuses on the importance of recognizing the possible need for change and assessing the strength of that need. The chapter defines the diagnostic process as well as critically evaluating the tools and frameworks that can be used as part of the process. This chapter provides the opportunity to take a step back and analyse the need for change.

In *Part Three – Planning, Communicating and Implementing Change* we review some specific issues that span organizations as a whole, such as learning, culture and structures. The process of moving from a recognized need for change to developing and implementing change is introduced in *Chapter 7 – Planning and Implementing Change*. This chapter focuses on the practical aspects of the 'how' of change. We consider a holistic approach to planning and implementing change and discuss the benefits of such an approach. The chapter critically evaluates linear models for planning and implementing change and illustrates what has worked in organizations, using a number of examples. The benefits of using a project management approach are also considered. We address some key questions, such as: How can we effectively plan a change initiative? How can we ensure the successful implementation of change? And what are the key issues that need to be considered when implementing change?

Chapter 8 – Organizational Development and Organizational Learning discusses the principles of Organizational Development (OD) and learning. This is an extensive chapter, which is split into two parts: first, we critically review different OD models and interventions, then the second part of the chapter focuses on organizational learning – what it is and why it is important in the context of change. We discuss the concept of a **learning organization** and why it is important and how to develop it. The chapter concludes by exploring how to create learning communities and learning contracts. We address some key questions such as: How can organizations harness and apply the knowledge and lessons learnt from OD interventions? How can a learning organization be developed? And how can we learn from failure? The originality of this chapter lies in its emphasis not so much on a theoretical perspective but on the practical side, through the inclusion of frameworks, tools and case studies. This is not a topic that is examined in such great depth in other textbooks on organizational change.

In *Chapter 9 – Changing Organizational Structures* we examine the rationale for structural change and some of the challenges associated with it. This is a subject that tends to be neglected in some of the literature on organizational change. In particular, we focus on restructures as a result of mergers and acquisitions. We also discuss the importance of **due diligence** as part of the process of a merger or acquisition. We address questions such as: How do formal structures and systems influence change in organizations? How can leaders and managers select the most appropriate structure for their organization? What needs to be considered when changing a structure? And what are the complexities of managing a merger or acquisition?

Changing anything inevitably entails communicating about it. *Chapter 10 – Communication and Change* focuses on communication as a key process that influences how effectively an organization sustains change. The chapter critically evaluates the impact of communication on gaining commitment to change and also on **trust** and uncertainty among individuals and teams in an organization. We address several key questions, including: How can managers communicate effectively during times of uncertainty? What affects the quality of communication? And what are the most appropriate communication strategies and tools available? Practical tools are included in this chapter to help you to develop a communications plan.

Part Four – People, Politics and Power during Change and Transformation explores the impact of change on individual behaviours as well as on the politics and power within organizations. In *Chapter 11 – The Nature, Impact and Management of Attitudes Towards Change* we examine the nature and management of attitudes towards change. The chapter discusses the impact of change on individuals and explores the transition issues they face. Specifically, we consider the impact of change on behaviour and motivation, how individuals react to change, their attitudes to change and what leaders and managers can do to effectively manage the impact of change on individuals. The chapter considers how to gain commitment to the change from individuals and the importance of involving them in the decision-making process.

Chapter 12 – Power, Politics and Conflict during Change explores the role of **power**, **political behaviour** and **conflict** during organizational change. The chapter provides a working definition of each concept and describes the roles of each in organizational change. The chapter discusses how power, politics and conflict are important to recognize and manage during change initiatives if change is to be sustained. The role of the change agent in relation to power, politics and conflict is also considered. The chapter concludes by providing some practical tools to analyse the power and influence of stakeholders in the change process. We address some key questions, such as: What are the positive and negative aspects of power, politics and conflict during change? How can political behaviour, power and conflict be managed effectively? How should the key stakeholders of change be identified and managed? What are the necessary skills to act as agents of change? And what are the key capabilities that change agents require?

In *Part Five* we aim to provide conclusions about *Sustaining Change and Transformation*. *Chapter 13 – Ensuring Sustainable Change through Monitoring and Measurement* focuses on measures for evaluating the effectiveness of change, and practical frameworks for achieving benefits and managing risks are provided. The chapter also examines the issues of declaring victory too soon and of people switching their attention and resources to other projects. It considers what to do if transformation fails and the strategies for turning the situation around. We address questions such as: How can organizations assess whether interventions are sustained as intended? How can leaders assess whether the chosen interventions are having the desired effect? And how can you ensure that the change plan continues to be valid? *Chapter 14 – Contemporary Issues in Change and Transformation* discusses the impact of megatrends on change at a global and local level and what this means for organizations. The chapter also examines the key issues of sustainability and business ethics for change and transformation. The need for future capability and capacity to cope with change and transformations is also considered, and key issues for the future of change are discussed. In the final chapter, *Chapter 15 – Conclusion* we attempt to synthesize our theoretical and practical perspectives on change and transformation and provide a summary of the issues we have discussed throughout the book.

In each chapter we have included the following: key issues, principal theories, relevant research, practical and tested tools, business examples, questions for discussion, activities and further reading, as well as practical conclusions and recommendations that point the way ahead for current and future managers and leaders.

This book is intended to provide a platform for the theory and practice of change, coalescing what is already known, identifying the priorities for what more needs to be known, and proposing how change can be sustained in organizations and benefits accrued from it. It attempts to address some of the key issues related to change from a practical and realistic perspective as well as a theoretical one. Experiences from individuals and organizations provide insights into what makes change successful and what makes it fail, as well as lessons learnt. We are pleased to share them with you.

Discussion Questions

1 From your experience, how valid is the claim that 'Organizations change all the time, each and every day' (Burke, 2002: xii).
2 In an organization you have either worked in or are familiar with, identify the changes that have been implemented in the past 12 months. How successful have they been?

Theoretical Approaches to Change and Transformation

2

Overview

- This chapter classifies change in organizations according to how it emerges, its magnitude, focus and level.
- Change can emerge through a planned approach. *Planned* change is deliberate, a product of conscious reasoning and action. In contrast, change sometimes unfolds in an apparently spontaneous and unplanned way (Lewin, 1947). This type of change is known as *emergent change* (Burnes, 2009a).
- The magnitude or scale of change can range along a continuum from small-scale discrete change (incremental) to a large-scale transformation. Incremental change aims to provide improvements. In contrast to incremental change, transformational change aims to redefine an organization's strategic direction, form, cultural assumptions and identity. This kind of change is also referred to as 'strategic', 'radical' or 'revolutionary' (Kanter et al., 1992; Weick and Quinn, 1999).
- An alternative position to viewing change as either incremental or transformational is punctuated equilibrium. This theory posits that organizations evolve through periods of incremental change, and periods of transformation, in which the deep structures of the organization are fundamentally altered (Gersick, 1991).
- The focus of organizational change can be *strategic* or *operational*. Pettigrew et al. (1992) distinguish between operational change as small-scale and relatively unimportant and strategic change as major and important structural changes.
- The level of the change process can be at an *individual, group, team* or *organization* level. The targets for this dimension of change tend to be behaviour, skills, knowledge and attitudes. Although the three levels are related, changes affecting each require different strategies and tactics.

The aim of this chapter is to provide an overview of the theories of change and to consider the contemporary debates that populate the literature on the nature of change. We do this by examining some of the theories relating to change and exploring the different types of change. Our aim is not to provide an in-depth, analysis as this has been done effectively elsewhere (for example, Hayes, 2010). The chapter considers questions such as: How can change in organizations be classified? How does change come about? What should the pace of change be – will it be easier if it is introduced quickly or over a longer period of time? And should change be driven by processes or people? We begin by defining what is meant by 'organizations', followed by an examination of the nature of change in organizations. The chapter explores next how change emerges, its magnitude, focus and level. The chapter concludes by examining whether change should be process- or people-driven.

Learning objectives

By the end of this chapter you will be able to:

- Appreciate the complex nature of change in organizations
- Critically evaluate the theoretical perspectives relating to the types of change that organizations may experience
- Identify what kind of change is needed as well as the magnitude, focus, level, pace and sequencing of the change

Organizations

Organizations pervade our physical, social, cultural, political and economic environment, offering jobs, providing goods and services, and contributing to the existence of whole communities. The products and services of organizations such as Google, Apple, Amazon, Starbucks and Toyota shape our existence and our daily experience.

Definition

An organization can be defined as 'a social arrangement for achieving controlled performance in pursuit of collective goals' (Buchanan and Huczynski, 2010: 8). This definition emphasizes that it is the preoccupation with performance and the need for control which distinguishes organizations from other social arrangements.

Gareth Morgan in his book *Images of Organizations* (2006) outlines eight metaphors, which invite the reader to view organizations through the following lenses:

- Machines
- Biological organisms
- Human brains
- Cultures or subcultures
- Political systems
- Psychic prisons

- Systems of change and transformation
- Instruments of domination

Morgan presents these metaphors as ways of thinking about organizations, as approaches to the diagnostic reading and critical evaluation of organizational phenomena. For instance, the metaphor of 'organization as machine' suggests an analysis of its component elements and their interaction. The metaphor of the 'psychic prison' suggests an analysis of how an organization constrains and shapes the thinking and intellectual growth of its members. Morgan suggests how, by using these different metaphors to understand their complex characteristics, it becomes possible to identify novel ways in which to design, change and manage organizations.

The nature of change

The idea that organizations are constantly engaged in change to a greater or lesser degree is not a new phenomenon. In 1947 Kurt Lewin postulated that life is never without change; rather there are merely differences in the amount and type of change that exist. Although change in organizations may be a constant, the nature of it is not always the same, as change comes in a variety of shapes and sizes and can be proactive or reactive depending on contextual factors.

Proactive and reactive change

Organizational change is triggered by a proactive or reactive response to something in the external environment or internally in the organization. *Proactive* change is initiated by leaders in an organization in response to a perceived opportunity as a result of their assessment or recognition of external or internal factors. For example, Howard Schultz perceived the opportunity to create an American version of the classic Italian coffee bar and transformed Starbucks in order to achieve that vision. Similarly, Madhavan Nayar, founder of Infogix, perceived the need for a new paradigm of information integrity and took steps to position his company for this emerging opportunity. Proactive change is an opportunistic change, in which the organization needs to create strategic advantage because of something present or anticipated internally or externally.

Reactive change is a response to factors in the external environment or within the organization that have already occurred rather than those that are anticipated in the future. The financial sub-prime crisis starting in 2007 and the Euro-crisis of 2010 created reactive change in the financial sector, such as the takeover of RBS by the UK government. Reactive change is something that has to happen to deal with an unexpected external or internal trigger.

A typology of change

Change in organizations can be classified according to it how it happens, its magnitude, focus and level, which form a typology of change as is illustrated in Figure 2.1. We will discuss each of these factors next.

How it happens	Magnitude
– Planned – Emergent – Contingency	– Incremental – Transformational – Punctuated equilibrium
Focus	**Level**
– Strategic – Operational	– Individual – Team – Organization

Figure 2.1 Typology of change

How change happens

There are different approaches to how change emerges and evolves over time. Sometimes change is deliberate, a product of conscious reasoning and action. This type of change is called *planned change*. In contrast, change sometimes unfolds in an apparently spontaneous and unplanned way. This type of change is known as *emergent change*.

Planned change

Planned change is an intentional intervention for bringing about change to an organization and is best characterized as deliberate, purposeful and systematic (Lippitt et al., 1958; Tenkasi and Chesmore, 2003). The traditional aim of planned change has tended to be continuous improvement and to focus on changing parts of an organization, rather than attempting to change the whole organization at once. The process of planned change is rational and linear, with leaders and managers the pivotal instigators of the change. Therefore it is usually change driven from the top (Carnall, 2007; Cummings and Worley, 2009; Kanter et al., 1992). The process of planned change may vary in the number of steps proposed and the order in which they should be taken. However, what reunites advocates of this approach is that change can be achieved as long as the correct steps are taken. For instance, Kotter (1996) maintains that although change is messy and full of surprises, his eight-step model will produce a satisfying result as long as the steps are followed. Similarly, Kanter and colleagues (1992) indicate that with their Ten Commandments for change, it is an unwise manager who chooses to ignore one of the steps. Such proponents of planned change argue in favour of change occurring through carefully phased or sequenced processes (we explore **linear models** further in Chapter 7). One of the classic models of planned change is that developed by Kurt Lewin.

Kurt Lewin's model of planned change

The fundamental assumptions underlying planned change are derived originally from Kurt Lewin (1947). Lewin's model is a key contribution to organizational change; indeed, if you scratch any account of creating and managing change, Lewin's model will not be far below the surface (Hendry, 1996). The model proposes three phases: unfreezing, moving and refreezing.

- *Unfreezing*. Lewin believed that the stability of human behaviour was based on a quasi-stationary equilibrium supported by a complex field of driving and restraining forces, hence his development of the **force field analysis**, which we discuss in Chapter 6. He argued that the equilibrium (the forces of inertia) needs to be destabilized (unfrozen) before old behaviour can be discarded (unlearnt) and new behaviour successfully adopted.
- *Moving*. This phase is about making the change happen.
- *Refreezing*. The final step in the model seeks to stabilize the group at a new quasi-stationary equilibrium in order to ensure that the new behaviours are relatively safe from regression.

Although there is evidence of the success of Lewin's approach in achieving behavioural change (Burnes, 2009b; Woodman et al., 2008), it is important to recognize that this approach is not meant to be used in isolation. For as Bernard Burnes (2013) points out, it needs to be recognized that Lewin intended his model to be used with the three other elements that comprise planned change – **field theory**, **group dynamics** and **action research**. Lewin saw the four as forming an integrated approach to analysing, understanding and bringing about change.

Although widely adopted and adapted, the idea that organizations are frozen, much less refrozen, has been heavily criticized. The main criticisms tend to focus on the following:

1. First, it is open to question as to whether organizations are as amenable to control as a block of ice (Grey, 2003). Dawson (2003a) and Kanter, Stein and Jick (1992) argue that the notion of refreezing is not relevant for organizations operating in turbulent times. They propose that organizations need to be fluid and adaptable and the last thing they need is to be frozen into some given way of functioning.
2. Second, Lewin's model is felt to ignore the human factor, treating individuals as automatons rather than active participants in the change process (Giddens, 1981). The model is also criticized for representing a singular, partial story told by senior management and consequently ignoring the many views of other individuals in the organization (Buchanan, 2003).
3. Third, Lewin's model is very much rooted in the North American assumptions of change. Marshak (1993) compares the assumptions of the model with assumptions behind an Asian model. In the Lewin model, change is linear, progressive, managed by people intent on achieving goals. In the Asian model, change is cyclical, processional, journey orientated, associated with equilibrium, and managed in a way that is designed to create universal harmony. So even if Lewin's theory is appropriate to North American organizations, it may not be appropriate to organizational change in other countries and cultures.

In summary, the critics of Lewin have concerns about how his model views organizations and individuals as well as the cultural assumptions embedded in it, which may limit its use across geographical and cultural boundaries.

Prochaska and DiClemente's change theory

In contrast to Lewin's linear model, Prochaska and DiClemente offer a cyclical model of change. The initial purpose of their model was to show where a patient was in their journey to change certain health behaviours. Prochaska et al. (1993) found that people go through a series of stages when change occurs. These are precontemplation, contemplation, preparation, action and maintenance. Progression through the stages is expressed as cyclical. This is because initially many individuals relapse in their efforts and do not successfully maintain the changes the first time around. Prochaska and DiClemente therefore created a spiral model to represent the various stages of their theory.

The first aspect of the model shows the movement of intentional change from precontemplation to contemplation of the issue. *Precontemplation* exists when an individual is unaware of the problems, or fails to acknowledge them, without engaging in any change process activities. Individuals in this stage do not want to change their behaviour and may insist that their behaviour is normal. *Contemplation* occurs when the individual becomes conscious of the issue. Individuals in this stage are thinking about changing their behaviour, but they are not ready to commit to the change process. The next stage of the model is preparation. *Preparation* is when the individual is ready to change their behaviour and plans to do so. The *action* stage follows next and is characterized by an increase in coping with behavioural change as the individual begins to engage in change activities. *Maintenance* is the last stage, where actions to reinforce the change are taken along with establishing the new behavioural change as part of the individual's lifestyle and norms. In this spiral model, individuals have the ability to exit at any time if they decide not to change. The model also takes into account a behavioural *relapse* or a return to the previous existing behaviour. In the case of a relapse an individual can revisit the contemplation stage and prepare for action in the future. The spiral pattern of the model suggests that many individuals learn from their relapses instead of circling around the issue.

So models of curvilinear or cyclic change assume that change in a certain direction creates the conditions for change in another (perhaps even the opposite) direction, whereas, linear models of change assume that change in a certain direction induces further change in the same direction.

Activity

Identify a change that you have personally experienced. Consider how the stages of the Prochaska and DiClemente model are applicable to the change?

Criticisms of planned change

Planned linear models can provide logical and sequential prescriptions for the processes of change. Such models map out the processes from the first recognition of the need or desirability for change through to the practicalities of implementation (Price, 2009). However, planned linear conceptions of change are increasingly being challenged. Buchanan and Storey (1997: 127) argue that those who advocate planned change are attempting to impose an 'order and linear sequence on processes that are in reality messy and untidy, and which unfold in an iterative fashion with much back-breaking'. The difficulty, according to Paton and McCalman (2008), is that most organizations view the concept of change as a highly programmed process which takes as its starting point the problem that needs to be rectified, then breaks it down into constituent parts, analyses possible alternatives, selects the preferred solution and applies this relentlessly.

The criticisms of the planned approach to change can be summed up as follows:

- The emphasis of the planned approach on small-scale and incremental change is not applicable to situations that require rapid and transformational change (Burnes, 2009a; Senior, 2002). Change is a complex and dynamic process that should not be solidified or treated as a series of linear events (Dawson, 1994). The planned change approach has, according to Vince and Broussine (1996), an over-emphasis on the rational and consequently does not take into account the complexity, ambiguity and paradox acknowledged to be an integral part of an organization.
- The planned approach is based on the assumption that organizations operate under constant conditions and that they can move in a pre-planned manner from one stable state to another (Bamford and Forrester, 2003). These assumptions are, however, questioned by those who argue that the current fast-changing environment increasingly weakens this theory and that organizational change is more an open-ended and continuous process than a set of pre-identified discrete and self-contained events (Burnes, 2009a).
- The approach of planned change ignores situations where more directive approaches are required. This may be a situation of crisis that requires major and rapid change (Burnes, 2009a; Kanter et al., 1992), such as the political uprisings in the Middle East in countries such as Egypt and Turkey in 2013.

Some critics of the planned approach prefer to see change as an emergent, ongoing process, which cannot be achieved in a highly planned and programmed way.

Emergent change

The 'emergent' approach to change has been defined by some writers as change 'as-it-happens' (for example, Burnes, 2009a). Pettigrew and Whipp (1991: 108), for example, state that 'the management of strategic and operational change for competitive success is an uncertain and emergent process'. Burnes (2009) points out that there are two common beliefs underlying what he terms as the 'emergent' approach. First, change is viewed as an ongoing emergent process with no finite end point. Second, change emerges from the actions and decisions of people in organizations; for example, as the outcome of conflicts between different vested interest groups, in an attempt to adjust the organization to changes in the external environment, or through attempts to construct and implement a new social reality on the organization. As such, change is viewed as a continuous process and, consequently, attempts to impose a linear sequence of planned actions on what are untidy processes that 'unfold in an iterative fashion with much backtracking and omission' (Buchanan and Storey, 1997: 127) are heavily criticized.

The 'emergent' approach starts from the assumption that change is not a linear process or a one-off isolated event but a continuous, open-ended, cumulative and unpredictable process of aligning and re-aligning an organization to its changing environment (Orlikowski, 1996). The rationale for this approach is that the nature of change is evolving and unpredictable, as Karl Weick says:

> Emergent change consists of ongoing accommodations, adaptations, and alterations that produce fundamental change without a priori intentions to do so. Emergent change occurs when people reaccomplish routines and when they deal with contingencies, breakdowns, and opportunities in everyday work. Much of this change goes unnoticed because small alterations are lumped together as noise in otherwise uneventful inertia. (2000: 237)

This is why the advocates of emergent change argue that it needs to be viewed holistically and contextually. Most importantly, proponents of emergent change view organizations as power systems and consequently see change as a political process whereby different groups in an organization struggle to protect or enhance their own interests. Consequently, Dawson states that:

> In managing these transitions practitioners need to be aware of: the importance of power politics within organizations as a determinant of the speed, direction and character of change; the enabling and constraining properties of the type and scale of change being introduced; and the influence of the internal and external context on the pathways and outcomes of change on new work arrangements. (1994: 180–2)

This view is supported by Pugh, who says that:

> Organizations are political and occupational systems as well as rational resource alloca- tion ones. Every reaction to a change proposal must be interpreted not only in terms of rational arguments of what is best for the firm ... The reaction must also be understood in relation to the occupational system ... and the political system (how will it affect the power, status, prestige of the group). (1993: 109)

Advocates of emergent change emphasize that it is the uncertainty of the external and internal environment that makes it more pertinent than the planned approach (Bamford and Forrester, 2003). According to Dawson (2003), the essential unforeseeable character of change means that the process cannot be predicted and that **outcomes** are often understood only in retrospect. To cope with uncertainty it is argued that organizations need to become open-learning systems where strategy development and change emerge from the way a company as a whole acquires, interprets and processes information about the environment (Dunphy and Stace, 1993). Burnes says:

> [This approach stresses an] extensive and in-depth understanding of strategy, structure, systems, people, style and culture, and how these can function either as sources of iner- tia that can block change, or alternatively, as levers to encourage an effective change process. Successful change is less dependent on detailed plans and projections than on reaching an understanding of the complexity of the issues concerned and identifying the range of available options. (1996: 13-14)

To outline an emergent and improvisational model for managing the introduction of change into organizations, Orlikowski and Hofman use the metaphor of a jazz band:

> While members of a jazz band, unlike members of a symphony orchestra, do not decide in advance exactly what notes each is going to play, they do decide ahead of time what musical composition will form the basis of their performance. Once the performance begins, each player is free to explore and innovate, departing from the original composition. Yet the performance works because all members are playing within the same rhythmic structure and have a shared understanding of the roles of this musical genre. (1997: 13)

This model assumes that change occurs through the evolution of an iterative series of steps that produces outcomes that management could not have predicted at the start. In this model, managers become nurturers and facilitators of the change process. Orlikowski and Hofman (1997), however, acknowledge limitations to their theory:

- It is most appropriate to open-ended, customizable technologies or for complex, unprecedented change.
- Some people are incapable of playing jazz. In other words, not everyone will have the skills or the inclination to participate in such an unplanned, open-ended approach to change.
- The model downplays the impact of differing interests and politics associated with change. People may be capable of 'playing jazz' but not willing to do so because it is not in their interests to engage in a particular change programme.

The emergent theory is criticized for a number of reasons. Bamford and Forrester (2003) say that the approach lacks coherence and creates confusion and uncertainty in an organization due to a lack of clear objectives. This uncertainty can be unnerving to people in an organization. The theory is also criticized by Dawson (1994) as consisting of a rather disparate group of models and approaches. The applicability and validity of the emergent approach depends on whether you believe that all organizations operate in dynamic and unpredictable environments, to which they constantly have to adapt.

Contingency model of change

According to Burnes (2009), advocates of the emergent approach tend to adopt a contingency perspective, although they do not always admit it. The contingency approach is founded on the theory that the structure and performance of an organization are dependent on the situational variables that it faces. Arguing that the complex nature of environmental conditions mitigates against the creation of a unitary model of change, the contingency school of thought proposes that 'managers and consultants need a model of change that is essentially a situational or contingency model' that indicates how to vary change strategies to achieve 'optimum fit' with the changing environment (Dunphy and Stace, 1993: 905).

Contingency theories of change share with planned change the assumption that change can be directed through a series of steps. However, they part company with the step approach in arguing that the nature of this direction depends on, or is contingent on, a range of organizational factors such as the scale of the change, the urgency of the change and receptivity to the change. There will therefore be different types of steps that managers will need to take, depending on the confluence of various factors.

The strength of the contingency theory is that it explains organizational change from a behavioural viewpoint where managers make decisions that account for specific circumstances, focusing on those that are the most directly relevant, and intervening with the most appropriate actions. The best course of action is the one that is fundamentally situational, matched to the needs of the circumstances. The contingency approach proposes no formulas or guiding principles for organizational change; instead the focus is on achieving alignment and a good fit to ensure stability and control.

Critics of the contingency approach argue that the theory assumes that organizations and managers do not have any significant influence and choice over situational variables and structure. Instead they argue that an organization does not necessarily have to adapt to the external environment. Burnes (1996) advocates an approach of choice, suggesting that there is certainly evidence that organizations wishing to maintain or promote a particular managerial style can choose to influence situational variables to achieve this. So rather than having little choice, rather than being forced to change their internal practices to fit in with external variables, organizations can exercise some choice over these issues (By, 2005). Despite such criticisms, the flexible nature of the contingency perspective means that change can be fast or slow, small or large, loosely or tightly controlled, driven by internal or external triggers, and appropriate to varying levels of uncertainty.

The processual perspective

The processual approach to change is often associated with emergent change. Patrick Dawson (2005), however, argues that this is a misrepresentation and that the emergent approach differs in a number of important ways from the processual perspective. The two main tenets that align are: first, that an understanding of power and politics is central to an understanding of the processes of organizational change; and secondly that small-scale incremental changes can over time lead to a major transformation in an organization. However, according to Dawson (2005), the claim that this approach equates with a contingency perspective (Burnes, 2005) in advocating that planned change is inappropriate in an uncertain environment misrepresents this perspective.

The processual approach does not view the non-linear dynamics of change as only being in evidence in turbulent environments, nor does it reject the notion of planning. The approach recognizes that there are often critical junctures that necessitate radical change – as illustrated by the Enron debacle – and that ongoing processes of change occur within organizations operating in relatively stable environments as well as those operating in dynamic business contexts (see Dawson, 2003b). The increasing number and rate of organizational change initiatives has drawn attention to the inadequacy of a one-best-way approach and the need for a broader understanding of the complex untidy and messy nature of change. But in so doing, the processual approach is not making a statement against planning for change, rather it is pointing out that change is unpredictable and therefore that there will be a need to accommodate and adapt to the unexpected, the unforeseen twists and turns, the omissions and revisions that are all part of managing the process of change over time. In seeking to make sense of the way that change unfolds, the processual approach also provides insight into processes of continuity, as well as the temporal reshaping of change (Dawson, 2005).

Dawson (2003) has developed a processual approach that consists of three main elements, namely politics, context and substance of change. The politics of change is taken to refer to political activities inside and outside the organization (see the discussion of politics and change in Chapter 12). The contextual dimension refers to the past and present external and internal operating environments, as well as the influence of future projections and expectations on current operating practices. While the third area – substance of change – has four dimensions: the scale and scope of the change; the defining characteristics of change; the timeframe of change; and the perceived centrality of change. The processual perspective developed by Dawson has some similarities to the framework proposed by Andrew Pettigrew (1985).

In his book *The Awakening Giant: Continuity and Change in ICI*, Pettigrew (1985) demonstrated the limitations of the theories that view change either as a single event or as a discrete series of episodes that can be decontextualized. In a comparative analysis of five cases of strategic change, the study illustrates how change as a continuous incremental process (evolutionary) can be interspersed with radical periods of change (revolutionary). These major change initiatives are associated with major changes in business market conditions, such as world economic recessions, in which managers develop active strategies that build on these circumstances in order to legitimize and justify the need for change. For Pettigrew, 'change and continuity, process and structure, are inextricably linked' (1985: 1). He argues that the intention is not simply to substitute a rational approach with a political process perspective, but 'to explore some of the conditions in which mixtures of these occur' (1985: 24).

In studying change, the processual perspective draws our attention to the temporal character of change (the before, during and after of change) and the need to examine the way this process is shaped over time. The elements of context, substance and politics are advocated as providing a useful analytical framework. Although, as Dawson (2005) points out, it is recognized that in practice these elements often overlap and interlock, they ensure that the importance of choice and human experience within the political context of organizational life is recognized.

Discussion Questions

1　Compare and contrast the main approaches to change discussed above. What are the advantages and disadvantages of each?
2　What are the implications of each of the approaches for managing change?

Magnitude of change

The second dimension of the organizational change typology is the magnitude or scale of change. The scale of change can range along a continuum from small-scale discrete change (incremental) to more 'radical' large-scale transformation. According to Burke (2002), nearly 95% of organizational changes are incremental. Incremental change aims to provide improvements. It is change that is constant, evolving and cumulative (Weick and Quinn, 1999). A key feature of this type of change is that it builds on what has already been accomplished and has the flavour of continuous improvement (known by the Japanese as *kaizen*). Incremental change tends to be quick and easy to implement and there are usually quick returns. The risk of failure tends to be low but so are the returns in terms of benefits.

Incremental changes are the outcome of the everyday process of management; they tend to occur when individual parts of an organization deal increasingly and separately with one problem and one objective at a time (Burnes, 2009a), such as the updating of processes, policies, methods and procedures (Hayes, 2010). Examples of incremental change include changing a product formula in such a way that customers would notice no difference (for example, Heinz changes the recipes of one of its soups by adding more herbs or less sugar); outsourcing a function, such as payroll (providing it does not lead to roles being made redundant); changing the format, but not the content, of written documents, such as policies, procedures or job descriptions.

Where change is incremental

The film *Groundhog Day* portrays a situation where change is incremental. In the film, Bill Murray plays a TV weatherman trudging off to remote Punxsutawney, Pennsylvania, to cover the annual 2nd February Festival (Groundhog Day). The next morning he awakens to discover that it is 2nd February again. He tries to break the pattern, through pranks, subversion and even eventually suicide attempts, but nothing changes. So Murray's trapped weatherman embraces his fate. As the weeks tick by he learns something new about the characters around him and the town and discovers how he can make the town a better place. *Groundhog Day* holds a deep moral about the importance of meaningful relationships and self-discovery. But perhaps a more important lesson is how the film – in highlighting the slow and deliberate nature of time and space – serves as an exaggerated example of an environment where change is incremental, predictable and certain.

According to Nadler and Tushman (1995), incremental changes are not necessarily small changes. They can be large in terms of the resources needed and their impact on people. For example:

- Adapting reward systems to the changing labour market conditions
- Enhancing IT systems
- Introducing a new type of commission on sales for how sales people will be rewarded
- Developing a new set of products or services for an emerging market on the basis of demographic shifts
- Implementing a new leadership programme for the top 150 senior managers in a company
- Modifying the structure of a specific department

Incremental changes can lead to major improvements and significant changes. Think of what has happened in discount retailing over the last ten years. Walmart's cumulative impact has been extraordinary, but the retailer developed that advantage by deepening existing customer and supplier relationships. In the financial sector, the example of Westpac Bank illustrates an organization that has effectively applied incremental change. Westpac is an Australia-based bank that offers general, commercial and industrial banking services as well as insurance and financial services. It has been rated the No. 1 performing bank on the Dow Jones Sustainability Index. Westpac has used incremental change strategies to build its capabilities and reputation in corporate sustainability and responsibility. This approach was initially seen as an effective way to mitigate risk and repair consumer confidence in banks, and Westpac's approach has since grown into a comprehensive strategic programme for achieving corporate sustainability. The bank's success at pursuing its incremental sustainability change strategy can be attributed to a variety of factors including:

- The development and incorporation of a values-and-goals statement that also elaborates on how the process of change should be managed and the integration of this into the mission and strategy of the organization
- The creation of a culture of constant **innovation**, including corporate sustainability and responsibility initiatives, such as the development of green products and a reduction of the organization's greenhouse gas emission
- The development of a workforce that takes initiatives both to shape the emerging business environment and to adapt rapidly and responsively to changing market, social and ecological conditions

The case of Westpac illustrates how incremental change can be used effectively. Incremental change therefore tends to be continuous and ongoing and for the most part impacts on the day-to-day operational processes of an organization.

The case of the John Lewis Partnership (below) illustrates that incremental change is about doing things better through a process of continuous tinkering, adaptation and modification. It is called 'logical incremental', in which change is implemented in small steps with lessons from each phase informing the next.

CASE STUDY

The John Lewis Partnership

The John Lewis Partnership – a chain of department stores – is known for its quality of service and value for money, including its policy of being 'never knowingly undersold'. Unusually, a trust owns the company on behalf of all employees, known as partners, who exercise a high degree of responsibility in managing the organization. In 2014, the partnership had 85,500 permanent staff, 40 John Lewis shops, 300 Waitrose supermarkets, an online and catalogue business, a production unit and a farm. The business had annual gross sales of over £9.5 billion. John Lewis has expanded mainly organically for six decades. In recent years, the challenge has been to maintain growth while confronting several developments: the advent of online shopping; keeping the 'not knowingly undersold' promise; intense competition from other retailers, including food retailers diversifying their offerings; and the general high street recession. John Lewis's success depends on innovation. It calls its approach 'logical incremental', in which change is implemented in small steps, with lessons from each phase informing the next. The partners play a key role by providing feedback and insights into consumers' changing needs.

In their article about the John Lewis Partnership, Nicholas O'Regan and Abby Ghobadian (2012) discuss the logical incremental strategy which the partnership employs. The strategy is applied in several areas:

- *Responding to customers' requirements*. This involves frequent renewal of a wide variety of products with a broad range of pricing. In 2012, Waitrose carried 4,600 new products, and John Lewis about 30 new brands. The supermarket's new own-labels included 'Heston from Waitrose' in a tie-up with chef Heston Blumenthal.
- *New store formats*. John Lewis's new 'At Home' is a smaller version of the classic format, being typically a third of the size, carrying two-thirds the amount of stock and for one-quarter of the cost (about £10m in 2009). The flexible format allows all the stock to be showcased in half the usual space and customers can use in-store technology to make purchases. Waitrose opened high street convenience stores – smaller, and often with longer opening hours – called Little Waitrose, in 2009. There are 30 classic John Lewis stores, nine At Home outlets, 255 Waitrose supermarkets, 35 Little Waitroses and 84,700 partners.
- *International expansion*. One of John Lewis's most remarkable moves has been international growth. With South Korean department store Shinsegae, it trialled a shop within a store in 2012, and plans to repeat this approach. A planned shop at London's Heathrow airport is intended to boost its international profile. Waitrose ventured overseas in 2008 through a licensing agreement with Spinneys of Dubai.
- *Online retailing*. From the start, the company aimed to extend its service ethos to online retailing, which meant ease of use, and reliable and speedy collection and return of items. The online platform is updated often to keep in step with new technology and customer expectations: in 2012, John Lewis spent £40m on it. Collection of items ordered online has been made progressively more convenient. Pick-up points were extended to Waitrose, and now John Lewis has teamed up with a service that will allow collection in the UK from more than 5,000 convenience stores. Online is helping the international push, with John Lewis online now serving 33 countries. Online sales rose by £278m to £958m and profits by 37.2% to £217m in the last financial year.

Adapted from O'Regan and Ghobadian (2012).

Discussion Questions

1 What are the benefits of the logical incremental approach to change used by John Lewis?
2 How might the incremental approach to change sustain the company's competitive advantage?
3 What lessons can be learnt from using an incremental approach to change?

Transformational change

The turbulent nature that characterizes the environmental context of the twenty-first century means that the slow, plodding process of incremental change is not sufficient for all organizations. Instead they rely on transformational change, which aims to redefine an organization's strategic direction, form, cultural assumptions and identity. This kind of change is also referred to as 'strategic', 'radical' or 'revolutionary' (Kanter et al., 1992; Weick and Quinn, 1999). For some organizations this is the only way for change to happen, for as Gersick (1991) points out, fundamental change cannot be accomplished piecemeal, gradually or comfortably. Transformational change can involve a paradigm shift and completely new behaviours not only in one company but also across an entire sector or even country – it means doing things differently rather than doing things better. It might even mean doing different things, such as when Amazon moved from being an e-commerce bookseller, to a content publisher, to a device producer. Similarly, Verizon – the technology communications company – experienced a transformational change when it invested billions in fibre optics to speed up landlines and partnered with Google to deploy Android smartphones, which required substantial change in the company's practices. An example of transformational change that has affected not only an organization or sector, but an entire country, is the case of the Chinese company Alibaba.

CASE EXAMPLE

Alibaba

Shopping in China can be a nightmare. First there are the hazards of simply leaving home – the smog, the traffic and the crowds. Then shoppers have two options: go to a modern shopping mall, where they can buy Western branded goods, made in China, for twice what they would pay for them in the West; or try their luck at the markets, where sellers haggle aggressively, overcharging everyone they can – and they never know if what they are buying is real or fake. What if someone could take this unpleasant experience and make it convenient and quick? This is what Jack Ma did, almost single-handedly, creating an e-commerce juggernaut known as Alibaba. The venture has taken the nightmare of shopping in China and transformed it into a painless, virtual experience, where sellers compete with each other and are rated by shoppers for quality and delivery. What Jack Ma did was to transfer the whole model online. Of course, it has not all been smooth sailing. Taobao – Alibaba's consumer-to-consumer sales portal, which is similar to eBay – has had to crack down on sellers after it gained a reputation for selling counterfeit goods.

Unlike Amazon, Alibaba has no inventory or logistics, and does not sell anything itself, aside from space on its servers and advertising for its search engine. Alibaba has been successful largely because it has leapfrogged offline shopping. Delivery companies run cheap, same-day delivery, and sellers compete in price wars with razor-thin margins, sometimes seemingly content to lose money in exchange for market share. Taobao and Tmall (Alibaba's websites) boast 80% and just over 50% cent of their respective markets.

The first competitor Alibaba saw off was eBay, which dominated China's e-commerce market but faltered when it switched traffic to US servers, resulting in slow performance. Users ditched eBay in droves, leading Ma to quip: 'eBay may be a shark in the ocean, but I am a crocodile in the Yangtze. If we fight in the ocean, we lose, but if we fight in the river, we win.'

Adapted from 'Ma's bazaar', Boldness in Business, *Financial Times*, supplement, March 24 2013.

Transformational change impacts on the deep structure of an organization. The key areas that represent an organization's deep structure are culture, strategy, structure, power distribution and the control systems (Tushman and Romanelli, 1985). Xerox is an example of a company which has gone through transformations that have affected its deep structure. When Anne Mulcahy took over Xerox in 2001, with the company in dire straits and $7.1 billion in debt, she implemented transformational change. Mulcahy restructured the company, downsized from 91,000 to 58,000 employees and made a strategic shift away from the black-and-white printer market. As a result of the transformational change, net earnings increased over 5 years to $1.2 billion.

Such transformational change is often triggered by external factors (see Chapter 5 for a discussion on the drivers for change and transformation). For example, technology innovations, such as Cloud computing, are driving significant change in companies that traditionally own their software and hardware and keep them on the premises in data centres and other specialized facilities. With Cloud computing, companies lease their digital assets, and their employees do not know the location of the computers, data centres, applications and databases that they are using. These resources are 'in the cloud' somewhere. Cloud computing is a sea change – a deep and permanent shift in how computing power is generated and consumed. According to Andrew McFee (2011), Cloud computing is as inevitable and irreversible as the shift from steam to electric power in manufacturing. And just as that transition brought many benefits and opened up new possibilities to factory owners, so too will Cloud confer advantages on it adopters. Another transformational change is 3D printing, also known as additive manufacturing. For instance, Nike and Adidas are embracing 3D printing to speed up their shoemaking process. They are using technology to make multiple prototype versions at a previously impossible speed. So technological advances are being exploited to drive transformational change.

An example of an industry that has implemented transformational change is the travel sector. The travel industry has always been and always will be a huge industry even though it has seen a lot of changes due to the internet. In the past, the only easy way to book a vacation or a business trip was through a travel agent. This has all changed, with so many different websites available that an individual can easily book a trip within a matter of minutes, and that includes booking everything – flight, accommodation, car rental and much more can all be done with a few clicks and a credit card. Travelling has been transformed in other ways, for example with technology such as iPhones and iPads it is easy to check on flight times and delays.

Such transformational changes vary in their magnitude. Flamholtz and Randle (2011) distinguish three types of transformational change:

- *Type 1* transformation occurs when an organization moves from an entrepreneurial to a professional management structure, for example the transformation of Apple Computers from an entrepreneurial company under its founder, Stephen Jobs, to a larger professional company under John Sculley.
- *Type 2* transformation involves the revitalization of an already established company. The organization remains in the same market but focuses on how to rebuild itself in order to operate more effectively. An example of this is Compaq Computers. In the 1990s this company faced a changing environment, including

changes in customer needs. The company re-engineered its operational systems, downsized, lowered its purchase and production costs, and placed more emphasis on teamwork.

- *Type 3* transformation involves change in which the organization fundamentally changes the business in which it is involved, such as the move from print to digital books, which is significantly transforming the publishing industry. The case of SECURICO – one of Zimbabwe's largest security companies – illustrates type 3 transformation.

CASE STUDY

SECURICO

The Harare-based firm SECURICO is a market leader in the provision of bespoke guarding services and electronic security solutions. In just over 15 years of doing business, SECURICO has risen to a $13m (revenues) company with over 3,400 employees – 900 of whom are women. In 2013 it was the winner of the prestigious Legatum Africa Awards for Entrepreneurship.

The company founder and managing director is Divine Ndhlukula, a Zimbabwean national who was keen to start her own business and saw an opportunity in the security services sector. The opportunity was prompted by what Divine had noted as a gap in the market for a quality-oriented security services provider. Divine identified two distinct groups of security organizations that existed at that time: the first group was comprised of the long-established and larger companies – there were about five of them. They had the market to themselves and did not see the need to meet customers' expectations as they could simply rotate the business among themselves in a cartel-like arrangement. The second group was the small emerging or submerging companies that did not have the resource capacity to service big corporations and multinationals. With next to nothing in capital and no security background, just armed with passion and determination to succeed in a predominantly male area, Divine founded SECURICO in 1998 in her small house in Harare, with four employees.

In 2008, at the height of the Zimbabwean economic crisis, SECURICO acquired an electronic security systems company – MULTI-LINK (PVT) LTD – as a going concern. It was transformed into a high-tech installer specializing in the latest innovative and cutting-edge electronic security solutions. The company has since established partnerships with suppliers in South Africa, China, Hong Kong and India. It has grown into the second largest company in Zimbabwe in the provision of electronic security systems such CCTV, access control systems, alarms, remote site monitoring and response services, and electric fences.

SECURICO has set a pace that has transformed the private security business in such a way that its brand has become the flagship. In the past the security industry in Zimbabwe was associated with people who had failed to make it into other careers. This resulted in an industry where employees had low self-esteem, which in turn affected the quality of services that were provided. SECURICO embarked on an initiative to shift this paradigm. This was achieved by a conceptual framework that Divine came up with and implemented in order to change that mindset. The security industry has since been transformed to one that is respectable, professional and one in which people are eager to build their careers.

Adapted from 'Africa's most successful women: Divine Ndhlukula', www.forbes.com (accessed June 2014)

Activity

1 Consider the different types of transformation discussed above. Identify the one that is most common in the organization in which you work or an organization which you are familiar with.

2 Explain why the type of transformation you have chosen is the most common approach used in the organization.

Change as punctuated equilibrium

Rather than focusing on either incremental or transformational change, an alternative position that has gained widespread currency is that more attention needs to be paid to the interplay between incremental and transformational change, which is known as **punctuated equilibrium**. This occurs when change oscillates between long periods of incremental change and short bursts of transformational change that fundamentally alter an organization's strategy, systems and structures (Brown and Eisenhardt, 1997; Gersick, 1991; Tushman and Romanelli, 1985). The inspiration for this approach arose from two sources. The first was from Gould (1978: 15), who, as a natural historian with an interest in Darwin's theory of evolution, argued that the evidence pointed to 'a world punctuated with periods of mass extinction and rapid origination among long stretches of relative tranquility'. The second source was the research of Gersick (1991), who defined the punctuated equilibrium as relatively long periods of stability (equilibrium) punctuated by compact periods of qualitative, metamorphic change (revolution).

A number of case studies offer empirical support for the punctuated equilibrium theory. In a study of AT&T, General Radio, Citibank and Prime Computers, Tushman and colleagues (1986) observed that periods of equilibrium were punctuated by brief periods of intense and pervasive change that led first to the formulation of new missions and then to the initiation of new equilibrium periods. An example of this can be seen in the UK banking systems. Traditionally the banking sector has been seen as cautious and by nature more likely to implement incremental change. Over the first 85 years of the last century, shareholders in the financial sector had a very dull time indeed. That picture was transformed over the next 20 years, when the banking sector made huge excess returns. Most startling of all perhaps was the rapid transformation of the old building societies in the UK, like Northern Rock, Halifax, and Bradford & Bingley. They decided to cash in the equity that had been built up over generations and to maximize value for their new shareholders, just about all of which was lost in the financial crisis that began in 2008. As a result of the crisis, banks had to go through another transformational change – with some moving from being privately owned to being owned by the government and the public.

Those who subscribe to the punctuated equilibrium theory of change argue that transformational episodes may affect a single organization or a whole sector (Abrahamson, 2004). For example, Marks & Spencer is an organization that has been faced several times with the need to reinvent itself when, after a long period of incremental change, it has found itself with declining profits. An example of a whole sector that has been faced with the need to change its deep structure is the publishing industry. In respond to the development of iPads, Kindles and other e-readers, publishing companies have had to change how they produce as well as distribute books.

Not only do organizations and sectors go through periods of continuous incremental and discontinuous transformational change, but also, according to Nadler and Tushman (1995), this pattern of change repeats itself with some degree of regularity. Patterns will vary across sectors, for example periods of discontinuity may follow a 20-year cycle in the education sector, but a two-year cycle in the technology sector. In almost all industries, the rate of change is increasing and the time between periods of discontinuity is decreasing.

Neither incremental nor transformational change works well in isolation. Brown and Eisenhardt (1997) point out that balancing tensions between transformational and incremental change tends to keep an organization 'on the edge of order and chaos' and so helps to sustain its innovative capability. Companies such as 3M or Apple have been able to sustain their innovative capabilities over long periods of time by finding a workable combination. Such organizations systematically invest in a wide variety of low-cost experiments to continuously probe new markets and technologies. They tend to pace the rhythm of change to balance chaos and inertia by applying steady pressure on product development cycles and market launches. They also maintain speed and flexibility by calibrating the size of their business units to avoid both the chaos that is characteristic of too many small units and the inertia that is associated with most large bureaucracies.

This kind of continuous innovation can be found not only in high-tech firms but also in so-called staid academic institutions. While universities may tolerate occasional bursts of transformational change, mostly they hum along, experiencing less-pervasive streams of small changes, here and there, pursuing a process that Eric Abrahamson (2004) has labelled 'dynamic stability'.

Dynamic stability is a process of continual but relatively small change efforts that involve the reconfiguration of existing practices and business models rather than the creation of new ones – what Eric Abrahamson (2004) refers to as 'tinkering' or 'kludging' (tinkering on a bigger scale), which are different from each other in scale. Dynamic stability requires implementing the transformational and incremental changes at the right level and right pace. Abrahamson (2004) cites the example of Lou Gestner who, at IBM, American Express Travel Related Services (TRS) and RJR Nabusco knew when to implement transformational change and when it was time to rest. At TRS he tinkered constantly to prevent the company from drifting into inertia; he played with the structure, with the compensation system and with TRS product offerings. But the unthreatening nature of the interim changes allowed the company to absorb more effectively new product launches and restructures when they were implemented. Managers and leaders are therefore confronted with an ever-greater need to manage between incremental and transformational change.

Focus of change

The third dimension of the organizational change typology is the focus of change, which can be *strategic* or *operational*. Pettigrew and colleagues (1992) distinguish between operational change as small-scale and relatively unimportant and strategic change as major and important structural changes. Similarly, De Wit and Meyer emphasize the difference between operational and strategic change in the following terms:

> Strategic changes have an impact on the way the firm does business (its business systems) and on the way the organization has been configured (its organizational system). In short, while operational changes are necessary to maintain the business and organizational systems, strategic changes are directed at renewing it. (2004: 163)

Strategic change includes restructures, mergers or acquisitions (which we discuss in Chapter 9). For example, PepsiCo made a strategic change through its largest international acquisition by purchasing Wimm-Bill-Dann Foods, a Russian food company that produces milk, yogurt, fruit juices and dairy products. It became the largest food and beverage company in Russia.

Operational change involves anything affecting day-to-day operations. For instance, when Apple replaced their acrylic displays that had information about the product with interactive iPad 2 displays, this was an operational change.

De Wit and Meyer (2004) acknowledge a tendency amongst commentators to depict revolutionary or radical change as strategic and evolutionary or incremental change as operational. However, Burke (2002: 67) suggests that 'more than 95 percent of organizational changes are evolutionary'. Other writers point out how the various approaches can be used in combination. Kotter (1996), for example, sees strategic change as comprising a series of large and small projects aimed at achieving the same overall objectives but which are begun at different times, can be managed differently and can vary in nature. This is also identified by Kanter et al. (1992) when discussing what they term 'long marches' and 'bold strokes'. They argue that bold strokes often have to be followed by a whole series of smaller-scale changes over a more extended timescale (long marches) in order to embed the changes brought about by the bold stroke. Consequently, as Burnes (2009) points out, when considering strategic changes, leaders and managers should be aware that they may have different elements at different levels, and at different times.

Pettigrew and Whipp (1993) propose a model for managing strategic and operational change that involve five interrelated factors:

1. *Environmental assessment* – organizations, at all levels, need to develop the ability to collect and utilize information about their external and internal environments.
2. *Leading change* – this requires the creation of a positive climate for change, the identification of future directions and the linking together of action by people at all levels in the organization.
3. *Linking strategic and operational change* – this is a two-way process of ensuring that intentional strategic decisions lead to operational changes and that emergent operational change influences strategic decisions.
4. *Human resources as assets and liabilities* – just as the pool of knowledge, skills and attitudes possessed by an organization is crucial to its success, it can also be a threat to the organization's success if the combination is inappropriate or managed poorly.

5. *Coherence of purpose* – this concerns the need to ensure that the decisions and actions that flow from the above four factors complement and reinforce each other.

For his part, not to be outdone by Pettigrew and Whipp's five factors, Dawson puts forward 15 'major practical guidelines which can be drawn from a processual analysis of managing organizational transitions' (1994: 179). These guidelines range from the need to maintain an overview of the dynamics and long-term process of change, to the need to take a total organizational approach to managing change. Such advice from the processualist-analytical camp has been criticized as being ' too general or cursory in nature and thus difficult to apply' (Burnes, 2009a: 386). Such critics tend to favour the more prescriptive camp has providing more substantial guidance to managers. However, these too can have their limitations, as we discuss in later chapters.

Level of change

The fourth dimension of the organizational change typology is the level of the change process, which can be at an *individual, group, team,* or *organization* level. The targets for this dimension of change tend to be behaviour, skills, knowledge and attitudes. Although the three levels are related, changes affecting each require different strategies and tactics. In addition, this dimension of change can often act like a 'waterfall'. What this means is that, if the target of change is the organization as a whole, the change intervention will frequently 'waterfall' (cascade) down to the teams that make up the organization. If the target of change is the team, the change initiative will frequently waterfall down to the individuals who make up the team.

The Coca-Cola company – the world's largest beverage company – has implemented organizational changes that have cascaded to different levels of the company. In 2012 the company consolidated leadership of its global operations under the Bottling Investments Group, Coca-Cola International and Coca-Cola Americas. Following this reorganization the company implemented further changes to streamline its focus and expedite its refranchising to independent bottling partners. The North American business was segmented into a traditional company and bottler operating model to suit the needs of the North American market. It consisted of two operating units: Coca-Cola North America and Coca-Cola Refreshments. As a result, a number of leadership changes took place throughout the company, including the Coca-Cola Americas operating structure ceasing to exist.

The business was reorganized to focus on key markets, streamline reporting lines and provide flexibility to adjust the business within these geographies in the future. The changes in Coca-Cola started at the organizational level, filtered down to the leadership team and then to individuals across the company.

Enabling Change

An organization needs to consider how to enable change to be effective. Questions such as the following have to be addressed: What should the pace of change be? Will it be easier if it is introduced quickly or over a longer period of time? How should the change be introduced? What should be the phases or sequencing of it?

We address each of these questions below, beginning with the pace of change.

Pace of change

Some researchers argue that change processes should be pursued at a slow pace while others argue that radical change needs to be made quickly (Beer et al., 1990). Sustainable change needs to be done with 'pace' rather than 'speed', says Steve Holliday, chief executive of the UK's National Grid: 'I think this is about wanting to do things with a bit of pace and urgency' (Prevett, 2013). Netflix is an example of an online company that was driven to implement transformational change with pace and urgency.

Netflix had to transform itself rapidly due to a great deal of negative publicity. Their CEO did a major restructuring and rebranding of the company, focusing on their two lines of businesses: DVD home delivery and video streaming. It was poorly managed, and in October 2011 Netflix announced that it had lost 800,000 US subscribers because of the poorly handled change. Since then Netflix has carried out a major transformation. The company has gone from being a home deliverer of discs to a producer of video content and streamer of video content to the homes of global subscribers, including a voice recognition system named 'max' that quizzes subscribers and gives movie suggestions. It has produced original series such as *House of Cards*, revived the TV series *Arrested Development*, and agreed a deal that involved DreamWorks producing more than 300 hours of original programming for them. By 2014, Netflix had more subscribers than HBO. This is from a company that, only a few years earlier, was a leader in distributing DVDs made by others to the homes of people on a subscription basis. In order to make this transformation the company changed its business model very quickly. Netflix has done what many other companies in the entertainment industry have been unable to do: execute a major change. One of its earlier competitors, Blockbuster, no longer exists because it was unable to do exactly that.

There are, however, those who caution against organizations following such courses of rapid change. Brown and Eisenhardt, (1997) argue that, in the experience of many firms, the whole notion of short, sharp bursts of change is erroneous and lacking. Amis, Slack and Hinings (2004) advocate that rapid change throughout organizations is not only insufficient to bring about radical change but even detrimental to its outcome. The case of Toyota is evidence of what happens when change is introduced too quickly. Toyota had for decades been a model to the whole world of manufacturing excellence and quality production. It seemed unimaginable that it could find itself facing a massive vehicle recall and the accompanying loss of customer trust, but this is what happened. In his written testimony to the US House Oversight Committee in 2011, chief executive Akio Toyoda said, 'I fear the pace at which we have grown may have been too quick' (*Financial Times*, 24 February 2010). Safety had always been the company's top priority, followed by quality and volume. Toyota's mission had become confused in the rapid expansion of the business. It had pursued growth over the development of its people and organization. As the story of Toyota shows, a continual rapid pace of change can be detrimental to a company. It can be difficult to sustain. Instead companies may follow a path of rapid transformational change followed by periods of slower more incremental change. Yet, in some industries companies who fail to match the speed of change may find themselves losing out to competitors.

Michael Schrage (2012) cautions against both moving too fast and moving too slowly. Schrage quotes examples such as Ron Johnson, CEO of JC Penney, as moving too fast and Meg Whitman of Hewlett-Packard, Jack Welch of GE, Bob McDonald of Procter & Gamble, as moving too slowly. This, Schrage says, is in contrast to IBM's Lou Gerstner's practised, cultivated deliberateness, which ensured that the right pace was employed.

So how fast the change is implemented depends on the nature, context and type of change.

Sequencing of change

Sequencing is related to the timing of change but refers specifically to the sequence in which different elements of the change are introduced. The available time for each stage or phase of change can be of importance because changes that are more fundamental require people to learn new behaviours, and often to adjust their norms and values. Such major adjustments take time and can be hindered when changes are implemented too quickly (Gravenhorst et al., 2003) or when there are individual differences and conflicting goals.

Dialectical theories focus on the conflicting goals of those involved in a situation. These conflicts give rise to a reactive sequence, in which one party challenges another party's attempts to secure a particular change. In reactive sequences, subsequent events challenge rather than reinforce earlier events. This may lead to deviations from the intended sequence of events. In some cases, negative reactions may lead only to minor deviations from the intended path but sometimes the reaction can block or radically transform the change. Mahoney (2000) refers to the possibility of a 'backlash' and Pierson (2000) observes that events can trigger counter-reactions that are powerful enough to move the system in a completely new direction.

Self-reinforcing sequences occur when a decision or action produces positive feedback that reinforces earlier events and supports the direction of change. This reinforcement induces further movement in the same direction. While self-reinforcing sequences can deliver benefits over the short term, managers need to be alert to the possibility that they may draw them into a path that will deliver suboptimal outcomes over the longer term. For example, Nokia stuck to a winning formula too long and failed to respond to new opportunities and threats as they emerged. Nokia focused on producing mobile phones (hardware devices) and missed the developments in software, which its competitors such as Apple were involved in. It was in danger of being squeezed out of what was becoming a highly profitable segment of the market. Growing profits from hardware and Nokia's dominant position in the mobile phone market had undermined its success. Just in time Nokia announced a new strategic direction, which involved a partnership with Microsoft to build a new mobile ecosystem. Nokia also announced that the Windows Phone operating system would be its primary smartphone platform (see Hayes, 2014: 11).

Managers need to consider introducing changes sequentially and at different tempos. Some researchers suggest that by implementing high-impact elements first, the symbolic effect on the organization, coupled with system dependencies, will secure the changes in other elements as well (Amis et al., 2004; Hinings and Greenwood, 1988). While other researchers argue that change, such as creating new services or products or entering new markets, needs to be made regularly and rhythmically through what Brown and Eisenhardt (1997) call 'time-pacing'. Time-pacing creates a regular, rhythmic and proactive approach to change that can increase the capacity for change. It gives people a sense of control because change becomes predictable, focused and efficient, and employees become more confident. Despite the regularity of changes, time pacing may not be appropriate for all kinds of organizational changes. Changes related to technological changes or more behaviourally oriented changes are perhaps less suited to being initiated at regular intervals.

As we will see in Chapter 7, several models do advocate a sequential progress of activities (for example, do X first, then Y, and finish the change process with Z), and many even suggest that to miss one step or to fail to do it justice before moving on to the next is a grave error. Yet there is little agreement on what steps should be taken first and what steps should follow. For example, should leaders first create a sense of urgency around the need for change and then set about designing the right change intervention? Or should there be an agreed plan in place before energizing the organization around it? Similarly, when should the phase of institutionalizing the new changes begin: should it be done from the outset or only once a 'critical mass' moment or 'tipping point' has been reached? Or should it be done only once they have been proven to work? When considering different models and theories it is important to examine the presumed sequence implied and why this might be expected to work.

Process-driven or people-driven change?

Organizational change has often been an either/or proposition: either process-driven to create economic value for stakeholders, or people-driven, potentially to develop an open, trusting culture in the long term. Beer and Nohria (2000) say that it is important to consider the extent to which the process of change should be process-driven, which they call Theory E, or person-driven, Theory O.

Theory E, they argue, advocates a process focus – a systems-driven strategy motivated by the need to achieve clear economic gains. The explicit goal of Theory E change is to dramatically and rapidly increase shareholder value, as measured by cash flow and share price. Popular notions of employee participation and the learning organization take a back seat to this over-arching goal. As a financial crisis is usually the catalyst for this approach to change, Theory E proponents rely heavily on mechanisms likely to increase short-term cash flow and share price, such as performance bonuses, headcount reductions, asset sales and strategic reordering of business units. Theory E advocates that all implicit contracts between the company and its employees, such as lifetime employment, are suspended during the change effort. Individual units whose activities fail to demonstrate tangible value creation and return on investment, such as corporate planning or training and development, are particularly vulnerable. With Theory E the CEO and the leadership team drive change from the top.

In contrast, Theory O is a person-driven approach in which organizational capabilities are built by investing in people and creating motivation and commitment. Companies that follow this approach attempt to invigorate their cultures and capabilities through individual and organizational learning. This approach was employed by Johnson & Johnson in 1990s when the company's performance was flagging. The Theory O approach requires high levels of employee participation, flatter **organizational structures** and strong bonds between the organization and its staff. As employee commitment to change and improvement are vital for Theory O change to work, implicit contracts with employees are considered too important to break – quite the opposite of what happens with Theory E. Leaders who advocate Theory O change are less interested in driving the success themselves than in encouraging participation from employees and in fostering employee behaviours and attitudes that will sustain change.

So which is the best theory to adopt? Unfortunately neither approach guarantees success. Theory E, which aims for rapid improvements in profitability, often succeeds in the short run but does so at the expense of future vitality. By reducing employee roles, it often leaves survivors demoralized. Any commitment employees had to the company may evaporate and the talent the company had hoped to retain are often the first to snap up redundancy packages and look for a job in another company. Theory O is not an ideal solution either. Reorientating corporate culture around employee commitment and learning is a noble endeavour but a long-term proposition. A successful programme may produce smarter, more adaptive employees in four to five years but companies that really need change cannot wait that long for results. Beer and Nohria (2000) conclude the best approach is a mix of Theory E and Theory O. For change in organizations is rarely black or white but more a fusion of different colours. Instead, the authors advocate that:

> Companies that effectively combine hard and soft approaches to change can reap big payoffs in profitability and productivity ... Those companies are more likely to achieve a sustainable competitive advantage [and] ... reduce the anxiety that grips whole societies in the face of corporate restructuring. (2000: 134).

General Electric (GE) is an example of a company that has employed both approaches in turn. When former CEO Jack Welsh took over he initially implemented a host of redundancies and got rid of under-performing work units through draconian Theory E methods. He then followed with Theory O change initiatives designed to improve the competitiveness of the company's culture by making it faster, less bureaucratic and more customer-focused. Companies that combine both theories can achieve huge benefits in profitability and productivity.

To help you think through the pros and cons of each theory, Table 2.1 summarizes the two archetypal change approaches and their combination in terms of key factors.

The models and approaches outlined in this chapter are all useful in capturing aspects of a complex whole. They do, however, need to be adapted to the context in which they are being applied.

Table 2.1 Key factors in Theory E and Theory O change – adapted from Beer and Nohria (2000)

Dimensions of change	Theory E	Theory O	Theories E and O combined
Goals	Maximize shareholder value.	Develop organizational capabilities.	Embrace differences between economic value and organizational capability.
Leadership	Manage change from top down.	Encourage participation from bottom up.	Set direction from tope and engage people below.
Focus	Emphasize structure and systems.	Build corporate culture.	Focus on structures, systems, and culture.
Process	Plan and establish programmes.	Experiment and evolve.	Plan for spontaneity.
Reward system	Motivate through financial incentives.	Motivate through commitment.	Use incentives to reinforce change but not to drive it.
Use of consultants	Analyse problems and shape solutions.	Support management in shaping their own solutions.	Expert resources who empower employees.

Implications for leaders and managers

Consider what kind of change is needed

Beyond the issue of what kind of change is needed and when it should be introduced, managers and leaders need to consider how to enable change to be effective. This involves choices to be considered such as the sequence and pace of the change, as well as how to develop a people and process driven approach.

Review the sequence of the change

A change process involves a number of events, decisions and actions that are connected in a sequence. They are connected in the sense that each event is influenced by earlier events and also helps to shape subsequent events. In the sequence A>B>C>D>E, event B is both a response to event A and a factor that shapes event C, which in turn affects D and so on. The way an earlier event will impact later events depends on how others respond.

Several models do advocate a sequential progress of activities (for example, do A first, then B, and finish the change process with E), and many models even suggest that to miss one step or to fail to do it justice before moving on to the next is a grave error. Yet there is little agreement on what steps should be taken first and what should follow. When considering different models and theories it is important to examine the presumed sequence implied and why this might be expected to work.

Pace of change

Along with the sequence of change, managers and leaders also need to identify the pace of change. As outlined in this chapter, fast-paced changes will contribute in releasing more energy. On the other hand, changes that are made too quickly may constrain problem-solving and adaptation to the new situation. Slow-paced change facilitates learning and allows all organizational members time to understand what needs to be changed and how. When done effectively, slow-paced incremental change can be a crucial part of short-term success. However, if a change process takes too long, the change may lose salience and people will not notice anything happening. A slow pace can also allow time for mobilization of power and increased resistance, which is often one of the main arguments behind implementing large-scale changes as rapidly as possible. Fast-paced change over a long period may also lead to change fatigue. So how fast the change is implemented depends on the nature, context and type of change.

When considering what kind of change is needed and the magnitude, focus and pace of it, you also need to take into account the organization's readiness and need for the change, which we discuss in the following chapter.

Discussion Questions

1 As an employee, would you prefer to work in an organization that favoured a planned approach to change or an emergent approach to change?
2 How realistic do you think it is to categorize types of change within an organization? What might be the advantages and disadvantages?
3 Is there a change theory that you have greatest affinity with? Explain why.
4 What are the implications of what you have learnt in this chapter for how you might design a change initiative?

Activity

1 Identify an organizational change that you are aware of, either in an organization in which you are working or in an organization you are familiar with (such as your university, a sports club, church, mosque or similar organization).

   a. Choose one of the change theories discussed in this chapter that best describes the type of change the organization went through or is going through.
   b. Discuss why this theory is the most appropriate.

2 Using the internet, find two companies that have undergone change and describe them in terms of types of change they have used. Were they successful? Why or why not? What could they have done differently?
3 Look at the business section of a recent newspaper and see how many references to change you find. What are the similarities? What type of change are they describing?

Further reading

Diefenbach, T. (2007) 'The managerialistic ideology of organizational change management', *Journal of Organizational Change*, 20(1): 126–44.

Ghobadian, A. (2013) 'Growth by small-change innovation: John Lewis' logical incremental style', *Financial Times*, July 23, p. 12.

Miles, R.H. (2010) 'Accelerating corporate transformations (Don't lose your nerve!)', *Harvard Business Review*, 88(1/2): 68–75.

Plowman, D.A., Baker, L.T., Beck, T.E., Kulkarni, M., Solansky, S.T. and Travis, D.V. (2007) 'Radical change accidentally: The emergence and amplification of small change', *Academy of Management Journal*, 50(3): 515–43.

Reeves, M. and Deimler, M. (2011) 'Adaptability: The new competitive advantage', *Harvard Business Review*, 89(7/8): 134–41.

Toms, W.M., Kovacs, E.B. and Immordino, K.M. (2011) 'Planned radical change in organizations: Unintended consequences on roles and continuity', *Journal of Enterprise Transformation*, 1: 98–118.

Zakaria, F. (2008) *The Post-American World*. London: Allen Lane.

Leading Change

3

Overview

- Leading change is one of the most challenging functions and requirements of leaders in organizations. It entails showing the way and helping or inducing others to pursue it.
- We present a model of six core themes and practices of leadership that attempts to integrate the diverse and fragmented body of existing leadership research and theories under one umbrella as an over-arching model. We describe how this model can help to understand and carry out sustainable organizational change and transformation. The six core themes and practices in leading change concern vision, purpose, values, strategy, empowerment and engagement, which are each explained and illustrated in turn.
- Effective leaders of change define and communicate a valid and appealing vision of the future. A vision for change is the state that the organization wants or needs to achieve as the outcome of the change. The chapter discusses why organizations have a vision for change, and why it is necessary to have one, its characteristics, and how a vision for change can be developed and implemented.
- Effective leaders of change define and communicate a valid and appealing purpose for change. We describe how effective leaders are people who evoke a clear, consistent purpose for change that attracts followers. We summarize research findings on purpose in relation to change in organizations. The characteristics of well-crafted and useful statements of purpose, their development and their linkage to vision, values and strategy are explained.
- Effective leaders of change identify, display, promote and reinforce shared values that inform and support the vision, purpose and strategies for change. Values are principles or standards that are considered to be important or beneficial, and moral or ethical values are those that are deemed to be 'good' or 'bad' or 'right' as opposed to 'wrong'. We describe how values are part of organizational culture, which may need to be strengthened through change or itself changed. Change initiatives must reflect and be informed by the organization's core

values, and we discuss the key values required in the leadership of organizational change and transformation.

- Effective leaders of change develop, communicate and implement rational strategies for change that are informed by shared values. The chapter discusses the nature of strategy as applied in organizational change and transformation programmes and how strategies for change are developed.
- Effective leaders of change empower people to be *able to do* what needs to be done. Empowerment is giving people the knowledge, skills, self-confidence, opportunity, freedom, authority and resources to manage themselves in a change programme and be accountable for their performance. We discuss issues that arise in seeking to empower people, and review key findings from research into empowerment that have implications for sustainable change.
- Effective leaders of change engage people in the change effort by influencing, motivating and inspiring them to *want to do* what needs to be done. Engaging people in a change effort is perhaps the most difficult part of leading organizational change but of critical importance to its success and sustainability. Managers and employees who are engaged with an organizational change initiative devote discretionary effort to it willingly, even eagerly. The ability to engage people requires the appropriate use of power, which in turn requires an understanding of human motivation and satisfaction. It also requires behavioural skills, in particular the skills of inspirational speech.
- Engagement of employees encourages **creativity**, and innovation is a potential and desirable outcome of creativity. The key to success in encouraging creativity and thereby enabling innovation is *learning* from failure and then putting the lessons into practice.
- Transformational leadership research and theory have much to offer leaders of change, particularly with respect to empowerment and engagement of themselves, managers and employees in the change process.
- The chapter concludes with a brief comment on applications of the leadership model, implications and questions for leaders involved in organizational change and transformation, and how leading change and managing change are different but mutual processes: each is necessary, but neither is sufficient alone.

Learning objectives

By the end of this chapter you will be able to explain:

- Why understanding the nature of leadership can help us to carry out sustainable organizational change and transformation
- The six core themes and practices of leading change: vision, purpose, shared values, strategy, empowerment and engagement
- How to apply the leadership model for sustainable change
- How leading change and managing change are different but mutual processes: each is necessary, but neither is sufficient alone

Why effective leadership and management are critical to sustainable change

Leading change is one of the most challenging functions and requirements of leaders in organizations. 'Our organizations are littered with the debris ... of yesterday's [change] initiatives,' said Andrew Mayo (2002). The reason for this, we contend, is most likely a lack of effective leadership: good management of change is necessary (as we will see in Chapter 4), but it is not sufficient (Gill, 2003). Management needs effective leadership to be effective: 'Change is created, inspired, explored and embraced by leaders' (CCL, 2012).

John Kotter says:

> In failed transformations, you often find plenty of plans and directives and programs ... [with] procedures, goals, methods, and deadlines. But nowhere was there a clear and compelling statement [a vision] of where all this was leading. Not surprisingly, most of the employees with whom I talked were either confused or alienated. [The 'managerial' approach alone] did not rally them together or inspire change. In fact, [it] probably had just the opposite effect ... (Kotter, 1990a)

Patricia McLagan points out that taking a purely rational and technical approach to change, 'making sure it's technically sound and offers economic advantage to the organization', tends to lead to the false assumption that the organization will naturally absorb change (McLagan, 2002). In his classic statements on management and leadership, John Kotter says that management produces orderly results that keep something working efficiently, whereas leadership creates useful change; neither is necessarily better or a replacement for the other (1990a, 1990b). Both are needed if organizations and nations are to prosper, but he makes this distinction:

> Management's mandate is to minimize risk and to keep the current system operating. Change, by definition, requires creating a new system, which in turn always demands leadership. (1990a)

> The simple insight that management is not leadership ... is better understood today [November 2012], but not nearly as well as is needed. Management makes a system work. It helps you do what you know how to do. Leadership builds systems or transforms old ones. It takes you into territory that is new and less well known, or even completely unknown to you. (Kotter, 2012b: vii)

Anne Stoughton and James Ludema (2012) highlight the crucial role of leadership in infusing a culture of sustainability. They point out that top-level leaders in organizations provide a framework for sustainable change by communicating their commitment to it, adopting reporting systems and prioritizing issues for attention. But they also demonstrate how middle-management leadership is important too: middle managers need to adopt new ways of thinking and behaving to translate the organization's vision for change into action. Furthermore, Stoughton and Ludema argue that employees at large 'need to adopt and internalize the new practices in order to make them effective'. All in all, this 'holistic web of power and influence is how ... [sustainable] change happens'. Moreover, change can be initiated anywhere in the organization – at any level – and permeate downwards, laterally and even upwards.

Dean Anderson and Linda Ackerman Anderson (2010a) argue, in a call for 'conscious **change leadership**', that a cohesive change process that leads to change that is sustainable is achieved only through addressing mindset, culture, behaviour and systems. That effective and sustainable change is characterized by effective leadership as well as management is illustrated and endorsed by Dean Anderson and Linda Ackerman Anderson (2010a) in their successful multi-dimensional, process approach to organizational change that focuses on organizational, team, relational and individual levels. They also provide a highly acclaimed 'how to' guide to using their methodology, with praise for it from Microsoft, Group Healthcare Cooperative, PeaceHealth, the US House of Representatives and many others (Anderson and Anderson, 2010b).

What is change leadership?

What is meant by 'leadership' is still contested: there is no commonly accepted definition and there are therefore many different views put forward by scholars and practitioners alike that have led to confusion (Gill, 2011: 2–11). For the sake of clarity, we use a general definition of leadership proposed by Gill (2011: 8–9) that reflects its etymology: 'leadership is showing the way and helping or inducing others to pursue it'.

We argue that leading change and transformation effectively – showing the way and helping or inducing others to pursue it – entails envisioning and communicating a desirable future as a result of the change, promoting a clear purpose for the change, supportive values, intelligent strategies for the change effort, empowering those involved in leading or managing change to be *able to do* what needs to be done, and engaging all those concerned to *want to do* what needs to be done. This is a model for leading change and transformation that we now elaborate.

A model of leadership for sustainable change

A model of six core themes and practices of leadership has been proposed that attempts to recognize and integrate the diverse and fragmented body of existing leadership research and theories under one umbrella as an over-arching model (Gill, 2011). The model's six core themes and practices comprise vision, purpose (or mission), values, strategy, empowerment and engagement (see Figure 3.1). The chapter discusses how these six core leadership themes and practices may help to explain, enable and establish effective and sustainable organizational change and transformation.

Leadership, change and vision

Effective leaders define and communicate a valid and appealing vision of the future (Gill, 2011: 108). Effective leadership is the key to making change effective because it provides the vision and the rationale for change (Seel, 2000). People want to know the reason for change, as Arleen Tony says:

> People are looking for meaning in what they do, no matter what kind of organization it is or what benefits they receive from it, people still want reasons for what they do. (2007: 47)

What is a vision for change?

Vision, according to the *Concise Oxford English Dictionary*, is 'a mental image of what the future will or could be like'; it involves 'the ability to think about or plan the future with imagination or wisdom' (Soanes and Stevenson, 2004: 1615). Vision defines what

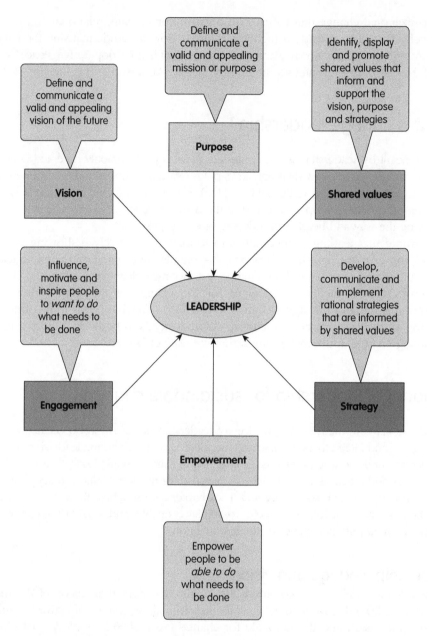

Figure 3.1 A model of six core themes and practices of effective leadership (Gill, 2011: 101)

or where the organization wants or needs to be. It is a statement of the likely, necessary or desired future of a group, organization or nation. Vision is fundamental to effective leadership and, at the corporate level, is the driving force for all organizational change in the organization. A vision for change is the state that the organization wants or needs to achieve as the outcome of the change.

James Kouzes and Barry Posner (1991: 135) depict vision as the 'magnetic north', and Stephen Covey (1992: 96) suggests that a vision provides a 'compass' for people in the organization. We need to keep this compass in view at all times for a clear sense of direction in our change efforts.

Why have a vision for change?

Jill Strange and Michael Mumford (2002), in reviewing vision studies, concluded that a vision serves five purposes:

- Specifying direction, purpose and uniqueness of a venture
- Providing a motivational force by organizing action around an evocative future goal
- Providing a meaning for the work that needs to be done and a sense of identity
- Enabling coordination of activities by providing a framework for action
- Providing a basis for developing [new] norms and structures

Envisioning the future is not just a cognitive or intellectual exercise but an emotional – and motivational – one too. Psychologist Scott Cole (2013) says:

> The act of mentally envisioning ... a hypothetical future scenario, or of ... envisioning a single event set in a specific time and place in the future ... has become a hive of psychological activity ... Recent work on mental time has found that when asked to rate the emotion of past and future events, [people] judge future events as more emotionally positive than past events.

Cole suggests that the probable reason for the optimism about the future is that put forward by Dorthe Berntsen and Annette Bohn (2010), namely that 'positive future bias maintains a sense of motivation, driving us toward novel experiences'. Envisioning the future can – and should – be motivational. A vision for change therefore can, and should, be motivational. In what way?

Characteristics of an effective vision for change

A vision for change has to be aligned to the needs and expectations of the organization's stakeholders. Where strongly held personal visions are not aligned among a number of individuals, they will resort to political means to pursue their own visions. This will leave the organization without a sense of direction and less capable of responding to the need for the change (Van der Heijden, 1993: 142). Positioning the organization for change is essential to the leadership role (Flanagan, 2000).[1] Warren Bennis says that is not just a matter of communicating the vision – explaining or clarifying it – but creating the meaningfulness of intentions (Bennis, 2010: 20), in respect of both the organization as a whole and change initiatives within it.

Visions for change must have an explicit ethical or moral component to them (Nanus, 1992); they must be in line with corporate values, says Lindsay Levin,

---

1 Sir Ronnie Flanagan was Chief Constable, Royal Ulster Constabulary (which was replaced by the Police Service of Northern Ireland) during a period of significant change and later Chief Inspector of Constabulary of the UK (excluding Scotland).

Chairman of the Whites Group (Levin, 2000). Visions may even be expressed in terms of values: Kees Van der Heijden (1993: 137–50) quotes the example of Levi Strauss's vision – 'To be a company that our people are proud of'. Stephen Zaccaro and Deanna Banks (2001: 188) suggest that the ethical and moral aspects are perhaps the most important features of a vision. Boas Shamir (1995) shows how a vision is most effective when it is congruent with followers' personal values. Subordinates or followers judge vision in terms of what is 'good' and 'right'. And values (which we discuss further later), are central to vision because they create passion and conviction about it (Senge, 1990).

According to the long-standing view of John Kotter (2012b: 74), a good vision in general has six characteristics:

- Imaginable – conveying a picture of what the future will look like
- Desirable – appealing to the long-term interests of all stakeholders
- Feasible – realistic and attainable
- Focused – clear enough to provide guidance in making decisions
- Flexible – general enough to allow individual initiative and differing responses in the light of changing conditions
- Communicable – easy to communicate and explainable effectively within 5 minutes)

In particular, a good vision for change:

- Is a coherent and powerful statement of what the 'future state' can and should be
- Builds a compelling case for change, showing how it supports business goals
- Clearly establishes both a direction and a destination
- Describes a realistic and credible future state
- Is flexible and able to adapt to changing circumstances
- Is translatable into actions by managers and employees that will produce tangible results
- Is compatible with, indeed is informed by, the core values of the organization

There has to be some compelling need, whether from inside or outside the organization, that provides the 'push' from the current state, and there has to be some solution – how the organization will respond to that 'push' – to reach a new, future state. A good vision for change captures all these elements.

Getting commitment to a vision for change is 'part and parcel' of the process of engaging people in the work and future of the organization or nation. John Kotter and Lorne Whitehead say:

> Anyone who is trying to help an organization, public or private, to go through large-scale change ... needs to communicate the new vision in a way that helps people not simply to understand it but to buy into it. (Kotter and Whitehead, 2010; Chynoweth, 2010a: 4)

This means *emotional commitment*, as well as intellectual understanding as a result of 'winning hearts and minds'. Reasoning using data and logic is no substitute for appealing to people's feelings: neither is sufficient on its own; both are necessary. The goal is gaining people's commitment to a vision so that it becomes a *shared* vision for change. Kotter (1997) makes the important point that, for organizational change, only an approach based on vision works in the long term. He says a shared vision:

- Clarifies the direction of change and ensures that everything that is done – new product development, acquisitions, recruitment campaigns – is in line with it
- Motivates people to take action in the right direction
- Helps to align individuals and coordinate their actions efficiently

Joed Carbonell-López (2013) says that lack of a clear vision for the organization leads to a sense of being lost, of not even knowing the destination: 'Without vision, a people perish', the Bible notes (Proverbs 29: 18). Vision must be communicated to people in a way that they can relate to in respect of their role in the organization (Patterson and Winston, 2006). A vision for change has the same requirements. In Chapter 7 we discuss the **Fionnphort model**, which helps us to analyse and close gaps between what people say and what they do, including a lack of understanding or clarity about direction of change – the vision for change.

Dennis Gioia and colleagues (2012) make the case for ambiguity in expressing future aspirations as visions specifically in the context of initiating major organizational *strategic* change because doing so 'enables a sense of alignment between local and larger organizational goals that eases the political path to successful change'. Ambiguous vision statements, they say, help rather than hinder strategic change. However, Gregory Shea and Cassie Solomon (2013a: Chapter 1) disagree. They say:

> A detailed, even granular, vision of the future can dramatically increase the odds of getting there. Abstract or ephemeral visions wrapped up in corporate speak do not. A specific vision can provide local meaning. It can clarify communication, motivate and direct action, aid planning, facilitate debriefing, guide revising, and revitalize by occasioning celebration of progress. Above all, a specific behavioral vision helps change leaders redesign the work environment to foster the behaviors and the change. (2013a: 16–17)

In settling this disagreement we need to separate the two ideas: the vision for the organization (or for the department, product, service, etc.) and the vision for change. The vision for the organization can be more abstract, though not couched in clichés or 'corporate speak'. It should nevertheless be appealing, better still inspiring. Yet it should provide not only for alignment between local and organization-wide goals during strategic change but also for long-term development of the organization without compromising its core values and purpose. The vision for change needs to be meaningful and therefore motivating but behaviourally be more specific, for example in terms of what people will be doing better or differently, and it should also support and facilitate pursuit of the over-arching organizational vision.

Why is a vision for change necessary?

Having a dynamic and inclusive vision for an organization is associated with its success. For example, Sydney Finkelstein and colleagues (2007: 145–6, 156–64) describe how Harley–Davidson transformed itself from industry follower on the verge of collapse to thriving industry leader through revitalizing its vision, purpose and consequential strategies.

A vision of change can determine survival. Examples of national visions for transformation are Malaysia's and Nigeria's. In the 1980s, then Prime Minister Mohamed Mahathir's 'Vision 2020'[2] for Malaysia was that Malaysia would be a fully developed nation by 2020 according to OECD criteria in respect of literacy, education and health. And the Nigerian government's 'Vision 2020' for the nation in 2008 was:

> By 2020 Nigeria will be one of the 20 largest economies in the world, able to consolidate its leadership role in Africa and establish itself as a significant player in the global economic and political arena. (Government of Nigeria, 2008)

A vision for change is necessary because it is the driving force for change.

Developing and implementing a vision for change

A vision is not the preserve of top management only, but a feature of effective leadership at any level, in any function, in an organization. The nature and content of visions vary at different levels, in different functions and for different kinds of change in any organization but they must be compatible with, and support, the overall corporate vision for there to be a shared sense of unity. The top-level leader or board of directors defines a broad, long-term (often ambiguous) vision for change or transformation and translates it into specific organizational strategies. The middle-level leader translates the organizational vision into a departmental vision or goals and more short-term strategies. And the lower-level leader in turn translates these goals and strategies into more short-term goals and operational plans and tasks (Kotter, 1990a; Kelly, 1993).

Developing a vision for change involves the following steps.

1. Clarify the need for the change

This addresses what is wrong with the way we are now, and what the *drivers for change* are. There may be obvious problems with the current state, such as out-of-date technology or high levels of employee turnover. Or the drivers may be external, such as customers demanding faster or better service, or a threat from competitors. The driver may be one over which the business has no control, such as a change in legislation with which the company must comply. Whatever the drivers are, they need to be captured in a way that makes it clear why the current state is unacceptable and organizational change is necessary. We elaborate the need and drivers for change in Chapters 5 and 6.

2. Describe the future state and its benefits

The more detailed you can make this description the better, although at the start of a change process it may have to be fairly high level. One way of doing this is to look at different aspects of the organization, and make a comparison between now and the future (for an overview of the Future–Present model see Chapter 6). Other ways of

---

2 An apt metaphor: '20/20' vision in optometry represents perfect vision.

defining the future state include a 'story board' showing an end-to-end process, such as the new start-to-finish of a customer transaction, or, for example, 'A day in the life of a customer agent', after the change is complete.

This process may include designing new ways of working, such as mapping and redesigning processes. Workshops or focus groups can be used to enable you to develop this aspect of the change in more detail. Involving people who are affected by the change will help ensure that your future state definition is realistic, as well as starting to engage people in the change process. When doing this type of analysis, you need to start thinking about what new skills and behaviours will be needed and how they will be developed. What training and support will need to be built into the project plan? Management skills, as well as the operational skills needed by front-line employees, may need to be developed.

3. Identify what the change will mean to the people involved. How will their lives change?

The business benefits of the change will have to be identified at the outset in order to justify going ahead with the project (we discuss this further in Chapter 13). Benefits to the business, while clearly important to employees in the long term, may not seem initially attractive in view of the disruption and uncertainty involved in the change. So you need to focus more closely on what it will mean for employees – 'what's in it for them'.

4. Outline the path for transition between the current and desired states

This will enable you to identify the actions you will need to build into your implementation plan (the force field analysis can be helpful for this – see Chapter 6). The step is particularly important if some of the changes are perceived as negative.

5. Assess and reinforce the power and relevancy of the change vision

Identify any significant shortcomings in the vision, the need for change, or the way the vision is currently understood. These will need to be addressed for the change to succeed. Some tools and techniques for this include:

- Visioning workshops with leaders and senior managers to help them to understand and agree the nature of the compelling need and to build and articulate a shared vision for change
- Senior management interviews to check their visions for the change, the consistency of these visions and to assess the level of management resolve
- Analysis of the organization's performance and the reasons behind that performance to identify the most important levers for change
- Management workshops to help promulgate the vision for change and gain additional information and buy-in from others in the organization once the vision is clear and you are ready to engage others in the organization with it
- Communication planning to identify key messages and appropriate communication methods (see Chapter 10 for some practical tips for developing a communication plan)

Engaging other people in developing a vision for the organization (or any part of it) increases the likelihood that it will be embraced by them (Kohles, 2012), and this is true for a vision for change too. Perhaps nowhere is this more important than in global or multinational organizations operating in different cultures – and especially in military coalitions. Carbonell-López (2013) gives the example of the vision of a safe and secure Afghanistan that was shared by the 42-nation International Security Assistance Force and had to be shared for any action to be effective and not dysfunctional.

Carla Miller and colleagues (2012) say that leaders of change not only need to have a vision for the change but also must make sure that the vision becomes a reality through setting priorities, compromise and choice – indeed through effective management. However good a vision is, change – at group, organizational, national or global level – can come only through effective implementation of the vision. This entails adequate resources and effective management, which we discuss in the next chapter, on managing change.

Discussion Questions

1   How can you create a vision for change that all stakeholders share?
2   How can you ensure that the people affected by or involved in the change understand and are committed to the vision for change?

A vision for change without purpose is doomed to fail. To be effective, vision for change has to be translated first into a mission or purpose for the organization, or part of it, and then into specific goals or objectives and action plans. Next, therefore, we consider sustainable change in relation to leadership and purpose.

Leadership, change and purpose

Effective leaders define and communicate a valid and appealing purpose (Gill, 2011: 136). As with vision, while this statement refers generally to the organization (or group or nation) as whole, it equally refers to a change or transformation in the organization. 'Purpose is preparation for doing what is right and what is worthwhile,' says Nikos Mourkogiannis (2006: 16) in a seminal book on purpose. Together with vision, it is the organization's *animus* – its driving force – for change. Effective leaders, Mourkogiannis (2006: 43) says, are people who 'evoke a clear, consistent purpose [for change] that attracts followers'.

The *Concise Oxford Dictionary* defines 'purpose' as 'the reason for which something is done or for which something exists ... resolve or determination' (Soanes and Stevenson, 2004: 1167). The UK's Chartered Institute of Personnel and Development (CIPD) defines an organization's purpose as '[its] identity, the reason why it exists and the golden thread to which its strategy should be aligned' (CIPD, 2011: 3). We address strategy as a core theme in leading change later in this chapter. The purpose of change, then, is the reason why it is to be carried out or is done.

Are purpose and goals the same? Marshall Goldsmith explains it thus:

> Goals are specific objectives we strive to achieve, usually within defined parameters of space, time and resources. Purpose is the 'why' behind any thought or deed. Purpose is not about achieving a goal – it's more a way of life. Purpose is enduring, whereas goals can be created, adjusted and discarded ... Purpose should be what the goals serve ... a greater overarching aim, one that benefits all stakeholders. (2008)

A sense of shared purpose for an organization should extend to all stakeholders, including, of course, employees. Shared or common purpose, however, is a regrettably rare phenomenon, according to Joel Kurtzman (2010), but it can be achieved and recognized:

> [Common purpose is displayed] when a leader coalesces a group, team, or community into a creative, dynamic, brave, and nearly invincible we. It happens the moment the organization's values, tools, objectives, and hopes are internalized in a way that enables people to work tirelessly toward a goal. (2010: xii)

The chief executive of the UK's National Grid, Steve Holliday, clearly understood the practical leadership challenge in organizational change. Creating and communicating a clear vision of what they are trying to achieve and then disseminating the message throughout the company is, Holliday, says, the role of a leader:

> To move the whole organization in one direction, you go on and on communicating that message and enthusing people, and explaining why that's the right thing to do. (Prevett, 2013)

Research in the UK by the CIPD (2011: 18) revealed that a sense of shared purpose of an organization is strengthened when shared values, objectives and actions are integrated into employees' goals as part of a performance management process. The implication is that this should also apply to change initiatives. A shared purpose is even more important in periods of uncertainty and change. In contrast to this, a sense of shared organization-wide purpose may be weakened by changes in the organization's environment such as globalization or when there are competing goals or conflict between departments in the organization. This requires, the CIPD (2011: 19) says, 'leaders ... to reassert the wider organizational purpose and ... vision [of the future]'. Changes in the environment, of course, may well call for change within the organization, and such change always needs to be initiated and conducted in the context of the wider organizational purpose (and vision).

The CIPD says: 'Shared purpose is closely aligned to both leadership and engage-ment' (CIPD, 2011: 20). In our model of leadership, shared purpose and engagement are not merely 'aligned' to leadership but are core themes and practices in effective leadership and in leading change in particular.

The CIPD research identifies three benefits of a strong sense of shared organiza-tional purpose, which also apply specifically to the purpose of change initiatives (CIPD, 2009a: 5):

- High levels of employee engagement through absorbing and meaningful work, motivation and commitment to the organization – a sense of shared purpose is strongest, the CIPD also says, when employees develop an emotional relationship with the organization's purpose (CIPD, 2011: 17), which again also applies to a purpose of change.
- A strong sense of community – a shared purpose engenders collaborative working.
- Effective teams – fostering both 'local' team spirit and 'global' commitment and enabling distributed leadership.

Characteristic drivers of a truly shared purpose, according to the 2009 CIPD research (2009a: 4), are:

- The purpose is invigorating – it is uplifting and deliverable.
- The purpose is brought to life through using crafted language and storytelling.
- The purpose is at the heart of the organization's vision and strategy [and the vision and strategy for change].
- Employees are consulted on key issues and decisions.
- Employees understand what is expected of them, receive clear performance feedback, receive coaching and discuss their training and development needs.
- Other common practices – such as quality management – exist in the organization and transcend functional and physical boundaries.

In two pieces of action research on leadership in strategic business units, Leopold Vansina (1988, 1999) found that successful general managers engaged in large-scale organizational change 'direct their efforts towards the "embodiment of purpose" within the *whole* company', shaping or strengthening corporate identity. Major structural or strategic change, such as a merger or acquisition, requires a review of corporate direction (vision) and identity (purpose) (Mourkogiannis, 2006: 21–2).

Intrinsic to a sense of purpose for change is resolve or determination (Soanes and Stevenson, 2004: 1167), and, often associated with this purposefulness, a sense of urgency, which is often lacking. According to John Kotter (2012b: viii):

> The problems created by complacency ..., and the power of a sense of urgency, are bigger today than they were a decade ago. I truly believe it is impossible to overstate the severity of the challenges caused by an inadequate or unaligned sense of urgency. And very experienced, very smart people fail here – with consequences that may not be clear for a year or even more – when needed action is delayed or slows down, and train wrecks (or their equivalent) start to become visible.

Urgency, Kotter says, does not have to mean panic, anxiety or fear but instead a situation in which people are 'always looking for both problems and opportunities, and in which the norm is "do it now"'. Urgency, Paul Taffinder (1998: 178–9) says, may be forced upon an organization whose leaders have been indecisive or 'rudely awakened by sudden changes in their environment'. In this case failure is a serious risk if any plan for change or transformation ignores the organization's future purpose. Taffinder suggests that failure to define the purpose of change may sometimes be due to a CEO's unwillingness to drive changes in the top team because of a lack of unity.

Creating a statement of purpose for change

Key questions to be considered in creating a useful statement of organizational purpose suggested by Kim Kanaga and Sonya Prestridge (2002) can be modified to help us create a statement of purpose for organizational change as follows:

- What purpose does the change serve?
- Who are the 'customers' of the change?
- What do they have to gain from it?
- What is our vision for the change?
- What are the distinctive competencies needed for the change?
- What energizes the change?
- How do the organization's core values inform our vision and purpose for change?
- What legacy should the change be intended to leave?

Following Kim Kanaga and Sonya Prestridge's approach, these questions are subjected to a brainstorming process:

1. One sheet on a flip chart is devoted to each question. Members of the group call out ideas, either randomly or in turn, that relate to each question, considered one at a time. All suggestions are recorded, regardless of quality or repetition, and this process is continued until ideas dry up.
2. The sheets are posted around the room. All members study them and then identify and report patterns and themes, looking for common words and repetition.
3. The themes and patterns are then discussed to identify the key ideas for a statement of the purpose of change.
4. All members individually write a statement of the purpose of change.
5. Members form groups of three or four and share their statements and create a common statement.
6. The whole group reconvenes, shares the small groups' statements of purpose, and creates a single, agreed statement. A sub-group may be assigned to add the finishing touches for approval by the whole group if desired.

Discussion Questions

1 How can you create a purpose for organizational change that all stakeholders share?
2 How can you ensure that people throughout the organization understand and are committed to the purpose for change?

Activity

Think of a change initiative in your organization or an organization known personally to you, define and evaluate its purpose for change and consider how it could have been expressed better.

This activity may be carried out by you alone or by all members of a group who then share their conclusions and identify what these have in common and which are unique and why.

Linking the purpose of change to core organizational values and strategies for change

Dr Reto Francioni, CEO and Chairman of the Executive Board of Deutsche Borse, links purpose to strategy: '..true transformation of an organization depends on ... anchoring strategy to purpose ... Strategy that has no purpose is merely tactics ...' (Mourkogiannis, 2006: ii). As we mentioned at the start of this section, the CIPD (2011: 3) endorses this view, as do we, and we discuss this further after the next section.

The purpose of a change initiative also must reflect the core values of the organization, modelled by those in leadership positions. Now, therefore, we turn to the place of values in leading change. Values both underpin and reflect an organization's vision, purpose and strategies and, consequently, both incremental and transformational change.

Leadership, change and shared values

Effective leaders identify, display, promote and reinforce shared values that inform and support the vision, purpose and strategies (Gill, 2011: 161). As with vision, purpose and strategy, this general proposition equally describes what effective leaders do with respect to organizational change and transformation. Shared values are an essential characteristic of a strong organizational culture, and organizational culture is an essential consideration – as a facilitator, inhibitor or focus of change itself – in organizational change or transformation.

What are values?

Values are principles or standards that are considered to be important or beneficial (Soanes and Stevenson, 2004: 1597). We evaluate aspects of our existence – objects, behaviour, events, activities, motives, intentions, goals and outcomes – on the basis of our values (Roe and Ester, 1999; Schwartz, 1992: 2). 'Moral' values are values that are regarded as 'good' as opposed to 'bad', 'right' as opposed to 'wrong'. **Moral values** are the basis for a system of **ethics** and professionalism. They serve as a 'normative regulatory guide' for individuals (Meglino and Ravlin, 1998). 'Values', Jo Silvester (2010) says, 'determine where individuals invest effort.' And values, together with their associated systems of ethics, are an important determinant of both corporate and national culture.

In the context of leading change, values provide us with a sense of the desirability of – and therefore a preference for – a particular new state of existence – a specific result of the change, a clear vision of the intended outcome, and instrumental and purposeful behaviour. Leadership is about showing the way and inducing or helping others to pursue it. Ethical behaviour is an increasingly important aspect of leadership in general and leading change in particular – for the greater good of individuals, organizations and society at large. And **moral intelligence** (Lennick and Kiel, 2008) – the ability to distinguish between right and wrong – is an underlying **competency** in leading change effectively.

Personal values and corporate values are different though they may overlap. Personal values, Stephen Covey (1992: 19) says, are individual, subjective and internal, whereas corporate values, which he calls 'guiding principles', are impersonal, objective and external. The 'corporate values' defined by many companies are guiding principles for people's behaviour in the organization. Metaphorically speaking, personal values come from the 'heart'; guiding principles come from the 'head'. Nevertheless, the corporate values officially espoused and promoted by an organization do reflect somebody's, if not everybody's, personal values. They are beliefs about what is good for its business and accordingly how people in the organization are expected to behave.

In a survey carried out for the CIPD in the UK in 2010, only 5% of respondents said they did not know their organization's values and only 4% said their organization did not have any stated values (CIPD, 2010). Moreover, in a study of a culture change programme in a large engineering company in the UK, Sharon Turnbull (2001) discovered that the content of the company's new corporate values was less important than the fact that corporate values now existed: employees apparently wanted to identify with *something*.

Peter Drucker, the grandfather of modern management, gives a practical example of differences in values that many companies will identify with:

> In any conflict between short-term results and long-term growth, one company decides in favour of long-term growth; another company decides ... in favor of short-term results ... this is not primarily a disagreement on economics. It is fundamentally a value conflict regarding the function of a business and the responsibility of management. (1999a: 177)

This distinction implies that differences in values influence the nature and effectiveness of organizational change or transformation – what is sustainable (long-term) in contrast to what is pragmatic or expedient and consequently transient (short-term), sub-optimal or, very often, an outright failure.

Patrick Lencioni (2002) usefully defines several types of values that have different kinds of validity:

- *Core values*. Inherent, sacrosanct values that distinguish a company and serve as guiding principles for everybody's behaviour. They are often the values of the founders, as with Hewlett–Packard's 'The HP Way'.
- *Aspirational values*. Values that an organization needs to be successful in the future but currently lacks. Lencioni quotes an example of a *Fortune 500* company who cited 'a sense of urgency' as a core value because employees were complacent: this is not a core value but an aspirational value.
- *Permission-to-play values*. Like core values but merely reflect the minimum behavioural standard required of all employees. It is these – such as integrity, teamwork, quality, customer satisfaction, innovation – that we see as common to many companies, but they do not create distinctive identity.
- *Accidental values*. Arise spontaneously, reflecting the common interests or values of employees, such as dress code, thus creating a sense of inclusivity, but they may limit a company's opportunities and development by being too exclusive. They are false core values.

Another useful way of classifying values is as moral values and instrumental values. Moral values emphasize intentions, behaviour, actions and their consequences as 'good' or 'right'. Instrumental values emphasize intentions, behaviour, actions and their consequences that are 'effective' in the context of a wider vision and purpose.

Societal culture influences organizational values and culture both directly and, indirectly, through its influence on individuals' values and on the nature of tasks in the organization, such as aggressiveness in competition, the nature of the organization's industry and dominant professions, and access to the internet (Sagiv and Schwartz, 2007). There are cross-cultural organizations that promote values-based leadership. For example, Simon Webley (1999) quotes the International Chamber of Commerce based in Paris and the Caux Principles,[3] which were published in 1996 reflecting a stakeholder model and promoting the shared values of the common good (*kyosei*) and human dignity.

Shared values in leading sustainable change

The more personal values and corporate values (guiding principles) are aligned, the more effective building a strong, favourable culture will be, says Stephen Covey (1992). Effective leadership entails creating and sustaining shared values in the organization and ensuring these guide organizational change and transformation. Emmanuel Ogbonna and Lloyd Harris (1998) concluded from their study of three retail companies that 'any change initiative which is based solely on head office values and perceptions is likely to be ineffective'.

Congruence between employee values and organizational culture as a whole is positively related to employee commitment (Chatman, 1991). And value congruence among group members is associated with lower conflict in their relationships and their enhanced performance and satisfaction (Jehn et al., 1997). As one of this book's co-authors says elsewhere:

> It is well established, but maybe not sufficiently well known, that action based on shared values is that most likely to bring peace and harmony. Political, ethnic and religious strife is invariably the consequence of behaviour reflecting values unique to a specific ideology, culture or religion. The effective way forward is for people to work together on what they agree on, not on what they do not. (Gill, 2012: 21)

Shared values also have a clear economic benefit, says Mark Tannenbaum (2003):

> An analysis of these successful companies and their competitors demonstrated that focusing first on alignment of values and strong cultural norms were distinguishing factors with measurable bottom-line revenue and profitability results.

A study of 11 US insurance companies showed that those whose managers did not share the same perception of corporate values performed less well than those with shared values (Gordon and DiTomaso, 1992). Ann Nicotera and Donald Cushman (1992) point out an ethical issue with this:

---

3   *Principles for Business*, Caux Round Table, The Hague, 1996.

If the value systems of individuals do not complement the value system of their organization, those individuals will eventually be faced with insoluble ethical dilemmas.

Peter Drucker (1999b) highlights the poor performance and frustration that can result from incompatibility between the individual's values and the organization's values:

> To work in an organization the value system of which is unacceptable to a person, or incompatible with it, condemns the person both to frustration and to non-performance … Organizations, like people, have values. To be effective in an organization, a person's values must be compatible with the organization's values. They do not need to be the same. But they must be close enough to coexist.

In leading changes in their organization some leaders and entrepreneurs may make decisions that cause harm to the environment in which they operate. For example, Dean Shepherd and colleagues (2013) explored the role of their personal values and agency in such decision-making with respect to the natural environment. They found that such leaders, in certain circumstances, do perceive opportunities that harm the environment as very attractive and therefore suitable for exploitation. The extent to which leaders disengaged from their pro-environmental values was stronger in those with low rather than high entrepreneurial self-efficacy. It was also stronger when 'industry munificence' – abundance of needed critical resources – was perceived as low. Knowing this may help to increase self-awareness and enhance decision-making among leaders of organizational change that has potentially harmful environmental effects in the context of the **triple bottom line**.

Leaders may face an emotional challenge in handling the 'difficult' thoughts and feelings associated with dilemmas that they face and resolving them when confronted by a clash between personal values and expectations and demands of a change initiative. Susan David and Christina Congleton (2013) explain how effective leaders do not willy-nilly try to either accept or suppress these thoughts and feelings: they use what they call 'emotional agility' – dealing with them in a 'mindful, values-driven and productive way', posing specific questions to themselves. This ability is just one aspect of **emotional intelligence**, which we discuss later.

Value congruence mediates the relationship between leadership style and performance outcomes (Jung and Avolio, 2000). When the values of the leader and the followers coincide, the leader gains legitimate power through credibility. Legitimate power is the ability to motivate people because of their belief in the leader and in what the leader is trying to accomplish (Covey, 1992: 102), an important element in leading change – in showing the way from what may well be a strongly entrenched 'comfort zone' to the unknown, or at least to a situation that is less than certain.

Shared values relating to work are important for the performance of team members and their satisfaction with cooperation among them. This was demonstrated in a study of 411 members and their team leaders in 72 Taiwanese corporate teams by Li-Fang Chou and colleagues (2008). Trustworthiness was found to mediate the relationship between shared values and team-member performance, and trustfulness to mediate the relationship between shared values and satisfaction with cooperation.

Discussion Questions

1   How should a leader in an organization who disagrees with the purpose or process of a change initiative that he or she is expected to champion handle the situation?
2   How would you apply the principle of the triple bottom-line to organizational change initiatives?
3   How important is it to gain 100% consensus among all directors, managers and employees on the need and process for a particular organizational change?

Leadership, change and strategy

Effective leaders develop, communicate and implement rational strategies that are informed by shared values (Gill, 2011: 200). Without strategies, vision is a dream. Philip Atkinson (2003) underscores the importance of the core leadership themes and practices of vision, purpose and values as a basis for effective management of change, in particular for creating the organization's strategy and business plan for change.

In a celebrated lecture at the Harvard Business School in 1931, Alfred North Whitehead, the eminent philosopher, identified strategic foresight as 'the crucial feature of the competent business mind' (Fiol and O'Connor, 2002). By this he meant the ability to anticipate future developments – to reflect on change and novelty, see through confusion, foresee trends, see emerging patterns, and understand social currents that are likely to shape future events.

What is a strategy for change?

Strategy is about *how* to get from where we are now to where we want to be. It is a journey plan for the change initiative and a route map for travelling to the destination (represented in a vision). Effective strategy also serves an organization's purpose and is informed by its core values and purpose or mission. Table 3.1 shows how.

Strategies, as a core theme and practice in leadership and a link between leadership and management, are ways of pursuing the vision and purpose, identifying and exploiting opportunities, anticipating and responding to threats, and not only *responding* positively to the need for change but also *creating* change.

Table 3.1   Statements of purpose and strategic principles for change compared*

Statements of purpose	Strategic principles
Inform a company's culture	Drive a company's strategy
Aspirational: something to strive	Action oriented: enable for action *now*
Intended to inspire people	Enable managers and employees to act quickly and make strategically consistent choices

*Based on Orit Gadiesh and James Gilbert (2001) 'Transforming corner-office strategy into frontline action', *Harvard Business Review*, 79(5), May, 72–79.

Effective leaders ensure that strategies for organizational change or transformation are developed, implemented and sustained during their life. This entails showing the way and enabling and ensuring commitment to it through ownership of it as well as the control mechanisms that are part and parcel of 'management'.

Moshe Farjoun (2002) defines strategy as:

> the planned or actual coordination of the firm's major goals and actions, in time and space, that continuously co-align the firm with its environment.

Goals state what is to be achieved and when results are to be accomplished, but do not state how the results are to be achieved (Quinn, 1980). Actions are 'resource deployments, initiatives, responses, moves, deals, investments, and developments' (Farjoun, 2002). Coordination refers to goals and means for achieving them, resources and administrative infrastructure. Co-alignment refers to adapting to, and at times adapting, the environment (Bourgeois, 1984; Itami and Roehl, 1987: Pfeffer and Salancik, 1978; Porter, 1991). Strategy thus is a matter of content (goals and action), coordination and context, and it is interactive, adaptive and integrative (Farjoun, 2002).

As with vision, purpose and values, strategies for change require intellectual validity, spiritual meaning and emotional appeal in the minds and hearts of followers for them to engage people. Good strategies for change result from the organization's vision and statement of purpose, and good strategic planning reflects the values of the organization and its environmental realities (Covey, 1992: 166–7). Psychologist Leonard Goodstein (2010: 45–6) argues that corporate strategic planning should include clarifying the organization's core values. Strategic decisions about change reflect such values.

Developing the strategy for change

A global survey of some 2,000 multi-business company executives conducted in December 2010 revealed that more than a quarter felt their companies lacked a consistent process for developing strategy (McKinsey & Company, 2011). James Champy (1997) says 'mere consultation and the broadcasting of messages' are not sufficient for achieving commitment to and ownership of strategy. Peter Linkow (1999) makes the point that organizations that do not involve employees in the strategy process in what Kees Van der Heijden (1996) calls 'strategic conversation' – simply conversation among people in the organization intended to contribute to its strategy – will not survive. The usefulness of strategic conversation is supported by empirical research findings (Johnson, 2005).

Gerry Johnson and colleagues (2005: 41–58) say that innovative strategies result from more than experience – from diversity and variety of ideas. Organizations therefore respond to the often rapidly changing and uncertain business environment through a process of 'logical incrementalism' in change initiatives – learning by doing – which relies more on emergent strategy than on top-down direction and control. Encouraging strategic conversation in the context of distributed leadership in the organization has the potential to enhance innovation in strategy and sustainable change.

There are several models for implementing change, including Rosabeth Moss Kanter's and John Kotter's, which are reviewed in later chapters (Eden, 1993: 117; Goodstein, 2010: 46–53; Nolan et al., 2008). Linking to these, developing a strategy for organizational change or transformation might usefully comprise the following steps:

1. Identifying the need for change based on an analysis of the issues facing the organization
2. Preparing for the strategic planning process – clarifying core values, assessing readiness, those to be involved, timeframe and communication of progress
3. Articulating the vision and purpose of change
4. Generating options and building scenarios
5. Identifying stakeholders and their possible response in relation to their own goals
6. Developing goals for the change
7. Setting action plans within the context of the goals
8. Integrating action plans to establish a strategic programme
9. Developing strategic controls and contingency plans
10. Implementing the strategic plan for change or transformation
11. Managing strategy: monitoring, feedback and correction of action or change of strategy

Thomas Stewart (2010), former editor of the *Harvard Business Review*, says that 'strategy without execution is daydreaming'. The Hay Group, management consultants, surveyed 100 senior managers just below board level in FTSE 350 companies and found, in the respondents' view, an astonishing failure of CEOs to execute strategy properly (Stern, 2008). Nearly 80% did not believe their businesses would achieve the CEOs' targets; 33% did not understand the CEOs' strategies well enough to carry them out; more than 25% disagreed with messages from the CEO; and some 25% were 'just plain bored'. Caution is needed in interpreting the findings because of the small sample and possible response bias (more contented senior managers may not have responded). Stefan Stern, who reported these findings, suggests that the problem is poor communication: the need for clearer, simpler and honest messages – both down and up.

Implementing a strategy for change, then, is above all a process of communication. The aim of communication about change strategy is gaining understanding of and commitment to it. This is required for joined-up thinking and action and effective teamwork in the implementation process. This means reaching not just managers throughout the organization who are involved or affected by the change but all involved or affected employees and in the different ethnic and national cultures in which they live and work (Garten, 2001: 147–9). In Chapter 10 we further explore the importance and nature of communication in respect of sustainable organizational change.

Discussion Questions

1 Should a strategy for organizational change or transformation be geared solely or largely to maximizing shareholder value? If so, why? If not, what should strategy chiefly be geared to?

2 How can commitment to strategies for change or transformation among those involved or affected by it be achieved?

3 What part do you see strategy playing in ensuring that organizational change or transformation is sustainable?

4 What differences, if any, do you see between leading and managing a strategy for change or transformation?

The vision, purpose and strategies for change and transformation, informed by core values, need to be turned into a reality. This requires the ability and desire of people to do so. We therefore now turn our attention, in the context of organizational change and transformation, to our two remaining themes and practices of effective leadership of change and transformation: the empowerment and engagement of people.

Leadership, Change and Empowerment

Effective leaders empower people to be *able to do* what needs to be done (Gill, 2011: 231). The 'best' leaders have followers or employees whom they empower and whose motivation, satisfaction and effectiveness come, in part but significantly, from a sense of self-efficacy – the feeling of capability or competence to perform a task – and the feelings associated with achievement. Successful and sustainable change depends on people empowered to achieve it.

What is empowerment?

The essence of empowerment is giving people power. This entails giving people the ability (through education, teaching, training or other opportunities for learning) or allowing or enabling them to do something or act in a particular way. 'Power' has connotations of vigour, energy, authority, influence, which we explore further in Chapter 12.

Leaders of change need to understand position power (authority) and personal power, where power resides in the organization, how to mobilize support, and how to respond to **resistance to change**. Tim Morris of Oxford University's Said Business School says:

> Personal power such as that of the chief executive is important when you are kicking off change, but it will not take you all the way along the road ... You have to reinforce it with other forms of organizational power to make sure that the change is sustained. You have to build a coalition of support among other key players, and you have to manage the opposition through influence and other tactics. (Chynoweth, 2012)

It should be noted that the use of influence *is* a form of personal power. And Morris's suggestion that one may coerce people resisting change 'who are relatively powerless' is questionable as the best way of handling them, though he does admit that coercion in the case of very strong 'negative power' is 'a risky tactic', where, he says more promisingly, 'consultation and compromise are likely to be more effective ways of neutralizing opposition'.

Effective leadership entails enabling people to do what needs to be done to pursue a vision, purpose, objective or strategy and to fulfil their potential. Robert Heller (1997) sees empowering people as 'setting them free to think for themselves'. Richard Olivier (2001: 37) says: 'Alignment happens when the right "thing" (outside) is linked to the right "feeling" (inside).' And, in this respect, as Goethe (1749–1832) said: 'Whatever you can do, or dream you can, begin it. Boldness has genius and power and magic in it' (Anster, 1888).

One of the first books about empowerment, written in the genre of a modern fable and a best-seller, is that by William C. Byham. Byham (1988) defines empowerment as '[having] responsibility, a sense of ownership, satisfaction in accomplishments, power over what and how things are done, recognition for ... ideas, and the knowledge that [one is] important to the organization'. The idea of empowerment has evolved to encompass sharing power, energizing employees, enhancing self-efficacy – belief in one's own capabilities to do what needs to be done – by reducing powerlessness, and increasing opportunities for intrinsic motivation at work (Menon, 2001).

An attempt to synthesize the range of key ideas and research findings in the practitioner and scholarly literature about empowerment is the basis for the following suggested definition (Gill, 2011: 231, 236):

> Empowerment is giving people the knowledge, skills, self-confidence, opportunity, freedom, authority and resources to manage themselves and be accountable for their performance.

A key aspect of empowerment for organizational change that is often overlooked, much to the cost of performance and achievement, is resources. Many a change initiative (particularly and very visibly in governments and the public sector) has failed or suffered because of a lack of appropriate or sufficient resources – people (human capital), money (funds/budgets), materials, equipment, facilities, technology, information, time, natural resources and reputation.

Along with empowerment comes accountability for behaviour and performance. Just as rights entail responsibilities, power entails accountability. So this definition of empowerment includes accountability for one's behaviour and performance. Rob Lebow makes an interesting point:

> unless you link accountability and responsibility ..., you'll never get accountable employees. It's the 'strings' that are placed on employees – policies, incentives and performance standards – that destroy accountability. (Creelman, 2003b)

The definition of empowerment also includes 'opportunity'. Nannerl Keohane, a distinguished leader in business and academia in the USA, criticizes the lack of opportunity associated with a lack of empowerment: 'Micromanaging subordinates', she says, 'gives them little opportunity to develop leadership skills of their own and reduces the energy available for the work of the organization' (Keohane, 2010: 62).

Leadership issues with empowerment

Amin Rajan (2000a) quotes a senior director involved in an empowerment initiative:

> We made a mess of our empowerment initiative at the outset. We did not think about the changes in corporate values that would be needed to make it work. We simply thought our people would be glad to have a job in this once-proud organization and thus go along with our blueprint for change ... we forgot to ask the basic question: 'Why would staff want to be empowered in a climate of exponential change?' But more than that, we forgot to ask, 'What's in it for the staff?'

'What's in it for the staff' in a change initiative may be either appealing or unwelcome. Chris Argyris (2000) points out a problem with empowerment that potentially has adverse consequences for organizational change: the conflict between employees' 'internal commitment' and 'external commitment'. This is the inconsistency of asking employees to 'own' situations and problems and to behave like owners (internal commitment), yet expecting them to meet job requirements as specified by bosses (external commitment). The problem occurs when managers ask for internal commitment and the organizational system rewards external commitment. Asking people to act like owners when they have not set the objectives is a psychological paradox. Argyris (2000) says:

> When someone else defines objectives, goals, and the steps to reach them, whatever commitment exists will be external. Employees may feel responsible for producing what is required of them, but they will not feel responsible for the way the situation is defined.

Micromanagement – practised by 'control freaks' – may reflect a lack of recognition and use of creativity in people who may have much to contribute to organizational change, innovation and transformation. Joe Prochaska (2002) believes that creativity is often misunderstood by top management in an organization:

> The biggest roadblock to creativity is that it is not precisely defined or well understood as a managerial practice that can have an attractive return on investment when put to work in an organization. It is especially misunderstood among top management, from whom a high level of support is needed to sponsor any change in an organization.

Nurturing the creativity of gifted people entails empowering them. What do we mean by 'creativity'? Creativity is the ability to generate new and original ideas, associations, methods, approaches and solutions – a process known as 'ideation' – and to relate them to a given problem. Creativity – popularly associated with the right hemisphere of the brain – is characterized by artistic, intuitive, conceptual, emotional, holistic, 'divergent' and 'lateral' thinking and the associated behaviour. Analytical thinking – 'left-brain' – in contrast is logical, rational, mathematical, technical, controlled, administrative, 'convergent' and 'vertical'.

The intelligence shown by creative people is evident through their conceptual fluency and flexibility, originality and preference for complexity (Steiner, 1965). Conceptual fluency is the ability to generate many ideas rapidly. Conceptual flexibility – 'dimensionality' – is the ability to 'shift gears', to discard an approach or a frame of reference in favour of another. Originality is the ability to give unusual interpretations or responses to situations. And creative people display a preference for complexity as an enjoyable challenge. This preference has important implications for leading creative people, especially in the context of organizational change.

Creativity should be contrasted with *innovation*. Innovation is not invention: that is creativity. Innovation is a process of implementation, Prochaska (2002) says; it is 'identifying an existing resource and, through knowledge, elevating it to a new level of utility and value to the customer'. He believes:

> The biggest roadblocks to innovation are a lack of understanding of when to take intelligent risks ... and insufficient knowledge of the skills and principles needed to develop innovation into a managerial practice ... innovation is largely knowledge driven. (Prochaska, 2002)

Activity

Think of an attempt to empower people as part of a change initiative in your organization or an organization known personally to you, identify the issues that arose and the reasons for them, and consider how these issues could have been avoided or at least minimized.

This activity may be carried out by you alone or by all members of a group, who then share their conclusions and identify what these have in common and which are unique and why.

Key findings from empowerment research

One barrier to empowerment, according to research by Robert Quinn and Gretchen Spreitzer (1997), is a bureaucratic culture that emphasizes maintenance of the status quo and thereby impedes change. Organizational change and transformation inevitably entail employees – and managers – having to perform existing tasks differently or new tasks. Eric Lamm and Judith Gordon (2010) in their study found important needs that people have in this respect:

- People want to know that changes in their work routines will occur gradually and that they will have the necessary time to adjust to them.
- Communication and justification of management's vision for change to get employee commitment to it is less important to people than that reassurance.

Organizational change inevitably also brings with it the unexpected. Teams and their leaders have to resort to improvisation to deal with unexpected occurrences. Massimo Magni and Likoebe Maruping's study of 48 work teams produced three interesting and useful findings:

- Empowering leadership positively moderates the relationship between improvisation and performance.
- Work overload attenuates the relationship between improvisation and performance.
- Improvisation is most positively related to performance when empowering leadership is high and overload is low. (Magni and Maruping, 2013)

For change to be sustainable, therefore, empowerment is a key practice by leaders in maximizing the positive impact of improvisation on performance in dealing with unexpected occurrences, and it must take account of work load. Work overload is common during change initiatives. It may be disempowering because it adversely affects self-efficacy. For example, empowerment includes having the resources necessary to perform work and the sense of being able to do so.

In their study of managers in the USA, Alan Randolph and Edward Kemery (2011) found a positive relationship between empowerment practices and psychological empowerment that is mediated by employees' perceptions of how their managers use power, which we explore in Chapter 12.

Spreitzer and Quinn (1996) found that managers with low levels of self-esteem, negative feelings about their jobs and poor support from their colleagues and bosses were less likely to display leadership during organizational change. Self-esteem, for the nineteenth century psychologist and philosopher William James (1890), is 'the ratio of a person's successes to his or her pretensions', where pretensions are viewed as goals, purposes or aims. Self-esteem is a powerful motivator, but too much self-esteem may lead to conceit.

What specific actions, behaviour or characteristics in change leaders constitute empowerment? Our review of the literature suggests the following:

- Self-awareness of one's strengths and limitations, interests, preferences and motivational drivers, and values, beliefs and attitudes
- Delegation of challenging tasks and the authority to make decisions and take action
- Stimulating people's intellects, imagination and intuition, questioning the status quo, and getting them to do likewise
- Providing the opportunity, resources and support for people to perform
- Sharing knowledge and rewarding *learning* as well as performance
- Coaching and training for skills acquisition or improvement
- Encouraging self-determination and autonomy – the freedom of people to manage themselves, with responsibility (sense of duty or obligation) and accountability (willingness to admit to being the source of actions or decisions that cause given outcomes)

Empowering others by helping them in this way requires courage and conviction in those leading change. Indeed courage and conviction are self-empowering. As David Roche, president of the global lodging group at Expedia, says:

> Endless lecturing about leadership is not going to produce any more of it. The world is not only changing very quickly but the rate of change is accelerating. Someone has to stand up and say: 'We can't continue like this.' They have to use their courage and conviction to bring about change. (Roche, 2013)

Discussion Questions

1 When should coercion be used in introducing organizational change in preference to influence and persuasion?
2 Is empowerment universally applicable and effective? What are the cross-cultural considerations?
3 Can leading change be effective without empowering other people?

Leadership, change and employee engagement

Effective leaders engage other people by influencing, motivating and inspiring them to *want to do* what needs to be done (Gill, 2011: 255). Engaging people in a change effort is perhaps the most difficult part of leading organizational change. Large companies in the UK appear to be making more of an effort to engage with their employees, though there are still concerns about whether meaningful change would result (Sutherland, 2010). Senior executives see employee disengagement as one of the three biggest threats facing their businesses yet, according to 43% of them, issues concerning morale and motivation are rarely discussed at board level and some 90% of their companies simply choose to ignore the problems caused by disengaged staff. Asks Brian Amble (2010): could this be due to ignorance, admitted or otherwise, of how to deal with it?

What is engagement?

We define engagement as the intellectual, emotional and spiritual commitment to what one is doing, shown by discretionary attention and effort devoted to it. The UK's CIPD defines employee engagement as 'a combination of commitment to the organization and its values plus a willingness to help out colleagues (organizational citizenship) ... [going] beyond job satisfaction and ... not simply motivation' (CIPD, 2009b). Managers and employees who are engaged with an organizational change initiative devote discretionary effort to it willingly, even eagerly.

Engaging people by influencing, motivating and inspiring them to do what needs to be done is the central idea in many theories of leadership. An example is Beverly Alimo-Metcalfe and Robert Alban-Metcalfe's model – Engaging Transformational Leadership (Gill, 2011: 87–90). Empowerment and engagement, as we define these two core themes and practices in our model for leading change, incorporate the concept and practice of transformational leadership. Perhaps the most widely accepted and, indeed, durable contemporary model of transformational leadership is that of Bernard Bass and his associates that forms part of his **full-range leadership (FRL) model** (Bass, 1985, 2008: 618–648). The FRL model comprises **transformational leadership, transactional leadership** and **laissez-faire leadership** requirements (see Gill, 2011: 81–7).

Laissez-faire leadership is really non-leadership: ignoring problems, avoiding taking a stand, not following up and refraining from intervening. It can be seen as 'hands-off', uninvolved and abdication. Transactional leadership is a way of influencing or motivating people to do what is wanted by **managing by exception** (e.g. focusing on errors, mistakes and deviations from requirements) and **contingent reward** (rewarding performance that meets or exceeds requirements). Transformational leadership, however, raises people's motivation to higher levels whereby they are willing and even keen to transcend their own immediate self-interest in favour of a greater good, e.g. that of the organization. Its components are individualized consideration, intellectual stimulation, inspirational motivation and idealized influence. These components contribute to the concepts and practices of empowerment and engagement in our model of leadership.

Engagement among employees is linked in part to the personality traits of adjustment (absence of neurosis), conscientiousness (prudence), altruism and agreeableness, which, Adrian Furnham (2010) says, means that 'some people are thus easy to engage by head and heart, and others not'. Engagement is significantly determined by effective leadership, whereby people see how their work fits into the 'big picture' and they feel they are listened to and dealt with fairly. As Furnham says, 'those who are intrinsically motivated don't need very much extrinsic motivation'. Effective leaders create the conditions for people to be motivated and even inspired – to be *engaged* with what they do.

Engaged employees are motivated to exert effort, perform the work that needs to be done and more besides. Understanding how this happens entails:

- Understanding *what* motivates people at work
- How it does so
- What leaders do when they motivate employees
- How they create the conditions in which motivation can emerge to the extent that employees are engaged with change initiatives in their work and the organization. (Gill, 2011: 260–5).

A report by the CBI and IPA (2011) in the UK provides several case studies and makes a compelling case for employee engagement as an essential component of leadership for transformation that public sector leaders need to be able to accomplish. It sets out four areas of practice in employee engagement for public sector leaders:

- Managers need to be empowered to engage employees
- Strong strategic leadership is essential
- Employees must be informed and given voice
- Organization must embed integrity at the heart of what they do

Business leaders gathering for a roundtable discussion on organizational transformation in Nice, France, in June 2012 were unanimous that engaging managers and employees in change initiatives is essential for effective and sustainable change (The Transformation Alliance, 2012). One participant, Anne Lalou, a non-executive director of several companies, said:

> Top management can clearly see the opportunity that transformation offers ... [but] the middle management ... become stuck in the middle trying to deliver the vision [for change] as well as the regular business.

Businesses headed by effective leaders have employees who are significantly more engaged, creative and innovative, and these businesses make more money than those run by less effective leaders, according to research carried out by Kenexa, surveying some 29,000 employees in 21 countries (Chynoweth, 2010b; Kenexa, 2010; Top-Consultant, 2010). Using an employee engagement index, the research found that engagement ranged from 91% where leaders were rated as effective to 17% where they were rated as neutral or ineffective: employee engagement is five times higher in businesses with effective leadership.

In a McKinsey survey, virtually all of the executives surveyed who characterized their companies' change initiatives as 'extremely successful' said that employees contributed ideas to shape the efforts (McKinsey & Company, 2010). Nearly 25% of the extremely successful transformations were planned by groups of 50 people or more, compared with 6% of unsuccessful transformations. The involvement and engagement of people is a key leadership process in organizational change and transformation.

How leaders engage employees in organizational change

Myeong-Gu Seo and colleagues (2012) explored the effects of their managers' transformational leadership on employees' responses to change. They also explored the role of employees' affective experiences (positive feelings) in shaping their commitment and behavioural responses to – their engagement with – organizational change at its start and then 12 months later. Their findings included the following:

- Unsurprisingly, employees' commitment and their supportive, resistant and creative behavioural responses to change were found to be strongly related to their affective experiences.
- Employees' affective experiences at the start of organizational change predicted both commitment and behavioural response to change 12 months later.
- Managers' transformational leadership shaped both employees' affective reactions and commitment to change at the start and their behavioural responses later.

Clearly managers, in exercising their leadership role during change, need to foster positive affect as much as possible during organizational change. Ways of doing this that Seo and colleagues suggest include the following:

- Providing a compelling vision for change
- Reminding employees of favourable outcomes of any previous change initiatives
- Reducing uncertainty, fear and anxiety through timely, frequent and accurate communication
- Education and training to ensure employees' ability and confidence to do what needs to be done differently as a result of change
- Including employees in decisions about change to increase their sense of control and fairness during the change process
- Showing support and appreciation for them and generally displaying transformational leadership
- Providing the opportunity for airing their grievances or negative feelings

A 'perfect example' of how employee *disengagement* can damage a business comes from British Gas (BG) (Goldsmith, 2010). The majority of the 3,000 unionized employees who responded to a trade union survey in BG voiced several serious complaints. These related to the company's management style, being overworked, being made to 'over-sell' to customers – 'Now it's all profit and no customer service' – and being micro-managed and subjected to draconian discipline over the slightest infringements, including missing performance targets for the first time. Such disengagement was the basis for an impending strike ballot. Yet a BG statement in response to these complaints referred only to an accusation of job cuts, apparently

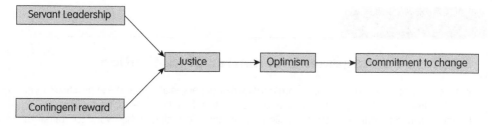

Figure 3.2   The relationship between commitment to change and servant leadership and contingent reward

Based on Marjolein Kool and Dirk van Dierendonck (2012)

ignoring the issue of disengagement. Sadly, in the past the company had been seen as a great place to work.

Leaders reap what they sow. This has far-reaching consequences in the context of organizational change. Robert Rubin and colleagues (2009) found that leaders who are highly cynical about change (a) convey their **cynicism** to their followers and this contributes both to cynicism in them too and a decrease in their followers' commitment to the organization and (b) themselves perform less well and display less citizenship behaviour. Cynical leaders are more likely to have disengaged employees.

Commitment to change is a determinant of sustainable change. We explore commitment to change further in Chaper 12. Using an approach to leadership theory that posits two underlying dimensions – task focus and relationship (people) focus – Marjolein Kool and Dirk van Dierendonck (2012) explored how **servant leadership** (with a people focus) and contingent reward (with a task focus) influence commitment to change. Servant leadership in the context of organizational (or national) change is leadership that reflects the desire to serve the needs and interests of followers and the people involved (Gill, 2011: 68–71; Greenleaf, 1977). Contingent reward is the practice of promising and delivering rewards in exchange for achieving desired or expected performance, mostly reflecting a form of position power (in respect of material reward) though also a form of personal power (in respect of approval, praise and recognition), and it is an aspect of transactional leadership in Bernard Bass's Full-Range Leadership model (Bass, 1985: 121–34).

Servant leadership and contingent reward were found to contribute to a stronger sense of justice[4] and an optimistic attitude[5] that results in greater commitment to change (Figure 3.2) (Kool and van Dierendonck, 2012).

Kool and van Dierendonck say: 'Leaders who are able to combine in their style servant leadership with contingent reward leadership are more likely to create an environment that helps their followers to embrace change in a positive way' (2012).

---

4 Justice is defined as the use of honest and sufficient explanations of decisions and procedures (informational justice) and the extent to which followers are treated with dignity, politeness and respect in carrying out procedures (interpersonal justice).

5 Optimism is defined as a positive attribution of about succeeding now and in the future.

CASE EXAMPLE

Employee engagement – a matter of motivation

What does employee engagement from a motivational perspective look like in practice? John Smythe, from the Engage for Change consultancy, offers two scenarios to illustrate it. Imagine two different employees, called Ruby and Geraldine, who work for different businesses.

Scenario 1

In the first scenario, Ruby is invited to attend a morning meeting titled 'Help our recovery'. 'The invitation confirms recent open communication about the poor performance of all parts of the company, and that its parent is unable to subsidise it, let alone provide more cash for investment, and that fast action must be taken to stabilise the situation,' Smythe explains. 'But it also says there are no secret pre-hatched plans for radical action. It says: "We want you and your colleagues to take ownership with management to solve the crisis, recognising that unpalatable options will have to be on the table".'

Ruby is both concerned and flattered. She arrives at the meeting feeling like a player rather than a spectator. A two-month timetable is laid out in which she and her colleagues are invited to use their knowledge to find achievable cost savings without harming key business areas.

In this process, Smythe says, there are three good questions employees can be asked. What would they do if they had a free hand in their day job? What would they do if they were a director of the company? What would they do if they had survived a takeover but were given two months by the acquirer to propose small but radical changes? In this way, employees can own the decisions that are necessary, and not become disengaged or demotivated even as tough measures are put in place.

Scenario 2

The alternative scenario, which concerns Geraldine, is less appealing. She is also invited to a meeting described as a 'cascade briefing'. Rumours have been spreading, directors have gone to ground and communication from the company has been sparse.

'At the "cascade", her fears are confirmed when, in a PowerPoint presentation, the full extent of the dire state of the business is revealed for the first time,' Smythe says. 'Detailed top-down plans for restructuring and efficiencies are revealed. The focus is all on reduction with no hint of new business opportunities. Geraldine feels less like a spectator and more like a victim. To varying degrees, her colleagues leave the meeting in shock and immobilised.'

These examples are based on real situations, Smythe says. 'The first adult-to-adult example resulted in very fast action from a large group of workers, who all, or nearly all, felt they were driving change where they worked, and fast results were achieved. The second disenfranchised those who could contribute, resulting in a huge task of execution by an overworked "change team",' he says.

'When have you have felt most engaged, most valued and most implicated in a successful project or period at work?' he asks. 'Absolutely none of us is going to report that it was more like Geraldine's experience.'

Engagement means sharing power, which can scare some managers. It also means developing a culture of 'distributed leadership': selecting and developing leaders at every level who engage people in the decision-making and change process.

'A culture of distributed leadership means challenging assumptions about the primacy and effectiveness of a command-and-control approach to leadership,' Smythe says. 'It primarily means individual leaders assessing how they have learnt to make decisions, how they engage others in decision-making and how they transition from being a "god" with all the answers to being a "guide" helping to liberate the creativity of others.'

This case example first appeared in 'Share the Power' by Stefan Stern, *FT.com* (*Financial Times*), on 22 March 2010 (www.ft.com) and it is reproduced with kind permission of the author and copyright holder, John Smythe of consultancy Engage for Change (www.engageforchange.com/make_contact.html).

Leading change through engaging people

Power in its various forms pervades human relationships. So how does it relate to engagement – to gaining people's attention, interest, cooperation, commitment, enthusiasm and dedication? And how do effective (and ethical) leaders use power in influencing, motivating and inspiring people and providing the conditions in which people can be engaged with work generally and in particular with change?

'Transformational leaders', Bernard Bass and Bruce Avolio (1994: 3) say, 'inspire those around them by providing meaning and challenge to their followers' work.' They display **spiritual intelligence** and spiritual leadership. Inspiring leaders are often regarded as charismatic – they are perceived to have a special talent or power to attract followers and inspire them with devotion and enthusiasm. One view is that charismatic leaders are emotionally expressive, self-confident, self-determined and free from internal conflict (Bass, 1992). They also show empathy with followers, they use compelling, emotive language, they display personal competence, they display confidence in their followers, and they provide followers with opportunities to achieve (Behling and McFillen, 1996). Effective leaders engage people in change initiatives by the way they talk about it.

Inspirational speech contains simple language, imagery and plays on words in a colourful way. It is delivered with sincerity and passion, with confidence and conviction, and often with expansive body language – in particular facial expressions, gestures of the hand, head movements and eye contact. Eye contact gives the listeners the impression of spontaneity and being addressed directly and personally (Atkinson, 1984). Inspiring leaders express emotions through their body language. For one CEO, John Robins of Guardian Insurance, 'leadership is about communicating emotions and excitement' (Rajan, 2000b).

Central to inspirational language are two skills – **framing** and **rhetorical crafting** (Georgiades and Macdonnell, 1998; Gill, 2011: 279–85) – which are important in engaging people in change. Framing is connecting your message with the needs and interests of those whose commitment you need (Conger, 1999). This means first knowing your audience. Framing is the management of meaning, which requires careful thought and forethought (Fairhurst and Sarr, 1996). Examples of framing are:

- Linking the message with the benefits for everybody involved
- Reflecting their values and beliefs
- Talking in their language

- Matching body language with words
- Moving from 'I' statements to 'we' statements
- Making positive comparisons of their situation with that of others
- Expressing confidence in people's ability to achieve

Rhetoric is the art of verbal expression. Inspiring leaders not only frame their language; they also craft their rhetoric. Rhetorical crafting of language consists of giving examples, citing quotations, reciting slogans, varying one's speaking rhythm, using familiar images, metaphors and analogies to make the message vivid (Martin Luther King's allusion to 'the jangling discords of our nation' in his 'I have a dream' speech comes to mind), waxing lyrical and using repetition. Bernard Bass (1988) describes how inspirational leaders substitute simple words, metaphors and slogans for complex ideas, such as *glasnost* and *perestroika* representing complex social, economic and political change in the former Soviet Union.

Inspirational language, however, is not the exclusive domain of the speaker's podium or rostrum. The skills of framing and rhetorical crafting apply just as much in any one-to-one conversation between leader and follower, manager and subordinate, or indeed between any two people – where the purpose is to motivate or inspire. The way we speak may either engage or disengage other people, as Jim Gray says:

> The ability to speak convincingly to others – to compel them – has to rank as one of the most important skills in business and in life. It's the mark of a true leader. For many who occupy positions of leadership, it's the one missing element that prevents them from fully realizing all that they can be. Audiences in today's communication-saturated age ... are more demanding and critical than ever. They want leaders who can address them with clarity and authenticity. (2010: 9)

Activity

Think of an initiative to engage people as part of a change initiative in your organization or an organization known personally to you, identify the issues that arose and the reasons for them, and consider how these issues could have been avoided or at least minimized.

This activity may be carried out by you alone or by all members of a group, who then share their conclusions and identify what these have in common and which are unique and why.

Applying the leadership model for sustainable change

The model of six core themes and practices of leadership has been used in leadership development programmes in the UK in several organizations concerned with change and transformation: a manufacturing company, a private mental healthcare company, a public sector defence agency, the top management teams of two universities, a youth charity, and an insurance and emergency-assistance company. In most cases change using the model was led from the top. But does it have to be? Can – and should – change be led 'horizontally', in a shared manner, or even 'bottom up'? Robert House and Ram Aditja argue for a collaborative approach to leading change:

The process of leadership cannot be described simply in terms of the behavior of an individual: rather, leadership involves collaborative relationships that lead to collective action grounded in the shared values of people who work together to effect positive change. (House and Aditja, 1997)

Paul Aitken argues for a collective-leadership approach to organizational change:

Change leadership is more about implementation than endless debates about policy or strategy. How you do that is through distributed leadership – you connect people up across the system. (Jayne, 2010)

Various references in the literature have been made to leadership that is shared, distributed, distributive, dispersed, collective or institutional. For clarity, distributed leadership may be defined as the (hierarchically) vertical dispersal of authority and responsibility and **shared leadership** as their 'horizontal' dispersal. (Gill, 2011: 30)

There are leaders at all levels in organizations – those in formal positions of leadership and those who do or can (if permitted or encouraged) exercise leadership informally. All these leaders, at all levels, can promote a vision for change, a purpose for change, shared values that inform the change and the change strategy itself; they all *can* empower and engage people in the pursuit of change and transformation.

Former US president Harry S. Truman is on record as saying:

where there is no leadership, society stands still. Progress occurs when courageous, skillful leaders seize the opportunity to change things for the better. (Whitson and Clark, 2002)

Organizational change requires effective leadership – effective leaders with altruism, courage, wisdom and skill. We have argued that such leaders embrace the need for vision, purpose, shared values, strategy, empowerment and engagement and put these practices into practice in achieving sustainable organizational change and transformation.

Implications and questions for leaders of change

- Review and redefine your role in leading change as showing the way and helping or inducing others to pursue it. How, and to what extent, do you 'show the way' in a change initiative? How do you help others to pursue it? What do you understand by 'inducing' others to pursue the change? How do you do this? How effective is it? How can you do all this better?
- Focus on having a vision and a purpose for change, underpinning values, having a strategy for change, and empowering and engaging those involved or affected by change so that they are able and willing to contribute to the change effort. Check that you address all these core practices in your change initiatives and efforts.
- Review whether and how you define and communicate a valid and appealing vision of the future that is intended as a result of a change and how a vision for the change is to be developed and implemented. How can you do these better?
- Review whether and how you define and communicate a valid and appealing purpose for a change and its linkage to the vision, values and strategy for change. How can you do this better?

- Review to what extent you know and share the core values of the organization and whether and how you identify and personally display, promote and reinforce shared values that inform and support the vision, purpose and strategies for change. In identifying the shared values, consider the principles or standards that are considered to be important or beneficial in leading change efforts and, in particular, those that are deemed to be 'good' or 'bad' or 'right' as opposed to 'wrong'. How can you better ensure you accurately know and personally display, promote and reinforce shared values that inform and support the vision, purpose and strategies for change?

- Review whether and how you develop, communicate and implement rational strategies for change or transformation that are informed by shared values. How can you do this better?

- Review whether and how you empower people to be *able to do* what needs to be done by giving them the knowledge, skills, self-confidence, opportunity, freedom, authority and resources to manage themselves in a change programme and be accountable for their performance. To what extent do you know each of your team members, both collectively and individually, in respect of their knowledge, skills, self-confidence, feelings and attitudes? How can you do all this better?

- Review whether and how you engage people in the change effort by influencing, motivating and inspiring them to *want to do* what needs to be done, to devote discretionary effort to it willingly, even eagerly. To what extent do you know what motivates and inspires each of your team members, both collectively and individually, in their everyday work and in times of uncertainty and change? How do you use your position and personal power, including the use of inspirational speech and language? How can you do all this better?

- Sustaining change requires the sharing of power through distributed leadership. Leaders need to assess their own feelings about being in control, sharing power and taking responsibility: change in organizations can be led from the top, the middle or the bottom. Organizational transformation, to be effective and sustainable, is led from the top. Consider how you feel about the notion that there can be – and are – legitimate leaders at all levels in an organization. How do you feel about sharing power, at times following rather than leading, and accepting responsibility and accountability for the initiation, process and outcomes of change?

- Sustainable change and transformation can be achieved only through ethical and socially responsible leadership. Key issues for you to consider, therefore, are economic impact; the well-being, satisfaction and commitment of employees during and after a change process; the clarity and intention of a vision for change; integrity with respect to organizational core values; allowing, indeed encouraging, employee voice; and providing meaning and value in employee work. How do you measure up in each of these areas? How can you do better?

- Leading change means changing ourselves, what we do and how we do it as well as changing others. Practitioners of change therefore need humility and receptiveness as well as **resilience** and persistence. Willingness to take risks and experiment and to learn *and apply* the lessons from both success and especially failure starts with oneself as a role model and then continues and succeeds by helping others to do the same. How can you do all this better?

Further reading on leading change

Barbour, J-A.D. and Hickman, G.R. (eds) (2011) *Leadership for Transformation*. San Francisco, CA: Jossey-Bass and International Leadership Association.

De Smet, A., Lavoie, J. and Hioe, E.S. (2012) 'Developing better change leaders', *McKinsey Quarterly*, April.

Kouzes, J.L. and Posner, B.Z. (2010) *The Leadership Challenge Vision Book*, 4th edn. San Francisco, CA: Jossey-Bass.

Nohria, N. and Kumar, R. (eds) (2010) *Handbook of Leadership Theory and Practice*. Boston, MA: Harvard Business Press.

O'Connell, D., Hickerson, K. and Pillutla, A. (2011) 'Organizational visioning: An integrative review', *Group & Organization Management*, 36: 103–25.

Rush, S. (ed.) (2012) *On Leading in Times of Change*. Greensboro, NC: Center for Creative Leadership.

Shea, G.P. and Solomon, C.A. (2013) *Leading Successful Change*. Philadelphia, PA: Wharton Digital Press.

Managing Change

4

Overview

- Change management is universally seen by managers as important to the success of their organizations. It is complementary to the leadership of change and, together with leadership, necessary for effective and sustainable change. However, its perceived importance is not matched by its actual success, often because of poor management. We describe how change is often poorly managed in many ways and the ghosts of past failures return to haunt us.

- The chapter discusses the role of managers in the change process and the competencies required of them in managing change.

- We consider several aspects of managing change, including the purposes of change management, managerial responses to the ability and willingness of people to adapt, theories of change management, structural and process aspects of managing change, and political considerations.

- Managing change requires action that translates vision, purpose, values and strategies into reality through action plans, accountabilities, objectives, key performance measures, tasks, action and, ultimately, outputs and outcomes.

- We discuss organizational capabilities and strategies for managing change and we provide examples.

- Ethically and socially responsible change is a necessary ingredient in managing for sustainable change in terms of the intentions, methods, results and consequences of the change process. **Employee social responsibility** is part and parcel of corporate social responsibility on managing change.

- Strategies and methods for developing change-management competencies are discussed.

- Organizational change is often the purpose of large-scale leadership and management development programmes, focusing on a few critical attributes and behaviours for managing change.

- Change is inextricably associated with risk and uncertainty and hence the possibility, indeed likelihood, of mistakes, errors and failures, as we discussed in relation to leading change. We argue further that these are golden opportunities for learning, improvement and development towards a dynamic learning culture and ultimately sustainable organizational success and competitiveness.

Learning objectives

By the end of this chapter you will be able to:

- Distinguish between leading change and managing change and relate them to each other in explaining effective organizational change
- Explain why change initiatives so often fail or fall short because of poor management
- Explain what is meant by 'strategies for change'
- Produce a model of change management
- Explain the competencies required for managers to carry out change initiatives successfully
- Explain the ethical and moral issues that arise in change initiatives and how they may be resolved
- Use learning opportunities to manage change effectively according to best practice
- Use the information and ideas in this chapter to manage organizational changes effectively or to contribute to the effective management of change initiatives and programmes in an organization

Change management is universally seen by managers as important to the success of their organizations (Gentry et al., 2013). However, its perceived importance is not matched by its actual success. Indeed, *'plus ça change, plus c'est la même chose'* (Karr, 1849) – 'the more things change, the more they stay the same' – an unfortunately suitable epigram for change management (Sirkin et al., 2005). Trying to change is fraught with difficulty. Change often fails because of poor strategic management of change, poor day-to-day management skills and sometimes unethical behaviour – the subject of this chapter.

Take, for example, the banking and finance sector. Following one of its most turbulent periods in its history, it has been facing more complex and dramatic change than ever before. Moorhouse Consulting says that UK and global regulatory requirements have been forcing banks and finance organizations not only to change their structures, processes and procedures but also to change the way they operate (Moorhouse Consulting, 2012a: 3). Moorhouse's Financial Services Survey 2012 revealed some issues in managing change:

- Senior leaders were not fully committed to the required changes, staff did not have the capacity to deliver change and front-line staff could not cope with the volume of change.
- Over half of the organizations surveyed displayed duplication of activities across departments.
- Only 11% measured return on investment from all of their change projects, leading to billions of pounds of untracked spend.
- Nearly half of the organizations are not coping with the volume of regulatory change (40% of all change projects).

Moorhouse Consulting (2012a: 3) – a management consultancy company – has recommended improvements in managing change in the financial services sector by:

- Defining and maintaining a single strategically aligned portfolio of change activity in which projects are aligned to strategy and vision (two of the core leadership themes and practices that we discussed in the previous chapter)
- Tracking, measuring and managing portfolio delivery through performance management (which we discuss more broadly later in this chapter)
- Making strategic improvements to the capability to deliver and sustain change
- Taking proactive steps to influence and shape the future of the industry

Large-scale organizational change initiatives often fail because of their complexity. Change management in these cases is challenging and daunting. Larry Hirschhorn (2002) suggests that a three-pronged strategy – he calls these three elements political, marketing and 'military' campaigns – increases the likelihood of success:

- A political campaign takes the form of building of alliances, first with enthusiasts and then with consensus builders, and changing both formal and informal organizational structures.
- A marketing campaign comprises working with employees in identifying and building on existing good practices and engaging employees in spreading them throughout the organization, using catchy themes for them.
- A military campaign focus on overcoming resistance to change by 'securing supply lines' and 'choosing beachheads' – paying attention to 'insurgents' and redirecting their initiatives and passion and focusing on selected targets and winning them over with success that others then want to emulate.

Hirschhorn illustrates the campaign approach with helpful examples from Hewlett–Packard, Bristol–Myers Squibb, ASDA and a consulting company.

Managers need to deal with constant change, says Edward Lawler (1986). But Robert Paton and James McCalman (2008: 3) go further:

> Management and change are synonymous; it is impossible to undertake a journey, for in many respects that is what change is, without first addressing the purpose of the trip, the route you wish to travel and with whom. Managing change is about handling the complexities of travel. It is about evaluating, planning and implementing operational, tactical and strategic 'journeys'.

We have argued in Chapter 3 that it is *leadership* that is intrinsically about change, about showing the way in the journey of change from A to B. *Management* is about ensuring that processes and people are working efficiently and effectively, about making it happen, which concerns not only maintaining the status quo but also changing it. In the latter case managing change *is* about making the journey from A to B, about dealing with the needs, problems, difficulties and solutions in making that journey.

Management can be thought of as a function that is part of an organization's formal structure, as in the four-fold characterization of management by Laurie Mullins (2010: 425) as:

1. Taking place within a structured organizational setting and with prescribed roles
2. Directed towards the attainment of aims and objectives
3. Achieved through the efforts of other people
4. Using systems and procedures

Management consists of roles that managers play – what managers actually do (Kotter, 1990a; Mintzberg, 1979). This chapter therefore also addresses questions such as the following. What is the role of managers in the change process? What do managers need to do to manage change no matter its source or impact? What are the capabilities required to effectively manage change?

While managers in organizations themselves have an important part to play in change programmes, Milan Kubr (2002: 85) points out that change is the 'raison d'être of management consulting'. Management consultants, he says, help clients to understand change and carry out change that is needed to survive, improve, develop or prosper in an environment in which 'change is the only constant'.

On the other hand, change management is an activity that practising managers, not human resources specialists or external consultants, should handle, and it comprises a set of skills that practising managers need to have, according to consultant Ron Ashkenas (2013). However, he says, while we do have a good understanding of change as a process and well-known techniques to carry it out, 'the managerial capacity to implement it has been woefully underdeveloped'. Companies should ask themselves the following questions. Are there a common framework, language and set of tools in place to facilitate change? Are plans for change properly included in overall business goals? Who is responsible for managing change within the organization?

The 2009 survey of companies' change programmes by Moorhouse Consulting (2009) and the *Financial Times* revealed several issues to do with organizational change, among them the following:

- A widespread failure to achieve the intended and sustainable benefits from change programmes
- A lack of a systematic approach or strategy for delivering the benefits
- Very differing beliefs about the success of change programmes between board members and middle-level managers – 37% of board members believing that planned benefits were delivered at least most of the time; 5% of middle managers believing so
- Needs for improvement in the delivery of benefits from change focusing on more resources, improved awareness and training, greater involvement of the business in delivering change, usage of relevant tools and techniques, and harmonizing perspectives across the organization

Moorhouse later found, in its 2012 'Barometer on Change' survey of 200 UK boardroom directors, that only 7% said that their company's change project worth an average of £10m and critical to the company's future had been fully successful (CIPD, 2012). Reasons for such a poor success rate were badly managed projects based on poor foundations, a lack of buy-in from key stakeholders, and a lack of methods to track or measure results. Moreover, Moorhouse's 2013 survey found that, while 31%

of respondents cited culture change as a key challenge, only 13% had programmes in place to address it (Moorhouse Consulting, 2013: 12).

Change programmes often fail specifically because of poor management: poor conceptualization, communication, planning, organization, direction, implementation, monitoring and control, as well as a lack of resources and know-how and incompatible corporate policies, practices and culture. Good management of change is a *sine qua non* for change to happen. While leadership of change is about showing the way and *enabling* it to happen, management of change is about *making* it happen. And managing change entails deploying important management processes and competencies.

A good case for effective management in the change process is made by Thomas Guskey in an interview with Guy Todnem and Michael Warner:

> People can be encouraged to change, but if the structure of the system in which the individuals work does not support them or allow enough flexibility, improvement efforts will fail. Similarly, if the organization's governance, policies, structures, timeframes, and resource allocation are changed but the individuals within the organization do not have opportunities to learn how to work within the new system, the improvement effort will fail. (Todnem and Warner, 1994)

Change must be managed – it must be defined, communicated, planned, organized, directed, implemented, monitored and controlled – and this is a necessary condition for successful change (Gill, 2003, 2006: 322–6; 2011: 22–5). We now explore how change is mismanaged so that we can draw some useful lessons for managing change effectively.

How change is mismanaged

How change is poorly managed is well known. Change efforts may fail because of poor planning, monitoring and control, focusing more on the objective than on the steps and process involved, a lack of milestones along the way, and failing to monitor progress and take corrective action. Change efforts often lack the necessary resources, e.g. budget, systems, time and information, and the necessary expertise – knowledge and skills (and wisdom). Corporate policies and practices sometimes remain the same and become inconsistent with the aims and strategies for change. For example, the performance criteria used in appraisal and reward policies may not support and reinforce a desired performance-driven, teamwork-oriented culture, resulting in a disincentive or lack of incentive to change behaviour. A large European study found that the most successful organizations make mutually supportive changes in terms of changes in roles, governance structures and strategies (Whittington et al., 1999): there needs to be an internal consistency among changes desired, changes achieved and their 'knock-on' effects.

Change is all too often regarded and conducted as a 'quick-fix'. This usually fails to address sufficiently the real requirements of change and their implications for the organization as a whole and therefore causes unforeseen and unacceptable disruption. Related to this, change initiatives are often the result of the naïve adoption of management fads. Such fads frequently deal with only one aspect of an organization's functioning without regard to their implications for other aspects, such as culture.

Managing change effectively requires management skills of a high order. For example, lack of communication or inconsistent messages and the resulting misunderstanding of the aims and process of change encourage rumours that demoralize people, with a consequential lack of commitment to change.

Change initiatives fail not only because of lack of such skills but also because of the use of incomplete change models and overlooking the organization's capacity to support large-scale change, according to Willow Dea (2013). For example, Peter Smith, a vice-president in Parexel International, a contract-research organization in the life sciences sector, says that, in his company's experience, the most commonly encountered problems in managing change are insufficiently researched impact assessments and poorly maintained documentation of the change process (Drakulich, 2012).

Another way that change is mismanaged is impatience. The Center for Creative Leadership (CCL) in the USA says that the challenge of transition – the process or period of adapting to change – is often underrated:

> A change that takes 12 weeks to plan and implement typically takes 100 to 120 weeks to integrate. Poorly planned, it may take 200 weeks. Yet managers and consultants rarely allow more than 26 weeks! Without providing time and attention to transition, organizations fail to see desired benefits of change efforts. (CCL, 2012)

Bart Perkins (2012) notes that change management is largely ignored in many organizations until problems crop up and they have to invoke it. And then they have to do so too quickly. There are, he says, other reasons too why management fails or refuses to recognize the need for change:

- The assumption that people will adopt new systems because they are better in some way
- Inadequate or non-existent analysis
- Limitations on resources
- The perception that the time and money required for change management is wasteful
- Political forces that inhibit change management owing to deeply entrenched interests in the status quo

Activity

Share with colleagues your experience of how change has been mismanaged in your organization or in one known to you personally.
   What similarities and differences are there in your accounts?

Discussion Questions

1 What do you think is the most serious way in which change is mismanaged?
2 Why?
3 How can this be prevented?

Perspectives on managing change

Organizations today face the pressure for change from many sources. Many changes are small but some are organization-wide. CCL (2013: 7) says: 'An organization's mission may change, as well as its focus, strategy, culture, and market. Such changes can have a serious impact on … leader[s].' CCL's research indicates that the most frequently mentioned success factor in change is the ability of people to adapt.

Knowing that organizational change can be a frightening prospect for employees, CCL produced a very useful short guidebook to help both managers and leaders in an organization adapt to a wide variety of situations, opportunities and environments. It shows how change affects them, their thoughts and their emotions. It provides them with management tools and strategies to allow them to take action not only to survive change but also to thrive in it (CCL, 2013). To the guidebook's readers, CCL says:

> Change is a constant in today's workplace, and leaders [and managers] must learn strategies to deal with change successfully, or otherwise face derailment. To succeed you must first understand how changes within your organization are affecting you, and use that understanding to help manage the transition from the old way to the new way of doing things. This transition typically occurs in three distinct phases: the ending, where you accept the conclusion of the old way of doing things; the neutral zone, where you begin to adapt to the confusion of the new way of doing things; and the new beginning, where you accept the new way of doing things and begin to successfully move forward in the new environment. Furthermore, by understanding how you and other individuals perceive your organization, you can gain a greater awareness of how to specifically manage the transition. Once you have done this, you will be able to move forward, helping yourself and the individuals you lead to survive and thrive. (2013: 6)

One aspect of managing and sustaining change, therefore, is preparing managers who are going to lead it. McKinsey consultants (De Smet et al., 2012) describe how a global industrial company placed leadership development at the heart of a major programme of operational improvement involving change to the production system across 200 plants around the world.[1] They offer insights into the lessons they learned that make it possible to sustain a profound transformation:

- Tie leadership training to business goals, whereby the goals of training clearly support or directly contribute to the vision, purpose, values, strategies and specific business goals and plans of the organization
- Build on strengths – train those managers already positively influential in change and skilled in desired behaviour
- Ensure training participants have access to senior-executive sponsors to discuss how they lead change and 'hard truths' about it
- Create networks of change leaders who use the same 'vocabulary' and encourage collaboration globally

---

1 The leadership development programme took four months, comprising two one-week offsite courses and, for each participant, ongoing coaching on how to apply what was learned to the workplace.

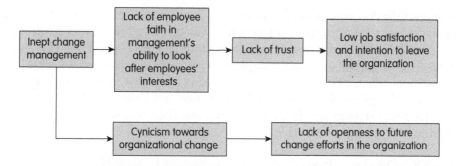

Figure 4.1 Cause and effect in change attitudes and behaviour, based on Bordia et al. (2011)

How a 'new' UK university prepared and developed leaders and managers for organizational change is the subject of a extensive case study accompanying this book.

In the Moorhouse 2013 'Barometer in Change', based on a survey of more than 200 UK board members and their direct reports, respondents were focused overwhelmingly on cost reduction (54% on cost reduction and 22% on performance improvement), and only 19% claimed they were addressing new products or services despite 72% citing new products and services as a major strategic challenge (Moorhouse Consulting, 2013). Moorhouse's analysis concluded that companies need to align their change initiatives to the broader strategic challenges they face and that they need to engage with their staff more effectively to foster a positive attitude towards change that embraces new skills. This is a question of organizational capability, to which we return later in this chapter.

The history of change in an organization shapes employees' attitudes towards future change and their resulting behavioural responses to it: 'once bitten, twice shy' is a well-worn adage. Managing change entails addressing and resolving this issue before proceeding with new change initiatives to avoid a strong likelihood of derailment later.

Two studies explored this phenomenon in the Philippines, one in a property development firm that was merging with another and the other in an educational institution that was undergoing extensive restructuring (Bordia et al., 2011). The cause-and-effect chains summarized in Figure 4.1 were hypothesized by Prashant Bordia and colleagues based on extant theory.

In a questionnaire survey of 155 employees in the property development firm (a sample of just under 50% of the total number), eight items measured aspects of poor change management (for example: 'In my experience, past change initiatives have failed to achieve their intended purpose'). Trust was measured using seven items and cynicism was measured using eight items taken from previously validated questionnaires (Robinson, 1996; Wanous et al., 2000). Inept change management was found, as predicted, to be inversely related to trust and directly related to cynicism.

In the educational institution, the same procedure was followed with a sample of 124 employees (a response rate of 62%), but with two additional aspects investigated. In the implementation of previous changes, staff had not been consulted and management had acted in an autocratic manner, leading even to lawsuits by some disaffected staff. Job satisfaction was measured using three items, turnover intentions were measured by four items, and openness to change was measured using four items, again taken from validated instruments (Cammann et al., 1983: 71–138; Fried et al., 1996; Wanberg and Banas, 2000). Data on employee turnover were collected two years later. The results for trust and cynicism were the same as in the first study. In addition, trust was found to be positively related to job satisfaction and inversely related to turnover intentions. And cynicism was found to be inversely related to openness to change.

   Bordia and colleagues (2011) write:

> as when driving a car, changing the direction of an organization should involve a 'rear view' inspection of the change management history. We recommend that leaders pay attention to employee change beliefs arising from the history of change in the organization.

Ineptly managed change, therefore, clearly has dysfunctional consequences. It causes negative attitudes towards both change in general and the organization itself. A vicious cycle results, whereby employees will avoid participating in change initiatives, consequently prejudicing future changes and thereby reinforcing negative attitudes and behaviour. *Déjà vu*: how the ghosts of changes past return to haunt us!

   There is no doubt that what Harold Sirkin and colleagues (2005) term the 'soft' aspects of organizational change – leadership, culture and employee motivation, for example – are critical to its success. In a study of 225 companies they found a significant correlation between the success or failure of change programmes and four 'hard' (management) factors, which need to be addressed first:

- **D**uration – planning and conducting frequent progress reviews (the more frequent, the better)
- **I**ntegrity – ensuring the integrity and capabilities of the project team
- **C**ommitment – ensuring the dedication of both senior executives and line managers to the change programme through its visible endorsement from the top down and the constant communication of the purpose and meaning of the change
- **E**ffort – ensuring that employees' workload is not increased too much – no more than 10% – which may entail removing some non-essential tasks from some employees or using temporary workers or outsourcing (the less extra work and effort, the better). (2005: 83(10), 108–118)

Sirkin and colleagues call these factors '**DICE**' and say that their use in assessing and managing change programmes has held up well in more than 1,000 change initiatives. While this model of change management provides a common language for change and clearly has real practical value, theoretically it includes what more accurately should be regarded as 'leadership' rather than management. Commitment from top management clearly is part and parcel of effective leadership, and commitment of line managers and employees affected by the change clearly is a consequence of top management's leadership and commitment. Moreover, the additional effort displayed by employees is also a consequence of effective leadership. And John Kotter argues that:

> Task forces, 'work streams', and project management organizations are still the most common vehicles used to drive significant change efforts. These structures can help, but they have tendencies that can lead toward wrong processes, and they simply don't have

sufficient power for an extremely difficult set of tasks … Leading change competently is the only answer. (2012b: viii–ix)

We would argue, however, that 'leading change' is not the *only* answer: leadership of change and management of change are each a *sine qua non* for effective change and transformation.

Mariannunziata Liguori (2012) investigated how organizations manage the process of change and why only some achieve radical change, using as examples change in accounting systems and structures in Canadian and Italian municipalities. The dimensions of change that she explored were the pace (evolutionary or revolutionary change), sequence (time order of key elements in the change process) and linearity (reorientation, discontinuance or lack of resolution in the change process).

Liguori found that radical change takes place independently of both linearity in the change process, namely oscillations and reversals, and pace, namely both evolutionary change and revolutionary change, and that radical change is primarily associated with the sequence of the key elements of the process. One implication of her findings, Liguori suggests, is that managers need to allow a 'settling time' between different changes so that new values and changes in systems and structures can be absorbed. A strong professional culture may have values that are inconsistent with managerialism, thereby adversely affecting, even halting, the change process.

Looking at the gap between planning change and doing it, Duane Dike, a manager at Disneyland in California, says that 'just about every change theorist will tell us that … questioning how we do things is the most significant sign of potential success … change isn't in the big things; change is the little learning stages along the way' (Dike, 2012). The stage between is exploration – 'thinking, mistaking, learning, testing, supporting and struggling'. An example he gives is the development sequence under Steve Jobs's leadership of Apple Macs, Pixar, iMacs, iPods, iPhones and then iPads. Change, Dike says, is 'not unlike the transformation of data to knowledge. Change is a progressive state of gathering knowledge', and indeed creating understanding and wisdom:

Data ⟶ Information ⟶ Knowledge ⟶ Wisdom

Managing the emotions and politics – scepticism, fear and panic – that inevitably accompany change is critical to its success. We discuss each of these further in Chapters 11 and 12. Ellen Auster and Trish Ruebottom (2013) suggest a tried-and-tested five-step process that can be tailored to particular contexts:

1. Map the political landscape of who will be affected by change
2. Identify the key influencers – those who have the skills and interest to influence and convince others of the benefits of change – within each stakeholder group
3. Assess influencers' receptiveness to change
4. Mobilize influential sponsors and promoters – those who have the skills, connections and insights to champion change
5. Engage influential positive and negative sceptics

Receptiveness to change tends to follow a pattern of diffusion – innovators, early adopters, the early and late majority, and the laggards (Rogers, 1962), important to the 'tipping point' (Gladwell, 2002) in a change process. Auster and Ruebottom (2013) recommend recasting diffusion in terms of sponsors, promoters, indifferent fence-sitters, cautious fence-sitters, positive sceptics and negative sceptics. Positive sceptics, they say, are valuable in the change process in offering perspectives and insights into challenges and risks. And negative sceptics are also important to work with: they represent anxieties and worries that need to be addressed.

In the case of a sustainability initiative, Auster and Ruebottom (2013) say:

> Key external stakeholders might include suppliers, customers, communities, government entities, other social sector organizations and informal grassroots activists. Formal internal stakeholder groups tend to follow the organization chart. In a sustainability initiative, they might include people at different levels as well as functional and product divisions or geographic regions. Informal groups might also emerge according to tenure in the organization, social demographics, spatial proximity or personal stance on sustainability issues.

Middle-level managers potentially play an important role in organizational change as change agents. However, as the interface between top-down and bottom-up changes, they are prone to experience additional workload and stress and display ambivalence towards it. Edel Conway and Kathy Monks (2011) show how, paradoxically, this ambivalence towards top-down change may actually stimulate initiatives in their areas of responsibility that allow the change to succeed. In their research in the Irish health service they found that middle managers' enthusiasm for their own changes, in contrast to their lack of it for top-down change, often led to solutions that the top-down change was intended to achieve, such as reductions in waiting lists and improvements in patient care.

And, finally, there is the question – what exactly is it that we change? If there is not a fit between, on the one hand, what we are or what we are doing and, on the other hand, what is needed, then what do we change? In the words of American feminist, journalist and activist Gloria Steinem (1984): 'If the shoe doesn't fit, must we change the foot?' Why, she asks, do we always try to change what we are or what we are doing rather than changing what is needed? The change literature scarcely addresses this aspect of change. And it is something for leaders and managers of change to ponder on.

Discussion Questions 1

1   How can we prevent the 'ghosts' of changes past that return to haunt us from doing so?
2   What impact on employee trust and receptivity to change would this have?

Discussion Questions 2

1   Why do you think the majority of companies (72%) cite new products and services as a major strategic challenge yet only a small minority (19%) say they are using change initiatives to address it?
2   Why (if it is true) do we tend to try to change what we are or what we are doing rather than changing what is needed?

Capabilities, competencies and strategies for managing change

Dynamic capability theory has a contribution to make from a strategic point of view to our understanding of how to manage change. Constance Helfat and colleagues (2007) define dynamic capability as 'the ability of the firm to purposefully create, extend, or modify its resource base to address a rapidly changing environment'. They argue that the three processes of coordination, learning and strategic competitive response are important activities that facilitate change within an organization and illustrate this with examples from a number of businesses:

- Coordination concerns identifying and integrating valuable existing resources in a way that shapes new competencies
- Learning concerns exploring, experimenting and exploiting lessons and successes
- Strategic competitive response (strategic flexibility) is the ability of the organization to scan the environment, identify new opportunities, assess its competitive position and respond to competitive strategic moves

A study by Aimilia Protogerou and colleagues (2008) using structural equation modelling supports this claim, suggesting that dynamic capabilities are antecedents to functional competencies (marketing and technological) that in turn have a significant effect on performance. Dynamic capabilities are important in managing both external environmental change and internal change (Barrales-Molina et al., 2013).

In response to a request by a well-known client company in the insurance industry, the second co-author developed a model of management, specifically showing the management steps in getting from the vision for the organization and its associated purpose or mission to the desired reality. This model is shown in Figure 4.2.

This model in part resembles Prisca Collins and Rodney Hopson's model in a mixed-method approach inspired by the W.K. Kellogg Foundation to evaluating

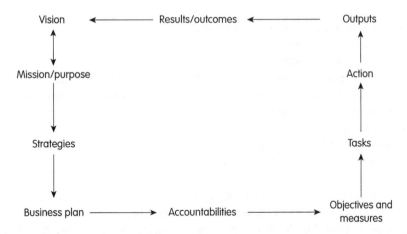

Figure 4.2   Management: turning vision and purpose into reality

leadership development programmes at individual, organizational and community levels in terms of resources/inputs, activities, outputs, outcomes and impact (Collins and Hopson, 2007: 173–98). It can serve as a basis for managing change too. Effective leadership underpins a change initiative, with a clear, shared vision, mission or purpose, and corporate values that show the way, and empowerment and engagement that enable and help change to be managed effectively. And in our model, strategies are a core leadership theme and practice, and they are the basis for managing a change programme.

So organizational change requires both leading and managing. Failure to understand this can result in failure in the change process. Victoria Grady (2013) says: 'Change management focuses on the change process, the steps taken, and the tools used to facilitate change.' And change management according to the American Society for Training & Development (now known as the Association for Talent Development) (ASTD, 2013) concerns applying 'a systematic process to shift individuals, teams, and organizations from current state to desired state'. According to the ASTD model, this entails:

- Establishing sponsorship and ownership for change
- Building involvement
- Creating a contract for change
- Conducting diagnostic assessments
- Providing feedback
- Facilitating strategic planning for change
- Supporting the change intervention
- Encouraging integration of change into organizational culture
- Managing consequences
- Evaluating change results

High-level cognitive and behavioural skills pervade the following nine steps of a 'road map' that Willow Dea (2013) proposes as characterizing successful and sustainable transformations:

1. Preparing
2. Creating an organizational (change) vision
3. Assessing design requirements
4. Designing the desired state
5. Planning and organizing for implementation of the change, including ensuring that the organization's managers are able to effect and sustain its implementation
6. Implementing the new state
7. Analysing the impact
8. Celebrating and integrating the new state
9. Course correcting as the new state takes hold

This model overlaps with the leadership aspects of change, in particular creating the vision, but all other steps in the roadmap are aspects of management.

Moorhouse Consulting (2008: 1) describes the conventional approach to managing change as top-down:

- Determining the vision for change
- Shaping the strategy that will deliver it
- Deciding the major activities required to deliver the strategy (the portfolio)
- Forming the building blocks (programmes)
- Designing the work required to drive the change (projects)

However, two issues arise in this approach, Moorhouse Consulting says, that hinder delivery. One issue is that 'business as usual appears to get in the way':

> Many organizations embarking on the route to change are inclined to regard business as usual as separate from change activity. The types of comment we hear from staff in these organizations are 'I don't have time to commit to change because it gets in the way of the day job' or 'I'm involved with a project, so don't need to worry about the day to day activity of the business'. (2008: 9)

The second issue is that in-house expertise, usually project management rather than programme management or portfolio management, mostly resides 'bottom-up'. Moorhouse Consulting (2008: 1) recommends a more pragmatic approach:

- Strategic alignment by integrating top-down and bottom-up thinking about how change is delivered
- Creating ownership of change throughout the organization and linking the way benefits are pursued and managed to a tested business case
- Adopting a consistent organization-wide approach to managing change, creating a core of expertise, and making the delivery of change a core skill and rewarding it accordingly

We discuss the use of project management in managing change further in Chapter 7.

Tenets for creating successful change, according to Gregory Shea and Cassie Solomon (2013a) are: 'Focus on the behaviors you want from people. Design the work environment to foster those behaviors.' They suggest there are eight factors that make up the work environment that influence work behaviour: organization, the physical workplace, work flow/processes, people's skills and orientations, rewards and punishments, metrics, information distribution and decision allocation (Shea and Solomon, 2013b). They quote the case of Hyundai, whose Chung Mong-Koo's leveraging of those factors transformed the car manufacturer.

To address the issues and shortcomings of change programmes they discovered in their 2009 survey, Moorhouse Consulting (2012a: 25) developed the approach termed Benefits Realisation Management (BRM). This comprises:

- A clear framework providing a common language and a route map to follow
- Available staff resources with the relevant skills, tools and techniques
- A clear and consistent statement of the nature of the benefits, defined in detail at the outset and agreed within the business
- Performance management using accurate, timely data
- A clear strategic linkage shaping the change programme to ensure the business strategies are delivered
- Full engagement by the change programme with the business, facilitated by a business change manager

Moorhouse Consulting rightly says: '[Change] programmes don't deliver benefits: businesses realise benefits enabled by the capabilities delivered by [change] programmes ... new capability is not, in itself, a benefit' (2012b: 25). We explore the identification, management and realization of benefits further in Chapter 13.

Deciding what to change is one thing; deciding *how* to change is another. The following case study describes a novel approach to doing this.

CASE STUDY

Deciding *how* to change

Gail Longbotham and Roger Longbotham (2006) describe how the powerful methodologies of process improvement and experimental design, commonly used in determining *what* needs to be changed, were applied to deciding *how* to change in a company with 150 stores throughout the USA. They claim that this approach provided an objective basis for decision-making about change. The change that was needed in the company was replacement of the commission-based pay scheme that was discovered to be dysfunctional with a salary-based scheme to minimize employee attrition and increase sales revenue. The experimental design chosen for identifying how to change was a fractional factorial design with replication. Seven factors were identified that were thought to be helpful in minimizing resistance to change and maximizing buy-in (+ and – indicate opposites or options, with + anticipated to be preferred):

A. Top management presentation of the change in person (+) or via video (–)
B. Implementation of change in stages (+) or simultaneously (–)
C. Lead time for initiating change after announcement of one week (+) or three to four weeks (–)
D. Context for announcing the change: meeting plus celebration (+) or meeting only (–)
E. Focus of corporate announcement: future health of company (+) or long-term benefit to employee (–)
F. Involvement of middle management with each sales associate: one-to-one meeting (+) or no meeting (–)
G. Minimizing attrition: incentive (+) or no incentive (–)

Two performance measures were used: employee attrition and sales. Using combinations of these seven factors and two treatment conditions and computations for sales and attrition, the effects of the factors on attrition and sales and their statistical significance were calculated. Based on this analysis, a plan for implementing the change was drawn up, as shown in Table 4.1.

Table 4.1   Actions used in implementing change

	Factor	Reason
A+	Personal visit from top management	Increased sales revenue
B+	Staged implementation	Minimized employee attrition
C–	Longer lead time	Increased revenue
D+	Do the celebration	Did not significantly affect revenue but it helped morale
F+	Conduct one-on-one meetings	Minimized attrition

According to Longbotham and Longbotham (2006):

Organizations have used rigorous methodologies to identify improvements necessary to remain viable and competitive in today's turbulent business environment. However, they have rarely used the same level of rigor in the implementation of the identified improvements. Using the same level of rigor as an approach to implementation is appropriate when successful implementation is uncertain, potential gain is high, and implementation is done at a large enough scale to warrant a test on a smaller scale.

One might question the particular factors, treatment conditions and performance measures used in this study and perhaps develop them, replace some or add more. But as an example of a rational basis for change management, it is worthy of consideration.

Case study questions

1   What are the benefits and drawbacks of using the Longbothams' approach to deciding how to change?
2   What is your overall conclusion about its rationale and usefulness?

Written by Roger Gill.

What factors determine the success of a change initiative? A survey of 181 senior executives in the heavy manufacturing industry in the USA with personal experience of a successful change initiative revealed the factor rankings and responses shown in Table 4.2.

We see here a mix of management and leadership factors that give a sense of the priorities that senior executive feel are important for successful change.

Table 4.2   Perceived determinants of success in change initiatives*

Rank	Factor	Responses (%)
1	Participation, teamwork and ownership	82
2	Clear focus, direction and goals	72
3	Trustworthy leadership	65
4	Speed and a sense of urgency	59
5	Ongoing measurement, feedback and adjustment	55
6	Clearly defined improvement process or plan	43
7	Follow-up and accountability	36
8	Effective training or education	31
9	Accurate data and effective analysis	29
10	Clearly defined roles and strong execution	26
11	Rewarding progress and celebrating success	25
12	The right people	24
13	Real commitment to improve or change	22

*Based on Longenecker, Papp and Stansfield (2006)

Ashley Harshak and colleagues (2010) at management consultants Booz & Company (renamed Strategy& in 2014) describe five key success factors in managing change that is sustainable:

1. Understanding and spelling out the impact of change on people

   - Roles and responsibilities
   - Skills and knowledge
   - Behaviours
   - Performance management

2. Building the emotional and rational case for change

   - Why are we changing?
   - What is changing?
   - What are the benefits?
   - What is staying the same?
   - What's in it for me?
   - What's against my interests?

3. Role modelling the change as a leadership team

   - Displaying the new behaviours
   - Holding one another to account for their successful adoption
   - Explaining what the top management were discussing and doing and progress being made

4. Mobilizing people to own and accelerate the change

   - Leveraging the informal organization – the network of peer-to-peer interaction
   - Focusing on shared values, communities and pride

5. Embedding the change in the fabric of the organization

   - How can we continue to engage and involve employees over the long term?
   - What lessons have we learned?
   - How can we institutionalize best practices to capture the full benefit of this change and any future changes?
   - Align HR systems, structures, processes and incentives with the goals of the transformation, e.g. performance management, recruitment and selection, learning and development, workforce strategy

Booz & Company's approach to change management therefore is people-focused and systemic and uses both formal and informal levers:

1. Define and articulate business objectives and a clear vision and goals for change
2. Understand how things work today by identifying change enablers and barriers in the current state
3. Define the case for change from a people perspective
4. Plan and manage the change programme, delivering a tailored programme of interventions in the formal and informal organization
5. Measure progress against change outcomes, focusing on people leading, adopting and sustaining the change to realize the business benefits

Table 4.3 Key attributes of change managers

Attribute	Score*
Empowering others**	88
Team building	82
Learning from others	79
Adaptability and flexibility	69
Openness to new ideas	64
Managing resistance	58
Conflict resolution	53
Networking	52
Knowledge of the business	37
Problem solving	29

*Based on Delphi-style panel members' ratings of importance from 1 to 10 resulting in a maximum potential score of 100.

**This attribute we classify as a core leadership theme and practice I (see Chapter 3 on Leading Change), but we include here because Caldwell classified it as an attribute of managing change.

In planning a change initiative there is much benefit to be gained by focusing on those employees who are most involved in, or who have the most influence over, the particular activities that need to change, which McKinsey consultants illustrate from their work with a European retail bank (Gardini et al., 2011).

McBer, a consultancy organization, developed a competency model of the successful change agent, emphasizing a combination of interpersonal, diagnostic, initiation and organizational skills (Cripe, 1993). More recently Bob Thames and Douglas Webster (2009) proposed 13 specific change competencies: leadership, commitment, accountability, forward thinking, innovation, communication, risk tolerance, organizational learning, trust, diversity, empowerment, adaptability and dynamic stability.

Key attributes (competencies) of change managers, according to research by Raymond Caldwell (2003), are shown in Table 4.3.

A team approach to implementing organizational change is recommended by Monica Higgins and colleagues (Higgins et al., 2012). Implementation teams are responsible for implementing change, whereas conventional teams in organizations are usually strategic decision-making bodies or operate as targets of change. Higgins and colleagues explored over a period of two years how learning by team members, an important factor in sustaining organizational change, was associated with positional and tenure diversity and work context in American school districts. They found that it was not so much team-membership stability as the stability of team members' roles that was important. The fact that team members may rotate or change in team roles is less important than the stability of the roles they perform. Higgins and colleagues believe that their findings concerning role stability may be more often the case than the exception in many settings, for example musical orchestras, military organizations and professional athletic teams.

James Evans (2012) describes in the following case study how a change programme addressed communication problems and dysfunctional departments that were causing confusion and enmity throughout the administration in a US art college.

CASE EXAMPLE

Improving communication and collaboration in a US art college

Communication problems and dysfunctional departmental silos were causing confusion and enmity throughout the administration in a US art college. This required an organization-wide change programme focusing on improving communication and collaboration, thereby providing better service to students and improved relations among departments.

A learning and development (L&D) advisory board was set up to provide support and direction. Programme outcomes were:

- Creation of an intranet devoted to information sharing and communication, including a directory of employees and their primary functions to help students link to the appropriate administrative resources
- Videos of inter-departmental awareness sessions used as an onboarding tool
- Improvements developed by staff members during cross-functional brainstorming workshops that included better communication among departments about student enrolment and financial status
- An employee-recognition programme.

Key lessons learned were that:

- Maintaining a high level of engagement with the change process can be difficult for L&D advisory board members as they balance their primary job responsibilities with the demands of their advisory board roles, and regular meetings to stay connected and a flexible approach from all involved are needed to maintain momentum
- Documenting the group's activities and sharing progress towards the initiative's goals motivates members and builds grassroots support
- Maintaining patience is paramount: organizational change is difficult, and it takes time, and this needs to be kept in mind to help people stay focused and positive when rough spots come, as they inevitably will

Written by Roger Gill.

Management essentially concerns the effective planning, organization, communication, and monitoring and control of work performance, entailing effective policies, resourcing, operational procedures and practices. Managing work performance – performance management – includes monitoring and control as an essential element. The ideas behind monitoring and control are that work performance should be tracked against objectives and plans and, where there is adverse deviation from them in progress or achievement, corrective action should be taken in a way, of course, that is emotionally intelligent and motivating. This view is rational and therefore represents common sense and 'good' management.

However, this view may be seriously counter-productive. The reason is that 'adverse deviation' may be regarded as a mistake, error or failure, and mistakes, errors and failure should be avoided at (almost) all cost and their cause – a human being – should be identified, blamed, punished and corrected. In managing change, this is particularly significant: change is about doing something new or in a new way and therefore is less predictable and more risky than merely maintaining the status quo. Therefore errors, mistakes and failure are more likely.

The interesting thing about errors, mistakes and failure is that they are potentially the greatest source of learning and development for human beings. Such potential for performance improvement and successful innovation, such capability for development – and for organizational change and transformation – can be fulfilled, however, only in a culture of accepting and then responding positively and constructively to such errors, mistakes and failure as opportunities to learn (which we also comment on in Chapters 3 and 8). For example, as Schumpeter said in *The Economist*:

> James McNerney, a former boss of 3M, a manufacturer, damaged the company's innovation … by trying to apply six-sigma principles (which are intended to reduce errors on production lines) to the entire company, including the research laboratories. (2011: 75)

Big errors, mistakes and failure, however, like defects on the production line or mistakes in the hospital operating theatre, Schumpeter says, obviously cannot be tolerated. 'Rampant experimentation' and exhortations by (some) management gurus to 'fail as much as you can' to provide maximum learning opportunities are as much an exaggerated and slavish attachment to a management fad as is the universal application of Six Sigma.

Once a learning culture that encourages and ensures learning from errors, mistakes and failure is established – and this is a huge transformation challenge in itself – the chances of success for change in the organization are vastly increased (see Chapter 8). Managing change therefore requires a performance management system that is embraced by enlightened and skilful managers and incorporates performance planning, progress monitoring, coaching for knowledge and skill improvement, counselling for problem solving, and reinforcement of improvement and progress.

Activity

1 In a group, share your experiences of how mistakes, errors and failures were handled in an organization you are familiar with.
2 Summarize the different ways they were handled.
3 Critique the ways they were handled and suggest how they could have been handled better to identify lessons for learning how to avoid or minimize such risks in future.
4 What would need to be done to make sure these lessons are actually applied in future?

Discussion Questions

1 What are the benefits and problems in using performance management to manage change initiatives?
2 What is your overall conclusion about its usefulness?

Ethical aspects of managing change

Sustainable change in organizations is a consequence of applying its members' collective knowledge and skills, and the influence of their collective attitudes in change initiatives. Ethical and socially responsible change, in terms of both the change process and the goals and outcomes of change, contribute to the well-being of all organizational stakeholders and society at large. Managing change responsibly entails ensuring that intentions, goals, performance measures, processes, actions, outcomes and consequences are ethical and socially responsible.

Investing in education and training in ethics is undoubtedly worthwhile in managing change (Gill, 2011: 162–4, 167). Education and training are always potential contributors to the corporate culture as well as to individuals' knowledge, ability to act effectively and desire to do so ethically. An ethical culture – a culture of ethical shared values and individual responsibility to act ethically – is characterized by employee attitudes that display this desire to act ethically. An ethical and socially responsible culture is the necessary setting for sustainable change in organizations. The following Raytheon Company case example shows the thinking and strategy in these respects in a company in an ethically challenged industry.

CASE EXAMPLE

The Raytheon Company

The Raytheon Company in the USA, a major American defence contractor and an industrial corporation with core manufacturing concentrations in weapons and in military and commercial electronics, is clearly in an industry challenged by ethical issues and dilemmas. Patti Ellis, a vice president in the company, says that the risk of not having developed an ethical culture is much greater than the risks of not having developed other areas of business, leadership and management (Ellis, 2013). She argues that an effective ethics education programme not only reinforces a company's code of conduct and corporate values but also shows how to engage ethically at multiple levels and both internally and externally, which is required in organizational change efforts.

The Raytheon Company has an ethical decision-making model that helps employees to assess whether a particular action is 'the right thing to do' (and cautions that not taking action may have serious consequences). The company's annual ethics education programme, 'Take an Ethics Check', encourages employees to pause when confronted with a work problem and consider it from an ethical point of view; then to contact a company ethics helpline, speak to a supervisor or manager, or consult a subject specialist before deciding what to do. This approach offers employees an opportunity to ask questions concerning the ethics of a problem without fear of reprisal. Having a current, evolving and interactive ethics-education programme, Ellis says, serves to uphold a company's principles of compliance, ethics and governance. It also strengthens its corporate culture as a whole. Such a programme can be a valuable contribution in preparing for organizational change that is sustainable.

Written by Roger Gill.

Whether or not a company behaves ethically is essentially the result of the decisions and actions of individual people taken every day, not the consequence of the company's **corporate social responsibility** (CSR) policy in itself, says Donna Sockell (2013). She argues for an emphasis on 'employee social responsibility' (ESR). We generally do not, she says, train employees at all levels to think about how they make decisions and how they act in relation to values they personally hold. She says: 'companies serious about customer satisfaction ensure this is at the forefront of every decision an employee makes. We need this for ESR, it needs to be part of every discussion, decision, action'. We can say the same about ESR in carrying out a change initiative.

Sockell (2013) proposes six steps to strengthen the relationship between CSR and ESR:

1. Publicize the dependence of CSR on ESR
2. Carry out empowerment and training to help individuals understand their own values, how they fit with corporate core values, and how to base decisions and action on them.
3. State that social responsibility must be part of every decision and action, and support, recognize and reward it.
4. Ally CSR and HR in organizational changes in meaningful ways, making ESR part of them.
5. Include ESR in assessment and recruitment criteria: 'Employees evaluate you on CSR; evaluate them on ESR'.
6. Make sure that managers invite, encourage, recognize and reward critical thinking about social responsibility.

Including CSR and ESR in change initiatives is a necessary part of change leadership and change management.

Discussion Question 1

If managers are responsible for carrying out what leaders decide, *who* is morally responsible for *what* in leading and managing change?

Discussion Question 2

'Sustainable change in organizations is a consequence of applying its members' collective knowledge and skills and the influence of their collective attitudes in change initiatives.' In what ways is this true (or not)?

Activity 1

Based on the information you have from this chapter on managing change and the previous chapter on leading change, create a synthesized set of criteria for assessing and developing the characteristics needed for a manager to be able to lead and manage change effectively.

Activity 2

Based on the results of Activity 1 and information you have gained from the previous chapter on leading change, create a generic development programme for leading and managing change and explain your rationale for it.

Developing effective managers and leaders of change

Morten Hansen (2012) asks: 'How do you get leaders, employees ... even yourself to change behaviors? Executives can change strategy, products and processes until they're blue in the face, but real change doesn't take hold until people actually change what they do.'

Here is a very short story from Dave Ulrich and Norm Smallwood (2013):

> a group of turkeys ... attend a two-day training program to learn how to fly. They learn the principles of aerodynamics and they practice flying in the morning, afternoon, and evening. They learn to fly with the wind and against it, over mountains and plains, and together and by themselves. At the end of the two days, they all walk home.

How sustainable would this learning be? How sustainable would the behavioural change be? Why didn't the turkeys fly home? Sustainable change comes not from learning alone but from applying the learning in everyday behaviour.

Sustainable change requires behavioural change. Hansen (2012) advises: focus on one behaviour to change at a time; define goals for behavioural change in concrete and measurable terms, e.g. '"Listen actively" is vague and not measurable. "Paraphrase what others said and check for accuracy" is concrete and measurable; and "Paint a vivid picture ... of 'where we are now' and a better vision of a glorious new state", taps into people's emotions, using stories, metaphors, pictures, and physical objects. Hansen tells the story of British celebrity chef Jamie Oliver's mission to the United States:

> When celebrity chef Jamie Oliver wanted to change the eating habits of kids at a US school, he got their attention with a single, disgusting image: a truckload of pure animal fat ... When Oliver taught an obese kid to cook, he showed how cooking can be 'cool' – walking with head up, shoulders back, and a swagger while preparing food. This gave the boy a positive image he could relate to. (Hansen, 2012)

Sharon Turnbull (2001) studied an organizational change programme for leaders in a large global organization aimed at their adoption of a new set of organizational values as they progressed through the programme over 18 months. She found that the extent to which the ideas were adopted varied considerably across the different parts of the organization. Turnbull found that much of the variation in programme impact on individuals and units was explained by context, culture and sub-cultures – many businesses within the organization were acquisitions rather than the result of organic growth.

Organizational change is often the purpose of large-scale leadership development programmes. However, it is difficult to evaluate their impact owing to its complexity. Organizational context and culture have a mediating effect. Gareth Edwards and Sharon Turnbull (2013) found that participants in such programmes usually report individual improvements in aspects of leadership such as awareness, understanding, self-confidence, self-reflection, knowledge, attitudes, beliefs and values but that these aspects are personal whereas organizational change is essentially about the 'sum of cumulative individual changes'. They say:

> Even where a program is designed with individual change in mind … we have observed that the organizational impact of these cumulative individual changes will always be mediated by the cultural context: the structure, style, power, controls, communication networks, products, technology, and existing leadership style of the organization. These elements of both design and evaluation of leadership development programs are too often overlooked, and yet there is significant anecdotal evidence of leaders who are highly successful in one culture or context failing badly in another. (2013)

Jon Katzenbach and colleagues (2012) endorse Hansen's advice of concentrating on a few critical behaviours during a change effort. They describe how Aetna achieved a sustainable culture change by doing this rather than striving for a comprehensive cultural transformation. This enables the positive aspects of the company's culture to be tapped in facilitating change in an evolutionary and therefore sustainable way. Building on this approach, Kevin Martin suggests that 'leadership agility' – 'being able to [role-]model from the top down' in respect of critical behaviours – is invaluable in change management (Institute for Corporate Productivity, 2013).

Coaching and mentoring can help to facilitate change, as we discuss in Chapter 8. Janet Harris (2006) showed this in respect of a public sector organization dispersed through many sites in the UK. Her framework used neurolinguistics programming (NLP) techniques to enhance communication in coaching and mentoring and **action learning** as the vehicle for study.

Homan Blanchard (2012) suggests that many people in leadership positions in organizations do not feel they have enough support to initiate major change because they are expected to be able to do so on their own because they are senior. She says: 'there are some principles that can be applied to development that will facilitate and sustain change':

- Provide leaders with a compelling argument for change in the form of unequivocal information linking it with business performance and the opportunity for dialogue about it.
- Clarify how their own efforts to make and sustain change will contribute.
- Use a blended learning and development approach customized to each leader's learning style.
- Show leaders how refusal to engage with change and take personal development seriously will have consequences.
- Those who are supporting leaders in their personal development and change efforts need to have or earn their respect through themselves acting as role models for growth and change.
- Change that will be effective and sustainable cannot be rushed: in addition to leaders' ability and willingness to learn and change and 'a steady dose of partnering to provide clear direction, conversation, support and accountability over a long period of time', patience is necessary.
- Ask rather than tell: involvement, dialogue and a resulting sense of ownership of ideas gain commitment better than telling does.

The box below shows what Homan Blanchard (2012) calls useful 'power questions' that typify effective questioning.

Leading change: 'power questioning'

- What are you trying to achieve?
- How are you going to achieve it?
- What is the most important thing to do now?
- What are the other most relevant things to do?
- What are you doing at present?
- How well is it working?
- What challenges do you anticipate?
- How will you handle them?
- If you do X, what do you expect to see?
- Why do you expect that to happen?
- How well organized are you for change?
- What support do you need?
- What resources do you have access to?

Leading change entails helping or inducing people to do what needs to be done. Inducing people to do this may be more difficult than some of us appreciate. For example, Amy Lewis and Mark Grosser (2012) suggest, students attending management and leadership courses, 'especially [those] who have [no or] limited managerial or workplace experience' (e.g. on undergraduate programmes), 'may underestimate the difficulty of convincing others to work towards change'. They have developed a useful exercise, 'The Change Game', to simulate the complexities of leading a change initiative and to illustrate the application of change leadership and management theories learned in the classroom, such as Lewin's and Kotter's. Particular aspects of change that the exercise illustrates are handling resistance to change, communication and the use of power.

Other experiential exercises helpful to learning how to lead change include a simulation that requires participants to deal with emotions and solve problems arising in a change effort concerning a hospital merger (McDonald and Mansour-Cole, 2000) and one that illustrates structural and procedural change and the importance of communication (Rollag and Parise, 2005).

Activity

Identify with your colleagues any experiences you have had of leadership development programmes that have focused explicitly on organizational change and discuss:

1 What it aimed to achieve
2 How it aimed to do so
3 How well it achieved its aims
4 How it could have been better

In his description of how Babson College in the USA transformed itself from 'a modestly known regional college to one that is consistently ranked in the top tier of business schools for all its programs [especially entrepreneurship]', Allan Cohen (2003) says that key learning points that emerged with respect to radical curriculum reforms were that:

> To sustain change ... the organizational system needs to be aligned with the vision ... [and] governance structure, rewards, evaluation, hiring, meeting arrangements, fund allocation, and leadership vehicles all had to change to support the radical curriculum reforms.

As Cohen says, 'Significant change is unusual enough in higher education to make it worth mining successful accomplishments for possible insights that can help others.' So we have included in the resources accompanying this book another case study in higher education, this time in the UK, focused on leadership development for organizational change, 'Developing Leaders and Managers for Organizational Change in a "New" UK University'.

Implications and questions for managers of change

- With regard to organizational change, leadership and management are complementary processes. Without *managing* change effectively, change initiatives and efforts will fail or disappoint, however 'good' leadership is. So as a manager of change you first need to make sure you understand and support the organization's vision, purpose and strategies for change and also the underlying values that will inform it. How well do you do so? What do you need to do to resolve any areas of doubt?
- You need to understand and practise effective management of the change process. This comprises several sets of skills: communicating, planning, organizing, directing, implementing, monitoring and controlling the various aspects of change. How well do you do so? What do you need to improve? How can you do so?
- You will also need to understand the meaning of tasks, action and outputs and their consequences and to understand and formulate accountabilities, objectives and key performance measures. How well do you do so? What do you need to improve? How can you do so?
- Using your knowledge of the competencies for managing change effectively, you have the opportunity to assess yourself against them with a view to capitalizing on your strengths and monitoring and developing these competencies where improvements can be made. How well do you do so? What do you need to improve? How can you do so?
- In change management it is important to have an understanding and acceptance of corporate social responsibility and ethical principles, including the organization's espoused core values. And it is particularly important for you, involved in managing the change process, to accept such responsibility in your own decisions, actions, methods and intentions, and their consequences. Review your experiences in taking on new responsibilities for, during and after change and ask yourself how you could have acted better.

- Review the various strategies and methods for developing change-management competencies. Leadership and management development programmes are one major strategy. Explore the relationship between the capabilities and competencies required by effective leaders and managers of change, and the learning and development methods used in such programmes, focusing on those in your own organization if appropriate. What improvements can you identify? And how might they be implemented? Also consider how these programmes are managed and how this might be improved.
- Effective managers understand that change brings with it risk of errors, mistakes or failure. Effective managers also understand that these risks bring with them something positive, namely the opportunity for both themselves and their staff to learn, improve and develop. Contributing in this way to a healthy and positive learning culture is part and parcel of being an effective and virtuous corporate 'citizen'. Review your own experiences in responding to errors, mistakes and failure, both in yourself and in the team that reports to you, and ask yourself how you could have responded better.

Further reading

Cameron, E. and Green, M. (2012) *Making Sense of Change Management*, 3rd edn. London: Kogan Page.

Lewis, A.C. and Grosser, M. (2012) 'The change game: An experiential exercise demonstrating barriers to change', *Journal of Management Education*, 36(5): 669–97.

Price, D. (ed.) (2009) *The Principles and Practice of Change*. Basingstoke: Palgrave Macmillan and The Open University.

PART TWO
Recognizing the Need for Change

The Drivers for Change and Transformation   5

Overview

- A trigger or driver of change is a catalyst for recognizing the need for a change to be initiated. Drivers of change can be internal or external to the organization.
- Recognizing the potential need for change can be done through conducting an analysis of the external environmental and an internal assessment of the organization.
- Leaders may fail to recognize the need for change because they pay insufficient attention to what is happening in the external environment. Even if they are aware of what is happening they may fail to recognize the implications for their organization. This can lead to complacency or to what Nadler and Shaw (1995) call the Trap of Success, or the organization becoming learning disabled.
- Encouraging innovation can help avoid becoming complacent or entering the 'death spiral'.

In Pasteur's words, change favours the 'prepared mind'. It is also true that organizations with high levels of readiness for change favour change. Leaders and managers need to be cognizant of the drivers for change, in order to be prepared to address the relevant ones that affect their organization They also need to be aware of how ready or not the organization is for change, especially the people within it. This chapter examines the contextual dimensions – external and internal – to explain what drives the need for change in organizations. We begin by discussing what are commonly referred to as the drivers of change, that is, those forces that have the potential to make organizations alter the way they do things. We examine the following external factors: globalization; the global economy; climate change; demographic shifts; technology and innovation; the political and social environment; competition and the knowledge economy. The chapter explores how the potential need for change can be identified through conducting an internal and external analysis of the environment in which an organization operates. The chapter concludes by considering the concept of **learning disabled** – when organizations fail to recognize the need for change – and critically evaluates what happens when organizations fail to change.

Learning objectives

By the end of this chapter you will be able to:

* Identify the external and internal drivers for change in organizations
* Examine reasons why organizations fail to learn how to change, or to realize what needs to change
* Critically evaluate the concept of organizational complacency and identify how it can be addressed
* Identify innovative approaches that will work in organizations

A catalyst for change

The first author of this book was in Riyadh, Saudi Arabia, in 2013 delivering a leadership programme for professional women. On the afternoon of the second day of the programme the sky suddenly became very dark. Slightly concerned, one of the participants said that it was a sand storm. Within minutes of the darkness rolling in, thunder and lightning erupted. The building began to shake and without warning the room in which the training was taking place was covered in a dusting of sand as it was blown through gaps in the window frames. The programme organizer told the women to quickly leave the building. As they were on the seventh floor, this was a terrifying experience: the building was swaying, sand was blowing in and thunder was crashing overhead. Despite the uncertainty and fear, the situation was straightforward: there was a need for immediate change. The sudden transformation in the weather demanded immediate action, and the required action – to evacuate the building – was understood. Most of the participants knew the key actions to take: where to exit and how to avoid panic.

In many situations, however, the need for change is vague and appropriate action is unclear. For example, even in an emergency, if there have been no 'storms' for some time, people may become complacent and warning systems may be ignored. A parallel to this might explain the lack of action with the sub-prime mortgage meltdown in the USA in 2007. Some experts had raised concerns as early as 2003 over flawed financial practices and regulations. Despite this, the warnings about the need to regulate mortgage lenders were largely ignored. The view of the US government was that regulations needed to be minimized because they got in the way of free markets and the generation of personal wealth. Before the financial meltdown, the need for change was evident to only a few people, which resulted in action being delayed and the ensuing global financial crisis. Both the above stories illustrate the need to take notice of the drivers of change.

The contexts of change

What one writer refers to as a trigger or driver of change, another writer may refer to as the context of change. The difference tends to be that while the former places emphasis on factors triggering and driving change, the latter emphasizes the context in which senior management make decisions (Hughes, 2006). One of the key exponents of examining change in a contextual manner is Andrew Pettigrew. Pettigrew defines a contexualist analysis as drawing on the 'phenomena at vertical and horizontal levels of analysis and the interconnections between those levels through time' (1990: 269). He summarizes the key points of analysing change in a contextualist mode as:

- The importance of embeddedness, in terms of interconnected levels of analysis
- The importance of temporal interconnectedness, in terms of past, present and future
- The importance of context and action, in terms of context as the product of action and vice versa
- The importance of causation, in terms of causation as neither linear nor singular

Daft (1995) identifies major contextual dimensions that characterize an organization as size, organizational technology, environment, goals, strategy and culture. He acknowledges that 'contextual dimensions can be confusing because they represent both the organization and the environment in which structural dimensions occur' (1995: 16). Dawson echoes this and highlights the need for examining both internal and external drivers for change:

> The contextual dimension refers to both the past and present external and internal operating environments, as well as to the influence of future projects and expectations on current operation practice. (2003a: 47).

So the contextual dimension – external and internal – explains what drives the need for change in an organization.

The external environment

Ring road issues

In its report on *Global Trends 2030: Alternative Worlds*, the National Intelligence Council (2012) identifies what it calls 'ring road' issues – the key drivers of change that will affect the lives of everyone on the planet over the next 30 years. We will discuss each of the following **ring road issues** and examine how organizations are responding to them:

1. Globalization
2. Global economy
3. Climate change

4. Demographic shifts
5. Technology and innovation
6. Competition

To this list we also add the knowledge economy.

1. Globalization

Globalization is a much-used word that is generally thought of as a larger worldwide marketplace made smaller by enhanced technologies and competition. It is often associated with protestors and marches outside government buildings or at World Trade Organization meetings, and with the exploitation of children in 'sweat shops'. Yet globalization long predates industrialization, much less sweatshops. Globalization is the process of intensifying social and economic transactions (Scherer et al., 2009). It is accompanied by a dissolving of territorially bound social, economic and political activities and the development of stronger worldwide interconnections (Crane and Matten, 2007). Globalization is an ongoing process that is triggered by several factors:

1. Technological developments in the field of communication, media and logistics enable a worldwide interconnection and make global trade economically profitable
2. Political decisions and events, like the breakup of territorial power blocks (for example, the Soviet Union), the reduction of trade and tariff barriers, or the establishment of free trade areas (such as the EU) accelerate the process
3. Emergence of socio-cultural processes such as an increasingly mobile workforce, pluralistic societies and an ongoing individualization of people's lifestyles (Sennet, 2006)
4. Awareness of global risks, such as environmental hazards, global warming, worldwide diseases or epidemics, nuclear threats and economic risks such as financial crises, which fosters cross-border coordination of activities and the incorporation of non-state actors like NPOs (Non-Profit Organizations) and multinational corporations into the decision-making processes (Scherer et al., 2009)

Accelerating rates of globalization are changing how people across the globe work. Over one billion people are now on Facebook, and 500 million-plus tweets are sent every day. Approximately 74% of the $2.8 trillion mergers and acquisitions industry is in cross-border transactions and one in eight people now lives and works in countries other than where they were born. In the old world, many of us developed, marketed and sold products and services and had bosses and colleagues all based in the same postcode. Today, companies have to develop, market, sell and collaborate across time zones, organizations and cultures. Globalization is no longer a game for multinationals. A 50-person SME (small and medium-sized enterprise) one of the authors of this book has worked with has offices in four countries, across seven time zones, and customers in Europe, the USA, Middle East, Asia and Africa. Some of the most successful outsourcing efforts have been done by SMEs, which have developed into global, virtual collaborations that cross geographical and organizational boundaries. The ability to collaborate with partners rather than outsource, provides these SMEs with a competitive advantage over larger organizations struggling to foster innovation and collaboration.

In future decades the number of such transactions, conducted irrespective of physical distance, is likely to increase. Such an expansion will shape the life of organizations.

Globalization means that the world is smaller and flatter, and it has led to changes in the way that companies do business. For example, it is cheaper for a company to host its IT infrastructure in Mumbai than in New York, while investing in a Chinese business may pay higher returns than investing in sluggish European competitors. During the economic crisis that began in 2008, the BRIC countries (Brazil, Russia, India and China) propped up the world economy as Western economies floundered (although the BRICs are now facing their own challenges – for instance in 2013 Brazil's economy had slowed down considerably, expanding by less than 2%). In the mid-twenty-first century the MINT countries (Mexico, Indonesia, Nigeria and Turkey) are predicted to become major players in the global marketplace.

From a market perspective, this implies the need to move to new territories and marketplaces and redesign products and services to meet local demands. HSBC captures this sentiment in its slogan *The World's Local Bank*. Changes in customer tastes and local competition from emerging markets are a major driver for change. A master of adaptation is the Swiss food giant Nestlé, which has created an array of products that incorporate differing regional flavors and cater to local tastes in coffee, chocolate, ice cream and even water. Nestlé's country managers are empowered to say no to the head office if a product or a campaign does not suit their local regions. As a result many consumers around the world believe Nestlé is a local company. Other companies are following a similar strategy. KFC is opening one new restaurant a day in China, on average, with the intention of reaching 15,000 outlets. The company has achieved this success by abandoning the dominant logic behind its growth in the USA: a limited menu, low prices and an emphasis on takeout (see Bell and Shelman, 2011). Similarly, Kraft has changed its Oreo cookies for China.

Kraft's Oreo cookies first went on sale in China in 1996, but sales were lacklustre and by 2005 it was clear that one of the world's largest biscuit brands was falling far short of expectations in China's fast-growing retail market. Research revealed that Kraft's positioning of the brand had missed the mark. First, its sales and marketing strategy had simply been replicated from the USA. Advertising and in-store displays were translated directly, and the pricing structure and packaging were largely the same as in the USA. Second, Kraft had paid too little attention to what the local market preferred. For example, the biscuit was too sweet for Chinese tastes.

To address the issues, Kraft adopted the following approach. It introduced a less sweet version called LightSweet Oreo and the size of the packet was reduced. The team expanded distribution beyond grocery stores and hypermarkets to include convenience stores, a fast-growing outlet for consumer packaged goods in China. Manufacturing, packaging, distribution and marketing were aligned with the Chinese market and sales soared from $20m in 2005 to more than $400m in 2012. Oreo's experience illustrates the dilemma faced by a multinational brand entering a new market. There are different consumer tastes and local sensibilities to cater to but international brands often rely on the parent product's strategies because they have worked well over long periods in established, familiar markets. This case illustrates how globalization is impacting on how and where companies operate and how they adapt to local tastes and needs.

Activity

1   Search the internet to find companies that have adapted their global products to the consumer tastes of local markets.
2   Identify the challenges the company has faced with this approach.
3   How has this approach created sustainable growth for the company?

2. Global economy

The economic crisis of 2008 and its long 'tail' raise the prospect of an extended crisis that will continue to undermine the social and political fabric in many countries and create long-term destabilizing effects, causing unprecedented challenges on a global scale. For the West, the challenge will be to ensure that the recent slow or stagnating growth, driven by de-leveraging – paying debts – does not lead to a prolonged slump or, worse, more financial crises. The McKinsey Global Institute's 2012 study of debt and deleveraging indicated that in the years since the onset of the financial crisis, major [Western] economies have only just begun deleveraging (McKinsey & Company, 2012). Total debt has actually grown for most major Western economies with the exception of the USA, Australia and South Korea, where the ratio of total debt to GDP has declined. Previous episodes of deleveraging have taken close to a decade. The McKinsey report concludes that this pattern is likely to continue, as no single country has all the conditions in place to revive growth. Most of the leading Western countries could therefore suffer the consequences of low economic growth that lasts longer than anticipated.

In the case of many European countries and Japan, the challenge will involve finding ways to sustain growth in the face of rapidly aging populations. For rising states such as China and India, the main challenge involves sustaining economic development and not falling into the 'middle-income trap' – a situation in which per capita income does not increase to the level of the world's advanced economies. To avoid such an outcome, the rising powers will need to consider implementing wide-ranging changes to political and social institutions.

A key feature of globalization is the continuing internationalization of markets for goods, capital, services and labour, which integrates geographically dispersed consumers and suppliers. This is likely to be an engine for accelerating economic growth, but also a source of risk, as local markets become increasingly exposed to destabilizing fluctuations in the wider global economy. These developments are driven by advances in global telecommunications, resulting in a pervasive information environment in which much of the global population is able to be online all the time. There are also winners and losers in a global economy led by market forces, especially in the field of labour, which is subject to the laws of supply and demand. As a result, everyday life for organizations is affected by continuous change, coupled with a lack stability and certainty.

For example, one sector that has been affected by the global economy is the luxury brands market. In their book *Luxury Talent Management: Leading and Managing a Luxury Brand*, Giles Auguste and Michel Gusatz (2013) describe how luxury brands such as Cartier, Louis Vuitton, Hermès, Swatch, Armani are in the midst of a sea change simply because those who have led the industry so successfully are now facing the challenge of 'going global'. Being a global player now demands that businesses focus on every major continent in terms of customers, market trends and new or emerging competitors. The companies that dominate the luxury brand industry need to:

- *Update customer service.* Luxury brand customers are different from mass-market customers. Clients of luxury firms expect shopping by appointment, the availability of a personal sales shopper, delivery of purchases and handwritten thank-you notes as part of the luxury brand experience. This concièrge-level service requires a professional career track that recognizes and rewards the importance of this role. Today, however, the luxury brand industry is more about creating masterworks and not about mastering the customer experience. Developing ways to boost customer loyalty through new levels of customer relationships is central to the challenge of sustaining any luxury brand.
- *Hire Asian executives.* Because countries such as China and India cannot be ignored by any luxury brand hoping to remain a global player, companies need to find ways to develop executives who understand Asian preferences. And those preferences differ from country to country. For example, in China, luxury brands are going to need to learn how to tap into local entrepreneurs, to train employees at middle and junior levels who probably have little experience in how luxury brands operate, and to actually understand Chinese consumers and local cultural trends. Such requisites mean that luxury brand companies need to create leadership duos. This means that they need to pair an Asian executive with a European/American business leader so that both can learn from each other while establishing the brand within a targeted part of the Asian economy.

Overall, firms in the luxury brand industry are facing some special challenges in the coming years. Auguste and Gusatz (2013: 243) quote Domenico De Sole, the former Chairman of Gucci Group, as saying that 'You can have the best strategy in the world; the difference between the excellent and the incompetent is execution, execution, execution …'. He is right. But execution is all about people who know the industry, know the marketplace, know the customers and know how to get things done. Most large organizations are ill equipped to compete in the changes in the economy, in which globalization and the shift in power in the marketplace from seller to buyer have put the customer in charge. They are focused principally on maximizing short-term shareholder value. Many organizations are currently over-capitalized and yet unable to find productive uses for the money in a stagnant economy. In his book *Fixing the Game* (2011), Roger Martin argues that the focus of companies must shift back to the customer and away from shareholder value. He states that the shift necessitates a fundamental change in the prevailing theory of the firm. The current theory holds that the singular goal of the corporation should be shareholder value maximization. Instead, Martin says that companies should place customers at the centre of the firm and focus on delighting them, while earning an acceptable return for shareholders. Martin goes onto say that companies must master the management principles needed for continuous innovation. This means that a radically different kind of management needs to be in place, with a different role for the managers, a different way of coordinating work, a different set of values and a different way of communicating. Steve Denning refers to it as radical management in his book *The Leader's Guide to Radical Management* (2010). He points out that companies in the global economy like Apple, Amazon, or Salesforce are leading the way in this, while those organizations that opt not to change will not survive.

3. Climate change

The physical environment is a trigger for change across the globe. The pictures of BPs oil well gushing millions of gallons into the Gulf of Mexico, oil-coated pelicans, as well as drought, extreme heat, disappearing ice masses, and torrential rain and winds are forcing the message that change is urgently needed. Such pressures will only intensify in the years ahead as evidence indicates that the atmosphere will continue to warm at an unprecedented rate throughout the twenty-first century. This warming will affect production, availability, storage and the use of energy, food and freshwater. Concerted attempts to reduce emissions of greenhouse gases, including carbon dioxide, methane, nitrous oxide and others, in addition to potential limits on availability of readily accessible hydrocarbon resources, will stimulate intensive investment in research to develop low-carbon energy production, as well as a focus on conservation.

However, there is uncertainty about the rate and magnitude of climate change over the next century. Climate change will affect the land, the atmosphere and the oceans, and may be an unstable and unpredictable process, involving both progressive evolution and sudden instabilities. The impact was seen in 2013 with the destruction caused in the Philippines by the typhoon and in 2014 with the torrential rain and winds that caused severe flooding in the UK and Indonesia. Major changes are likely to include melting ice caps, progressive thermal expansion of the oceans, and increasing acidity of seawater as carbon dioxide transfers from the atmosphere. These changes will have consequences that vary over time and geographical extent. For example, some regions will experience desertification, others will experience permanent inundation, and tundra and permafrost are likely to melt, releasing methane, possibly in large amounts. Land available for habitation is likely to reduce, and patterns of agriculture are likely to change. The scarcity of strategic resources like water, minerals and fossil fuels could trigger price hikes and operational costs. Organizations are being forced to lower their eco-footprint, adapt to rising operational costs and restructure along sustainable lines. Although these developments raise questions for governments, institutions and individuals, it is organizations that are their common categorical denominator, and which therefore have the greatest need to address them.

The drive to drastically reduce emissions has already seen some companies take the initiative by changing the way they design, manufacture and market their brands and goods, such as Toyota's Prius hybrid car. The first generation Prius, at its launch in 1997, became the world's first mass-produced gasoline–electric hybrid car. In constructing the Prius, Toyota used a new range of plant-derived ecological bioplastics, made out of cellulose derived from wood or grass instead of petroleum. While Swiss Re, one of the world's largest reinsurers, has taken the task of adapting to the risks of climate change into its core business. The company has developed a collaborative approach with like-minded institutions and formed the Economics of Climate Change Working Group, which is a partnership between GEF (Global Environmental Facility – a UN body), the European Commission, the Climate Works Foundation, the Rockefeller Foundation, and companies like Standard Chartered Bank. The aim is to develop further the systemic understanding of resilience and climate change. The Group has developed a methodology that helps decision-makers in regional and national economies think about climate-related costs, investment options, and how to measure and achieve the costs and benefits.

To address the issues of climate change will involve organizations making significant changes to their purpose, operations, behaviour and, above all, the ethical values that underpin these. Leaders will need outstanding cognitive skills to balance the competing demands of financial success, social responsibility and environmental custodianship, and must act as change agents, advocating environmentally responsible business practices. As By and colleagues (2011) argue, only leaders and organizations with a strong moral compass are likely to be able to resist the siren call of short-term expediency in order to promote long-term sustainability. However, as they also argue, one cannot compel or trick people into behaving ethically; they have to choose to do so. This requires an approach to change that is ethical and allows individuals, groups and organizations to assess their own situation and make their own choices.

The economic as well as the ethical challenges can no longer be addressed by organizational solutions alone. The constantly changing business environment cannot be countered solely by institutionalized procedures, as it requires the flexibility to address unforeseen events. Leaders are the focal people in organizations. They have the positional power, and the discretion, to implement legitimate solutions within the organization to address climate change issues.

4. Demographic shifts

The Development, Concepts and Doctrine Centre (DCDC) (2010) identified that by 2040 the global population is likely to grow from 6.9 billion in 2010 to 8.8 billion, and around 65%, or 6 billion, of the world's population will also live in urban areas, attracted by access to jobs, resources and security. The greatest increases in urbanization will occur in Africa and Asia. No state, group or individual can meet these challenges in isolation, only collective responses will be sufficient. The struggle to establish an effective system of global governance, capable of responding to these challenges, will be a central theme of the era. Population-driven resource demand is therefore likely to increase in intensity out to 2040 before gradually subsiding later in the century as technological and organizational innovations take effect, and the rate of population growth declines (DCDC, 2010).

Four demographic trends will fundamentally shape, although not necessarily determine, most countries' economic and political conditions and relations among states. These trends are: ageing both for the West and increasingly most developing states; a still significant but shrinking number of youthful societies and countries; migration, which will increasingly be a cross-border issue; and growing urbanization, which will spur economic growth but place new strains on food and water resources (National Intelligence Council, 2012). The aging population means demographic imbalances are rapidly emerging, leading to skills shortages. For organizations, this means the war for talent will continue to rage; leaders will need to attract, motivate and retain increasingly diverse teams and find ways to develop and promote the growing numbers of international migrants, women and older people into leadership positions.

5. Innovation and technology

Innovation and technology will continue to facilitate change. Innovation will create new opportunities and generate value, by successfully exploiting new and improved technologies, techniques and services, overcoming cultural and process barriers. It will occur when invention reduces costs to a point where an explosive growth cycle is realized or where a new market is created. For example, over the past 20 years the reducing cost of mobile telecommunications has made mobile phones readily available. Scientific advancement or invention is likely to produce breakthroughs in several disciplines, primarily in Information and Communications Technology (ICT), though developments will also be observed in biotechnology and energy management. Examples of such advances include: growth in biotechnology pharmaceuticals, stimulated by an ageing population and energy management advances driven by the need to reduce carbon usage and reliance on fossil fuels. The complexity and interdependence of physical, social, and virtual environments will increase, and successful innovation is likely to require a collaborative, networked approach to development.

The pervasiveness of ICT will enable more people to access and exploit sophisticated networks of information systems. The internet and associated technologies, together with digitized portable communications, will increasingly become the means by which a rapidly expanding array of audio, visual and written information products are distributed. For many people, group membership will extend beyond physically proximate communities, reflecting the ability to sustain relationships and identities over distance through globalized communications and travel. The increasing size of available networks will also increase economic and finance opportunities for individuals and smaller communities through initiatives such as micro-finance. This may transform how business is conducted, with a shift away from traditional hierarchical structures to smaller, networked structures that favour more even distribution of profit.

By 2040 it is likely that the majority of the global population will find it difficult to 'turn the outside world off'. ICT is likely to be so pervasive that people could be permanently connected to local or global networks. ICT investment will be driven by new business models that help sustain the insertion of new technologies. Significant changes are likely to be observed in applications, mobile devices and tailored information and interaction modes rather than in infrastructure. The evolution of ICT devices will be driven by their increasingly wide range of applications and rising demand by society. Emerging technologies such as second-generation wireless communications (smartphones) are also likely to accelerate the empowerment of individuals, introducing new capabilities to the developing world in particular. The second wave of wireless communications engenders a reduced need for developing countries to invest in and build expansive, costly communications infrastructures. Such technologies will reduce the urban–rural split that characterized first-wave technologies. The spread of smartphones in Africa during the past few years – 65% of the continent's population now has access to them – has been particularly impressive.

Now millions of Africans are connected to the internet and the outside world, and they are using such technologies to mitigate deep-seated problems such as water-borne illness, which have slowed development.

Today's social networking technologies help individual users form online social networks with other users, based on factors that can include shared interests, common backgrounds, relationships, geographic locations and so on. In many respects, social networks are becoming part of the fabric of online existence, as leading services integrate social functions into everything else an individual might do online. The kinds of networks and interactions that social network services foster vary greatly. In many cases, members have developed uses for their social network services that go far beyond what the service providers themselves may have intended. Innovative uses for such services range from controlling home appliances remotely to managing restaurant reservations in real time, and analysts widely cite Twitter (along with other social network services) as having been a significant contributor to the Arab Spring protests.

Social media is accelerating the process of individual empowerment. This is particularly seen in the Middle East, where Muslim women have historically lagged in educational skills and integration into the market economy. More recently, they have become prolific users and consumers of social media. Muslim women are using online communities to reach beyond their everyday social networks into safe spaces to discuss such issues as women's rights, gender equity and the role of women within Islamic law. Participation in online and social media platforms hinges on income, literacy and access. As these expand a growing number of Muslim women are likely to participate in online forums, potentially affecting their societies and governance. The spread of innovations in technology will give individuals and groups unprecedented capabilities to collaborate in new ways.

New manufacturing and automation technologies such as additive manufacturing (3D printing) and robotics have the potential to drive changes in work patterns in both the developing and developed worlds. In developed countries these technologies will improve productivity, address labour constraints and diminish the need for outsourcing, especially if reducing the length of supply chains brings clear benefits. Nevertheless, such technologies could still have a similar effect as outsourcing. They could make more low- and semi-skilled manufacturing workers in developed economies redundant, exacerbating domestic inequalities. For developing economies, particularly Asian ones, the new technologies will stimulate new manufacturing capabilities and further increase the competitiveness of Asian manufacturers and suppliers.

Technology will continue to blur the boundaries between private and work lives, will broaden generational divides, and will shift power to employees with extensive digital skill, particularly the rising class of knowledge workers who can work anywhere. As organizations become increasingly virtual, leaders must recognize and harness the critical skills required to exploit technology.

Technology is also playing a key part in changing the face of communication. The social media revolution has been a key driver for the change in strategy for many companies. For example, see below the case of Burberry. Although we are not aiming to catalogue all new and emerging technologies in this section, we are aiming to highlight the importance to managers and leaders of paying attention to technological drivers for change and the impact that they will have on organizations, now and in the future. As a result of these forces, product development and life cycles are short-ened and managers must respond in a timely fashion. Leaders need to be aware of technological trends and to be proactive in their consideration of how to respond to those that are relevant for their organization (Cawsey et al., 2007).

CASE STUDY

Burberry

The fashion house Burberry was founded in 1856 when 21-year-old Thomas Burberry, a former draper's apprentice, opened his own outdoor clothing store in Basingstoke, Hampshire, England. Soon after, the company introduced gabardine, a water-resistant but breathable fabric, and started producing the trench coats that would become famous in England and around the world.

In 2009 Burberry was feeling the pressure of the economic downturn, even though its financials had been strong over the previous decade. Revenue growth dropped from 18 and 15% respectively in the previous two years to 7% that year, excluding the impact of foreign exchange rates, while operating profit margin shrank from about 15% to 9.8%. In this harsh retail environment, Burberry recognized the potential value of the digital media. In March 2009, with 175 million users on Facebook and 600,000 more joining it each day, Burberry began allocating marketing and public relations spend and dedicated personnel to pursue tech-age marketing. Building a social media presence seemed critical, but the question was, 'how'?

Burberry had already joined Facebook, but wanted to do something more, something distinctive and unique to the brand. It looked to other iconic brands such as Nike, Apple, and Google. These brands were hitting social media hard, and Burberry wanted to follow suit. The mandate was simple: to develop a campaign that was innovative and would engage younger consumers.

The idea for the Art of the Trench campaign was born. A website was launched where existing customers could share photos of themselves wearing their Burberry trench coats, giving them their '15 minutes of fame' as models on the site, and allowing other customers to admire their sense of style. Customers could upload photos of themselves in their Burberry trenches, and customers and aspirational customers alike could comment on them, 'like', and share the photos via Facebook, email, Twitter or Delicious. Users could also sort photos by trench type, colour, gender of the user, weather, popularity and the where the photo originated and click-through to the Burberry site to make a purchase. Rather than explicitly market the Art of the Trench, Burberry opted to rely largely on public relations and word of mouth, and users sharing their submissions on Facebook and Twitter. In the year following the launch of the Art of the Trench, Burberry's Facebook fan base grew to more than one million. E-commerce sales grew 50% year-over-year, an increase partially attributed to higher web traffic from the Art of the Trench site and Facebook. The site had 7.5 million views from 150 countries in the first year. Conversion rates from the Art of the Trench click-through to the Burberry website were significantly higher than those from other sources. By all metrics, quantitative and qualitative, the campaign was a success.

The success of the Art of the Trench affirmed Burberry's strategic focus on digital. By 2012, Burberry had moved 60% of its marketing budget to digital. Burberry has since executed many other digital innovations, setting the bar for online customer engagement. Each of these initiatives has built on the digital strategy Burberry kicked off with the Art of the Trench, and has led to the brand's pre-eminent status as a tech-savvy brand. Financially too, the strategy seems to be paying off, with company sales more than doubling. Rivals have tried to keep pace with varying levels of success, but none has gone full throttle like Burberry.

Despite Burberry's success, there are those who doubt the sustainability of the brand's digital strategy and wonder if letting fashion take a backseat may lead to the company's downfall. Sales, profit, and share price growth have all begun to slide this year. Growth in China, Burberry's largest market, has been hit hard. The CEO Angela Ahrendts has defended her strategy: 'I've seen what happened to brands like Kodak that did not keep up with digital change. That's a lesson in what to avoid.'

Adapted from 'How Burberry capitalized on the social media revolution', *Business Today*, 3 February 2013.

Discussion Questions

1 What are the benefits of Burberry's social media strategy?
2 To what extent do you think that the social medial strategy was responsible for Burberry's return to market leadership?
3 Is the strategy the right one for the company or is it a strategy blindly, excitedly pursued that may be too great a deviation from the company's core business?
4 How might Burberry sustain the impact of their social media strategy?

6. Competition

Increasing competition is another driver for change. For instance, some of the biggest threats to financial services organizations are coming from supermarkets such as Tesco and Walmart. Competition drives companies to change. For example, in 2006 American Online (AOL) core customers, internet subscribers, were cancelling their service and getting free email accounts from competitors such as Google. As a consequence, AOL made many of its services free and changed its strategy from generating revenues via customer subscription to sales via advertising on its site. In 2007 Telco (a European owned telecoms company) was operating in a saturated market with intense price competition. It was faced with 30–40% reduction in markets. The company implemented a number of changes, including reducing operating costs through consolidation, standardization, redundancies and outsourcing. Telco also introduced a new global business model and organizational structure, segmented around customer enterprise. Sony is another company that has made changes triggered by an increasingly competitive environment. The company experienced a major downturn in sales in mature markets and growth in Eastern Europe due to intensified price competition in the early 2000s. In response to this, Sony implemented cost reductions through global and regional economies of scale, synergies and a transformation of its business processes. Such examples illustrate how competition can significantly drive change in companies.

As described in the sections above, some of the factors that can affect the context in which organizations operate and can trigger change include: globalization, the global economy, climate change, demographic shifts, technology and innovation, and competition, linked in to each of these factors are social and political elements. To this list we will also add the knowledge economy.

7. The knowledge economy

The knowledge economy can, according to Ian Brinkley, be prosaically defined as what you get when firms bring together powerful computers and well-educated minds to create wealth (2006: 3). At its heart, the knowledge economy refers to activities that create value from exploiting knowledge and technology rather than physical assets and manual labour. The impact of the change the knowledge economy has triggered has been recognized across the globe. In 2008, Barack Obama said in one of his campaign speeches:

> This long-term agenda ... will require us first and foremost to train and educate our workforce with the skills necessary to compete in a knowledge-based economy. We'll also need to place a greater emphasis on areas like science and technology that will define the workforce of the 21st century, and invest in the research and innovation necessary to create the jobs and industries of the future right here in America.[1]

According to Levy and colleagues (2011), progress towards the global knowledge economy will not be reversed. They cite the change as being underpinned by three fundamental drivers:

1. *Consumer demands are changing* – as consumers become richer, more sophisticated and more diverse, they increasingly buy intellectual content and technologically advanced products and services. This is driving up the demand for knowledge-intensive products and service.
2. *Technological progress* – the development of new technologies both increases productivity and creates new products and jobs. In particular, the proliferation of powerful cheap computing power and the internet has made many knowledge-intensive ways of working possible.
3. *Globalization* – increasing flows of ideas, knowledge and goods from around the world have accelerated the transition towards a knowledge economy.

The key features of the knowledge economy and knowledge economy organizations, according to Brinkley (2006), are:

- The knowledge economy represents a 'soft discontinuity' from the past – it is not a 'new' economy operating to a new set of economic laws.
- The knowledge economy is present in all sectors of the economy, not just the knowledge-intensive industries.
- The knowledge economy has a high and growing intensity of ICT usage by well-educated knowledge workers.
- A growing share of GDP is devoted to knowledge intangibles compared with physical capital.
- The knowledge economy consists of innovating organizations using new technologies to introduce process, organizational and presentational innovation.
- Knowledge economy organizations reorganize work to allow them to handle, store and share information through knowledge management practices.

---

1 Remarks of Senator Barack Obama: 'Change That Works for You,' 9 June 2008, at www.barackobama.com/2008/06/09/remarks_of_senator_barack_obam_76.php.

Knowledge-intensive work can be most easily thought of as activities that depend on the use of high-level tacit knowledge that resides in people's minds. This tacit knowledge takes the form of expertise and/or experience. Examples of knowledge-intensive tasks include bespoke statistical analysis, system maintenance, graphic design or software design (Levy et al., 2011). In the UK, employment in knowledge-intensive market-based services (such as information and communication; professional, scientific and technical services; financial and real estate; administration and support activities; and arts, entertainment and recreational services) went up by 93% between 1979 and 2010 (Brinkley, 2010)

So progress towards the knowledge economy is transforming the world of work. Knowledge-intensive work depends on the use of tacit knowledge that resides in people's minds in the form of expertise or experience, rather than being written down in manuals, guide lists and procedures. Productivity here depends on deriving value from intangible assets such as research and development, IT, branding and advertising, and organizational development. The knowledge economy is therefore a key trigger for change within organizations.

External factors such as those described above can either create a need to change in order to survive or create an opportunity that leaders wish to exploit. The economic globalization of the world, the demographic shifts, technological opportunities and political and economic uncertainties, and the growth of the knowledge economy form the reality of the environments in which organizations operate. Leaders need to be aware of how these external events impact on their organization. There are some helpful analytical tools that can be useful in analysing the external environment for opportunities and threats.

External analysis tools

Popular tools for anticipating the nature and extent of future changes in the external context include **PESTELI** (see Chapter 6 for details of this and other diagnostic tools). The PESTELI analyses the Political, Economic, Social, Technological, Environmental, Legal and Industry factors. It is a popular and simple tool to use, but it is open to criticism. For instance, Worthing (2003) identifies its limitations as including dependency upon the process of information gathering and evaluation, unanticipated events occurring and the analysis becoming an end in itself. Dawson is quite philosophical about the outcome of using not only this tool but also about doing any other analysis exercise and says, 'the essential unforeseeable character of change means that the process cannot be predicted and that outcomes are often only understood in retrospect' (2003b: 179). However, this does not negate the need to consider the external context and drivers for change. For as we discuss later in this chapter, those organizations that are not aware of what is happening in the external environment and ignore drivers for change may find themselves in the 'death spiral'.

Strebel (1996) developed a tool that managers can use to anticipate technological and economic changes in the environment and to help them initiate changes that will enable their organization to remain one step ahead of the competition. Strebel argues that there is an evolutionary cycle of competitive behaviour and that different phases of the cycle are marked by break points. He also suggests that, given proper attention to competitive trends, these break points can be predicted in advance. The two phases of the cycle are innovation and efficiency.

The start of the innovative phase of the cycle is characterized by a sharp increase in divergence between what competitors are offering and begins when an innovation by one competitor is seen to create a new business opportunity. This triggers others to innovate and gives rise to a greater variety in the offerings (such as products and services) available to customers. This process continues until there is little scope for further innovation that offers suppliers or customers much in the way of added value. At this point, the divergence of offerings begins to decline as the best features of past innovations are imitated by competitors.

The next phase of the cycle begins when one or more providers begin to turn their attention to efficiency rather than innovation. Cost reduction is seen as the route to maintaining market share and increasing profit. They achieve this by improving systems and processes to reduce delivered cost. While each phase of the cycle can present opportunities for some, it can also pose threats for others. In the efficiency phase of the cycle, only the fittest survive and inefficient competitors are driven out of business.

When most of the opportunities for gaining competitive advantage from improving efficiency have been exploited, attention might switch once again to innovation, and the cycle will repeat itself. Strebel notes that convergence, when organizations turn their attention to efficiencies, is usually easier to anticipate than divergence, because it involves a move towards greater similarity in existing products and services, whereas divergence is based on potential new offerings and their existence might not be known until a competitor offers them to customers.

As well as focusing on the alignment of their organization with its external environment, using tools such as PESTELI, leaders and managers also need to consider internal alignments and how internal drivers can trigger change.

The internal environment

Greiner's life cycle model

Greiner (1972) cautions managers against merely focusing on the external drivers for change. He asserts that, for many organizations, the most pressing issues are embedded in the organization's past decisions rather than in the present events and external dynamics. His view is that an organization evolves through five predictable stages of development and each stage brings with it a set of alignment-related issues that have to be managed if the organization is to be effective. The five phases that Greiner identifies are:

1. Growth through creativity leading to a crisis of leadership
2. Growth through direction leading to a crisis of autonomy
3. Growth through delegation leading to a crisis of control
4. Growth through coordination leading to a crisis of 'red tape'
5. Growth through collaboration

Each phase of the organization life cycle involves a prolonged period of evolutionary growth during which changes tend to be small and incremental and these phases create their own issues, due to internal misalignments, that end with a period of turmoil and transformation. Greiner argues that it is internal issues which trigger crises and cause discontinuous change. The way these crises are managed determines whether or not the organization will survive and move forward to the next phase of evolutionary growth. Managers need to be aware of where their organization is, in terms of the five stages of development, and recognize the kinds of issues that need to be addressed.

Internal drivers for change

Drivers for change emanating from the internal environment of an organization are often those related to people wanting to improve the things that they do: developing new and better ways of working to solve problems with current practice; improving operational efficiency; cost reduction; and improving the quality of products and ser-vices, as well as processes. Dawson (2003a: 47) cites the work of Leavitt (1964), who suggests that internal drivers for change include human resources, administrative structures, technology and product or service, as well as an additional category labelled the history and culture of the organization.

Internal drivers for change can also be based on improving the working conditions and physical environment for staff. This was a key driver for the relocation of offices in the case study below written by Ritienne Bajada. Internal drivers for change can also include: changes in ownership, which may occur through divestitures, mergers or acquisitions. In such situations the new owners will normally bring their own views about the company and what needs to change. Change is also likely to be triggered with the arrival of a new leader. Like a new owner of an old house, a new leader will want to alter or remodel the existing structure and business processes (see Chapter 9 for further discussion on restructures).

This was certainly the experience of the first author of this book, who previously worked for an international organization that had offices in countries across the globe. Each office was led by a country director who would generally move to a different global location every 3–5 years. The locally engaged staff referred to it as the 'new broom concept', which meant that when a new director took up his/her role they would immediately instigate changes (sweep out the old ways of doing things and bring in new ways) in how the local office was run. In practice, new managers and leaders always want to make their own mark on their departments, divisions and/or teams.

Internal analysis tools

In an attempt to provide a framework that can be used to analyse the internal drivers of change, Hughes (2006: 43) proposes the following factors are considered:

- *Human resources*: what are the skills, abilities, attitudes, values and beliefs of the employees?
- *Administrative structure*: what is the structural form of the organization, and what are the implications of this form for: leadership, authority, responsibility and communications?
- *Product or service*: what products and/or services does the organization provide?

- *Technology*: what technology is uses to deliver the product and/or service?
- *History and culture*: what is the history of the organization, and what cultures are evident within the organization?

Such questioning encourages a more dynamic approach to understanding the internal triggers and context for change.

Other tools that can be used to analyse the internal context include popular ones such as **SWOT** and the Seven-S. We discuss these tools and others in Chapter 6.

CASE STUDY

Relocation

Background

The change consisted of the relocation of offices for a department of 40 employees. Having had no previous experience of this kind of change, I assumed it would be a relatively easy project considering that alternative office space had already been secured. However, I later realized that a lot of detail and preparation is required in order to ensure that this type of change is accepted and supported by all individuals who are directly affected, as well as any stakeholders who will be indirectly affected.

The drivers for the change

There were several drivers that instigated this change and discussions had been going on for a while prior to the launch of this project. The main reasons that pushed management to look for an alternative office space were that the 'old' office was small and had originally been designed to seat around six individuals in an open plan environment with small meeting rooms all around, a reception for visitors, a small kitchen and two toilets. As the team expanded, desks were added in the open plan section resulting in little personal space for individuals sitting in this area and minimal space to walk around the office. The issue of lack of space resulted in another problem as the department expanded further and individuals within the same team were located in different buildings as there was no more space available in the main open plan office. This caused a lot of time inefficiencies as team members found it difficult to communicate with each other and had to book more 'official' meetings to discuss work-related issues that could otherwise have been discussed in a few minutes, had they been sitting within the same space. This brought about another issue, which was a lack of meeting rooms. Priority was given to individuals within the team who required a private space for meeting with clients on a one-to-one basis. During busy times, other team members found it impossible to book meeting rooms for internal meetings.

One other major driver for change was that the current space did not look very professional and was an inappropriate environment in which to welcome clients and other visitors. The location of the offices also made it difficult for clients who were unfamiliar with the site to find us as it was off the beaten track at the far end of the site.

Another driver for change was the lack of natural light and fresh air. The open plan main office did not have any windows that could be opened and the only door overlooked a main road, which resulted in loud traffic noises when opened. This made the office environment unhealthy and unpleasant for those spending a minimum of eight hours a day in it.

What the change involved

The change involved various major stages, the first and most important one being the appointment of a project manager to ensure that a project plan was put in place and, more importantly, that all stakeholders directly or indirectly affected were involved or updated about decisions. The second stage was to look at the different choices available in terms of alternative space. These choices were relatively limited and there was a very obvious choice that management identified from the very early stages. This required the redesign and renovation of the new office space. Various negotiation talks were required with the space planning department in order to ensure that the changes were in line with the department's requirements. In addition to this, all the furniture needed to be procured and seating plans needed to be prepared showing where each individual team member would be sitting. It required negotiation and discussions with various team members to ensure that, where possible, everyone was happy with where they were sitting. Another important aspect of the change was the effect on various key processes used by the department and other stakeholders, including external deliveries to the department, visitors getting access to the building and a meeting room bookings system.

The challenges faced

As with any significant change, there were several challenges that needed to be tackled prior to, during and after the relocation had taken place. The most important challenge was selling the idea to and getting the support of those involved. In this case, some individuals favoured the change whilst others were dubious on whether the new space was an appropriate option and had concerns as to whether it met their individual requirements and those of the department and their clients. There was also a substantial amount of concern around how the new processes would be handled and what would be the impact on the individuals of using them, as well as the customer experience. Another challenge was around informing all the relevant stakeholders and keeping them updated in an efficient and effective way about the changes taking place without slowing down the process.

Sustaining the change

During the 'running in' phase there were various minor issues that needed to be resolved; however, there were no major unexpected problems that threatened the sustainability of the relocation. In this case sustaining the change translated into whether the team and stakeholders were happy with the change introduced and the repercussions this had on the various processes. To help run things smoothly, the project management team ensured that the move was planned to every minute detail, that everyone had information on when personal belongings needed to be packed and moved and that a support team was put in place in the new office space to deal with minor issues, ensuring that everyone knew who to report any issues to as they arose. Regular communications were sent out to other departments and stakeholders, letting them know when the move would take place and all other necessary information. A house-warming party was also planned, and used as a PR tool and opportunity for external stakeholders to see the new offices and for the team to celebrate the completion of the project.

(Continued)

(Continued)

Lessons learnt

Looking back and reflecting on the feedback gathered from all those involved in the process, the first lesson to be drawn from the experience is the importance of the way the idea was sold to all those directly involved – this can make or break the success of any change being introduced. Ensuring that the majority of stakeholders support the change being proposed has a huge impact on the success of the project. The second lesson concerns the involvement of individuals in the decision-making process and ensuring that they feel their ideas and concerns are being given the required attention and addressed accordingly. The third lesson is the importance of having a good project manager who can provide clear direction and take decisions, and finally, it is important to involve key stakeholders in the project team, in order to ensure that all individuals are being fairly represented.

© 2015 Ritienne Bajada, Senior Sector Manager for the Energy Sector, Career Services, London Business School.

Discussion Questions

1 Identify the main drivers of the change for the company.
2 What were the key lessons learnt?
3 Consider changes in an organization in which you have worked or one you are familiar with. Identify the changes. What were the internal and external factors that triggered them? Review each change and explore if it was anticipated, and if so, how and by whom.
4 Consider what would trigger an organization to stop changing.

The Resource-Based model

When discussing the internal drivers for change it is helpful to consider the Resource-Based View (RBV). This model focuses on a change strategy building on competencies and thereby driving change rather than adjusting to the PESTELI type environment and being reactive. The model is a counter to the traditional 'outside-in' approaches, in which the starting point for thinking about change and competitive advantage is the external environment. The work of Michael Porter is most associated with this outside-in perspective. The RBV on strategy, and by extension on change, sees the fundamental and indeed only sustainable route to competitive advantage as arising from how an organization puts together unique and enviable contributions of internal resources.

The focus of the RBV model is on the relationship between an organization's resources and its performance. The RBV sees above-average profitability as coming from the effective deployment of superior or unique resources that allow organizations to have lower costs or better products, rather than tactical manoeuvring or product market positioning (Fahy, 2000). Such resources include tangible assets, such as plant and equipment, and intangible assets, such as patents and brands; and capabilities such as skills, knowledge and aptitudes of individuals and groups (Wernerfelt, 1995). Resources such as these are not free-standing assets that an organization can obtain or dispose of easily or quickly, but are deeply embedded in an organization's processes and as such are very difficult for others to replicate (Ordanini and Rubera, 2008). Proponents of the RBV see organizations as being heterogeneous in respect of their resources, i.e. no two organizations possess exactly the same combination of these (Burnes, 2009a). An organization's success is seen as coming from distinctive capabilities. Hax and Majluf state that:

> The essence of the resource based-model ... [is] that competitive advantage is created when resources and capabilities that are owned exclusively by the firm are applied to developing unique competencies. Moreover, the resulting advantage can be sustained due to the lack of substitution and imitation capabilities by the firm's competitors (1982:10).

The RBV challenges the view that competitive advantage arises mainly from external factors. Instead, it maintains that the possession of valuable, rare, inimitable and non-substitutable resources may result in sustained superior performance (Furrer et al., 2008).

Such a perspective has led some writers to argue that the way organizational cultures and therefore organizational change are managed is what differentiates organizations (Pfeffer, 1998). Thus the RBV has strong links with ideas on learning organizations and organization learning (Easterby-Smith et al., 2000), subjects that we explore in Chapter 8.

There are, however, criticisms that have been raised against this Resource-Based View, including the lack of empirical support, complex and ambiguous definitions of resources, and that it is merely a rehash of the SWOT analysis (Fleisher and Bensoussan, 2003). A further criticism is that the concept of what constitutes a valuable resource is based on a tautology. For example, Priem and Butler (2001) note, the main method of identifying a valuable resource is that it already has value. In addition, Burnes (2009a) points out that because resources cannot easily or quickly be acquired or developed, in the short run, firms are stuck with the ones they have. Therefore, depending on the circumstances, and how they change, these organizational specific assets can either be a boon or a curse. This is echoed by organizational ecologists who argue that, because these competencies take so long to develop and external environments change so quickly, any beneficial match between an organization's competencies and its environment is likely to be accidental or fortuitous rather than the result of deliberate or foresightful actions by managers (Hannan and Freeman, 1988).

Internal and external perspectives

'Inside-out' theories such as the RBV have a tendency to offer a one-best-way solution regardless of context. As Porter (1996) has contended, resources in and of themselves are of no competitive value; it is how and in what context such internal resources are used that leads to value creation. The answer to this lies somewhere in the middle, with both the external and internal perspectives having something to offer. This is why there is a need for organizations to consider not only the internal but also the external factors that drive change.

When considering the drivers for change, it is worth noting that the external and internal factors that create the need for change seldom arrive as single events or issues. For example, when changes in the economic environment result in interest-rate rises, the costs for an organization also rise. To deal with those increased costs the organization may decide to change working practices to improve efficiency. Changes in the rate of interest will also increase the cost of living for people working in the organization. As a result they may demand higher salary increases. The increase in interest rates is one single event that may occur at the same time as new legislation is brought in, new governmental targets are launched, or a new humanitarian aid crisis arises. Leaders need to be aware of the demands of the external environment. Those who detect and anticipate external drivers of change will be ready to respond to them and view them as an opportunity, as well as a challenge. At the same time they should not neglect internal drivers for change. Internal and external drivers do not, however, in themselves bring about change and transformation. They simply create the need for change.

Discussion

Sometimes it is relatively easy to anticipate the need for change. For example, companies can anticipate the impact of new government regulations. However, occasions arise when organizations are confronted with changes that are difficult to anticipate, such as the effects of the 9/11 terrorist attacks on the World Trade Center in New York or the financial and economic crisis of 2008/9.

1   What drivers for organizational change have arisen recently that have been a surprise to you?
2   What factors are more influential in driving organizational change – internal or external factors?
3   How do the contexts in which organizations operate change over time?
4   What would trigger an organization to stop changing?

Recognizing the need for change

Organizations are challenged to grow and change with the world around them. To achieve this organizations must first recognize that change is desirable and feasible. Leaders must get people to recognize that changes are needed. There is a famous story in a company that Colin Carnall (2007) writes about and which is known as the 'The Chairman's rice puddings'. The story illustrates when the need for change is not recognized:

> A senior manager had been given the task of leading a review of head-office systems and procedures. As he and his team proceeded with the review, all manner of good ideas

were identified and implemented. Then, one day, the team examined the chairman's kitchen. They found that every day two rice puddings were made at 12:15. The same two rice puddings were thrown away at 14:45. When asked about this the chef said that they had always made two rice puddings. No one had ever eaten one to his knowledge. This had been happening since he joined the company eight years before. They never included the rice puddings on the menu! Further investigation revealed that 17 years before, the then chairman had chosen, on a whim, to visit the kitchen. In conversation with the chef of the day he had said that his favourite dessert was sweet rice pudding. When he left the chef gave instructions that two rice puddings were to be made each day but not included on the menu. The head waiter could then offer the chairman a rice pudding. Being a shrewd character the chef asked for two, thinking that if the chairman did ask for one, then so would someone else. Four years later the chairman had retired, five years further on the next chairman died. But eight years later on the chef still made two rice puddings every day. (Carnall, 2007: 189)

If you look around the world today, you will see a number of organizations that have stalled or are in a state of atrophy, still making 'rice puddings', as they have not recognized the need to change. **Recognizing the need to change** involves complex processes of perception, interpretation and decision-making, which, if not managed carefully, can lead to inappropriate outcomes.

One such organization is the Girl Scouts of the USA. The 101-year-old institution is struggling to change and remain relevant when the world around it is shifting from campfires to iPads. In an article entitled, 'Will the girl scouts earn a badge for change leadership?', Russell Roath (2013) writes that with the advent of the new traditional family (dual working parents, lower birth rates, work and family priorities being redefined), there have been fewer volunteer troop leaders and fewer young girls expressing interest in the organization, all of which had contributed to a 20% drop in membership over several decades. This had created a creeping budget shortfall, which had been addressed with layoffs and early retirements. The CEO, Anna Maria Chávez, had a tough job ahead of her. As Roath (2013) points out,

> [a]ny improvements will be incremental and unsustainable unless she takes on the type of leadership the organization will respect and embrace. The first challenge Chávez has in front of her is to establish a clear understanding of this opportunity across the organization and that in order to stay afloat they need everyone on board. She needs to establish a sense of urgency. There seems to be a dearth of pride for this venerable institution. If Chávez cannot find a way to both fix these challenges, and accelerate the changes that are needed to take the organization forward, she may not be there long.

An organization, like the Girl Scouts, may be failing to change when it needs to. Leaders may fail to recognize the need for change because they pay insufficient attention to what is happening in the external environment. Even if they are aware of what is happening they may fail to recognize the implications for their organization. At an organizational level this can lead to strategic drift – a gradual change that occurs so subtly that it is not noticed until it is too late. At a departmental or team level it can lead to a lack of alignment and ultimately inefficiencies.

As Nadler and Shaw (1995) point out, one of the paradoxes of organizational life is that success often sets the stage for failure. This is illustrated in the Trap of Success cycle in Figure 5.1, which shows that after a prolonged period of success organizations

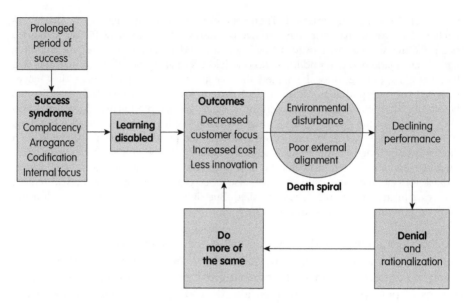

Figure 5.1   The trap of success (adapted from Nadler and Shaw, 1995)

become locked into the patterns of behaviour that produced the original success. These patterns become codified or institutionalized and are rarely questioned and can lead to complacency, arrogance and an internal focus. As a result, it is taken for granted that the relation between the company and its environment will automatically be successful. Nadler and Shaw (1995) refer to the organization becoming 'learning disabled' – it becomes incapable of looking outside, reflecting on success and failure, accepting new ideas and developing new insights, it decreases its customer focus, and costs increase.

If unchecked, the ultimate outcome of this trap of success can be what Nadler and Shaw (1995) refer to as the 'death spiral'. This spiral involves a decline in performance, denial about what is happening and more of the same behaviours and approaches that result in a negative impact on customer focus, cost and innovation. For example, IBM was once so successful that it achieved an amazing 90% market share. But success turned to arrogance, a 'we know best' mindset – which people inside the company often did not see – which led to little listening from others who wondered if they should be trying new things. Then the world changed on them, first with Ken Olson and Digital Equipment Corporation, and then with the PCs. IBM reacted slowly and late. The size of their market, the big mainframes, stopped growing as fast. But IBM still made money. Then incredibly faced with more and more data that they were in trouble, they did little to change. Ultimately they were saved by Lou Gestner, who came in from outside and changed the company radically. Without this, who knows what might have happened to IBM.

General Motors is an example of another company that fell into the 'death spiral'. The company filed for bankruptcy in 2009 and brought to an end over 100 years of steady-state and assured motor car production. Once the largest manufacturing company in the world, General Motors (GM) had come to the position in which it found itself, through a combination of factors, in a position of having an inability to: control costs; innovate in motor car production; recognize and respond to changing environmental concerns; and respond to changing market demands. Instead it continued to produce cars that nobody wanted to buy.

All these factors can be summarized as the inability to change. In particular, GM failed to recognize the opportunities that each of the above factors presented, namely the opportunity to: pioneer and develop a full range of fuel-efficient cars of the type that the market would want to buy; change the organization structures and culture to move with the times; and to use the capabilities of the workforce to change and develop existing production and operational processes.

GM's problems had become apparent some months earlier, when it became clear that the financial crisis and ensuing recession of 2008 was going to mean a sharp reduction in people's willingness and capability to buy new cars. In an attempt to get support from the US government, the top management of Ford and Chrysler and the senior GM team flew to Washington, DC to meet with the President and other senior politicians in their own private airplanes. This action brought the top managers of each of these companies into ridicule, since flying in an executive jet to a meeting to ask for a government bailout for the companies was hardly the best way of going about things. It also caused industry and market analysts to begin to take a real interest in the strengths and weaknesses of the companies. What they found reinforced the image created by the use of the private planes – that top and senior management were detached, complacent and either unwilling or unable to develop and grow their organizations for the future and were therefore failing.

Alastair Dryburgh (2013) cites Kodak as an archetypal example of another organization that failed to change. Dryburgh describes how Kodak, who he says 'really wrote the book on how not to manage change', after having invented digital photography in the 1970s, then sat on the technology to protect its legacy film business, with disastrous, if entirely predictable, results.

The history of retail, like that of the car industry, is littered with brands that shone brightly but then lost their lustre. Some, such as Sears and JC Penney, the US mid-market department stores, are struggling in a crowded market. They have a surfeit of physical space and are being attacked by online retailers. It is a problem shared by discount or mass-market department stores as far afield as Australia and Germany. It is not the brands themselves that become tired, but their product mix, or the way they fail to respond to customer wants and needs. For example, Argos – a catalogue merchant based in the UK and Ireland – has seen its sales flag and has only belatedly entered the online shopping market and moved to integrate digital elements into its traditional print channel. The hypermarket is another prime example. In developed markets, the ageing hulks operated by Walmart, Metro, Carrefour and Tesco are undergoing a midlife crisis, as many staple products migrate from store shelves to shoppers' laptops. Retailers need to be constantly recalibrating. They need to be continually examining who their customers are, who they think their competitors are, and then adapting. Failure to do this can lead to lost sales, or worse still, failure. Some store groups have managed to adapt. For instance, Target, the US mid-market retailer, has turned to designer collaborations to stay ahead. While River Island, the British private fashion retailer, has departed from its Chelsea Girl incarnation which was a regular fixture on high streets in the 1970s and 1980s. The rapid and constant drive for change in sectors such as retail and technology should foster an attitude of preparedness among leaders. They need to keep asking: what is our Kodak moment and how can we avoid it?

> **Discussion Question**
>
> Consider some of the issues that might constrain managers when they are forced to react to an urgent and pressing need for change.

Challenging complacency

The trap of success or death spiral raises an important question: does an organization have to wait until a change is needed? The answer is no, as leaders can raise concerns about a current problematic situation and urge management to challenge the complacency that fosters it without resorting to crisis-mode tactics. According to Beer (1988), there are four ways of doing this:

1. Using information about the organization's competitive situation to generate discussion with employees about current and prospective problems
2. Creating opportunities for employees to educate management about the dissatisfaction and problems they experience
3. Creating dialogue on the data that should aim for joint understanding of a company's problems
4. Setting high standards and expecting people to meet them, since setting high standards creates dissatisfaction with the current level of performance

If it is not addressed, complacency can be a barrier to change. When people are comfortable with the way things they are more likely to be oblivious to the things that need to be changed. Some of the signs of complacency to be aware of are outlined in Table 5.1.

> **Discussion Question**
>
> What are some of the examples of complacency in your organization that you need to look out for?

Innovation

Innovation can help avoid complacency. One company that has focused on innovation and fundamentally changed the way that it does business, rather than face eventual

Table 5.1 Signs of organizational complacency

Organizational complacency	
Signs of complacency	**Examples**
No highly visible crisis.	The company is not losing money; no big layoffs are threatened.
The company measures itself against low standards.	The company compares itself to the industry average, not to the industry leader.
Organizational structure focuses attention on narrow functional goals instead of broad business performance.	Marketing has one measurement criterion; manufacturing has another that is unrelated. Only the CEO uses broader measures (such as return on invested capital, economic value added.).
Planning and control systems are rigged to make it easy for everyone to make their functional goals.	The typical manager or employee can work for months without encountering an unsatisfied or frustrated customer or supplier.
Performance feedback is strictly internal. Feedback from customers, suppliers and shareholders is not encouraged.	The culture dictates that external feedback is either without value or likely to be uninformed. 'Customers really don't know what they want. We do.'
Evidence that change is needed results in finger pointing.	'It's manufacturing's problem, not ours.'
Management focuses on marginal issues.	'The ship is sinking. Let's rearrange the deck chairs.'
The culture sends subliminal messages of success.	Plush offices, wood panelling and fine art adorn corporate offices.
Management believes its own press releases and mythology.	'We are the greatest ad agency in the country. We set the standard for our industry.'

Source: Adapted from John Kotter (1996), *Leading Change,* Boston, MA: Harvard Business School Press, 39–41.

extinction, is ArcelorMittal, the steel company. The company has 1,300 scientists working to make its products more sustainable and has instituted a lot of measures to 'lift and shift' innovations made in one location across its global operations.

Elements of innovation

David Magellan Horth and Jonathan Vehar (2012) of CCL identify four elements to innovation: process, context, output and people. These are described as follows:

- *Process* – ensuring people have a common framework and language enabling them to work together
- *Context* – creating a climate and culture that nurtures and promotes one another's innovation competencies
- *Output* – configuration (profit model, networking, structure and process), offering (product performance, product system) and experience (service, channel, brand, customer engagement)

To help to apply these concepts and foster a culture of innovation, companies are using external experience to help them foster a culture of innovation. Procter & Gamble, for instance, have sought the help of outside innovators through collaborative

crowdsourcing – a strategy that is now responsible for 50% of its new products. Chlorox, 3M, Johnson & Johnson and Amazon have also adopted crowdsourcing, while Google acquires a lot of smaller companies because it recognizes that it has to look outside to develop new products as well as foster innovation from within. Sooner or later a company will need to transform itself in response to triggers and shifts in the marketplace, ground-breaking technologies or disruptive start-ups.

In an article in the *Harvard Business Review*, Clark Gilbert and colleagues (2012) describe how most companies will need to reinvent themselves in response to drivers for change. The authors propose an approach that rests on two insights:

1. Major transformations need to be two different efforts happening in parallel: (i) Transformation A should reposition the core business, adapting its current business model to the altered marketplace; (ii) Transformation B should create a separate disruptive business to develop the innovations that will become the source of future growth.
2. The key to making both transformations work is to establish a new organizational process called capabilities exchange through which parallel efforts can share select resources without changing the mission or operations of either.

Gilbert and colleagues cite the example of Barnes and Noble, who, threatened by the advancement of e-books, closed all underperforming megastores and aggressively expanded into the textbook segment, acquiring a leading USA contract operator of college bookstores. By focusing on higher margin gifts, gift books, children's books and textbooks, the company found a way to make its brick and mortar operation profitable. They recruited an e-commerce expert to head Barnes and Noble.com and to launch their Nook e-reader.

Innovation, such as that implemented by Barnes and Noble, is a key imperative that does not just happen through top-down investment in Research and Development (R&D) but involves people across the company identifying and acting on opportunities. It manifests itself in a wide variety of outcomes, from new products and services to new business models and new ways of working. Employee-led innovation, while alluring in principle, is difficult to manage in practice. Everyone has ideas about ways their company's products and internal processes could be improved. But the reality is that most of these ideas never even get out of the starting gate and those that do often get bogged down in formal procedures, or held up by short-term oriented management.

Employee-led innovation

Innovation, as a bottom-up activity, is about trying to do things that go beyond an individual's job description. By definition, it is about taking time to try something that offers uncertain pay-offs, at some time in the future. But companies still struggle with how to overcome these obstacles without compromising today's business. A recent study into employee-led innovation by Julian Birkinshaw and Lisa Duke (2013) at London Business School, identified four enablers to make innovation happen: Time Out, Expansive Roles, Competitions and Open Forums. The following is based on their descriptions of these enablers:

Time Out

Time Out is about setting aside some time for people to work outside their formal role. Over the years, many companies have experimented with the idea of formalizing this sort of arrangement — 3M, the Post-it Notes to medical products company, popularized the notion of 15% innovation time, and Google rebranded it as 'Innovation Time Off', whereby its software engineers are allowed to spend up to 20% of their time on pet projects.

Expansive Roles

A different solution to the same problem is the idea of giving employees much less specific job descriptions. A celebrated example of this principle comes from the American company W. L. Gore, manufacturer of Gore-Tex fabrics. In *The Future of Management*, Gary Hamel (2007) describes how new recruits at Gore-Tex are deliberately hired into broad roles, such as R&D Engineer or Business Development Leader, and in the first few months they circulate among several teams, seeking to find the best fit between their skills and the needs of the business. Expansive Roles help employees to make connections, and to see the bigger picture, and these are vital ingredients in the innovation process.

Competitions

A third enabler is the use of competitions as a way of getting employees' innovative ideas flowing. The success of the TV show *Dragons' Den* over the last decade has helped people to relate to the idea that innovation in business involves trial-and-error, competitiveness and even a little showmanship. But of course the idea of using competitions and tournaments to spur innovation is an old one.

Open Forums

The fourth enabler is the old-fashioned notion of a town hall meeting or open forum, in which information about the company is shared with employees, and they in turn are encouraged to ask questions, challenge the senior executives, and take responsibility for helping to improve things. Open Forums are a vital way of retaining the personal touch, and creating the transparency and trust that is necessary for innovation to take place. So these enablers are critical to the creation of a supportive culture, one that reinforces the importance of innovation, experimentation and risk-taking.

Implications for leaders and managers in identifying the drivers for change and transformation

There are a number of implications for leaders and manager in terms of identifying the drivers for change and transformation.

Understand the context in which the organization operates

In order to sustain organizational change there is a need to understand the context in which changes take place. As highlighted in this chapter, external factors may be identified using a PESTELI analysis but leaders and managers also need to take into account the unexpected turbulent factors that may suddenly occur without warning, such as financial crisis, terrorist attacks, countries invading other countries and political revolutions. Leaders and managers who detect and anticipate external drivers of change will be ready to respond to them and view them as an opportunity, as well as a challenge. At the same time they should not neglect internal drivers for change. When considering the internal drivers for change it is helpful to consider the Resource-Based View (RBV). This model focuses on an inside-out approach driving change rather than adjusting to the PESTELI-type environment and being reactive. However, managers and leader must not ignore the 'outside-in' approaches, in which the starting point for thinking about change and competitive advantage is the external environment. What is required is a mix of the two. Being aware of the internal and external drivers for change is vital and it is important to proactively assess what is happening both outside and inside the organization and what factors may trigger the need for change.

Recognize the need for change early

Whether the need is for incremental or transformational change, the earlier the need is recognized, the greater the number of options managers will have when deciding how to manage it. Whenever managers are forced to react to an urgent and pressing need for change, they are relatively constrained in what they can do. As Hayes (2014) points out: there is less time for planning; there is unlikely to be sufficient time to involve many people; there will be little time to experiment; and there will be little opportunity to influence shifts in markets and technologies.

Creating the belief that change is needed

Review how ready or not the organization is for change, especially the people within it. Today there are many organizations that have stalled or are in a state of atrophy, still making 'rice puddings', as they have not recognized the need to change. Recognizing the need to change involves complex processes of perception, interpretation and decision-making that, if not managed carefully, can lead to inappropriate outcomes. This requires showing how the current performance of the organization differs from the desired future state, which will be brought about by the change. It is important to emphasize the drivers external and internal to the organization, in justifying the need for change.

Encourage innovation

When seeking to make their organization more innovative, many leaders fall back on structure and process: do we have an efficient process for evaluating and reviewing our innovation projects? Have we allocated money to the right types of activities? Do we have a board-level sponsor for innovation? These are all valid approaches, but as Birkinshaw and Duke (2013) point out, they slightly miss the point because they do not encourage the spontaneous development of new ideas from the bottom of the organization. Consider how you can encourage innovation in your organization – perhaps by using the four enablers outlined above (Time Out, Expansive Roles, Competitions, Open Forums). These enablers will, of course, have to be adapted to the context of the organization in which they are being used.

Further reading

Auguste, G. and Gusatz, M. (2013) *Luxury Talent Management: Leading and Managing a Luxury Brand*. London: Palgrave.

Bell, D. and Shelman, M. (2011) 'KFC's radical approach to China', *Harvard Business Review*, 89(11): 137–42.

Brown, B. and Anthony, S.D. (2011) 'How P&G tripled its innovation success rate', *Harvard Business Review*, 89(6): 64–72.

Buchanan, D.A. (2011) 'Reflections: Good practice, not rocket science – understanding failures to change after extreme events', *Journal of Change Management*, 11(3): 273–88.

Gilbert, C., Eyring, M. and Foster, R.N. (2012) 'Two routes to resilience', *Harvard Business Review*, 90(12): 65–73.

Hope Hailey, V. and Balogun, J. (2002) 'Devising context sensitive approaches to change: The example of Glaxo Wellcome', *Long Range Planning*, 35: 153–78.

Styhre, A. (2002) 'Non-linear change in organizations: Organizational change management informed by complexity theory', *Leadership and Organizational Development Journal*, 23(6): 343–51.

Diagnosing the Need and   6
Readiness for Change

Overview

- Organizational **diagnosis** is a process of research into the functioning of an organization that leads to recommendations for improvement. Diagnosis is not, however, a one-off activity. It can be carried out using tools such as **COPS**, **Seven-S** and **Burke–Litwin**.
- Component diagnostic models focus on particular aspects of organizational functioning such as motivation, decision-making, group dynamics and organizational structures. Whereas holistic models consider the organization as a whole.
- Readiness for change refers to organizational members' beliefs, attitudes and intentions regarding the extent to which changes are needed and the organization's capacity and capability to successfully make these changes.
- Managers and leaders need to create readiness for change – an environment where people understand why change is being introduced, what difference it will make to them personally, and the part they will play in it, in order to gain commitment to change.
- Commitment to change is the 'glue' that brings people and change together – it helps people to understand the purpose of change and, as a consequence, can increase employees' individual efforts to implement and sustain change.

Today's changing economic, social and political environments are responsible for rapid and often radical change in organizations. The importance of determining the direction for organizational change cannot be overstated. Organizational diagnosis is the critical first step in planning change interventions (Burke, 1994; Spector, 2007). Failure to develop appropriate strategies for change can reduce organizational effectiveness, waste limited resources and, in extreme cases, result in organizational decline and collapse. Organizational diagnosis is critical to understanding organizational problems, identifying the underlying causes and selecting appropriate interventions regardless of whether the change process is planned or emergent, as well as identifying whether or not change is needed. In the absence of a rigorous diagnostic process, consultants and organizational leaders are likely to address the wrong problems and/or choose the wrong solutions (Meaney and Pung, 2008).

Diagnosis enables organizations to recognize the need for change and critically reflect on whether it is always necessary. The recognition that external events – such as the 2008 economic crisis, the effects of 9/11 terrorist attacks, or the Ebola epidemic of 2014 – or internal circumstances – such as the retirement of key staff or the development of a new product – require a change to take place. Recognition involves complex processes of perception, interpretation and decision-making that, if not managed carefully, can lead to inappropriate outcomes, for example the organization might fail to change when it needs to or it may change when change is not required. As discussed in Chapter 5, leaders sometimes fail to recognize the need for change because they pay insufficient attention to what is happening in the wider environment. Even where organizational members are aware of what is going on outside, they may fail to recognize the implications this could have for the organization.

The purpose of this chapter is to focus on the importance of recognizing and diagnosing the need for change and critically reflecting on whether it is always necessary. The chapter provides the opportunity to take a step back and analyse the need for change, and we begin by discussing whether change is always necessary. The chapter focuses next on diagnosis by defining the diagnostic process and critically examining diagnostic models. Following recognition of the need for change, the next step involves translating the need into a desire for change. We therefore conclude this chapter by examining the need to create a readiness for change, which involves alerting organizational members to the need for change and motivating them to let go of the status quo and move into a state of transition with the change.

Learning objectives

By the end of this chapter you will be able to:

- Critically reflect on the need for change
- Use diagnostic tools to identify the need for change
- Critically assess the readiness for change in an organization
- Address the following questions using relevant frameworks: How can we understand complexity, interdependence and fragmentation? Why do we need to change? Who and what can change? How can we make change happen?

Is change always necessary?

In an article in the *Financial Times* on Monday, 8 July 2013, Lucy Kellaway described the set the Rolling Stones had played at Glastonbury at the weekend as nearly identical to one they had played 40 years earlier. The only difference, Kellaway pointed out, was that you could actually hear it, as the sound at rock concerts is so much better than it was:

> There they all were, ginormous and wearing just the sort of clothes the Stones ought to wear and playing 'Gimme Shelter' just as it sounds on the 1969 LP *Let It Bleed*. It's true that you could also see the deep furrows on their faces but those merely served to mark time and make the lack of any other change all the more remarkable.

Kellaway says that the Stones' tour should be made into a business school case study on when change is called for and when it isn't. She concludes that change is good if it means being better, faster, cheaper and if it leads to clearer sound and cleaner images, but in anything that touches our emotions, change is a very bad thing indeed.

As Kellaway points out, it is as important to recognize when not to change as it is to identify when there is a need for change. Perhaps one of the major myths that pervade the literature on change is that, when changes are inevitable, change initiatives should not be questioned but embraced as they are ultimately vital to the success of the organization (Dawson, 2003a). Konnopke's Imbiss is an example of a company that has recognized the need *not* to change (see study below).

CASE STUDY

Konnopke's Imbiss

Konnopke's Imbiss is one of the most famous snack bars in Berlin, Germany. This family business was set up in 1930 and is famous for its currywurst, a Berlin speciality of fried sausage served with ketchup, chilli sauce and curry powder. By 2010, the snack bar had been run in the same location for 34 years by Waltraud Ziervogel, who took over from her father, Max Konnopke, who started the business and ran it until 1976. Its main branch is in Prenzlauer Berg, considered to be one of the coolest districts of Berlin.

In 2010, Waltraud learnt that the snack bar would have to close for a year because of nearby construction work on a subway station. The proposed disruption offered an opportunity for some fundamental rethinking about the positioning and marketing of Konnopke's Imbiss, not to mention the business model. Should it move to a spot with even more tourists and potential customers? Should it have a healthier menu? Should it raise its prices and extend the opening hours. Many other businesses would have taken the opportunity to make changes with the product, price, place and promotion. Instead Waltrud rebuilt her stand in exactly the same place with almost the same 1960s look and feel, save for a refurbished, bigger seating area and a slightly different outward appearance. The menu remained unchanged, as did the opening hours and the prices. By not radically changing, Konnopke's positioned itself as Berlin's most authentic snack bar.

Case written by Julie Hodges and adapted from Mueller and Etzold (2012).

Discussion Questions

1   What were the benefits for Konnopke's Imbiss of not changing?
2   What would you suggest should have been changed and why?
3   Which organizations do you know of that have not changed? What has been their ration-
    ale for staying as they are? Will they be able to sustain this strategy longer term?

To answer the question about whether change is necessary, leaders and managers
need to take two critical steps. The first step is to recognize the possible need for
change and the second is to assess the strength of that need. The recognition that
change needs to take place is only the starting point. Much like a physician identifying
the source of a symptom in a patient, the second step is to make an accurate diagnosis
of what is causing the problem so that changes can be made to deal with it effectively.
Initiating changes that do not resolve or improve the underlying issue is sometimes
worse than making no changes at all.

Recognizing the need for change

Proactive recognition

Recognizing the potential need for change can be done through conducting an analysis of the external environmental and an internal assessment of the organization.
Completing the external environment analysis involves collecting and analysing information on areas such as political, economic, social, technology, legal and environmental factors as well as the market, competitors and key trends that might positively or
negatively affect the organization's continued success. Completing the internal organizational assessment involves identifying the company's strengths and limitations.
Information can be gathered via activities such as spotting trends in sales and actively
seeking the opinions of stakeholders, such as shareholders, customers and employees.

Starbucks is a company that actively focuses on spotting trends by proactively
studying various ways to retain its current customers and attract the next generation
of young coffee drinkers. The company also asks customers what they think needs to
change. As a result of finding out what a group of 20-year-old volunteers really
thought about Starbucks, the company established Starbucks Express. Starbucks
Express allows customers to email their orders to the store they patronize. The stores
then have the coffee waiting for the customers in a personalized cup when they arrive.

Individuals within an organization can also be proactive in recognizing the need
for change. According to Pitt et al. (2002), issues emerge and are shaped to form the
need for change through various forms of individual initiative. Thompson (2012) echoes this view and asserts that those employees who interact directly with customers
can be the first to learn about product or service shortcomings or pick up on what
competitors are doing to increase their market share. Thompson goes on to say that
people throughout the organization can have value insights about opportunities for
change, but all too often, those potential contributions are lost.

Pitt et al. say that if ideas and concerns are to have any impact on what the organization does, they must receive some minimal level of collective attention and be recognized as having sufficient priority to deserve further consideration. Personal concerns compete for collective attention and interpretation:

> Whether and how fast a concern crystallizes into an issue or item on the agenda depends on who is involved and the opportunities they have to interact and construct the issue through conversation and debate (Pitt et al., 2002: 157)

Thompson (2012) says that recognizing and using the valuable information that is scattered around the organization constitute one of the key business challenges of the modern age.

One way to collect internal as well as external data is to use diagnostic tools. We will examine some of those tools in the next section. The result of conducting a diagnosis is the identification of key issues that the organization needs to address, and therefore changes that the organization needs to make. Typically this will result in a proactive planned approach to managing change. Even when there is a systematic process in place for diagnosing the internal and external environment there will be times when an organization needs to react to drivers for change that could not have been anticipated, such as major shifts in a competitor's strategy, natural disasters, economic crises and the sudden and unexpected loss of key leaders from within the organization. In these situations, organizations that have a formal process to assess internal strengths and limitations will be better placed to make necessary changes than those whose understanding of their internal and external environment is less clear.

Diagnosis

Identification of the appropriate strategic and organizational changes comes from diagnosis, which means analysing the organization in its environment, understanding its strengths and limitations, examining the various parts of the organization at each level and how they affect and are affected by one another and by the whole, and analysing the implications of anticipated changes. Postma and Kok (1999) define organizational diagnosis as a process of research into the functioning of an organization that leads to recommendations for improvement.

This definition highlights that diagnosis is a formal process that enables leaders and managers to understand an organization better and to identify areas for improvement. This formal approach to diagnosis is important because managers and leaders in an organization carry around in their heads their own views as to how things work and what causes what within the organization. In this sense, diagnosis exists whether or not models are used. Although these views may not be explicitly stated, as implicit models they still have a powerful capacity to guide how leaders and managers think about situations that they face in their organizations, how they talk about these situations, and what they think are appropriate interventions. While implicit approaches may provide valuable insights based on accumulated experience, they do have limitations. They are likely to be based on the limited experience of one or a few individuals, so their generalizability is questionable, as it can be subjective.

Explicit, formal diagnosis involves the collection, integration and analysis of data about the organization and its environment. Burke (2008) suggests that the diagnostic

study of change is assisted by the use of models or frameworks that allow the catego-
rization of enormous amounts of data into manageable chunks that 'help us to be more
efficient and to be more rational as we attempt to understand and to change an
organization' (p. 192). Burke (2008) goes on to identify that such models for collecting
data can be useful for:

- making the complexity of a situation where different things are going on more
  manageable by reducing that situation to a manageable number of categories
- helping to identify what aspects of an organization's activities or properties are
  those most needing attention
- highlighting the interconnectedness of various organizational properties, such as
  strategy and structure
- providing a common language with which to discuss organizational characteristics
- providing a guide to the sequence of actions to take in a change situation.

Component and holistic models

Component models focus on particular aspects of organizational functioning, such as
motivation, decision-making, group dynamics, and organizational structures and so
on, whereas holistic models consider the organization as a whole. Nadler and
Tushman (1980) acknowledge the utility of component models but caution against
combining, in some additive way, the specific assessments they provide because they
may produce an incomplete or misleading view of the organization. They argue that
there are properties of the whole that cannot be understood by simply adding
together the component parts. Indeed, part of the dynamic of the whole concerns the
nature of the interaction among the different components of organizational behaviour.

A useful starting point can be to use holistic models to provide an overall assessment before focusing attention on specific issues using a component model. This will
provide a more complete view of the organization.

A method for diagnostic frameworks

While recognizing the utility of component models we have chosen to use a method
that clusters some of the holistic models around a small number of key questions. This
is because these questions are likely to be at the forefront of the minds of leaders and
managers whenever they attempt to make links between the immediate pressures of
organizational life and change interventions. The four questions used are:

1. How can we understand complexity, interdependence and fragmentation? *What
   frameworks can help with thinking constructively about living with this kind of
   complexity?*
2. Why do we need to change? *What frameworks can help to share an understanding
   of why change is needed?*
3. Who and what can change? *What frameworks can help to identify the key areas for
   attention?*
4. How can we make change happen? *What frameworks can help to create a change
   initiative that will really deliver the results that are needed?*

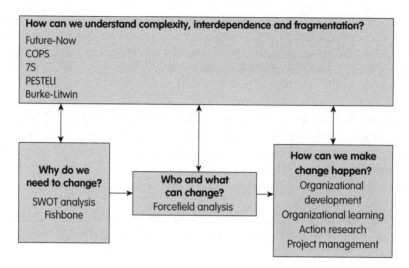

Figure 6.1 Diagnostic tools, models and approaches

The questions and the clusters of models under each question are set out in Figure 6.1. It is not suggested that these questions and clusters are the only way to organize the models nor that all relevant models are included. Neither are they intended to be a prescription for managing the process of change. Their purpose is purely to make the models and frameworks more accessible.

1. How can we understand complexity, interdependence and fragmentation?

To address this question we need to consider the frameworks that can help with identifying the current situation in the organization and what needs to change.

Future–Present model

A basic framework to use is the **Future–Present model** (Wardrop-White, 2001), which focuses on identifying what the current situation is and what the future situation should be (Figure 6.2). The left-hand box (The Present) is defining what the current situation is. While the right-hand box (The Future) is about what the future situation should be. There is debate about whether the process should start with looking at the present or the future. The argument with starting with the present is to ensure that the change is not conceived as a utopian leap to an unrealistic future that cannot be reached from the current situation. While on the other hand, focusing too heavily on the present may limit horizons and lead to the goals for change being too cautious and constrained by current experience. It can also lead to getting too bogged down in what is wrong with the current situation rather than focusing on what the future should look like.

The present state of the organization can often only be understood in terms of the context of its history, its external environment, and the reactive and self-reinforcing sequences that have contributed to the current situation. Common reasons for reviewing the present state are to: help identify the required change by diagnosing the cause

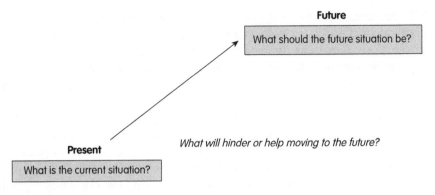

Figure 6.2 Future–Present model

of a problem; identify current deficiencies or clarifying opportunities; establish a baseline so that it is clear what is changing; and help define the future direction.

What is required when identifying the future state depends on the kind of change (incremental or transformational) to be carried out. Defining the future state may be about developing a view or vision of what the organization (or team/department) ought to look like in the future and the likely impact of the change.

Some of the key questions to ask when using this framework are:

- What should the future situation look like or what would 'better' look like? How will we know when we get there? What will it look like, feel like?
- What is happening in the present situation?
- What is the context in which things are happening?
- What will hinder progress towards that future?
- What will help progress towards that future?

This is a simple model and does therefore have limitations. It provides only an initial analysis of the situation and at a relatively high level. It can, however, be used effectively with teams and groups of individuals at different levels in an organization to gain an overview of the current situation and what the future should look like. As with all such frameworks they are more effective when used in conjunction with other models, such as COPS or Seven-S.

The 'COPS' framework

The COPS framework (Wardrop-White, 2001) can be used for scanning an organization internally to establish how healthy the organization is and whether the different elements are aligned with one another. Four separate aspects of the organization are considered and the relative strengths and weaknesses of each are assessed. The four elements of the COPS framework are:

C = Culture (beliefs, values, artefacts, manifestations)
O =Organization (structure, job roles, reporting lines)
P = People (staff, competencies, experience)
S = Systems (processes and procedures)

The COPS framework can be used to establish how healthy the organization (or team) is and how aligned the four elements are with the strategy and with one another. It can also be used as a basis for data-gathering activities, such as interviews, focus groups or questionnaires. Questions can be designed for each of the four areas (for example, How would you define the Culture in this organization?). The four elements can also be used to structure and present the data gathered about the organization.

COPS is a framework which can be used to do a 'quick and dirty' analysis. It does therefore have some limitations. While it may be tempting to build a picture of what is going on in an organization by looking at the various components separately, the picture this produces may be incomplete. The systems nature of organizations implies that there are properties of the whole that cannot be understood simply by adding together the component parts. Indeed part of the dynamics of the whole concerns the nature of the interaction among the different parts.

Seven-S framework

A framework that does focus on the interaction of different parts of an organization is the 'Seven-S' model which was developed by Pascale and Athos (1981) and further honed by Peters and Waterman (1982), and eventually became known as McKinsey's Seven-S model. The premise of the model is that successful change is based on the interdependence between seven elements: strategy, structure, systems, staff, style, skills and shared values.

- *Strategy.* The purpose of the business and the way the organization seeks to enhance its competitive advantage.
- *Structure.* Division of activities; integration and coordination mechanisms; nature of the informal organization.
- *Systems.* Formal and informal procedures and processes for measurement, reward, resource allocation, communication, resolving conflicts and so on.
- *Staff.* The organization's employees' experience, skills, knowledge, education and attitudes, as well as demographics.
- *Style.* Typical behaviour patterns of key groups, such as leaders and managers and other professionals, and the organization as a whole.
- *Shared values.* Core beliefs and values, and how these influence the organization's orientation towards customers, employees, shareholders, the external community and other key stakeholders.
- *Skills.* The core competencies and distinct capabilities of organizational members.

Managers using this model can draw on their knowledge of the seven elements in the organization to construct a Seven-S matrix to assess the degree of alignment between each of the elements. This analysis might point to areas where it is necessary to use component models to design an intervention to change an element. However, changes to one of the elements can affect all the other components, as they are an interconnected set of levers. For example, if changes are being made to the information systems in order to make the organization more customer-responsive, managers making the changes need to carefully consider the implication on the other elements and be prepared to manage the change in a holistic fashion. Making changes to one of the elements while ignoring the implications on the others is a recipe for disaster. The Seven-S model is useful as part of the data-gathering process as it helps to ensure that the key components are covered when assessing the internal factors. However, this focus on internal factors is also a limitation because leaders and managers also need to consider the external environment. The model does not contain any external environmental variables. It is a description of the seven internal elements and shows how they interact to create organizational patterns, but there is no explanation of how each element affects another or how the seven dimensions are affected by the external environment.

PESTELI

A framework that covers the external factors is PESTELI (Iles and Sutherland, 2001), originally known by the acronym 'PEST', which stands for:

- *Political*. Political forces and influences that may affect the performance of, or the options open to, the organization
- *Economic*. The nature of the competition faced by the organization or its services, and financial resources available within the economy
- *Societal*. Demographic changes, trends in the way people live, work, and think
- *Technological*. New approaches to doing new and old things, and tackling new and old problems

More recently the list has been expanded to PESTELI, and in addition includes:

- *Environmental factors*. A definition of the wider environmental system of which the organization is a part and consideration of how the organization interacts with it
- *Legislative requirements*. Originally included under political, relevant legislation now requires a heading of its own
- *Industry analysis*. A review of the industry of which the organization forms a part

More commonly a PESTELI+ is used, which includes reviewing competitors and customers as well as the traditional PESTELI parameters.

To provide an analysis of internal and external factors, however, the PESTELI does need to be used in conjunction with a tool that diagnoses the internal environment, such as the Seven-S model.

Combining internal and external frameworks: the 'outside to inside' frameworks

It is possible to use two or more frameworks together, as in the example in Figure 6.3, where the Seven-S and the PESTELI frameworks come together. This allows managers and leaders to consider the link between what is happening in the outside world and how it will be dealt with in the organization.

Burke–Litwin model

The Burke–Litwin (Burke and Litwin, 1992) model seeks to address the complexity and interdependence of the internal and external factors affecting change. It illustrates how the external environment affects the performance of the organization and how

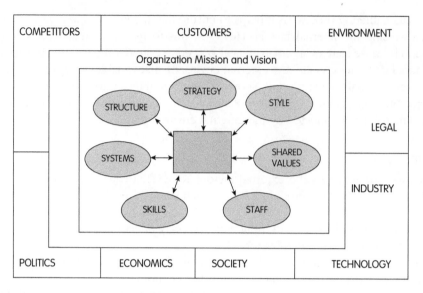

Figure 6.3   An outside-to-inside analytical framework

organizational performance affects the external environment. The model is predictive rather than prescriptive in that it specifies the nature of causal relationships and predicts the likely effect of changing certain elements rather than others (Figure 6.4).

It also differentiates between two types of change: transformational change, which occurs in response to important triggers in the external environment, and transactional/incremental change, which occurs in response to the need for more short-term transactional improvement. The variables located in the top half of the model (environment, leadership, mission and strategy, and organizational culture) are identified as the *transformational factors*. Changes to these organizational factors are seen as likely caused by interactions with the external environment. Initiatives in this area are difficult to manage because they challenge core beliefs and assumptions about the organization and what it should be doing. They entail significantly new behaviour by organizational members and major alterations to other variables in the model. However, when fundamental reorientation and re-creation are a necessity, they may represent the only viable approach to organizational rejuvenation and long-term success.

The remaining variables are identified as the *transactional factors* because they are more directly involved in the day-to-day activities of the organization. Changes of an incremental nature can occur without necessarily triggering changes in the transformational factors. This can be seen in on-going quality improvement initiatives, management development programmes, work realignment and other incremental interventions aimed at refining and improving internal practices in order to enhance fit and, therefore, performance.

A brief description of each of the 12 variables is outlined below:

- **External environment.** The key external factors that have an impact on the organization must be identified and their direct and indirect impact on the organization should be clearly established.

- **Mission and strategy.** The vision, mission and strategy of the organization, as defined by the top management, should be examined in terms of the employees' point-of-view about them.
- **Leadership.** An analysis of the leadership structure of the organization should be carried out, which clearly identifies the chief role models in the organization.
- **Organizational culture.** An organizational culture analysis should seek information on the explicit as well as the implied rules, regulations, customs, principles and values that influence the organizational culture.
- **Structure.** The analysis of the structure should not be confined to hierarchical structure; rather it should be a function-based structure focusing on the responsibility, authority, communication, decision-making and control structure that exists between the people of the organization.
- **Management practices.** This would entail an analysis of how well the managers conform to the organization's strategy when dealing with employees and the resources.
- **Systems.** Systems includes all types of policies and procedures with regard to both the people and the operations of the organization.
- **Work unit climate.** This involves an assessment of how the employees think, feel and what they expect. The kind of relationships the employees share with their team members and members of other teams is also an important aspect of work unit climate.
- **Tasks and individual roles.** This involves an understanding of job roles, and skills and knowledge that an employee must have in order to fulfil the task responsibilities of their role.
- **Motivation level.** Identifying the motivation level of the employees will make it easier to determine how willing they are to achieve organizational goals. This would also involve identifying motivational triggers.
- **Individual needs and values.** This variable seeks to explore employees' values and needs, as well as their opinion about their work so as to identify the factors that will result in job satisfaction.
- **Individual and organizational performance.** This variable examines the level of performance, on individual and organizational levels, in key areas such as productivity, quality, efficiency, budget and customer satisfaction.

Burke and Litwin (1992) present an impressive, if somewhat selective, summary of studies that provide empirical support for the causal linkages hypothesized by their model. One of the benefits of the model is that it provides a conceptual map of the organization, with a set of variables that help explain organizational dynamics. By separating variables into transformational and transactional, the model provides a way of examining the impact of changes on different variables. However, this complexity makes it difficult to keep track of all variables and develop clear action plans. Additionally, while the model does have both the environment and individual/organizational performance as variables, these are viewed as just two of the 12 variables. As a result there is no direct flow from environment to organization to performance.

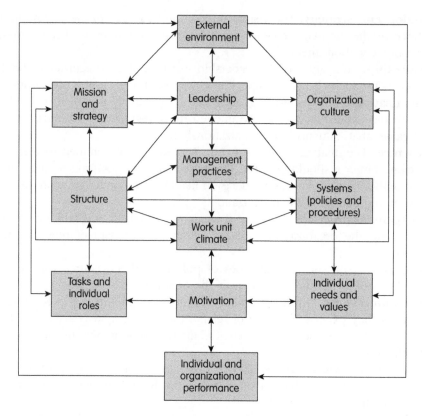

Figure 6.4   Burke–Litwin model (adapted from Burke and Litwin, 1992)

Activity

Use the Burke–Litwin model to analyse a change you are considering either at a team or organizational level:

1   Is the change you intend to make transformational change or incremental change, or is it a blend of both? What kind of change does the organization really need?
2   What elements of the model have you not yet considered in your change plan?
3   In which 'boxes' will you have problems?

---

2. Why do we need to change?

Tools that can be used to address the question, 'Why do we need to change?' include SWOT and the Ishikawa diagram.

SWOT

SWOT is an acronym for examining an organization's Strengths, Weaknesses, Opportunities and Threats, and using the result to identify priorities for action (Selznick, 1957). The main principle underlying SWOT is that internal and external factors must be considered simultaneously when identifying aspects of an organization that need to be changed. Strengths and weaknesses are internal to the organization; opportunities and threats are external. Many leaders and managers will have experience of working with this framework. The strengths and weaknesses should be identified first, preferably using a checklist such as the Seven-S model, and then the opportunities and threats, using a checklist for the external environment such as PESTELI. On its own this information is rarely helpful or usable and must be considered further. This requires asking questions about each of the factors listed under the four headings.

For *strengths* and *weaknesses* the questions to ask are:

1. What are the consequences of this? Do they help or hinder us in achieving our mission/purpose?
2. What are the causes of this strength (or weakness)?

For *opportunities* and *threats* the questions are slightly different:

1. What impact is this likely to have on us? Will it help or hinder us in achieving our mission/purpose?
2. What must we do to respond to this opportunity or threat?

SWOT is one of the most widely used tools. However, in a review of its use in 50 UK companies, Hill and Westbrook (1997) found that SWOT often resulted in over-long lists, descriptions, a failure to prioritize issues, no attempt to verify any conclusions and the outputs, once generated, were rarely used. So if not used effectively then SWOT can be translated into a Substantial Waste Of Time. In order to overcome such limitations it is important that actions to exploit the strengths and opportunities are identified as well as actions to reduce the weaknesses and threats (see Box 6.1). These need to be put into an action plan with specific, measurable, agreed and time-bound objectives, with the accountability for achieving each objective identified.

Box 6.1

Internal factors			
Strengths	Ways to exploit	Weaknesses	Ways to reduce

External			
Opportunities	Ways to exploit	Weaknesses	Ways to reduce

Fishbone (Ishikawa) diagram

The Ishikawa diagram can be used to help understand the root causes of problems or opportunities. It was devised by Kaoru Ishikawa (1985), who pioneered quality management processes in the Kawasaki shipyards in Japan. The diagram is also known as the **fishbone diagram** because of its resemblance to the skeleton of a fish. It can be used to help think through all of the possible causes of a problem and what needs to change. The model provides a cause-and-effect analysis, which aims to identify the causes, factors, or sources of variation that lead to a specific event, result, or defect in a product or process.

The effect or problem being investigated is shown at the end of a horizontal arrow; potential causes are then shown as labelled arrows entering the main cause arrow. Each arrow may have other arrows entering it as the principal causes or factors are reduced to their sub-causes. Brainstorming can be effectively used to generate the causes and sub-causes. The various causes are grouped into categories and the arrows indicate how the causes cascade or flow toward the end effect.

The steps to carrying out a cause-and-effect analysis are:

1. Define the effect. Be specific.
2. Choose categories. The most common set of categories are Equipment, Process, People, Materials, Environment, Management. Categories can be added to or removed based on the specific case.
3. Brainstorm possible causes for each category in turn.
4. Ask why? To find the root causes ask 'Why?' or 'Why else?' over and over until possible root causes are identified. 'Improper safety procedure' is not a root cause, while 'Failing to wear a safety helmet' might be closer to a root cause. But, you could still ask 'Why was he/she not wearing a safety helmet?' with the possible response 'There were none available.' It is a lot easier to take action against the inventory problem than just the generic 'improper safety procedure'.
5. Investigate. After the possible causes have been identified, gather data to confirm which causes are real or not.

The cause-and-effect model encourages people to think about the issues that provoke the problem rather than focusing attention simply on the effects of that problem; as such it allows people to tackle root causes rather than just the symptoms. The effectiveness of the model is, however, dependent on people being able to accurately identify the causes of the problem; where the causes are not properly identified, the focus of any subsequent changes will be inappropriate and therefore likely to fail to achieve desired outcomes.

3. Who and what can change?

To gather data to address the question of 'Who or what can change?' frameworks such as the force field analysis can be used.

Force field analysis

The force field analysis, developed by Kurt Lewin in 1947, is a diagnostic technique which can be used in identifying the forces that will help or hinder a change. It is based on the concept of forces, a term that refers to the perceptions of people in the organization about a particular factor and its influence. Driving forces are those forces affecting a situation and which are attempting to push it in a particular direction. These forces tend to initiate change or keep it going. Restraining forces are forces acting to restrain or decrease the driving forces. A state of equilibrium is reached when the sum of the driving forces equals the sum of the restraining forces.

Constructing a force field diagram
The approach to using the force field analysis comprises four steps:

1. Think through the current situation and the desired future state (using the Future–Present model).
2. Write down a definition of the change to be implemented – the solution as you see it. Draw a line down the middle of the page and head the left-hand column 'Driving Forces' and the right-hand column 'Restraining Forces'.
3. List the 'Driving Forces' and by each force draw an arrow pointing to the right. Next list the forces that will work against the solution being achieved. List these forces in the 'Restraining Forces' column and draw an arrow pointing to the left.
4. In both cases identify the most important drivers and restrainers to address. Create a strategy to weaken each of the key restrainers and a strategy to strengthen each of the key drivers. See Appendix 6.1 for an advanced force field analysis.

Once the analysis is complete the next step is to identify the actions to take for each of the forces identified, as outlined in Table 6.1.

The force field analysis provides a picture of a given moment in time. It is therefore useful to use the tool at various stages of the change process and also to use it with other frameworks. For instance, it can be used with the Future–Present model to identify what will help and hinder moving to the desired state. It can also be combined with the COPS framework. A combination of frameworks is helpful in beginning to identify what needs to change. Figure 6.5 shows how the Future–Present and PESTELI models can be combined. This approach provides a deeper analysis.

Table 6.1 Actions to address drivers and restraining forces

Driving forces	Actions to take
Customer wants new products quicker	Inform customer about plans to change systems.
Improved speed of purchasing	Identify benefits for stakeholders of new system.
Low maintenance cost	Carry out cost-benefit analysis and measure benefits. Share information with stakeholder.

Restraining forces	Actions to take
Staff afraid of losing their job	Involve staff in selection of new systems and responsibility for implementing it.
Staff fearful of new systems	Brief all staff on benefits of new system and provide training in how to use it.
Cost	Carry out a cost-benefit analysis and measure benefits.

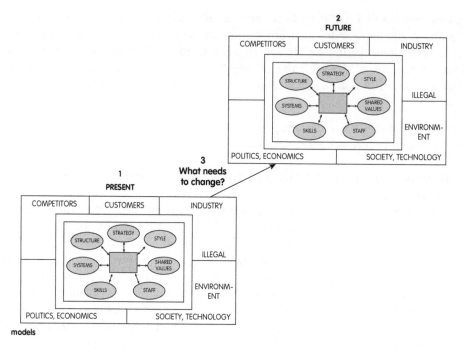

Figure 6.5   Combination of models

Activity

Think of an organization that you are familiar with and analyse it using one of the frameworks we have discussed in this section.

Based on your analysis consider the changes that you believe would improve things.

---

4. How can we make change happen?

The final question in our model is 'How we can we make change happen?'

Frameworks that can help to create a change initiative and that will really deliver the results that are needed include but are not limited to organizational development, organizational learning, action research and project management. We examine each of these in later chapters.

Diagnosing where an organization is in the present is a prerequisite for identifying its future direction. Addressing the question of 'why change' is a precondition to being able to define the desired future state or the vision. If the question 'why change?' is never addressed, no one should expect the emergence of any sense of a shared vision. The answer to 'why' is a prerequisite to the 'what' and 'how' of change.

Diagnosis should not be a one-off activity but ongoing. It can begin with a review of the total organization and then a review of its different functions, departments and teams. However, you should develop a healthy scepticism towards the utility of different models and constantly reassess which is most appropriate for the intended purpose. All models are simplifications of the real world, and the utility of any particular model, in the context of change, needs to be judged in terms of whether or not it provides a helpful conceptual framework for the change process. The choice of model is often one of personal preference. Frameworks should be customized to meet the needs of the situation.

In the following case study Simon Haslam shares his experience of using a matrix that can be customized to suit the needs of different organizations.

CASE STUDY

In praise of the 'Four Box Grid'

This story is based on two separate strategic change discussions that happened within days of each other. Each concerned a different organization but what they shared was the 'matrix' approach to framing the change issue. The 'matrix' approach involves the creation of a simple diagram to show the relationship between two independent variables. The matrix diagram, if well designed, strengthens the ability of a complex change issue to be summarized and clarified. Such matrices are not without their critics. 'Too simple', 'There's more than two factors', are regularly voiced concerns. But, I have found their vulnerabilities are outweighed by their strengths. Here are the two examples.

Context 1 – 'the agency'

This organization is a business support agency. Its remit is to support smaller businesses in its local area, and its primary funding to do this comes indirectly from government (in this case via the local council). This particular agency manages premises owned by the local council (business units and office space) which are rented to local small firms. Being a landlord and property manager is a major source of income for the agency. The last time I met the Chief Executive of the agency, he spoke of his organization's possible move into microfinance, to help small businesses with funding gaps. This was in response to what he saw as a tightening up of lending policy by the main retail banks. Such a move would require a change to the agency's skill set, which would not necessarily be an easy journey, but would help meet the needs of some of the new start-ups and small businesses that were his agency's main market. He also mentioned that the council had not yet renewed its contract for the agency to manage the property portfolio and had picked up on the grapevine that the council had reviewed its purchasing procedures and were moving other contracts from smaller suppliers like the agency, to larger, more integrated services organizations. The Chief Executive was able to frame the strategic issue for his board with the help of a four-box grid (see Figure 6.6). The horizontal axis related to whether the council would renew the property contract with the agency and the vertical axis related to whether the agency should expand its services into microfinance.

The matrix helps those making decisions, and thus shaping the change direction, by providing a more structured way of looking at the possibilities and options. Accepting that the council's property management decision and the possible move into microfinance are separate decisions, they need to be considered together as they both relate to the same organization and both have implications on that organization's resources etc. Figure 6.6 gives a summary of the matrix with the main strategic options shown.

(Continued)

(Continued)

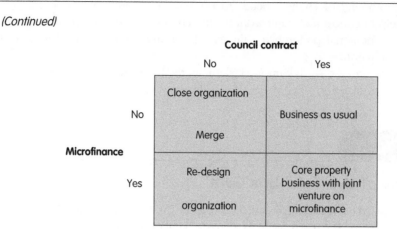

Figure 6.6 The 'agency's matrix'

Context 2 – 'the manufacturer'

The second example comes from a directors' 'away day' I was facilitating for a consumer goods manufacturing business. The business's channel to market is via high street retailers. The retailers enter into a six-year agreement with the manufacturer which gives each retailer territorial exclusivity and branding support. There are about 120 retailers with whom the manufacturer has a commercial relationship, and the majority of these are independently owned. The manufacturer's dilemma relates to the varying degrees of enthusiasm for their products among the different retailers. In the words of the manufacturer's Chief Executive, *'We've made a lot of people [retailers] very rich, but when someone has ten million in the bank their keenness to earn the eleventh becomes diminished.'*

One of the outputs from the away day was a way for the manufacturer to move its current retail network to a more strongly performing one. This way was facilitated in part using a two by two matrix (see Figure 6.7). On the horizontal axis is the degree to which the retailer was enthusiastic. On the vertical axis is the scale (low–high) of the retailer's business with the manufacturer – above and below £40,000 per annum. The matrix is shown here in summary form.

	'Enthusiasm'	
	No	**Yes**
High	Convert or replace by alternative	Encourage/enable extension of reach
Low	De-list	Possible to raise sales

Scale (on the vertical axis labelled between High and Low)

Figure 6.7 The 'manufacturer's matrix'

'Because they are good at PowerPoint'

The value of both matrices is similar. In both cases, the simple diagram enabled a group of people to visualize the issue to the point they were able to have productive conversations and explore options for taking their enterprises forward. Another client of mine asked his boss why their firm used McKinsey& Company as consultants so much. His boss's reply was 'Because they are good at PowerPoint.' This boss went on to explain that one of the skills the McKinsey team brought to the client situation was the ability to crystallize a messy array of data into a simple visual model. Once created, this visual provided the platform for further discussion and deliberation, but to a greater level than would have been possible without the visual model.

The strategist Richard Rumelt, in his book *Good Strategy, Bad Strategy* (2012), writes that a good strategy should be a cohesive response to an important challenge and that good diagnosis of the situation is a necessity. What I particularly like about the above two examples is that the matrices are customized to each client's situation and focused only on a summary of the diagnosis of that client's context and its challenges. And as a client's important challenges are likely to change over time, both these matrices are likely to have short lives. There are 'industry standard' matrices, such as Ansoff's matrix, the BCG matrix and the 'readiness for change' matrix, but whether such generics can be as helpful in practical terms, is probably open to debate.

© 2015 Dr Simon Haslam, Director, FMR Research Ltd.

Discussion Questions

1 How helpful are such matrices?
2 Identify a challenge you are facing in your work or personal life and produce a matrix to diagnose the challenge.

Readiness to change

There is a Chinese proverb which says that you should 'dig a well before you are thirsty'. In other words, we should deal with change by getting ready for it. This is what Sir Ernest Shackleton did before setting off on his transAntarctic expedition in 1914. He advertised for men to take part in a hazardous journey in the bitter cold with long months of complete darkness, constant danger, with safe return doubtful, honour and recognition in case of success, and minimal wages. The expedition resulted in 27 men being stranded on Elephant Island off the Antarctic coast, awaiting rescue that in all likelihood would never come. But after 22 months, all the men survived. They had each been recruited individually with the view to being ready for the change ahead of them. The aim was to have individuals who would each contribute to and drive the expedition, not just the leader.

The role of individual actors has often been ignored in change accounts; those studies that have examined individual roles have often favoured a leader-centric perspective that focuses on the strategic and/or personal nature of transformational leadership. This has often been at the cost of focusing attention on those lower down the organization whose decision-making and subsequent actions will likely have a determining impact on the overall effectiveness of any change programme (Armenakis and Bedeian, 1999; Armenakis and Harris, 2009; Ford et al. 2008). Importantly, a developing body of literature, focused on the readiness of individuals to engage with, and realize, change, has begun to address this gap in our understanding (Armenakis et al., 1993). Thus, research that has focused upon readiness for change has provided welcome actor-centric insights into how change takes place.

Readiness for change refers to organizational members' beliefs, attitudes and intentions regarding the extent to which changes are needed and the organization's capacity to successfully make those changes (Armenakis et al., 1993). Gregory Stevens (2013) refers to terms such as 'openness', 'receptivity', 'commitment' and 'attitudes towards change' when defining readiness for change. Readiness encompasses the extent to which employees have positive views about the need for change and believe that these changes have positive implications for themselves and the wider organization (Goh et al., 2006). Thus readiness for change denotes employees' beliefs that the organization can initiate a change and also engage in the practices that lead to it being successfully implemented.

Antecedents of readiness for change

Imran Hameed and colleagues (2013) show empirically that the identification of employees with the organization – the psychological bonding between an individual and his or her organization – has a significant positive effect on readiness for organizational change. This is consistent with the earlier arguments of Rousseau (1998) and Cherim (2002) and suggests that to facilitate effective change organizations should focus on developing the strong attachment of employees to the organization. Yet during change efforts many companies communicate poorly, fail to deal with uncertainty, impose decisions on employees and fail to reassure employees of their worth to the organization, leading to a decrease in organizational identification. A decrease in the level of employees' organizational identification can decrease their readiness for change. In turn this may cause employees to oppose change at a time when the organization really needs their support (Madsen et al., 2005).

Alannah Rafferty and colleagues (2012) say that, while there is substantial agreement about the key cognitions that underlie change readiness, there is a lack of research evidence both for its affective aspects and for possible variations in change readiness at different levels of analysis – individual, group and organization-wide. They propose that an individual's self-perceived readiness for change is a function of the individual's belief that change is needed, that he or she has the capacity to undertake change successfully and that change will have positive outcomes for his or her job or role.

Change readiness at the group and organizational levels, Rafferty and colleagues suggest, is a function of the shared beliefs and emotional responses of individuals. They argue that an organization's leadership, identity and culture are likely to contribute to the development of consistent collective affective responses to organizational change events. They conclude that readiness for change is created through a culture of openness, trust and flexibility that influence the degree to which its members are adaptable and generally open to new ideas.

Discussion Questions

1　What might an organization do that would lead you to think that it was ready for change?
2　What might an organizations do that would lead you to think that it was not ready for change?

Assessment of readiness for change

The assessment of readiness for change allows an organization to tailor efforts to make success more likely. Armenakis and colleagues (1999) identified the following as indicators of an organization's readiness for change: the need for change is identified in terms of the gap between the current state and the desired state; people believe that the proposed change is the right change to make; the confidence of organizational members has been bolstered so that they believe they can accomplish the change; the change has the support of key individuals that the organizational members look to; and the 'what is in it for me/us?' question has been addressed. Judge and Douglas (2009) used a more rigorous approach to assessment, with the identification of the following eight dimensions related to readiness for change:

1. Trustworthy leadership – the ability of senior leaders to earn the trust and credibility of others
2. Trusting followers – the ability of stakeholders to willingly support the change
3. Capable champions – the ability of the organization to attract and retain capable champions
4. Involved middle managers – the ability of middle managers to effectively link the change proposed by leaders with the rest of the organization
5. Innovative culture – the ability of the organization to establish norms of innovation and encourage innovative activity
6. Accountable culture – the ability of the organization to carefully steward resources and successfully meet predetermined deadlines
7. Effective communication – the ability of the organization to effectively communicate vertically, horizontally and with customers
8. Systems thinking – the ability of the organization to focus on root causes and recognize interdependencies within and outside the organization's boundaries

Along with such lists there are a number of generic approaches to readiness assessment that organizations can use singly, in concert or in multiple combinations. These approaches, which help gauge the readiness for change, include:

1. Conducting an audit of the thoroughness of the content and strategies used in communication about change (Armenakis et al., 1999).

2. Observing employees for behaviour that will reveal their reactions. Observation should be relatively unobtrusive. It involves being attentive to rumours, increases in absence or turnover, or any unusual behaviour associated with denial or opposition to change.
3. Discussing with employees their reactions toward the change, either in one-to-one interviews or in focus groups.
4. Conducting an organizational survey, consisting of responses to Likert-style items and open questions (such as 'what …?', 'why …?', or 'how …?'

When conducting readiness assessments it is important to be cognizant of the behaviours that demonstrate readiness and non-readiness for change. These behaviours are illustrated in Table 6.2.

Table 6.2 Behaviours describing organizational readiness and non-readiness for change

Commitment of leaders to change

Leaders are decisive with respect to organizational goals, priorities and strategies concerning the change.

Leaders themselves have bought into the change and promote it by behaving in a manner consistent with the change.

Leaders define the course of change over time and stay the course.

There is a champion of change at the most senior level of the organization.

Competence of change agents

Change agents have done research to select the right type of change that addresses the underlying causes of organizational problems rather than just symptoms.

Change agents provide valid arguments to justify the change.

Change agents have considered different options for implementing change.

Change agents are competent to answer employees' questions about the change.

Support of immediate manager

Managers are held accountable for passing information on the change to their staff.

Managers acknowledge the impact that the change may have on their staff.

Immediate supervisors encourage their staff to participate in the change process.

Poor communication of change

The outcomes and benefits of the change are not well explained.

The reasons for the change are not well explained.

There is no vision for the change that everybody in the organization understands.

Adverse impact of the change on work

The change process does not involve the phasing out of old duties and employees are expected to perform both the old and the new duties.

Workloads do not permit people to get involved in the change initiatives.

People are discouraged from saying 'no' to work, even when the assigned task is not a priority.

(Adapted from Cinite et al., 2009)

Activity

Consider a change that is currently being implemented in your organization or one with which you are familiar:

1 What is the need for change? What are the consequences to the organization of changing or not changing? Are people aware of these risks?
2 How are managers demonstrating the need for change?
3 What are the benefits of the change?
4 If individuals believe the benefits outweigh the costs, do they also believe the probability of success is great enough to warrant the risk-taking, including the investment of time and energy that the change will require?
5 What other change interventions would they prefer? What is it about their costs, benefits and risks that make them more attractive? How should these alternatives be addressed by leaders?

Implications for leaders and managers for diagnosing the need and readiness for change

Several practical implications for managers and leaders can be drawn from the areas we have discussed in this chapter.

Use a variety of tools for diagnosis

Organizational diagnosis is a process of research into the functioning of an organization that leads to recommendations for improvement. Diagnosis is not, however, a one-off activity. It can be carried out using tools such as COPS, Seven-S and Burke–Litwin. When using diagnostic tools, consider the implications of changing one part of an organization, for example the structure – review what the implications will be on the other parts of the organization.

Identify what influences readiness for change

Readiness for change refers to organizational members' beliefs, attitudes and intentions regarding the extent to which changes are needed and the organization's capacity to successfully make those changes (Armenakis et al., 1993: 681). Managers and leaders need to be aware of what influences employees' readiness for change, such as existing organizational conditions, the nature of the change, and individuals' belief in their ability to change. Existing organizational conditions (such as culture, management and leadership style) can affect employee loyalty, commitment or other feelings toward an organization and its leaders, consequently influencing readiness. Effective management practices (planning, delegating and communicating) have been found to influence employee cooperation and perceived equity and to be associated with higher employee readiness for implementing improvements in procedures and problem-solving. In contrast, ineffective practices are associated with lower readiness to change

(Fox et al., 1988). The nature of the change may also affect individuals' readiness for change. Transformational change, such as changing from a functional form to a strategic business unit organization or from an assembly line to an autonomous workgroup arrangement, requires different behaviours from individuals and the development of new skills. On the other hand, incremental change, such as rearranging desks to a more efficient layout, requires lesser modifications of behaviours and a simple fine-tuning of working arrangements.

Creating readiness involves proactive attempts by leaders and managers to influence the beliefs, attitudes, intentions and ultimately the behaviour of employees. By considering what is promoting and inhibiting change readiness, actions can be taken to enhance readiness. Developing change readiness is an important aspect to laying the foundations for sustaining change.

Consider whether change is necessary

To answer the question about whether change is necessary, leaders and managers need to take two critical steps. The first step is to recognize the possible need for change and the second is to assess the strength of that need. The recognition that change needs to happen is only the starting point. Initiating changes that do not resolve or improve the underlying issue is sometimes worse than making no changes at all.

When considering whether or not an organizational change is necessary, leaders and managers may want to consider the following questions, which we have adapted from the work of Weisbord (2012). Answer each of the questions then rate each one at the end.

1. Is there a good **business reason** for making this change?

   a. How much pressure is there for change?
   b. What is the business reason?
   c. What are the benefits, risks and costs?
   d. How do the costs and benefit of this change compare to those of other changes the organization is making now or could make?
   e. To what extent does the organization have the capacity to implement the change?

2. Is there **committed leadership** for the change?

   a. How willing are you as a leader/manager to take risks to achieve this change?
   b. To what extent are other levels of leadership supportive of the change?
   c. To what extent is there a clear and shared vision of the goal and direction?
   d. How much effective liaison and trust do you have?

3. Are those people affected by or doing the work involved **energized** to take this change on?

   a. What are the costs and benefits of the change to the staff?
   b. What are the costs and benefits of the change to other key groups who are affected by the change?

c. How does this change compare to other changes that staff are facing?

d. How does the change compare to other changes that stakeholders are facing?

e. How able are the staff to come together to understand joint concerns and to act together in meeting them?

f. To what extent do we have capable people and resources to take on and cope with the change?

g. To what extent do we have suitable rewards and defined accountability?

h. To what extent is there a will and the power to act?

Consider your answers to each question and enter an overall rating of high, medium or low, according to the chart in Figure 6.3.

Use your ratings to identify strategies for action:

Table 6.3 Rating the need for change

Key question: To what degree do we have this ingredient present in forecasting success in fulfilling this change initiative?	Overall rating		
Business reason	Low	Medium	High
Committed leadership	Low	Medium	High
Energized people	Low	Medium	High

For low ratings: What can you do that would lead you to improve your ratings?

For medium ratings: What strategies for action does this key response suggest?

For high ratings: How can you put this asset to use? How can it be used to improve areas with lower ratings?

Appendix 6.1: Force identification and labelling template

Table 6.5

Force	Resisting or supporting	Importance (low, medium, high)	Ease of changing (low, medium, high)	Priority (numerical rating or low, medium, high)

Further reading

Cohan, P.S. (2008) *You Can't Order Change: Lessons from Jim McNerney's Turnaround at Boeing*. New York: Penguin.

Eby, L.T., Adams, D.M., Russell, E.A. and Gaby, S.H. (2000) 'Perceptions of organizational readiness for change: Factors related to employees' reactions to the implementation of team-based selling', *Human Relations*, 53: 419–42.

Hope Hailey, V. and Balogun, J. (2002) 'Devising context sensitive approaches to change: The example of Glaxo Wellcome', *Long Range Planning*, 35: 153-78.

Jarrett, M. (2009) *Changeability: Why Some Companies Are Ready for Change – and Others Aren't*. Harlow: FT/Prentice Hall.

Lehman, W.E.K., Greener, J.M. and Simpson, D.D.D. (2002) 'Assessing organizational readiness for change', *Journal of Substance Abuse Treatment*, 22: 197–209.

Lyons, J.B., Swindler, S.D. and Offner, A. (2009) 'The impact of leadership on change readiness in the US military', *Journal of Change Management*, 9(4): 459–75.

McFillen, J., O'Neil, D.A., Balzer, W.K. and Varney, G.H. (2013) 'Organizational diagnosis: An evidence-based approach', *Journal of Change Management*, 13(2): 223–46.

Pellettiere, V. (2006) 'Organization self-assessment to determine the readiness and risk for planned change', *Organization Development Journal*, 24: 38–43.

PART THREE
Planning, Communicating and Implementing Change

Planning and Implementing Change 7

Overview

- Linear models for planning and implementing change provide a structured but simplistic approach. What is often missing from them is making the change stick – sustaining it in the organization so that benefits can be realized. In contrast, the cyclical approach enables leaders and managers to verify the change protocols and ensure that anchorage to the change interventions is maintained. It is therefore more realistic to see the planning and implementation of change as a cyclical rather than a linear process.
- Project management provides an approach for the planning and implementation of sustainable change. It comprises the activities of planning, communication, setting clear, measurable objectives for the change, and evaluating their achievement by using clearly defined success measures as well as monitoring that all intended potential benefits are delivered.

All too often the idea and vision of change assume more importance than the change itself. It is easier to 'talk a good game' than to focus the mind on ensuring successful planning and implementation. There is often a tenuous relationship between those who create the vision for change and those who implement it. In the words of David Magellan Horth and Jonathan Vehar of the Centre for Creative Leadership in the USA:

> those who prefer to challenge the status quo and generate radical ideas are typically not skilled at execution and implementation. They tend to be averse to structure or completely ignore it. Implementation is the skill of those attuned to shaping ideas, navigating organizational systems and structures, and transforming ideas into useful processes, products and services. (2012: 7)

As Horth and Vehar point out, those who are good at creating the ideas and vision for change may not be so good at the implementation of it. The planning and implementation of change needs to be done by managers and follow a favourable assessment of change readiness (as discussed in Chapter 6). The likelihood of an organization being able to implement change successfully without being change-ready is arguably like a toddler trying to walk before being able to crawl: it might be possible for some, but impossible for others (Armenakis et al., 1993). Planning and implementation are the 'how' of change. It is the 'how do we get the organization to change?' It is the 'here is how we will go about changing'.

This chapter focuses on the practical aspects of the 'how' of change. We consider a holistic approach to planning and implementing change and discuss the benefits of the approach. The chapter critically evaluates linear models for planning and implementing change and illustrates what has worked in organizations, using a number of examples. The chapter also considers the benefits of using a project management approach. We address some key questions such as: How do we get the organization to change? How can we effectively plan a change initiative? How can we ensure the successful implementation of change? And what are the key issues that need to be considered when implementing change?

Learning objectives

By the end of this chapter you will be able to:

- Appreciate the holistic approach to planning and implementing change
- Develop an implementation plan for change
- Monitor and control the implementation of change initiatives
- Identify success factors for implementing change in an organization

Linear models

There are hundreds of models and checklists for planning and implementing change. The majority of these models tend to consider change as a step-by-step process. In Table 7.1 we compare four of the most well-known and written-about models from Beer (1990), Kanter and colleagues (1992), Kotter (1996) and Luecke (2003).

The models in Table 7.1 tend to have similar approaches, although they may use different language to describe the same activity and suggest a slightly different order for each step. The proposed approaches in each of the models can be synthesized into four main stages, which we have illustrated in Figure 7.1.

Stage 1: Define the need for change and develop a vision
This involves identifying a performance gap between what the organization is currently doing and should be doing by using one of the diagnostic models we discussed in Chapter 6. By recognizing the gap, managers and leaders are able to define what

Table 7.1 Change models

Beer's Six Steps for Change (1990)	Kanter and colleagues Ten Commandments for Change (1992)	Kotter's Eight Step Process for Successful Organizational Transformation (1996)	Luecke's Seven Steps for Change (2003)
Mobilize commitment to the change through joint diagnosis.	Analyse the organization and its need for change.	Create a sense of urgency.	Mobilize energy and commitment through joint identification of business problems and their solutions.
Develop a shared vision of how to organize and manage for competitiveness.	Create a shared vision and a common direction.	Form a guiding coalition.	Develop a shared vision of how to organize and manage for competitiveness.
Foster concerns for the new vision, competence to enact it, and cohesion to move it along.	Separate from the past.	Develop a vision and strategy.	Identify the leadership.
Spread revitalization to all departments without pushing it from the top.	Create a sense of urgency.	Empower broad-based action.	Focus on results not on Activities.
Institutionalize revitalization through formal policies, systems and structure.	Support a strong leader role.	Communicate the change vision.	Start change at the periphery, then let it spread to other units without pushing it from the top.
Monitor and adjust strategies in response to problems in the revitalization process.	Line up political sponsorship.	Generate short term wins.	Institutionalize success through formal policies, systems, and structures.
	Craft an implementation plan.	Consolidate gains and produce more change.	Monitor and adjust strategies in response to problems in the change process.
	Develop enabling structures.	Anchor new approaches in the culture.	
	Communicate, involve people and be honest		
	Reinforce and institutionalize change.		

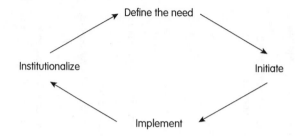

Figure 7.1 Change cycle

changes need to take place and therefore define the vision for change. Building support for the need for change comes through communication and the involvement of key stakeholder groups in the decision-making process.

Stage 2: Initiate the change

This is the stage at which the plans for change are defined. Leaders can adopt solutions that they have either previously used or seen used elsewhere, or alternatively, create new and innovative solutions. The approach taken will be governed by the magnitude, level and focus of change required (see Chapter 1). To initiate the change, leaders need to build a team to support them to build commitment for the change.

Stage 3: Implement the change

Implementing change is about putting into practice the vision and specific goals that address the need for the change. It is also about influencing and involving key stakeholders and employees and dealing with their reactions to the change.

Stage 4: Institutionalizing the change

This is when the change becomes the norm – business as usual – and is no longer an initiative, programme or a project but the way that things are done in the organization. It becomes part of the way that people work and behave in the organization. This is about sustaining the change and continuing to monitor and measure the benefits and costs as well as manage the risks.

The linear approach to change is popular because it creates a narrative of change as a manageable, even if a somewhat uncertain process. All it requires is a perceived urgent need for change. In this narrative, at each step of the process a different, but largely foreseeable, set of issues and challenges present themselves so that, with the appropriate guidance, leaders and managers can anticipate how they can instil sufficient direction and coordination into the change process. The idea that change can be a linear process of managed temporary transition is extremely compelling. Craig Smith's experience of using Kotter's model illustrates this point in his story outlined below. Following this, Steve Taylor describes how he has used Kotter's model to implement change in a European outdoor development centre.

Using Kotter's model to implement change

The company which I was working with as an external consultant wanted to develop the ability of leaders within the business to understand the impact of people and to improve employee engagement across its manufacturing sites. The company had been receiving continuously low employee opinion scores and had tried many interventions without success. They had big issues with quality, cost and service KPIs and were clear that a disengaged workforce was the root cause. The change was sponsored by the Vice President for the European business but was also championed by site leaders across the business. The business also had a strong internal Organizational Capability Manager who had partly initiated the change. The organization had a fairly patchy track record of change. There had been many well-thought-out and well-resourced interventions. The organization was poor at institutionalizing change and often relied on crude measurement systems to try to do this.

The change involved the introduction of a new framework for assessing the performance of 32 operational sites against 50 standards. These standards were defined as the factors that had the biggest impact on employee engagement from the standard of the canteen facilities all the way through to clarity of the site vision and values. The format we ended up with was that all site leaders would be trained as assessors and would assess each other's sites. Results would be for developmental purpose and we would not compare sites against each other in order not to create a culture of hiding bad news. The change was to be implemented over a six-month period but it was realized that it would take many years to fully embed.

Working with us, the Organizational Capability Manager set up a Guiding Team (GT) to lead the change effort. We pulled in the managers who had originally advocated the change and also senior users with credibility and power. There were 10 people in this team and the senior operations leaders from the business sponsored the team. The team had strong characters who had different styles and approaches. Meetings had to be well facilitated and also trust and candour had to be high. Our role was in the facilitation of GT meetings and in helping to come to consensus. The sponsors had faith in the team and supported it.

The change was implemented and the assessments succeeded in a number of levels. They drove the right actions to improve engagement. Those who took part in the assessment process understood it better and were therefore able to use it at their own sites more effectively. Sponsorship remained high throughout the project. As a result, the changes are still in place, several years later. The success was dependent on the following: the set-up of the GT was crucial. Had we used HR professionals or consultants to lead the change it would have been seen as another 'fad' and would have lacked credibility. The people in the GT were strong, well respected and great advocates of the process.

While the change was a success, complacency is easy to generate and difficult to destroy. The organization made a conscious effort to ensure that the change was part of a journey and not a final destination to reach. The programme has been through many iterations and it is a constant challenge to keep it relevant and fully supported. The most difficult parts were around resources and, in particular, time dedicated to the process and to follow up on improvement opportunities at the sites. The benefits achieved from the change were greater employee engagement, better retention and improved business performance.

Kotter's change model was used to lead the change effort. The GT was a great success. The way the organization institutionalized the change was strong. Assessing became a critical experience required for promotion and the senior team did a great job in role modelling many of the leadership aspects we were trying to reinforce.

If there was one area we really struggled with, it was the vision. It was hard to articulate an end state when there were so many standards and when we knew there would not be a point at which we would be done. We did create a vision but, in my opinion, it was a weak one.

© 2015 Craig Smith, Senior Consultant and Director Flint Consulting.

CASE STUDY

Using Kotter's model in a European outdoor education and management training centre

The company I recently led through change as CEO is one of the leading European outdoor education and management training centres, which has its roots in the 1920s. It had always had a traditional approach to education and a focus on skill areas, rather than a client-focused approach. As a result, the company had lost a great deal of opportunity development. This, coupled with a 150-year-old parent charity and a local management committee steeped in the old ways of providing youth development, had led to a lack of action over a long period of time. Not everything was broken. The organization had a good reputation both in the UK and abroad. It had a loyal client base and successful client outcomes. It led on key issues in the industry and had an excellent capital development record in the area of youth development. The financial model, however, was increasingly unsustainable. Whilst funding to build accommodation for youth clients was relatively easy to obtain, funding for general capital development, course revenue and profitability was difficult to and the organization was falling behind competitors in the quality of its resource and thinking.

The driver for the change was principally economic but the financial imperative was felt alongside other drivers that happened to exert their effects at about the same time. For example, the introduction of the national minimum wage added to the financial burden at the same time that the government introduced regulation into the industry (Adventure Activities Licensing Authority). Drivers that demand action are always multi-faceted and usually it is not until there is no choice that action is taken. The challenge was to create a win–win situation where the staff team, the clients and the business moved forward.

The proposed new business model was simple to use to create a client-focused departmental structure and expand the client base. This would allow us to take the profit from professional management courses and use it to provide subsidy for the youth work as well as put resource back into the site.

There were two immediate issues to resolve. The first was that the entire physical structure of the organization was not going to deliver the new business model. Staff lived in the best accommodation for the young people and the youth work was done in the best accommodation for the management work. The very best parts of the infrastructure, the Chapel and the Environmental Centre, were effectively occupying the best locations and only very occasionally used for their intended purpose. Secondly, staff worked for the organization because of its values, history and for the delivery of outdoor education skills. Rather than seeing these skills as a vehicle for personal development they were seen as an end in themselves. Creating a vision that staff would not only buy into but also contribute to was critical. It had to be a compelling future vision as well as be urgent (Kotter's Create a sense of urgency).

The drivers for the change really helped to create a compelling vision for the team to get around and to contribute to. The intention was to move staff out of the centre and pay them a living wage in order to create a sustainable professional staff team who were more than just seasonal. The drivers for this were the national minimum wage and the Adventure Activities Licensing Authority. This would free up useful accommodation that, with a little investment, would start to generate income immediately (Kotter's Generate quick wins). The other areas of the centre were similarly reorganized to generate income and help the staff restructure. This second challenge was the most difficult as it involved people changing a way of being and thinking.

There were several important considerations in the success of this:

1   The timing of the change. We chose the winter following a busy summer. This meant less clients and staff were on site.
2   The message. We were clear about the vision (Kotter's Develop a vision and strategy) and the values and the reason for the change (Kotter's Communicate the change vision). We sold the benefits to the staff through clear and effective messaging.
3   The senior team. It was essential to have a dedicated unified team that took responsibility for their area of change (Kotter's Create a guiding coalition). The change was seen to be a centre-wide creation though effective management of the teams and their input through the senior team (Kotter's Empower broad-based action). This way, staff knew who was responsible and accountable without having any one person to 'blame' for the changes.

These three factors were extremely helpful, if not critical, in making the change effective (Kotter's Consolidate gains and produce more change). The creation of the client-focused teams necessitated organization-wide restructuring and redundancies. It was important to be both efficient and effective in this new structure. As much as was possible we sought to keep and develop the existing staff team but this was not entirely possible, and in the end some staff chose to move on. Throughout the process, staff team meetings were held first thing on a Monday morning. These were as much as possible compulsory for staff. Communication was such an important part of the change process that this was not just a core practice but was part of our core purpose too. In order to make these meetings effective we had a formula that included as much inspirational, informative and instructive input as we could from a range of staff members. As staff saw the changes take place and have a positive impact on them, as well as on the client and the profits, the change took on a life of its own (Kotter's Anchor new approaches in the culture). This was helped by two things. First, the departure of negative staff who wanted to derail the process, and secondly, the extremely positive feedback from all of our clients (22,000 young people and 8,000 professionals).

The following lessons were learnt though the change process:

• Have a clear vision for the change as well as a business model.
• You cannot over-communicate.
• Timing is critical.
• Understand what is driving the change in order to make the right decisions.
• Know your stakeholders and understand what they need.
• Build and sustain an excellent team that can implement the change.
• Trust the process and the people.
• Don't give up early until it is completely embedded and effective, otherwise it will all be wasted and will lead to a situation that is worse that when you began.
• Every business has both a culture and a power base. It is essential to understand both prior to embarking on a major change initiative.

Prior to being appointed CEO to the organization, I had just completed a Master's degree in people management and leadership, and due to this had been able to understand both the marketplace and the organizational structure. I had a good knowledge of what needed to be done and was able to communicate this effectively especially through the building of a senior team. What I did not know was the process by which to implement the change. With the help of a number of internal and external resources, we used our planning and decision-making skills to create a process. In this case study I have linked our thinking to Kotter's eight-step model of change. We found our self-developed process to be remarkably similar to his. In other change situations, I have found a model or framework, adopted or adapted, to be rather like rail tracks on which the train travels and, as such, the choice of such directional and guiding structures to be essential for all involved.

Discussion Questions

1 Compare and contrast the benefits of the linear approach used in both the cases outlined above.
2 What might be the implications of not creating a vision for change, as described in Craig Smith's case?
3 What else might have been done in both situations to implement change effectively?

Using linear models

The linear approach to change underpins the standard organizational-change methodology that was regularly used by one of this book's authors when employed some years ago as a senior manager in a major global consultancy. A classic three-phase approach was used.

In the first phase, the consultant would carry out a diagnostic exercise, typically using one of the tools described in Chapter 6. Data were gathered from stakeholders, analysed then fed back to the client with recommendations for an intervention to address the key issues. In the second phase, a team of consultants would scope out a proposed intervention and the overall outcomes in terms of expected benefits, costs and risks. A pilot would then be run to test the proposed change to ensure that it would deliver the expected business benefits. The third phase entailed the roll-out of the change across the whole or the relevant parts of the organization. Typically, much effort was put into minimizing disruption to daily business during the first and second phases. Almost always this would involve a few carefully selected employees from their normal line duties to work alongside the consultants. A change programme office would be established, either in an off-site location or in a well-secured area on-site. Since it was impossible to hide from the rest of the organization that change was being planned, these phases would be accompanied by a communications programme designed to assuage fears and to counter rumours about the scale of change being planned. Since no amount of secrecy and communication can ever hope to counter or contain rumours, fears and speculation, the emphasis in the communication during these first two phases tended to be: to reiterate the need for change; to reaffirm that, despite any speculation to the contrary, none of the details of the changes had been finalized yet; to reaffirm that staff views were being taken into account; and to assure employees that the process was being managed in an effective and timely manner with clear dates set for reporting, decisions and implementation.

As the change project moved from the second to the third phase, the communications would more strongly reinforce the urgent necessity for change and the impossibility of carrying on as usual. Outlines of the planned changes would be provided and highly visible displays of strong leadership commitment to the changes would be engineered. Employees would be presented not with a change programme whose aims, objectives and content they could help to shape, but with a programme of pre-designed changes on which they were being invited to provide feedback. A lack of commitment to the change programme was perceived often as lack of a commitment to the future success of the organization.

For anyone involved in change management consultancy, this is doubtless a familiar stereotypical model of an organizational change programme. It closely follows Bullock and Balton's four-phase linear model of Exploration, Planning, Action, and Integration (Carnall, 2007: 71). The first three phases align with the stereotypical consultancy model described above, although the phases would more usually be named as scoping (exploration), design (planning) and implementation (action). The final phase represents a transition at the end of the change programme, as the consultants withdraw from the organization.

These step-change models have lost none of their potency over the years. Much of the advice is general, which is why many authors have concluded that change cannot be managed. It can, however, be understood and led, and leadership does make a difference, as we discuss in Chapters 3 and 4.

Despite the linear models being open to criticism, they are useful. They provide a consistent structure for planning and implementing change. They also reduce the risk that some key parts of the change process might be missed, and linear models also tend to be easily understood. What is, however, often missing from them is making the change stick – sustaining it in the organization so that benefits can be realized (we discuss this further in Chapter 13).

Activity

Think of a change that has recently been implemented in an organization in which you work are or in one with which you are familiar. It may or may not have been successful.

   In your experience, what are the things that helped and hindered the implementation of the change?

Approaches to Planning Change

There are different approaches to planning change. For instance, Quinn (1993) suggests an incremental approach. He argues that reflecting on progress and building on the experience gained can be effective because it:

- improves the quality of the information used in key decisions
- helps to overcome the personal and political pressures resisting the change
- copes with the variety of lead times and sequencing problems associated with change
- builds the overall awareness, understanding and commitment required to ensure implementation.

Based on his observations of senior managers in Xerox, GM and IBM, Quinn concludes that often, in practice, by the time change plans begin to crystallize, elements of them have already been implemented. He says that by consciously adopting an incremental process, managers can build sufficient momentum and gain commitment to change plans 'to make them flow towards flexible and successful implementation' (1993: 83).

While recognizing the importance of planning, Nadler and Tushman (1989) caution against developing an uncompromising commitment to an implementation plan. Early actions will have unintended consequences, some welcome, some not, and it is inevitable that some unforeseen opportunities as well as problems will be encountered. They assert that to ignore unanticipated opportunities just because they are not in the plan could be foolish. Planned change involves learning and constant adjustment. Planning needs to be balanced with what they refer to as 'bounded opportunism'. Managers should not feel compelled to respond to every problem, event or opportunity, because doing so could involve adopting courses of action that are inconsistent with the intent to change, but within certain boundaries, being opportunistic and modifying plans can deliver benefits.

Change requires managing (as we discuss in Chapter 4) and one way of doing this is to use a project management approach.

Project management

Change initiatives essentially are projects, and project management, which we consider here, is a specialized activity in its own right. Project management provides an approach for the planning and implementation of sustainable change (Boddy, 2002; Martin and Cheung, 2002). It comprises the activities of planning, communication, setting clear, measurable objectives for the change, and evaluating their achievement by using clearly defined success measures (or 'KPIs' – Key Performance Indicators), as well as monitoring and control to keep the project focused and on track through to completion so that all intended potential benefits are delivered.

A project can be described as having three features:

1. An objective that has three dimensions: performance specification, time and cost
2. A degree of uniqueness: in that it is carried out once, is temporary and usually involves a new group of people coming together to implement it
3. Resources: people, materials and a budget

Key aspects of the project management approach to change

Adopting a project approach to organizational change encourages managers to articulate and be explicit about key aspects of the process. Typically these include:

- Purpose: an understanding of why change is needed.
- Goals: an outline of what the project seeks to achieve. The project is defined in terms of scope and objectives, and analysed in terms of context, constraints, stakeholders and risk.
- Plan: a map of the sequence, duration and interdependencies of the specific steps required to achieve the project's objectives in terms of milestones (intermediate objectives), activities (work to be undertaken) and resources (people, materials and budget required).
- Monitoring and control processes: regular assessment of the project's progress compared to the project plan will highlight the need for corrective actions. Such

actions may involve the provision of extra resources or time in order to achieve original objectives or may involve the redefinition of project objectives.

- Evaluation: upon completion, a review of whether the project objectives and benefits have been achieved. Evaluation should not be seen as an optional add-on but as a crucial part of the project and should be planned from the outset. Evaluation helps identify lessons and experience that contribute to individual and organizational learning (which we discuss in Chapter 8).

Project management tools

In order to manage the complexity inherent in most projects, a number of tools have been developed. We review briefly some of the tools that are widely used.

- *Work breakdown structure (WBS)*. This defines the scope of the project, specifying the work that falls within its remit. WBS is used to break objectives down into detailed elements of work until activities or tasks that can be undertaken by project team members are defined. WBS is the first step in the production of the project's plan and, if costed, can be used to identify the necessary budget.
- *Milestone plan*. This shows the deliverables that build towards the final objectives of the project. By linking dependent milestones it shows the sequence of states a project will pass through.
- *Responsibility chart*. This defines the responsibilities of various groups involved in the project, differentiating between: those who execute the task; those who take decisions about it; those who need to be consulted or kept informed; and those who can provide advice and expert guidance.
- *Gantt chart or activity schedule*. This is a combination of the milestone plan and responsibility chart. It shows each task in terms of estimated duration, the activities on which it depends in order to be completed and subsequent tasks that depend on its completion to proceed.
- *Network diagram*. This involves mapping of the dependencies between the tasks in the change process. This should enable the identification of a critical path of activities that need to be completed on time if the overall project is to meet its deadline.
- *Risk matrix*. This plots the likelihood of the occurrence of an adverse event against the impact on the project if it does occur. The development of a risk matrix encourages managers to look for possible consequences of change. It facilitates the development of **risk management** strategies either to reduce the likelihood of unfavourable consequence or to develop contingency plans to deal with effects if the risk is realized (we discuss this further in Chapter 13).
- ***Stakeholder analysis***. This requires indentifying all key stakeholders, how influential they are and assessing whether they support the change (see Chapter 12).

Extremely complex projects, such as large engineering, IT or significant organizational transformations, often comprise a series of projects, grouped together into a programme. In these cases, discrete sets of activity and constituent parts of the overall project management process (the process of defining objectives and analysing context, constraints, stakeholders, and risk) may be viewed as stand-alone projects.

There are also specialized forms of project management for particular types of change. For instance, the PRINCE project management approach is used to guide the introduction of IT systems across a number of sectors.

The advice to managers that worry about being unable to manage large transformational change projects is to break them down into smaller pieces carried out over shorter periods. Long-running change programmes need to be stage-gated – the norm for big oil and gas projects – to ensure contractors do not move to the next phase before assessing progress. On big building projects, such as the One World Trade Center in New York, or the Burj Khalifa tower in Dubai, architects and contractors used simulations to show how changes in design would affect the timing and cost of the programme.

In the 1990s IBM realized that it would have a competitive advantage if it improved its project management skills. It set up a 'centre for excellence' that develops managers to handle ever-more complex and interconnected programmes. Many companies still underestimate just how important some projects may be to their future. BP's Deepwater Horizon disaster was an example of a complex risky project gone fatally awry; while the poor project management of the building of the Sydney Opera House resulted in a 1,400% cost overrun. An example of ineffective planning happened recently at Heathrow airport in London. In the early summer of 2012 long queues were forming at Heathrow, the UK's busiest airport. They were caused by a lack of effective planning amid job cuts. Limited resources were not being matched to the demand at the airport, with border control agency staff signing off at the start of busy periods. Organizational changes such as the introduction of team-based working, a new shift-working system and the amalgamation of immigration and customs roles had suffered from a lack of effective planning. Resources were not matched to demand, management oversight and assurance was lacking in many areas and staff were not always properly trained to undertake their duties. There had been far too much organizational change during Heathrow's busiest time of the year, with a lack of coherent planning and a consequent effect on the agency's ability to maintain an effective and efficient border control system.

Project management methods are designed for change projects in which there is a defined beginning and end and in which a discrete and identifiable set of sub-tasks must be completed to achieve the change. They allow monitoring of completion of those activities. So project management can increase efficiency, reduce risks and improve customer satisfaction.

Change plan

Developing a change plan involves thinking through what needs to happen if a change target (work group, department or organization) is to be moved towards a desired end state.

According to Beckhard and Harris (1987), the characteristics of effective plans are that they are:

1. Purposeful: the planned activities are clearly linked to the change goals with priorities
2. Task-specific: the type of activities involved are clearly identified rather than broadly generalized

3. Integrated: the discrete activities are linked
4. Temporal: events and activities are timetabled
5. Adaptable: there are contingency plans and ways of adapting to unanticipated opportunities and problems
6. Agreed: by senior management, and other key stakeholders, as required
7. Cost-effective: to avoid unnecessary waste

A high-level change plan should include the following eight phases:

1. Current state research: this involves assessing the current situation (using diagnostic tools outlined in Chapter 6) and making recommendations to the board about next steps.
2. Communication and engagement: if the company has locations across the globe, it has to identify communication strategies for different locations.
3. Design: this phase is about identifying the project team, key roles and responsibilities; and carrying out a stakeholder map and involving key stakeholders in the design process.
4. Preparation: this involves carrying out an impact analysis and preparing for the implementation.
5. Final design: this phase involves identifying how any changes will impact on other departments, processes and systems across the organization. It is also about identifying and monitoring the benefits and costs of the change.
6. Communication, education and engagement: this phase is about raising awareness across the organization of the change.
7. Re-align processes, begin measurement: this phase involves evaluating the impact of the change, putting the measures in place and identifying any new or existing processes which need to be changed.
8. Development and reward: this includes ongoing communication about the change, as well as ensuring performance management and reward systems are in place to recognize changes in behaviour.

Each phase should be divided into key activities and deliverables, and have a completion date.

The benefits of having a plan are evident in the case of toy company Mattel – maker of brands such as Barbie, Fisher-Price and Hot Wheels.

CASE STUDY

Mattel's plan for rapid change

In July 2007 evidence was found of toxic lead paint in Mattel toys. Lead paint, which had been outlawed in the USA and Europe for decades, had found its way into an unknown number of Mattel toys made in China.

(Continued)

(Continued)

Within a few days of initially hearing about this, Mattel employees had identified the factory that produced the tainted toys, stopped production and launched an investigation to determine the scope of the problem. That investigation concluded by the end of July and by 2 August the company had alerted the public and begun taking back about 1.5 million toys. Mattel then voluntarily expanded the scope of its investigation and issued two more recalls, one on 14 August and another on 5 September. In the 14 August 14, Mattel decided to head off another potential safety problem by recalling 18 million toys with magnets that could hurt children if they became dislodged and were ingested. To prevent any future lead paint issue, Mattel adopted a new test procedure where every production batch of every toy had to be tested before it could be released to go on sale. It also named publicly the contractors in China that had been involved in producing the toys with lead paint, severed many supply relationships and installed more Mattel people in contract manufacturers' facilities.

During this period Mattel also created a post of senior vice-president of corporate responsibility to oversee audits of all subcontractors. It also called for more regulation and for more resources to be allocated to the Consumer Product Safety Commission in the USA. The company consistently communicated with all stakeholders and communications generally began with 'I'm sorry…' as the company acknowledged the failure of trust. Mattel was praised by the media and in Congressional hearings for facing the crisis with speed, honesty and a laudable lack of corporate denial or defensiveness.

The key lessons from the case of Mattel are: first, have a plan. When a company's actions radically diverge from expectations, such as safety failure, corruption, deception, permitting fraudulent or criminal behaviour, its revelation can go viral. When the crisis hit Mattel, the company was ready with a crisis plan. Second, put doing the right thing for regulators, retailers, customers and suppliers ahead of damage control or profits. Mattel's investigations were rigorous and expanded as needed; additional recalls were undertaken as the facts warranted them. This publicly aligned Mattel's interests with those of parents and regulators. Third, communicate often, sincerely and transparently. Mattel's communication helped retailers and parents feel the company understood it had violated trust and that it was determined to make it right. Mattel sought the help of regulators in making genuine change rather than stonewalling them.

Fourth, there are nearly always systemic flaws that allow such trust failures: be ready to investigate the root causes and take action.

Written by Julie Hodges, adapted from Hurley (2012).

Discussion Questions

1 Evaluate the approach to change used by Mattel. What were the key parts of their plan that helped mitigate the risks?
2 How did Mattel build trust again with its customers?
3 How might you apply the lessons learnt to a project you are working on?

Change readiness and implementation

As discussed in the previous chapter, readiness for change is a prerequisite for considering the planning and implementation of change. Oakland and Tanner (2006;

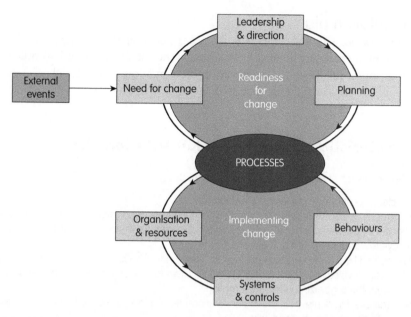

Figure 7.2   The interaction of readiness and implementation of change. (Reproduced with kind permission from Professor John Oakland. (Oakland, J.S. and Tanner, S.J. (2006) 'Quality management in the 21st century – implementing successful change', *International Journal of Productivity and Quality Management*, 1(1–2): 69–87. Oakland, J. (2014) *Total Quality Management and Operational Excellent: Text and Cases*, 4th edn. Routledge: Oxford. www.Oakland Consulting.com)

Oakland, 2014) have devised a framework that shows how readiness interacts with the implementation of change (Figure 7.2).

The framework starts with the impact of *external events* that drive the *need for change*. As we mentioned in Chapter 5, it is important to understand what the external drivers for change are, as well as the internal drivers, so that the need for change may be understood and articulated. Clarity on the need for change is vital as from it derive *leadership and direction* to turn the need into expectations, aims and priorities. Robust *planning* then allows the priorities to be translated into objectives and targets. This then influences the organizational *processes*. The processes drive the way the *organization* works, and how resources are deployed. The resources then support the organization's *systems and controls*. The systems and controls impact on *behaviour*, including what people say and do in an organization.

The 'Figure of 8' in the framework closes with the behaviours linking to the process, as it is individual behaviour that makes the processes work, resulting in the change being embedded in the organization. This cyclical approach means that taking another trip around the Figure of 8, after the initial one, will verify the change protocols and ensure that anchorage to the change strategies is maintained (Oakland and Tanner, 2006; Oakland, 2014). This approach links readiness for change to the implementation of change.

Implementation plan

A.G. Lafley, former CEO of Procter & Gamble, said that the challenge in achieving excellent implementation is learning to 'unpack' the idea (Gupta and Wendler, 2005). The starting point for this is to devise an implementation plan. The characteristics of a good implementation plan are outlined in the box below.

Characteristics of a good implementation plan

The characteristics of an implementation plan are that:

- It is clear, realistic and adequately resourced.
- It is simple: overly complex plans may confuse and frustrate participants, so if the flowchart of activities and milestones looks like a wiring diagram for the space shuttle, rethink it with an eye towards simplicity and coherence.
- It is created by people at all affected levels: there should be joint development of the plan, as a plan devised solely by strategists is less likely to reflect the realities of the business and what the organization can accomplish.
- It is structured in achievable chunks: overly ambitious plans are usually doomed to fail.
- It specifies roles and responsibilities.
- It is flexible: it should be a 'living' document open to revision.

The key questions to ask when devising a plan, are outlined in Appendix 7.1 and a validation checklist is provided in Appendix 7.2. One way of validating a change plan is to perform a simple 'reality check' to ensure that nothing important has been missed so far. One way of doing this that is quick, and that you may find of help, is the SMARTIES approach (see Appendix 7.3).

Despite all the best preparation and planning, change projects almost never proceed according to plan. All types of unanticipated problems occur as people move forward. Developments in the external environment can affect what is going on inside an organization, while internally, issues may arise such as key staff leaving the organization, or a sudden and unexpected cut in project resources. Plans must therefore be sufficiently robust to accommodate alterations in the schedule, and sequencing of change activities. The effectiveness of the plan must be reviewed, which involves monitoring whether the selected interventions are being implemented as intended (see Chapter 13).

Activity

Reflect on changes you have been responsible for implementing:

1   Did you have an implementation plan that worked? If yes, in what ways did it work?
2   What could you have done to improve the implementation plan?

The Fionnphort model

A common experience in implementing change is to reach a point where you realize that the change is not working in the way that was anticipated. There may appear to

be a gap between what people say they will do and what they actually do. It is important to identify where the gaps lie and what needs to be done to move forward. At
this stage it may be useful to apply the Fionnphort model (Wardrop-White, 2001).

This model was developed from the experience of two colleagues of one of the
authors who are involved in supporting change programmes. It is named after a small
beach on Iona, in the west of Scotland, where the two colleagues were waiting for a ferry
and discussing a dilemma about the implementation of a change project they were working on. In an effort to depict the implementation of change, they began to draw pictures
in the sand. The resulting model identified three areas: direction, leadership and energy.

Direction. This focuses on having a clear and understood direction. It can be
addressed by questions such as:

- What is the direction of the implementation plan?
- How clear is it?
- How is this known, and how is it going to be measured, if it is to be understood
  by others in the organization?

We discuss the question of the direction of change further in Chapter 3, where we
discuss vision as a core theme in leading change. Vision is direction in the sense of
being a mental image of where we want to be or need to be in the future.

Leadership. This is about appropriate behaviour being demonstrated by leaders in
the organization. Questions to consider here are:

- What is the required behaviour of different leaders for the implementation to be a
  success? Is there a gap between this requirement and what they are actually doing?
- Is there a need for different behaviours from different leaders?
- Is there a need for different behaviours at different stages in the implementation?
- How will leaders be coached on what they need to continue to do differently?

Energy. This element focuses on having sufficient energy to effectively implement the
change. Questions to consider are:

- How much energy and desire to change exist in the organization?
- What other requirements need organizational energy right now? Is there enough
  energy and resources to do all that needs to be done?
- How is the reaction to the change influenced by the experience of previous or
  other existing change programmes?
- Do people understand the benefits of change?
- What can be done differently, if anything, to increase the amount of available
  energy and resources for implementing the change?

The Fionnphort model is a quick and easy framework to use. It can be used both as a
planning tool and as a simple measure for assessing the effectiveness of the
implementation process, in a way that is similar to the Balanced Business Scorecard
approach (see Chapter 13). However, it does have limitations in that it can provide only
a 'quick and dirty' analysis and covers only three areas. For a more detailed analysis than
can be given by the Fionnphort model, it is worth using the Implementation Compass.

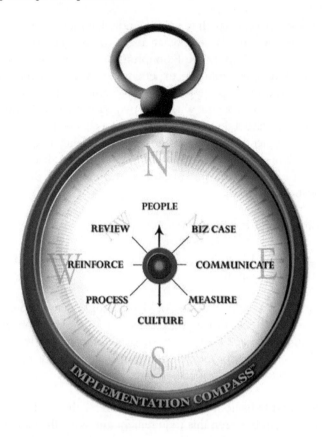

Figure 7.3   The Implementation Compass (Bridges Consultancy)

The Implementation Compass

The Implementation Compass was developed by Bridges Consultancy[1] to provide the structure for an implementation strategy. It helps to assess the current status in preparing to implement a change and to maintain momentum throughout implementation. Each of the eight compass points has a number of prompts to help guide leaders and mangers through effective implementation (see Figure 7.3). The degree of importance of each direction varies for each organization. For example, one organization may spend more time on measurement while another will focus more on communication.

The compass points are described below, with questions for guidance:

1. *People.* This point emphasizes the important of *nurturing those who do the work, the people not the leaders*:

    *   Is the right calibre of people on board with the change?
    *   Do they have the skills and knowledge to execute the new strategy?
    *   How much are they engaged in the implementation?

---

1   www.bridgesconsultancy.com/consultancy/proprietary.html#ImplementationCompass

2. *Business case*. This point is about the *rationale for the change*:
   - Do employees know what the change is?
   - Do they understand why it is important?
   - Are staff motivated to participate in the implementation?

3. *Communicate*. This point is about *explaining what needs to be done and constantly updating people on progress*:
   - Do employees know the new actions they must take to implement the change?
   - Are leaders talking about the change at every opportunity and communicating what is going on?
   - Have messages about successes, best practices and lessons learned from the implementation been communicated on an ongoing basis?

4. *Measure*. This point is about *tracking the implementation's progress with the right measures*:
   - Have the measures for the change been identified to track the implementation success?
   - Are leaders adopting new measures in meetings?
   - Do the new measures drive the right actions?

5. *Culture*. This compass point focuses on *allowing the culture to drive the way in which the change gets implemented*:
   - *How prepared is the organization to adopt the change?*
   - *Does the current culture support the change?*
   - *Do all the leaders understand the culture and how it impacts the implementation?*

6. *Process*. This involves *changing the way people work by aligning processes*:
   - *Do the processes support the change?*
   - *Are managers ready to redesign relevant processes?*
   - *How well do managers know which processes need to be redesigned?*

7. *Reinforce*. This point is about *reinforcing the expected behaviours so they are repeated continually*:
   - Are employees recognized and rewarded for changing behaviour?
   - Do leaders and managers encourage employees to keep demonstrating the right actions?
   - Are leaders and managers supporting and encouraging staff performance by being visible (walking around and leading by example)?

8. *Review*. Review constantly to *ensure the right actions are taken to deliver the right results*.
   - Is the implementation reviewed and adjusted when required?
   - Are the actions taken producing the right results?
   - Do leaders and managers know what has been learned from the implementation in the last 90 days?

The compass provides a useful checklist for leaders and managers for implementing change. However, as with all such tools, it has its limitations in that it covers only certain elements. And it should be adapted to the context in which it is being used.

In the following case study, Martin Gray shares his experience of implementing change in local government in the UK.

CASE STUDY

Commissioning for children in change in Gateshead Council

Local councils in England are becoming organizations that convene and commission services, and are moving away from a historical model in which they provide services themselves. At the heart of this change is an increasing focus on a commissioning model. This model places a greater focus on outcomes, and involves a continuous process of reviewing the design of services and the range of potential delivery models, including in-house, competitive tender, partnership or joint venture. This is, in part, driven by the financial climate for greater efficiencies and also by the need to review the role of the council in the direct provision of services. It also reflects the longer journey of change – of challenging established approaches and thinking more fundamentally about the role of the council.

When a new commissioning approach to the delivery of children's services was introduced in Gateshead Council in Newcastle-upon-Tyne it represented a fundamental change to the business and delivery model and led to significant organizational and structural change. It represented an example of how the local council was responding to changing policy and a decrease in funding from central government. The changes proposed included the establishment of a new service, under a new Head of Service, and a reshaping of services. It was a response to wider changes across public authorities in England and a proactive approach to creating a fundamentally new business model.

The changes heralded the development of a commissioning council model, whereby all services would be assessed using a commissioning framework, based on an assess–plan–do–review methodology, which prioritized outcomes, value for money and aimed to build community capacity. Consequently, it challenged long-established ways of working.

The Director of Children's Services took a proactive decision to introduce the new model into the Gateshead Learning and Children Group (the term given in Gateshead to a collection of services, known elsewhere as a directorate or department), as a forerunner for wider change in the Council. This represented a fundamental shift in the business model of the Group, and was accompanied by a review of the management structure. The Strategic Director was keen to plan for business continuity as well as fundamental change. The change involved the creation of a new service to lead the implementation of a commissioning approach. It brought together a number of existing teams into a new management structure. It also included the consolidation of commissioning functions, such as quality, performance, regulation and strategic planning. It focused on a commissioning model at the heart of a new business model, and heralded a shift towards a clearer separation of commissioning functions from provider roles within the Council.

With this change came requirements for efficiencies, which resulted in a number of employees leaving the Council through a voluntary redundancy scheme. It involved a continuous process of review of business process and delivery, whereby every aspect of the group's activities was assessed against the new commissioning approach. There have subsequently been a number of other structural changes, with a number of teams being consolidated into the new Children's Commissioning service, and a gradual shift of financial responsibility and budget management into the new service, with other services becoming the provider.

The significant changes to the business model were implemented at a time of shrinking resources. Change was needed to respond to the financial position, but there were little available resources to bring in external expertise to provide guidance on the planning and design stage. Employees were therefore asked to continue to deliver their daily activities and to take part in the change process. There was suspicion and resistance to change in some areas, which resulted in some changes taking longer to implement than others. There still remains reluctance by some people to embrace a commissioning model in full, as this is equated to an agenda around the outsourcing of services. Training programmes were developed to support new skills for commissioning, such as increasing market awareness, development of service specifications and contract management. Provider services also received training around marketing and the development of service offers to prepare them for external challenges.

There are some clear lessons to be learnt from this change process. It was initiated by senior managers, which was not universally popular at the time, partly because there was not a definitive blueprint of what changes might happen and why. It was based on the anticipation of change and the acceptance that there was a risk to the survival of the service (it could be outsourced) if change did not happen. But the ultimate end point was never clearly defined. Implementation has required persistence and a willingness to refine the approach. The introduction of the new business model was not implemented in isolation, particularly given the increasingly tight financial climate for local government; there were many other changes happening which were causing stress among the workforce. Implementation was only possible with an ongoing process of dialogue and communication. This was not always successful, but there was a commitment to transparency and a willingness to engage staff in implementation, whenever possible.

© 2015 Martin Gray, Service Director – Children's Commissioning, Learning and Children Group, Gateshead Council, UK.

Discussion Questions

1   What might the Council have done to improve its implementation plan?
2   What key lessons can be learnt from this case and applied to the planning and imple-mentation of change in other sectors?

Implications for leaders and managers for planning and implementation change

A number of practical implications can be draw from the areas discussed in this chapter.

Readiness for change is a prerequisite for considering the implementation of change

Oakland and Tanner (2006; Oakland, 2014) have devised a framework that shows how readiness interacts with the implementation of change (see Figure 7.2). The cyclical approach outlined in the framework enables leaders and managers to verify the change protocols and ensure that anchorage to the change strategies is maintained. This approach links readiness for change to the implementation of change. Review readiness for change before you embark on implementing change.

Develop a plan to measure and assess progress

An implementation plan should strike the right balance between being too vague to be useful and too detailed to be flexible (see Appendices 7.1 and 7.2) for checklists to use when developing a plan). It is important also to identify likely implementation risks and costs and to prepare contingency responses for addressing them. The plan should also include mechanisms for monitoring and evaluating the change and its impact. An implementation plan should answer the following questions: who is going to do what, by when and how? The plan should carefully lay out the path that must be taken to turn the change vision into reality. Furthermore, the plan should include objectives, milestones, performance measures, benefits, costs and risks. Details are important in the plan, as this is the document that people will adhere to in executing it. According to Carlos Ghosn (2002), who transformed Nissan, 'You need to devise a plan with quality and depth – one that is detailed enough to execute … when it is time for action'. Despite the importance of a detailed plan, managers must also recognize that the plan is a living document that should be constantly scrutinized, adjusted and changed as a result of the progress of the project. Thus planning needs to be viewed as a more open-ended, iterative process that emerges and evolves over time. As plans are implemented, they need to be tested before further steps are taken.

Understand the complexity of implementation

At the heart of implementation is changing the behaviour of employees. This is no simple task. Inertia and habit can counter attempts to change behaviour. Given the opportunity, most people will happily fall back into their comfortable ways of working and behaving. Behaviour change takes a lot of energy and deliberate action from leaders and managers. A further complexity of implementation occurs when employees have to spend substantial time and effort in making the planned changes in addition to their 'day jobs'. Employees who oppose the change will create obstacles that could be devastating in the implementation stage, especially if people do not feel they are getting the results they expected. We address, in more depth, reactions to change in Chapter 11.

Ensure employee commitment and involvement

Implementing change is also about influencing and involving key stakeholders and employees and dealing with their reactions to the change. Involving employees in the implementation will help gain their commitment to the change process. Review how you can involve individuals in the change process.

Appendix 7.1: Plan for change

The questions in Table 7.2 can be used to assess what is required when planning a change. You might want to use it as a checklist.

Table 7.2

	Agree		Disagree		
	1	2	3	4	5
There is a compelling need, widely agreed, that the business must go ahead with this change.					
There is a clearly articulated and attractive vision for this change that is consistent with and obviously linked to the overall corporate vision.					
The quantified benefits of this change, and when they will be delivered, are clear.					
The behavioural and technical changes required to deliver business benefits are clear.					
The organization has the capacity to succeed with this change and the other initiatives that are in progress or planned.					
The structure and plans for the change have taken into account the style and preferences of the organization.					
The need for quick wins or other implementation options has been considered and used in developing the structure of the change.					
The past history of change programmes in the organization has been considered and steps taken to reproduce past successes, learn from past mistakes, and put that learning into practice.					
There is an integrated project plan that pulls together the technical aspects of this change and the associated organizational and behavioural changes.					
The steps in this plan and responsibilities for delivering those steps are clear, documented and agreed by those responsible for delivery.					
It is clear who has authority to start this initiative and see it through.					
The people who have responsibility to make the change happen are aware of their roles and they are ready and equipped to undertake them.					
There are plans for leadership of the change to be shared and cascaded down the organization as the initiative progresses.					
We know how to go about winning the commitment required from people to make this change succeed.					
There is a defined programme in place to communicate the changes to the organization.					
The need to change performance management, reward and other HR systems to underpin the change is understood.					
The changes in culture required for this change are defined and there is a plan in place to bring them about.					
The changes in the organization design required for this change are defined and there is a plan to bring them about.					
Sufficient time and resources have been provided to ensure the success of the change programme.					

Appendix 7.2: Validating an existing change plan

We have studied a number of organizations that have gone through major change and developed the following generic list of critical success factors for a change plan. You might wish to use it as a checklist.

Degree to which this is present in the organization

- Shared vision of the desired future   Low |_|_|_|_|_| High
- Unified management   Low |_|_|_|_|_| High
- Concerns allowed to surface   Low |_|_|_|_|_| High
- Content *and* process management   Low |_|_|_|_|_| High
- Realistic time and resources   Low |_|_|_|_|_| High
- Regular and open communications   Low |_|_|_|_|_| High
- Systems and rewards support change   Low |_|_|_|_|_| High
- Commitments are honoured   Low |_|_|_|_|_| High
- Right people in key roles   Low |_|_|_|_|_| High
- Involvement of those affected   Low |_|_|_|_|_| High
- Leaders offer support   Low |_|_|_|_|_| High
- Measurement   Low |_|_|_|_|_| High
- Appropriate skills, knowledge and attitudes of staff   Low |_|_|_|_|_| High
- Effective organizational 'scaffolding (a good transition management plan)   Low |_|_|_|_|_| High

Appendix 7.3: SMARTIES: a reality check

Another way of validating a change plan is to perform a simple 'reality check' to ensure that nothing important has been missed so far. The SMARTIES approach is one quick and helpful way of doing this.

- **Specific** – what are you changing? Does it relate completely to the results of the data-gathering/diagnostic process?
- **Measurable** – how will you know you have changed effectively?
- **Achievable** – is this 'Mission Impossible'?
- **Relevant** – Is the implementation plan relevant and will it actually help implement the change required? How?
- **Time-bound** – what are the milestones to achieve and the key dates?
- **Integrated** – is the change linked to other projects?
- **Externally linked** – does the plan link to external drivers? How?
- **Sponsored** – who is championing the project? How keen are they? How will you keep them involved?

Further reading

Applebaum, S.H., Habashy, S., Malo, J-L. and Shafiq, H. (2012) 'Back to the future: Revisiting Kotter's 1996 change model', *Journal of Management Development*, 31(8): 764–82.

Cameron, E. and Green, M. (2012) *Making Sense of Change Management: A Complete Guide to the Models Tools and Techniques of Organizational Change.* London: Kogan Page.

Kerzner, H.R. (2013) *Project Management: A Systems Approach to Planning, Scheduling, and Controlling.* Hoboken, NJ: Wiley.

Tabrizi, B. (2007) *Rapid Transformation: A 90 Day Plan for Fast and Effective Change.* Boston, MA: Harvard Business School.

Organizational Development (OD) and Organizational Learning

8

Overview

- Organizational Development (OD) is the process for initiating, implementing and sustaining change through the facilitation of individual, team and organizational interventions.
- Dialogic OD methods, such as **Appreciative Inquiry, Open-Space Technology,** and Knowledge, or **World Cafe**, have developed in response to criticisms of the traditional OD approaches.
- An organization can proactively sustain change by making continuous learning part of its culture, by becoming an organization that learns – a learning organization. A learning organization is an organization that has developed the continuous capacity to adapt and change (Senge, 1990).
- The ability to tolerate failure is a hallmark of an innovative organization (Kuyatt, 2011). When change does go wrong, it is important to evaluate what happened. For example, the change message may not have been properly communicated, necessary changes may not have been implemented swiftly or thoroughly enough, or managers were not decisive enough in their decisions (Greenwood and Hinnings, 1996). The important point about change and transformations that fail is that managers and leaders take the time to learn from them and ensure that the learning is shared with relevant stakeholders.

Learning and change are inter-related. Change is a learning process and learning is a change process (Beckhard and Pritchard, 1992). At the heart of organizational change is the facilitation of learning through **Organizational Development** (OD) interventions. OD operates at all levels of an organization: individual, team and organization-wide. It is a process for initiating, implementing and sustaining change. This chapter examines varied OD methodologies and how to select the most appropriate method given the nature of the change being implemented. We review different OD models, as well as OD interventions. The second part of the chapter focuses on organizational learning – what it is and why it is important – and addresses questions such as how can we learn from failure as well as what works well. The chapter concludes by discussing how to create **learning communities** and build capability for change.

The emphasis in the chapter is not so much on a theoretical perspective but on the practical side through the inclusion of frameworks, tool kits and case studies. The originality of this chapter is that this is not a topic that is examined in such great depth in other textbooks on organizational change.

Learning objectives

By the end of this chapter you will be able to:

- Define organizational development in the context of change in organizations
- Discuss appropriate organizational development interventions and explain their strengths and limitations
- Select, implement and review development interventions to help facilitate effective change
- Appreciate what is meant by organizational learning in the context of sustainable change in organizations
- Identify the necessary capabilities that are needed to manage different change initiatives
- Apply the key concepts for developing a learning organization

What is organizational development (OD)?

Organizational development (OD) is an interdisciplinary field with contributions from the behavioural sciences, including psychology, human resource management, anthropology, sociology and management. Within the OD field, there are a number of major theorists and practitioners who have contributed their own models and techniques to its advancement (for example, Beckhard, 1969; Blake and Mouton, 1964). The OD movement grew out of, and became the standard bearer for, Kurt Lewin's pioneering work on behavioural science in general, and his development of planned change (see Chapter 2), in particular (Burnes, 2009a; Cummings and Worley, 2009).

Up to the 1970s, OD tended to focus on group/team issues in organizations, and sought to promote Lewin's humanistic and democratic approach to change in the values it espoused. However, with the oil shocks of the 1970s, the economic turmoil of the 1980s and the rise of Japanese competitiveness, organizations became less interested in group-based change and more concerned with transformational change (Burnes, 2009a). According to French and Bell (1999), this resulted in a major broadening of the scope of OD. Instead of focusing mainly on group-based incremental change, it began to embrace more fundamental, organization-wide transformation initiatives. In the past 20–30 years, OD has moved from its roots in group-based planned change and now takes a far more organization- and system-wide perspective of change.

Not surprisingly for a subject with such diverse roots there are many definitions of OD, which have evolved over time. One of the most frequently cited definitions comes from Richard Beckhard, an early leader in the field:

> Organization development is an effort which is (1) planned, (2) organization-wide, and (3) managed from the top, to (4) increase organization effectiveness and health through (5) planned interventions in the organization's 'processes', using behavioral science knowledge. (1969: 9)

French and Bell provide a more comprehensive definition that includes the role of top management, and the use of applied behavioural science methodologies and tools to improve the organization's ability in respect of visioning, empowering, learning and solving problems:

> Organizational development is a long-term effort, led and supported by top management, to improve an organization's visioning, empowerment, learning, and problem-solving processes, through an ongoing, collaborative management of organizational culture – with special emphasis on the culture of intact work teams and other team configurations – using the consultant-facilitator role and the theory and technology of applied behavioral science, including action research. (1999: 25–6)

French and Bell (1973) identify four core values of OD:

1. There is a belief that the needs and aspirations of individuals provide the prime reason for the existence of organizations within society.
2. Change agents believe that organizational prioritization is a legitimate part of organizational culture.
3. Change agents are committed to increased organizational effectiveness.
4. OD places a high value on the democratization of organizations through power equalization.

In a later survey of OD practitioners, Hurley and colleagues (1992) found these values were clearly reflected in the five main approaches they used in their work: empowering employees to act; creating openness in communications; facilitating ownership of the change process and its outcomes; the promotion of a culture of collaboration and; the promotion of continuous learning.

In recent years there has been a shift in OD being defined as a group-based intervention to one focused on increasing organizational performance. This has led to the view by Anderson that OD is:

> the process of increasing organizational effectiveness and facilitating person and organizational change through the use of interventions driven by social and behavioural science knowledge. (2012: 3)

This definition proposes that an outcome of OD interventions is organizational effectiveness. It also emphasizes the applicability of knowledge gained through the social and behavioural sciences to organizational settings. It views OD as a process for instigating, implementing and sustaining change which has two important characteristics: (i) it is a process of change with a framework of recognizable phases that take an organization from its current state to a new, more desired future state and (ii) within and across these steps, the OD process can be perceived to be a collection of activities and techniques that selectively and accumulatively help organizations and/or its parts to move through these phases (Senior and Fleming, 2006).

There are therefore a range of OD perspectives, from the alignment perspective – the effectiveness of an organization will be determined by the level of congruence between people, processes, structure, values and the environment – to the evolution/revolution perspective – the effectiveness of an organization depends on the extent to which it can develop competencies to engage both in incremental (evolutionary) and transformational (revolutionary, radical) change.

OD interventions

OD interventions are focused on individuals, teams, groups or the whole organization. They include a wide variety of activities that range from the redesign of an organization's structure to team-building activities to individual mentoring and coaching. Argyris (1970: 15) defines an intervention as, 'entering into an ongoing system of relationships, in order to come between or among people, groups or objects, for the purpose of helping them'. Anderson (2012) notes that there are three points to stress about this definition: (i) the system is *ongoing*: that is, an intervention enters into the ordinary and continuous stream of organizational life and, as such, it is influenced by all of the complexities inherent in organizations, such as politics, power, organizational goals and workload, and physical environmental constraints, interpersonal relationships, past history and more. Because the intervention does not occur in a vacuum, the OD practitioner must be conscious of the relationship between the intervention and the organizational context; (ii) interventions *come between* or deliberately interrupt existing processes, thinking, people, groups and relationships. As they often try to unsettle current practices, interventions may be uncomfortable for people who are not ready to change. Understanding readiness to change, as we have discussed in Chapter 6, is an important part of identifying interventions; and (iii) the *purpose* of interventions is to help or improve the effectiveness of organizations, groups, teams and individuals. If interventions are improperly selected and poorly defined and managed they will not sustain the change, instead they could actually hurt it.

Types of interventions

In this section we discuss some of the different types of interventions that can be applied in organizational development and associated learning activities and processes at individual, team and organizational levels.

Individual interventions

Individual interventions can be very influential in changing behaviour and include:

- *Coaching*. This is a one-to-one intervention in which an individual works with a coach to improve a specific behaviour or skill or to take action to reach a desired future goal. The role of the coach is to use questioning to enable an individual to identify for themselves what they need to do differently, rather than telling them. The GROW model (Landsberg, 1996) (Figure 8.1) provides a framework for coaching. The types of questions coaches can use are outlined in Table 8.1.
- *Mentoring*. This involves a relationship between a protégé (mentee) and a skilled and knowledgeable expert (mentor) who can provide guidance. Unlike a coach, mentors may provide explicit advice or direction rather than wait for a mentee to find the answer themselves.
- *360-degree feedback*. Multisource or 360-degree feedback systems enable individuals to receive feedback from a wide range of people with whom they work. It can be a powerful source for reflection and personal change. Questionnaires are usually used to gain anonymous feedback. The data are then analysed and fed back to an individual. Generally, 360-degree feedback is used for individual development, most often for managers and leaders of organizations, although some organizations use 360-degree feedback as part of their annual performance management process or for team development interventions.
- *Career planning and development*. Many organizations have developed career development systems to attract, motivate, develop, promote and retain individuals. The concept of career development originated from the interests of organizations in balancing what employees want for their own career and personal development, and what organizations need from them to achieve their strategic objectives. Most organizations believe that the primary responsibility for career growth and development rests with the individual. Given the frequent **downsizing** and restructuring in organizations, as well as changes in the employment 'contract', it makes sense for individuals to be conscious of their own career plans and development. Career development programmes and one-to-one career interventions can help individuals through a forced transition such as a merger or acquisition. They can also help individuals proactively choose to take required action in anticipation of a change in the future, such as seeking out new skills required for a change of role (Anderson, 2012).

The types of questions used for each part of the GROW model during coaching are shown in Table 8.1.

Individual interventions can help employees through the **transition.** For example, 360-degree feedback can provide information to an individual about his or her own style and behaviour, as well as others' perceptions of them. This can prompt reflection on strengths and areas for development and can encourage individuals to think about how they wish to change. Coaching can enable an individual to identify options for change and what they need to help them change; mentoring can help individuals learn new skills and reflect on their actions; while career development interventions help individuals to focus on the challenges that they

What will you do?   What do you want?

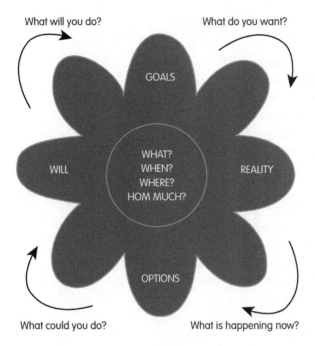

GOALS

WHAT?
WHEN?
WHERE?
HOM MUCH?

WILL   REALITY

OPTIONS

What could you do?   What is happening now?

Figure 8.1   The GROW model, adapted from Landsberg (1996)

face at various points in their career and how to move forward in their career and make changes to it.

Individual change is not on its own a sufficient method for achieving organizational change as organizations are comprised of many processes and systems, as well as teams with strong cultural values and beliefs. Therefore individual interventions need to be supplemented with team-based and/or organization-level interventions.

Team interventions

The effective functioning of teams is central to the performance of organizations. Teams play a central role in the implementation and sustaining of organizational change. Team interventions are amongst the most common OD techniques and one of the earliest was T-groups.

T-groups

T-groups were built on Lewin's (1947) work on the social psychology of groups. The first T-groups were unstructured, agenda-less groups of strangers who learnt from their own interactions and the evolving dynamics of the group (Bradford and Burke, 2005). The purpose of these small unstructured groups was to meet and, without a formal leader, agenda or purpose, to begin exploring personal and interactive behaviour within the group. As a consequence of the depth of emotional involvement, interaction and feedback generated during the process, members learnt about themselves and their behaviour. The intention was for the individuals within a group to be

Table 8.1   Questions using the GROW model

GOAL
- What is the aim of this discussion?
- What do you want to achieve in the long term?
- How much personal control or influence do you have over your goal?
- What is your short term goal?
- When do you want to achieve it by?
- Is that positive, challenging, and attainable?
- How will you measure it?

REALITY
- What is happening now?
- What, where, when, how much, how often?
- Who is involved (directly and indirectly)?
- When things are going badly on this issue, what happens to you?
- What happens to the others directly involved?
- What is the effect on others?
- What have you done about this so far?
- What results did that produce?
- What are the major constraints to finding a way forward?

OPTIONS
- What options do you have?
- What else could you do?
- What if ...?
- Would you like another suggestion?
- What are the benefits and costs of each option?

WILL
- What options will you do?
- When will you do them by?
- What help do you need to implement them?
- What might get in your way of successful implementation?
- How will you know you have been successful?

able to use the understanding they had gained to connect with one another in a more meaningful way and so be able to engage in a change process more effectively. The T-group approach is often referred to as 'sensitivity training', because it sensitizes participants to their own behaviour. Today such an approach is often adapted and used as the first stage in teambuilding activities.

Teambuilding

Interventions to enhance team effectiveness include team development and teambuilding events. Team development events proactively encourage teams to develop in a positive manner. They are often opportunities to allow teams to identify more effective ways of working. In contrast, team interventions employ a problem-solving approach that helps establish the identity of teams and address obstacles and constraints to high performance. Often they involve teams in activities (indoor and outdoor) where they have to work together to solve a problem (such as building a tower out of paper). Whether they are addressing a team development or team problem, most of these interventions go by the general label 'teambuilding'. The purpose of teambuilding sessions tends to be to improve a team's effectiveness, relationships among its members and the team's contribution to the performance of the wider organization.

Organization interventions

Organization interventions are designed to address issues that affect the whole organization. The most common interventions include:

- *Organization restructuring* (see Chapter 9 on changing organizational structures)
- *Quality and productivity interventions – Quality Circles.* A Quality Circle is a small group of between three and 12 people who do the same or similar work, voluntarily meeting together regularly for about one hour per week, usually under the leadership of their own supervisor, and trained to identify, analyse and solve some of the problems in their work, presenting solutions to management and, where possible, implementing solutions themselves.
- *Business Process Re-engineering*: the fundamental rethinking and radical redesign of business processes to achieve dramatic improvements in critical, contemporary measures of performance, such as cost, quality, service and speed.
- *Total Quality Management*: a holistic approach to the management of quality that emphasizes the role of all parts of an organization and all people within the organization to influence and improve quality.
- *Six Sigma*: a philosophy of improvement that recommends a particular approach to measuring, improving and managing quality and operations performance generally.
- *LEAN*: an approach to operations management that emphasizes continued elimination of waste of all types.
- *Leadership development programmes*: leadership development programmes usually begin at board level.

Such large-scale interventions are used for a number of reasons: reducing costs, increasing productivity, speeding up the cycle time of product and service development, clarifying direction, improving morale and meeting the expectations of stakeholders. Organizations often approach large-scale interventions consciously and intentionally, such as when they are developing a strategic plan or acquiring or merging with another company. They may be applied when change is forced on the organization due to political, economic, social, technological, legal regulatory, environmental or stakeholder requirements, competition, or due to internal drivers for change, such as an unexpected departure of a senior executive. Organizations will often choose a large-scale intervention when the task is complex or urgent or when multiple people are required to accomplish it (Bunker and Alban, 1992).

The purpose of organization-wide OD interventions, such as those described above, is to make lasting change in the character and performance of the organization

(Cummings and Feyerherm, 1995). Large-scale interventions significantly affect integral aspects of the organization's strategy, structure, people and processes. They are visible, wide-ranging and require the commitment and attention of leaders and managers. In her description of change in the case study of a European life and pensions business, Fiona Sweeney describes an organizational intervention to develop strategic capabilities to support the business drivers for change.

CASE STUDY

Strategies for organizational transformation in a European life and pensions business

Within the operations arm of a leading European life and pensions business, a current state assessment had identified key challenges that the company needed to address. The key issues identified were:

- Customer management processes were deeply flawed
- The operations arm was in trouble across most of its existing business offerings
- People were 'maxed out' and 'change fatigued'
- The operating structure was inappropriate for current and expected market conditions

The organization had a clear vision to be recognized by their customers for delivery of a consistent, quality, cost-effective service in comparison to its major competitors. Its aim was to move from a service- and volume-based model to a value-based model by:

- Being clear about the service promise it made to intermediaries and policyholders
- Re-engineering its processes and excelling at performing them
- Delivering through the quality of its people
- Aligning technology and focusing on 'fit for purpose', not on 'world class'
- Using different sourcing options (such as offshore/outsource) where appropriate for reasons of quality and cost.

Following this strategy would create a radically different future organization and the challenge of achieving it would require a significant transformation from the current state. The focus moving forward was to build on and refine the core change levers:

- *Process excellence.* Extend LEAN and Six Sigma to cover the entire Operations business and build a sustainable capability to continue this improvement.
- *Technology.* Focus on delivering the required customer proposition.
- *Business Processing Outsourcing (BPO).* Reconsider its appropriateness as the outsourcing market develops.
- *New levers.* People and communications; contact strategy; process/product rationalization.

In Operations' view, these five areas would lead towards a new way of doing business with wide use of automation and multi-sourcing strategies. The key characteristics of the organization that they needed to support were:

- Fulfilling the need to transform the business

  - Process excellence
  - Multi-sourcing
  - Delivering technology changes
  - Responding to market and regulatory change

- Being clear about the service promise made to intermediaries and policyholders

  - Clear customer focus
  - Aligning service to value
  - Relationship management

- Excelling at performing the processes

  - Focus on continuous improvement
  - Consistency and efficiency focus to drive out costs
  - Realizing economies of scale wherever they occur

- Retaining and developing core capability

  - Retaining knowledge workers who deliver competitive advantage
  - Transforming the business to empower people to deliver of their best

The key dimensions of the change journey were to:

- Ensure that change in Operations was connected and consistent with wider organizational strategy
- Develop change leadership capability to allow effective delivery of the transformation
- Reduce headcount in a way that retained capability and the high performance that was needed in future
- Evolve the organization's structure to realize economies of scale, avoid duplication and increase flexibility
- Implement process management to evolve the way to measure and manage process performance
- Develop and recruit capabilities to bridge key strategic and core capability gaps
- Develop roles, career structures and an employment proposition to reflect the evolving capability needs
- Evolve the location picture to retain manageable and effectively structured teams in key locations
- Develop effective partnerships with outsourcing and offshore partners
- Evolve methods of performance management, recognition and reward to reflect increasing process and customer focus

The transformation programme that the Operations arm was planning coincided with extensive operational changes within the European life industry. Leadership was vital to ensure that transformation was effective. As well as this there would be and continue to be significant demands on HR to shape, deliver and support the transformation activity for operations over a three-year period. HR would be key players in determining the delivery of a 'new world' organization that would be cost-efficient. The scale of the transformation would most likely change the employment landscape and therefore the employment proposition. The 'showstoppers' were nearly all about people. There was also recognition that to achieve their vision a number of core and management capabilities needed to be in place. The organization's business drivers required it to develop a number of strategic capabilities:

- *Change leadership*

  - The ability to lead the organization through a period of very significant change
  - Expertise in strategic priority areas, such as process excellence

- *People management and leadership*

  - Ability to motivate teams and effectively manage performance

(Continued)

(Continued)

- *Commercial management*
  - Focusing on commercial drivers and ruthlessly driving out cost
  - Governance, control and benefit management
- *Supplier management*
  - Effective partnership with and performance management of offshore and out-sourced delivery units
- *Technology management*
  - Need to define their technology needs and prioritize with much greater clarity

Careful consideration was given to how to manage the change journey, and a number of measures were put in place, including:

- A governance for the change programmes involving representatives of each business area;
- A head of change in each business area to coordinate activity;
- A communications team centrally communicating about change to give information about ongoing initiatives
- Project steering groups managing individual change levers, such as process excellence
- Project teams throughout the business making the change happen, such as 'lean' events, offshoring project teams

The key lessons learnt from the transformation were:

- Make sure activity is driven by a sense of urgency, not by fear and anxiety.
- Identify and communicate real, individual benefits of change.
- Link change delivery to managers/staff measures, rewards and recognition.
- Reinforce required behaviours and remove negative behaviours.
- 'Leadership, leadership and leadership.'
- Create a compelling, involving reason for change and its intended end-state.
- Ensure consistency and alignment between the behaviours required in the 'to be' state. Such behaviours were to be driven by the organization's value set and to be rewarded by the organization's performance management system.
- Ensure strong programme management support.

© 2015 Fiona Sweeney, People Director, Virgin Active.

Discussion Questions

1 Consider how the challenges identified could be effectively dealt with.
2 How might the lessons learned be applied to a change initiative you are familiar with?

Selecting interventions

Interventions may function differently in different organizations, so adapting any intervention is a necessary skill for those implementing change. Depending on the organizational structure, processes, age, technology and cultural factors, such as organizational members' tolerance for ambiguity and/or flexibility, what has worked for one organization may not work for another. Selecting the right approach is more than just finding the best OD technique to address the issue. According to Anderson (2012), an intervention strategy will be more effective and sustain the necessary change if it takes into account the following factors.

1. Matching the intervention to the data and diagnosis

One of the most important criteria for selecting an intervention is what Bowers, Franklin and Pecorella (1975: 406) call the Principle of Congruence: 'Change activities must be matched appropriately with the nature of the problem and their cases and with the nature of the organizational units under consideration.'

The intervention needs to be matched to the diagnosis and designed to address the need for change. OD practitioners need to consider what type of method is suited for the organization's particular problem. The best advice is that of Hanson and Lubin, who say that:

> Regardless of how attractive some of these techniques are consultants must always ask themselves, 'Is this exercise appropriate or relevant to the learning goals of this organization or to the situation being addressed, or is it just one of my favorite interventions?' (1995: 114)

One test is that a given intervention is likely to be well matched to the diagnosis if it results in a high probability that the problem will be solved with the least probable recurrence (Argyris, 1970). In other words, the OD intervention will solve the issue.

2. Readiness for change

As we discussed in Chapter 6 'readiness for change' refers to the involvement, willingness, energy, time, capability, and motivation of the organization to change (Armenakis et al., 1993). If the individual, team or organization is not ready or willing to change, then any intervention is unlikely to be successful. If there is a willingness to change in a certain direction and not another, or there is a preference of one intervention over another, then it is best to start where the energy is for the change.

Readiness may also concern the organization's capability and competence to change. For example, a team may not be capable of changing if a manager does not have the budget to purchase the new tools for employees that are necessary to make change happen or employees may not have the necessary skills or competence to implement a change effectively. For example, before implementing a new sales process that requires employees to aggressively sell a variety of new products and negotiate discounts, appropriate negotiation training will be necessary. Managers need to ensure individuals are ready for change.

3. Where to intervene first

It is often recommended that organizations start with task interventions, then move on to people and relationship interventions (Harrison, 1970). Focusing first on the tasks and processes, such as structures, roles, communications, decision-making, meetings and so on, can help build trust and credibility before going into deeper personal and emotional issues. Task-related interventions are often easily sold to individuals because they are often seen as more tangible. However, as Beer and Eisenstat (1996) note, interventions that focus on harder elements of structure and systems typically do not develop the softer elements of skills, values and leadership. A better approach is therefore an integrated approach that focuses on tasks as well as people issues.

4. The depth of the intervention

How deep the intervention needs to be in order to sustain the change has to be considered. Clarifying roles and responsibilities and developing new skills are surface-level interventions. A deeper intervention might be to address job dissatisfaction, low morale, expectations or leadership and management styles. Still deeper might entail focusing on a team's level of openness and trust, accountability, or commitment to the success of the change.

5. The sequence of activities

When a change intervention consists of a number of separate activities there is a need to think about how those events are sequenced in order to achieve benefits. Beer (1980) lists six considerations for how different interventions should be sequenced in an overall intervention strategy:

- *Maximize diagnostic data*. Interventions that provide data about the organization should be conducted first to allow better customization for those that follow.
- *Maximize effectiveness*. Initial interventions should build enthusiasm for change and confidence in success so that later interventions can be more effective.
- *Maximize efficiency*. Interventions should conserve time, energy and money as much as possible.
- *Maximize speed*. Interventions should be constructed so that they do not interrupt the desire for the pace of change in the organization.
- *Maximize relevance*. Interventions should be chosen so that the primary problem is addressed first.
- *Minimize psychological and organizational strain*. Early interventions should be safer and produce minimal anxiety.

Choosing the right intervention therefore involves a number of stages. Listing the possible interventions and analysing them together with such considerations will help identify which are the most appropriate.

Reviewing OD

Despite the obvious benefits of OD in facilitating and sustaining change, it is not without its critics. Based on his study of strategic change at ICI, Andrew Pettigrew (1985: 17) rejected OD, arguing that 'Planned change and innovation [are] both an inadequate way of theorizing about what actually happens during change processes and an overtly simple guide for action.' Pettigrew goes on to identify what he considers to be the shortcomings of OD:

- It is too rational, linear, incremental and prescriptive.
- It does not pay enough attention to the need to analyse and conceptualize organizational change.
- It fails to recognize that change processes are shaped by history, culture, context and the balance of power in organizations (Pettigrew, 1985).

In its place, Pettigrew (1987) argues for an approach that sees change as a complex political and cultural process of challenging and changing the core beliefs, structure and strategy of an organization.

Others have criticized OD as having a Western bias. Writers such as Adler (1997) warned that not all change methods and techniques are transportable across national boundaries to other parts of the world or even to different ethnic groupings within single countries. According to some writers, such as Senior and Fleming (2006), this is particularly true with regard to the range of techniques associated with OD as a philosophy and a methodology for bringing about change. One consequence of these reservations about the degree to which OD approaches can be used to help facilitate change is that there is a need for OD interventions to be tailored not only to the organizational culture in which they are being applied but also to the culture of the country in which the organization operates.

The fundamental issue, however, is not that OD itself is being attacked but that newer approaches to organizations and to organizational change are emerging that challenge the validity of its participative approach – and offer other options. In recent years a number of OD practitioners have been doing OD in a way that deviates from some of the basic tenets of the field, most notably the tenet that a diagnosis should precede any intervention. For example, Bushe and Marshak (2008) have called their alternative approach 'dialogic'. What they label as a dialogic change process does not seek the facts, analysis of the facts, solution of a predefined problem or use of a diagnostic model. Their metaphor or image of an organization is more that of an ongoing conversation. They propose that OD is found in the following set of common values:

1. *Greater systems awareness is encouraged and facilitated.* The change method works to increase the knowledge of employees about the organization, usually through facilitating events where the organization is an object of enquiry and discussion.
2. *Concern for capacity building and development of the organization.* An OD method attempts not only to achieve a change target but also to develop the organization's efficacy and increase its capacity to survive and prosper.
3. *Consultants stay out of content and focus on process.* OD practitioners would probably not be providing advice or an opinion on decisions. Instead they would emphasize their neutrality and encourage employees to decide for themselves.

Examples of dialogic OD methods are **action research, action learning, Appreciative Inquiry, Open-Space Technology** and **World/Knowledge Cafe**. We discuss each of these in turn.

Action research

Action research is about involving all relevant key stakeholders and is a process for facilitating change aimed at getting individuals, teams and organizations to perform better. It has been widely applied in management research in various forms and has been used to identify and implement change (French and Bell, 1999). It is a way of using research in an interventionist way so that the person carrying out the research is both a discoverer of problems and solutions and is involved in decisions about what is to be done and why. Action research sees organizational change as a cyclical process where theory guides practice and practice in turn informs theory. The concept of action research can be traced back to Kurt Lewin (1947). It elaborates on the transitional model of unfreezing, moving and refreezing, adding feedback loops between the stages and promoting iteration between the thinking and acting processes of change. Action research puts into practice Lewin's (1947) assertion that theory should not only be used to guide practice and its evaluation but that, equally important, results of evaluation should inform theory in a cyclical process of fact-finding, planning, action and evaluation.

Action research results from an involvement by the person doing the research with members of the organization over a matter that is of genuine concern to them and in which there is an intent by the organization to take action based on the intervention (Eden and Huxham, 1996). It incorporates the belief that for change to be effective it must take place at the group or team level and must be a participative and collaborative process of discussion, debate and experiment that involves all of those concerned (Bargal and Bar, 1992). Though action research is often characterized as a diagnostic process (French and Bell, 1999), it is also about creating a dialogue that allows individuals to reach a common understanding of the context in which their behaviours take place (Burnes, 2009a). In simplified form action research involves the following steps:

1. A perception by leaders/managers of the issue(s) that need to be addressed
2. Consultation with an OD practitioner/consultant (or whoever is carrying out the research) about the issue and the need to gather data about it
3. Data-gathering and preliminary diagnosis (see Chapter 6 for details of diagnostic tools)
4. Feedback to key stakeholders
5. Joint agreement of the issue(s) and the change required
6. Joint action planning
7. Implementation of agreed actions
8. Reinforcement and assessment of the change

In this way, action research is a combination of research and action. It entails gathering data relevant to the issue, feeding back the results to those who need to take action, collaboratively discussing the data to create an action plan, and finally taking the relevant action.

Systemic action research is an approach for whole-system change (Burnes, 2009a). It helps people gain meaningful insights into events, behaviour and structure. It enables an understanding of an organization's environmental context, business strategy, culture and operations and their impacts on one another. This is where the underlying structural solution to the change problem can be developed. According to Senge (1990), the structural solution is the least common and most powerful as it focuses on the causality of the patterns of behaviour. This is important because only the structural solution addresses the underlying causes of behaviour at a level that patterns of behaviour can be changed. As structure induces behaviour, so changing underlying structures can produce different patterns of behaviour. Thus the dynamic nature of the context for change requires systemic understanding of all of the factors to understand the relationship between organizational and contextual factors affecting proposed change.

This has been demonstrated in a study by John Molineux (2013), who carried out a longitudinal assessment of organizational cultural change from 1995 to 2010 based on a major action research project carried out in a large Australian public sector agency from 1998 to 2002. The aim for the agency was to shift the organization toward a performance culture that would result in a more effective and responsive workforce and enable the organization to achieve its future challenges. The study found that the implementation of a systemically designed Strategic Human Resource Management (SHRM) intervention had a positive and sustained impact on an organization's culture. Through systemic action research an appropriate strategy was developed to shift the culture.

Action research is not a one-off event that ends when a change has been completed but an iterative or cyclical process that is continuous. Each of its parts – diagnosis, data-gathering, feedback to the key stakeholders, data discussion, action planning and implementation – may be used to form each of the phases that make up a typical OD process. These components may, collectively, form cycles of activity within each stage of the OD process. The OD approach to change is firmly embedded in the assumption that all who are or who might be involved in any change should be part of the decision-making process to decide what that change might be and to bring it about.

CASE EXAMPLE

Changing leadership behaviour

The first author of this book led an action research project with a global business software company. She analysed the concept of leadership and how it was enacted across the globe, using structured interviews with leaders, customers, executive board members and staff, as well as a review of company documents. A summary of findings was provided to the executive board. Feedback from staff about the findings, their implied meanings and the analysis, was also encouraged. From this interaction with staff, new questions were raised for the researcher to investigate and slowly ideas about how to improve the leadership were generated. Workshops were held with senior leaders from across the globe to define leadership behaviours. This was then fed back to board members for comment.

Initially leaders were defensive of the findings, feeling criticized, and resisted changing

(Continued)

their behaviour. They explained why the findings were not accurate and that the language used was inappropriate to describe leadership language and behaviours across the globe. Changes were made as a result of their input. Eventually they came to realize the benefits of adapting the behaviours to their local context. In later interviews, leaders were less defensive of the proposed change in the leadership behaviours. Instead they were more likely to include requests for advice about how to adapt their behaviour in different situations. Eventually positive feedback about the proposed changes was received and a development programme was delivered to help leaders identify how to change behaviours.

Case written by Julie Hodges.

Action learning

The purpose of action learning is that a group of peers, each seeking to bring about change, meet regularly to discuss where they are each experiencing difficulty and then test in action the ideas that arise from the discussion (Revans, 1982). In organizations today action learning is usually practised through action learning groups or sets. The groups tend to consist of a small number of people, usually four to seven, working on separate projects, who meet regularly to discuss the problems they are each encountering, the objective being to learn with and from one another. At each meeting the time is usually split equally so that everyone can focus together on the issues of each person in turn. Each meeting has a clear structure. The group meetings, however, are only one part of the process. The other part is the testing of the ideas in action, which happens during the time between the group meetings. The group helps each individual in turn to reflect on the outcomes of his or her recent actions and to develop ideas for overcoming obstacles that are getting in the way of progress. In this way action learning is about experimenting with the application of existing and new ideas in a safe yet challenging environment.

Appreciative Inquiry

The essence of Appreciative Inquiry is the generation of a shared image of a better future through a collective process of inquiry into the best of 'what is' – what the future would be like if the best of 'what is' becomes the norm (Reed, 2007). By understanding what has worked in the past, an organization can choose to focus on these positive elements and build on the strengths of their past successes to create a competitive organization. Appreciative Inquiry uses a 'Four-D' model:

1. *Discovering* the best of what is
2. *Dreaming* of the best possible future, from the best of what is
3. Creating *Destiny*
4. *Delivering* ideas into practice

In practice the model can be used as follows:

1. *Discovering*: The issue to be addressed needs to be defined in a way that focuses attention on the positive rather than the negative aspects of people's experience.

For example, if the issue is a high turnover of staff, rather than focusing on why people leave the organization, the inquiry might focus attention on why people choose to stay. People are asked to tell stories about the best of what is. This might involve pairs of people interviewing each other or a core of interviewers each interviewing a number of others and then sharing their findings and identifying key themes.

2. *Dreaming*: Dreaming involves drawing on the themes identified in the discovery phase and envisioning what the future would look like if the best of 'what is' becomes the norm.

3. *Discovery*: The dream or vision needs to be translated into 'provocative proposi-tions'. These are statements of intent – what might be – challenging the status quo and current assumptions to create design principles that can be used to identify the type of structures, processes and practices that will deliver the dream.

4. *Destiny*: Destiny is about identifying how the organization moves towards the desired future state (the dream or vision). We discuss vision as a core theme and practice in leading change in Chapter 3.

Appreciative Inquiry has been used successfully in a wide range of different situations (Sorensen et al., 2003). Projects vary in terms of scale, organizational context and focus. Hayes describes an Appreciative Inquiry in Médecins Sans Frontières (MSF). The secretary-general of the company launched an organization-wide programme to 'unlock potential'. Eight cross-functional working groups were set up to look at how the organization functioned and identify what MSF was best at doing in order to con-solidate successes as a basis for leveraging further development. The *discovery* phase involved eight working groups collecting information through interviews and surveys and cascading this approach down the organization in order to ensure that everybody had the chance to contribute to defining best practice and developing ideas (*dream-ing*) about how to evolve new practices and procedures that would enable MSF to respond to new challenges *(discovery)*. MSF adopted this approach because it wanted to maintain its passion, maverick character and ability to help where others were unable to do so (Hayes, 2014: 354).

The main concerns that tend to be voiced about Appreciative Inquiry are whether or not it really is any different from other change techniques and whether, if it does not focus on problems, this means that they do not exist. Despite such criticisms, Appreciative Inquiry is appealing because it provides a proactive and optimistic approach to change by accentuating the positive and therefore what the organization can build upon. It can stir up moments of energizing success creating a new energy that is positive and synergistic. Participants walk away with a sense of commitment, confidence and affirmation that they have been successful (Hammond, 1998).

Activity

Using the internet, find three organizations that have used Appreciative Inquiry. What are the similarities among the three organizations? What are the differences? What conclusions can you draw from this?

Open-Space Technology

Open-Space Technology (OST) is a scalable and adaptive method devised by Harrison Owen (2008). It can be used in meetings of anything from five to 2,000 people. OST is most distinctive for its initial lack of an agenda. This sets the stage for the meeting's participants to create the agenda for themselves in the first 30–90 minutes of the meeting.

Typically, a meeting will begin with short introductions by the sponsor, the official or acknowledged leader of the group and usually a single facilitator. The sponsor introduces the purpose, and the facilitator explains the 'self-organizing' process called 'open space'. Then the group creates the working agenda as individuals post their issues in bulletin-board style (using Post-It notes on a flipchart). Each individual facilitator of a breakout session takes responsibility for naming the issue, posting it on the bulletin board, assigning it a space and time for people to meet, and then later showing up at that space and time, initiating the conversation and taking notes. These notes are compiled into a proceedings document that is distributed physically or electronically to all participants. Sometimes one or more additional approaches are used to sort through the notes, assign priorities and identify what actions should be taken next. Throughout the process, the facilitator is described as being 'fully present and totally invisible', 'holding a space' for participants to self-organize rather than managing or directing the conversations.

The OST approach is characterized by the following steps:

1. A broad, open invitation articulates the purpose of the meeting.
2. Participant chairs are arranged in a circle.
3. Issues and opportunities are posted by participants on a bulletin board.
4. Participants move freely in a 'marketplace' between breakout areas, learning and contributing as they 'shop' for information and ideas.
5. A 'breathing' or 'pulsating' pattern of flow takes place between plenary and small-group breakout sessions.

There are several desired outcomes from an OST event:

- The issues that are most important to people are discussed.
- The issues raised are addressed by the participants who are most capable of getting something done about them.
- All of the most important ideas, recommendations, discussions and next steps are documented in a report.
- When sufficient time is allowed, the report contents are prioritized by the group.
- Participants feel engaged and energized by the process.

The process works best when the following conditions are present:

- There is a real issue of concern – something worth talking about.
- There is a high level of complexity, such that no single person or small group fully understands or can solve the issue.
- There is a high level of diversity in the skills and people present, to aid a successful resolution.

- Real or potential conflict exists, which implies people genuinely care about the issue.
- There is a high level of urgency for action.

The recognition of these conditions by leaders and managers typically implies some level of letting-go of control of an issue and a willingness to open it up to others to address. Owen (2008) has articulated the 'principles' that are typically quoted and briefly explained during the opening briefing of an OST meeting. These principles describe rather than control the process of the meeting. They are:

1. Whoever comes are the right people.
2. Whenever it starts is the right time.
3. Wherever it happens is the right place.
4. Whatever happens is the only thing that could have happened.
5. When it's over, it's over.

To ensure the principles are adhered to, Owen (2008: 64) recommends his one law, also called the 'law of two feet' or the 'law of mobility', which he describes as, 'If at any time during our time together you find yourself in any situation where you are neither learning nor contributing, use your two feet, go someplace else.'

In this way, all participants are given both the right and the responsibility to maximize their own learning and contribution, which the law assumes only they can ultimately judge and control. When participants lose interest and get bored in a breakout session or have accomplished and shared all that they can, the approach is to move on. In different ways and to varying degrees, leaders convening open-space meetings acknowledge that they personally do not have the answer to whatever complex, urgent and important issue(s) must be addressed, and they put out a call – an invitation – to anyone in the organization who cares enough to attend a meeting and try to create a solution. So an open-space meeting attracts those who are most concerned with the issue and willing to participate in contributing to and identifying potential solutions.

World Cafe

A 'World Cafe' or 'Knowledge Cafe' is a type of meeting or workshop that aims to provide an open and creative conversation on a topic of common interest to identify collective knowledge, share ideas and insights, and gain a deeper understanding of the subject and the issues involved. The method was developed by Elizabeth Lank, who created the concept of a physical and mobile cafe area in the 1990s using small round tables, each covered with a checked tablecloth, with a vase of flowers, a block of paper and coloured pens. The main principles of a World Cafe are:

1. *Setting.* Creating a special environment, with small round tables, paper and pens, with an optional 'talking stick', which is held by the person who is talking and is then passed to another person when he or she wants to talk.
2. *Welcome and introduction.* The sponsor or facilitator begins with a welcome and an introduction to the World Cafe process, setting the scene and sharing the 'cafe etiquette'.

3. *Small-group conversation rounds.* The process begins with the first of three or more 20-minute rounds of conversation for each small group seated around a table. At the end of the 20 minutes, each member of each group moves to a different table. Each group chooses whether to leave one person as the table host for the next round who welcomes the next group and briefly fills the members in on what happened in the previous round.

4. *Questions.* Each round is prefaced with a question designed for the specific context and desired purpose of the session. The same questions can either be used for more than one round or be built upon each other to focus the aim of the conversations or guide their direction.

5. *Harvest.* At the end of the event (and/or between rounds, as desired) individuals are invited to share insights or other results from their conversations with the rest of the plenary group.

In this way the World Cafe process has been used by people around the world to tackle issues.

OD is more than a toolkit

OD is more than a toolkit. It offers more than a procedure for moving from point A to point B. It involves being attuned to the social and personal dynamics of the organization that usually require flexibility in problem-solving, not just a standardized set of procedures or tools. OD is so much more than a short-term training toolkit.

In recent years serious questioning has emerged about the relevance of OD for leading and managing change in organizations. The need for 'reinventing' the field has become a topic that even some of its 'founding fathers' are critically discussing (Bradford and Burke, 2005). With this call for reinvention and change, scholars have begun to examine OD from an emotion-based standpoint. For example, deKlerk (2007) writes about how emotional trauma can negatively affect performance. Owing to downsizing, outsourcing, mergers, restructuring, continual changes and abuses of power, many employees experience the emotions of aggression, anxiety, apprehension, cynicism and fear that can lead to a decrease in their performance at work. deKlerk (2007) suggests that, to heal such trauma and increase performance, OD practitioners must acknowledge the existence of the trauma, provide a safe place for employees to discuss their feelings, symbolize the trauma and put it into perspective, and then allow for, and deal with, the emotional responses. One method of achieving this is by having employees draw pictures of what they feel about the situation and then having them explain their drawings to one another. Drawing pictures may be beneficial because it allows employees to express emotions they may not be able to put into words.

The development of such approaches helps to emphasize that OD is not a 'one-size-fits-all' approach to organizational change or a methodical set of rigid practices and procedures. Instead it consists of multiple methods, perspectives, approaches and values that influence how it is practised. OD interventions can help employees maintain a clear focus on their goals, confront and resolve interpersonal problems in a proactive, preventive way and help to sustain organizational changes at individual, team and organizational levels.

Learning and development do not take place just in the classroom. Ongoing learning at work is fundamental to creating sustainable change. In their research into what makes for a consistently high-performing workforce, Spreitzer and Porath (2012) found that happy workers who are more than just satisfied and productive are also engaged in creating the future and are less susceptible to stress. Spreitzer and Porath (2012) believe that learning is a vital component to achieve this because people who are developing their abilities are likely to believe in their potential for future growth. The implications of their research reinforce the need for organizations to create opportunities for employees to learn and grow by fostering practices that encourage individual and organizational learning. This view is supported by Keller and Price (2011), who add that 'healthy organizations' (as defined by their capacity to adapt and change more quickly than their competition) do not merely learn to adjust themselves to their current context or to the challenges that lie just ahead: they also create a capacity to learn and change.

Organizational learning

What is a learning organization?

In his book *Images of Organization*, Gareth Morgan (2006) outlines the notion that there are a number of organizational metaphors.[1] One such metaphor he describes is of an organization as a brain – storing, transmitting and manipulating knowledge, and becoming, in the process, a learning organization.

Garvin (1993) defines a learning organization as an organization that has developed the continuous capacity to adapt and change. Chen (2005) builds on this definition and says that it is an organization that is skilled at creating, acquiring and transferring knowledge, modifying its behaviour to reflect new knowledge and insights and adjusting itself to adapt to internal and external environmental changes, thereby achieving both sustainability and development.

In the 1990s, the idea of a learning organization was popularized in a seminal work by Peter Senge (1990). In his book *The Fifth Discipline*, Senge (1990: 4) advocates the concept of a learning organization as possible because 'deep down, we are all learners … Learning organizations are possible because not only is it our nature to learn but also we love to learn.' Senge (1990) defines the learning organization as an organization where people continually expand their capacity to create the results they seek, where new and expansive patterns of thinking are nurtured, where collective aspiration is set free, and where people are continually learning to learn. This definition implies a specific kind of organizational culture that enables risk-taking, continuous personal development, experimentation and the influx of new ideas, concepts and ways to manage and develop the business. This cultural element is also implicit in the definition of the learning organization put forward by Rowden (2001),

---

1 Organizations as machines; organizations as organisms; organizations as cultures; organizations as political systems; organizations as psychic prisons; organizations as flux and transformation; organizations as instruments of domination; organizations as brains.

who defines the learning organization as a model of strategic change in which everyone is engaged in identifying and solving problems so that the organization is continuously changing, experimenting and improving, thus increasing its capacity to grow and achieve its purpose. The basic rationale for such an organization is that in situations of change only those organizations that are flexible, adaptive and productive will excel. For this to happen, Senge (1990) says that organizations need to increase people's commitment and capacity to learn at all levels. Studies (such as Edwards and Usher, 2001) have built on Senge's approach and, using the experience of leaders in organizations, have identified the following five pillars as the basis for a learning organization:

1. Vision
2. Infrastructure
3. Culture
4. Learning dynamics
5. Training and development

Vision

In a learning organization, the organization's clarity of vision exists to the extent that learning is part of that vision. The organization's vision plays an important role in creating and sustaining a learning organization (O'Connor and Kotze, 2008; Vardiman et al., 2006). The role of vision in leading and sustaining change is discussed in Chapter 3.

Infrastructure

The sharing of information and knowledge (infrastructure) consists of making knowledge accessible and comprehensible to people in the organization. For this to happen there must be 'exteriorization' – conversion of tacit knowledge into explicit knowledge (Pankakoski, 1998). The ability to gather information and use that same information to alter behaviour is the pillar of effectiveness in a learning organization (Franco and Almeida, 2011). Information and knowledge need to be made available in suitable means for use by people in the organization.

Culture

Corporate culture influences all aspects of organizational performance, including learning (Brown and Duguid, 1991). Culture is considered as the basis of the learning organization because all individuals need to share organizational values. The creation of a culture based on the construction of knowledge and learning is therefore important in creating a learning organization (Goh et al., 2006). In Chapter 3, we discuss shared values as a core theme and practice in leading change.

Learning dynamics

Individuals need to help one another and share knowledge and professional experience to create important synergies (Claver et al., 2001). Various researchers believe that one of the most important characteristics of organizations that learning is *continuous* learning (Leitch et al., 1996). A system of effective organizational learning challenges people to think and act with a wider perspective and to look for deep causes, patterns and interdependence. As a result, people learn to think systematically about the impact of their decisions. From another aspect, it is important to stress that a learning organization has a learning atmosphere based on freedom. Employees are not afraid to speak, errors are accepted and mistakes are not punished (Barrett, 1995). These organizations, besides optimizing their own experience, examine the experience of others and use it for their own benefit (Franco and Almeida, 2011).

Training and development

Learning can be developed through training and development, which focuses on the acquisition of knowledge, skills and attitudes. This can have a number of benefits, such as improved work, individuals' adaptability to new technology and the growth of individuals' competencies within the organization. Training and development enable an organization to be more adaptive and flexible and to tap the learning of individuals to improve organizational performance and enhance learning across the organization (Rijal, 2010).

Single- and double-loop learning

To become a learning organization, leaders and managers must create an environment that enables double-loop learning to avoid being trapped in single-loop learning. 'Single-loop learning' is adaptive learning, that focuses on how to improve the status quo. Involving incremental change, it narrows the gap between desired and actual conditions. Single-loop learning is the most prevalent form of learning in organizations. 'Double-loop learning' is generative learning, aimed at changing the status quo. Members of the organization learn how to change the existing assumptions and conditions within which single-loop learning operates. Double-loop learning can lead to transformational change (Argyris and Schon, 1978). Argyris and Schön (1978) have taken this a step further and identified 'deutero-learning', which is learning how to learn. The learning is directed at the learning process itself and seeks to improve both single- and double-loop learning.

Argyris and Schön (1978) go on to suggest that most individuals appear to operate within their organizational context according to the following rules: strive to be in unilateral control; minimize losing and maximize winning; minimize the expression of negative feelings and be rational. These rules and strategies underpin what is known as Model I theory-in-use and are effective only in encouraging single-loop learning. Conforming to Model I often leads to defensiveness and 'learning disabilities' such as withholding information and feelings, competition and rivalry, and little public testing of assumptions about organizational processes and performance. At a collective level, these defensive routines result in the development of organizational malaise, characterized in individual members by hopelessness, cynicism, distancing and blaming others and at an organizational level by mediocre performance.

A more effective approach, called Model II, is based on values that promote valid information, free and informed choice, internal commitment to the choice and continuous assessment of its implementation. This results in minimal defensiveness with greater openness to information and feedback, personal mastery, collaboration with others and public testing of theories-in-use. Model II is necessary for double-loop learning, where theories-in-use are changed, and for deutero-learning, where the learning process itself is examined and improved. Organizational learning interventions are aimed at helping to secure a change from Model I to Model II thinking in organizational members. An example of a company that has attempted to make this move is L.L. Bean. The case study below illustrates how the company has relied on inquiry as a source of learning to deepen its understanding of customer needs.

CASE STUDY

L.L. Bean

L.L. Bean, Inc. is a leading multichannel merchant of quality outdoor gear and apparel. The company L.L. Bean was founded in 1912 by its namesake, avid hunter and fisherman Leon Leonwood Bean, in Freeport, Maine. The company began as a one-room operation selling a single product, the Maine Hunting Shoe. Bean had developed a waterproof boot (a combination of lightweight leather uppers and rubber bottoms) that he sold to hunters. He obtained a list of non-resident Maine hunting licence holders, prepared a descriptive mail order circular, set up a shop in his brother's basement in Freeport, and started a nationwide mail-order business. By 1912 he was selling the 'Bean Boot', or Maine Hunting Shoe, through a four-page mail-order catalogue, and the boot remains a staple of the company's outdoor image. Defects in the initial design led to 90% of the original production run being returned. Bean honoured his money-back guarantee, corrected the design and continued selling the boots. While its business has grown over the years, L.L. Bean still upholds the values of its founder, including his dedication to quality, customer service and a love of the outdoors.

The company relies on inquiry as a source of learning to deepen its understanding of customer needs. Rather than collect impressions second- or third-hand, L.L. Bean goes to those in the know – experienced users who have lived with the product, often under demanding conditions, who then act as field testers. Testers are sent several samples, one from L.L. Bean and at least one from a competitor, to use for three months. During the test period, Bean encourages extensive feedback at all times, and formally solicits feedback at three points: when the product is first received, at the midpoint and at the end of the test. The midpoint evaluations are especially revealing because of the creative approach the company employs. The company structures these around an outdoor activity such as hiking or cross-country skiing. For example, when sales of the once best-selling Crest Hiker began to decline, L.L. Bean assembled groups of testers, product designers, marketers and suppliers for a two-day hiking trip to test a new version of the boot. Participants were put in groups based on foot size, given two to three pairs of boots – the new Cresta Hiker, as well as the very best competitive offerings – and were instructed to hike, switching pairs every one and a half hours as they made their way up the mountain. After the two days' testing, and constant interactive feedback, the design team returned to headquarters and were immediately debriefed and key learnings extracted. Prototypes were quickly developed and sent to testers for their reactions. They approved, and the new Cresta Hiker was launched. The results were significant. Sales rose more than 85% over the previous year and the initial shipment sold out within weeks.

Case written by Julie Hodges and based on *L.L. Bean: Our Story* http://www.llbean.com/customerService/aboutLLBean/images/110408_About-LLB.pdf (accessed April 2012).

Discussion Questions

1   What are the benefits of the learning approach used by L.L. Bean?
2   How might this approach be adapted to an organization with which you are familiar or one you have worked in?
3   What else might L.L. Bean do to be defined as a learning organization?

Concerns with the learning organization

One of the concerns with the concept of the learning organization is that there are very few organizations that come close to the combination of characteristics that Senge identifies as necessary for the learning organization. His vision of companies and organizations turning wholeheartedly to the cultivation of the learning of their members has come into fruition in only a limited number of instances. While the leaders of organizations will look to their long-term growth and sustainability, they do not always focus specifically on developing a learning organization. The focus may be on enhancing brand recognition and status (Klein, 2001); developing intellectual capital and knowledge (Leadbeater, 2000); delivering product innovation; and ensuring that production and distribution costs are kept down. As Will Hutton (1995: 8) has argued, the priorities of companies 'are overwhelmingly financial. What is more, 'the targets for profit are too high and time horizons too short' (1995: xi). Such conditions are hardly conducive to building the sort of organization that Senge proposes. So in organizations where the bottom line is profit, a fundamental concern with the development of a learning organization is that it is simply too idealistic and too time- and resource-intensive to build and maintain.

Although there is the question of whether Senge's vision of the learning organization and the disciplines it requires has contributed to more informed and committed action with regard to organizational life, Senge's work does provide leaders and managers with a comprehensive model of what a learning organization should be. John Van Maurik (2001: 201) has suggested that Senge is ahead of his time and that his arguments are insightful and revolutionary. Van Maurik goes on to say that it is a matter of regret 'that more organizations have not taken his advice and have remained geared to the quick fix'.

Activity

Think about how you will review and learn from your latest experience of change:

1   How well did you do it?
2   To what extent do you think the organization as a whole has learnt from the change?
3   What is the most important lesson that has been learnt? .
4   What should have been learnt but probably has not been learnt?

Learning from failure

The April 2011 issue of the *Harvard Business Review* was devoted to failure, featuring, among other contributors, A.G. Lafley, a successful ex-boss of Procter & Gamble (P&G), who proclaims that 'we learn much more from failure than we do from success.' IDEO, a consultancy, has coined the slogan 'Fail often in order to succeed sooner'.

There are good reasons for the 'failure fashion'. Success and failure are not polar opposites: you often need to endure the second to enjoy the first. Failure can indeed be a better teacher than success. It can also be a sign of innovation. Businesses cannot invent the future – their own future – without taking risks. Entrepreneurs have always understood this. Thomas Edison performed 9,000 experiments before coming up with a successful version of the light bulb. Students of entrepreneurship talk about the 'J-curve' of returns, which illustrates that failure comes early and often and the successes take a little more time.

A more tolerant attitude to failure can also help companies to avoid destruction. When Alan Mulally became boss of an ailing Ford Motor Company in 2006, one of the first things he did was demand that his executives own up to their failures. He asked managers to colour-code their progress reports – ranging from green for good to red for trouble. At one early meeting he expressed astonishment at being confronted by a sea of green, even though the company had lost several billion dollars in the previous year. Ford's recovery began only when he got his managers to admit that things were not entirely green.

Companies need to learn how to manage failure. Amy Edmondson (2011) in an article on 'Strategies of learning from failure' argues that the first thing companies must do is to distinguish between productive and unproductive failures. There is nothing to be gained from tolerating defects on the production line or mistakes in the hospital operating theatre. Schumpeter (2011) recounts how James McNerney, a former boss of manufacturer 3M, damaged the company's innovation engine in his efforts to apply Six Sigma principles (which are intended to reduce errors on production lines) across the entire company, including the research laboratories. Companies must also recognize the virtues of failing small and failing fast. Peter Sims (2012) likens this to placing 'little bets', in a book of that title. Placing small bets is one of several ways that companies can limit the downside of failure. Chris Zook of consultancy Bain and Company urges companies to keep potential failures close to their core business – perhaps by introducing existing products into new markets or new products into familiar markets (Schumpeter, 2011).

But there is no point in failing fast if you fail to learn from your mistakes. India's Tata group awards an annual prize for the best failed idea. Intuit, the software company, and Eli Lilly, the pharmaceuticals firm, have both taken to holding failure parties. P&G encourages employees to talk about their failures as well as their successes during performance reviews. Leaders should remember how often failure paves the way for success. Henry Ford got nowhere with his first two attempts to start a car company, but that did not stop him (Schumpeter, 2011). Ignoring failure can limit the understanding of the theory and practice of organizational change (Thorne, 2000: 305). Leaders and managers need to show that learning from failure can be positive and can encourage innovation. As Alan Kuyatt says:

fear of failure inhibits innovation by hiding failures, suppressing new ideas, and avoiding risky concepts. Leadership practices that discourage innovation must be replaced with ones that encourage innovation, including accepting risk, viewing failure as a learning opportunity, allowing sufficient time for innovative ideas to develop, and encouraging champions to help overcome resistance and find resources. Management needs to make the organization an ambidextrous operation that can continue to improve the efficiency of current products and services with incremental innovation, while simultaneously encouraging the discovery, adoption, and implementation of radical innovations, without the fear of failure ...'. (2011: 31)

This quote highlights that the ability to tolerate failure is a hallmark of an innovative organization. When change does go wrong it is important to evaluate what happened. For example, the change message may not have been properly communicated, necessary changes may not have been implemented swiftly or thoroughly enough, or managers may not have been decisive enough in their decisions (Gill, 2003; Greenwood and Hinnings, 1996). Alternatively, or additionally, reasons for failure of a change initiative are regularly located on the side of employees and lower management. For example, employees are allegedly not ready for change, middle managers do not support the strategic change initiative, and/or their individual or collective, overt or covert resistance to change creates major barriers (Ford et al., 2008; Oreg, 2003).

A more recent focus has been on poor leadership (By and Burnes, 2013). Thomas Diefenbach (2013) investigates some of the possible reasons for managers' and leaders' failures and shortcomings with regard to change leadership. In particular, he focuses on incompetence and immorality. We explore the ethical issues of change further in Chapters 3 and 4.

The important point about change and transformations that fail is that managers and leaders take the time to learn from them and ensure that the learning is shared with relevant stakeholders.

Activity

Consider your organization or one with which you are familiar:

1   Is it a learning organization? If it is, consider the factors that make it capable of learning?
2   If it is not at present a learning organization, consider the changes that would need to be made to enhance learning and create a learning culture. What policies and processes would aid in knowledge acquisition and retention?
3   Using the internet, find two organizations that have successfully created learning organizations. What factors contributed to their success?

Learning communities

Learning communities offer the opportunity for learning not only within an organization but also across organizations. Learning communities are networks of people who share a common interest in a specific area of knowledge or capability and are willing to work and learn together over a period of time and share that knowledge. They are based on the premise that learning is largely a social activity in which people learn best in groups.

For example, although PwC has invested in considerable formal knowledge management databases to share learning and knowledge, 'Kraken' is an informal and unofficial email list that is highly effective at doing just the same globally across the company. Named after a mythological sea monster in a poem by Alfred Lord Tennyson, Kraken is a sort of global glue, sharing knowledge and learning across the firm. Knowledge sharing via Kraken is a manifestation of community in practice. In fact, the majority of the messages sent via Kraken begin with, 'Does anybody know …?' or 'Has anyone any experience of …?' Such questions often result in long responses. The first author of this book used Kraken many times while working for PwC: it provided insights, lessons learnt, approaches used and models that worked as well as those that did not.

The characteristics of effective learning communities are that:

- Membership is voluntary.
- They have a specific focus.
- There is no expectation of tangible results that can be measured.
- Their existence is defined by group members and they last as long as members want them to last.

Learning communities exist in some form in every organization, whether or not they have been deliberately created and labelled as such. The challenge for managers is to support them in such a way that they make a positive contribution to creating and sharing organizational learning.

Implications of organizational development and learning for managers and leaders

Several practical implications can be drawn from the issues we have discussed in this chapter.

Develop a culture of learning in the organization

As we discussed in this chapter, an organization can proactively sustain change by making continuous learning part of its culture, by becoming an organization that learns – a learning organization. To test if an organization is a learning organization, Garvin (2000) suggests that the following litmus tests can help determine whether or not the organization qualifies:

Does the organization have a defined learning agenda?

Learning organizations have a clear picture of their future knowledge requirements. They know what they need to know, whether the subject is customers, competitors, markets, technologies, or production processes, and are actively pursuing the desired information. Even in industries that are changing as rapidly as telecommunications, technology and financial services, broad areas of needed learning can usually be mapped with some precision. Once they have been identified, these topics are pursued through multiple approaches, including experiments, simulations, research studies, post-audits and benchmarking visits, rather than education and training alone.

Is the organization open to discordant information?

If an organization regularly 'shoots the messenger' who brings forward unexpected or bad news, the environment is clearly hostile to learning. Behaviour change is extremely difficult in such settings, for there are few challenges to the status quo. Sensitive topics – dissension in the ranks, unhappy customers, preemptive moves by competitors, problems with technology – are considered to be off limits, and messages are filtered, massaged and watered down as they make their way up the chain of command.

Does the organization avoid repeated mistakes?

Learning organizations reflect on past experience, distill it into useful lessons, share the knowledge internally and ensure that errors are not repeated elsewhere. Databases, intranets, training sessions and workshops can all be used for this purpose. Even more critical, however, is a mindset that enables companies to recognize the value of productive failure as contrasted with unproductive success. A productive failure leads to insights, understanding and thus an addition to the commonly held wisdom of the organization. And unproductive success occurs when something goes well, but nobody knows how or why. There is a peculiar logic at work here: to avoid repeating mistakes, managers must learn to accept them the first time around.

Apologies offered and actions taken to correct or prevent further problems can be very powerful. According to Kouzes and Posner (2011), this approach can work well even in the face of repeated mistakes or failures. Of course, even the most forgiving and trusting people may become disenchanted with a long record of failure. The best prevention for the onset of cynicism about organizational change is successful, well-communicated change. But because organizations and the people in them are not perfect, mistakes are inevitable and corrections essential. Until the past is accounted for, that is until someone admits the mistake, people may find it difficult or impossible to let go of mistrust.

Does the organization lose critical knowledge when key people leave?

The story is all too common: a talented employee leaves the company, and critical skills disappear as well. Why? Because crucial knowledge was tacit, unarticulated and unshared, locked in the head of a single person. Learning organizations avoid this problem by institutionalizing essential knowledge. Whenever possible, they codify it in policies or procedures, retain it in reports or memos, disperse it to large groups of people, and build it into the company's values, norms and operating practices. Knowledge becomes common property, rather than the province of individuals or small groups.

Does the organization act on what it knows?

Learning organizations are not simply repositories of knowledge. They take advantage of their new learning and adapt their behaviour accordingly. Information is to be used; if it languishes or is ignored, its impact is certain to be minimal. By this test, an organization that discovers an unmet market need but fails to fill it does not qualify as a learning organization; nor does a company that identifies its own best practices but is unable to transfer them across departments or divisions.

To achieve the aims outlined above, consider creating an environment that enables double-loop learning to avoid being trapped in single-loop learning (Argyris and Schön, 1978). The task of realizing this in practice is a challenging one and very much one that leaders and managers must see as a work in progress.

Accelerate learning

Dealing with the ambiguity and complexity of change fundamentally changes the type of learning experience organizations need to create. It means moving more into accelerated learning.

Organizations have begun to focus on accelerating learning. Johns Hopkins University Teaching Hospital, for example, has worked with Duke University to implement accelerated learning. It started with this question: 'Where does learning at work occur in a planned and disciplined way?' Working with the doctors at the hospital and with PwC, Duke University found that a number of the routines embedded in the training of physicians could actually accelerate the learning, development and engagement of teams (Duke Corporate Education, 2011). This is referred to as team-based learning (TBL). TBL instills learning-centred routines into the day-to-day work of teams in a way that is similar to the learning routines that are regularly used to train physicians at teaching hospitals. It puts specific behaviour and simple processes to work to ensure that for every moment on the job, individuals can exploit the potential for learning. TBL is a change in behaviour, the way employees are coached and the way teams collaborate with one another. The model creates more lasting learning experiences for staff and earlier development of their skill set. The more organizations use accelerated development at work, the quicker learning is applied and impacts positively on business results.

Reflect on and learn from experience

Reflection has a key role to play in helping individuals become more aware of and able to review their learning. Reflection needs not only to review what has happened but also to identify possibilities for improvement. According to Hayes (2014), reflecting on one's own and others' behaviours can enable leaders and managers to make sense of situations, identify cause-and-effect relationships, develop corrective routines and challenge beliefs and assumptions that guide their attempts to secure intended outcomes. Learning logs can be an effective way of reflecting on, and identifying and examining, patterns of behaviour. Gold and colleagues (2010) advocate the use of learning logs to help individuals develop the meta-reflection skills that can help them identify and understand key themes and persistent patterns of behaviour. Learning logs are especially useful for individual reflection, while for collective learning, leaders and managers may want to consider using AAR – 'after action review'– which was developed by the US army. AAR reviews the intent (stated at the start of a change) and compares it with what subsequently happens. It involves addressing the following questions: What was supposed to happen? What actually did happen? Why did it happen this way? And what are we going to change? This approach can be used at a team or organizational level.

Build learning contracts

A **learning contract** is a useful way to help sustain learning in organizations. A typical learning contract is a formal written agreement between an employee and his or her manager that specifies (Knowles, 1975):

- What the individual needs to learn.
- The resources needed and strategies available to assist in learning it.
- What will be produced as evidence of the learning having occurred.
- How the outcome will be assessed: what the individual will be doing or saying that is different.

A learning contract can provide a means of monitoring the learning progress. It can be amended to suit individuals and their particular circumstances. Learning contracts can also be agreed with colleagues in an action learning group and with managers during performance management reviews. A contract usually includes:

- A statement of intent – for example: 'By [date] I will have learned the following …; experienced the following … ; gained the following … ; tested new and different ways of working/relating to others …; have achieved …'
- Resources and help required: 'What I will need from others to help me is …?'
- Outcomes: 'How I will know when I have achieved the proposed learning objectives …'

There are, however, several issues raised in the literature about the use of learning contracts. The ways in which employees are introduced to learning contracts is a recurrent concern (Hammond and Collins, 1991; Lane, 1988). To address this concern careful attention is needed to orientate employees and develop their skills in using contracts; otherwise, the use of contracts may cause anxiety or frustration. Another concern is that contracts may not be suitable when the subject matter is new to the learner because decisions about what needs to be learnt can be difficult to make and the resources and strategies available may not be readily identified (Knowles, 1986). Again it is important to ensure that individuals are made aware of the purpose of contracts and have the skills to devise and use them effectively.

Despite such concerns, learning contracts can be a useful learning and evaluation tool to help sustain change in organizations, if facilitated correctly between managers and individuals. They can also be used at a team level to identify team-learning objectives. Learning contracts can engender a sense of ownership of the learning process. And by specifying objectives in advance, both managers and employees have an agreed understanding of the expected outcomes and development objectives.

Organizations will often build in a personal development plan as part of their performance management process. The purpose of this plan is similar to that of a learning contract in that it enables employees to identify development needs such as what skills, knowledge and capabilities they need to learn, how, by when and what the outcomes will be. Personal development objectives are then set and reviewed regularly with employees and their managers. These plans can be beneficial to the personal growth of individuals and can help them identify what they need to change and how they will change their behaviour. If they are used as an active part of performance management they can help sustain behavioural change and ensure individuals have the support they need.

Characteristics of a learning contract proposal

1 Clear objectives, strategies, resources needed and evaluation criteria.
2 Based upon the learner's identified development needs.
3 Involves a range of learning activities (blended learning).
4 Develops skills of learners in how to learn.
5 Involves learners in monitoring both their own progress and outcomes.
6 Includes realistic tasks and goals achievable within the proposed timeframe and availability of resources.
7 Requires learners to engage in a deep approach to their learning.
8 It is actively negotiated and agreed between an individual and their manager.
9 Objectives in the contract should be 'SMART': specific, measurable, agreed, realistic and time-bound.

Several benefits have been identified for learning contracts, with regard to the development of learners, their relationship to learning and the strengthening of their skills. Learning contracts can help foster independence and the development of problem-solving skills (Tompkins and McGraw, 1988) as well as being flexible in meeting different learning needs, styles and pace of learning (Galbraith and Zelemark, 1991).

Further reading

Aldred, R. (2009) 'From community participation to organizational therapy? World Café and Appreciative Inquiry as research methods', *Community Development Journal*, 46(1): 57–71.

Brown, D.R. and Harvey, D. (2004) *An Experiential Approach to Organizational Development*. Upper Saddle River, NJ: Prentice Hall.

Brown, J. and Issacs, D. (2005) *World Cafe: Shaping our Futures through Conversations that Matter*. San Francisco, CA: Berrett-Koehler.

Burnes, B. and Cooke, B. (2012) 'The past, present and future of organization development: Taking the long view', *Human Relations*, 65(12): 1–35.

Bushe, G.R. and Marshak, R.J. (2009) 'Revisioning organizational development: Diagnostic and dialogic premises and patterns of practice', *Journal of Applied Behavioural Science*, 45(3): 348–68.

Cooperrider, D.L., Whitney, D. and Stravros, J.M. (2008) *Appreciative Inquiry Handbook*. Brunswick, OH: Crown.

Fagenson-Elan, E., Ensher, E.A. and Burke, W.W (2004) 'Organization development and change interventions: A seven-nation comparison', *Journal of Applied Behavioural Science*, 40(4): 432–64.

Lines, R., Sáenz, J. and Aramburu, N. (2011) 'Organizational learning as a byproduct of justifications for change', *Journal of Change Management*, 11(2): 163–84.

Oswick, C. (2013) 'Reflections: OD or not. OD that is the question! A constructivist's thoughts on the changing nature of change', *Journal of Change Management*, 13(4): 371–81.

Changing Organizational Structures 9

Overview

- Any discussion of organizational change needs to pay careful attention to the role of formal systems and structures since they influence what gets done, how it gets done, the outcomes that are achieved, and the experiences of the people who come into contact with the organization.
- Each form of organizational structure possesses unique strengths and weaknesses that make it appropriate for some situations and not for others. To adjust to the rapid changes in the environment today more flexible structures are being implemented, such as networks.
- Reorganizing or restructuring is a common change intervention in organizations. Some organizations are restructuring in the right way and improving people's experience of them, in others a restructure can creates uncertainty and lower morale.
- Structuring an organization involves making well-considered choices among the various alternatives available. Organization design is the process of making these choices.
- Mergers and acquisitions (M&As) present a complicated challenge as they involve the combination of separate companies, departments, functions and units. The benefits of a merger or acquisition can be considerable, such as economies of scale, greater sales revenue and market share, broader diversification and increased tax efficiency. However, the reality of managing a merger or acquisition is complex. We discuss the complexities in this chapter.

In 1957 Charlton Ogburn said:

> We trained hard, but it seemed that every time we were beginning to form up into teams we would be reorganized. Presumably the plans for our employment were being

changed. I was to learn later in life that, perhaps because we are so good at organizing, we tend as a nation to meet any new situation by reorganizing; and a wonderful method it can be for creating the illusion of progress while producing confusion, inefficiency and demoralization. (Charton Ogburn Jr., 1957)

This quote is still as insightful to us today as it was then. More recently Sir Roy Griffiths, a previous managing director of the supermarket chain J. Sainsbury, said, 'Reorganizing is the thing you do when everything else has failed' (Timmins, 2007). A restructure is often the last resort for many organizations, for example, Air France, the Franco-Dutch airline. The company had suffered six consecutive years of losses. Due to its high cost base, it had to contend with big fuel bills and fierce competition from low-cost carriers. The company was on the brink of collapse and was left with no other alternative but to restructure.

Contingency theory tells us that as circumstances change (as in the case with Air France) an organization must adapt to remain relevant and appropriate because it provides the foundation for everything that goes on within the company. An organization's current structure, whether functional, divisional, matrix or incorporating one or more inter-organizational collaborative relationships, is not therefore permanent, but subject to regular revisions. Restructures can create uncertainty and lower morale, if not managed correctly.

The aim of this chapter is to look at changes to the structures of organizations. We examine the rationale for changing structures and consider how to implement such changes in a way that is not demoralizing for employees. In particular, we focus on structural changes that can occur as a result of mergers and acquisitions. We begin by providing a brief overview of the types of structures in organizations.

Learning objectives

By the end of this chapter you will be able to:

- Identify the characteristics of different types of organizational structures
- Compare and contrast the different types of structures in organization
- Examine the key components for designing organizational structures
- Critically assess why structures are resistant to change
- Apply key approaches to managing mergers and acquisitions
- Appreciate how organizational structure relates to sustaining change in organizations

The nature of an organization's structure

Any discussion of organizational change needs to pay careful attention to the role of formal systems and structures because they influence what gets done, how it gets done, the outcomes that are achieved and the experiences of the people who come into contact with the organization. Sometimes systems and structures represent what needs to change. An organization's formal structure is defined by how tasks are formally divided, grouped or coordinated, in essence the social structuring of people and processes (Senior and Fleming, 2006). Wilson and Rosenfeld offer the following definition of an organization's structure:

> The established pattern of relationships between component parts of an organization, outlining ... communication, control and authority patterns. Structure distinguishes the parts of an organization and delineates the relationship between them. (1990: 215)

Bartol and Martin add the element of 'designed by management' to this definition:

> The formal pattern of interactions and coordination designed by management to link the tasks of individuals and groups in achieving organizational goals. (1994: 283)

Like Bartol and Martin, Stacey draws attention to the role of management in the creation of the structure:

> The structure of an organization is a formal way of identifying who is to take responsibility for what; who is to exercise authority over whom; and who is to be answerable to whom. The structure is a hierarchy of managers and is the source of authority, as well as the legitimacy of decisions and actions. (2007: 62)

These definitions give a sense of the objectives of an organization's structure as well as the process through which these objectives can be met. A structure reflects the aims and objectives of an organization, the size and complexity of its purpose, the nature of the expertise to be used, the preferred management and leadership styles, and the means of coordination and control. The structure must provide effective channels of communication and decision-making processes and provide also for the creation of professional and productive relationships among individuals and teams. Departments, divisions and functions are created, as required, to achieve aims and objectives together with the means and methods by which they are coordinated and harmonized (Pettinger, 2010).

Organizations also have informal structures that are not designed by management but are the outcome of groups and individuals linking together as a result of interests, politics and power relationships. Such relationships are discussed further in Chapter 12.

Like the skeletal system of the human body or the steel framework of a building, an organization's structure differentiates among its parts even as it helps to keep those parts interconnected. In doing this it creates and reinforces relationships of interdependence among the people and the groups within it. Balancing this structural integration and differentiation is a challenge facing many leaders. The ability to create a workable balance between the two can determine whether a company succeeds in organizing work activities in a way that allows something meaningful to be accomplished (Wagner and Hollenbeck, 2010).

An organization's structure should enable the people within it to work together, and accomplish things beyond the abilities of unorganized individuals. To help their employees achieve this feat in the most effective manner, leaders need to know how to structure their organization in a way that will enhance employees' performance, control the costs of doing the work, and keep the organization ahead of changes in the external environment, as well as being able to respond to internal triggers for change. Leaders need to develop an understanding of how existing structures are currently influencing outcomes and how they are likely to facilitate or impede the proposed changes. They must understand the design and specific features of the different types of structures that they might choose to implement and be aware of the likely advantages and disadvantages of each structural type. Once that understanding is developed, leaders need to put that awareness to use to promote and enact change.

Conventional types of structures

Organizational charts describe the structure. They are useful in showing the formal relations and staff deployment between departments. The charts tend to depict: hierarchy – the number of levels of the chain of command; specialization – the division of tasks and who is responsible for the tasks at each level. Organizational structures try to balance the need to specialize with the need for coordination. There are a variety of ways an organization can be structured including, functional, divisional, matrix and flat. We examine each of these next.

Functional structures

Functional structures tend to have centralized control and separate functional departments, such as marketing, production, human resources, IT and customer service. Employees within a functional department tend to perform a specialized set of tasks. For instance, the finance department will be staffed with accountants, who focus on financial efficiencies. The functional structure is best suited to an organization that is a producer of standardized goods and services in large volumes. Activities are integrated vertically so that products are produced, sold and distributed quickly and at low cost. A small business, with a functional structure, for example, will make components used in the production of its products instead of buying them (Snow and Miles, 1992).

General Motors (GM), the US car manufacturer, built itself on a multi-functional structure in the 1940s. The multifunctional form (also called the unitary form or U-form) separates the various inputs to a firm's business operations and organizes them accordingly. This form is viable where products share common production methods and technologies, and it allows employees to become highly specialized in their work.

Functional structures tend to work best in organizations that are relatively stable, such as hospitals, and have a small number of products and/or services with relatively easy coordination across specialized units. This structure is also best suited to routine technologies in which there is interdependence within functions and to organizational goals emphasizing efficiency and technical quality (Cummings and Worley, 2009).

A criticism of the functional approach is that it can potentially lead to poor communication among the different functional groups. So when change is being implemented within such a structure it is vital that there is a communications strategy that ensures communication goes up, down and across all functions. We discuss communications further in Chapter 10.

Divisional structures

The divisional structure groups all relevant organizational functions into individual divisions. Each division contains all the necessary resources and functions within it. Divisions can be formed on a geographical basis (an Asian division and a European division, for example) or on a product or service basis (such as different products or services for different customer groups such as households or companies). For example, in the product-based form, divisions look after all aspects of the production of a particular product, that is, from purchasing materials through to manufacturing and distribution. Each division may have its own research and development, marketing and finance departments. For example, Toyota is made up of separate divisions for textile machinery, compressors, vehicles, engines, material handling and technology development. The energy company BP, which employs over 100,000 people and operates in more than 100 countries, has four divisions: Exploration and Production; Gas, Power and Renewables; Refining and Marketing; and Petrochemicals. Each of these divisions contains several business units that report to the Chief Executive. Multinational enterprises may structure their divisions based upon the geographic regions in which they operate, such as North America, Latin America, Europe, Asia, Africa and the Middle East. This type of structure enables companies to serve geographically diverse markets and to produce and distribute goods locally, allowing managers to meet local market preferences arising from cultural differences (Brooks, 2009).

The limited degree of independence afforded the divisions within a divisional structure allows one division to stop doing business without seriously interrupting the operations of others. For example, the division of aerospace manufacturer Boeing – that fulfils military contracts could stop doing business without affecting the work in the firm's civilian aircraft division. However, as each division in such a structure is itself organized like a functional structure, a particular division cannot change products, locations or even customers without incurring serious interruptions in its own internal operations. So a decision at Boeing to service NASA contracts in the military division would require substantial reorganization of that division (Wagner and Hollenbeck, 2010). As each unit in a divisional structure is designed to fit a particular niche, the structure adapts well to uncertain conditions. Divisional units also help to coordinate technical interdependencies across functions and are suited to organizations promoting product or service specialization and innovation (Cummings and Worley, 2009).

The flexibility that is the main strength of divisional structures comes at the price of increased costs from the duplication of effort across divisions. For example, every division is likely to have a separate sales force, even though that structure means that salespeople from several different divisions visit the same customer. Similarly, if several divisions operate their own purchasing function there may be duplication and a lack of shared information about purchasing that could lead to inefficiencies.

The primary weakness of divisional structures is that they are, at best, only moderately efficient owing to duplication of effort. A divisional structure works best in conditions almost opposite to those for a functional structure. The organization needs to be relatively large to support the duplication of resources and effort across the different units.

Matrix structures

The distinguishing feature of a matrix structure is its flexibility and ability to change more rapidly than other structures. In a matrix structure employees have two and sometimes more reporting relationships. One line of authority, often the functional area, manages the formal side of the employment contract, such as performance management and salary negotiations. The other lines of authority are used to involve employees in projects and other change initiatives.

A matrix structure is beneficial when there is a need for staff to spread their time across a range of different activities as they can help to push forward progress on a number of fronts simultaneously and allow staff to reap the benefits of working together from different functional areas. Starbucks has developed a matrix structure that combines functional and product-based divisions, with employees reporting to two managers. A multinational matrix that maintains coordination among products, functions and geographic areas is common in global companies, such as Procter & Gamble and Unilever.

One of the benefits of a matrix structure is that it does not have to apply to the whole organization. John Kuprenas (2003), for instance, describes the positive effect of the introduction of a matrix structure within the Bureau of Engineering in the City of Los Angeles public services.

Matrix structures are appropriate under three main conditions. First, there must be external drivers for a dual focus. Organizations that choose matrix structures and function effectively are generally those that face transformational change that would destroy them if they could not easily adapt to the dynamic environment in which they operate. Organizations that attempt a matrix structure but later abandon it tend not to face the degree of change required to justify the costs of the matrix approach (Wagner and Hollenbeck, 2010). Second, a matrix structure is appropriate when the organization must process a large amount of information, such as when: the external environmental demands change unpredictably; an organization produces a broad range of products and services or offers those outputs to a large number of different markets; and the relevant technologies evolve quickly. In each case, there is considerable complexity in decision-making and pressure on communication and coordination systems. Third, there must be pressure for shared resources. When customer demands vary greatly and technological requirements are strict, valuable human and physical resources are likely to be scarce. The matrix structure works well under those conditions because it facilitates the sharing of scarce resources. If any one of these conditions is not met, a matrix structure may well find it difficult to survive (Cummings and Worley, 2009).

Despite the benefits they offer, matrix structures are open to a number of criticisms. First, since the functional line manager has position power over the project manager(s), there is a danger that unproductive power struggles can occur (Brooks, 2009). The focus of attention, the project or the customer can be lost in such struggles as priorities shift towards self-interest and political posturing. Second, matrix structures are costly to operate. The expense stems partly from the proliferation of managers in a matrix structure. Matrix structures also incorporate the same sort of duplication, such as multiple sales forces that make divisional structures so expensive to operate. Third, because employees have more than one reporting line, working in a matrix can be stressful. This stress can lead to absenteeism, turnover and ultimately lower productivity and higher human resource costs (Burns and Wholey, 1993).

Flat structures

A flat structure has relatively few levels of hierarchy. Its aim is to: improve the focus on customer needs and the speed of response; to reduce the levels of bureaucracy in the organization; to facilitate greater empowerment; and to reduce dysfunctional status differences. The flat structure is common in small companies, start-ups and online companies. A flatter organization, such as that in Google, may also be more open to innovation. Communication is usually more effective as there are fewer layers to communicate across.

This is evidence in Morning Star – the world's largest tomato processor – where the structure is flatter than a pancake levelled by a steamroller. There are no managers, no directives from above, no promotions and no titles. Instead, there is the philosophy promulgated by Morning Star's founder, Chris Rufer, who called this self-management. But it is also mutual management. Employees' decisions about what they will do are determined largely by their commitments to others. Those commitments are embedded in peer-to-peer contracts known as colleague letters of understanding, or CLOUs. The importance of each CLOU is a personal commercial mission crafted by each employee to describe their contribution to Morning Star's success. The terms of how everyone will work with everyone else are negotiated by the people doing the work. In Morning Star autonomy extends beyond the deliverables. If equipment is needed to do their job then employees can buy it. If they see a process that would benefit from different skills then they can hire someone. Colleagues consult one another and then simply act. The ballast to this autonomy is accountability. In a company with no promotions, people earn more by getting better at their jobs. Employee-elected compensation committees set pay levels after measuring the performance of colleagues against their CLOUs. Morning Star pays 15% more in salaries and 35% more in benefits than the industry average because it is not paying managers and productivity is so high.

Creating a flat structure in an existing organization with a divisional or functional structure involves removing layers in an existing structure (often middle management). Simply taking levels and people out of the structure and expecting the remaining employees and managers to absorb the consequences is unrealistic and liable to end in disaster. Simply removing slack from the organization means there is less spare capacity to deal with any change that arises.

Emerging organizational structures

In recent years many organizations have found it necessary to become more flexible in their structure. This is partly due to the impact of globalization, which has meant that some companies employ staff across the globe as well as changes in routes to market, such as the expansion of online retail.

As a result, they have begun to experiment with different structures. We examine two such structures below – network and **virtual structures**.

Network structures

A **network structure** – also known as a spider's web, starbursts or cluster organizations – aims to manage the diverse, complex and dynamic relationships among multiple organizations and units, each specializing in a particular business function or task (Snow et al., 1992). Although traditional structures, such as divisional or functional, tend not to change from year to year, the network can morph with ease. In the absence of bureaucratic layers, this type of network permits a level of individualism, creativity and innovation that not even the least bureaucratic hierarchy can provide. Populated with employees from across the organization and up and down its ranks, the network liberates information from silos and hierarchical layers and enables it to flow with far greater freedom and accelerated speed (Kotter, 2012a).

The essence of networks is the relationships among organizations that perform different aspects of work. In this way, organizations are able to do the things that they do best, such as manufacturing or distribution logistics. Network organizations use strategic alliances, joint ventures, research and development consortiums, licensing agreements and wholly-owned subsidiaries to design, manufacture and market advanced products, enter new markets and develop new technologies. Companies such as Amazon, Apple, Benetton, Google, Facebook, Sun Microsystems, Liz Claiborne, Nike and Merck have implemented network structures (see Figure 9.1). The advantages that such companies gain from a network structure are that they are highly flexible and adaptable to changing conditions, which means that they can adapt to the triggers for change quickly. The ability to form partnerships with various organizations permits the creation of the 'best of the best' to exploit opportunities, often global in nature. This enables each member company to exploit its distinctive capabilities. It can provide sufficient accumulated resources and expertise for large complex tasks that single organizations cannot perform. Perhaps most important, network organizations can have synergistic effects where members build on one another's strengths and competencies, creating a whole that exceeds the sum of its parts.

Network structures are complex and managing the complexity can be a disadvantage. Other disadvantages of network structures include the difficulties in motivating organizations to join such structures and of sustaining commitment over time. Potential members may not want to give up their own autonomy to link with other organizations. And, once linked, they may have difficulties in sustaining the benefits of joining together. Joining a network may also expose a company's proprietary knowledge and skills to others.

Network structures are best suited to environments where multiple capabilities and flexible responses are needed and where there are complex tasks or problems involving high interdependencies across organizations.

Virtual structures

Since time and distance are no longer the barriers they once were, for organizations across the globe, virtual structures can be created that are geographically distributed but are held together and enabled by technology. In a virtual structure, several organizations achieve the performance capacity of a single, much larger organization while retaining flexibility and efficiency (Desanctis and Monge, 1998). Clases and colleagues

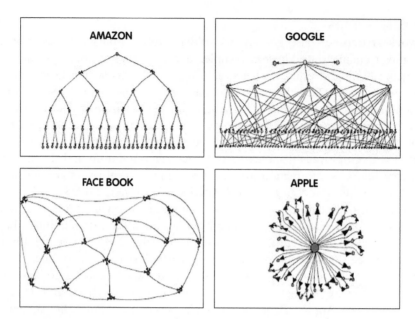

Figure 9.1 Network structures (drawing by Manu Cornet downloaded from www.bonkersworld.net)

(2003) define virtual structures as a set of economically independent organizations operating together to meet the needs of customers or other stakeholders. Such an organization structure is a culmination of an information-based and constantly evolving enterprise. In this way, virtual structures are essentially like a network of connections into individuals, groups, teams and parts of formal organizations. They are suited to rapid exchanges of information for solving problems or locating resources. Virtual structures can be short-lived, and because of their loose structure, dissolving one can occur rapidly.

The virtual organization has no shared physical location. It exists within a network of alliances, using the internet. This means that, while the core of the organization can be small, the company can still operate globally. During its temporary existence, a virtual structure resembles a loosely coupled functional structure where each department is an otherwise autonomous company. Connecting the various companies is an intranet of systems. Levi Strauss and Dell Computer are two of the better-known companies that have implemented aspects of a virtual structure approach.

The temporary nature of the virtual structure is the source of its flexibility, because companies can be added or removed as the situation warrants. In the face of this flexibility, the virtual structure's efficiency comes from each company's singular focus on doing what it does best. For example, IBM, Apple and Motorola combined forces to design a new computer memory chip and to introduce it to computer manufacturers throughout the world. Once this had been achieved the companies disbanded their joint operations and retrieved the resources they had loaned to the project.

The virtual structure does, however, have some drawbacks. Considerable efficiency may be sacrificed owing to the cost of coordinating efforts spread among several otherwise independent companies. These costs inhibit the use of virtual structures in all but the most turbulent situations. Two further challenges for virtual structures are the creation of trust among people who do not know one another and who rarely or never meet and the building of relationships that will work over different time zones, culture and distances (Briscoe, 2004). It is therefore interesting that Peter Zimmermann and colleagues (2008), in a survey of 419 technical engineers working as members of virtual teams at Shell Global Solutions International, found that most task-oriented and relationship-oriented leadership behaviours are considered by them to be more important in virtual settings than in face-to-face settings. And the greater the degree of virtualness in team members' daily work, the greater the relative importance of many leadership behaviours.

Two structures, one organization

Traditional hierarchies and processes that together form an organization's operating system do a great job of handling the operational needs of most companies, but they are often too rigid to adjust to the quick shifts in today's marketplace. In order to address this, some organizations are using more innovative structures within their traditional structure. One example of this is Skunk works.

Skunk works

As it has become increasingly important for organizations to be innovative, not just to gain competitive advantage but to survive, some organizations have turned to incorporating a skunk works into their structures.

A skunk works is a structure designed to encourage the employees of large organizations to come up with original ideas. It usually consists of a small team taken out of their normal working environment and given exceptional freedom from their organization's standard management constraints. The name is taken from the moonshine factory in a famous Al Capp cartoon series called 'Li'l Abner'. Skunk works are defined by Single and Spurgeon as a 'method of managing the innovative process, characterized by extremely efficient use of time by a small group of creative engineers' (1996: 39). Terrence Brown (2004: 134) says that 'a true skunk works is an isolated and highly skilled team designed to accelerate the research but especially the development of innovative products and/or services'.

All skunk works are modelled on the Lockheed aircraft company's secret research-cum-production facility where, in the 1940s, staff were removed from the corporate bureaucracy and encouraged to ignore standard procedures in the hope that they would come up, in the first instance, with a high-speed fighter plane that could compete with those produced in Germany by Messerschmitt. So successful was the concept that the company continued with it, and its skunk works came up with a number of other innovative products, including the notorious U2 spy plane. The idea was soon copied by other large companies, including IBM.

It is generally the case that most skunk work-like programmes in large firms are mandated and created by top management. In establishing these programmes good management takes the responsibility for ensuring they have adequate resources, especially human and financial. However, instead of being mandated by top management directive, skunk works can often emerge. Individuals or teams somewhere in the organization begin working on solutions to problems they believe are important. They generally use the 'beg, borrow and steal' method of acquiring resources to further their work. While organizations may sometimes have unspecified resources that are available for unspecified projects, most attract resources, including human and financial, as the project gains attention and support, albeit usually quietly (Gwynne, 1997). For example, in a story described by Field (2001), a group of rogue engineers at Compaq thought they could develop a high-density computer by reducing some of the extra features and by using mostly parts from their current AlphaServer DS10. Although top management seemingly liked the idea, the funding request was turned down, because the DS10 was the company's top focus and hope for the future. However, the 'rogue' engineers continued to work on the high-density server in their own time and, unofficially, top management did not discourage the project. In a short time, the group was successful and their persistence resulted in a multimillion dollar global business for Compaq (Brown, 2004).

A list of the factors required for skunk works to be deemed successful is provided by Brown (2004). This list is not complete, nor is it inclusive; however, it does further the debate about the value of skunk works:

1. The corporation needs to have a special culture that allows the existence of a counterculture entity associated with it (Gwynne, 1997). Not every organization will allow a foreign entity to exist within it. It is analogous to a body allowing a virus to exist without trying to destroy it. The successful organization must not only allow the skunk works to exist and flourish, it must sometime create the entity itself.
2. There needs to be a strong sense of urgency. The Second World War drove the urgency of the original skunk works. The successful skunk works must also be driven by a sense of urgency, such as the threat of competition.
3. The skunk works should have a powerful top management supporter, sponsor or champion. This champion has an important multi-functional role. First, the champion must protect the skunk works from the rest of the organization. Second, the champion must make sure that the required resources are available. Finally, the champion may play a role in transitioning the project to the corporate mainstream.
4. The skunk works must have freedom from the regular organizational processes and bureaucracy.
5. The skunk works need a special hands-on leader, who is not only respected for his/her technical skills and intellect.
6. A successful skunk works is one characterized by informal processes with close personal interaction. One task of the leader is to spur the creation of this type of environment.
7. There must be a strategy for commercializing the skunk works output (Single and Spurgeon, 1996). The first skunk works was also driven by customer satisfaction; and had only one demanding client, the US War Department. Accordingly, skunk works needs to be customer- and product-orientated. The more well defined the customer, the better.

8. The organization and the skunk works must have the ability to understand and handle the important transitions: the market and the organization.
9. Innovations fail more often than they succeed; as a result, skunk works that are designed on a 'one-shot deal' basis face huge odds. Successful skunk works should be long-term programmes with the portfolio approach in mind (Gwynne, 1997).
10. The skunk works should not only be culturally distant from the rest of the organization, but physically/geographically distant as well. The distance is in part symbolic, but it has other effects. For example, the distance and isolation helps, among other things, to rapidly create group cohesiveness, which can be instrumental in group dynamics and performance.

The establishment of a skunk works is typically an admission by management that their organization is no longer capable of competing with other organizations, especially smaller, entrepreneurial ones, in the production of innovations. As stated above, skunk work programmes can be symptomatic of organizational and management dysfunction instead of organizational and management success.

There is evidence, albeit anecdotal, that large corporations are having success with skunk works. Much of Motorola's Razr mobile phone, for example, was developed in a new laboratory that the company set up in Chicago, 50 miles from its main R&D facility in suburban Illinois. With lots of bright colours and no dividing walls, the building and design of the laboratory's workspace was very different from Motorola's main offices. Google has also created a skunk works – Google X – a laboratory whose mandate is to come up with technologies that sound more like plot contrivances from *Star Trek* than products that might satisfy the short-term demands of Google's shareholders. Although shrouded in secrecy, some of the projects Google X is supposedly working on include bringing internet access to undeveloped parts of the world.

There are, Brown (2004) points out, two partially related organizational challenges for skunk works. First, in order for them to occur on a frequent basis, the organization needs to foster a special type of culture, that allows independent creative action as well as tolerance and acceptance of failure. Secondly, nearly all skunk works require isolation and a counterculture environment, which are hard to maintain within the reach of the large corporation. It can be difficult to have a group inside the organization that has its own set of rules. Assuming it can be done, are the resulting innovations transformation or just incremental? A third challenge is the basic incongruity of skunk works, which, has been pointed out by Gwynne, is the fact that 'for maximum effectiveness skunk works need to operate in secrecy, but concurrently new technologies, innovations, new products and so on, must get rapid corporate acceptance and significant market exposure and publicity' (1997: 19). These are some of the challenges that have to be addressed when considering whether the skunk works is the right structure for an organization.

Accelerator structure

John Kotter (2012a) has redefined the concept of a structure within a structure, in order to unleash employee innovation. Kotter proposes that the most agile, innovative

Hierarchy

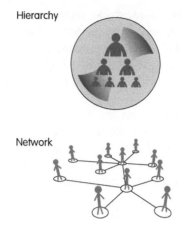

Network

Figure 9.2   Hierarchy and network structure working together

companies add a second operating system, built on a fluid, network-like structure, to continually formulate and implement strategy (see Figure 9.2). The second operating system should run on its own processes and be staffed by volunteers from throughout the company.

Kotter (2012a) proposes that there are processes – 'accelerators' – which enable such structures to work. The eight accelerators are:

1. *Creating a sense of urgency around a single big opportunity.* This is absolutely critical to heightening the organization's awareness that it needs continual strategic adjustments and that they should always be aligned with the biggest opportunity in sight. Urgency starts at the top of the hierarchy and it is important that leaders keep acknowledging and reinforcing it so that people will wake up every morning determined to find some action they can take in their day to move towards that opportunity.
2. *Building and maintaining a guiding coalition.* The core of a network is the guiding coalition (GC), which is made up of volunteers from throughout the organization. The GC is selected to represent each of the hierarchy's departments and levels, with a broad range of skills. It must be made up of people whom the leadership trusts, and must include at least a few outstanding leaders and managers. This ensures that the GC can gather and process information as no hierarchy ever could. All members of the GC are equal; no internal hierarchy slows down the transfer of information.
3. *Formulating a strategic vision and developing change initiatives designed to capitalize on the big opportunity.* The vision will serve as a strategic direction for the dual operating system. A well-formulated vision is focused on taking advantage of a big make-or-break opportunity. The right vision is feasible and easy to communicate. It is emotionally appealing as well as strategically smart. And it gives the GC a picture of success and enough information and direction to make consequential decisions, without having to seek permission at every turn.
4. *Communicating the vision and the strategy to create buy-in and attract a growing volunteer army.* A vividly formulated, high-stakes vision and strategy, promulgated

by a GC in ways that are both memorable and authentic, will prompt people to discuss them without the cynicism that often greets messages cascading down the hierarchy. If done properly, with creativity, such communications can go viral, attracting employees who buy in to the ambition of the message and begin to share a commitment to it.

5. *Accelerating movement toward the vision and the opportunity by ensuring that the network removes barriers.* For instance, Kotter (2012a) gives the example of the case where a sales representative receives a customer complaint about the bureaucracy in the company which he does not know how to fix or have time to think about. Someone in the network hears about this and says, 'I've seen that. I volunteer. I'll put together a group to address the issue.' That person writes up a description and sends it out to the volunteer army, and five people immediately step forward. They set up a call to begin learning why this is happening, figuring out how to remove the barrier and designing a solution – a better CRM system, perhaps. The team probably includes someone from IT who has technical expertise and can help identify where the money for the new system might come from. The team works with additional volunteers who have relevant information – from whatever quarter may be germane – to act quickly and efficiently. The time between the first call and this point might be two weeks, which Kotter (2012a) defines as a model of accelerated action. The network team settles on a practical solution that properly supports the sales team. Then its members take their thinking to their boss, who gives feedback and may offer the budget and the resources.

6. *Celebrating visible, significant short-term wins.* A network's credibility will not last long without confirmation that its decisions and actions are actually benefiting the organization. Sceptics will erect obstacles unless they see proof that the dual operating system is creating real results. As people have only so much patience, proof must come quickly. To ensure success, the best short-term wins should be obvious, unambiguous and clearly related to the vision.

7. *Never letting up.* This means that organizations should keep learning from experience and not declare victory too soon. They must continue to carry out strategic initiatives and create new ones, to adapt to shifting business environments, and thus to enhance their competitive positions.

8. *Institutionalizing strategic changes in the culture.* No strategic initiative, big or small, is complete until it has been incorporated into day-to-day activities. A new direction or method must sink into the very culture of the enterprise and it will do so if the initiative produces visible results.

The model above is based on Kotter's eight-step change process. The difference with the accelerator model is that it is cyclical – a much better way to show the process of change.

Organizational design

The fact that many different kinds of organizational structure exist, as outlined earlier in this chapter, suggests that no one type will be suitable for all organizations. Instead, each form of organizational structure possesses unique strengths and weaknesses that make it appropriate for some situations and not for others. Structuring an organization involves making well-considered choices from the various alternatives available. Organization design is the process of making these choices. In this process managers diagnose the change confronting their organization and then select and implement the structure that seems most appropriate, within the context in which the organization operates.

This is the contingency approach to organizational design. It recognizes that the organization is a complex, open system in an equally complex environment. There is therefore no optimal design. The mix of hierarchy, flexibility, centralization, working teams and so on will be unique, with every principle somewhere in the structure. The contingency approach recognizes common elements and themes but stresses the unique nature of the situation. To improve or change the structure the various contingencies need to be examined, including the relationships between the various variables – externally and internally to the organization (see Chapter 6).

So the process of organization design is consciously adaptive and is guided by the principle that the degree to which a particular type of structure will contribute to the effectiveness of an organization depends on contingency factors that impinge on the organization and shape its business (Priem and Rosenstein, 2000). The process is complex, requiring considerable thought into the links between the organization and its environment.

Environmental uncertainty and organization design

The aim of organizational design is to redesign the organization in order to address changes in the external and internal environment. Two important studies have examined how organizational structures adjust to changing environments. The first study was conducted by Burns and Stalker (1961), into diverse bases of internal structure; and the second one was carried out by Lawrence and Lorsch (1967), who applied the ideas of differentiation and integration.

The key contribution of the study by Burns and Stalker (1961) is the typology for characterizing how organizational structures adapt to change. The study identified *mechanistic* organizations, which have rigid structures in contrast to organic organizations that are flexible and adaptable to change. Mechanistic structures are highly formalized and centralized. Communication tends to follow formal channels and employees are given specific job descriptions delineating their roles and responsibilities. These forms have the downside of inhibiting entrepreneurial action and discouraging the use of individual initiative on the part of employees. Not only do mechanistic structures have disadvantages for innovativeness, but they also limit individual autonomy and self-determination, which will likely lead to lower levels of intrinsic motivation on the job (Colvin and Slevin, 1988). The main advantage of a mechanistic structure is its efficiency. Therefore, in organizations that are trying to maximize efficiency and minimize costs, mechanistic structures provide advantages. Examples of organizations using mechanistic structures include schools and universities.

In contrast to mechanistic structures, organic structures are flexible and decentralized, with low levels of formalization. In organizations with an organic structure, communication lines are more fluid and flexible. Employee job descriptions are broader and employees are asked to perform duties based on the specific needs of the organization at the time as well as their own expertise levels. These structures tend to be conducive to entrepreneurial behaviour and innovativeness (Colvin and Slevin, 1988). For example, Google has an organic structure.

Burns and Stalker (1961) found that in stable environments, mechanistic organizations were more successful; and in unstable and uncertain environments, organic organizations did better. The implications of this are important. Although, as Naylor (2004) points out, we should not react to the descriptions of mechanistic and organic by saying that the first is bad and the second good. In reality, organizations vary from these ideal types. First, functions may be mixed; for example, an organization may run its operations in a mechanistic style and its Research & Development organically. Second, organizations may face diverse parts of the environment in different ways – consumers against business customers. Third, organizations may adapt their structures as the environment changes. In today's changing environment, many successful organizations run on organic lines. At the same time many mechanistic structures exist which serve the needs of their customers.

Lawrence and Lorsch's contingency approach

Paul Lawrence and Jay Lorsch (1967) conducted a series of studies into the appropriate structure and functioning of organizations using what has become known as the organization and environment approach, described in their seminal book of that title. Lawrence and Lorsch began their analysis with the question of why people seek to build organizations. Their answer is that organizations enable people to find better solutions to the environmental problems facing them. This explanation immediately highlights three key elements in their approach to understanding organizational behaviour: (i) people, not organizations, have purposes; (ii) people have to come together to coordinate their different activities into an organization; and (iii) the effectiveness of an organization is judged by the adequacy with which the members' needs are satisfied through planned transactions with the environment.

Lawrence and Lorsch found that to cope effectively with their external environments, organizations must develop segmented units, each of which has as its major task the problem of dealing with some aspect of the conditions outside the firm. For example, in a manufacturing firm with production, sales and design units, the production unit deals with production equipment sources, raw materials sources and labor markets; the sales unit faces problems with the market, the customers and the competitors; and the design unit has to cope with technological developments, governmental regulations, and so on. This differentiation of function and task is accompanied by differences in cognitive and emotional orientation among the managers in different units, and differences, too, in the formal structure of different departments. For instance, the development department may have a long-term time horizon and a very informal structure, whereas the production department may be dealing with day-to-day problems in a rigidly formal system, with the sales department facing the medium-term effects of competitors' advertising with moderate formality. Even so, the organization is a system that has to be coordinated so that a state of collaboration exists to obtain for members the benefits of effective transactions with the environment. This is the required integration, and it, too, is affected by the nature of the external conditions.

The basic necessity for both appropriate differentiation and adequate integration to perform effectively in the external environment is at the core of Lawrence and Lorsch's model of organizational functioning. They looked at the structures of ten companies in the plastics industry, food industry and container industry, to assess their degrees of differentiation and integration, and found that:

- the organizations that did best had internal structures that permitted high differentiation while promoting matching integration;
- organizations needed to match their differentiation to their environment – more complexity meant higher differentiation; and
- more differentiation required more attention to integration.

The research of Lawrence and Lorsch emphasized that the appropriate organizational structure will depend on the environmental demands, thus taking a contingency approach, and rejecting the formulation that one particular structural form is always best. Their conclusion was that appropriateness is the key.

Assessing existing structures – the star model

The Star model, developed by Jay Galbraith in the 1960s, provides a holistic and integrative approach to organization design. The framework consists of a series of design policies that are controllable by management and can influence employee behaviour. The policies are the tools with which management must become skilled in order to shape the decisions and behaviours of their organizations effectively. The first policy is *strategy*, which determines direction. The second is *structure*, which determines the location of decision-making power. The third is *processes*, which have to do with the flow of information; they are the means of responding to information technologies. The fourth is *rewards* and reward systems, which influence the motivation of people to perform and address organizational goals. The fifth category of the model is made up of policies relating to *people*, which influence and frequently define the employees' mindsets and skills.

There are a number of implications of the Star model, which Galbraith highlights. The first is that organizational design is more than just structure. Most design efforts invest far too much time drawing the organization chart and far too little on processes and rewards. Structure is usually over-emphasized because it affects status and power, and a change to it is most likely to be reported in the business press and announced throughout the company. The second implication is that different strategies lead to different organizations. Although this seems obvious, it has ramifications that are often overlooked. There is no one-size-fits-all organization design that all companies – regardless of their particular strategy needs – should subscribe to. There will always be a current design that has become fashionable. But no matter what the fashionable design is – whether it is the matrix design or the virtual corporation – trendiness is not sufficient reason to adopt an organization design. All designs have merit but not for all companies in all circumstances. The design, or combination of designs, that should be chosen is the one that best meets the criteria derived from the strategy. A third implication of the Star model is in the interweaving nature of the lines that form the star shape. For an organization to be effective, all the policies must be aligned and interacting harmoniously. An alignment of all the policies will communicate a clear, consistent message to the company's employees. The Star model therefore provides a guiding framework for organizational design. It shows the levers that managers and leaders can control and as a result can affect employee behaviour. It also shows that managers can influence culture, but only through design polices that affect behaviour.

Tests of fitness

Michael Goold and Andrew Campbell (2002) have identified tests of fitness to assess existing organizational structures (see Table 9.1) and tests to use for general good organizational redesign principles (see Table 9.2). Considering these tests of fitness may help to assess the current strengths and limitations of an existing structure and define what a restructure should address.

Table 9.1   Test of fitness to assess existing organizational structures

Drivers of fitness	Tests of fitness
Service strategy	Service advantage test: does the design pay sufficient attention to the priorities in each service area?
Corporate strategy	Parenting test: does the design pay sufficient attention to the strategic initiatives and add value to the organization?
People	People test: does the design adequately reflect the motivation, strengths and weaknesses of the available people?
Constraints	Feasibility test: does the design take account of constraints that might make the proposal unworkable?

Table 9.2   Design tests

Design principles	Design tests
Specialization	Specialist culture test: do any units have or need a specialist culture? And do these units have enough protection from the dominant culture?
Coordination	Difficult links test: does the organization need any coordination that is difficult to achieve on a networking basis?
Knowledge and competence	Redundant hierarchy test: do all levels in the organization's workforce hierarchy add value?
Control and commitment	Accountability test: does the design enable economical and motivating control processes?
Innovation and adaptation	Flexibility test: will the design help the development of new strategies and be flexible enough to adapt to future changes?

Activity

Examine your organization, or one you are familiar with, using the questions in Tables 9.1 and 9.2. If any of your answers fall short of your ideal, consider how they might be addressed.

Changing structures

In this section we discuss some of the common structural changes, such as downsizing, as a form of organizational restructure, and also mergers and acquisitions. We provide examples of companies that have confronted such changes and also draw from our own experiences to identify the key issues and challenges faced when restructuring. In his book *Inside Story*, Greg Dyke, the former Director-General of the BBC, writes that 'there is no perfect organizational structure and constant rethinking is healthy for any organization' (2004: 162). Dyke describes how he set about transforming what he saw as a deeply unhappy organization:

> We either change or we simply manage decline gracefully. The changes happening in technology, in the wider society, and in our competitive environment, make this one of these times when change at the BBC is essential. (2004: 160)

Dyke went on to remove management layers, disband divisions, centralize functions such as marketing, and merge the old executive committee with the BBC's Board of Management to create one management group running the BBC. The reorganized structure – known as the 'One BBC'– was drawn up on paper as a series of colourful petals, with Dyke at the centre to demonstrate a less hierarchical organization.

Changes in the structure of an organization, such as the BBC, can be triggered by external or internal events. The triggers may result in the need for a restructure, or may create the driver for a merger or acquisition. For example Airbus, formerly known as EADS, the European aerospace group, carried out a significant reshaping of its corporate structure by reducing the group to three core divisions, through a radical shake-up and rebranding of its defence businesses. The changes followed the collapse of a €36 billion merger with BAE Systems. The significant restructuring of its diverse defence operations was an attempt to make them more profitable and competitive. Three operations were being merged into one Airbus defence and space division, based in Munich: Cassidian, the current Munich-based unit; Astrium, the space division headquartered in Paris that makes ballistic missiles for the French military; and Airbus Military, based in Madrid. It was not a comfortable transformation for the company's state shareholders. France and Germany were nervous about the future of the core defence technologies and there was a fear of job losses. However, the restructure was necessary to move the business forward.

When Maersk – the container shipping company – decided to restructure it also faced significant challenges. Benjamin Paul outlines the challenges and approach that Maersk took in the case study below.

Customer-facing organization restructuring in the Maersk Line in Vietnam

Container shipping is an intensely competitive industry. Price competition between shipping lines combined with the volatility of the global economy has resulted in poor profitability for all the key industry players over recent years. Maersk Line is the market leader in container shipping. Maersk Line's strategy is to maintain its leading position and achieve higher profitability than its competitors by delivering the highest level of service, with the most competitive operating costs in the industry. Maersk Line has offices in 125 countries, each with a dedicated customer-service function.

One project that helped to deliver on this strategy was the reorientation of the global customer service organization. Maersk Line also operates a number of global service centres in India, China and Philippines, where back office functions are carried out. The aims of the project were to remove transactional and labour-intensive tasks from the front-line customer service organizations and centralize them in the service centres. At the same time, the role of the country-based customer service organization would change to become less administrative and more focused on adding value to customers through enhanced service delivery.

Each country was tasked with running the change project themselves, under the guidance of a steering committee that included stakeholders from the Global project team. The Country project teams were to first review their processes and identify those that could be moved and those that would remain based on the global guidelines and local practices. They were then to design and implement the new customer service model, which would first of all include the transfer of tasks to the service centres staff, whose roles would shift in focus from an administrative to a more consultative role. In Vietnam, the project team was led by the Country Customer Service Manager, Trang. During the initial analysis phase, 82 tasks were identified to be moved from the front office to the shared service centres. The project included a number of significant challenges.

Due to the reduction in transactional tasks, the number of customer service staff in Vietnam was to be reduced by 14 people, from 45 to 31. The new model also meant that there would be dedicated people in Manila who would now work exclusively for the Vietnam organization. Although there would be a separate manager in Manila for that team, the team would have a 'one team' approach to ensure consistency of service delivery towards the customers. The challenge was to ensure an effective new organizational structure and seamless processes between two sites, whilst improving the services offered to customers.

The changes required significant training and competence development. The staff at the Manila service centre would need to be trained in the new processes. The staff that remained in Vietnam would need to develop new skills in order to become more customer-focused. The changes demanded several cultural shifts. Processes had to be split between two different country sites. The move towards a more customer-focused organization involved changing attitudes and approaches.

The project was initiated in March 2012. The organizational changes and handover of processes were conducted over a 6-month period and signed off by the steering committee in October 2012. At sign off, the project was considered to be extremely successful. Staff engagement had actually increased and reached a record high. Customers remained as happy as they had been before the change and the new processes run between the two sites were delivering in line with the targets set.

(Continued)

(Continued)

The success can be attributed to several elements. First, there was strong alignment between all stakeholders towards the change. All of the management team spoke with one voice in support of the project and continuous communication of the benefits that it would bring internally. The impact on individuals was also managed extremely well. Those that were not to have a role in the future organization were offered extensive support both financially and emotionally. Every effort was made to reposition people within the organization, or if that was not possible, support was given to help them to find jobs outside the company. For those that were to remain, excitement was generated through communication of an enticing vision of the future where their roles would be more interesting and customer-focused. With a team that was already engaged around offering service excellence, the opportunity to spend more time on value-adding tasks was received positively. Continuous communication and dialogue was the hallmark of this change. Opportunities for feedback and continuous updates to staff meant that they were involved in every step of the change. Management of the handover of tasks to the service centres was planned and executed well. Structures were built to effectively manage the new processes, including clear key performance indicators and service level agreements that were focused around customer outcomes and process capabilities. Regular meetings, multi-level dialogue and escalation processes were established. Culturally, much was done to encourage a one-team approach, with front-line staff from Vietnam being involved in training the staff in the Philippines. Joint teambuilding was conducted to develop social bonds. Care was taken to encourage use of the right language in both organizations, for example the use of 'we' instead of 'us and them'.

Strong leadership and meticulous planning were the key elements underpinning the success of the project. The project leader enjoyed a high level of credibility in the organization and was able to command trust from her staff. Although this was a project that was initiated as a top-down exercise, the execution was bottom-up, from identifying processes to migrate to handover and training. The entire team was involved and their input was considered throughout. Following the sign-off of the new structure, it was recognized by the organization that this was not the end, but only a milestone in the change process. Sustaining the changes will include continually working to improve the ability of the new structure to meet the long-term aim of delivering a better level of customer satisfaction. Continuation of leadership alignment, staff engagement and continuous communication of priorities will be important in reaching these goals.

© 2015 Benjamin Paul, Country Manager, Maersk Line.

Discussion Questions

1   What made this a successful project in Maersk?
2   What did Maersk do to ensure the changes were sustained?

Downsizing

Downsizing refers to interventions aimed at reducing the size of the organization. This typically is accomplished by decreasing the number of employees through redundancies,

Table 9.3   Types of downsizing (adapted from DeWitt, 1998)

Type of downsizing	Characteristics
Retrenchment	This is done by centralizing or specializing a firm's operations to sustain or improve productivity. It is brought about by reengineering jobs and amenities. This form of downsizing may increase the economies of scale and help maintain a competitive advantage.
Downscaling	This is constituted by permanent alterations to employment and tangible resource capacity. This reduces the firm's economies of scale and competitive market share.
Downscoping	This is when the firm divests activities or markets in which it operates. This is done by reducing the vertical and/or horizontal differentiation.

attrition, redeployment or early retirement, or by reducing the number of organizational units or management layers through divestiture (see the case study below of Sterling Software and CNS) or outsourcing. As can be seen in Table 9.3, there are a variety of approaches to downsizing, including retrenchment, downscaling and downscoping. The reasons for organizations undertaking this type of change are varied. They include the closing or selling of a business unit, increased productivity through greater efficiency and effectiveness, and coping with external pressures, including economic recessions and downturns, technological change and increased competitive pressures through greater globalization of business.

The prime reason for downsizing tends to be to reduce costs. Iberia, the Spanish airline, for example, announced it would axe 22% of its workforce in 2013 as part of a series of cost-cutting measures; while in 2012 Hewlett–Packard announced they were to lay off 27,000 employees. In the same year UBS, the Swiss bank, initiated the most significant overhaul of an investment bank since the 2008 financial crisis. The shake-up aimed to cut UBS staff numbers by a sixth and its risk-weighted assets by a third and leave the bank focused on its wealth management business supported by a much smaller investment bank. According to Cummins and Worley (2009), planned downsizing interventions tend to proceed with the following stages:

Stage 1: Clarify the organization's strategy. As a first step leaders need to specify the strategy and communicate how downsizing relates to it. They need to provide opportunities for employees to voice their concerns, ask questions and obtain support when required from the human resources department.

Stage 2: Assess downsizing options and make relevant choices. Once the strategy is clear the options for downsizing need to be identified and assessed. Often organizations will choose the obvious solutions such as redundancies because they can be implemented quickly. This action tends to create a climate of uncertainty and fear as staff focus on whose roles will be made redundant and who will leave the organization. Rather than going for the first obvious and quick option, leaders should involve employees in the decision-making process, and consider other ways of addressing the issues. This can help create a sense of urgency for identifying and implementing options for downsizing rather than the obvious reaction of redundancies. Participation will also provide employees with a clearer understanding of the rationale for the downsizing and increase the likelihood that whatever choices are made are perceived as fair and employees are committed to them.

Stage 3: Implement the changes. This stage involves implementing the methods for reducing the size of the organization. Specific areas of inefficiency and high cost need to be identified and targeted. The morale of the staff can be hurt if departments or teams known to have a decline in their performance are left untouched. Specific actions should be linked to the organization's strategy. Employees need to be reminded consistently that downsizing activities are part of a plan to improve the performance of the organization. Leaders and managers also need to communicate frequently using a variety of media. This keeps people informed and helps to lower their anxiety about the downsizing.

Stage 4: Address the needs of the survivors and those who leave the organization. Managers need to give attention to staff who are staying with the organization as they will feel concerned about seeing their colleagues leave the company, the security of their own job and the increased workload they may have to take on as a result of fewer employees. For staff who are leaving the organization, it is important that they have outplacement support to help them find another job.

Stage 5: Follow through with growth plans. This final stage of downsizing involves implementing a process of organizational renewal and growth. Failure to move quickly to implement growth plans is a key cause of ineffective downsizing. Leaders and managers must ensure that employees understand the renewal strategy and their new roles in it. Employees need reassurance that, although the organization has been through a tough time, their renewed efforts can help move it forward.

Human challenges of downsizing

Downsizing can be difficult for all who are involved and there are almost always employee morale issues to deal with as a result of downsizing. The three main groups affected are employees who leave the organization, survivors (those who remain in the organization) and the managers of the two groups. The reactions of each of the groups will be different. Being aware of the impact of managing the change on the individuals and responding to concerns, as well as providing communications and next steps after the downsizing is complete, is a crucial managerial responsibility.

Employees who leave the organization

Staff who lose their jobs will experience the fear and uncertainty of how they are going to be able to find new employment, particularly in a tough economic climate. This may lead them to question how the decision was reached to make their roles redundant. Unsatisfactory answers may generate anger. It is vital to emphasize that it is the roles that are being made redundant, not the people. Individuals who have lost their job need time to look for redeployment opportunities in the company or jobs externally. Outplacement support needs to be provided for such employees to help them find another job.

Survivors

The staff who remain in the organization – the survivors – may also experience fear about the uncertainty of their jobs and what the future holds for them in the organization. This can lead to low morale, anxiety, mistrust of management and a drop in productivity. This type of reaction, known as 'survivor syndrome', can affect the realization of the benefits from the downsizing. Managers need to reassure staff and identify ways of improving their morale by addressing their uncertainties and fears. Staff that remain may be anxious about being overburdened with an excessive workload. There should be an expectation that people can say 'this is too much' and that they will be given help to prioritize and cope with any additional work. Survivors need the opportunity to vent their worries, but they also need to be given the opportunity to articulate what their professional ambitions are for the future and, importantly, identify what practical steps, however small, can be taken towards achieving that goal.

It is important that the staff who remain with the organization see and feel that the redundancy process is handled appropriately. They have to see that those who were forced to exit the organization were looked after and given an opportunity to say goodbye.

When cutting costs, it can be tempting to cut non-staff costs to avoid making redundancies but the staff who survive will need to be supported in any new roles they are taking on or additional work they are given, so managers have to ensure that there is a training and development budget that can be used soon after the restructuring. This provides a good opportunity to engage the employees who remain and show that they are valued members of the organization.

Managers

Leaders and managers who employ downsizing need to question whether these measures will benefit their organization and create an improved structure. If they feel they do then managers need to identify good practice in downsizing rather than employing knee-jerk reactions such as hasty cost-reduction techniques. Managers responsible for making roles redundant and managing the remaining staff may find their team demoralized and demotivated. It is important that managers are given support from human resources staff to address such issues. Studies have suggested that, where downsizing programmes adopt appropriate OD interventions they generate more positive results for individuals and the organization (for example Cameron, 1994; Ryan and Macky, 1998). However, success depends on identifying the right interventions at an individual, team or organizational level and evaluating the effectiveness of them (see Chapter 8 for more information on OD interventions).

Whether they are maintaining existing structures or implementing new ones, managers and leaders need to know about the different types of structures, as well as their appropriateness and their strengths and weaknesses. In addition, they must be able to diagnose and react to the various factors that influence the effectiveness of each type of structure. They must also be able to recognize how a particular organization structure fits their company's specific business situation and needs.

The case of Sterling Software and CNS, written by Jonathan Reeves, illustrates how a divestiture can be successful.

Divestiture at Sterling Software and CNS

In 2002 CNS split away from Sterling Software. CNS was a software manufacturer that created mobile business applications, that is to say software that manages a company's external data environment for end users. Sterling, the world's third largest software company, had acquired CNS a few years previously, amidst a great fanfare. Sterling, now IBM, sells high-end CRM software solutions to large corporate clients. Their acquisition of CNS was to grant them a competitive edge and a slice of the dynamic mobile applications market. Thereafter they became Sterling's Managed System Division. Personal Data Assistants, similar to iPad and iPhones, had not yet been invented. Palm pilots and a myriad of other hand-held data devices started appearing and the mobile market was set for an explosion, as evidenced a decade later.

CNS's marriage was not a happy one. The bride did not exactly look ugly in the morning but she was never fully understood. Sterling Software's senior management had a problem that was largely of their own making. Sterling, for all its size, was really four separate and autonomous business units located under one communal roof. Each division had a niche and sold independently of the other. This made amalgamating CNS into the collective a tall order and one that was never issued. In today's market such a merger is unlikely to have been enacted and would not have survived due diligence. However, during the dotcom boom, speculative purchases were common place. Large corporations, buoyed by record share prices and their associated resources, adopted a predatory posture, acquiring firms lower down the food chain.

In 2002 the dotcom bubble burst. A few industry analysts, like Gartmore, had been predicting this for some time and even more afterwards. The 'new' economy, sharing the hallmarks of recent events, was thought to be bullet-proof and immune to the mechanizations of a more classical market. Investors scrambled for safe havens, withdrew funds and the Nasdaq collapsed. Sterling was hit, but not terminally. The senior management had to undertake a period of rationalization and overdue sobriety. They determined that CNS did not fit with Sterling's future core business focus. CNS was divested four months later.

Change for CNS manifested into three major components: the psychological, physical and financial. Emotionally you either welcome it or are adverse to the concept, depending on your natural disposition. *Psychological* portrays how your firm is perceived, not only internally but also by the wider market. These, essential stakeholders, consist of customers, suppliers and competitors. The *physical* depicts sourcing new offices and relocating servers and other equipment. The *financial* component reflects the impact that change has on the corporation's resources. This affects budgets and salaries. These three components are by-products of each other and are not mutually exclusive.

Working for a large MNC (multinational corporation) carries a certain amount of kudos. They seek to attract the best in their relentless war of talent. Working for a global leader makes the incumbent employees more desirable and regular targets for head-hunters. The transition to SME (small, medium enterprise) status is a little like being downgraded. Leveraging industry recognition is an important weapon in an MNC's arsenal. This is why dominant industry leaders deploy vast marketing resources to lock in their positions. Marketing, PR and other activities make prospective clients and partners more receptive to the firm's agents. CNS's divestiture removed many of the capabilities that they currently enjoyed and would impact on their ability to compete thereafter.

As touched on previously, CNS was never actually fully embedded into Sterling Software. This made leaving no great upheaval. Thus, the physical detachment process became the salient feature. The indigenous teams all worked together and had minimal interaction with the other divisions. There was no pervasive dominant culture, with each unit having their own independent hierarchy. The management systems did not have to be altered, to any great extent, as they were not integrated. This made the MSD (Managed Systems Division) a firm within a firm. That played well for the divestiture and partly explains why they were divested. New offices had to be sourced, which would not be as comfortable as Sterling's Stockley Park, complete with a golf course and Japanese fighting fish.

From the financial perspective, CNS could not afford to lose key people. This was potentially one of the biggest threats to the change. However, the freefall of the technology sector made finding better employment an unlikely proposition. Most were buttoning down the hatches to ride out the storm. Had the divestiture taken place in a more buoyant period, CNS would have suffered a mass exodus. At the very least, they would have had to commit considerable resources to retain their best employees. As things stood, they lost very few employees and could jettison through redundancy those that were surplus to requirements. Most of the senior management team stayed on or those that left were rapidly replaced.

Continuity in a sea of change is crucial, especially if the waters are tepid. CNS's directors attempted to manage the story as best they could. They needed to keep their employees and clients happy. Potential customers would have to be informed without jeopardizing any unsigned contracts. The divestiture was spun in a positive light and positioned as hard-won independence. CNS would have their own resources and could act autonomously free from the bureaucracy and centralization. Once the *message* had been internally crystallized and accepted, it was then ready for external proliferation. Special efforts were expended in consulting with key partners and clients. The directors intervened where necessary to fire-fight. Communication and transparency were the main objectives. In a disruptive environment rumours can spring from nowhere and only have to be repeated enough to be cemented as fact.

In reality, CNS's exodus was fairly painless. They had always retained their SME mentality and never lost their identity. Essentially, it was business as usual. The goal of managing the change was continuity of business against a backdrop of uncertainty. To migrate control from Sterling without affecting the core business functions that lie underneath was the real challenge. Planning and good execution were key features of this success. The motivation of the staff and management in making sure everyone was 'on message' and consistent. It was in everyone's interest to succeed when your collective value has been brought into question. That can inspire loyalty, spirit and a togetherness that few companies could ever hope to emulate. After a successful divestiture, CNS was acquired by another software manufacturer in 2006.

© 2015 Jonathan Reeves, Partner at Act Partnership Ltd.

Discussion Questions

1 What helped to make the divestiture of CNS relatively painless?
2 What factors could have hindered the divestiture?
3 What key factors need to be considered when managing a divestiture?

Mergers and acquisitions

Mergers and acquisitions (M&As) present a complicated challenge, as they involve the combination of separate companies, departments, functions and units. The benefits of a merger or acquisition can be considerable, such as economies of scale, greater sales revenue and market share, broader diversification and increased tax efficiency. However, the reality of managing a merger or acquisition is complex. We discuss the complexities in this section. We begin by clarifying what is meant by the terms 'merger' and 'acquisition'.

Definitions of mergers

Definitions of what constitutes a merger vary. According to Sudarsanam (2003), a *merger* takes place when two or more companies come together to combine and share their resources to achieve common objectives. The shareholders of the combining companies often remain as joint owners of the combined entity. In contrast, Sherman and Hart (2006) define a merger as a combination of two or more companies in which the assets and liabilities of the selling company are absorbed by the buying firm. While Gaughan (2002) says that a merger is a process in which two companies combine and only one survives, and the merged company ceases to exist, or there is a combination of two companies where both the companies cease to exist and an entirely new company is created. From the various definitions it would appear that a merger involves the mutual decision of two relatively equal companies to combine to become one legal entity with the goal of producing a company that is worth more than the sum of its parts. In a merger of two corporations, the shareholders usually have their shares in the old company exchanged for an equal number of shares in the merged entity. The case study below, which is written by David Wardrop-White, describes his experience of a merger between two hospitals.

CASE STUDY

Merging two hospitals

This case study concerns the closing of a hospital specializing in maternity care – in this instance, healthcare for mother and infant during and after the birth. The hospital was the smallest in the group of three urban maternity units and, while physically connected to the largest by a link corridor, it retained its own identity as a quieter, more home-like place in which to give birth. It also offered accommodation in single rooms (opposed to hospital wards shared with numbers of other patients) as a matter of course rather than solely on medical grounds. But the key difference between this hospital and its two larger sister units was in clinical care: here the baby was delivered by the family doctor – the 'general practitioner' (GP), in the public health service – rather than by a specialist in obstetrics and gynaecology (O&G), as was the case in the other two units and indeed through most of the health service in the country. This same GP or GP partnership would probably have cared for the mother and her family for several or many years before the birth and would continue to do so afterwards as part of their 'whole family' medical care.

The key driver for closing Queen Anne's Hospital was the increasing concern on the part of the O&G specialists about the risks to mother and baby which arose as a result of this different, less specialist clinical care. Patients coming to Queen Anne's were under the care of their GP from the start of their pregnancy, through delivery, to the care of the child in his/her early years. However, if complications arose during or after childbirth, the mother and/or her child would be speedily transferred to the adjacent major hospital and to the clinical care of an O&G and/or paediatric specialist. The increased frequency with which such transfers were occurring, coupled with the fact that they by definition presented as emergencies, was causing anxiety amongst the hospital's O&G and paediatric specialists. In addition, advances in diagnostic tools and approaches to treatment were opening a gap between what was routine for the hospital specialists and what was normal for the GP caring for a mother-to-be or mother and baby. Finally, the number of pregnancies in the country and in the city was falling, reducing further the already limited opportunities available to GPs to care for a mother in and after childbirth and develop their clinical experience as a result.

Accordingly, the decision was taken by the health authority that Queen Anne's should be closed and all births and aftercare accommodated in the adjacent main hospital. I was responsible for the non-clinical administration of both hospitals and for managing the changes involved.

The closure of Queen Anne's involved several key elements:

- *Hospital O&G and paediatrics staff agreeing with GPs an alternative approach that enabled the GP to continue as far as possible to care for his/her patient.* This was initially difficult: GPs wanted to continue attending their own patients in and after childbirth, but now in the major hospital. The O&G team were very wary of this concept, seeing the potential for 'two-tier' obstetric care and a continued flow of emergency transfers to their clinical care, albeit without the hasty transit along the corridor linking them to Queen Anne's. Eventually, following some hard work by my clinical leadership colleagues (on a doctor-talking-to-doctor basis) agreement was reached on protocols that satisfied both groups, managed their concerns and the risks they perceived, and provided a good service to the patients involved.
- *Reassigning or relocating staff currently working in Queen Anne's.* The staff working in Queen Anne's were, with one exception (see Lessons Learnt), successfully integrated into the major hospital. Many had worked in both locations and their physical proximity meant little personal disruption for most of them. Some nursing staff in particular welcomed the greater opportunities for building their experience and skill through permanently working in the larger unit.
- *Communicating with patients, the community, staff in the major hospital, and other stakeholders.* I was fortunate that effective communications systems (oral and written) already existed within the hospitals and that the GPs were committed to informing their own patients of the planned changes. Together with my clinical colleagues, I increased the number of staff briefings and visited a number of GP practices personally for one-to-one updates.

The biggest challenge was to build sufficient trust between two key groups of stakeholders (GPs and hospital O&G specialists) so that together they could find a new way of working that met the needs of both. While all were members of a relatively small medical community in and around the city, their opportunities for building relationships, other than through the referral on paper of patients to each other, were limited. Conventional concepts of hierarchy were also less evident in the medical profession than in many others, which meant that much had to be achieved by peer influence and persuasion rather than through command and control.

Professional respect provided a good initial basis for building trust, but additional interventions were needed to accelerate the development of these key relationships. Accordingly, I arranged a series of meetings, workshops, presentations, one-to-one and two-on-two meetings, often with refreshments or a meal, to provide opportunities for this. Choosing the locations (initially, a neutral one), structuring and facilitating or leading the event carefully, and pitching the hospitality/catering at an appropriate level were all material factors in achieving this rapid rise in trust and collaborative working. I found it very helpful to

(Continued)

(Continued)

start the discussions with my clinical leadership colleagues about the design of a workshop or meeting by looking thoroughly at the perspectives, aspirations and concerns of the people who would be attending, and building the shape and style of the event on that platform. I also set up a project steering group, representing key stakeholders, which oversaw the changes and acted as a conduit for communications and feedback with the communities they represented.

Physically closing Queen Anne's ensured one part of the change was sustained – no more babies would be delivered there – but sustainability in the longer-term of the new way of working together required continued commitment, energy and time from the key stakeholders. Both groups (GPs and O&G specialists), to their considerable credit, explicitly recognized that they had to continue to approach this as a shared learning experience rather than a battle for power or control. Very soon, practitioners in each group recognized that there were unexpected and welcome benefits in the new process: GPs were seeing cutting-edge approaches to obstetrics in action while O&G specialists were gaining valuable first-hand insight in depth into the patient's medical history, family and background. It was also evident to both groups that, overall, fewer risks now attended childbirth. The steering group was wound up, and GPs were integrated into the regular meetings of the O&G specialists in the hospital.

Lessons learnt

First, the level of investment in building relationships was a key factor in achieving this change smoothly. I learned quickly that sending communications and building relationships are not synonymous: the time spent meeting key stakeholders on a one-to-one basis, and listening rather than talking, was critical.

Second, I worked hard to build a small core team across the key clinical disciplines, so that we could support, encourage and challenge each other, and produce good decisions.

Third, with dismay and hindsight, I learned that thorough mapping of stakeholders is crucial to sustaining an effective change. Somehow, I had not identified Jane as a stakeholder and I did not manage her well. Jane worked part-time for another organization in the city that provided baby milk products to new mothers, and she had been housed in Queen Anne's hospital some years previously simply because we had spare accommodation. She was therefore not in any of the chains of command or communication in the hospital, and I overlooked her. Too late, I realized that I didn't have the space she needed in the main hospital, and she spent many miserable weeks issuing baby milk to mothers from a desk stranded in our chilly main entrance hall, until we found a better solution. Attention to detail in identifying and understanding stakeholders was, I learned, critical to successful, sustained change.

Discussion Questions

1 What type of merger was carried out between the hospitals?
2 What key lessons can be learnt from this case about how to sustain change?
3 What could have been done differently and better?

Definition of acquisitions

An *acquisition* is the purchase of an asset such as a factory, a division or an entire company. Sudarsanam (1995) defines acquisition as an 'arm's-length deal', where one company purchases the shares of another company and the acquired company is no longer the owner of the firm. LinkedIn is a company that has grown through acquisitions. With more than 161 million subscribers to LinkedIn in 2013 it was significantly ahead of its competitors Viadeo (35 million) and XING (10 million). LinkedIn has acquired the start-up Rapportive, which created a browser plug-in that takes contact information from social networks such as Twitter and Facebook and places them into Google's Gmail. It has also acquired SlideShare, deemed 'the YouTube of slide shows', for $119 million. The purchase aimed to give LinkedIn members a way to discover people through content. Facebook is also an acquisitive company, having purchased virtual reality headset maker Oculus for $2 billion in cash and stock, as well as the messaging system WhatsApp for $19 billion in 2014. There have also been significant acquisitions in other parts of the globe. For example, Shoreline Energy International, a Nigerian conglomerate with interests that span oil and gas, power generation, commodities trading, infrastructure and construction across sub-Saharan Africa, partnered with UK-based Heritage Oil in acquiring a stake in OML 30, an oilfield asset in Nigeria for a reported $850 million.

According to Gaughan (2002), acquisitions are friendly transactions in which the senior management of the companies negotiate the terms of the deal and the terms are then put to the shareholders of the target company for their approval. The takeover of the British engineer Invensys for £3.4 billion by France's Schneider Electric was unanimously backed by the Invensys board. Sir Nigel Rudd, the company's chairman, said there was a 'strong strategic fit' between Invensys and Schneider.[1] With a combined workforce of more than 4,600 staff in the UK, and almost 160,000 staff worldwide, Schneider hoped the deal would raise its industrial automation business to the level of the world's main players, such as Siemens and Mitsubishi. However, it warned of wider job losses as it revealed plans for cost savings of around €140 million a year by 2016.

An example of another friendly acquisition is the Walt Disney Corporation's purchase of Pixar Animation Studios. In this case, Pixar's shareholders all approved the decision to be acquired. This approach is in contrast to a hostile takeover, where a different set of communications takes place between the target company and the acquirer. A company can initiate a hostile takeover of a smaller firm, which essentially amounts to buying the company in the face of resistance from the target company's management. This is what happened with Kraft's hostile takeover of Cadbury.

Drivers for mergers and acquisitions

When a little-known investment company called 3G Capital said it would buy the Miami-based fast-food chain Burger King for about $4 billion in 2012, an obvious

---

1   Szu Ping Chan, 'Invensys agrees £3.4bn takeover by Schneider', *The Telegraph*, 31 July 2013, www.telegraph.co.uk/finance/newsbysector/industry/engineering/10213147/Invensys-agrees-3.4bn-takeover-by-Schneider-Electric.html (accessed June 2014).

question that arose was: why are they doing this? Every merger or acquisition has its own unique reasons why the combining of two companies is a good business decision and adds value. Such reasons include: positioning; gap-filling; organizational competencies; broader market access; bargain purchase; competition; diversification; short-term growth; undervalued target and financial. We examine each of these next.

- *Positioning.* When companies need to position themselves to take advantage of emerging trends in the marketplace they can take advantage of future opportunities by merging with or acquiring another company. For instance, a telecommunications company might improve its position for the future if it were to own a broadband service company. Amazon began to build its position in the mapping business by acquiring 3D mapping start-up, UpNext. For Amazon, the acquisition marked a move into new territory that would help the company offer native mapping capabilities on its apps.
- *Gap-filling.* This enables a company to fill gaps in its offerings. For instance, one company may have a major weakness (such as poor distribution), whereas the other company has some significant strength in this area. By combining the two companies, each company closes strategic gaps that otherwise may prejudice long-term survival. For example, Microsoft acquired Yammer, a leading provider of enterprise social networks, for $1.2 billion in cash. Yammer added enterprise social networking to Microsoft's gap in its portfolio of cloud services. Similarly, to fill a gap in its programmes of enterprise applications, Oracle bought more than 30 firms for about $25 billion in total.
- *Organizational competencies.* Acquiring human resources and intellectual capital can help improve innovative thinking and development within a company. For example, Facebook has acquired talented staff and additional expertise from a number of companies it has bought, including enhanced content development (FriendFeed, Face.com), IP (Tagtile), location awareness (Gowalla) and e-commerce (Karma).
- *Broader market access.* Acquiring a foreign company can give a company quick access to global markets: for example, Tata's acquisition of Tetley tea (see case study below). While the merger between Exxon and Mobil allowed both companies a larger share of the oil and gas market.
- *Bargain purchase.* It may be cheaper to acquire another company than to invest internally. For example, if company A is considering expansion of facilities, and company B has very similar facilities that are idle, it may be cheaper for company A to acquire the company B with the unused facilities than to build new facilities itself.
- *Competition.* When faced with competition companies may well attempt to purchase the competitors' company. Facebook is known for buying its competition: for example, when Instagram threatened its image and mobile space, Facebook bought the company.
- *Diversification.* It may be necessary for a company to enter new markets to achieve more consistent long-term growth and profitability. For example, in 2012 IBM announced plans to spend $20 billion on acquisitions that would focus on

software rather than hardware for the next few years. Diversified groups are becoming the dominant form of business in many emerging markets, including Chile, Indonesia, Mexico, Pakistan, Thailand and India. The Tata Group has projected a new type of company onto the global stage which is more diversified than Western firms (see case study below).

- *Short-term growth.* Leaders may be under pressure to turn around sluggish growth and profitability. Consequently, they may decide on a merger or acquisition to boost poor performance in the short term. This is what CISCO did with the purchase of Pure Digital, the parent company of the bestselling camcorder, Flip. Having owned the company for less than two years, CISCO announced that it was shutting it down, in spite of Flip's enduring popularity. It had given CISCO the short-term entry it needed into the consumer market.

- *Undervalued target.* Some mergers are executed for 'financial' reasons and not strategic reasons. The target company may be undervalued and therefore represents a good investment. For example, Kohlberg Kravis and Roberts acquire poor performing companies. They replace the management team in the hope of increasing depressed values.

- *Financial.* Financial gains are a key driver for M&As for many companies. In 2013 Vodafone sold its 45% stake in Verizon Wireless to US telecoms group Verizon Communications for $130 billion in one of the biggest deals in corporate history. It was the third biggest corporate transaction, behind Vodafone's deal to buy Germany's Mannesmann and AOL's purchase of Time Warner. The reason for the sale was to allow Vodafone to invest money in its businesses, especially high-speed mobile phone networks.

When it comes to reasons for being acquired, Burger King has experienced them all: falling profits and sales, angry franchise owners, mediocre innovation and growing competition. 3G said it would be able to trim costs (though no more than 10%) and increase international expansion to make the deal work. Hence the 'Number 2' fast-food chain was taken over by a little-known company with a 'hands-on' management approach and an intention to invest in the brand. The first priority of 3G was a push to cut costs by starving the Burger King brand of capital and by making a large percentage of the staff roles redundant in Burger King's Miami headquarters. Not only did 3G not invest any capital in the company, it sucked $295 million out of the business. 3G eventually listed Burger King on the New York Stock Exchange, in a complex deal that resulted in the private equity firm owning 71% of Burger King with the rest owned by Justice Holdings, a special purpose acquisition company owned in part by hedge fund, Pershing Square Capital.

As in the case of Burger King, the outcomes of acquisitions can vary. On the one extreme, an acquired company may be left to operate similar to the way it has done in the past, except for minimal governance or operational changes. At the other extreme, an acquired company may be subject to a complete overhaul in its governance structures, human resource systems, financial systems and other operating systems, bringing these in line with the acquiring company. For other companies being acquired means that they are sucked into the acquiring company and disappear.

Due diligence

A key part of any M&A process which can help lead to its success and sustainability is known as 'due diligence'. Due diligence aims to explore every facet of the company that is to be acquired or merged with – the target company – in as much detail as possible prior to the final agreement. An over-riding question for due diligence is: will this merger or acquisition work? To answer this question, leaders must determine what kind of fit exists between the two companies. The types of fit and examples of the questions to be considered for each are outlined in the box below.

Types of fit

- *Investment fit.* What financial resources will be required; what level of risk fits with the merger/acquired organization?
- *Strategic fit.* What management strengths are brought together through this merger/acquisition? Both sides must bring something unique to the table to create synergies.
- *Marketing fit.* How will products and services complement one another between the two companies? How well do various components of marketing fit together – promotion programmes, brand names, distribution channels, customer mix and so on?
- *Operating fit.* How well do the different business units and production facilities fit together? How do operating elements fit together, such as workforce, technologies, production capacities?
- *Management fit.* What expertise and talents do both companies bring to the deal? How well do these elements fit together, such as leadership styles, strategic thinking, ability to change?
- *Financial fit.* How well do financial elements fit together, such as sales, profitability, return on capital, cash flow?
- *Cultural fit.* How well do the two cultures fit? What challenges might there be if attempts are made to merge the cultures?

Due diligence must be broad and deep in order to identify risks as well as the likely synergies. It also needs to be well structured and proactive. Failure to perform due diligence effectively can be disastrous. A classic case of what can go wrong is the merger between Hewlett–Packard and Autonomy (a business software company). Acquiring Autonomy was part of an attempt by HP to strengthen its portfolio of high-value products and services for corporations and government agencies. Among other things, Autonomy made search engines that help companies find vital information stored across computer networks. When Hewlett–Packard (HP) bought the company it was forced to take an $8.8 billion write-down against earnings tied to alleged accounting improprieties at Autonomy. This was largely due to poor due diligence that failed to show the accounting value of Autonomy with its real value. The size and scope of the charge was staggering, given that the $8.8 billion financial hit was nearly as large as the $10 billion that HP paid for the company. Due diligence is therefore absolutely essential for uncovering potential problem areas, exposing risk and liabilities, and helping to ensure that there are no surprises after the merger or acquisition is announced.

Cross-border mergers and acquisitions

There has been a substantial increase in cross-border M&As as a result of globalization and deregulation. Cross-border mergers and acquisitions can be complex owing to differences in the political, economic, social, technological, regulatory and legal environments in which companies operate as well as their country and organizational cultures. This was evident in the acquisition of Tetley tea by Tata.

CASE STUDY

Tata's acquisition of Tetley tea

In March 2000 Tata Tea bought Tetley for £305 million. What made this deal special was the fact that it was the first-ever leveraged buy-out (LBO) and also the largest cross-border acquisition by an Indian company. The major driving force for the deal was that Tetley fitted into Tata Tea's globalization strategy. The acquisition brought with it a greater market penetration, which helped Tata Tea's operating efficiency, as Tetley's operating margins were superior in comparison to Tata Tea's (20% versus 14% in 1999–2000). The acquisition provided a number of benefits for Tata, including access to Tetley's strong brands and products and to its worldwide distribution network as well as Tetley's proven expertise in the area of product innovation. The acquisition was one of the most challenging Tata had embarked on as it landed Tata Tea in debt. Tata Tea had acquired Tetley for £271 million and it was clear that it paid too much – £100 million more than the next highest bid.

There were several challenges that Tata Tea had to deal with as a result of the acquisition:

- *Culture.* Tata Tea was half the size of Tetley in terms of revenue and number of senior managers and it feared a domination of Tetley's corporate culture. There was also a great deal of concern about how British employees would react to Indian managers.
- *Finance.* Financial constraints, such as legal and capital control in India that made the listing of Tetley shares in India unattractive.
- *Integration.* Problems with the integration of processes of both the companies within their supply chains.

To address these concerns, Tata Tea focused first on identifying common beliefs across the companies. An international consulting firm was commissioned to identify the common beliefs of the two companies and to suggest ways to bring them closer. Secondly, two major structural changes were made. First, there was the separation of the branded and plantation operations into independent economic centres. This was followed by the integration of the sales and marketing operations. Through those initiatives, by 2006 Tetley's worldwide business was integrated with Tata Tea and the new group, Tata Tea Group, was later renamed Tata Global Beverages.

Case written by Julie Hodges.

Tata is not the only Indian company to have completed a series of high-profile overseas acquisitions. One of the largest Indian acquisitions of a US company was the acquisition by Apollo Tyres of Cooper Tyre and Rubber, the world's eleventh largest tyre producer. Avantika Chilkoti (2013), in an article in the *Financial Times* entitled 'India plc goes shopping', identified three trends that were emerging from Indian companies that had successfully navigated foreign deals. First, Indian businesses are often looking for a technology or a brand that sells internationally, both of which require the knowledge and training of employees at the acquired business. So they are unlikely to bulldoze operations. Second, Indian companies have experience dealing with diverse cultures. The Indian market alone is comprised of 28 states and there are 22 officially recognized languages. This means companies often adopt a moderate approach to ease cross-cultural suspicion. Third, Indian businesses generally look to international expansion once they have an established business in their home country. So they are likely to have capital to invest in the foreign business.

One of the best-known cases is Tata Motors' acquisition of Jaguar Land Rover (JLR). At the time of the purchase the deal was widely criticized. What could an Indian brand, out to produce the world's cheapest car, the $2,500 Nano, do for the producer of quintessentially British luxury vehicles? And how could it add value that Ford, JLR's previous owner, had not? The deal is now considered a success. How did Tata achieve this? Operations were left largely untouched. Only one person from Tata was installed on the board of JLR, to provide financial control. And to help with integration, exchanges were organized for corresponding teams in the UK and India to network and swap notes. At JLR's production plant, which adjoins Tata Motors' facility in Pune, UK employees were brought in to train local workers. A lot of money was put into the business, including into product investment.

Another quality that Indian companies bring to acquisitions is experience of a market that is hypersensitive to price. Nicholas Piramal, the pharmaceuticals arm of the Piramal Group, bought a production facility at Morpeth, in northeast England, from Pfizer. Since the Indian company took over, overall revenue per employee has increased 20% and operating margins have grown by almost 600 basis points. Using its networks in Asia – the China office, in particular – Piramal has brought cheaper suppliers to Morpeth and material costs have fallen 6%. Contracts for site maintenance, insurance and energy have been renegotiated. And within six months of taking over, Piramal had replaced the multiple, overlapping IT programs used at Morpeth with an SAP system managed in-house. The company also did not overhaul the management team. Before the deal closed, the head of the Morpeth site declared that he wanted to move on, but instead of parachuting in a Piramal executive, a replacement was chosen from within the existing team. Team leaders at Morpeth now report to the corporate office in India as well as site heads. And cross-cultural training programmes have allowed staff to build relationships with their peers abroad.

These strategies are not limited to Indian companies' acquisitions in developed markets. Mahindra and Mahindra, the India carmaker, bought South Korea's Ssangyong Motor for $466 million and adopted similar approaches. One method they have used to achieve this is 'synergy councils' set up to allow the companies to learn from one another and create economies of scale in sourcing, product development and network development. Mahindra has also recruited new staff in product development and started a second shift on existing production lines. The company did not challenge the Korean culture. They also did not send senior managers from India to change the business. They retained the Korean CEO and almost all of the first two layers of management. So the management succeeded by retaining the existing culture and not attempting to change it.

Individuals' responses to mergers and acquisitions

A fundamental factor that contributes to the success of M&As is people – their expertise and the organizational culture (Cartwright and Cooper, 1995). In an article in the *Financial Times* entitled 'Shared vision is key to changing a vision', Sarah Neville (2013) quotes Judith Smith, head of policy at the Nuffield Trust, a London-based think-tank, as saying that integration must be given time to work as, 'We often have this short-termist nature, wanting the quick fix. It takes time to change professionals' behaviour and get people working in different ways.'

Many of the benefits that are anticipated when an acquisition or merger is being planned depend on employees' commitment to the new organization and their willingness to work together to deliver high performance (Buono and Bowditch, 1989).

Employees will respond to acquisitions and mergers in many different ways. Some identify and welcome opportunities for career development, greater challenges and more opportunities for varied work. Others may see it differently. Employees of the acquired company might feel that they have been 'sold out'. Members of both companies may be concerned about job security and redundancy. This can have a significant adverse impact on morale and motivation and can lead to anxiety, stress, a reduction in performance and an increase in absenteeism and turnover (Hayes, 2010). The reaction of employees to mergers/acquisitions is partly dependent on how they adapt to the new organization – their *acculturation.*

Acculturation

Berry (2005) defines acculturation as the dual process of cultural and psychological change that takes place as a result of contact between two or more cultural groups and their individual members. Malekzadeh and Nahavandi (1988) have applied theories of acculturation to the study of how organizational members adapt to acquisitions and mergers. They identify the different ways in which employees of acquired and acquiring organizations can combine their organizational cultures, practices and systems. These include: Integration, Assimilation, Separation and Deculturation. We will examine each of these briefly.

- *Integration* involves some degree of change for both organizations but allows both of them to maintain many of the basic assumptions, beliefs, organizational practices and systems that are important to them and make them feel distinctive.
- *Assimilation* is a unilateral process in which employees from one company willingly adopt the identity and culture of the other.
- *Separation* involves employees of the acquired organization seeking to preserve its own culture and practices by remaining separate and independent of the acquiring organization. If allowed to do so, it will function as a separate entity under the financial umbrella of the parent company.
- *Deculturation* involves employees rejecting cultural contact with both their own organization and the other organization. It occurs when employees do not value their own culture, perhaps because the company has failed, and do not want to be assimilated into the acquiring company.

According to Malekzadeh and Nahavandi (1988), the process of acculturation that occurs depends on the degree of congruence between the acquired and acquiring organizations' preferred modes of combining and the ability of each organization to impose its preference. There are a number of ways in which managers and leaders can promote the acculturation of employees. At an early stage in the M&A process, the acquiring company can pre-screen potential target organizations for cultural compatibility. The due diligence process can include a cultural audit to gather data on the similarities and differences. This data will help inform the integration strategy. It will also guide how the various aspects of the integration process can be managed and adapted: for example, involving, at an early stage, those managers who will be responsible for managing the acquired business and focusing their attention on potential people issues; ensuring adequate communications are in place about the changes and how they will be implemented; involving staff from both companies in joint task forces to plan how particular aspects of the organizations will be combined; and exploring transition arrangements that will ease the introduction of common terms of employment, such as reward, recognition and pensions.

A merger or acquisition creates huge change issues. The integration process is vital to help to mitigate the risks and ensure the deal is a success.

Unholy alliances – failure of mergers and acquisitions

There have been big mistakes made in M&As, owing to companies' being attracted to them. Feldman and Spratt warn of the seductive nature of M&A activity:

> Executives, everywhere, but most particularly those in the world's largest corporations and institutions, have a knack of falling prey to their own hype and promotion … Implementation is simply a detail and shareholder value is just around the corner. This is quite simply delusional thinking. (1999: 21).

The car industry has seen its share of catastrophic purchases. In 2000 GM swapped 6% of itself for 20% of Fiat and the two agreed to work together. But things quickly went awry. As the Italian company continued to lose money, GM balked at the possibility of having to rescue it and ended up paying $2 billion to wash their hands of the deal. The supreme car alliance disaster was DaimlerChrysler. It was supposed to be a 'merger of equals', but ended up as a bonfire of investment. Executives sparred and cultures clashed. In 2007 the companies separated. Chrysler was bankrupt within two years. VW and Suzuki are still fighting legal battles over their partnership that went sour. Most alliances fail, industry executives say, because of a lack of patience. Product cycles are typically more than five years long, meaning that companies can take the best part of a decade to align their model strategies in order to share designs, factories and parts. But with new technologies such as electric and hybrid cars and self-driving vehicles needing huge, long-term investments, many see no alternative to alliances. In an article in the *Financial Times* (11 December 2013), Henry Hoy quotes, Stefano Aversa, managing director at AlixPartners, a consultancy, as saying that the main driver of future alliances will be 'to share the huge costs of developing these mega platforms that will be dominating the auto industry in the next decade. If you go outside your core product area, you are almost obliged to find alliances.'

Getting it right is important. Yet approximately half of all mergers and acquisitions are estimated to be failures (Ravenscraft and Scherer, 1987) with the synergies projected for them not achieved in approximately 70% of cases (Galpin and Herndon, 2000). Exactly which elements of the acquisition process produce a greater chance of success is still open to debate. It is, however, unlikely that just one element causes success or failure. Sudarsanam (1995) and Damodaran (2001) propose the following reasons for the failure of many mergers and acquisitions: poor strategic fit; lack of clarity about the objective of exercise; cultural differences; inexperience; poorly managed integration; paying too much and over-optimism.

Hayes (2010) points out that many of the potential problems with mergers and acquisitions can be avoided, or at least minimized, if careful attention is given to: specifying the objectives of the acquisition or merger; developing an acquisition/ merger overview to provide a bridge between the objectives and what needs to happen if they are to be achieved; elaborating this overview to develop an implementation plan and avoiding a heavy-handed way of managing the implementation. There is, however, often tremendous pressure to make a deal quickly before a competitor does, so much so that success becomes completion of the deal rather than the longer-term programme of achieving intended benefits.

Activity

Consider an acquisition or merger which you have either been involved in or with which you are familiar:

1 What did the acquiring organization or merger partner seek to gain? List the objectives.
2 To what extent were the intended benefits achieved?

Implications of restructures for leaders and managers

There are a number of implications for practising and aspiring leaders and managers from what we have discussed in this chapter.

Consider the best type of structure for the organization

As Mullins (2007: 648) points out, 'Organizations cannot, without difficulty, change their formal structure at too frequent an interval.' Whether leaders and managers are maintaining existing structures or implementing new ones, they need to know about the different types of structures, as well as their appropriateness and their strengths and weaknesses. In addition, they must be able to diagnose and react to the various factors that influence the effectiveness of each type of structure. They must also be able to recognize how a particular organization structure fits their company's specific business situation and needs. So the best approach depends on the context in which the organization is operating.

Address the people issues raised by a restructure

A restructure can be difficult for all who are involved in it and affected by it. There are almost always employee morale issues to deal with as a result of a restructure such as downsizing. Leaders and manages need to be aware of who will be affected, including employees who leave the organization, those who remain in the organization, and the managers of the two groups. The reactions of each of the groups will be different. Being aware of the impact of managing the change on the individuals and responding to concerns is a crucial managerial responsibility.

Studies have suggested that, where restructures adopt appropriate OD interventions, they generate more positive results for individuals and the organization (for example Cameron, 1994; Ryan and Macky, 1998). However, as we discuss in Chapter 8, success depends on identifying the right interventions at an individual, team or organizational level and evaluating the effectiveness of them.

Consider how the merger or acquisition will be implemented

As outlined in this chapter, approximately half of all M&As are estimated to fail (Ravenscraft and Scherer, 1987) with the synergies projected for them not achieved in approximately 70% of cases (Galpin and Herndon, 2000). Exactly which elements of the acquisition process produce a greater chance of success is still open to debate. With mergers and acquisitions leaders and managers must carefully consider several issues, including the following: how fast to integrate; how much disruption will be created; how disruption can be minimized; how people can be helped to continue focusing on customers, safety and day-to-day operations; and how best to communicate with all the main stakeholder groups (such as shareholders, employees, customers and the public).

Reorganizing a company's structure is a little like turning an oil tanker into a cruise ship while being at sea: it is disruptive and complex. So restructures should not be done unless the benefits outweigh the real costs of disruption.

Further reading

Ashkenas, R., Francis, S. and Heinick, R. (2011) 'The merger dividend', *Harvard Business Review*, 89(7/8): 126–33.
Bower, J. (2001) 'Not all M&As are alike', *Harvard Business Review*, 7(3): 93–101.
Cascio, W.F. (1993) 'Downsizing: What do we know? What have we learned?' *Academy of Management Executive*, 7(1): 95–104.
Cascio, W.F. (2005) 'Strategies for responsible restructuring', *Academy of Management Executive*, 1(4): 39–50.
Dyke, G. (2004) *Inside Story*. London: HarperCollins.
Eriksson, M. and Sundgren, M. (2005) 'Managing change: Strategy or serendipity – reflections from the merger of Astra and Zeneca', *Journal of Change Management*, 5(1): 15–28.

Hamel, G. (2011) 'First, let's fire all the managers', *Harvard Business Review*, 89(12): 48–60.

Kavanagh, M. H. and Ashkanasy, N.M. (2006) 'The impact of leadership and change management strategy on organizational culture and individual acceptance of change during a merger', *British Journal of Management*, 17: S81–S103.

Kuprenas, J.A. (2003) 'Implementation and performance of a matrix organization structure', *International Journal of Project Management*, 21(1): 51–62.

Marks, M.L. and De Meuse, K.P. (2005) 'Resizing the organization: maximizing the gain while minimizing the pain of layoffs, divestitures, and closings', *Organizational Dynamics*, 34(1): 19–35.

Taylor, A.C. (2013) 'Enterprise's leader on how integrating an acquisition transformed his business', *Harvard Business Review*, 91(9): 41–45.

Vermeulen, F., Puranam, P. and Gulati, G. (2010) 'Change for change's sake', *Harvard Business Review*, 88(6): 70–6.

Communication and Change

10

Overview

- Communication is integral to sustaining change. Research shows that those who have information about change are more committed to a change effort (Herold et al., 2008; Wanberg and Banas, 2000).
- Communication enables leaders and managers to create a shared sense of direction, purpose and values, establish strategies, plans and priorities, reduce uncertainty, build trust, and empower and engage people in doing what needs to be done.
- Communication is an ongoing activity and should be adapted to the nature and stage of the change. The methods, messages, audiences and feedback are all vital parts of the communication process during change.
- Management by storytelling is a technique for inspiring and motivating staff by telling them fascinating stories (DuBrin, 2012). Storytelling helps to bring out the need for change. Stories engage people's interest and can help to communicate the vision, purpose and values behind change and transformation in a meaningful way that others can relate to.

Imagine this. It is time for the big announcement. The employees have filled the staff restaurant. The CEO approaches and delivers a rousing speech about a proposed change, building up to a conclusion and asking for everyone's support. Following the speech, the communications campaign begins. A pre-recorded version of the speech is sent to all company locations across the globe via the company's intranet site. An online site goes live for handling employee questions. An email is sent to every employee. Leaders visit all locations carrying a personalized message about the importance of the change and how it will affect employees. Adding a little razzmatazz, posters with change slogans are hung in the company lifts.

The unwritten assumption of this communication campaign is that employees are most likely to change if the same message is scattered across the company in different ways first by the CEO, then by various leaders, followed by the company intranet site, e-mails and so on. Yet is this approach really effective? It certainly provides quantity but not necessarily quality communications.

The quality of communication has a substantial impact on the sustainability of change. Aristotle told us, in 350BC, that if communication is to change behaviour, it must be grounded in the desires and interests of the receivers. In the more than 2,000 years since then, there has been no major change in this idea. To be effective, communication must contain something that interests and engages individuals to change their behaviour. The quality of change can also affect whether the need for change is recognized in good time and can have a significant impact on the quality of organizational learning.

This chapter considers the role of communication during organizational change. It begins with a discussion of the importance of communication. The value of a communications strategy is discussed and some of the issues that need to be considered when formulating a coherent approach to communicating change are examined, including the content, message, medium, audience and feedback. The chapter then explores the impact of communication on uncertainty and trust, and how communication can be used to affect both of these factors positively. The chapter concludes with some practical implications about developing and planning a communications strategy.

Learning objectives

By the end of this you will be able to:

- Identify the factors that enable quality communications during change
- Appreciate how uncertainty and trust during change are affected by communications
- Develop and implement a communications plan for a change initiative

The importance of communication

Communication can be defined as the messages, stories, information, ideas and emotions transmitted through various verbal and non-verbal methods. It may be intentional, such as a carefully phrased email, or unintentional, such as inferences another person may make, correctly or incorrectly, about an individual's body language. Communication is integral to implementing and sustaining change. As Barrett (2002: 19) points out, 'without effective employee communication, change is impossible and change management fails'. This is supported by Covin and Kilmann (1990), who emphasize that failure to share information or to inform people adequately of what changes are necessary and why they are necessary can have a negative impact on how people react to change. Communication is therefore vital to the effective sustainability of organizational change.

Several studies have shown the importance of the impact of communication during change in organizations (such as Lewis and Seibold, 1998; Schweiger and DeNisi,

1991; Smeltzer and Zener, 1992). For example, a study conducted by Nelissen and van Selm (2008) explored the correlation between responses of survivors of a restructure and the role of communication. The study found that employees who were dissatisfied with the communication provided by management had negative attitudes towards the organizational change, including a lack of confidence about its successful implementation. Another study, conducted by Frahm and Brown (2007), investigated whether communication during organizational change was linked to employees' receptivity to change. This study showed that frustrated employees typically felt this was owing to a lack of involvement in the change process and a lack of information regarding the change. The failure to provide employees with adequate information about change can affect whether or not the change is a success or failure.

In order to avoid the failure of change, CEOs need to provide open and honest communication. This is what Hewlett–Packard's CEO, Meg Whitman, did when she sent a video announcing job cuts of 27,000 employees and other changes she was making to her 350,000 staff. In her message she laid the bad news on the line:

> At the end of 2009 we reported a workforce of about 304,000. At the end of 2010 we had almost 325,000 employees, and at the end of 2011 that number had ballooned to nearly 350,000. Over that same period we saw year-on-year revenue growth of 10% in 2010, of 1% in 2011, and so far in 2012, revenues have been declining. We are struggling under our own weight. And we've got to restore our healthy balance in order to return HP to its position as a growing, thriving, innovating industry leader. That's what this is all about. And the workforce reduction is only one piece of a comprehensive effort. We see a lot of opportunity to remove complexity, streamline and reduce costs in a number of areas across HP.[1]

Meg Whitman's message is an example of how to tell employees the truth in order to remove uncertainty about what is happening and build trust. We will examine uncertainty and trust in relation to communicating about change next.

The Notion of Uncertainty

Within the context of organizational change, research has demonstrated that uncertainty is often a major consequence for employees (Ashford, 1988; Schweiger and DeNisi, 1991). Uncertainty is the individual's felt inability to predict something accurately (Milliken, 1987). Research has identified that this inability to predict events can be attributed to ambiguous or contradictory information or to a simple lack of information (Putnam and Sorenson, 1982). Uncertainty has traditionally been considered to be a non-preferred state that motivates people to engage in coping strategies aimed at reducing their uncertainty (Berger and Bradac, 1982).

Geert Hofstede (2001) identified 'uncertainty avoidance' as one of the cultural dimensions in relation to perceptions, feelings and attitudes across different cultures.

---

1 Downloaded from www.forbes.com/sites/timworstall/2012/05/27/why-meg-whitman-needs-to-shrink-hewlett-packard/

Hofstede defined uncertainty avoidance as the extent to which the members of a culture feel threatened by ambiguous or unknown situations. In some cultures people tolerate ambiguity and uncertainty quite readily. If things are not clear they will improvise or use their initiative. In other cultures people tend to be more reluctant to act or make decisions without clear instructions and communications.

During organizational change, employees are likely to experience uncertainty in relation to a range of different organizational issues, including the rationale behind the change, the process of implementation and the expected outcomes of the change (Buono and Bowditch, 1989; Jackson et al., 1987). Research has also indicated that employees may experience uncertainty regarding the security of their position and their future roles and responsibilities (Bordia et al., 2004a). Consequently, organizational change can be a major stressor during which employees seek to gain some understanding about events and situations in order to minimize their uncertainty (Sutton and Kahn, 1986). Researchers generally agree that communication or the provision of information constitutes a vital component of any successful change initiative (Schweiger and DeNisi, 1991). Yet, despite the general acceptance that communication is important during organizational change, strategies implemented by managers often fail to fulfil their purpose of providing quality information to employees.

Organizations will encounter difficulties in reducing employee uncertainty during change if the nature of their communication strategies is one-way (top-down) and predominately focuses on providing employees with information regarding strategic issues. While this approach may be effective during the initial stages of the change process, it is unlikely that it will remain successful as employees' concerns shift to more job-related issues. A continued focus on strategic issues surrounding a change may serve only to heighten employee uncertainty. Employees are then often left seeking additional job-relevant information through alternative sources, such their line managers or co-workers (Allen et al., 2007; Brown and Cregan, 2008).

It is important that how the change impacts on the role, responsibilities, tasks and career opportunities of individual employees is communicated. Changes in the organization therefore need to be translated into the implications for each job and employee. Young and Post (1993: 41) say that this is 'the only way you can get support'. While information about the individual impact of the change will increase understanding and acceptance, a lack of understanding of the individual impact of the change may trigger uncertainty and anxiety and cause low acceptance of the change. Information that directly affects an individual's job is likely to be listened to and retained, whereas information about the organization in general may be forgotten more easily or not even listened to at the outset (Klein, 1996).

Two important aspects of the impact of the change that need to be communicated are the benefit of the change and any potential risks (see Chapter 13 for a discussion on benefits and risks). The benefit of the change should be communicated because recipients are unlikely to support a change that they do not perceive as beneficial. Quirke (1996) points out that without explicitly addressing the benefit of the change, recipients will view the change as an unfair violation of their actual or implicit contract with the organization. Potential difficulties or risks of the change should also not be played down because communicating challenges and negative aspects increases the believability of the message. Larkin and Larkin (1996) argue that uncertainty is even more painful than bad news and Young and Post (1993: 39) found that 'when bad news is candidly reported, an environment is created in which good news is more believable'.

The sharing of information about change helps employees understand the reason for management decisions and to see things from management's perspective (Wanous et al., 2000). When leaders and managers share information in a timely manner, employees are less likely to be surprised by organizational changes. A lack of knowledge about current and future events undermines an individual's ability to influence or control those events, which ultimately results in lower performance and reduced commitment and professionalism (Bordia et al., 2004b). Employees who possess information feel more prepared and able to cope with change and are more likely to commit to the change (Gagnon et al., 2008).

The mere provision of quantity of information is unlikely to be sufficient to reduce employee uncertainty, because employees' attitudes towards change are also influenced by the perceived *quality* of the information they receive about the change (Bordia et al., 2004b). High-quality communication can facilitate openness and positive attitudes towards change and help to address uncertainty, as well as to develop trust (Allen et al., 2007; Bordia et al., 2004a). The direction of communication will also have an impact on uncertainty in an organization.

The direction of communication

Change is often experienced as a top-down process, with those responsible for managing the change informing others lower down the organizational hierarchy about the need for change, what is going to happen and what is required of them. Allen et al. (2007) say that the reason why many organizations encounter difficulties in reducing employee uncertainty during change is because of this one-way, top-down pattern of communication. Effective change communication is up, down and laterally across the organization. Upward communication is essential because it provides leaders and managers with valuable information that can help them clarify the need for change and help them develop and implement plans for change. Beer (2001) identifies poor quality upward communication as one of his six 'silent killers' that block change and learning.

Lateral communication is vital. The quality of lateral communications can have a powerful impact on an organization's level of performance and its ability to innovate and change. Brown and Eisehardt (1997) argue that intense and open lateral communication is an essential requirement for continuous improvement. This information-sharing contributes to the identification of issues and the development of new possibilities. Hargie and Tourish argue that 'when groups work in isolation, with people sharing minimal information …. the locomotive of change slows to a crawl' (2000: 7). They report that poor interdepartmental communication is linked to feelings of isolation and dissatisfaction and low levels of involvement in the decision-making process. In their opinion, 'poor information exchange exacerbates uncertainty, increases alienation and produces a segmented attitude to work that is inimical to the spirit of innovation' (Hargie and Tourish, 2000: 7). So communication needs to be up, down and across the organization in order to build commitment, reduce uncertainty and also to develop trust.

Communication and trust

Employees need to trust the communication which they receive. The believability of the information is a necessary condition for its use but ensuring believability is a big challenge because recipients may not trust the communicator, they may not believe the message content or they may consider the communication activity as inappropriate (Quirke, 1996). Several authors (such as Kotter, 1995) argue that, with growing frequency, employees interpret change messages for hidden meaning because, having gone through change before where the truth was not fully told, they are 'less likely than ever to accept information from their companies at face value' (Lippitt, 1997: 20). Recipients ask themselves why management should tell the truth this time.

A study by Rousseau and Tijoriwala (1999) of a restructure in a hospital examined how employees perceived the information presented by management regarding the reasons behind the change. The results demonstrated unsurprisingly that the relationship between reasons used to justify the change and employee perceptions of the legitimacy of the reasons were weaker under conditions of low trust. When employees have experienced a lack of communication in previous change projects, trying to gain their trust through improved communication can be difficult. Shontelle Bryan shares her experience of how an attempt to improve trust failed in an organization despite an improvement in communication, in her case study.

CASE STUDY

Communication during a restructuring in a manufacturing company

A manufacturing company in Barbados, where I worked in the early 2000s, went through a massive restructuring exercise in which a third of employees were made redundant. As a result, workload was significantly increased and feelings of resentment and anger were felt towards management who were thought to be at the helm of the upheaval. The restructure was seen by management as the solution for bringing the company back to profitability and making it more competitive in the marketplace.

A year after the exercise, when the books were examined, the CEO realized that profitability had not significantly increased. He therefore contacted an external consultant to review the situation. After meetings with the CEO and executive management, the consultant issued a survey to employees which asked for feedback about areas such as communication, job satisfaction and trust. The survey revealed that communication and trust were the two main issues employees had with management. The consultant decided to explore this avenue further to ascertain if these areas impacted on profitability. Interviews with employees confirmed this and also showed that these areas were linked to the restructuring exercise a year previously. Hence the change initiative was born to improve communication, bridge the gap between management and employees, and create an environment that was focused on employees.

In the change initiative, managers and supervisors were trained in skills to help them deal with employee issues and to enhance communication. An 'open-door' policy was also strongly emphasized for managers to encourage employees to discuss feelings and issues. Many

(Continued)

(Continued)

employees still harboured resentment towards senior management as they felt the restructuring was unfair and targeted only the employees at the bottom of the organizational structure and that management's expectation from staff was 'move on and get on with business as usual'. The past restructuring exercise therefore was discussed in open forums where employees were able to air their views and management could rectify any misconceptions. Committees were formed to deal with conflict and to organize activities with the aim of fostering cohesiveness and bridging the gap between management and staff. Some employees felt that that they would be victimized if they were to openly speak their mind, so a suggestion box was also was put in place where employees could submit their views anonymously.

The CEO drove the change across the organization and expected to be kept informed of any initiatives and issues. The organization had been through several change programmes in the past, but changes did not stick. Hence the CEO was adamant that this programme would be successful. Many of the employees, however, thought the attempts to change were a waste of time because of past experience. The consultant tried to change mindsets and create change agents who could push the initiatives forward, but this proved to be difficult.

It was now three years since the change programme started and the general consensus among employees was that nothing had significantly changed. There was still the gap between management and employees, and communication had not improved. Trust and confidence in management are still a major problem. And to make things worse, employee turnover created new posts with many of the people recruited to them lacking proper management skills. The change agents also lost their drive over time, and many reverted to their old way of thinking, which was that the change effort was useless.

Making change stick in the organization, where there was a history of failed change programmes, was difficult. Extra effort was therefore needed from senior management, and they needed to be willing to change their behaviour to see results. In addition, new managers should have been carefully chosen and brought up to speed with what needed to be achieved from the programme, and it should have been stressed that their buy-in was essential in order to make the initiative successful. The consultant should have continued to play an active role throughout the change process and mentor the managers so they could remain enthusiastic and drive the initiative forward.

© 2015 Shontelle Bryan, Project & Operations Consultant.

Discussion Questions

1 Why do you think that this change failed?
2 How could the issue of employees feeling victimized about speaking out have been resolved?
3 What could have been done differently with the communications strategy?

Communication strategies

Communication plays a vital role in the change process. It is a prerequisite for recognizing the need for change. And communication enables leaders and managers of change to create a shared sense of direction, purpose and values; establish strategies, plans and priorities; reduce uncertainty and build trust; empower and engage people in doing what needs to be done; and facilitate learning.

Leaders and managers, however, often give insufficient attention to the role of communications (Hayes, 2010). Philip Clampitt and colleagues (2000) suggest that communication strategies often emerge from existing practices with little hard thinking about communication objectives or processes. Managers make choices about the content of communications. They also make decisions or unconsciously act in ways that impact on the shape of the communications network. For example, they may communicate with some organizational members but not with others, and they may authorize or encourage certain others to communicate with one another. They may also influence, if only by example, preferred channels for passing on particular kinds of information.

On the basis of their experience in several organizations Clampitt et al. (2000) define the following communication strategies.

Spray-and-pray. This is a communication strategy that involves showering employees with all kinds of information in the hope that they will feel informed and have access to all the information they require. The communications strategy is based on the assumption that more information means better communication, which in turn contributes to improved decision-making. It is also based on the implicit assumption that all employees will be able to sort out the significant information from the insignificant. In practice, some employees may attend only to the information that is related to their own personal agenda, while others may be overwhelmed by the amount of information with which they are confronted.

Tell-and-sell. With this strategy, leaders and managers communicate a more limited set of messages that they believe address core organizational issues. First, they tell employees about the key issues, and then they sell to them the wisdom of their approach. Leaders and managers who adopt this approach often spend the majority of their time planning sophisticated presentations, but they devote little energy to fostering meaningful dialogue with employees about concerns related to their proposals. Assuming that employees are passive information receivers, these managers rarely think that feedback is necessary. They may also believe that they are in the position to know all the key organizational issues and they place little value on input from others.

Underscore-and-explore. Like the tell-and-sell approach, this strategy involves managers focusing on a few core messages. But unlike the tell-and-sell approach, leaders and managers give others the creative freedom they need to explore the implications of the issues. Those who adopt this approach are concerned not only with developing a few core messages but also with listening attentively for potential misunderstandings and unrecognized obstacles.

Identify-and-reply. This strategy is different from the first three in that the primary focus is the concerns of organizational members. It is a reactive approach that involves a lot of listening to employees to identify and then respond to their concerns. It is concerned with helping employees make sense of the change. But it is also mindful of their concerns because it assumes that organizational members are in the best position to know what the critical issues are. However, this may not always be the case. Clampitt and colleagues (2000) suggest that often organizational members may not know enough even to ask the right questions.

Withhold-and-uphold. Leaders and managers following this strategy withhold information until it is necessary to disclose it and, when confronted by rumours, they uphold the party line. Secrecy and control are often the implicit values of those who embrace this strategy. Those who adopt this approach often assume that information is power, and they do not want to share power with anyone else. Others assume that employees are not sophisticated enough to grasp the vision.

The spray-and-pray strategy provides employees with a great deal of information, while the withhold-and-uphold strategy provides very little information. Both strategies make it difficult for employees to understand and make sense of the intended change and its consequences. The strategies such as tell-and-sell, and identify-and-reply tend to offer employees more guidance by prioritizing communications and providing specific and relevant information. These strategies also tend to be the most sensitive to employee needs, although they make different assumptions about the nature of those needs. Clampitt and colleagues (2000) argue that the most effective strategy is underscore-and-explore. This is because it includes elements of the tell-and-sell strategy and allows leaders and managers to shape the change agenda. It also incorporates aspects of the identify-and-reply strategy that responds to the concerns of employees.

To ensure that the relevant communication strategy is implemented, managers need to develop a **communications plan**.

Developing a communications plan

Communication plans need to be developed for a number of reasons, including: to ensure the need for change is understood throughout the organization; to enable individuals to understand the impact of the change on themselves; to communicate any structural and job changes that will influence how things are done; and to build trust and reduce uncertainty about change.

The critical components of a communications plan are illustrated in Figure 10.1, which shows the key quadrants of the framework: message, methods, audience and feedback. These are the four aspects of communication where managers and leaders must make active decisions about the best approach to adopt. The four elements need to be considered holistically.

Methods of communication

The choice of the most appropriate method of communication is important because different methods can differ markedly in their capacity to convey information. The method of communication can enhance or distort the intended message. The method must therefore fit the content and complexity of the message that needs to be communicated (Kitchen and Daly, 2002).

Face-to-face is the richest method of communication because it has the capacity for direct experience, multiple information cues, immediate feedback and personal

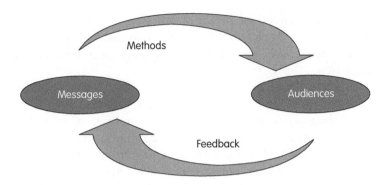

Figure 10.1 Communications framework

focus. Smeltzer (1991) even argues that it would be ideal if all big changes were communicated by means of one-to-one communication that was face-to-face. According to Klein (1996), one of the advantages of face-to-face communication is it influence on recipients' emotions. Emotions can be conveyed more easily via personal communication because non-verbal cues can be used whereas too much information can get lost in e-mails. Quirke (1996) argues that direct contact between the implementers and the recipients of change creates familiarity, and familiarity creates good relationships and trust.

The importance of face-to-face communication, however, does not obviate the need for other communication efforts. A benefit of e-mail communication is its reach. It is possible to convey information to many employees at different locations. Another benefit is that the information is available any time. Quirke (1996) found that employees want information on demand, not when it suits the deliverer to send it, and that employees want to know that they can find certain information, even if they do not need it immediately. An additional benefit of electronic communication is the speed at which topical information can be conveyed to large audiences. Clampitt et al. (2000) say that, during times of uncertainty, speed is sometimes more important than complete two-way communication. A key limitation of e-mail communication, however, is that it rarely provides an opportunity for ensuring the feedback and debate that is necessary for increasing understanding and acceptance of changes. It also tends to be designed for consumption by a broad audience and, therefore, not tailored to specific groups.

An important issue regarding the choice of the method of communications is the relation between the method and the message. A communication programme is more likely to be successful when communication activities and message content fit together compared to when there is a random approach to distributing information. Smeltzer (1991) found that messages about change that would have serious implications on people in the organization could be alienating when delivered via electronic communication and perceived as impersonal and distant. It may therefore be better to communicate the need for change and the vision face-to-face, whenever feasible.

A newer method of communication – social media – has been identified as a way to facilitate faster and better change. This can provide the opportunity for real-time communication and feedback from and to an audience. Inevitably there are concerns about this form of communication. Typically, concerns include: How will we 'police' the postings? And should we really be sharing this information? As we discuss later in this chapter social media does provide the opportunity for a more innovative communication approach.

A number of methods of communication are therefore available to managers and leaders. The choice of method should fit the significance and complexity of the message being communicated as well as the stage in the change process. Using various methods can be of benefit. Evidence of this comes from a study by Schweiger and DeNisi (1991) that investigated two groups of employees involved in a merger. One group was informed of the merger through a newsletter, access to a telephone hotline, group meetings with management, and individual meetings with other employees affected by the change. A second group received information about the merger only through a letter sent by the CEO of the organization. The results of this study found that both groups experienced increases in stress and decreases in satisfaction as a result of the merger. However, the group that was given information from multiple sources coped better with the change.

The methods of communication used can influence the thinking and feelings of individuals. Fox and Amichai-Hamburger (2001) say that, while leaders seem to perceive employees' emotional reactions to change as one of the burdens that they must endure, emotions are in fact a potential tool for securing the willingness and commitment of employees in the change process. This idea is supported in a study conducted by Huy (2002), which found that middle managers' efforts to pay attention to employees' emotions contributed to successful change efforts. Fox and Amichai-Hamburger (2001) suggest that, if change leaders are to influence both feelings (emotions or affect) and thinking (thoughts and beliefs) they need to use various forms of communication and influence. For example, when seeking to influence thinking and beliefs, the main forms of communication that should be used include words, arguments, rationales, analyses and numbers. In contrast, when seeking to influence individuals' emotional responses, leaders need to consider using different means of communication, such as pictures, colours and music.

Remember Martin Luther King, who did not stand up in front of the Lincoln Memorial and say 'I have a great strategy' and illustrate it with 10 good reasons why it was a good strategy. He said those immortal words 'I have a dream', and then he proceeded to show the people what his dream was. He illustrated his picture of the future and did so in a way that had high emotional impact. Leaders and managers need to recognize that different forms of communication need to be used to influence the beliefs and emotions of individuals prior to and during change. This is evident in the case of how communication was used in the merger between PostBank and ING Bank.

When PostBank and ING Bank, two subsidiaries of the Dutch ING group, merged they used internal and external communications to gain understanding, acceptance and support of the merger:

1. *Internal communication.* The first phase of the internal communications strategy was to explain the merger to employees. To do this communication took place through meetings, informal get-togethers and through the Chief Executive's blog. Next was

the integration communication phase: the aim of this phase was to unify employees from both banks around the consolidated organization. The core message was to appreciate the combination of the banks' strengths. The communications team also introduced a new internal name that staff at both banks could identify with – NWE Bank (the New Bank) – and installed a countdown clock. In the final phase of communication – living the brand – the focus was on creating momentum. The team devised 10 countdown episodes before the merger in January 2009. In each one, staff were given items such as a video or pencils bearing the new logo.

2. *External communication.* The aim of the external communication was ensure that customers were aware of what was happening. As different customers had different questions, communications were used to reach them in different ways, such as using surveys to understand their needs, sending welcome packages and personalized letters, and calling them in person, as well as through television and print adverts.

ING's communications strategy worked because it understood the situation from the customers' and employees' viewpoints; it took time over the implementation; and it found ways such as the informal discussion meetings and the CEO blog to capture the attention of internal and external stakeholders.

Audiences

The change plan should also take into account the audiences who will receive the communications. Target groups critical to the change must be identified. A stakeholder analysis is a useful tool to use here (see Chapter 11).

Knowledge about the audience is an important prerequisite for effective communication. Palmer and Fenner (1999: 54) say that 'a key feature of dissemination activities is to tailor the message and the choice of media to the target groups' needs and interests'. Hutchison (2001) elaborates that knowledge about the audience includes general tolerance for change, degree of agreement with the change initiative, need for information and preferred communication activities for receiving the information. Knowledge about the audience becomes even more important when the change is of major importance to the organization and/or when the change is controversial (Lewis et al., 2001). The challenge in addressing recipients' needs is that different groups of employees are likely to have different needs, partly because they are affected by the change in different ways at different times (Hutchison, 2001). Without knowledge about the target groups, it is difficult to provide the information that individuals need to fully understand the change and to provide the meaning and justification individuals are seeking.

Individuals who are affected by change, but not personally involved in planning and conceiving it, are seekers of meaning. They try to make sense of the change by trying to guess the true motives behind the change and how it will affect their own personal values and goals (Lines et al., 2005). They are looking for justification for the change. If such a justification is perceived as adequate, and it is provided at the right time, several positive outcomes may result, including perceptions of procedural fairness, organizational citizenship behaviours, preservation of organizational commitment, trust in leadership and, more specifically, positive attitudes and behaviours towards change (Lines, 2004). Unfortunately many leaders and managers fail to provide explanations for change, or they provide explanations that are so general that they lack real information content. This often means that, when leaders and managers do write and talk, recipients do not always listen (Folger and Skarlicki, 2001).

Communicating involves paying attention to the differing needs and interests of different audiences to persuade them of the appropriateness of the change or, if necessary, to modify the change to produce the best outcome in the given situation. Critical listening skills, including evaluating feedback, are needed to be receptive to issues that may impact on the proposed change and to make informed judgements about the issues. Providing persuasive accounts of the need for change, along with enhanced negotiation skills, is required to win over key audiences. This may involve persuasion through deals, including selling change upwards and downwards throughout the organization (Dutton et al., 2001).

Leaders and managers should be aware that people differ in their ability to understand written and spoken communications. To address this there is a need for repetition, which can help in messages being listened to and remembered and in building a commitment among key audience members. Repetition increases the odds that everyone will at least hear the core messages. Individuals' memories can be increased by diffusion and repetition of the message through several media, leading to message retention. Kotter (1996) emphasizes that the change message needs to be repeatable as ideas sink in deeply only after they have been heard many times. A degree of fortitude is necessary to recognize that, even though the message has been delivered a hundred times before, it may well be the first time some employees have heard it.

Messages

Messages must be clear and consistent. Individuals need to understand the context as to why certain priorities are important and an explanation of not only how the organization will benefit but also how they personally will benefit. This will help create readiness for change. Armenakis and Harris (2002) identified three message strategies that can be used to convey change messages and create readiness for change:

1. *Persuasive communication* (direct communication efforts)
2. *Active participation* (involving people in activities designed to have them learn directly)
3. *Managing internal and external information* (making the views of others available)

In *persuasive communication*, the manager or leader is directly communicating the change message through primarily verbal means. For example, a CEO who travels to various corporate locations in order to discuss the need for change is demonstrating persuasive communication. This allows not only the message itself to be communicated but also the importance of the issues to be symbolically magnified by the fact that time, effort and resources are used to communicate the changes directly.

Active participation includes three forms:

1. Enactive mastery – gradually building skills, knowledge and efficacy through successive involvement and practice

2. Vicarious learning – observing and learning from others
3. Participation in decision-making

The active participation strategy is perhaps the most effective one in communicating messages because it capitalizes on what Fishbein and Azjen (1975) define as 'self-discovery'. Self-discovery, when combined with the symbolic meaning of organizational leaders demonstrating their confidence in employees through participation, can produce a genuine feeling of employees working in partnership with management on the development and implementation of change.

The *management of information* refers to using internal and external sources to provide information about change. A message generated by more than one source is considered to be more believable, especially if the source is external to the organization. Sources may include sharing press articles about industry trends or competitor successes and failures, sharing the organization's financial records to demonstrate a cost-management problem, or bringing in speakers to inform people about external drivers for change that affect the operations of the organization.

Armenakis and Harris (2002) say that a successful change message must address five key areas: *discrepancy, appropriateness, efficacy, principal support* and *personal valence*. First, the *discrepancy component* involves explaining the gap between the current state of the organization and the desired state. Management may choose to point out that the organization will not survive in the long term if the current state of operations continues. The *appropriateness* component is more specific and conveys the idea that the proposed change (i.e. its content) is appropriate in bridging the gap between the current state and the desired state. Communications should focus on the factors guiding the choice of a given change effort in comparison with other possible courses of action. *Efficacy*, the third component, entails expressing confidence in the organization's ability to successfully implement the change. Employees need to have confidence in the ability of both themselves and others to successfully implement the change and in knowing that the leaders of the organization are behind the change. The *principal support* component supports the latter point in emphasizing that it is important for managers to demonstrate that they are serious about the change and that this attempt is not just another 'programme of the month'. Finally, *personal valence* helps to clarify the benefits of the change to the employees. Employees should clearly see the personal benefits of successfully implementing the change. For example, they may be able to perform their job better, pay might increase, or long-term job security may increase. The ability of the management team to address these five message components is influential in the ultimate commitment of individuals to the change.

Messages must resonate with the key audiences on three levels: *strategic, tactical* and *personal:*

- *Strategically*, communication is the means of aligning action with strategy. Words and ideas enable audiences to understand and commit to the change. It is through this commitment that an organization can realize the benefits derived from the change.
- *Tactically*, communication carries the specific messages of what actions are desired for whom, when, why, where and how. Targeted audiences must receive

effective communications in order to understand what they need to do to implement the change.

- *Personally*, communication motivates individuals when the message carries a credible 'what's in it for me'.

The content of the message needs to focus on what information is conveyed to employees before, during and after the change initiative as well as what information is sought from employees. Kitchen and Daly (2002) identified three types of information that affect employees during change:

- What employees *must* know, including job-specific information.
- What employees *should* know, including desirable information about the organization.
- What employees *could* know, including relatively unimportant office gossip. Employees will want to know as much information as possible in order to minimize uncertainty.

The purpose of the content of the message has been described in various ways, such as spreading a vision, involving employees by seeking their input to the process and content of the change, minimizing uncertainty, overcoming barriers to change, gaining employee commitment and challenging the status quo (Kitchen and Daly, 2002; Kotter, 1996). Different changes are likely to produce different reactions and, therefore, the content of change communication activities depends on the change at hand (Carnall, 2007; Dunphy and Stace, 1993). Lundberg (1990: 10) states that 'each type of change has implications both for communication content and communication process'.

Consider the film industry. Movie trailers last only about two minutes for a reason. They convey the broad concepts to a wide audience while still providing a meaningful plot and the opportunity to engage people in the story. Movie trailers do not waste time explaining the intricacies of cast selection, the fine print of pay structures or the legalities of foreign rights. They also do not present the details of film crew's break schedules or of the lighting procedures. This is important information that would be contained in an overall communication plan. But for a general audience, this would be meaningless 'noise', drowning out the core message. It is important to provide people with the right information at the right time so that they can make an informed decision. Whether the change being crafted could be described as a drama (system change), an adventure (acquisition/new product line), or even a horror show (downsizing), an organization will be best served by clarity and brevity of message. This will help employees decide whether this movie is worth staying for – whether the message is worth listening to and accepting.

Feedback

As part of a communications plan, managers should seek feedback on the effectiveness of the communication in order to measure its impact. As Barrett says:

> The effectiveness of the company's communication needs to be measured company-wide formally and frequently against defined goals on an ongoing basis and throughout the key stages of any major change (2002: 222).

Regular feedback provides real-time data about individuals' understanding and acceptance of the change. Toterhi, and Recardo (2012) suggest that the effectiveness and impact of communications can be measured by gauging:

- *Timeliness*: were the communications completed in a timely manner?
- *Usefulness*: did the communications address questions or issues that were meaningful to the stakeholder group?
- *Understandability*: did the audiences understand the intended message?
- *Believability*: did the audiences believe what was communicated?

Such feedback can provide leaders and managers with information about which messages have been delivered most clearly, which methods are most effective and whether the appropriate target audiences have been identified. Changes can then be incorporated into the existing communications plan. It is critical that an organization does something with the feedback it requests and receives from individuals, as this shows that the views of individuals are valued and that management are willing to listen to them. Proactively eliciting feedback can also help to eradicate silence about how employees feel about the change (see section below on 'Silence as a killer of change') and prevent individuals seeking information through informal channels.

Activity

Consider a change intervention with which you are familiar and consider the following questions:

1 How was the need for the change communicated?
2 Was it communicated to all those affected by the change? If not, who was left out?
3 How might communication have been improved?

The role of informal communication

In addition to the available formal methods, research has also highlighted the importance of informal communication networks during change (Kitchen and Daly, 2002). Formal communication is 'concerned with the flow of information through the authorized channels in the organization, including supervisory relationships, work groups, permanent and ad hoc committees and management information systems' (Poole, 1997). Informal communication is 'concerned with the flow of information outside the authorized channels in the organization' (Gallagher et al., 1997: 584). The informal communication system is often referred to as the 'grapevine' or 'the rumour mill'. A rumour can be defined as 'an unverified statement about an issue of current interest to people' (Bordia et al., 2000: 2309). The role of informal communication such as rumours can be significant during change. Authors such as Crampton et al. (1998) and Quirke (1996) estimate that recipients may receive up to 70% of their information through informal networking. While respondents in a study by Glover (2001) ranked the grapevine on the same level of effectiveness as events and group meetings. As a result, formal communication activities were often supplemented and, in some cases, usurped by the grapevine. Richardson and Denton (1996: 203) found that 'the most commonly cited reason for failure of a change effort was the presence of inaccurate and negative rumors'.

Informal communication can fill the information vacuum when formal communication fails to reduce the uncertainty and anxiety that typically accompanies organizational change (Kitchen and Daly, 2002). It provides explanatory control – why something may be happening – and predictive control – what may be happening in the future. Crampton and colleagues (1998) found that individuals are likely to use informal communication even if formal communication activities provide the desired information because informal networks are a natural consequence of people interacting.

There are, however, several limitations to informal communication. One is that it may not reach all employees within an organization. Distribution through the grapevine is uneven and certain individuals may be left out of the circuit. Another limitation is that rumours are not an effective means of reducing uncertainty and anxiety because they tend to focus on negative and often inaccurate information (Schweiger and DeNisi, 1991). Furthermore, even if informal information is accurate, individuals do not know whether the information is accurate. Therefore, they may be cynical about the ability of the informal communication system to relay reliable information and prefer receiving information from formal sources (Glover, 2001).

Informal networks can be developed face-to-face or through online social media networks. While social media networks are increasingly used as communication channels, they may meet with mixed success due to the informal and spontaneous nature of such groupings (Cross and Prusak, 2002). However, leaders and managers should not ignore them as they are becoming more prolific both in and outside organizations as a method of communication that reaches a wide array of audiences.

Silence as a killer of change

Silence can kill employee commitment and energy for change. A climate of silence exists when employees believe that speaking up about issues is not worth the effort or that voicing their problems and concerns is risky, even dangerous. **Organizational silence** is described by Morrison and Milliken (2000) as the withholding of opinions and concerns about organizational problems by employees. This highlights a challenge for change in that employees may choose not to change, yet remain silent. According to Morrison and Milliken (2000), a climate of silence in organizations will develop, firstly, when leaders and managers fear negative feedback from subordinates and try to avoid it or, if this is not possible, dismiss it as inaccurate or attack the credibility of the source. Secondly, when leaders and managers hold a particular set of implicit beliefs about employees and the nature of management that make it easy for them to ignore or dismiss feedback. Such beliefs are that employees are self-interested, untrustworthy and effort-averse; management knows best and therefore subordinates should be unquestioning followers, especially because they are self-interested and effort-averse and therefore unlikely to know or care about what is best for the organization; and dissent is unhealthy and should be avoided, and unity, agreement and consensus are indicators of organizational health.

Such beliefs can give rise to structures, policies and managerial behaviours that not only create an environment that discourages upward communication but also foster a climate of organizational silence. Organizational silence can have destructive outcomes for employees, with knock-on effects for the organization. Employees may feel undervalued and this may affect their commitment to the organization and engagement with the change, leading to lower motivation, satisfaction, psychological withdrawal or the decision to quit. When discouraged from speaking up, employees may feel that they lack sufficient control over their working environment. This lack of empowerment can also lead to low motivation, low satisfaction and possibly attempts to regain some control through acting in ways that are destructive to organizational change, such as engaging in sabotage. Employees may also experience cognitive dissonance because of the discrepancy between their beliefs and behaviour, leading to anxiety and stress (Hayes, 2010).

One constructive response to organizational silence is to involve employees in the communications. Upwards as well as downwards and across the organization, communication can generate a dialogue throughout the company, fostering a sense of participation that can make even the largest companies feel smaller in the hearts and minds of employees. To make this happen leaders need to actively encourage daily dialogue with all audiences about the change process. They need to constantly reinforce the case for change. It is imperative that leaders make time to talk with their staff about their experience of the change process. And this needs to be an organized effort that is formally coordinated, thereby raising the profile of the change efforts throughout the organization.

Another way of addressing organizational silence is to encourage **purposeful conversations** – conversations for action rather than idle talk (Dervitsiotis, 2002). Purposeful conversations allow the sharing of meaning and ideas, are driven by the vision, deepen mutual understanding and create purposeful action. They can be facilitated in meetings, workshops and online discussion forums.

For instance, a purposeful conversation can begin by asking people to imagine what the change will look like in the workplace after implementation. This gives them the opportunity to express any confusion or ambiguity, ask for clarification and articulate possible stumbling blocks they may think of, as well as moving into accountability and solution mode. Such conversations leave little room for ambiguity or misunderstanding and at the same time create real thinking space for individuals and teams. The more the change is a topic of conversation, the greater its implied urgency (Kotter, 1995). Purposeful conversations create new opportunities and generate action, leading to what Lloyd and Maguire (2002) describe as a quickening of the 'corporate pulse' – information flow increases and individuals become more able and willing to share information and feelings and to engage in the change process.

Storytelling

Management by storytelling is the technique of inspiring and motivating staff by telling fascinating stories (DuBrin, 2012). Storytelling helps to bring out the need for change. Stephen Denning, a former manager at the World Bank, explains how storytelling helped him persuade leaders at the bank to adapt knowledge sharing as a key strategy:

In June of 1995, a health worker in a tiny town in Zambia went to the website of the Centers for Disease Control and got the answer to a question about the treatment of malaria. Zambia is one of the poorest countries in the world – and this town is 375 miles from the capital city. But the most striking element in this picture, at least for us, was that the World Bank wasn't in it, despite its know-how on poverty. Imagine if it were. Think what an organization it could become. (2008: 130–1)

This simple story prompted World Bank staff to envision a different future and become a world leader in knowledge management (DuBrin, 2012). Such a story can elicit a future scenario in the minds of the listeners: the listeners start to imagine what the future could be like if they implemented the relevant change idea embodied in the story in their own contexts.

Leaders and managers should consider alternative ways of communicating such as storytelling. Stories can engage people's interest. They can communicate the vision, purpose and values behind the change in a meaningful way that others can relate to. If leaders keep their strategy locked behind the boardroom door and do not effectively communicate to people in a way that can help turn that strategy into reality, then their strategy may remain a mystery.

Not everyone will grasp statistics, data immersed in reports or bullet points in complex often tedious presentations. But stories can be cross-cultural and capture the imagination. So when leaders tell their strategy as a story, it can give it meaning across the organization (Gill, 2011: 121, 283–4). For example, think about how teachers struggle to control young children all day long but, come story time at the end of the day, the children all sit quietly of their own free will and listen with great curiosity and enthusiasm as the storyteller evokes their imaginations.

Studies have shown the benefits of storytelling. Roberto and Levesque (2005) studied six strategic initiatives undertaken over several years at Apparelizm Corporation. They demonstrated the importance of vivid communication, finding that a verbal picture is 'worth a thousand words', and emphasized the benefits of using metaphors, analogies and examples. By engaging in storytelling and symbolic action, the managers at Apparelizm created a compelling case for the initiative. They were also able to explain the specific changes that would be made. The use of metaphors served a number of purposes, such as relaying the details of the programme and creating excitement and support for it. The core team used an auto-racing metaphor. It compared a *National Association for Stock Car Auto Racing* (NASCAR) race crew to the store staff. A video was even created to solidify the metaphor. Roberto and Levesque concluded that the metaphor was effective. Employees understood the link between the need to be fast, responsive and highly knowledgeable, much like a NASCAR team. They also understood the importance of communication and teamwork within a NASCAR team, and they were then able to make the correlation with their role in the initiative. Links were drawn carefully for the connection to be easily made by the employees.

In his book *The Leader's Guide to Storytelling*, Stephen Denning (2010) highlights eight different story patterns that leaders and managers can use:

1. *Sparking action* – describes how a successful change was implemented in the past, but allows listeners to imagine how it might work in their situation. It involves posing questions such as 'What if …?' or 'Just imagine …'.

2. *Communicating who you are* – this involves providing some details about yourself ensuring the audience has time and the inclination to hear the story. Responses to it might be, 'I didn't know that about him!', 'Now I see what she's driving at.'

3. *Transmitting values* – this should feel familiar to the audience and will prompt discussion about the issues raised by the value being promoted. Believable characters and situations should be used and storytellers should ensure that the story is consistent with their actions. Responses might include, 'That's so right!' 'Why don't we do that all the time?'

4. *Communicating your brand* – this is usually about the product or service itself by customer word of mouth or by a credible third party. It might create a response such as, 'Wow! I've got to tell someone about that.'

5. *Fostering collaboration* – this involves recounting a situation that listeners have also experienced and prompts them to share their own stories about the topic. Storytellers should ensure that a set agenda does not limit the swapping of stories and that there is an action plan ready to tap the energy unleashed by this narrative chain reaction. Responses might include, 'That reminds me of the time ...' 'I've got a story like that.'

6. *Taming the grapevine* – this highlights through gentle humour some aspect of a rumour that reveals it to be untrue or unreasonable.

7. *Sharing knowledge* – this focuses on problems and shows, in some detail, how they were corrected, with an explanation of why the solution worked. Storytellers should solicit an alternative and possibly a better solution.

8. *Leading people into the future* – this evokes the future that the storyteller wants to create without providing excessive detail that will prove to be wrong.

Storytelling is a collective way to translate strategy into something more tangible that sticks in people's minds and creates a common expectation and retention of what it is all about. Different combinations of story can be woven together as an integrative narrative tapestry. Stories can inspire and evoke purpose, meaning and emotion – they can be both empowering and engaging. In her case study below, Karen Geary describes a global transformation at Sage, the business software company, and how stories were used as part of the communications strategy.

Communication plays a critical role in the change process. It is an essential prerequisite for recognizing the need for change. It enables managers to create a shared sense of direction. And it establishes priorities and can reduce uncertainty.

CASE STUDY

Business transformation at the Sage Group plc

The Sage Group plc is the global leader in business software for small and medium-sized businesses, operating in 23 countries worldwide. During 2010, the CEO of Sage retired, having successfully led the business for 15 years. During his time the business entered and maintained a position in the FTSE100, making him one of the most highly regarded CEOs

(Continued)

(Continued)

based on shareholder return during his tenure. His successor, an internal candidate, took up the reins in September of that year.

After first establishing his new leadership team, a new vision, brand and strategy were devised. These were designed to propel the company to fully embrace the technology disruption taking place in the market with the advent of cloud computing and a more digitally connected world. Crucially, the plan was to double the rate of current growth in a deep recession in the Eurozone countries.

The drivers for change were not readily evident as Sage was seen largely as a highly successful business. However, the rate of growth was lagging behind the competition and there were new and more agile competitors coming into the market, driven by lower barriers to entry. Establishing basic accounting solutions in the cloud and establishing presence were becoming easier. The vision, brand and strategy did not dictate a wholesale move into new products and markets and therefore the change involved was limited to an internal transformation, albeit on a global scale. The principal deliverables were:

1   A new suite of cloud-based products and services available globally. Historically, Sage products were largely developed locally to serve local needs. The development of the cloud meant that common platforms could be developed once and made available for localization.
2   A reduction in the product portfolio and, where appropriate, to include the disposal of businesses, products and services that were no longer seen to be core to the future success of the business.
3   A re-allocation of resources according to strategic need, which required prioritizing according to size of opportunity. This was a transformation that had to be self-funded, with margins maintained, if not improved.
4   A change to the pricing models the company operated, to offer customers greater flexibility in the way the products and services were used and, from a business point of view, to increase the lifetime value of the customer.

In order to achieve what was required, a fundamental change in the way the business was organized was necessary. The business had achieved great success historically over and above its competitors as it was highly decentralized in order to be close to the customer in the country. This meant that decisions were devolved as far as possible, and local leaders were free to run their 'kingdoms'. The proviso was that they operated within the principles and governance model set down by the company and that financial goals were met. This was a model that engendered a very strong culture – its fiercely decentralized way of working was much admired by its competitors. It was something the company was extremely proud of.

The underlying mindset of the local leader and the local executive team could be best described as entrepreneurial, with freedom and autonomy given in return for results. In order to build ownership, a new guiding coalition was formed comprising the most senior executives of the company – some 35 people from around the globe. This community was called the 'Global Leadership Team' (GLT) and was charged with executing the plan.

At its inaugural meeting, the CEO made a declaration that the business was to be less decentralized if it were to achieve its goal. He made it clear that he would not advocate moving to a fully centralized organization but that there were components of the strategy which meant that working differently would affect all of the leadership. The Group Human Resources Director, who doubled as the Transformation Executive, elaborated further on how the top initiatives would unfold and what leaders could expect in the short to medium term. One explanation that resonated particularly with the leadership team was through the use of Charles Handy's 'doughnut principle', which was used to explain that core responsibilities would remain largely unchanged, (the centre of the doughnut) but there was now a requirement to expand the leadership role outside of the core, which would bring each other into contact with other ways of working and with other people (the next ring of the doughnut).

Lessons learnt

Top-executive alignment. The key lesson was in getting the top team aligned. It was a 'team of champions', with executives running their own areas. But the team was now required to become a 'championship team', working together for a common cause, breaking down barriers and fostering more collaboration and innovation. Inevitably when there are 'rock stars' in teams, this process takes time, patience and strong leadership.

Identifying the right set of initiatives and avoiding initiative overload. Sage has a highly intelligent leadership team and, once the business planning cycle had commenced, the implications of what was needed became readily apparent. Well-intended enthusiasm created acute 'initiative overload'. This initially created a drag on the business as leaders struggled to make careful choices as to what should be tackled first and over what time. Global initiatives (a new phenomenon) were meant to replace local initiatives, but the reality was that local initiatives at the start of the change were not being discontinued, putting key people under considerable strain. Over time, executives became smarter and more discerning about what they were prepared to commit to. Each project required clear terms of reference in order to avoid scope creep and clear KPIs and milestones.

Getting rapid alignment. Executives were required to balance running of the business and developing the business simultaneously. This was something that proved to be challenging across all markets, principally because the resource allocation required in order to align the organization took far longer than anyone originally anticipated. Where initiatives stalled, it was usually due to lack of resources or skills or where resources were required to cover too much ground. Behaviourally, alignment meant a 're-wiring' of Sage's much-prized 'Leadership Standard' because different behaviours were required to drive the change. A project was undertaken to determine what was required, using external expertise, and 'The Confident Leader' emerged as the new leadership standard, aligned to the new brand and the requirements of the strategy.

Doing something symbolic. There were a number of symbolic actions taken to provide the organization with proof that Sage was serious about change:

- A change in key leadership. This was restricted to small changes, but nonetheless signalled the intent of change. Those with the desired mindset were asked to play a part in the key initiatives.
- A new Global Programme Management Office was created, designed to drive the transformation.
- The introduction of a commercial matrix structure on a pan-European basis to include a pan-European structure to address one specific market segment. This broke the country-led model.
- The introduction of a global brand and visual identity, designed to propel the strategy commercially, while creating consistency in the way the company behaved.
- Communicating the strategic intent to financial institutions to include disclosing of targets. This was a 'first time' for Sage.

Making it meaningful. Significant investment was made in communications to both leadership and employees. A communication 'burning platform' toolkit and road show were

(Continued)

(Continued)

created that could be used globally. To accompany this, managers were trained in storytelling techniques so that they could personalize what they were communicating and better deliver the 'So what?', and 'What it means to me' with greater authenticity.

Building ownership. There were a number of global commercial initiatives and enablers, such as brand. Each one of these initiatives was sponsored by a member of the executive team and teams of key talent who were required to operate globally rather than locally in order to fast-track some initiatives and to build global consistency.

At the time of writing, the change is still under way. The markets will ultimately judge if Sage has been successful in its attempt to transform its business and ultimately demonstrate higher growth than in previous years. However, the change required of local leadership to play the role of an executive on a more global stage, where there is more sharing, collaboration and co-ownership, is a long road and, while many are already thriving, for some it may be a change too far from the days of local autonomy.

© 2015 Karen Geary, Chief People Officer of WANdisco plc.

Discussion Questions

1 How might you apply the lessons learnt to change within your organization?
2 What will the leaders need to do to share and collaborate across the globe?
3 Do you think this is a change too far for the company? Justify the reason for your answer.

Implications of communicating during change and transformation for leaders and managers

From this chapter there are some key practical implications for managers and leaders for communication during times of change.

The importance of communication

Most leaders and managers are familiar with the popular assertion that you cannot over-communicate during a change. This is true in theory, but the intricacies of a well-fashioned communication plan merit more than just a philosophical 'one-liner'. To build support and maintain the perception of transparency, leaders and managers often overwhelm employees with unnecessary details of a change initiative without properly segmenting their audience(s) affected by the change and the type of media and communications they will need. People want information. Understanding exactly what to say and to whom is the key to a successful communications strategy.

Develop a stakeholder communications plan

Effective communication for stakeholders needs to be a four-way process – up, down and across the organization (left to right and vice versa). It is always more powerful

Audience	Message	Media	Frequency	Responsibility	Feedback	Performance measure

Figure 10.2   Stakeholder communications plan

than one-way communication. This approach allows for involvement, resolves ambiguities and increases the chances of the communicators connecting adequately with individuals. It also enables individuals to feedback to management their thoughts, feelings and ideas about the change.

The stakeholder communications plan shown in Figure 10.2 can be used to ensure that managers identify what communications activities are required to build and maintain the support of stakeholders. It should be completed after the stakeholder analysis and mapping exercises (outlined in Chapter 12) and reviewed regularly as part of the project management for the change. It might also be helpful to use the checklist in Appendix 10.1 to review any intended communications.

Keeping people informed

People need to be fully informed and educated about the necessity for change, the progress and challenges associated with change processes, and the outcomes of change. Information minimizes misinformation, where employees fill in the blanks of missing information for themselves, often resulting in the misperception that change has been a failure when it has not. The need to blame somebody is lessened, pessimism is reduced and cynicism about organizational change is minimized. People need information most whenever they are likely to be surprised by events. A sudden announcement of a new change programme to improve customer service, for example, would catch most employees by surprise. Among their questions might be:

- Why is the change programme necessary?
- Why this particular programme?
- Why now?

- Why here and not some other location?
- Whatever happened to the last programme that was supposed to improve quality?

If these questions are not thoroughly answered at the time the change programme is announced, people will begin to fill in their own answers either independently or through interaction with co-workers, most of whom may be equally uninformed. People who feel more informed and involved are less likely to possess cynical attitudes. Routine notice about what is happening, and especially why it is happening, prevents anyone being caught off-guard. If done correctly communication can help provide clarity, facilitate the development of trust and assist the sustainability of change. Communication is not just about providing timely information. It is about creating a participative dialogue and feedback, up, down and across the organization.

Use social media

Social media platforms (such as blogs, Twitter, Facebook sites) are ideal mechanisms to facilitate change because much of change is about ongoing dialogue and conversations in an organization. Leaders and manages should consider starting a blog as a way to reach people in the organizations. It can provide an opportunity to engage and collaborate by asking and answering questions on the blog. Polls can also be taken on the blog. The blog can be used to capture the reasons why change is needed. It can also be used to capture what people think about the change. Employees who support the change could be asked to be a guest blogger and asked to write about the change.

Torben Rick on his website www.Torbenrick.eu provides a number of suggestions for how social medial can be used to communicate about change. His suggestions include the following:

- *Improving employee involvement and engagement.* Social media allows information to flow in multiple directions, rather than just from the top down. For example, using microblogs applications for sharing short bursts of information, leaders and managers can 'crowd-source' ideas and involve employees more directly in change initiatives. Organizations can actively build greater trust and loyalty by actively soliciting continuous feedback on issues related to the change.
- *Building collaboration.* Acceptance of change can be accelerated across the organization through real-time sharing of experiences. Social networking is an effective way of bringing employees together to perform new ways of working and to share experiences. People can form communities to learn from and support one another
- *Idea generation.* Social technologies or simple suggestion boxes in the form of blogs or message boards with comments can provide opportunities to share, generate and build on ideas in collaborative, open format that has visibility across the organization.
- *Establishing effective two-way communication.* By monitoring and participating in online discussions mangers can see where any issues are and take steps to address them.
- *Storytelling.* Social media tools provide an effective medium to tell a story.

Table 10.1

Area to assess	Assessment	Action for improvement
Why?		
• ... are you communicating?		
(e.g. just to keep people informed, to prepare them for an event, or to engage them in the change process)		
Who?		
• ... is the target audience?		
This will dictate the tone, style and content of the message.		
• ... will deliver the message?		
This influences how the message is received. Assess their authority, rapport and credibility with the audience.		
What?		
• ... are you trying to say?		
In no more than two lines, explain the core of what it is you are trying to convey? (If you can't capture it, what makes you think that your audience will?)		
When?		
• ... are you planning on telling them?		
Too late and it will appear as a *fait accompli* decided behind their back, so be ready for resistance. Too soon and it may give them time to fret over an event that may be insufficiently thought through.		
How much?		
• ... information will they be given?		
Consider the information you are holding back and be able and ready to explain why.		
How?		
• ... is the message to be conveyed?		
To all employees together at the same time – information that directly impacts on them all equally and that you do not want to circulate on the grapevine.		
On a one-to-one basis – information that is sensitive or needs explaining or that impacts individuals to varying extents.		

(Continued)

Table 10.1 *(Continued)*

Area to assess	Assessment	Action for improvement
How accurate?		
• ... is the information?		
Is it:		
– Up-to-date?		
– Correct?		
– Accessible to the entire target audience?		
Which method?		
• ... will you use to convey the message?		
Does it suit the kind of information you have to convey, e.g. too impersonal, too casual, or too public?		
What is the impact?		
• ... has the communication generated?		
This raises questions of feedback:		
– What mechanisms are in place for employee feedback?		
– How positive or critical is it?		
– What do you do about it?		

- *Creating learning experiences.* Social media can be used to deliver personalized learning experiences related to the change initiative, for example live web meetings can bring together employees for a learning experience; user-generated content platforms, such as YouTube, allow staff to provide short videos or audio training segments relevant to a change programme.
- *Sharing current practice through a knowledge network.* Knowledge networks can be formed using Twitter, Yammer and Facebook. These networks can be used to share innovative practices and receive answers in a timely manner.
- *Assessing progress and receiving feedback.* Social media can provide real-time feedback by providing a platform for immediate survey-based feedback, or by conducting facilitated online feedback sessions.

Appendix 10.1: Communication checklist

Use the checklist in Table 10.1 to review your intended communication, your assessment of effectiveness, and how it could have been more effective.

Further reading

Argenti, P.A. and Barnes, C.M. (2009) *Digital Strategies for Powerful Corporate Communications.* New York: McGraw-Hill.

Butcher, D. and Atkinson, S. (2000) 'Stealth, secrecy and subversion: The language of change', *Journal of Organizational Change Management,* 14(6): 554–69.

Groysberg, B. and Slind, M. (2012) 'Leadership is a conversation', *Harvard Business Review,* 90(6): 76–84.

Patterson, K., Grenny, J., McMillan, R. and Switzler, A. (2012) *Crucial Conversations.* New York: McGraw-Hill.

PART FOUR
People, Politics and Power during Change and Transformation

The Nature, Impact and   11
Management of Attitudes
Towards Change

Overview

- To understand why people react to change the way they do, leaders and managers need to view the change from other people's perspectives to understand the concerns people have about change.
- Responses to change will vary depending on the nature and impact the change has on individuals.
- Attitudes to change range from positive acceptance to scepticism and cynicism to outright opposition. Many individuals do respond positively to change.
- Trust is a condition for successful change. Employees' trust in leaders and managers, as well as in the organization, is an expression of confidence in their reliability and honesty in times of change and uncertainty (Zeffane and Connell, 2003). Organizational change initiatives can significantly erode trust both in the organization and in its management (Morgan and Zeffane, 2003).
- Gaining commitment and involving people in the change can build trust and positive attitudes towards the change. Participation in the change process is important for helping to reduce negative responses to change by reducing anxiety, creating a stronger sense of ownership and enabling individuals to actively contribute to the shaping of change.

People are at the core of sustaining change in organizations and also represent the greatest challenge to the mastery of change. Structures, systems, processes and strategies are relatively simple to understand and even fix. People, however, are more complex. They have different backgrounds, abilities, personalities, dispositions, 'hang-ups', interests, motivations and aspirations. Change can have a different impact on each individual, all of which can cause different attitudes and reactions. The complexities of human responses to change are often ignored when change is planned. According to Woodward and Hendry (2004: 164), one-third of senior managers acknowledge that the people aspects are ignored in their change programmes. This is quite a shocking statistic, for as Jick and Peiperl (2003) point out, any organization that believes change can take hold without considering how people will react to it is in deep delusion. Choi (2011) echoes this and observes that change often fails because those leading the change pay insufficient attention to how change affects individuals.

Leaders need to be aware of the attitudes towards change of their employees, such as:

- What might be their anticipated emotional and attitudinal reactions to the change?
- What determines employees' willingness to change and how can it be influenced?
- What different responses can be expected from different people?
- How can this information be used in planning the change?

Leaders often gloss over such issues, yet it is human behaviour that ultimately will sustain change in organizations. Yet as Bridges (1980) points out, many managers are wise about the mechanics of change but are often unaware of the dynamics of the transition that people go through. Leading people through change therefore requires an understanding and respect of how change affects individuals. No organization can institute change if its employees will not, at the very least, accept the change. No change will work if employees do not help in the effort, as change is not possible without people changing their behaviours.

The aim of this chapter is to examine the impact of change on people and explore how leaders and managers can manage people more effectively during transitions. The chapter begins by discussing the impact of change on individuals and explores the transition issues which they face. Specifically, we consider the impact of change on behaviour and motivation, how individuals react to change, their attitudes to change and what leaders and managers can do to effectively manage the impact of change on individuals. We examine individuals' response to change as a progression through a number of stages of psychological reaction. The chapter also considers how to gain commitment to the change from individuals and the importance of involving them in the decision-making process. The benefit of viewing resistance to change as valuable feedback rather than a threat that has to be removed is explored. Finally we review the implications for managers and leaders of the key issues discussed in the chapter and identify steps that they can take to motivate others to change.

Learning objectives

By the end of this chapter you will be able to:

- Appreciate how people at all levels in an organization react to change
- Identify what leaders and managers can do to minimize or overcome any opposition to change
- Appreciate the meaning and theories of resistance to change
- Discuss the concepts of cynicism and trust, and how cynicism and trust affect change
- Implement approaches for managing how people react to change

Individual reactions to change

Most of us are creatures of habit. We do not always appreciate changes in our daily routine, in our working practices and working environment. We may become unhappy about any loss of freedom to do certain things, for example changes in shift patterns or hours of work, or changes in our standard of living and buying power. Such reactions have been evident in the angry demonstrations in Greece against the Greek government's severe austerity measures in 2012, in the demonstrations in Egypt and Turkey in the summer of 2013 and in the Ukraine in 2013 and 2014, as well as the one-day strike in July 2011 in the UK against the government's plans to extend retirement ages and increase pension contributions in the public sector. For individuals there is often a sense of security in the past, the way things have always been done and which appear to have been done reasonably well (Pilbeam and Corbridge, 2006). As a result, change when it is imposed on people can trigger a range of intense emotional reactions (Bartunek, 1984; Fugate et al., 2008; Huy, 2002; Kiefer, 2005), which, in turn, can influence how people behave, depending on how they view the proposed change.

The view from one's 'hilltop'

How individuals perceive the impact of change depends on their own personal view of it, from their own perspective – their 'hilltop' (see Figure 11.1). Leaders and managers will be looking at the change from their own personal **hilltops** in the organization, and what they see below may be different from what members of their staff may see who are elsewhere in the organization and looking down from their hilltops, and *their* views may differ from person to person. To appreciate how staff view the change, leaders and managers need to move across to the hilltops that their employees are standing on. This is a simple but effective model that has been used by one of the authors of this book with many different leaders of change in different countries. The most recent example was with professional women in the Middle East who

Figure 11.1 Hilltops
Reproduced with permission of the copyright holder, FMR Research Ltd

were attempting to understand how not only women but also men from the region saw the changing role of women in society. The model has also been used very successfully with international bankers who were attempting to improve relationships with their customers whose small and medium enterprises (SMEs) were experiencing financial difficulties. Both groups – the women in the Middle East and the bankers – were encouraged to consider the view of the world from their hilltops, the view from the hilltops of others, and how their different perspectives made each group view change differently.

Employees' concerns about change

To understand why individuals react to change the way they do, leaders and managers need to view the change from other people's perspectives (hilltops) as well as understand the concerns they may have about change. In his TedxTalk called 'Embracing Change', Jason Clarke, Co-Founder of the Centre for Sustainability Leadership, talks about the real reasons why people resist as being:

- Feeling too full of emotion and fear
- The change being a shock to them
- Being scared of the transition rather than the idea
- Not being able to see how they fit into the change
- Being fed up with phoney change that goes nowhere

Clarke proposes that people audit their understanding of change through an analysis of what they see as the positive aspects of the status quo and the negative aspects of the change. The status quo (A) is known and certain, whereas the future (B) is unproven and uncertain. Individuals may fear that moving from A to B will cause failure, loss, rejection, ridicule, risk, anxiety, blame or pain. Any of these can cause fear and anxiety, which can inhibit change. Battistelli and colleagues (2013) identify concerns that stimulate fear and propose a model that includes three specific concerns:

- Concerns about the content of change
- Concerns about the benefits of change
- Concerns about mastering the change

Concerns about the content refer to worries about the impact of the occurring change on an individual's role and the loss it may bring. For many employees their reactions to change are driven by a concern about a sense of loss (Burke, 2002; Jick and Peiperl, 2003), such as a loss of decisional power or a degrading of their position within the organization or loss of earnings or even one's job. Losses can also be intangible or even imaginary but no less personal and painful. For example, someone whose job becomes routinized and marginalized as a result of changes introduced by the organization might see this change as a loss of status or a loss of their identity.

When experiencing *concerns about the benefits of change* employees may worry that the change will not bring the expected benefits for individuals or the organization. For example, employees might fear their change efforts will not be adequately rewarded or that too much time will pass before they will get the desired benefits. The perceived fairness of the outcomes resulting from a change will therefore influence individuals' reactions (Armenakis et al., 2007).

Finally, *concerns about mastering change* refer to employees' worries about not being able to successfully face the change, such as properly fulfilling new tasks, learning new ways of doing things and being enabled to effectively contribute to the change initiative. Levels and forms of concerns can vary across individuals, depending on change efforts by provoking negative consequences on a number of change-related processes and outcomes (such as commitment to change) at both the individual, team and organizational levels (Battistelli et al., 2013).

Activity

Consider a change you have personally experienced:

1 Identify the concerns you had about the change.
2 Describe how you dealt with them.
3 Explain what you would do differently if you were able to do it again.

Responses to change

During change employees tend to make a personal assessment of the impact that the change could have on factors such as their levels of responsibility and authority, their status and career prospects, their salary and job security, and the range and quality of their social relations at work (Greasly et al., 2009; Iverson, 1996). These personal assessments are likely to colour individuals' attitudes towards the change that in turn can be expected to affect their overall reaction to the change (Elias, 2009).

When change is perceived as personally beneficial, individuals will exhibit a more positive reaction to it. For example, changes in working practices such as the introduction of flexi-time and increased opportunities to work partly from home are often well received. The greater the perceived benefits of the change, the more positive individuals' attitudes towards the change can be expected to be and, therefore, the lower their resistance to the change is likely to be (Giangreco and Peccei, 2005).

Responses to change will vary, depending on the type of change. Some people will fight the change 'to the death', constantly denying that the change is necessary; while others will embrace the change readily and be willing to adjust to it. Most people are usually somewhere in between (Burke, 2002).

Cynicism

We often hear that people hate change. If this is true then we have to tell the fashion industry, because it is based entirely on the idea that people want to change how they look. Likewise, we need to tell all the people in gyms or those who are having cosmetic surgery in order to change how they look. And the politicians who fight elections to change governments. So, it would seem that people do want change but they are fed up with change that is imposed on them and does not work. This type of change can create cynicism.

Cynicism about change involves an individual's negative attitude towards the purpose or potential success of change efforts. According to Dean and colleagues:

> [Organizational cynicism is] a negative attitude towards one's employing organization, comprising three dimensions: 1) a belief that the organization lacks integrity, 2) negative affect [emotional bond] toward the organization, and 3) tendencies to disparaging and critical behaviours toward the organization that are consistent with these beliefs and this effect. (1998: 346)

Cynicism involves a loss of faith in leaders, resulting, for example, from the experience of organizational change as a result of the latest management fad or a quick-fix attempt to address a problem (for example Reichers, Wanous, and Austin, 1997). Cynicism is a formidable adversary for any change. However, Reichers and colleagues (1997: 50) offer hope by considering cynicism as a response that 'may simply help people to make sense of puzzling events'. But if it is not dealt with, the price of cynicism can be high and include reduced satisfaction, less organizational commitment, less motivation to work hard, more accidents and errors, less willingness to engage in change initiatives, and the diminished credibility of leaders (Walker et al., 2007). This is illustrated in the case study (below) written by Lynne Smith about changes at the British Aerospace site at Dunsfold.

CASE STUDY

British Aerospace Dunsfold

Several years ago British Aerospace (now BAE systems) owned Dunsfold Aerodrome near Cranleigh in Surrey, UK, where the Harrier jump jet was originally conceived and built. My role was as Department Administrator for the Aerodrome Engineering Department, responsible for the maintenance and upkeep of the whole site. When I first assumed this role, the Department Manager asked me to develop and implement a change-management programme for the re-skilling of the workshop employees. The existing workers consisted of electricians, carpenters and millwrights. There was a strong cultural demarcation between the jobs that they would carry out. Thus, for example, an electrician would not unblock a toilet, while a carpenter would not change a light bulb. The aim of the re-skilling programme was to make these craftsmen more multi-skilled. The reasoning behind this was that British Aerospace was looking to change to a facilities management operation at the Aerodrome. There were two options for achieving this: either to completely disband the existing Aerodrome Engineering Department and replace it with outside contractors or to change the skills of the existing workforce.

The Department Manager had already tried to implement this change and failed. As I began to explore the situation and formulate a training programme, I uncovered the reasons behind the Department Manager's failure to achieve change and a high level of resistance to what I was trying to implement. There was a strong lack of trust in the Department Manager due to a failure on his part to deliver previous promises of change that had been suggested by the craftsmen. This was coupled with a great deal of cynicism about the change to facilities management. It had been talked about for over 12 months and was now regarded as a 'false threat' and something to 'beat the workforce with'. The most interesting aspect of this scenario was that the main resistance to change was led by one particular person, who applied peer pressure to the rest of the workforce, trying to get them not to cooperate in attending training courses. Part of the re-skilling also included training in the use of a new computer-based maintenance system. There was also strong resistance to it. As time progressed, the focus of mistrust was shifted from the Department Manager to me: I was now regarded as his messenger. The other major factor in the force field of resistance was that most of the craftsmen had been employed with the company for a long time (one electrician for more than 20 years) and did not perceive any benefit in changing their working practices. Time had lulled them into a false sense of security.

My main concern was not for the resistance 'ringleader' but for the other employees who would have benefited greatly from the retraining schedule. External circumstances changed the picture completely. After its merger with Marconi Systems, British Aerospace announced the closure of Dunsfold. The company implemented a number of measures to deal with the future of the site workforce. The primary one was trying to redeploy them at other sites, with generous relocation packages. Another was a £1 million budget for training courses. The redeployment process involved interviewing all employees individually, determining what route they wished to pursue, whether they wished to retrain and finding the most suitable course(s) for their needs (which even included driving lessons for non-drivers who wished to find jobs further afield).

I relocated to BAE Systems' main site at Farnborough Aerospace centre but still kept in touch with my old department at Dunsfold, which remained in place to the very end of the site-closure process. Most of the craftsmen were successful in gaining new employment and I was told that some felt the change was the best thing that could have happened to them. I did successfully implement some change, in that the level of department training increased dramatically. The presence of the change resistance 'ringleader 'was very stressful to deal with, especially as I had no or very little support from the Department Manager. This person used personal criticism as a weapon to try to derail whatever I was attempting to achieve. It is very difficult to communicate the benefits of change when the people involved have been working in the same situation for a very long time. If you engage people in a change dialogue, you must deliver your promises; otherwise trust and cooperation very quickly disappear.

© 2015 Lynne Smith, Business Manager, Heritage Trust.

Discussion Questions

1 How could the benefits of change have been communicated better?
2 How would you deal with someone who is irrationally determined to undermine any positive change and its advantages and benefits to a team?
3 How would you manage cynicism about a change initiative?

People do not deliberately become cynical, pessimistic or blaming. Rather, these attitudes result from experience and are sustained because they serve useful purposes. Cynicism persists because it is selectively validated by the organization's mixed record

Table 11.1   Strategies to manage and minimize cynicism about organizational change

1	Keep people involved in making decisions that affect them.
2	Emphasize (and reward) relationship-oriented behaviour for supervisors.
3	Keep people informed of ongoing changes: when, why, how
4	Enhance the effectiveness of timing.
5	Keep surprising changes to a minimum.
6	Enhance credibility, ensure managers communicate who are liked, trusted and credible, use positive messages that appeal to logic and consistency, use multiple channels and repetition.
7	Deal with the past. Acknowledge mistakes, apologize and make amends.
8	Publicize successful changes.
9	Use two-way communication in order to see change from the employees' perspective.
10	Provide opportunities for employees to express feelings, receive validation and reassurance.

of successful change and by other people in the organization who hold and express similar views (Reichers et al., 1997). Reichers and colleagues (1997) offer a 10-point checklist for managing and minimizing cynicism (see Table 11.1).

Managing cynicism about organizational change involves providing timely, appropriate and credible information. Cynicism can be minimized by admitting mistakes when they occur, apologizing and quickly taking appropriate corrective action. Two-way communication, whereby managers become aware of employee perceptions of change and their feelings about it, is critical to success. Addressing people's fears helps them to 'let go' of their concerns long enough to give change a chance of success. The approach taken by managers has the potential to counteract the negative consequences of employee cynicism. Individuals may be much more likely to commit to organizational change if they are properly prepared for the change.

Resistance to change

Resistance to change has been described as an ongoing problem for leaders and managers and is believed to lie at the heart of most change programmes (Stickland, 1998). Oreg (2003) defines such resistance as an individual's tendency to resist and avoid making changes, to devalue change generally and to find change aversive across diverse contexts and types of change. From this perspective resistance is linked with negative employee attitudes or with counter-productive behaviours, and it is frequently perceived as intentional (Bovey and Hede, 2001). It is therefore described as a form of organizational dissent that individuals engage in when they find the change personally unpleasant or inconvenient (Peccei et al., 2011). This dissent can take a variety of forms. One form is a failure to cooperate with those responsible for the change, in the sense of failing to engage in behaviours that involve sharing commitment to the change. Another form is to avoid engaging in behaviours that promote the value of the change to others inside and outside the organization (Herscovitch and Meyer, 2002).

The concept of 'resentment-based workplace resistance' is introduced by Folger and Skarlicki (1999) to describe the reactions of disgruntled employees against the perceived unfairness of the change. Resentment-based resistance behaviours can range from subtle acts of non-cooperation to industrial sabotage. From this definition we learn that resistance to change can vary in terms of intensity. This idea of conceiving resistance on a continuum of intensity is also evident in Coetsee's (1999) work. He conceives resistance as a continuum that ranges from apathy (indifference) to aggressive resistance, i.e. destructive opposition. Between these extreme poles he distinguishes two intermediate forms of resistance: passive resistance and active resistance. *Passive resistance* exists when mild or weak forms of opposition are encountered which are demonstrated by the existence of negative perceptions and attitudes. Examples include blocking or impeding change by voicing opposing views and rejecting the change in public.

Such resistance to change may also be displayed through storytelling by those who perceive that they are adversely affected. Patrick Dawson and Peter McLean (2013) describe how this occurred in an Australian colliery among miners who felt that management were imposing a performance appraisal system on them in a way that threatened their identity of what it meant to be a miner. Dawson and McLean say that the many stories were reflexive, subjective, sometimes partial, incomplete and prospective, sometimes providing after-the-event retrospective narratives with characters, plots and endings. Such stories are not only ways of making sense of change but also ways of exercising political leverage, in this case to subvert the appraisal system.

Active resistance is characterized by opposing behaviour such as trying to undermine the implementation of change by working to rule and slowing down activities. It may also result in personal withdrawal, which involves different distancing behaviours and cognitions ranging from intentions to quit to more subtle psychological neglect, such as not fully concentrating on work. Such withdrawal is often due to individuals' concern or uncertainty about the proposed change and not being ready for it (Wacker et al., 2003). The following case illustrates a change programme in a business school in Northern Europe, which ultimately failed owing to opposition to change.

CASE STUDY

Resistance to change

A colleague of one of the authors of this book was recruited to a senior role – as Director of Executive Education – at a university business school in Northern Europe, in order to improve the reputation, brand and quality of its Executive Education programmes. The Executive Education programmes had been neglected by the previous Director and been left to be run by a Programme Manager, who was running them in very much her own way. The arrival of a new Dean at the school, with objectives to increase the profile of the school and create leading-edge Executive Education programmes, had resulted in the appointment of the new Director, who had been approached by the Dean for the role, which had not been internally or externally advertised. The Dean had announced the

(Continued)

(Continued)

appointment at a Christmas party and positioned the new Director's arrival as if she were a 'knight on a white horse', charging in to save the day – or at least the Executive Education programmes. On her first day, the Dean came up and put his arms around her and said, 'I am so glad you are here'. All seemed to go well in the early days, but it was not long before it became evident that there were serious issues and challenges to be addressed.

The first challenge was with the Executive Education team. The team had never been led and had managed to survive by working on their own and doing what they wanted. The portfolio of programmes had not been changed for more than 10 years, the quality of teaching was patchy and had not been monitored or properly evaluated. The result was declining student numbers, programmes that were stale and out of date, and a lack of reputation in the marketplace. The previous Director had preferred a laissez-faire style of management and allowed the Programme Manager to run the Executive Education programmes somewhat like a private club – holding soirées with copious amounts of wine and cheese. There was little innovation in the programmes, and it was clear that, with numbers of applicants declining, there was an urgent need for change.

The new Director began by consulting key stakeholders, including the Executive Education team, faculty, students, alumni and senior management in the business school, about the current situation and the desired future of the programmes. The Director developed a vision for the programmes, along with a strategy for making the vision real. The strategy was then drafted and circulated to key stakeholders, including the Executive Education team, for comment, although there were no comments forthcoming from the team. Adjustments were made to the vision based on feedback from the stakeholders, The document was presented to the School Advisory Board, who were very supportive of the recommendations. The strategy was agreed and signed off by the Board and the school's senior management team. The Director then set up a meeting to discuss the implementation with the Executive Education team. At the meeting there was no response from any of the team members, except nods that they agreed with it. A plan was drafted by the Director, circulated again for comment to the team; but again no comments were received. A meeting was then held to discuss the plan and actions. Everyone agreed to the plan and the actions. But nothing happened. No actions were implemented. Nothing changed. Everyone continued to do what they had always done.

The Director ensured that the Executive Education team were consulted and kept informed of all proposed changes, and their ideas were frequently encouraged. Every attempt was made to engender trust and cooperation with transparent and frequent communication through regular team meetings, one-to-one meetings and feedback from senior management meetings. However, as the time approached to implement the strategy (implementation was not a strength of the school in the past), the barriers to change began to emerge. The recommendations in the strategy had included changes to the structure of the Executive Education team, the portfolio of programmes offered and marketing of the programmes, including changes to the website. When a meeting was held with the Executive Education team to scope out a potential structure, the Programme Manager erupted in floods of tears. The meeting was a disaster, as she refused to discuss the structure. Shortly after the meeting the Deputy Dean refused to allow any changes to take place with the structure. The status quo was being clung to by the 'old guard'. Without changes to the structure, the strategy would be hard to implement. The dark side of politics and power began to cast its shadow as the senior management team withdrew support for the changes, except for the curriculum review and a complete overhaul of the website.

The Programme Manager was to prove the thorn in the side of the new Director and a vehement opposer of change. Indeed, she eventually showed her true colours as manipulative and deceitful. She sat in meetings about proposed changes and conscientiously wrote down everything that was said by the Director, agreed with it and then did nothing to implement what she had agreed to. At the very first team meeting she had burst into tears and said that she could not move forward until all the issues in the team were dealt with. It was to be the first of many 'tear-induced' meetings whenever change was mentioned. Later, again in tears, she told the new Director that she made her feel inadequate and incompetent because of their different styles. The Director, she said, was business-like and professional. The Director spent many meetings with the Programme Manager attempting to involve her in creating ideas about what needed to change but was always met with an emotional response and 'But we can't do that ...'

Support from the senior management team began to be withdrawn. Its members began to use language such as '*your* Executive Education programmes' when talking to the Director, rather than '*our* Executive Education programmes'. The Director was called into several meetings to justify the recommendations, despite their having been signed off. The Dean appeared to be backtracking: he began to question what was being proposed and failed to make decisions when pushed about what had been signed off for implementation.

Internal politics were rife. The Programme Manager managed to convince those around her that the change was destructive and would not work. At heart she was fighting for her status and the enclave of power she had set up for herself. She had a staunch ally in the Deputy Dean.

Within a year the Director left. The culture had beaten her. The opposition to change was too great. It was beginning to affect not only her confidence but also her health. Within three months the Programme Manager had taken over the Director's role. The significant changes that had been made to the website for the Executive Education programmes were reversed and the site was back to advertising the curriculum as it had been before the changes were made.

Lessons learnt

When change was introduced, the internal historical culture of 'the old guard' and the organizational systems was left intact, creating a context in which lasting change was untenable. Metaphorically, this resembled bungee jumping, in which the organization was propelled in one direction until the cord was extended fully, whereupon it lurched back from the brink, finishing its journey within its own predetermined boundaries. Members of the senior management team were obstructive and there was strong opposition within the Executive Education team to embrace any change.

So what did the Director learn from this experience? On reflection it was tough: it made her realize that putting the theory of change into practice can be difficult because the hardest part of change can be the people part. Individuals bring their own agenda, and it can be hard to get them on side if they refuse to contemplate change. It also made the Director realize that ongoing support from senior management is vital. In this case the support was initially there – at least in terms of the right words and gestures – but as the senior management team dealt with its own internal politics and power struggles it began to backtrack on what it had initially agreed. When support disappeared, change was impossible.

Perhaps the approach to change was too transformational for the culture. Clearly there was an urgent need to do things differently, and in a short time the change had to have a fast pace, but within an environment that was used only to incremental change (if even that), the strategy to turn sinking Executive Education programmes into those that had potential to survive and grow was a step too far.

Written by Julie Hodges.

Discussion Questions

1 What could have been the reasons for the resistance to the change from the Executive Education team?
2 What might the new Director have done differently in order to gain commitment to the proposed changes?
3 To what extent was the strategy to transform the Executive Education programmes a step too far?

Resistance and the need to motivate people to change

Leaders and managers can do a number of things to minimize opposition and motivate individuals to change. Kotter and Schlesinger (1979) propose the following approaches:

- *Education and persuasion.* One of the most frequently used ways to reduce opposition to change is to present rational arguments and technical evidence to educate people about the need for change. People need to understand the logic and the need for change. Zaltman and Duncan (1977) refer to 'educative' strategies as those that provide a relatively unbiased presentation of the facts in order to provide a rational justification for action. This approach is based on the assumption that individuals are rational beings capable of discerning facts and adjusting their behaviour accordingly when the facts are presented to them.

  A related approach is to persuade people to change by appealing to their emotions, presenting passionate arguments and biasing the message to increase its appeal. Hayes (2014) points out that when the level of commitment to change is low, persuasive approaches are likely to be more effective than rational educative strategies. Persuasive approaches can increase commitment by stressing either the benefits of changing or the costs of not changing. The way a persuasive argument is framed is important. Thaler and Sunstein (2009) argue that individuals are more likely to be persuaded to change if attention is focused on what they will lose by not changing rather than on what they will gain if they do change.

- *Participation and involvement.* People will be more supportive of the change if they are involved in the development and design of it. This will help them feel that they are part of the change and that it is not just being done to them. When employees are involved in the change effort they are more likely to be committed to the change. Nadler (1993) points out that involving people in the collection, analysis and presentation of information can motivate them to change, as information people collect themselves is more believable than information presented to them by someone else. Hayes (2014) says that a potential benefit of participation and involvement is that it can excite, motivate and help to create a shared perception of the need for change within a target group. When change is imposed the target group is likely to experience a lack of control and feel the 'victim' of change. The more people are involved, the more likely they are to feel that the change is something they are helping to create. In addition to increasing motivation, participation and involvement can also produce better decisions because of the wider input and can help to sustain the change once implemented because of a greater sense of ownership. However, involvement can be time-consuming and if those who are involved have less technical expertise than those leading the change it can result in a change plan that may not be as effective (Hayes, 2014).

- *Facilitation and support.* Kotter and Schlesinger (1979) say that when fear and anxiety lie at the heart of resistance, an effective approach to deal with them is to offer facilitation and support. They suggest that this might involve the provision of training in new skills, giving time off after a demanding period, or simply listening and providing emotional support. Nadler (1993) suggests that individuals need to have the time and opportunity to disengage from the current state, especially when they feel a sense of loss or letting go of something they value or feel is an important part of their individual or team identity. One way of doing this is to facilitate group/team sessions where members are given the opportunity to share their concerns about the change. However, Nadler (1993) cautions that such sessions might also have the effect of increasing rather than decreasing resistance, for example by becoming an opportunity just to raise grievances. Ceremonies and rituals to mark transitions can also help people to move on and let go of the past. When staff at an international bank had to move from a building in the middle of a city to a new building on the outskirts of the city, they burnt a paper model of the old building. Teams then held lunch events where they all talked about the move – what they would miss and what they would gain. Rituals can help people manage the sense of loss that is often associated with change.
The provision of emotional support can be particularly effective in circumstances where feelings undermine people's ability to think clearly and objectively about a problem.

- *Negotiation and agreement.* Kotter and Schelsinger (1979) say that negotiated agreements can be a relatively easy way to avoid resistance when it is clear that an individual, who has sufficient power to resist a change is going to lose out if the change is implemented. Incentives can be offered to employees to overcome resistance. Individuals can also be offered incentives to leave the organization through early retirement packages or redundancy packages in order to avoid having to experience the change. The issue with this approach is that others, who may have been content with the change and to support it, may then see the possibility of negotiating a better position for themselves. The long-term effect can be to increase the cost of implementing changes and increase the time required to negotiate the change with key stakeholders.

- *Manipulation and co-option.* Manipulation is the covert attempt to influence others to change and it can involve the deliberate biasing of messages. It can also involve co-option. Kotter and Schlesinger (1979) state that co-opting usually involves giving an individual or team leader a desirable role in the design or implementation of the change. The aim is to secure their endorsement of the change. While this approach may be quicker and cheaper than negotiation, it runs the risk of those who are co-opted feeling that they have been tricked into supporting the change. There is also the risk that those who are co-opted steer the change in a different direction than originally intended.

- *Explicit and implicit coercion.* The ability to exercise power exists when one person or team is dependent on another for something they value. Coercive strategies involve managers using their power to force employees into accepting change by making clear that resisting the change can lead to actions such as losing jobs, being dismissed, or lack of promotion opportunities. While the result might be a willingness to comply with the change, an individual's commitment to the change may be low. Coercive strategies may be appropriate in situations where there is a low perceived need for change, where the proposed change is not attractive to the target individuals or teams, or where speed is vital. However, this approach lacks ethical justification and can result in individuals feeling threatened about what will happen if they oppose the change.
- *Goal setting.* Hayes (2014) adds to Kotter and Schlesinger's list by including goal setting. Hayes argues that goal setting can affect resistance to change and increase motivation to support it. Seijts and Latham (2012) say that attractive goals can affect priorities, effort, persistence and the search for effective ways of working. For example:

  o Most individuals have multiple demands on their time at work. Presenting them with compelling goals for change can help them set priorities.
  o Goals that are perceived to be of benefit and are challenging will motivate individuals to continue to work to implement and sustain the change.
  o When it is not clear what needs to be done, goals can help provide direction and clarity about what is expected.

Activity

1 What methods have you seen used in organizations to overcome opposition to change? Think specifically about a change instance and what was done, using:

   a Education and persuasion
   b Participation and involvement
   c Facilitation and support
   d Negotiation and agreement
   e Manipulation and co-optation
   f Explicit and implicit coercion

2 What were the consequences of using the different methods?
3 What worked and what did not work? Why?
4 What personal preferences do you have regarding these techniques?
5 Which ones do you have the knowledge skills to match?

A critical perspective on resistance to change

Much of the literature on change tends to see resistance to change as an irrational response from those who are managed. This assumption that resistance to organizational change is a problem that always requires management is open to challenge. Some scholars have questioned the value of this approach (Piderit, 2000) and others have begun to re-examine and reconceptualize resistance (Ford et al., 2008). One of the concerns when we label 'resistance' to change as a negative response is that it can be used to dismiss potentially valid employee concerns about proposed changes.

Employee resistance to change is often not a result of negative attitudes towards change but comes from a well-grounded understanding by employees of the implications of change that is different from the understanding that leaders and managers have. People will often resist change out of genuine self-interest, knowing that the change will have adverse effects on them and others in the organization. They may have well-informed grounds for considering them ill advised, and have other options which they think are better. Maurer (1996) points out that those who resist change often have something important to tell us. They may see other options that leaders and managers never dreamed of. They may understand problems about the minutiae of implementation that leaders never see from their lofty perch atop Mount Olympus.

Resistance is often seen as a form of conflict, yet when differences among people are surfaced, confronted and debated, improved decision-making results (Ford et al., 2008). In other words, the organizational change effort can progress, just not quite in the way that managers planned it or thought that it might proceed. So instead of seeing resistance as a form of conflict, we need to consider it as a way that differences among people are surfaced. The mantra of 'resistance to change' may therefore have taken us as far as we can go. Instead we should retire it in favour of employees' 'responses to change' and think about responses rather than resistance (Piderit, 2000).

Discussion Questions

1 What is the history of concerns about change in your organization or an organization with which you are familiar?
2 How have the concerns been dealt with?
3 What could be done to improve how concerns about change are dealt with?

Discussion Questions

1 What happens to an organization if individuals do not change as part of a change initiative?
2 What encourages and discourages us to change as individuals?
3 What are the tangible and intangible manifestations of negative reactions to change in organizations?
4 Why is resistance to change usually thought of as something that has to be overcome?
5 What alternative term to 'resistance' could be used? Why?

Stages of reactions to change

How people respond to change has been compared to the phases described by Elizabeth Kubler-Ross (1973) which people pass through when coping with personal

loss, grief, trauma or serious illness. These phases are: shock, denial, anger, resignation, acceptance and commitment.

- *Shock.* When a change is first announced, especially if it is without any warning, individuals can become immobilized and shut down to protect themselves. At this stage they may not be able to focus on their work.
- *Denial.* In this phase individuals feel threatened by the anticipated change and may even deny its existence: 'I will be Ok'; 'This is not happening.'
- *Anger.* Individuals may get angry and lash out at what has been done to them, even as they hold on to accustomed ways of doing things: 'Why me?'; 'It is not fair, how can this happen to me?'; 'Who is to blame?' They will attempt to keep a hold on the status quo while decrying the fact that changes are happening.
- *Resignation.* This is the stage when individuals reach a state of desperation and cannot see a way to accept the change and move forward. They may decide to look for a job elsewhere in the organization or even to leave the organization because they do not see themselves staying with it: 'I am so sad; why should I bother?', 'What is the point? I may as well go elsewhere.'
- *Acceptance.* Most people eventually internalize the change, make any needed adaptations, and then move forward with the change. Even if it is a grudging acknowledgement, they will start to consider the change for the best. In some cases, people will actively advocate what they had previously opposed. Acceptance and adaptation mean relinquishing the old ways of working and behaving, as well as the pain, confusion and fear experienced in the earlier stages of change: 'It's going to be OK', 'I can handle the change', 'I can't fight it, so I may as well prepare for it?
- *Commitment.* At this stage individuals will be committed to the change and begin to demonstrate the new behaviours and ways of working.

The reactions to each of these phases and suggestions for managing them are outlined in Table 11.2.

These phases can play a part in understanding the impact of change on people. There does, however, need to be a word of caution about they are used, as the phases that Kubler-Ross refers to do not always follow the sequence prescribed. Some people may skip certain stages. And some people may simply get stuck, for instance, in denial or anger. In such cases, people may be unwilling or unable to move forward. Some people will pass through each of the phases quickly; others will go slowly and may even go back to phases they have already experienced. When managing change it is important to recognize where people are on this curve and to respond accordingly. People get stuck for a number of reasons:

- Change is not a single event with neat and tidy beginnings and endings.
- Individuals' experiences of change may vary depending on their individual circumstances and experiences.
- To complicate matters, change often comes from two or more directions at the same time, which may add to the fear and uncertainty experienced by some individuals. For example, a division of a large company can be going through a restructure in which many roles are made redundant. The same division might then be sold to another company, which could result in a new leadership team, new policies and procedures, and a further restructure.

Table 11.2   Responses to change

Responses to change	Reactions	Suggestions for managing
Shock	• Inability to take in messages • Inaction – a lot of time spent talking in huddles • Anxiety – 'can I cope?' • Fear – 'what impact will it have on me?'	• Show that you understand their situation • Keep messages short and simple – complex argument will be wasted • Allow people time to digest information and share their feelings with others
Denial	• 'If we keep our heads down it will go away • Focus on 'business as usual'	• Gently and supportively confront what is being denied • Repeat messages • Arrange demonstrations on what the change will involve • Establish a timetable to provide milestones and evidence of change • Get people to do practical tasks related to the change
Anger	• This may be active: for example, challenging or disagreeing with management decisions • Or it may be passive: for example, not showing up at meetings or briefing sessions	• Encourage open communications – remember that bad news is better than no news at all • Listen and acknowledge feelings • Respond to concerns – be honest in recognizing the negative aspects of change, so don't oversell • Be clear on the givens, but highlight areas for negotiation and control – actively engage people in these aspects • Help rebuild self-esteem by identifying existing skills and experience that will be of value in the future
Resignation	• Increase in absenteeism • Exit –'I am off, this is not for me'	• Provide a series of specific next steps and follow-up frequently • Help individuals to identify options and benefits • Help them to focus on things they can do or can influence • Reinforce positive actions the individual can take • Consider coaching or counselling for the individual
Acceptance	• Express ownership for solutions • Focus on achieving benefits	• Use the individual as a coach or mentor for others and provide recognition • Recognize and reward achievement • Praise and support success • Provide feedback • Encourage networking
Commitment	Committed to making the change work 'This can work and be good'	• Use as role models for the new way of working • Recognize and reward achievement • Help them to build on successes • Broadcast their success • Get them to share their experience and learning

Models similar to the one from Kubler-Ross have been developed by Isabella (1990) and Bridges (1992). Isabella (1990) proposes that individuals go through the following stages in response to change:

1. *Anticipation* – this involves uncertainty, rumours and conducting 'sense-making' probes of what might be about to happen.
2. *Confirmation* – this involves being curious about what is happening and selecting a conventional explanation by an analogy in a way that standardizes the event ('It is an X kind of situation' or 'It is like when X happened') and personalizing the change.
3. *Culmination* – this is reconstructing one's viewpoint, testing it and learning the new reality, and searching for symbolic meanings in the new – from disorientation and confusion to understanding through to reconstruction.
4. *Aftermath* – this is accepting the change after it is over, especially its positive and negative consequences, the new strengths and weaknesses of the organization, and the winners and losers created by the change.

Isabella's model emphasizes that employees' reactions to change are multi-dimensional and multi-staged. The phases outlined in the model do raise some concerns. First, there is a passivity to Isabella's framework that is questionable. Individuals are not thought to get angry, alarmed or frustrated by changes. Indeed, the absence of hostility to the changes contrasts with other models, such as that of Kubler-Ross, which expressly includes an anger phase. Second, there is an assumed linear progression, from uncertainty and curiosity to reconciliation and acceptance. As mentioned with Kubler-Ross's model, this assumed linearity might not always be the case. Some employees will pass through the phases quickly; others may need time; but some will be unable to let go and they will get stuck in anger and resentment.

In contrast, Bridges (1992) proposes that individual reactions to change begin with an ending and then go on to a new beginning via a neutral zone:

1. *Ending phase.* This is a period of letting go of the current situation, characterized by disengagement and disenchantment with the organization or with one's work. This can be painful and upsetting. Until this has happened it is difficult for individuals to engage in new roles or change their behaviour. In this first transitional phase individuals need to be aware of how they have interpreted the change and how much of their response includes emotions of fear and loss. In this phase managers need to be aware of:

   o How individuals are responding to the proposed change
   o How much of their response is emotional

2. *Neutral zone.* This is when an individual completes the endings attached to the previous situation and starts tentatively to build energy and enthusiasm for change, characterized by disorientation, disintegration and discovery. This is still a period of confusion. The danger is that people may be so uncomfortable that they push prematurely for certainty and closure and ignore any possibility of a creative search for better alternatives. This is a phase that is necessary in order to summon the energy to embrace the new situation. The positive side of the neutral zone is

the tremendous opportunities to create new ways of thinking and acting. In this phase managers need to consider:

o How individuals can be encouraged to use the change to think and act differently
o How individuals and teams can be helped to see opportunity amid the change

3. *New beginnings*. This is a period in which individuals are able to align themselves with the new vision and the changes seem appealing. In this phase managers should recognize that individuals have accepted the change and are ready to move on. They should consider how they will continue to talk with their teams and the individuals within them about how they are feeling about the change and how they are adapting to it and what organizational support they need.

Bridges (1992) notes that many organizations are often in a hurry to force employees into the third phase before they have passed adequately through the prerequisite first and second phases. The term 'prerequisite' highlights the fact that the Bridges' model, as with those of Kubler-Ross and Isabella, is sequential. It is assumed that each individual must go through each phase in order, dealing with the consequences of each phase fully before advancing to the next phase. In reality this strict ordering may not be evident. The content of each phase, and progress through it, is subject to the employee's will and capacity. It is fundamentally a matter of employees' interpretation of the changes that determines how they react. Managers do need to be sensitive to where individuals are and what they are experiencing and not just expect them to move forward. Ultimately the employee needs to go through the process in his or her own time.

Using Bridges' (1992) model provides a simple framework for the stages of transition that describe natural emotional responses to change. Managers need to recognize that there will often be a time lag between the announcement of a change and an emotional reaction to it. It is easy to mistake the apparent calm of the first shock and denial phases for acceptance of the change. Different individuals will progress through the different stages at different rates and in different ways because the change will affect them differently. Managers need to beware that they themselves will go through the phases at a different rate from their staff. Managers will tend to know about the change before others and therefore may reach an acceptance of the change long before other organization members.

None of the models we have discussed on its own gives a complete picture of how people react to change. Therefore we propose combining both the Kubler-Ross and Bridges models to show a more realistic transition that individuals go through (see Figure 11.2).

How does change affect the psychological contract?

The combined effects of changes and the necessity for organizations to implement changes often quickly can significantly redefine employment relationships and have an impact on an individual's **psychological contract** with the organization in which they work. The psychological contract is defined by Rousseau (1990: 391) as 'the individual's beliefs about mutual obligations, in the context of the relationship between employer and employee'. According to this definition, a psychological contract consists of organizational obligations (to be fulfilled by the organization) and

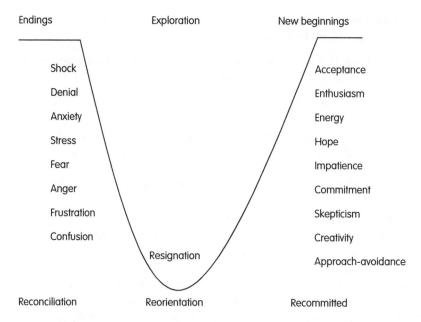

Figure 11.2   Transition individuals go through during change

employee obligations (to be fulfilled by employees), based on promises made by the employer and employee, respectively. The contract tends to be based on trust and defines the perceptions of the terms of an individual's relationship with their employer, and the organizational obligations to them.

The violation of the psychological contract increases during organizational transformations, since perceived organizational obligations tend to be fulfilled to a lesser extent, especially with regard to rewards, social atmosphere at work, career opportunities, job security, compensation and communication (Pate et al., 2000). Since much of the psychological contract is implicit rather than explicit, leaders and managers may be unaware when they implement organizational transformations of the impact the changes can potentially have on an individual's psychological contract. Often managers and leaders fail to realize that individuals may have a view that is very different from their own of what constitutes their psychological contract. Changes that impact on the psychological contract of employees can therefore result in a breach of trust if they are not considered in advance.

Activity

Think about a change initiative you are aware of. What happened or what will likely happen to the psychological contracts of those involved in the change?

1 What was the existing psychological contract?
2 In what ways did the change disrupt the existing contract?
3 What steps could have been taken to reduce the negative responses?
4 How should a new psychological contract be developed with affected individuals?

If you were affected by the change, what steps could you have taken to manage your way through the development of a new contract?

Trust and change

Trust is an important condition for successful change. In an organizational context trust is defined as the degree of confidence that individuals have in the goodwill of their leaders, specifically the extent to which they believe that their managers and leaders are honest, sincere and unbiased in taking their positions into account (Dirks and Ferrin, 2002; Kiefer, 2005; Mishra and Spreitzer, 1998). Employees' trust in leaders and managers, as well as in the organization, is an expression of confidence in their reliability and honesty in times of change and uncertainty (Zeffane and Connell, 2003). Such judgements about the reliability and honesty of management are shaped by everyday experiences at work. Organizational change initiatives can significantly erode trust both in the organization and in its management (Morgan and Zeffane, 2003).

Without trust, individuals are more likely to withdraw their involvement in the organization and the change project (Mishra and Spreitzer, 1998). Trust in times of change is based on two things: predictability and capability (Duck, 2001). In any organization, people want to know what to expect; they want predictability. Predictability consists of intention and ground rules: what the general goals are and how decisions will be made. The more leaders clarify the organization's intentions and ground rules, the more people will be able to predict and influence what happens to them, even in the middle of constant change.

The second part of the equation is capability. To trust an organization, both managers and their employees must define the capability that each is providing, and each side has to believe that the other is capable of playing the new role. To make this happen, managers and employees must identify needed capabilities and negotiate the roles and responsibilities of those involved in the process. To build trust in times of change, leaders and managers must demonstrate that they are capable of leading the change and that they will act with integrity, honesty and fairness (Mayer et al., 1995). The importance of building trust is emphasized in the following case study, written by Anthony Greenfield, concerning a major cost-reduction programme in a supermarket chain.

CASE STUDY

A major cost reduction programme at a supermarket chain

The situation

A large supermarket chain found itself losing market share. It was suffering from long-term underinvestment in infrastructure and innovation. A critical factor was its over-inflated cost base, estimated to be several hundreds of millions of dollars larger than that of similar competitors. Central to this cost base was the prices they paid for the goods, mainly food, which were sold in their stores.

The buying teams within the business had become too remote from their suppliers. They negotiated the price of finished goods delivered to their warehouses without much insight

(Continued)

(Continued)

into the underlying cost drivers. This meant that decisions they made about products, packaging, transportation and storage of goods often led to price inflation and growth in the cost base. Suppliers were reluctant to contradict such decisions, as they feared losing business. Buyers therefore got into the habit of dictating terms. Prices were often inflated surreptitiously. For instance, a supplier would use foreign exchange fluctuation as an excuse to increase prices or wait for a buyer to move jobs (which was a regular occurrence) and then take advantage of the new buyer's lack of information and experience to hike up prices.

The solution

After some initial analysis indicated the scale of the opportunity to shrink the cost base, an external consulting team was invited by the Buying Director to get to work on reducing the price of goods. They recruited a number of buyers and other supermarket employees to work alongside them in a joint effort. The backbone of the approach they pursued was to break down end-to-end supply-chain costs into their component parts to identify where cost could be taken out. For instance, the cost of a box of tomatoes might be made up of the cost of growing and harvesting the tomato plants, the cost of washing and packing the tomatoes, the cost of the packaging and labels, the cost of transport and storage and, finally, the cost of taking the box from the storage area in a store and placing it on the shelf ready for the customer. It is likely that at least one of these cost components could be significantly reduced.

Difficulties encountered

The project began steadily taking cost out of several products, for instance by changing packaging specification or simply calling suppliers to account on inflated prices. Savings measured in millions of pounds were achieved in a matter of months, but this was far off from the hundreds of millions of dollars that had been targeted.

The project was an uphill battle. The biggest barriers were internal to the company and stemmed from uncertainty, mistrust and a feeling that change was being imposed from the outside. The cost-reduction team were seen as outsiders despite the fact that the most of the team members were supermarket employees. There was a feeling that they could not be trusted not to upset supplier relationships or that they would focus too much on cost and not enough on quality. There was also resentment that they had the time and money to focus on improvement while the buyers still had their day job to do and that the team would take all the credit and the buyers would be made look incompetent. As a result, the cost-saving team did not get the support it needed from within the business to deliver the required savings. People resisted passively by simply being slow to help or through a variety of delaying tactics, and a few were openly hostile.

The breakthrough

In its first year of operation, the cost-reduction team became able to work effectively with the buying departments and with suppliers, and cost savings continued to rise steadily, but despite their best efforts, the pace of delivery increased only slowly.

The breakthrough came when the Buying Directors took a decision to train all of their people in the techniques that the cost-reduction team had been employing. Over a period of a few months every buyer, merchandiser and new product developer went on a three-day training course in how to take cost out of the supply chain.

The results

Some buyers used what they learned on the training course to reduce the cost of the products that they were responsible for, but these individuals were in a small minority. Most were too busy with their day job to take the time to work through the cost-saving process. However, as the techniques were now familiar to them, they realized that they made sense.

Trust between the buyers and the cost-reduction team increased as people felt more in control of the changes that were required to shrink the cost base. As a result, senior managers allowed the cost-reduction team into their departments. Likewise, the buyers provided support for their work or at least granted them access to work on their products and with their suppliers. Active and passive resistance largely fell away.

As for cost savings, the pace of delivery started to accelerate rapidly as the floodgates opened. In the first year of the programme, savings were just under $40m. In year two, when the training took place, $120m was saved, and in year three $300m was saved (a total reduction in the annual cost base of $460m).

Lessons learnt

People are wary of change that is seen to be imposed by outsiders and will oppose the change either actively or passively (through non-cooperation). Putting the tools of change into the hands of the people who are affected by it builds trust and gives them a sense of control over it, making it *their* change rather than someone else's. As a result, people actively support the change, or at least do not oppose it.

© 2015 Anthony Greenfield, Founder and Director of the 5 Forces of Change.

Activity

1   Consider the impact of a change on an organization you are familiar with and then analyse the impact of the change on the individuals affected. How would you describe the impact and its causes?
2   What were the perceived costs of change? Who perceived these? How accurate were the perceptions? How could they be influenced?
3   What were the perceived benefits of change? How accurate were these perception? What was the probability of achieving these benefits? How dissatisfied with the status quo were employees? Why? What were the costs of not changing?

Managing reactions to change

Participation

Involving people in the change process can help to generate positive attitudes and commitment to change. Starting with Coch and French's (1948) classic study at the Harwood Manufacturing Corporation, studies of participation have focused on the degree to which employees are involved in planning and implementing change. Such participation creates a sense of both contribution to the change and control over it. As a rule, employees who participate more tend to report greater readiness and acceptance of change, recognize change as less stressful and show more overall support for the change (Holt et al., 2007). Involvement in the early stages of the change can also decrease individuals' change-related stress (Holt et al., 2007), while participation during the change process has been linked with positive emotions, a greater understanding of the meaning of change and greater involvement in implementing behavioural changes (Bartunek et al., 2006). Participation in the change process is important for helping to reduce negative responses to change by reducing anxiety, creating a stronger sense of ownership and enabling individuals to actively contribute to the shaping of change.

Activity

Reflect on a change that you have experienced:

1 What evidence was there that those leading the change agreed with the participative approach?
2 In what ways, if any, were you able to participate?
3 How did that affect your attitude towards the change?

Commitment versus compliance

Whether change is achieved through commitment or compliance depends on the change that needs to be made. If a child was running towards a street with traffic you would not use a commitment approach and explain that the car will hurt them. You would pull them back and explain later. This is the same approach that is used in an organization for immediate compliance purposes. The opposite is also true. If you want a child to make a long-term, sustained change, such as eating more healthily, you would not just give them a raw carrot and expect them to eat it. You would make the child aware of the better options, help them understand what food is better for them, and reinforce what the benefits are for them in order to sustain the change. The same is true when we need to achieve sustained behavioural change in organizations. We need to gain commitment to the proposed change.

Organizational commitment plays an important role in employees' acceptance of change (Yousef, 2000) and their reactions to it. Several studies have found that employees who are committed to their organization are willing to exert effort on its behalf and are more accepting of the need for change (Oreg et al., 2011). Begley and Czajka (1993) also found that organizational commitment can serve as a buffer, dampening the detrimental effects of change-related stress. Furthermore, individuals' past experience of change can affect their level of commitment to the organization and their willingness to support further change (Hayes, 2014).

Commitment to change refers to the degree of an individual's willingness and desire to support the change that results from a sense of needing to reciprocate positive treatment received from the organization or a sense of moral duty rooted in loyalty to the organization (Herscovitch and Meyer, 2002). Employees with strong organizational commitment are more likely to develop positive attitudes towards organizational change and therefore be more willing to put more effort into a change (Iverson, 1996). Each individual determines through his or her perceptual filters whether change is a threat or a benefit. Each individual's unique schema of what change is or what change represents adds to the formulation of attitudes and reactions to change (Woodman, 1995). Individuals who are committed to their organization accept its values, are willing to exert effort on its behalf and wish to remain in it. They tend to report higher levels of readiness to change and acceptance of the change (Madsen et al., 2005; Mowday et al., 1979; Shapiro and Kirkman, 1999).

In any change process, managers and leaders have to decide whether they will achieve change through commitment or compliance. Compliance is about no-choice change: the system requires and enforces compliance. It may be relevant and necessary at certain times, such as having to comply with new legislation or regulations. In contrast, commitment is about choice-change: how one engages with change is a free choice.

Leaders must select the most appropriate approach for the change in their organizations. The route chosen depends on (a) the kind of change and (b) the level of commitment required for the change to be successful. Both incur cost but at different stages. With compliance, heavy costs can occur later on, especially if old habits return and the change is not sustained. With commitment, costs occur early on through involving people, communications and stakeholder management.

Implications for leaders and managers: strategies for managing the impact of change

There are a number of practical implications that can be drawn from the issues raised in this chapter.

Recognize the impact of change on people

For leaders and managers, change is often appropriate and necessary. But until everyone understands the what, why, when, who, where and how of the change, there is potential for negative reactions to the change. Individuals will have their own perceptions about the change. For instance, individuals may perceive it as threatening their status or adding extra work to their already overloaded work schedule. Individuals may then appear to oppose the change and as a result be viewed in negative terms – as 'resistors'. Leaders and managers need to recognize the impact of change on individuals and why they respond as they do. Leaders and managers need to see change from the 'hilltops' of others and be aware of where on the change curve individuals are.

Convince people that change is really necessary

The reality is that many people will react positively to change. People will embrace rather than resist change if the outcome is important to them and they have been convinced that they will be better off rather than worse off. People pay attention to the process and will want to know:

- The need for the change – in advance
- How the change is to be managed
- The vision for where the organization is going with the change
- The reasons for the change, clearly and fully explained
- What training and development will be provided to implement or take part in the change

People need to be convinced that change is necessary and that there is a need to move from the status quo. Leaders need to be able to show that there is a better alternative. Leaders and managers also need to be seen to have a process to move people from where they are to where they need to be and to be able to show that the benefits outweigh the costs.

Role modelling

Leaders and managers need to role model the change in behaviour they expect of others. As the Russian thinker, novelist and philosopher Leo Tolstoy said, 'Everyone thinks of changing the world, but no one thinks of changing himself.' When leaders and managers live by the principles they set out for change they gain credibility in relation to the change agenda.

Of particular importance to role modelling is the ability of leaders and managers to act as active participants in change processes and to have the courage to carry on with the change even when their role is under threat of redundancy. Leaders and managers will also need to think about where they are in the emotional stages of change so they can manage their own reactions to the change as well as those of other people. They may be further ahead than their staff, having accepted the change while their staff are still in denial about it.

Social support

Various forms of social support can assist employees in coping with change. Research that originated in the 1980s found that social support could help individuals to cope with and alleviate the negative effects of stress caused by change (Cohen and Wills, 1985). Social support is a positive or helpful interpersonal interaction with someone such as a manager, colleague, friend or relative, which House (1981) says involves one or more of the following:

- Emotion – showing concern and listening
- Information – providing information and advice
- Instrumental – providing active help with issues, such as workload
- Appraisal – providing information relevant to individual performance

Employees who perceive management as supportive and who feel respected are more receptive to suggested changes and more willing to cooperate with the change (Lawrence and Callan, 2011). In contrast, employees who perceive their work environment as generally unsupportive are more likely to have cynical reactions, suffer from negative emotions and ultimately reject the change (Kiefer, 2005). The more effective and supportive managers are in taking care of employees, the more employees will trust their decisions and accept change (van Dam et al., 2008).

Appendix 11.1: Understanding responses to change

Which groups of people will be impacted by the proposed change and what are their likely responses?

Table 11.3

Group of people	What is the impact of change on this group? (1 = low; 5 = high)	What is their likely response? (positive or negative)	How should change in this group be best secured? (commitment or compliance)	What level of investment is needed for this group to change? (1 = low; 5 = high)	When does this group need to be involved in the change? (early/later)

Further reading

Baraldi, S., Kalyal, H., Berntson, E., Naswall, K. and Sverke, M. (2010) 'The importance of commitment to change in public reform: An example from Pakistan', *Journal of Change Management*, 10(4): 347–68.

Barton, L.C. and Ambrosini, V. (2013) 'The moderating effect of organizational change cynicism on middle manager strategy commitment', *International Journal of Human Resource Management*, 24(4): 721–46.

Bernerth, J.B., Armenakis, A.A., Field, H.S. and Walker, H.J. (2004) 'Justice, cynicism, and commitment: A study of important organizational change variables', *Journal of Applied Behavioral Science*, 43(4): 303–26.

Caldwell, S.D. and Liu Yi (2010) 'Further investigating the influence of personality in employee response to organizational change: The moderating role of change-related factors', *Human Resource Management Journal*, 21(1): 74–89.

Millar, G. (2012) 'Employee engagement – a new paradigm', *Human Resource Management International Digest*, 20(2): 3–5.

Novak, D. (2012) *Taking People with You: The Only Way to Make Big Things Happen*. New York: Portfolio/Penguin.

Palmisano, S. (2004) 'Leading change when business is good'. Interview by Paul Hemp and Thomas A. Stewart, *Harvard Business Review*, 82(12): 60.

Peccei, R., Giangreco, A. and Sebastiano, A. (2011) 'The role of organizational commitment in the analysis of resistance to change: Co-predictor and moderator effects', *Personnel Review*, 40(2): 185–204.

Van der Smissen, S., Schalk, R. and Freese, C. (2013) 'Organizational change and the psychological contract: How change influences the perceived fulfillment of obligations', *Journal of Organizational Change Management*, 26(6): 1071–90.

Power, Politics and Conflict During Change

12

Overview

- Power is a dynamic variable that changes as conditions change (Yukl, 2006). Leaders and managers need to understand the difference between the different types of power and their characteristics in order to be able to use them appropriately. Understanding this can help in influencing and motivating people to do what needs to be done during change.
- Organizational politics are often described as a turf game involving a competition of ideas (Buchanan and Badham, 2009). There are two different perspectives on organizational politics. One views politics as a negative process that actively inhibits the effective running of an organization; the other sees politics in a more positive light. The latter view focuses on the waste of time and energy and the damage that politics can cause. Organizational politics can provide the stimulating force for change, and political forces can generate the energy for organizational change.
- Change can generate conflict. The Thomas–Kilman model provides a way for leaders and managers to understand how people react to and deal with conflict.
- Change is rarely dependent on the actions of a single key figure, whether it is a CEO or some other change agent, because change is a distributed phenomenon. The concept of change agency, therefore, is of more value than the notion of a single change agent (Buchanan and Storey, 1997; Denis et al., 2001). Change agency is emergent and fluid. The change agent is a member of this cast, formally appointed or self-appointed, seeking to drive a change agenda. The change agents needs the ability to identify and manage the power, politics and conflict that may arise from organizational change.

Understanding the power and political dynamics in an organization is critical to being able to sustain change. Political behaviour tends to be more intense in times of change because individuals and teams perceive the possibility of upsetting the existing balance of power. Some may be motivated to defend the status quo; while others may perceive change as an opportunity to enhance their position. Leaders and managers therefore need to be aware of the political dynamics and power plays that can impact on change.

Although power, politics and conflict are natural phenomena in any organization, they traditionally get a 'bad press' and tend to be shown to be to the detriment of those who have to experience change (Burnes, 2009a). How power is used can affect a change initiative either favourably or unfavourably, while political behaviour and conflict can stop change that is necessary or desirable from being implemented successfully in organizations (Lines, 2007; Senior and Fleming, 2006). The process of leading and managing organizational change more often than not creates or results in conflict and opposition. Despite this, power, politics and conflict tend to be overlooked in much of the literature on organizational change.

This chapter explores power, politics and conflict during organizational change. It provides a working definition of each concept and describes the roles of each of them in organizational change. The chapter discusses how power, politics and conflict are important to recognize and manage during change initiatives if change is to be sustained. The role of the change agent in relation to power, politics and conflict is also considered. The chapter concludes by providing some practical tools to analyse the power and influence of stakeholders in the change process.

Learning objectives

By the end of this chapter you will be able to:

- Explain the differences, similarities and relationships between the concepts of power, politics and conflict in the context of change
- Identify the power dynamics in an organization and the various sources of power
- Appreciate the role of change agents and change agency in change initiatives
- Identify key stakeholders involved in change initiatives and the power they hold
- Apply conflict-handling techniques, when required to do so, during change

Power

The prominent role power plays in organizational change is evident in the following sentiment from Kanter that no new change will occur 'without someone with power pushing it' (1983: 296). It is therefore important, as French and colleagues point out, 'to know who has power and from what sources that power comes, to know how to exercise power and how to resist other people's exercise of power' (1989: 414). Accordingly, there is a need to learn how to read the political context of a change initiative (Lewis and Seibold, 1998) – its political manoeuvring and informal social network (DeLuca, 1984) – in order to use the available power sources (Greiner and Schein, 1989; Schein, 1977) and 'bring about the outcomes desired' (Salancik and Pfeffer, 1977: 3).

Power is defined as the ability to change the behaviour of others (McClelland, 1975). It is the ability to cause others to perform actions they might not otherwise perform. Those in authority are those who are seen to have a legitimate right to influence others due to their position. Notions of positional power dominate traditional conceptions of management (see Pfeffer, 1992). Positional power is defined in terms of the right one has to dominate another through the exercising of authority. This is a view that stems from a bureaucratic mindset, where the authoritative right of control and power extends downward from superior to subordinate (see Weber, 1946); this hierarchical chain confers legitimacy and the right to dominate according to one's position (Morgan, 2006). According to Marshak (1993), planned change models, based on positional power, rest on five assumptions:

1. The linear assumption – movement is from one state to another in a forward progression
2. The progressive assumption – movement is from a lesser state to a better state
3. The goal assumption – movement is to a specific end state
4. The disequilibrium assumption – movement requires disequilibrium, for instance, an impelling, disruptive force
5. The separateness assumption – movement is planned and managed by people apart from the organization, rather than those within it

These assumptions can determine how power is exercised in implementing change.

In contrast to planned change models based on positional power, a relational conception of power and change engages quite different assumptions. Instead, Marshak (1993) points out that forms of control are not foisted a priori onto the participants' interaction but are embedded with the power relations emerging from those interactions and context. This perspective of power contrasts with positional power.

Power: A Radical View

In 1974 Steven Lukes published *Power: A Radical View*. Lukes maintains that power is one of those concepts that is unavoidably value-dependent, that is, 'both its definition and any given use of it, once defined, are inextricably tied to a given set of (probably unacknowledged) value-assumptions which predetermine the range of its empirical application' (Lukes, 2005: 30).

Lukes sketches three conceptual maps that reveal the distinguishing features of three views of power: the pluralist view (which he calls the one-dimensional view); the view of critics of pluralism (which he calls the two-dimensional view); and a third view of power (which he calls the three-dimensional view) (Lukes, 2005: 29). The distinctive features of these three views of power are summarized below.

- *One-dimensional view of power.* This view focuses on behavior, decision-making, key issues, observable conflict and interests seen as policy preferences revealed by political participation.
- *Two-dimensional view of power.* This view focuses on decision-making and control over the political agenda, issues and potential issues; observable conflict; and interests, seen as policy preferences or grievances.

- *Three-dimensional view of power.* This view focuses on decision-making and control over the political agenda; issues and potential issues; observable and latent conflict; and subjective and real interests.

According to the one-dimensional view, power is conceived of as intentional and active and can be measured through the study of its exercise. According to the critics of this view, power is not only reflected in concrete decisions. Individuals or groups can limit decision-making to relatively non-controversial issues by influencing community values and political procedures and rituals. Power may also be located in the capacity to create or reinforce barriers to the public airing of policy conflicts (Bachrach and Baratz, 1970: 8).

According to Lukes, the two-dimensional view of power is limited in that it focuses only on observable conflicts, whether overt or covert. Lukes claims that A can also exercise power over B by influencing, shaping, or determining his/her wants and preferences. A second criticism is that this view is too committed to behaviourism, that is to the study of concrete decisions, whereas inaction can also be the outcome of socially structured and culturally patterned collective behavior. The third point on which this view is seen as inadequate is in its claim that non-decision-making power only exists where there are grievances that are denied entry into the political process in the form of issues. In line with the previous arguments, however, Lukes argues that power can also be exercised by *preventing* grievances – by shaping perceptions, cognitions and preferences in such a way as to secure the acceptance of the status quo since no alternative appears to exist, or because it is seen as natural and unchangeable, or indeed beneficial.

The third dimension of power – the power to prevent the formation of grievances by shaping perceptions, cognitions and preferences in such a way as to ensure the acceptance of a certain role in the existing order – is a very contentious and, at the same time, fundamental view.

The three-dimensional view allows the consideration of the many ways in which potential issues are 'kept out' of politics, whether through individuals' decisions or through the operation of social forces and institutional practices. Lukes introduces and stresses the importance of the concept of latent conflict. A latent conflict consists in a contradiction between the interests of A (those exercising power), and the real interests of B, which are excluded. The conflict is latent because those subject to power do not express or even remain unaware of their interests. This means that the interests of B are very difficult to trace, because those concerned either cannot express them or are unable to recognize them.

So these different forms of power relationships can be deeply embedded in organizational structures and procedures, such that they come to be taken for granted. Embedded power relationships can operate by influencing the basic understanding and perceptions of individuals (Hardy and O'Sullivan, 1988). However, as Clegg and colleagues (2006) observe, delving deeper into the workings of power can become a highly abstract exercise. The main point is that power operates at different levels in an organization. Managers and leaders need to understand the different types of power and the modes of influence that are available to them and others.

The two faces of power

Traditionally power is seen as either negative or positive. At its most unsubtle, power is about forcing others to do things against their will (Kanter, 1979). This is emphasized by Dahl (1957: 202), who defines power as a relationship among individuals in which one individual (A) can get another individual (B) to do something they (B) would not otherwise have done. While this definition focuses on the behavioural effects of power, others have stressed that power can have an effect on attitudes in addition to behaviour (for example House, 1981).

The negative, unattractive face of power is characterized by a need to have dominance and control over others. In contrast, positive power derives from a need to initiate, influence and lead. Positive power recognizes other people's needs to achieve their own goals as well as the needs of management to achieve their goals (McClelland, 1975). An example of the difference is assertiveness (positive power) versus aggressiveness (negative power). Positive power seeks to empower both oneself and other people whereas negative power aims to empower oneself at the expense of others (French and Bell, 1999).

Another way to think about power is as a motivating force for managers. In 'Power is the great motivator', an influential article written by David McClelland and David Burnham and published in the *Harvard Business Review* in 1976, the authors laid out the findings of a survey of managers in a range of US corporations. They found that managers comprised three different motivational groups. The first group was affiliative managers, who wanted to be liked more than they cared about being effective. The second group was motivated by achievement and did not worry what others thought of them. The third and most effective group was institutional managers, who were most interested in power. They focused on amassing power through influence rather than their own achievements. The most important check on their aggression and ego was emotional maturity, which allowed them to exert power without coercion or bullying.

Ashforth (1994) found that the acquisition and use of power in particular tends to corrupt the power holder. Indeed, in Lord Acton's memorable phrase, 'power tends to corrupt; and absolute power corrupts absolutely' (Dalberg-Acton, 1887). The power holder can develop an exalted sense of self-worth while at the same time devaluing the worth of others. Over time, this leads to distorted images of oneself and others and corresponding attitudes and behaviours on the part of both the power holder and their employees. For example, the greater the power differential and the stronger and more controlling the influence (such as rewards, coercion), the more inclined the manager is to attribute employees' successes to managerial control rather than to subordinates themselves, and the less inclined employees are to openly question the manager. Accordingly the manager comes to believe that they can do no wrong, that they should not be bound by the same constraints as others and that employees must be closely supervised (Ashforth, 1994: 73).

When people with distorted personalities gain power via hierarchical positions, their insecurities, narcissism and power-and-control-orientation turn into management incompetence and permanent tendencies towards grandiosity (concerning themselves, their actions and ideas) and distrust (concerning others) (Maccoby, 2005). Positional power can lead to what Barbara Kellerman (2004) terms simply 'bad leadership'. Higgs (2013: 173) identifies a range of descriptions of bad leadership, which include the abuse of power. This encompasses the use of power to serve personal goals or achieve personal gain, reinforce self-image and enhance perceptions of personal performance (Ashforth, 1994).

Types of power

Different types of power can be identified. Hardy and Clegg (1996) differentiate three types of power:

1. *The power of resources* is linked to control over scarce resources. This type of power is exercised by the deployment of key resources on which others are dependent. With this power the outcome of decisions may be influenced through individual control and the management of resources such as information, expertise, budgets, rewards and punishments.
2. The *power of process* is related to influencing outcomes by controlling those who participate in decision-making processes and those who do not. The power of process is linked to the influence of outcomes by indirect participation. Who takes part in decision-making therefore is controlled rather than controlling the decision-making directly.
3. The *power of meaning* has to do with controlling or shaping perceptions, cognitions and preferences. This is possible by influencing what information is given, how it is given and to whom it is given. It has to do with controlling language symbols and rituals.

Leaders and managers need to understand the different types of power and their characteristics in order to be able to use them appropriately, in order to influence and motivate people to do what needs to be done during change. Several characteristics of power are described by Buchanan and Badham (2009):

- Power as a *property of individuals*, as expressed in terms of power sources and bases, either structural or individual.
- Power as a *property of interpersonal relationships* among organizational members, expressed in the perception that some individuals possess or lack particular **power bases**.
- Power as an *embedded property* of structures, procedures and norms of the organization, perpetuating existing routines and power inequalities.

The notion of power as a persuasive and embedded construct has three consequences. First, it highlights the tangible dimensions of power, existing in the taken-for-granted procedures and practices of the organization. Second, it emphasizes the wide range of both the methods and techniques available to leaders and managers and the potential responses from the targets of political tactics. Third, it highlights that the notion of what may be defined as 'power' in textbook terms may not be so unambiguously regarded in practice. Power in practice becomes a slippery concept when its users can credibly claim that they are applying custom and practice or accepted norms, rules or regulations. What may be regarded as the exercise of power from one perspective may be regarded as commonplace and routine from another (Buchanan and Badham, 2009).

Power bases

Power stems from an individual's personality and skills as well as his or her formal position in an organization. It differs along a set of dimensions known as power bases. In 1950s, Raven and French (1958) developed a now-classic model, which identified sources of power and, in so doing, replaced the traditional view that power primarily derived from formal authority.

Raven and French's sources of power are:

1. *Coercive power*, which is dependent on fear. People respond to this form of power out of fear of the negative results that occur if they fail to comply. It is characterized by the application or threat of physical or psychological sanctions that prevent or reduce the meeting of basic existential, physiological, safety or psychological needs of an individual.
2. *Reward power* is the opposite of coercive power. Compliance with the wishes of the power holder is dependent on the promise of outcomes that are perceived as rewards (concerning the pursuit of pleasure or happiness), such as monetary bonuses (material rewards) or recognition such as praise, publicity or fame (psychological rewards). Reward power derives from either of two sources: formal position of the power holder (known as position power or authority) or the power holder's personality or skills (known as personal power) (Gill, 2011: 266–71). An individual's formal position in an organization may carry with it the authority to dispense material rewards, whereas anybody, no matter what their position in an organization, may dispense psychological rewards.
3. *Legitimate power* represents the formal authority to control and use organizational resources and to insist on something being done. It is based on the power a person receives as a result of their position in the hierarchy of an organization.
4. *Expert power* is influence wielded as a result of expertise – knowledge, competence or special skill(s) – perceived by others.
5. *Information power* is related to expert power but concerns information rather than expertise: 'People are influenced by those who have information that they need or want for their work but do not have or [by those] who control access to it' (Gill, 2011: 269).
6. *Referent power* is based on the identification with a person who has desirable resources or attractive personal traits, for example charisma. It develops out of admiration for another person and a desire to be like that person.

Research suggests that expert and referent power bases are the most effective of these power bases (Robbins et al., 2010). They are derived from an individual's personal characteristics and experience. In contrast, coercive, reward, information and legitimate power are essentially derived from the organization. As people are more likely to enthusiastically accept and commit to an individual whom they admire or whose expertise they respect, rather than someone who relies on their position for influence, the effective use of expert and referent power relate positively to employee motivation, performance and commitment to change (Podsakoff and Schriesheim, 1985). Expert power especially appears to offer wide appeal, and its use as a power base has been found to result in high performance from individuals (Lines, 2007). It would therefore seem appropriate that, to implement and sustain change effectively, leaders and managers need to consider using a mix of referent and expert power.

Power tactics

Power tactics are used to put power bases into action. Tactics, which can be applied during change for each power base, have been highlighted by Yukl and Tracey (1992) are outlined in Table 12.1.

Robbins et al. (2010) have identified nine distinct influence tactics from the research, which are:

1. *Legitimacy* – relying on one's position of authority and stressing that a change is in accordance with organizational policies and rules
2. *Rational persuasion* – presenting logical arguments and factual evidence to demonstrate that a change is reasonable
3. *Inspirational appeals* – developing emotional commitment by appealing to an individual's values, needs, hopes and aspirations
4. *Consultation* – increasing an individual's motivation and support by involving him or her in deciding how the change will be achieved
5. *Exchange* – rewarding an individual with benefits or favours in exchange for supporting a change
6. *Personal appeal* – asking for compliance based on friendship or loyalty
7. *Ingratiation* – using flattery, praise or friendly behaviour prior to making a change
8. *Pressure* – using warnings, repeated demands and threats
9. *Coalitions* – enlisting the aid of people to persuade an individual or ensuring the support of others as a reason for an individual to agree to a change

Some tactics are more effective than others. Specifically, rational persuasion, inspirational appeals and consultation tend to be most effective, while pressure tends to backfire and is the least effective tactic (Yukl, 2006). Managers can increase their chances of success by using more than one tactic at a time. For example, using ingratiation and legitimacy can lessen the negative reaction that occurs from being told about changes.

Jeffrey Pfeffer (2010) in his book *Power: Why Some People Have It – and Others Don't*, says that what leaders need to do is to follow his 11-step plan (see box on p. 341), starting with handing out resources to anyone who will help to build a power base. This includes co-opting antagonists and removing rivals before moving on to persisting with what you are doing despite any setbacks, and making important relationships work, no matter what, and finally, creating a vision that is compelling enough for others to follow.

Table 12.1   Guidelines for using power bases

Power base	Uses
Legitimate	• Make polite clear requests.
	• Explain reasons for the request.
	• Do not exceed the scope of your authority.
	• Verify authority if necessary.
	• Follow up to verify compliance.
	• Insist on compliance.
Reward	• Offer the type of rewards that people desire.
	• Offer rewards that are fair and equitable.
	• Do not promise more than you can deliver.
	• Explain criteria for giving rewards.
	• Provide rewards as promised if objectives are met.
Coercive	• Explain rules and requirements.
	• Respond to issues promptly and consistently.
	• Investigate to get facts – don't jump to conclusions.
	• Provide oral and written warnings.
	• Stay calm and avoid hostility.
	• Express a desire to help individuals.
	• Invite individuals to suggest ways for improvement.
	• Use punishments that are legitimate and fair.
Information	• Provide information for the rationale for the change.
	• Provide information about the benefits of the change.
	• Direct employees to relevant information sources.
	• Communicate information regularly.
Referent	• Show acceptance and positive regard.
	• Act supportive and helpful.
	• Defend and backup individuals when appropriate.
	• Keep promises.
Expert	• Explain reasons for change.
	• Provide evidence that change will be successful.
	• Listen to concerns.
	• Act confidently and decisively in a crisis.

Pfeffer's rules for exercising power

1   Give resources to potential backers.
2   Shape behaviour through rewards and punishments.
3   Advance on multiple fronts.
4   Make the first move.

(Continued)

(Continued)

5   Co-opt antagonists.
6   Remove rivals – nicely, if possible.
7   Don't draw unnecessary fire.
8   Use the personal touch.
9   Persist in what you are doing.
10 Make important relationships work – no matter what.
11 Make the vision compelling.

Activity

1   What sources of power are you comfortable with, and which ones do you have access to?
2   Think of a change you are familiar with. Who had power? What behaviours were associated with their having power?

Powerlessness

Power is the energy needed to initiate and sustain action or, to put it another way, the capacity to translate intention into reality (Bennis and Nanus, 1985). A good idea is one thing but getting it implemented can be a challenge. Kotter (1985) traces the problem to what he describes as the 'power gap'. This is a discrepancy between the resources and authority attached to formal positions and the power needed to obtain cooperation and support from the different groups on which a successful change depends. This gap can lead to frustration from managers who see their superiors, colleagues or employees as obstructing change. In the face of opposition to change there is a natural tendency to attribute resistance to deliberate obstruction and to the active pursuit by others of their own agendas. At one level this is an understandable and appropriate acknowledgement of the surface dimension of politics – the cut and thrust of self-interest.

However, below this lies another reality, the more or less widespread experience of powerlessness. Rosabeth Moss Kanter says:

> powerlessness breeds bossiness and creates ineffective desultory management and petty, dictatorial rules-minded managerial styles. The complex web of embedded restrictions on the ability of individuals to pursue and realize goals often generates powerlessness. (1997: 135)

Few employees relish being powerless in their job and organization. Kanter (1997) notes that when people in organizations are difficult, argumentative and temperamental, it may be because they are in a position of powerlessness in which the performance expectations placed on them exceed their resources and capabilities. The successful implementation of change means overcoming not only powerful vested interests but also the powerlessness that can impede any initiatives. For the power to influence the actions and reactions of others is critical for achieving change.

Politics: power in action

Perspectives of organizational politics

Organizational politics are often described as a turf game involving a competition of ideas (Buchanan and Badham, 2009). As with power, there are two different perspectives on organizational politics. One views politics as a negative process that actively inhibits the effective running of an organization; the other sees politics in a more positive light. The latter view focuses on the waste of time and energy and the damage that politics can cause. In support of this, Ward argues that:

> To ignore organizational politics when managing change is to fail. What then is the alternative? Should one be political? The short answer is no. If you do become political, then professional integrity is sacrificed. You are just another silver-tongued hustler parading your wares while seeking to manipulate. This is the road to disaster. Politics does not add value. (1994: 143)

This dark side of politics is referred to by Ferris and Kacmar, who observe that:

> A fundamental issue in work on organizational politics concerns its largely negative interpretation. Most people perceive only the dark side of politics, and indeed there is a dark side, characterized by destructive opportunism and dysfunctional game playing. (1992: 113)

Ferris and King (1991) describe politicized decision-making as 'a walk on the dark side', which is echoed in Gerard Egan's (1994) book *Working the Shadow Side: A Guide to Positive Behind-the-Scenes Management*. Chanlat (1997) goes as far as describing politics as a 'social disease', which is often associated with high levels of stress, depression and other undesirable individual and corporate outcomes.

This negative view is, however, widely challenged by proponents of the positive perspective of politics. For instance, Kumar and Thibodeaux (1990) acknowledge and indeed advocate the use of political strategies in planned change. In support of their argument they identify three levels of change: first-level change, which involves improving unit or department effectiveness; second-level change, which involves introducing new perspectives to organizational subsystems; and third-level change, which concerns organization-wide shifts in values and ways of working. While first-level and second-level changes require political awareness and political facilitation respectively, third-level change entails political intervention. In other words, the more widespread the implications of organizational change, the greater the political involvement required by leaders and managers.

Organizational politics can provide the stimulating force for change, and political forces can generate the energy for organizational change (Hardy and Clegg, 1996). Political struggles usually play a role in resolving competing perspectives and interests in the context of organizational change (Frost and Egri, 1991). The history of conflicting interests, alignments and negotiations, argue Bacharach and Lawler (1998), is the history of change. To shut down political action is to remove this source of energy and creativity. While agreeing that the costs of eliminating politics are high, Jeffrey Pfeffer (1992) observes that the quality of debate in a politics-free organization is likely to be poor. Pfeffer points out that:

Politics concerns the creation of legitimacy for certain ideas, values and demands, not just actions performed as a result of previously acquired legitimacy. The management of meaning refers to a process of symbol construction and value designed both to create legitimacy for one's own demands and to 'delegitimize' the demands of opponents. (1977: 85)

This view of politics as natural and necessary highlights the need for leaders and managers to intervene in the political system of the organization in order to legitimize the rationale for change, particularly when they are faced with opposition to it. This requires them to demonstrate political behaviour.

Activity

Think of a change situation in your organization or an organization with which you are familiar. What types of power are evident? Who has position power? Who has personal power, and which kind?

Political behaviour

Political behaviour happens whenever people get together in groups and where an individual or group seeks to influence the thoughts, attitudes or behaviour of another individual or group (Robbins et al., 2010). Acting politically is part of negotiation as a means of overcoming resistance and resolving conflict. It can also be a cause of conflict when an individual or group seeks to affect adversely another individual or group. In contrast, power can be used to overcome conflict by averting it. Political behaviour is the influence, or an attempt to influence, the distribution of advantages and disadvantages within the organization. It is not normally part of an individual's formal role in an organization or defined in their job description. Political behaviour is therefore outside the specified job requirements of individuals: it requires the use of power bases. Politics is thus power in action, where individuals use tactics and other techniques of influence to foster their will or objectives in others (Hardy and Clegg, 1996).

Political behaviour during change

We have long known that change can trigger and intensify political behaviour (Schön, 1963). Change may threaten to push individuals out of their 'comfort zone', as well as jeopardize existing practices and routines, status hierarchies, information flows, resource allocation and power bases. Political behaviour can be triggered by a diversity of opinion, values, beliefs, interpretations and goals in the context of organizational change (Tushman, 1977). Individuals who believe that they will lose out in some way, or who feel that there are better ways to achieve the same result or better results, are likely to put up a fight. They may initially present a reasoned critical case or what they believe to be more effective options. If their voices are not heard, or when counter-proposals fail, some will give in and accept the change. However, where the stakes are high and the issues are important, some opponents are likely to continue their opposition through more covert, political means. Such political behaviour is not only inevitable in the context of organizational change but also necessary in stimulating creativity and debate (Frost and Egri, 1991).

Politics is a naturally occurring phenomenon in organizations and it is resistant to management attempts to stifle or eradicate it. So rather than attempting to do so, the more appropriate response is to manage it. Nadler (1988) proposes four actions for managing the political dynamics of change:

1. Ensure the support of key power groups (stakeholders) – a key element of change, which we discuss in more detail later in this chapter.
2. Use leadership behaviour to generate energy and enthusiasm in support of the change, thereby, adds Kotter (1995), building a coalition of support that can help manage political elements.
3. Use symbols and language to create energy and commitment for change.
4. Build in stability using power to ensure some things remain the same, such as location and hours of work. Such sources of stability are anchors for people to hold on to during change. People need to know what will remain stable and what is likely to change.

Managing politics actively in this way can help reduce the conflict created by change.

Conflict

The concept of conflict is by no means uncontentious because what one person calls conflict another person might call 'hard bargaining'. A number of definitions of conflict can be found in the literature. Robbins (2005) defines conflict as a process that begins when one party perceives that another party has negatively affected, or is about to negatively affect, something that the first party cares about. Mullins (2007) refers to conflict as behaviour intended to obstruct the achievement of some other people's goals. While Tosi and colleagues (1994) see conflict as a disagreement, tension, or some other difficulty between two parties. The parties in conflict often see each other as frustrating or about to frustrate the needs or goals of each other. Such definitions collectively include the following aspects:

• Conflict must be perceived by other parties.
• One party must be perceived as about to do, or actually doing, something the other party does not want.
• There must be opposition.
• Some kind of interaction must take place.

Conflict comes in many disguises but can be considered as something that disrupts the normal and desirable states of stability and harmony within an organization (Martin, 2005). By this definition, conflict is something to be avoided and if possible eliminated. Conflict is, however, an inevitable feature of human interaction, especially during times of change.

Table 12.2 Destructive and constructive consequences of conflict (adapted from Robbins et al., 2010)

Destructive consequences	Constructive consequences
Increase in employee turnover	Improved quality of decisions
Decrease in employee satisfaction	Stimulates creativity and innovation
Increase in inefficiencies between teams	Encourages interest and curiosity
Creates sabotage	Provides a medium through which problems and tensions can be aired
Increases work grievances	Fosters an environment of self-evaluation and change

Consequences of conflict

The consequences of conflict may be *destructive* or *constructive* depending on the situation (Robbins et al., 2010), as outlined in Table 12.2. The most obvious destructive consequences are increased employee turnover, decreased employee satisfaction, inefficiencies between work groups, sabotage and work grievances. In contrast, conflict may be constructive when it improves the quality of decisions, stimulates creativity and innovation, encourages interest and curiosity among people, provides the medium through which problems can be aired and tensions released, and fosters an environment of self-evaluation and change. Conflict can improve decision-making by allowing all points, particularly the ones that are unusual or held by a minority, to be taken into account when making decisions. Conflict may also be an antidote to 'groupthink' (Janis, 1982), as it does not allow a group to passively agree decisions that may be based on weak assumptions or inadequate consideration of relevant alternatives. Conflict may challenge the status quo and further the creation of new ideas. While often perceived in negative terms and regarded as undesirable, conflict may have the positive result of forcing issues into the open, stimulating wider debate and thereby leading to improved decision-making.

Conditions for conflict to surface

There are a number of conditions which, although they may not lead directly to conflict, are necessary for conflict to surface. For simplicity's sake, Robbins and colleagues (2010) have condensed them into the general categories of communication, structure and personal variables.

1. *Communication.* Communications can be a source of conflict. Different word connotations, jargon, insufficient exchange of information and a lack of clear messages are all barriers to communication and potential antecedent conditions to conflict (Thomas, 1992). Robbins et al. (2010) point out that the potential for conflict increases when there is too little or too much communication.
2. *Structure.* The greater the ambiguity in defining where responsibility for action lies during change, the greater the potential for conflict to emerge. Such jurisdictional ambiguities may increase intergroup fighting for control of resources and territory.

3. *Personal variables.* Personal variables include personality, emotions and values. Evidence indicates that certain personality types, for example individuals who are highly authoritarian and dogmatic, may create conflict more easily. Kennedy and Kray (2014) found that women feel greater moral outrage and they perceive less business sense in the decisions than men do when ethical values are compromised for social status and monetary gain.

Strategies for managing conflict

A comprehensive and practical approach to conflict resolution is the one devised by Thomas and Kilmann (1974), which identifies the following five styles or modes of handling conflict: competing; collaborating; avoiding; accommodating; compromising. As shown in Figure 12.1, each style is positioned on two axes representing two different concerns. The vertical axis represents a concern to satisfy one's own needs (assertiveness versus passivity). The horizontal axis represents a concern to satisfy the other person's needs in situations of conflict (cooperativeness).

1. *Avoiding* (uncooperative and passive) does not address the conflict but diplomatically sidesteps the issues or postpones handling them until a better time. This style is used when matters are trivial, when individuals need to regain their perspectives, or when the benefits of resolution are outweighed by the costs of addressing the conflict at the present time.
2. *Competing* (assertive and uncooperative) uses whatever power seems appropriate to get the desired result. Ranging from defending a position to simply trying to win, the style is effective in an emergency when unpopular actions need implementing quickly and on issues that are critical for the organization's welfare.

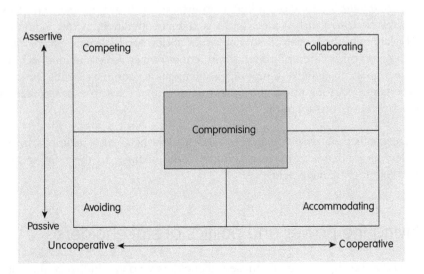

Figure 12.1 Thomas–Kilmann conflict resolution styles

3. *Accommodating* (cooperative and passive) may be either selfless generosity or yielding to the will of a more powerful individual. The style can be used when the importance of an issue is greater to one individual than the other, to preserve harmony, or to build credit for the future.
4. *Collaborating* (assertive and cooperative) involves working with others to find a solution that fully satisfies the agendas of all individuals involved. It requires time and effort for learning to take place. This style can be used to merge different perspectives on the same issue. It is a powerful tool for gaining commitment.
5. *Compromising* finds a mutually acceptable solution that partially satisfies the agendas of both parties. This style can be used when equally powerful individuals need to achieve a temporary agreement to complex issues or arrive at expedient solutions.

Leaders and managers should not assume that one approach for handling conflict will always be the best. Instead there is a need to select the most appropriate style for the situation. Like leadership style, conflict handling style is situational in its skilful application and its effectiveness. Thomas (1992) provides the following guidelines:

- Use *competing* when quick, decisive action is vital on important issues or where unpopular changes need to be implemented, such as cost cutting or downsizing.
- Use *collaborating* to find an integrative solution when concerns from all individuals are too important to be compromised, when the objective is to learn, to merge insights from people with different perspectives, to gain commitment to change, or to work through feelings about the change.
- Use *avoiding* when an issue is trivial or when more important issues are pressing, when potential disruption outweighs the benefits of resolution, to let people cool down and regain perspective, when gathering information supersedes immediate decision, or when others can resolve conflict more effectively.
- Use *accommodating* to allow a better position to be heard, to learn and to show reasonableness, to satisfy others and maintain cooperation, when harmony and stability are important, or to allow employees to develop by learning from mistakes.
- Use *compromising* when opponents with equal power are committed to mutually exclusive goals, to achieve temporary settlements to complex issues, or to arrive at expedient decisions under time pressure and as a backup when collaboration or competition is unsuccessful.

To manage conflict effectively, managers and leaders need also to know who their stakeholders are and what are their attitude to the change. In the next section we discuss stakeholder management.

Identifying the power and politics of stakeholders

Leaders need to be able to identify those stakeholders who can influence the outcome of the change, and therefore where the power lies. Freeman (1984) defines a stakeholder as any individual or group who can affect or is affected by the achievement of the organization's objectives. In the context of evaluating corporate performance, Clarkson (1995) widened the definition to include the government and the communities that provide infrastructure and markets – whose laws must be obeyed, and to whom taxes and other obligations may be due – as well as traditional stakeholder groups such as employees, shareholders, investors, customers and suppliers. Stakeholders can exercise considerable influence over the outcome of change initiatives.

Different stakeholders are likely to act in ways that maximize their own power and their ability to secure preferred outcomes. McCall (1979) suggests that individual stakeholders accrue power from positioning, timing, resources and past actions and that the most powerful are those who:

- Are in a position to deal with important problems facing the organization
- Have control over significant resources valued by others
- Are lucky or skilled enough to bring problems and resources together at the same time
- Are centrally connected in the workflow of the organization
- Are not easily replaced
- Have successfully used power in the past

How can these stakeholders be identified? Tushman and O'Reilly (2002) suggest asking the following questions:

- Who has the power to make or break the change?
- Who controls critical resources or expertise?
- How is the change likely to affect each of these individuals or groups?
- How is each one likely to react toward the change?
- Who will gain or lose something?
- Which groups or individuals are likely to mobilize against or in support of the change effort?

Stakeholder analysis

Stakeholders who have power can be identified through a *stakeholder analysis* (Brugha and Varvasovszky, 2000). A stakeholder analysis is a powerful technique to ensure that the key players are engaged and contributing to the success of change. It is particularly helpful at the outset of a change process. The purpose of a stakeholder analysis is to:

- Identify critical stakeholders, both individuals and groups
- Assess the effect of any proposed change on them and their concerns or perceptions
- Identify any need for outstanding data on specific stakeholders
- Support a structured discussion about the involvement of critical stakeholders within the change project plan in an objective way
- Enable a change project team to plan the involvement and commitment of critical stakeholders through the life of a project and to manage and review the management of key relationships as well as the content of the project

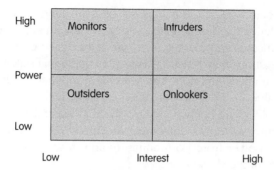

Figure 12.2 Power versus interest map (Price, 2009)

See Appendix 12.1 for a useful checklist of questions to use when analysing stakeholders. There are many ways to carry out a stakeholder analysis. One method to use is a power/interest map.

Power versus interest map

Power/interest maps have traditionally been used to consider the potential impact that stakeholders can have on decisions about change. The matrix in Figure 12.2, developed by Deborah Price (2009), can be used to map the relationship between power (the ability to intervene) and interest (the extent to which people are concerned) of stakeholders. The idea of mapping this relationship is to anticipate the responses of various groups to the changes being planned. This allows those directing the change to then make proactive decisions regarding the extent to which people are consulted about the change; the extent to which the change is communicated to them; or the extent to which people are simply subject to the change being implemented.

The power/interest map is divided into four categories: monitors, intruders, onlookers and outsiders.

Monitors

These are groups of individuals who are powerful enough to be able to support or undermine the change. They may be shareholders, commissioning bodies, funders or internal management. What is important to recognize is that they can work against the change, e.g. they can force plans to be altered, or they can work with the change, e.g. they can influence people around to support the change.

However, because they are mapped on the matrix in the 'low interest' category, in this particular context they are not really concerned about the nature of the consequences of the change being considered. For them neither the costs of the change nor the benefits that may be brought about by the changes are important. Because of this, rather than intervene in the change, they simply observe.

Intruders

These are individuals or groups or teams who are powerful enough to support or undermine the change and who are interested enough in the changes taking place to take action. As with monitors, they may be internal to the organization, for example trade unions or a senior manager, or they may be external to the organization, e.g. shareholders or local pressure groups. The important thing is that if these people are supportive they can be a great influence for change. However, if they disagree with the change they may intervene to force it to be altered or even prevent it happening.

Onlookers

Onlookers are groups of individuals or individuals who are very interested in the changes planned. The changes may have an impact on them personally or may have consequences for people or for things they care about. Despite being interested in what is happening, these people have very little power to do anything. They cannot influence the change in any way.

Outsiders

Outsiders are groups or individuals who rate low on both interest and power. However, they are still stakeholders and their position as 'outsiders' may change if plans are altered. The movement of stakeholders between categories is important to recognize, especially as change may not always follow the initial implementation plan. There is also rarely only one change taking place in organizations. Therefore people who find themselves in the 'outsider' category for one change may be in the intruder (or another) category for another change.

The first stage in using this map is to brainstorm a list of stakeholders. This can be done from an individual or group perspective. Next think about the extent to which each of the stakeholders will be interested in the change. Think about it from their perspective – their hilltop (see Chapter 11). What will be the impact of the changes on them? And is that important to them? Next think about what the stakeholders can legitimately do to stop the change or at least force the change to be delayed. Once the stakeholders have been mapped, action can then be identified for dealing with them.

A stakeholder's position on the grid shows the actions that have to taken with them:

- High-power, interested people: these are the people who must be fully engaged and whom managers must make the greatest efforts to satisfy.
- High-power, less interested people: these people need to be kept satisfied and involved and manages must ensure that they do not become bored with the message.
- Low-power, interested people: these people must be kept adequately informed and talked to in order to ensure that no major issues are arising. These people can often be very helpful with the detail of your project.
- Low-power, less interested people: these people need to be monitored but should not be bored with excessive communication.

This model helps us to think through the ways in which stakeholders and potential stakeholders may respond to proposed changes. This allows time to consider whether

Stakeholder	Stakeholder role	Action	Action category	Action owner	Timing	Performance measures
Stakeholder 1						
Stakeholder 2						
Stakeholder 3						
Stakeholder 4						

Figure 12.3 Stakeholder action plan

there are actions that need to be taken to address anyone who may block or oppose the change and how to deal with their concerns. The limitation is that it still involves a value judgement as to how stakeholders will respond and why.

By using such a framework to assess behaviour, leaders and managers can predict the influence and required support of stakeholders and the impact of the change effort on them and use that information to formulate political strategies and tactics that will help to implement and sustain change. This can be done using a stakeholder action plan (see Figure 12.3) to identify action for managing each stakeholder.

Stakeholder analysis, mapping and action planning are an iterative process and should be revisited throughout implementation to identify key players, to understand how they are affected by the change and their reaction to the change and to develop strategies and interventions for influencing stakeholders.

Activity

1 Consider one or more changes your organization (or an organization with which you are familiar) has faced in recent years and answer the following questions:

  o Who were the key stakeholders?
  o Which stakeholders exhibited the most and the least influence?
  o Who were the most powerful individuals or groups in your organization?
  o Why? What was the basis of their power?

2 Draw a power/interest map of the key stakeholders. Review your map and identify how you managed your relationship with stakeholders. Which stakeholders did you:

  o Proactively address – do a great deal to address their concerns?
  o Accommodate – take a less active approach to dealing with their concerns?
  o Ignore – do little or nothing to address their concerns?

3 What steps did you take to increase support for or reduce opposition to the change?

Change agents

Buchanan and Badham (2009) describe change management as a contact sport: 'those who do not wish to get bruised should not play'. Individuals who are involved in making change happen need to be able to manage the power, politics and conflict in an organization and to exercise leadership. Such individuals may be known by many names such as facilitators, project managers or programme managers. They are known commonly in the literature on organizational change as *change agents*, people who plan and support change.

Rogers (1983) describes change agents as people with one foot in the old world and one in the new – creators of a bridge across which others can travel. They help others to see what the problems are and to convince others that change needs to happen. Change agents are the individuals or groups of individuals whose task it is to effect change. They can be any members of an organization involved in facilitating, initiating, influencing or implementing change, whether or not they have an official title which recognizes or formalizes that responsibility.

Committed change agents inevitably become 'guardians' of the change agenda. As leaders they fulfil critical roles in a number of ways, including:

- Seeing and diagnosing the need for change
- Articulating the need for change
- Influencing, motivating or inspiring people to change
- Working through others in translating intention into action
- Fostering self-renewing behaviour in others so that they can 'go out of business' as change agents

The change agent can be an insider, a member of the system or subsystem (such as department of team) that is the target for change, or an outsider. Hayes (2014) points out that an insider might be chosen in situations where:

- The person responsible for managing the unit/team that is to be the initial target for change is committed to acting as change agent
- It is agreed that a particular internal individual has the time, knowledge and commitment to manage the change more effectively than an outsider
- The organization does not have the resources to employ someone external
- Issues of confidentiality and trust prohibit the use of an external individual
- There may be concerns that outsiders will not understand their business, its culture and its values and will simply create disruption
- It proved impossible to identify a suitable outside consultant

An outsider may be chosen where:

- There is nobody internally who has the time or competence to act as a change agent
- It is felt that all competent internal people have a vested interest in the outcome and therefore might be less acceptable to other parties than and neutral external person

Often the most value is in having a mix of internal and external change agents.

Change agency

Change is rarely dependent on the actions of a single key figure, whether it is a CEO or some other change agent, because change (like leadership) is a distributed phenomenon. The concept of **change agency**, therefore, is of more value than the notion of a single change agent (Denis et al., 2001; Buchanan and Storey, 1997). Change agency is emergent and fluid, and it is typically driven by what Hutton (1994) describes as 'a cast of characters'. The change agent is a member of this cast, formally appointed or self-appointed, seeking to drive a change agenda. Those who take the lead as change agents will themselves change over time as an initiative develops and matures, as other projects and individuals come into play, and as responsibility changes. Having the right skills is vital for anyone involved in change agency.

The effective change agent

According to the numerous lists of competencies that have been identified for change agents, they must possess 'near-superhuman' qualities. Kanter (1989) lists the following seven capabilities associated with an effective change agent:

1. Ability to work independently without power and sanction of the management hierarchy
2. Effectiveness as a collaborator and able to compete in ways that enhance rather than destroy cooperation
3. Ability to develop high trust relationships with high ethical standards
4. Possession of self-confidence tempered with humility
5. Respect for the process of change as well as the substance
6. Ability to work across business functions and units
7. Willingness to take rewards on results and gain satisfaction from success

When considering the attributes of an effective change agent, it is difficult to escape such competency lists. McBer, a consultancy organization, developed a competency model for a successful change agent, summarized in Table 12.3 (Cripe, 1993). This portrays a combination of interpersonal, diagnostic, initiation and organizational skills. It does not, however, mention stakeholder management or sustaining change, and it appears to be more appropriate for an external consultant as a change agent.

Robert Paton and James McCalman (2008) have attempted to synthesize the lists by identifying five key competencies that emphasize the planning process of change (see Table 12.4).

Such lists tend to provide the tasks that change agents need to do rather than the skills and attitudes they need. Successful change agents need to have analytical skills, creativity, judgement and implementation skills. Analytical skills are needed to be able to build an in-depth appreciation of the context of the change. Creativity provides novel or unique ideas, approaches and suggestions. And judgement is required to be able to assess the critical contextual enablers and constraints of the context. Implementation skills are to do with action – the phasing and synchronization of change interventions.

Change agents also need curiosity, which according to Jonathan Rowson of the Royal Society of Arts (2012) is a focused or exploratory inquisitiveness that motivates

Table 12.3   The McBer Competency Model for Change Agents (From Cripe, E. J. (1993) 'How to get top-notch change agents'. *Training and Development*, 47(12): 52–58.

Interpersonal skills

- Able to express empathy
- Have positive expectations of people
- Display genuineness

Diagnostic skills

- Knowledge of the principles of individual and organization development
- Able to collect meaningful data through interviews, surveys and observation
- Able to draw conclusions from complex data and make accurate diagnoses

Initiation skills

- Able to influence and market skills, and persuade internal customers to use services
- Able to present in a concise, interesting and informative way
- Able to manage group dynamics
- Problem solving and planning skills, to help improve goal setting and performance

Organization skills

- Designing adult learning and organization development exercises
- Administering resources such as personnel, materials, schedules and training sites.

Table 12.4   Activities constituting the role of change agents (Paton and McCalman, 2008)

- Identifying and managing stakeholders.
- Working on objectives – making sure they are clear and relevant.
- Setting an agenda – setting a holistic view and identifying challenges.
- Establishing a control system – ensuring communication flow is effective.
- Planning the process of change, ensuring the following:
  - Roles are clearly defined and allocated
  - Team building
  - Support is nurtured and apathy challenged
  - Relentless communication
  - Power bases are recognized
  - Change is sustained by ensuring hand-over

people to connect what they do not know to what they do know. Rowson says that curiosity is dually important for innovation, first in its link to creativity and divergent thinking, and second as an intrinsic motivator to sustain interest in a given area. He goes on to suggest that curiosity can be cultivated in people in several ways:

- Teaching for the development of competencies and dispositions, such as curiosity, as a learning goal in itself rather than merely as a collateral benefit
- Encouraging forms of mental attention, such as mindfulness, that make us more curious about things we previously had not noticed

- Promoting focal awareness and vital engagement by giving people a chance to learn something in considerable depth
- Experimenting with keeping learning outcomes open to make learning more exploratory
- Encouraging reflexive awareness of students' own natures and learning patterns
- Remaining vigilant about the impact of screen-based technologies on different kinds of curiosity

This requires experience and is something that change agents are likely to develop through time. As such, change agent training should be less about teaching individuals 'the ten rules of change', for example, and more about getting them to be inquisitive and to examine different change situations, what worked and what did not work within those contexts, and why.

Developing political and power skills

Lists of competencies for change agents tend to ignore organizational politics. Hutton (1994) argues that the change agent should be 'able to recognize and deal with office politics without becoming involved in the politics'. Just how this feat is to be achieved – addressing politics without involvement – is not explained.

There is, however, no shortage of advice on the use of political tactics in other literature, a tradition that dates from Machiavelli (1514) and *The Prince* through to *The Princessa: Machiavelli for Women* by Harriet Rubin (1997). Ferris and colleagues (2003) define political skill as an interpersonal-style construct that combines social astuteness with the ability to relate well and otherwise demonstrate situationally appropriate behaviour in a disarmingly charming and engaging manner that inspires confidence, trust, sincerity and genuineness.

There are many methods for developing political expertise. Courses and books can provide concepts and terminology and generate discussion and reflection through case analysis, self-assessments and other diagnostic tools. For those for whom acquiring and developing political skill does not come naturally, on-the-job experience of 'getting one's hands dirty' is necessary (Provis, 2004). Buchanan (1999) describes how involvement in a hospital re-engineering programme contributed significantly to the development of the political skills of the change agents who worked in and with the re-engineering teams. Such experience can help to lift individuals out of a narrow functional role and expose them to organization-wide issues.

Egan (1994) offers advice by suggesting that change agents plan their political campaign as follows:

- Learn 'the name of the game' in your organization: how are politics played here?
- Get to know the playing field, the informal organization and the communication networks.
- Identify key players and their main interests.
- Get organized, enlist your supporters early and form powerful alliances and a coalition.
- Use informal networks to gather intelligence and to send unobtrusive messages.
- Develop relationships with those who you know will support you.

- Know who owes you favours and call these in when necessary.
- Balance overt and covert action.
- Know when to go public and when to work behind the scenes.
- Learn how to use trade-offs and maximize flexibility without becoming 'slippery'.
- Use drama and 'theatre' sparingly, and use stirring gestures that do not cheapen the agenda.

There is much advice available that is similar to this to help change agents to build and maintain their credibility, reputation and influence. Table 12.5 summarizes the main themes of this advice under the headings: context, positioning, relationships and tactics.

According to Laver (1997), change agents can be viewed as political entrepreneurs deploying political tactics when necessary to advance combinations of personal and organizational agendas, in the face of potential opposition. Political skill is thus a key element in the behavioural repertoire of change agents. To achieve this, change agents require a combination of political awareness and the use of appropriate power tactics.

Table 12.5   Political skills for change agents

Organizational context

- Make sure that you have an agenda for enhancing organizational performance that is positive and legitimate.
- Get clearance for your initiative from senior management or the sponsor.
- Establish control of scarce and important resources, including information.
- Learn how politics are played, what works, and who the key stakeholders are.

Personal positioning

- Make sure you have a cause that colleagues will want to support.
- Look and act powerful, successful and decisive; radiate self-confidence; and project the image of someone who clearly knows what he or she is doing and why.
- Develop your communication skills: persuasion, influencing and selling.
- Highlight successes and achievements.
- Be visible.

Exploiting relationships

- Enlist supporters.
- Form a coalition with a powerful voice and develop and exploit your networks.
- Formalize your coalition when appropriate by creating a steering group, a committee and a task force.
- Barter, negotiate, trade, and compromise only on minor issues.

Tactical planning

- Decide when to push fast and when to hold back and delay.
- Use 'negative timing' to create deliberate delays when there are key issues to analyse, difficulties to overcome, problems to solve and implications to consider.
- Neutralize opponents by inviting them to participate in the change.
- Maintain flexibility and room for manoeuvre.

(Adapted from Buchanan and Badham, 2009: 270)

Pfeffer (1992) sets out a 'seven-point plan' for change agents for the effective exercise of organizational power:

1. Decide your goals.
2. Diagnose patterns of interdependence, focusing on those who are influential.
3. Establish their views of your goals.
4. Identify their power bases.
5. Identify the bases of your own power and influence.
6. Determine effective strategies and tactics for the situation.
7. Choose a course of action.

Change agents need to be able to use power skills and political skills. As they are faced with multiple stakeholders and perceptions and with change agendas that are often complex, multi-layered, pressurized, contested, politicized and shaped by changing management fashions. For as Carly Fiorina found to her cost when she took over as CEO at Hewlett–Packard, even as a change agent with the title and position, you can be effectively rendered powerless by people's collective decisions to maintain the status quo. Internal politics and power play ultimately led to Carly's downfall from Hewlett–Packard.

So a change agent needs to be able to use power and authority to intervene and mobilize people to change. An individual does not have to be the boss to be a change agent. A change agent must be able to stimulate a process where people tackle essential issues and modify their habits, practices, routines and ways of working in order to make progress. This engagement process can be difficult but it is necessary if a team, group or organization is to progress. It does need to be done, however, in a way that is ethical for all those involved.

Power, ethics and change

Ethics is a key issue in considering power and politics in organizational change. Marie McKendall (1993) says that most organizational change efforts actually serve to increase the power of leaders relative to others in the organization. This occurs for several reasons:

- Planned change, especially strategic change, typically is initiated by leaders and implicitly bears the message that leaders not only are in control but also have a right to be in control.
- Planned change creates uncertainty and ambiguity in the organization. Under these conditions, employees might seek stability through conformity to the wishes and desires of those who appear to be in charge.
- Efforts at organizational change involve leaders defining a new 'reality' for the organization's members. 'It reaffirms [their] right to define the order of the organization' (McKendall, 1993, p. 99). The basic question becomes one of how leaders can secure compliance with their wishes.

Obviously, stating the issue in this way makes more apparent the possible ethical dilemmas that leaders may confront in attempts to change or transform an organization.

At some point, change can become coercion, and influence can become manipulation – and there might be a very fine line between the two. Even though contemporary theories such as transformational leadership express a distaste for the old authoritarian biases of past leadership practices, there still are activities that leaders engage in that can have the effect of devaluing, and even dehumanizing, their employees. Being aware of some of the potential ethical dilemmas that are inherent in leadership, and especially in organizational change, can help leaders and managers to be more sensitive to the concerns of others in the organization and therefore to be more likely to act in a consistently ethical manner. The two main issues that leaders and managers need to consider are:

- Who determines the need for change and the intended outcomes?
- How can they instil change in a way that is both effective and ethical?

With regard to the first issue, a leader or manager who pursues organizational change exclusively for his or her own self-interest would be acting in an unethical manner. Any deliberate influencing of the behaviour of others would constitute a violation of their basic humanity. On the other hand, effective behavioural change involves some degree of use of power and control and a potential imposition of the change agent's values on other individuals. Certainly, by involving themselves in organizations, individuals give up some of their decision-making autonomy. But there are limits to the extent to which those in positions of power and authority should impose their will on others. Some such restraints are formal and specific, and they protect the rights of employees (e.g., prohibitions on sexual harassment). Others are more general, for example the emphasis on empowerment in organizations presents a significantly different answer to the question of power and control in organizations than that given by the early proponents of top-down scientific management. Some organizations are more open and involving of lower-level participants than are others. However, in either case there is an ethical question concerning the extent to which leaders should impose their values on employees.

The second issue is how leaders can bring about change in a way that is both effective and ethical. Unethical actions would coerce employees into certain behaviours. Coercion takes place when one person or group forces another person or group to act or refrain from acting under threat of severe deprivation, such as the loss of one's life, job or well-being. Overt acts of coercion tend to be objectionable. But there still are situations in which employees are told essentially to 'shape up or ship out'. Whether these actions are unethical is perhaps only possible to judge within the context of particular situations, but they certainly raise not just technical issues but ethical ones as well.

Manipulating employees against their will to change might also be considered unethical. Seabright and Moberg (1998) suggested that manipulation can be classified in two categories:

1. Situational manipulation, where the circumstances in which the target acts are structured so that the target sees no apparent alternatives
2. Psychological manipulation, in which the target's efforts to make sense of a situation are confused or misdirected

Seabright and Moberg (1998) say that manipulation operates by robbing the victim of autonomy either in choice (situational manipulation) or in self-definition (psychological manipulation) for the sole purpose of advancing the perpetrator's objective. The results are actions that are not freely undertaken. Examples of manipulation in an organization include fooling someone into doing something by the use of flattery or lies. As with coercion, manipulative tactics that involve deception, threats, fear, secrecy and dishonesty should be considered unethical. But manipulation sometimes is difficult to identify because it is so closely related to persuasion and facilitation, neither of which has quite the same negative connotation as manipulation. But in terms of organizational change, White and Wooten (1983: 691) argue that 'basically, manipulation and coercion can occur when the organizational development effort requires organizational members to abridge their personal values or needs against their will'.

It has also been argued that organizational change efforts can become dehumanizing and therefore ethically questionable (Woodall, 1996). This argument proposes that efforts at organizational change that suppress personal development or limit an individual's autonomy and independence raise ethical issues. As with coercion and manipulation, dehumanization raises not only ethical issues but also practical ones – dissatisfaction, lack of innovation, groupthink and the creation of an overly conformist culture in which conflict can be found. Woodall summarizes the ethical issues in organizational change in this way:

> The role of change agents, and above all the process whereby a cultural change is introduced, [is] surrounded by ethical dilemmas. These do not just concern the inherent worth of the exercise or its benefit to the organization. They also include the impact on individual motivation to comply and above all the infringement of individual autonomy, privacy, self-esteem, and equitable treatment. (1996: 35)

So how can efforts at organizational change be carried out in a way that avoids coercion, manipulation or dehumanization? One way is for leaders and managers to do those things that promote the autonomy and independent involvement of individuals. Indeed, one of the most significant ethical issues facing leaders and managers is how they can fully involve all of those individuals both within and outside of the organization who should play a role in decisions about change (Svara, 2006).

Power, politics and conflict exist in organizations at all levels. However, power does not always reside in the organizational charts, and the political reality of the workplace is not always evident. Power, politics and conflict are heightened in times of change and transformation, power balances change, conflict arises and opportunities are created for people to act politically. Leaders and managers therefore ignore the power, politics and conflict associated with change at their peril (Senior and Fleming, 2006).

Implications of power, politics and conflict for leading and managing change

There are several practical implications for practising and aspiring managers and leaders which arise from the issues discussed in this chapter.

Assess the power of individuals to oppose change

The power of any individual or group/team to block change can be gauged by considering whether the changes proposed will alter the degree of power held. If it is likely to be diminished, then individuals may oppose the change. To address this, leaders and managers need to assess the motivation of individuals to do so. This is not an easy task. Figure 12.4 shows a model developed by Senior and Fleming (2006) categorizing individuals or groups according to their power and motivation to block change. Each cell of the matrix shows a particular situation and a strategy to deal with it. So if an individual has no power to block change and, in addition, little motivation to do so, no immediate action needs to be taken (cell C). If there is both power to block change and the motivation to do so, this represents a serious situation in terms of the need to negotiate with those concerned and, if possible, reach a collaborative agreement (cell B).

A potential risk for any change is those individuals who fall into cell A – those with a high degree of power but little motivation to do anything about the change. This is because, if the situation changes, their interest could be increased and this might then move them into cell B. A strategy for such people is to keep them satisfied, which includes maintaining their awareness of how the change will benefit them.

The people in cell D represent a different challenge. They have high motivation to block change but no power to do so. It might be tempting to ignore them but because change situations are fluid, they might begin to gain power and thus move into the more contentious group represented by cell B. Consequently, these people should be kept informed of developments and effort made to persuade them of the benefits of the change.

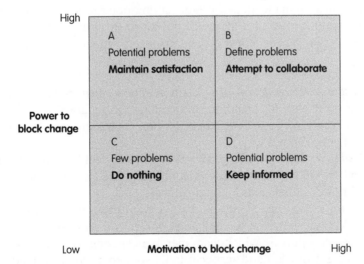

Figure 12.4   The power and motivation to block changes (Senior and Fleming, 2006)

Ascertain power bases

In getting things accomplished, it is critical to have a sense of the game being played, the players and what their positions are. One can get badly injured playing rugby in a tennis outfit or not knowing the attack from the defence. It is important for leaders and managers to ascertain the power bases of the other players as well as their own potential and actual sources of power. In this way managers and leaders can determine their relative strengths along with the strengths of other players. There are a number of questions that can be asked to gauge the power of others:

- What are their opinions of the change likely to be? How will they feel about what is being proposed?
- What are the power bases of influence of key individuals? Which of them is more influential in the decision-making process?
- What are your bases of power and influence? What bases of power and influence can be developed to gain more control over the situation?
- Which of the various strategies and tactics for exercising power seem most appropriate and are likely to be most effective, given the situation?

Understanding the sources of power is critical in diagnosing what is going to happen in an organization as well as in preparing what action to take. Leaders and managers should consider carefully the various tactics that are available to them as well as those that may be used by others involved in the process. These tactics help in using power effectively, and they can also help in countering the use of power by others.

Leaders and managers of change also need to listen to what the stakeholders have to say, modify their position accordingly and choose appropriate strategies and tactics to accomplish the change (see the case study by Keith Marriott).

Recognize and manage conflict constructively

The Thomas–Kilman framework is a useful starting point to identify how individuals will react in situations of conflict. Research published by Greer and colleagues (2011) suggests three further steps that leaders and managers can take to constructively manage conflict:

1. *Define, discuss and reinforce roles.* Team members need to have clear, accepted agreement over roles and standing, and continue to reinforce those as time goes by. Conflict can also be better managed when each team member's expertise is recognized and deferred to.
2. *Establish shared decision-making.* Members of teams feel less threatened by other team members when decision-making is shared. Shared power reduces the real or perceived power differentials among members.
3. *Provide conflict training.* Managers that have sufficient training in conflict management skills are better at recognizing conflict and addressing the real underlying issues. Recognizing which team members are engaged in a power struggle and resolving it quickly and respectfully is something leaders need to be able to do.

CASE STUDY

The purchase of VAX by TTI

Background

In 1999 TTI, the world's fourth largest manufacturer of vacuum cleaners and second largest manufacturer of power tools, based in Hong Kong, bought VAX, a UK-based vacuum cleaner manufacturer that had been larger than Dyson but which then had only a 2% UK market share by value, and that was declining.

VAX had been formed in the 1970s by an inventor (a little like James Dyson) called Alan Brazier and had been a private family firm that engendered great local loyalty in the West Midlands. The product invented by Brazier was a carpet-washing machine and at its height in the 1980s millions of units per year were manufactured at the factory in Droitwich. However, trends changed, people started to replace carpets more often (often now with hard flooring) and clean them less, and then they would often just hire one of the newly available professional carpet-cleaning machines.

VAX tried to replace declining sales by opening factories abroad: a joint venture in India and a subsidiary in Australia, which brought a very small amount of new business, and then a very expensive failure in the USA. Several disastrous new product launches followed, notably an upright version of the carpet washer, which was distributed with a catastrophic fault. Tens of thousands of units were returned and VAX's relationship with its customers was in ruins. The upshot was that VAX could no longer afford to continue and the company was sold to a venture capital company. The staff, however, did not change, and belief in the original product continued unwaveringly in the face of evidence to the contrary. The product was expensive to manufacture in the UK, seen as old-fashioned and diminishing in popularity, and the new company failed to successfully add any new products into the range. By 1999 VAX had not made a trading profit for 10 years.

TTI was a soaring success. In 1998, after only 10 years, it was turning over several hundred million pounds with very cheap labour but in very modern, high-quality, efficient Chinese factories and it was starting to supply technologically advanced vacuums and power tools to some of the world's largest brands. Horst Pudwill, the inventor founder of TTI, was hugely ambitious and wanted to acquire other brands in America, Europe and the UK as outlets for its massive production capacity and very large range of products. TTI was the fourth largest and fastest growing manufacturer of vacuums in the world, with low labour costs, huge economies of scale, access to money and world markets, and state-of-the- art technology.

Pudwill approached me when I was running Dirt Devil and Power Devil in the UK and asked me to start up a vacuum-cleaner company in the UK that would primarily be supplied by TTI. I suggested that TTI purchase VAX, a company we had already done due diligence on. This was agreed, and a strategy was planned whereby a worldwide joint venture between VAX and Bissell outside of the USA would be formed. This would be supplied primarily by TTI and Bissell USA (great product synergy and already working together on NPD), production would be moved from the UK to the Far East and the UK VAX operation would be scaled down (currently VAX had 150 direct employees including more than 20 managers and directors) to become more or less a simple marketing and distribution operation. I would join the VAX board to make the change as smoothly as possible.

Strategically VAX had identified the need for a 'star' product and had just initiated the concept stage of a technologically advanced upright cleaner to challenge Dyson's market

(Continued)

(Continued)

dominance. An investment appraisal was undertaken and the project was declared financially viable. TTI agreed to continue the project. There would initially be two versions of the product at different price points called the AVC1 and the AVC2. There was no legal contract between the companies – simply an internal service level agreement.

My initial impressions

My initial assumption was that TTI would subsume all functions where costs could be lowered and efficiencies made, introduce new products from the TTI range and simply leverage the VAX brand. It would also cut UK staff to the bone, probably retaining only sales and marketing, and warehousing and distribution functions.

TTI had to make continuous changes to our original plan for VAX, and the reasons were sometimes surprising and sometimes funny. It is an example of how the most unexpected things can cause change.

In this case factions with opposing agendas formed and strong personalities lined up against each other and were prepared to behave perhaps unethically and certainly ruthlessly to achieve their aims. But alliances shifted as new threats and opportunities became apparent. I came to realize that change is complex and needs an agile approach.

I was employed by TTI to join the board of VAX to facilitate change from the inside and I saw myself as a TTI man, not a VAX man, which was how I was perceived by the VAX board, who did not trust me and put obstacles in the way of my making changes. I shared the view of the TTI management that VAX's practices and products were outdated, and I also thought they gave too little emphasis to sales and marketing and therefore lacked skill in these areas.

My initial impressions were not contradicted by my early experience of the company. In the first week I walked into the conference room to join a meeting where the company's sole salesman (dealing with every major retail account in the UK) sat surrounded by managers who told him that, because his sales forecast was wrong again, he would have to come back in tomorrow and redo it. More surprising was the lack of understanding of the inefficacy of this approach of 'rearranging the deckchairs as the ship sank'.

The main product was large and complicated but technically excellent in concept. However, the practice in retail had changed and was now to display the product in boxes on the shop floor. Unfortunately, the product was delivered to the retailer in a plain brown box. The opportunity to use the large surface area of the box to advertise the benefits of the features of the product, of which there were many, had not been realized, despite the fact that above-the-line advertising expenditure had been reduced to zero as sales declined.

The fear of declining sales had manifested itself in some unfortunate ways. There was a lack of confidence in the existing abilities of the staff. Management consultants had been hired the previous year at great expense and they had produced a sales strategy 'based on' the book *The Japanese Art of War* by Sun Tzu. Among its recommendations was that 'there would be no serious consideration of a new upright until a reputation for successful new product launches was established'. It is worth pointing out here that the VAX products washed carpets, a product category worth less than 2% of the value of the market and declining. But upright vacuum cleaners accounted for 65% of the value of the market! It was a strategy that emerged from current practice, and it was short on detail and not radical enough. But one thing it did correctly identify was that there was a need to change the existing culture to empower employees and encourage innovation. There was also an idea for an 'advanced vacuum cleaner' (the AVC), but this was still intended to be wet and dry. The AVC became a key factor in this story.

Some straws were clutched at, and in a remarkable presentation to the major retail buyers, a new version of the wet-and-dry canister (predominantly used by women) had been launched – called 'The Mother Sucker'! You know how sometimes when things are going badly, they just get worse ...?

VAX and TTI cultures

Understandably the incumbent board felt defensive. In the call for change there was an implicit criticism of their performance. And it quickly felt as if two 'tribes' with very different cultures were forming. In the VAX corner they came from a point where they had believed they were right and the market was wrong and it would come back to them when it realized this. They had a glorious history based on existing practices and still believed in the superiority of existing product.

Practice was characterized by a rigour and an attention to detail to the point of distraction, and it was felt at TTI that the process at VAX was more important than the product. There was risk aversion and fear of failure within a blame culture. Research and development were focused on quality and technical improvements to existing products. Staff were highly controlled and not empowered. The management was seen as hierarchical, transactional and bureaucratic, and staff sitting next to each other would email rather than talk so that, in the words of one engineer, it could 'be seen that they were not to blame'.

In the TTI camp there was disbelief about the urgency of developing new products. We were customer-orientated and saw the irrelevance of VAX products to the market. We were characterized by our speed of reaction, agility and willingness to make mistakes and move on quickly. We were risk-takers with reward systems. Our attention was on system changes and removing obstructive behaviour. Our management was flat and transformational.

At this stage, in the TTI camp we recognized that the old ways needed to be changed quickly.

The change plan

We (TTI) had a strategy – an episodic plan to make the changes. We knew we had to clearly communicate this to the staff, often on a one-to-one basis, explaining the benefits of it with pay rises where necessary and the expansion of their departments as appropriate. We emphasized a Utopian vision, but pointed out the unpleasant consequences of failing to change.

We had a clear mission and strategy. We had economy of scale and could reduce overheads. All functions should be moved to the Far East, where efficiencies could be achieved. In the carpet-washing market VAX had one product and TTI 20 products. A joint venture between VAX and Bissell (outside of USA) would be formed.

We did not know how to best manage the change. We did not appreciate where we should have intervened at times, we didn't appreciate any behavioural science and the effect of staff attitudes to change. So often we were surprised when things did not turn out as we had assumed. The following are some examples of this, by department.

On the *factory floor* we predicted that there was likely to be a problem as we were moving the production tools to China and most of these staff would be made redundant. That was obvious, so planning went into preventing this from becoming a problem. There was a lot of communication, natural wastage replacement by temporary (indirect) labour, incentivization of leaders or, in the case of the production director, who resisted and instigated many diversionary tactics, redundancy, and it worked well. Quality control improved, and a limited production and a quality control facility remained. Eventually as sales volumes improved production space was given over to warehousing, and staff were retained as warehouse staff.

(Continued)

(Continued)

Engineering, we thought, would disappear to the TTI factory in Hong Kong, but, as the staff became more empowered and keen to come forward with ideas, it became apparent that there was a great design and research competency. Staff were given key project positions and regularly flown out to China to consult with production engineers there, and the department was upgraded to become a group centre for R&D.

Marketing was in a dreadful state. It was inward-facing and product-orientated, and the process had become more important than the product. And, as discussed, there was a deluded understanding of the external environment. However, the marketing manager presented us with an unexpected quandary. On the face of it, a classically blue-chip trained product manager with an excellent technical background in product quality and improvement and an academic understanding of marketing, he was an obstacle to the new strategy. Yet he embodied the very inward-facing, product orientation that we needed to change. Well, what actually happened was that, as my positioning changed, I came to appreciate his competencies and how his integrity and rigorous approach to product quality/development might act as a foil or counterbalance to a potential flaw in the execution of our strategy. This was the danger of the speed in the implementation of the plan leading to poor product quality and causing a nervousness about the lack of control. The answer was to make him product manager, with enough authority, and bring in a marketing manager who knew how to sell products. A position for a product-sourcing manager was created. The sales department, with 700 live accounts and one salesman, was expanded and distributors with sales forces taken on to deal with the smaller accounts.

Factors affecting the change

The major factors affecting the implementation of changes were the different cultural approaches of VAX and TTI and the lack of trust this engendered and the jostling for power that this caused.

The incumbent COO of VAX was an accountant by profession. He had no marketing experience and was product- not customer-orientated. He was very hard-working and proficient and had great rigour in product development and finance, frequently using the expression 'leave no stone unturned'. He worked long hours and persuaded the staff to work longer hours than they wanted to, and it was often apparent to me that jackets had been left over the backs of chairs. I felt the atmosphere was oppressive and that long hours were confused with productivity. The VAX board expressed great willingness to change practices but they were actually resistant to change in their behaviour. By contrast, Horst Pudwill (Chairman and CEO of TTI) was an engineer and entrepreneur with great ambition, used to fast growth and constant change, and, although also without marketing experience, he was very customer-orientated. My background as originally Commercial Director and ultimately as the sole UK Executive Director of VAX, was as a corporate entrepreneur. I had started in sales and marketing but had gone on to run another vacuum cleaner company (Dirt Devil) and started a power tool company from scratch for the Alba Group, which went on to turn over more than £25 million, and my approach was far closer to Horst's.

My approach was crucial in the development of the AVC. The AVC would now be a dry vacuum cleaner and would allow VAX to enter and take a significant share of that valuable upright market in the UK and USA. However, the project had become bogged down while looking for a technical solution to dirt compaction. I was determined that this was an innovation that would not give a good return on the investment of time and money that would be needed to achieve it and that the project must be speeded up. It was a huge project that involved our applying for many new patents and Dyson trying to prevent us from doing so.

We were happy that our product was technically superior. But I believed the battle would be fought in marketing, so the product also had to be aesthetically and ergonomically superior and we had to get that message across and persuade the retail buyers and the salesmen in the shops – currently receiving very large commissions from Dyson for selling Dyson models – as well as the public. I had already changed the rather industrial VAX logo to a softer, more domestically orientated shape and done extensive art design work for the existing products and packaging. Image change was a late addition to our strategy. This was not an area of expertise of TTI but of mine, and I believed it was essential as a part of culture change. This type of expenditure was not popular with TTI, which was not a marketing company, and they would limit the television advertising budget for the AVC launch to £1.5 million.

The COO had worked hard in reducing the product BOM (bill of materials) cost and was now being asked to accept a transfer cost from TTI, who would be manufacturing the product in the future. One manifestation of the lack of trust was that he could not accept that and insisted on an agreed maximum transfer cost. Culturally VAX felt that TTI had a sloppy attitude to technical quality. They were not quite right. As time went on I came to understand that TTI was high in conformance quality but low in specification quality. This was demonstrated when the speeding up of the project led to an oversight on the final colour of one of the AVC versions and TTI, without consultation, substituted an unattractive finish that was unacceptable to the retail buyers.

To protect the equity in the VAX brand, which was still seen as highly reliable and technically advanced, although slightly industrial, I introduced a sub-brand called 'VAX Selections' so that it would support the AVC. This allowed me to source products from TTI's existing ranges, and from other suppliers I had previously sourced products from, that could be quickly placed in the range to grow the business and make inroads into the dry-upright and cylinder markets while the AVC was being developed.

Could we have made it easier?

We had considered the content of change more than the process of change, especially with regard to culture. We did not know how ready staff were to change or how dissatisfied with the status quo they were. Little attention was paid to how staff perceived the changes. There was little knowledge of individual motivation, which turned out to be a serious gap as there was great resistance to change from the Chairman and COO. The VAX board tried to control me through diversionary tactics, including increased workload and bureaucracy, such as the demand for an unreasonable level of proof of concept before implementing new product development.

My relationship with the VAX board was deteriorating and power games were being played out. For example, the COO would call me at home over the weekend to ask me to 'consider' ideas for the board meeting on Monday afternoon. I would be difficult, replying when I got to a noisy rugby match and accidentally 'dropping' my phone, and he would try to move the board meeting to Monday morning, knowing that I would have difficulty making it in time. But this actually helped in the change process: we had demonstrated the need for change and the opportunity in the market and created anxiety that if we did not change the company would close. And now I, with my very different experience, became a rival mentor to staff who were more in favour of change.

Power constellations formed, altered and reformed around myself or the COO and Chairman as people evaluated where their personal interests would be best served. Of course, everyone wanted to safeguard their own position through company success, and at one stage the old VAX board sided with me when the market demanded costly national television advertising. TTI were unhappy, but I unveiled the campaign pitch, got agreed orders

(Continued)

on the back of an advertising schedule, and was backed by the VAX board, which realized the value of the investment. Something changed at this point and I, as the agent of change, became a 'double-agent': I started to value the success of VAX above the wishes of TTI.

However, the original momentum continued, and I went to a meeting with Horst to which the COO was not invited, where Horst asked me if the COO was a barrier to progress towards TTI's plans. Following that meeting, the COO was removed, leaving me as the only UK-based executive director. That was key in changing the culture at VAX. I changed working practices. There was a further decentralization of internal structures, moving away from 'silo' barriers between us and them and very separate departments, with mixed business unit committees everywhere. The operations at VAX and TTI were complementary and dovetailing nicely, but I began to feel a cultural backwash, appreciating the broad range of competencies of the newly empowered VAX staff over the narrow operations resource perspective of TTI, and I argued with TTI where I believed it was in the interests of VAX.

I was enjoying VAX's success: the product range was vastly expanded and revenue had doubled. Most production had been moved to China and with the cost base halved VAX had returned to profitable trading for the first time in 13 years. Five new export markets were opened, and every UK retailer stocked our products. Most importantly, the AVC had been delivered to the market at a price-point similar to the Dyson and was outselling the Dyson in many of the outlets, where it is was supported. I was proud of these achievements and now cared greatly about the brand.

My increasing loyalty to the VAX brand rather than to TTI grew with my increased responsibility for the brand, and it was strengthened further when TTI pulled the rug from under the VAX brand by selling the flagship AVC to Bosch in a power-tool deal: VAX had been offered as part of the package but was not wanted by Bosch.

On reflection the results of the purchase of VAX by TTI were positive for VAX but disappointing. VAX could not have continued as it was for long, so jobs and the brand were saved. The culture was changed and new expertise in research and design was created at VAX, and VAX eventually became the second-largest vacuum cleaner brand in terms of volume in the UK after Dyson. However, in the process, Bissell had been made a serious competitor and the AVC, a product that could have rivalled Dyson, had been dropped. This meant that VAX was repositioned so as never to be able to compete with Dyson.

The results were very positive for TTI. They gained some valuable engineering and design excellence that they were able to use across all of their brands. They gained an eventually successful company, which is a good outlet for their production in the UK and around the world. VAX was the number-one brand in Russia and Australia and very successful in many other states – but the chance was missed to compete with Dyson.

The story should also be viewed from the perspective of TTI because, of course, TTI was far more important to VAX than vice versa. TTI became a multibillion dollar conglomerate with global reach that had subsumed many of the world's largest brands in power tools – the most important part of TTI's business – and vacuum cleaners, producing millions of products each month. VAX was only ever worth a couple of per cent of TTI's revenue and, more important to TTI tactically, it was used to create relationships with brands that were very valuable to TTI, such as Bosch, Bissell and Dirt Devil (Royale).

Our approach mimicked that of Kurt Lewin: we saw VAX as an essential stable and ordered entity that needed to be unfrozen and then changed until it was 'like us'. Having gone through the change process, however, the idea of 're-freezing' such a fluid entity seems mad in such a turbulent environment when it was inflexibility in a fast-moving external environment that got VAX in trouble in the first place. This theory also neglects power and politics and, as you have heard, change is contested. And as much as anything else, this is a story of people with power and influence fighting for what they wanted.

Discussion Questions

1   Conduct a stakeholder analysis of the stakeholders identified in the case.
2   Identify the power bases. How did the author influence the different power bases?
3   What key lessons might be learnt from this case about power and politics during change?

Appendix 12.1: Stakeholder analysis

You may find this a useful checklist to use when conducting a stakeholder analysis as part of a change initiative:

- Who are the key stakeholders in the change initiative?
- Who are the formal decision-makers with the formal authority to authorize or reject the change project? What are their attitudes to the change?
- What is the commitment profile of stakeholders? Are they against the change, neutral (let it happen), supportive, or committed champions of the change? Do a commitment analysis of each stakeholder.
- What would change the views of stakeholders? Can the reward system be altered? What information or education would help?
- Who influences the stakeholders? Can you influence the influencers? How might this help?
- What coalitions might be formed among the stakeholders? What alliances might you form? What alliance might form to prevent the change you want?
- How might you satisfy the needs of those opposing the change?
- How can you continue to keep the supporters of the change on your side?

Further reading

Alfes, K., Truss, C. and Gill, J. (2010) 'The HR manager as change agent: Evidence from the public sector', *Journal of Change Management*, 10(1): 109–27.

Buchanan, D. and Badham, R. (2008). *Power, Politics, and Organizational Change: Winning the Turf Game*. London: Sage.

Ezzamel, M., Willmott, H. and Worthington, F. (2001) 'Power, control and resistance in the factory that time forgot', *Journal of Management Studies*, 38(8): 1053–79.

Ferris, G.R., Treadway, D.C., Kolodinsky, R.W, Hochwarter, W.A., Kacmar, C.J., Douglas, C. and Frink, D.D. (2005) 'Development and validation of the Political Skill Inventory', *Journal of Management*, 31(1): 126–52.

Jehn, K.A., and Mannix, E.A. (2001) 'The dynamic nature of conflict: A longitudinal study of intragroup conflict and group performance', *Academy of Management Journal*, 44(2): 238–51.

Munduate, L. and Bennebroek Gravenhorst, K.M. (2003) 'Power dynamic and organizational change: An introduction', *Applied Psychology: An International Review*, 52(1): 1–13.

PART FIVE

Sustaining Change and Transformation

Ensuring Sustainable Change through Monitoring and Measurement

13

Overview

- Successful change initiatives can be undermined because too little attention is paid to holding on to the gains once the change objectives appear to be achieved. Change may therefore fail to be sustained. When this happens the benefits from it evaporate and the organization will be left to suffer the costs.
- Building into the initial planning ways of sustaining the change rather than leaving it as an afterthought is vital. This should include the measuring, monitoring and reviewing of key objectives, benefits and risks.
- It is vital to monitor and review the implementation of the change in order to identify areas that need to be adjusted and adapted to ensure that the change is effectively implemented and that the intended benefits are achieved.
- Declaring victory too soon can encourage leaders and managers to switch their attention and resources to other change projects without sustaining the current change they are working on. So it is important that leaders and managers do not declare the change finished and a success too early.
- When transformation fails there are a number of strategies leaders and managers can consider for turning the situation around, including: ensuring that there is clarity about the aim and outcome of the change initiative; providing sufficient support and readiness for the change; ensuring that key players are performing; reviewing the implementation plan; focusing on the emotional commitment to the change; reviewing the communication strategy; and recognizing failure and mistakes and using them as opportunities for learning, improvement and development.

Change needs to have not only commitment and support from individuals but processes in place for sustaining it. Monitoring and control mechanisms are required that continue beyond the implementation of change (Jacobs, 2002). Bateman (2005) found this to be the case in a study of the manufacturing sector which highlighted the importance of processes for promoting contribution and buy-in during the early stages of implementation and for maintenance of standards and continuous improvement once the initial changes had been successfully implemented. One of the key processes that is vital for sustaining change is being able to measure its impact, especially by identifying and monitoring benefits and risks.

The *2012 Barometer on Change* survey from Moorhouse[1] found that many change programmes do not have their expected benefits measured or tracked. Participants in the survey included 200 UK board members or people reporting into the board working on transformation projects with a direct value of over £10 million. Respondents came from the FTSE 250 multinational and public sector organizations. Less than a quarter (24%) of respondents were found to measure the benefits of these projects properly after they had finished – equating to some £850 million in potentially wasted investment in projects that did not have clear resulting benefits or outcomes. Fewer than half (41%) of respondents felt very or extremely confident that projects would run to time or on budget. Only a third (36%) felt that stakeholders and key staff had 'bought into' to the project's aims and benefits, and a similar third felt that projects were under-resourced at their start. What is concerning about these results is the risk of the lack of monitoring and measurement of the impact of these projects, which are perceived as critical to the success of the business and cost significant amounts of financial investment.

This chapter focuses on how to measure the effectiveness of change, how managers can assess if the chosen interventions are having the desired effect and whether the change plan is still valid. The dangers of declaring victory too soon are explored and what to do if change or transformation fails. Strategies for turning the situation around are also discussed. The chapter concludes by looking at the implications for leaders and managers and providing practical advice.

Learning objectives

By the end of this chapter you will be able to:

- Identify the factors that contribute to measuring and monitoring organizational change and transformation
- Apply techniques for sustaining change
- Describe the pitfalls that can be encountered when seeking to sustain change
- Identify the benefits and risks of change
- Measure the impact of change

Measuring change

Measuring the impact of change is a key aspect of sustaining change for a number of reasons. First, it is a means of monitoring the progress of the change ('what gets measured

---

1 Downloaded from www.hrmagazine.co.uk/hro/news/1072845/less-change-projects-seen-successful-moorhouse-study#sthash.3HtATthJ.dpuf

gets managed'). Second, what gets measured is likely to have a significant impact on how people act. Third, it enables leaders to assess whether the chosen interventions are having the desired effect and whether the change plan continues to be valid and practical.

Wells Fargo provides an example of how a company uses measures to sustain change. In the lead-up to the financial crisis in 2008, the CEO of Wells Fargo – John Stumpf – knew the company needed to improve its performance, which was worsening. Stumpf was passionate about positioning the company for success in the longer term by creating a spirit and way of thinking in the company. He and his top team set out the aspiration of 'One Wells Fargo', which included equal focus on performance measures such as earnings growth, cross-selling and a culture of customer centricity and collaboration. This was monitored through a series of measures at organizational, team and individual levels.

As in the case of Wells Fargo, change needs to be kept on target, on time and within budget unless there are compelling reasons for not doing so. The process for measuring the impact of change should include establishing a clear aim, defining key measures, collecting base-line data, collecting data consistently and charting progress.

1. *Establish a clear aim.* Establish a clear overall aim or target of the change (for example, increase sales by 25 per cent by 1 December), which can then be broken down into specific measures.
2. *Define the key measures.* Establish clear definitions of measures prior to starting the change process. The measures should clarify the objectives and be agreed by key stakeholders. Objectives should be 'SMART' – specific, measurable, agreed, realistic and time-bound. This ensures that the results are interpretable and accepted within the organization. Responsibility and accountability for the objectives should be clearly allocated to individuals. The objectives should be reviewed with individuals and their managers on a regular basis.
3. *Collect baseline data.* Baseline data provide a starting point for the change. Such data should be collected before making any changes. This process anchors the change (pre-change) and enables measurement of the impact of the change over time (post-change).
4. *Collect data consistently.* Consistent channels for collecting measurement data should be established and data shared with relevant stakeholders.
5. *Chart progress.* As pre-change (baseline) and post-change data become available over time they should be shared with those involved in the change as well as with other stakeholders.
6. *Ask questions.* Measuring the impact of change does not stop here; in fact it is only the beginning. The most important step in the process is to ask questions such as: What are the data telling me about change in my organization? What do we need to do differently? This information will help identify which intervention is the most successful in meeting the overall aim of the change, as well as where there is a need for improvement. It will also help to identify any potential issues in sustaining the change.

By collecting data before, during and after the implementation of change, managers can measure, evaluate and compare progress with the objectives set out at the start of the change.

Effective implementation hinges on measuring whether or not progress is being made at an appropriate pace. The most popular tool for assessing progress is the

Balanced Scorecard, developed by Kaplan and Norton (1996). It is a carefully selected balanced set of measures that represent a tool for leaders to use in communicating strategic direction to the organization and to motivate individuals to change. The scorecard enables managers to review performance from four strategic perspectives, which are: financial, internal business process, learning and growth, and customers. Each perspective of the scorecard includes objectives, measures of these objectives, target values of those measures and initiatives, defined as follows:

- Objectives – major objectives to be achieved, for example, an increase in profits
- Measures – the observable parameters that will be used to measure progress towards reaching the objective, for example, the objective of an increase in profits might be measured by growth in net margin
- Targets – the specific target values for the measures, for example, +4% growth in net margin
- Initiatives – action programmes to be initiated in order to meet the objective

The measurements should be linked, consistent and be mutually reinforcing. Some generic measurements are presented in Table 13.1.

The benefits claimed for the scorecard are that it clarifies strategy, focuses the organization on priority issues, encourages continuous improvement, promotes teamwork, motivates individuals and focuses on targets and performance rather than data. Achievement of the scorecard targets is dependent on the actions and achievements of the teams and individuals in the organization.

Determining whether or not change has been sustained will involve measurement of the benefits achieved as well as management of the risks associated with the change.

Identifying the benefits of change

Change can be costly, disruptive and potentially dangerous. As Paton and McCalman (2008) point out, it would be unwise to embark on the journey without first establishing that success would be probable and beneficial. As part of the planning process

Table 13.1 Generic measurements in the balanced scorecard

Perspective	Generic measurements
Financial	Return on capital employed, economic value added, sales growth, profit, loss, revenues.
Customer	Customer satisfaction, retention, acquisition, profitability, market share.
Internal business process	Includes measurements along the internal value chain for: • Innovation – measures of how well the company identifies the customers' future needs. • Operations – measures of quality, cycle time, and costs.
Learning and growth	Includes measurements for: • People – employee retention, training, skills, job satisfaction • Systems – measure of availability of critical real time information needed for front line employees.

for sustaining any change, it follows that it is vital to identify the benefits to be achieved. The rationale for identifying benefits is outlined in the box below.

Reasons for identifying benefits at the start of a change initiative

- Benefits are identified, measured and the process is locked in from the start.
- The business case for change is identified in a quantifiable way.
- The reason for change is clear; the benefits provide a focus for everyone.
- Return on investment in change can be measured.
- Success can be identified, recognized and celebrated, thereby having a positive impact on future change initiatives.
- There is clear agreed accountability for sustaining change.
- Progress can be tracked, monitored and delivered.
- Stakeholders are clear about both current and expected performance.
- The credibility of the change is enhanced through realization and recognition of the benefits.
- The cost of implementation is calculated, understood and monitored.

The types of benefits that should be identified include financial (such as a decrease in staff costs), operational (such as an increase in stock availability), customer (for example, an improvement in product range), and employee (for example, an increase in retention rates). Once benefits are identified the next step is to ensure that they are realized.

Realizing benefits

Benefits realization depends on the process of organizing and managing so that potential benefits, arising from investment in change, are actually achieved. It should be the core management process of any change initiative. The key activities for realizing benefits comprise engaging stakeholders, developing a business case, identifying risks, developing tracking mechanisms, continually tracking benefits, communicating achievement of benefits, monitoring and reviewing progress against the benefits. In the box below are the key activities and the tasks for each of the activities.

1 Engaging stakeholders

- Stakeholder analysis, mapping and action plan
- Communications with stakeholders
- Feedback from stakeholders and involvement in decisions.

2 Developing the business case

- Identifying benefits opportunities
- Building and quantifying the case for the benefits (from the business case)
- Identifying accountability for achieving the benefits

(Continued)

(Continued)

3   Identifying risks

- Identifying the probability of risks, their impact, and how to mitigate them

4   Developing a tracking mechanism

- Developing and tracking benefits (using baselines)
- Developing a benefits realization action plan
- Assessing implementation readiness

5   Tracking benefits

- Executing the benefits realization action plan
- Reviewing progress

6   Communicating achievement of benefits

- Informing key stakeholders when benefits are achieved
- Asking for feedback from stakeholders

7   Monitoring and reviewing benefits realization

- Realizing results (measurement–review–action)
- Capturing and applying the lessons learned
- Reviewing and revising the benefits realization action plan as appropriate

Taking time to identify benefits may seem like an unnecessary distraction from getting on with the actual change. However, it prevents what Stephen Covey (1989) describes as 'getting to the top, looking out, and saying "whoops, climbed over the wrong wall"'. It is not about measurement for the sake of measuring, but about measuring the impact of the change so that adjustments can be made in order for change to be sustained.

In the following case study Alison Clare focuses on how benefits were measured and realized during the introduction of a clinical portal to provide a paperless records system to replace hard-copy case notes in a hospital.

CASE STUDY

Measuring and realizing benefits from introducing a clinical portal at the Royal Liverpool and Broadgreen University Hospitals NHS Trust

The Royal Liverpool and Broadgreen University Hospitals NHS Trust is implementing a clinical portal to provide a paperless records system and replace paper case-notes.

The Trust is among the largest university hospitals in the north of England, with an annual budget of over £400 million, more than 5,500 staff including 300 consultants, and serving almost one million patients a year from across the north-west and beyond. It provides general hospital services and specialist and emergency care, including a full range of medical, surgical, diagnostic, rehabilitation and therapy services. These include nationally and internationally recognized services such as ophthalmology, hepatobiliary surgery, gastroenterology and pathology.

Drivers for change

Like many other NHS organizations, staff rely on paper case-notes when seeing their patients. Case-notes, a traditional method of managing medical records, is inefficient and expensive. There are several problems with the paper records: they can be difficult to locate, labour-intensive to maintain, prepare and transport, and they can be in poor condition, with only one person at a time able to read the notes.

The Trust is not alone in its findings. Paper is inflexible and not conducive to information sharing or joined-up patient care. Analysis at the Trust has identified an average of 12% of case-notes are unavailable at the point of care because they are booked out somewhere else in the hospital. Clinical safety is compromised when doctors cannot see the most up-to-date records of their patients, and there is also an increased cost of care. Duplicate tests are expensive and inconvenient to patients who have to visit our hospitals more often than they would otherwise.

The solution

By developing new and improved IT systems and replacing paper case-notes with a clinical portal, efficiency will improve, and the hospital will become more cost-effective and most importantly be able to deliver improved patient care.

The Trust recognizes an electronic patient record is a better way to care for their patients. It has partnered with CSC and Carefx, leading interoperability platform providers, to implement the Carefx Fusion Clinical Portal. Given that the national programme no longer intends to replace systems wholesale and that the government's ICT strategy is to connect information rather than store everything in a single system, the Trust, rather than 'ripping and replacing' all their existing IT systems, has chosen to keep the assets it already has and re-work them into a portal.

Portals are a new cost-effective way to replace paper-based systems. The screen is divided into several portlets, each of which draws and displays live patient information from existing systems. By calling this data in real-time the portal puts it together in seconds and all the portlets show information about the same patient. So if a clinician searches for another patient, that data will replace the previous patient's data in all of the portlets. This context change ensures a clinician is only ever looking at a single patient's information.

Before committing to a full rollout, the Trust ran a pilot project to test the principle of paperless clinics and wards. This ran between June and September 2010 for 60 days, initially in two small haematology and dermatology clinics.

Clinical engagement

During the design phase of the pilot, in order to identify the screen layout and content, workshops with a variety of clinicians were set up at the start of the project. By discussing and demonstrating draft versions of the portal during its design, the Trust ensured its clinicians were involved at every point. Normal workflows were documented so that the existing paper case-notes journey could be reviewed and streamlined where possible, creating new more efficient business processes.

(Continued)

(Continued)

The time spent understanding these processes was invaluable in designing the portal and understanding exactly what information was important to the doctors and nurses and when they used it.

Giving clinicians a say in the portal design played a great part in gaining their commitment to the change. There was little evidence of resistance, and as a result of their input they found the portal simple to use. Basically anyone who is able to navigate the internet can use it with minimal training and, because the clinicians were already familiar with the underlying source systems, there was no additional training required.

Input from clinicians was also used to design different roles and access levels for GPs referring their patients, and nurse and doctor views driven by daily clinic lists. The portal design includes a facility to search for patients by name, NHS and hospital number at the same time as maintaining existing data protection and legitimate doctor–patient relationships. This restricted access to appropriate clinicians ensured patient confidentiality was not compromised. From design to implementation the project took three months, with live testing taking place for a further three weeks before the system was signed off for the pilot phase. Such a rapid implementation avoided any disruption to 'business as usual'.

Managing the change

Once the design phase was complete and developers began writing the interfaces to feed data between existing source systems and the clinical portal, the project team widened their communications to engage with clinicians who had not otherwise been involved in the project. Presenting at departmental meetings and demonstrating the product at key stages in the development enabled clinicians to identify what they liked and didn't like, and the project team was able to document future requirements. By mapping these requirements to each group of stakeholders, the Trust was able to identify the likely resistance to change, if any, in the future. Using this information the Trust developed communications to allay clinicians' fears and alleviate resistance to the change before it became a threat to delivery.

After user-acceptance testing by key clinicians, the portal went live in two clinics. Consultants, their registrars and specialist nurses were able to view patient medical history, key treatments, referrals and diagnosis and test results at the touch of a button on a single screen. And although paper case-notes were still available, they were not required by clinicians at all throughout the pilot.

Benefits realization

In order to determine if the project was successful, baseline measurements were taken. The technology was measured against system availability and speed, and information accuracy between the underlying source systems and the portal. The number of missing case notes was also measured to ensure this original driver remained valid. In all cases the baselines taken prior to 'go-live' were exceeded, and the project was so successful that it was extended to more clinicians and larger 50-plus patient clinics, which included patients with chronic conditions. This was intended to further challenge the portal and prove that it could be used in very busy clinical environments as well as support more complex patient care than the pilot originally intended.

The project ran for 60 days, during which time the success criteria were measured. Once the official pilot came to an end, clinicians requested that they continue to use the portal rather than return to case-notes. The benefits were clear: clinics finished on average 30 minutes earlier than when run with paper case-notes, nurses saved 12 minutes per 25 patients as a result of fewer administrative tasks, clinic clerks no longer had to search for missing files, accurate and up-to-date patient information was available instantly, resulting in reduced clinical risk.

Clinician feedback was excellent. One renal consultant said: 'Missing case-notes were a big frustration, though I had reservations about whether the portal was the answer. But it's brilliant and makes it so much easier to deal with patients properly.'

And because the portal incorporated 'single sign-on' functionality, clinicians needed only to remember one password to access multiple systems. So each clinician used a single set of credentials and their access rights were linked to their role.

Pilot outcomes

The pilot proved a complete success, with clinicians agreeing they could run clinics without paper case-notes. Patient safety increased by clinicians' having an electronic patient record at their fingertips and the removal of paper improved infection control. Frustrations with missing case notes were removed by the end of logging on to multiple systems, with the benefits of having to remember only one password. Basically, the clinical portal allowed clinicians to focus on patient.

Next steps

Following the pilot, the Trust went through a framework tender process and has now procured the Carefx portal solution from CSC. The Trust decided to opt for a portal solution as they found in the pilot it was easier and quicker to deploy alongside existing systems and would minimize disruption.

The portal was seen as a strategic decision to protect existing investments in IT systems as well as an effective and efficient way to reduce costs and administration, while simultaneously speeding up and increasing the throughput of patients.

© 2015 Alison Clare, Freelance project, programme and change manager.

Discussion Questions

1   What were the key drivers for the change in the hospital?
2   In your view, was a rapid implementation the best approach? What were the benefits and risks of this approach?
3   What approach could have been taken to address the resistance to the change?
4   How might the sustainability of the project be measured?

Activity

Consider an organizational change you are familiar with:

1   What benefits were expected?
2   Were the benefits realized?
3   If not, why not?

Management of risk during change

Determining whether or not change has been sustained will involve measurement of the benefits achieved as well as management of the risks associated with the change. A risk is the probability of an event or issue being realized that may lead to an undesirable effect on the organization or on the people in it. In his book *Managing Risk in Organizations: A Guide for Managers*, J. Davidson Frame (2003) outlines the key elements of risk management, which include the planning, monitoring and controlling of actions that will address the threats and problems identified so as to improve the likelihood of the risks not occurring. Risks need to be identified, managed and mitigated during change.

Identifying risks during change

Broadly, there are four main types of risk associated with change:

1. *External risks.* External events are mainly outside the control of managers or leaders. Examples include government regulatory changes; industry-specific procedures (new standards, issues); mergers and acquisitions; legal issues (disputes, lawsuits and court orders); new products and/or services; changes in the competitive market; and disasters such as fire, flood, earthquake or other natural disasters. Most of these risks are very difficult to control but can be identified and therefore managed. This means that managers must review the external environment regularly in order to identify potential risks.
2. *Cost risks.* Many of these types of risks are directly or indirectly under the manager's control or within his or her area of influence. Examples of cost risks include those arising from cost overruns by project teams, subcontractors, vendors and consultants; scope creep, expansion and change that has not been managed; poor estimating or errors that result in unforeseen costs; and overrun of budget and schedules.
3. *Technology risks.* Technology risks can result from a wide variety of circumstances. Typical examples are problems with immature technology, use of the wrong tools, software that is untested or fails to work properly, requirement changes with no change management, failure to understand or account for product complexity, integration problems, and software/hardware performance issues (poor response times, bugs and errors).
4. *Operational risks.* Operational risks can result in a failure to realize the intended or expected benefits of the project. Typical causes are inadequate resolution of priorities or conflicts, failure to designate authority to key people, insufficient communication or lack of a communication plan, and rollout and implementation risks – 'too much, too soon'.

The risk identification process consists of assessing the probability of the risk occurring and its impact on the change initiative, whether it is high, medium or low risk. Guidelines to assist in assessing the probability of a risk are:

- *High* (certain): the risk could happen at any time if no new or additional measures are implemented.

- *Medium* (possible): a risk could happen but circumstances are not yet clear or there exist a number of mitigating factors to reduce the possibility of the risk occurring.
- *Low* (remote): if a risk were to occur, it would require an unusual or exceptional combination of different factors or, alternatively, there is a wider range of mitigating factors to prevent the risk occurring.

Managing risks during change

In general, risk management is based on four steps: risk identification, risk analysis/assessment, risk treatment and the monitoring of risks.

1. Risk identification is the identification of risks and their causes.
2. Risk analysis/assessment is the estimation of the likelihood of risks occurring and their impact.
3. Risk treatment concerns the actions and mechanisms to minimize risks.
4. Monitoring and control comprise the continuous monitoring of risks and the actions to manage them.

The most common reasons for managing risks during a change process are outlined in the box below.

The most common reasons for managing risks

- Reduce or eliminate where possible the impact of a risk that has occurred.
- Increase the chance of success of change(s).
- Reduce or eliminate where possible the probability of a risk occurring.
- Reduce or eliminate where possible the financial impact of a risk that has occurred.
- Increase the visibility of risks to management and other staff.
- Secure successful continuity and profitability.
- Secure a stable working-environment for staff.

Mitigating risks during change

Managers need to decide on a risk management strategy for addressing risks once the probability is identified. This is the process whereby a decision is made as to whether the risk should be managed, contained or eliminated. The responses to risks tend to be:

- *Avoid*. Counter-measures are put in place that either stop the threat or problem from occurring or prevent it from having any impact upon the change.
- *Transfer*. A specialist form of risk reduction, where the impact of the risk is passed on to a third party via, for instance, an insurance policy or penalty clause, albeit at a cost.

- *Mitigate.* Where the response actions either reduce the likelihood of the risk developing or, if the risk occurs, limit the impact on the change to acceptable levels.
- *Accept.* There is acceptance of the possibility that the risk might occur.

The most appropriate response will be dependent on the following:

- The cost of minimizing the impact on the change initiative of any risk should it occur
- The costs of the risk management strategy in relation to the value (cost) of the risks
- The likelihood and probability of the risk occurring
- The availability of resources to avoid, transfer, mitigate or accept the risk
- The severity of the impact on the change initiative

Once the risk strategy has been agreed on, actions need to be allocated to individuals to address each one. These actions need to be monitored, controlled and the status of the risk and actions agreed updated on a regular basis, as events may occur to remove the risk or to reduce the impact and probability of the risk.

Monitoring change

Monitoring the progress of change needs to be ongoing and frequent if it is to be sustained. Buchanan and Storey (1997) argue that change can involve much backtracking. Burke (2002) echoes this view and argues that the change process is often more like a series of loops rather than a straight line, reflecting the reality that things rarely progress as planned, and even when plans are implemented as intended, there are often unanticipated consequences. There is often a need to fix things to keep the change on track. Seeking out and addressing feedback is essential if managers are to monitor whether or not the change plan is working. All too often those leading and managing change fail to deliberately seek out feedback and realize that change is failing or producing unintended consequences only when something unplanned happens to draw their attention to it.

Feedback

Several writers (Beckhard and Harris, 1987; Nadler, 1993) argue that tailored feedback mechanisms not only facilitate monitoring and control of change but can also help to sustain change. Managers can help to develop this kind of feedback by designing feedback mechanisms that can be used to monitor and manage the situation over the longer term.

Another way in which managers can achieve feedback is by 'managing by walking about' (known popularly as MBWA), although it is possible that individuals might be nervous about speaking up (recall 'organization silence' described in Chapter 10), in which case it may be necessary to use focus groups or some other means of collecting data, such as non-attributable feedback from surveys. Feedback on how the change is progressing can signal a need to think again about the change plan and the way it is being implemented.

Surveys

Surveys are helpful to capture people's attitudes, opinions and experiences at a particular time and then track these attitudes over time. Surveys can provide anonymity to the respondents and make it possible to capture the opinions of a larger proportion of participants than might otherwise be possible. For instance, in order to gauge the readiness for change (see Chapter 6 for a discussion about the readiness for change) surveys can provide feedback on aspects such as the participation and consultation practices as well as views on the proposed change. While during the implementation stage of change, surveys can provide feedback on the management of the change process. Feedback from employee surveys can help to stimulate discussion about what is working and what needs to be improved. It can also help to identify any required modifications to the change plan or the way it is being implemented or, if necessary, to a reorientation of the vision for the change.

Feedback provides information not only on what people are thinking and therefore doing but also on why. Knowing the why enables leaders and managers to identify which behaviours and actions need to be stopped or changed, either because the behaviours are representative of the past, or because they are new but creating unhelpful interpretations of the change, and which behaviours and actions need to be encouraged because they are fostering helpful interpretations. The 'why' enables leaders to engage with the issues of those involved in change and work with them (Balogun, 2006).

The design, administration and analysis of feedback require careful consideration. Although online survey packages such as SurveyMonkey.com and EmployeeSurveys. com provide an accessible design, delivery and analysis of survey data, the ability to frame good questions skilfully is a prerequisite to getting useful information. The same holds true for analysis and interpretation.

The findings from surveys can be used to create learning opportunities and contribute to the way that the change is dealt with. Encouraging discussions about the feedback provides a vehicle for individuals and teams to raise any issues, queries or ideas and help them to agree on commitments to various actions.

Leading a change project or programme without metrics and a risk assessment is like flying a plane without instruments. For a short flight on a clear day you might be able to reach the destination safely, but once you are in some clouds you will find yourself in serious trouble. Too often organizations avoid the discomfort of establishing a robust series of meaningful metrics and end up having to deal with the agony of a stalled change initiative, which results in wreckage.

It is vital to monitor and review the implementation of the change in order to identify areas that need to be adjusted and adapted to ensure that the change is effectively implemented and achieves the intended benefits.

For change to be meaningful in organizations, it needs to be sustained over time, and this implies a shift in the organization's habitual ways of being. Martin Davis outlines his experience of implementing handheld technology for a mobile workforce in the following case study. Davis describes what the challenges were and how the change was eventually sustained and the lessons he learnt from it.

Implementing handheld technology for a mobile workforce and sustaining the change

Traditionally, companies with a mobile workforce have relied upon paper job-sheets, two-way radios and mobile phones to control, dispatch and manage staff in the field. With the increasing capabilities of mobile technology this is rapidly changing. The growth of high-speed 3G and 4G networks plus devices like smart phones and the iPad have led to fully functional mobile solutions that enable real-time information flow and drive significant business improvements. These technologies can be applied in many situations from waste-management pick-ups to freight deliveries, a mobile sales force and repair crews. This case describes the change process when a dispatch company chose to implement handheld technology for its mobile workforce.

Traditional processes have considerable inefficiencies with mobile staff out of contact with their dispatcher or office for long periods of time. Mobile staff can often be found waiting for instructions or for their next job. Similarly dispatchers struggle to know who is free and located nearest when trying to assign a new task. All of this leads to waste and increased costs to the business. Additionally, customer satisfaction suffers as the company is guessing at arrival times based on incomplete and out-of-date information. The key drives for the change were:

- Real-time information – where are the mobile workforce and which tasks have they completed
- Improved customer service – ability to more accurately forecast arrival times at a customer site
- Increased ability to plan and utilize resources
- minimized, resource utilization is improved and ultimately business profitability is increased.

The original way of working in the company included the use of manually completed paper forms to track jobs assigned and work completed and to calculate customer charges and staff performance. These were replaced by using handheld devices, which communicated to control and digital mapping systems at the depots. These systems allowed the dispatcher to understand location and work status in real time, enabling better planning and resource management.

Even more significant than the use of technology was the change of work processes for the mobile workforce, the administrative staff and the dispatchers. While this may not be the most complex of technology implementations it had significant impact on the people involved and made many changes to their daily life. For example, dispatching a new job used to involve guessing at who might be nearest, calling them on the radio or cellphone and then relaying instructions orally, and of course completing the paperwork. Now it simply involves checking the digital map, seeing who is nearest and available and then assigning the job to them with a single click. The mobile staff are then alerted on their handheld device and press a button to accept the job. The device then calculates the route needed and provides the necessary guidance. Upon arrival the driver clicks a button to notify dispatch, completes the work and clicks another button to say 'finished', and enters any additional information related to extra work or charges.

In order to achieve success with this project the team spent as much if not more effort on change management compared with what they did on technology implementation. The change-management approach closely followed Kotter's eight steps for leading change in helping the staff to see the reasons for the project, guiding them towards the new reality and finally anchoring it into new working practices – what Kurt Lewin termed 'unfreeze – change – refreeze'.

Changing long-used processes comes with a number of challenges and, when combined with new technology, the problems multiply. The main challenges we faced were:

- Staff not used to using technology – there was a fear of technology leading to concerns and resistance. This required considerable effort, with face-to-face training, videos and online help. Not everyone was used to using a keyboard, a mouse or a handheld device every day.
- Long-ingrained traditional processes – when people have been doing their jobs in certain ways for many years, it becomes second nature to them and therefore very difficult to change. New processes had to be carefully designed, involving as many key workers as possible, coupled with thorough training and support. This was further assisted by removing the opportunity for staff to continue to use the old processes.
- Resistance due to fear of the unknown – people do not naturally resist change; in fact everyone likes to have variety. People do, however, fear the unknown, which leads to resistance. To combat this we used communication and involved everyone affected in the project.
- Short timescales – balancing the time to involve everyone with the need for urgency was a difficult trade-off. However, it was essential to a successful change that sufficient consultation and communication took place.
- 'Big brother is watching you!' Within the mobile workforce this generated more concern than was expected and required additional communications and discussions in order to resolve it. The bottom line though was that, unless people were misusing company vehicles, they had nothing to worry about.

As Kotter, Lewin and others have made clear, unless a change is anchored in the organization, then once the project team has gone, processes will start to revert to the old ways of doing things. So key to sustaining success was removing or dismantling the old processes, giving staff no option to go back to paper-based processes. Additional actions included ensuring that all communications happened via electronic dispatch messages – removing the use of the phone – and, finally, using key performance indicators from the technology in order to measure workforce performance.

Lessons learnt

The key lessons learnt were:

1 *Ambition.* Base the project around a sufficiently ambitious business change, of which IT is just one component. Is the change ambitious enough? Will it motivate the organization to alter and adopt new processes and systems?
2 *Project name.* Name the project carefully by choosing a word, phrase or acronym related to the business processes that are changing and the desired end-result. It may seem like a small thing but the name can set the mood for the whole project. Also do not choose the name of a technology, because that implies the project belongs to IT as opposed to its being a business project.
3 *Design a structured and coherent change programme.* To be successful you need a structured approach, such as Kotter's 'Leading Change' framework.

(Continued)

(Continued)

4   *Leadership.* The change requires strong leadership from senior management, painting a clear picture of the reason for change, leading the staff who are affected towards a new vision ('The Promised Land'!) and then anchoring that new reality in the organizational culture.
5   *Urgency.* The leadership and management teams need to emphasize the reason for change and create a real sense of urgency within the business. Without urgency it becomes just another 'management bright idea'. Urgency in the business motivates the staff to take action.
6   *Ensure it resonates with staff.* Make sure the staff understand and embrace the vision and the need for change. If it resonates with them as the way to move forward then they will start helping drive the future, and over time this will develop into the bottom-up change that you need to sustain. If you can achieve this, the battle is 50% won already.
7   *Involve everyone.* Have the employees affected by the change as part of the decision-making process. Helping to define the needs, the solution and the revised processes means they are far more likely to embrace change. It also goes a long way to reducing the fear factor. The problem for management becomes how to involve as many people as possible, keep the project moving forward and continue daily business.
8   *'What's in it for me?'.* Staff will become far more interested if they know how they might benefit. This can range from their ability to influence future directions to elevation of status, new opportunities, recognition and so on.

© 2015 Martin Davis, VP of IT for J D Irving Ltd.

Discussion Questions

1   Was the linear approach to change the right one to take within the context of the organization and the change required? Why?
2   What else could be done to sustain the change?

Changing the change

Just as it is important to be aware of the premature labelling of change as successful, it is also important to recognize that not all changes are a good idea. If change is not producing the desired outcome, it may be that the change needs to be reconsidered. In this regard, there may be the assumption that the failure of the change is due either to the lack of sufficient resources or to the change needing longer to prove itself. This may lead to a further commitment of resources, referred to by Staw and Ross (1987a) as 'escalation of commitment'. Staw and Ross identify four factors (determinants) that can lead to escalation:

1.   *Project determinants.* Commitment is likely to increase where the lack of progress is considered to be due to a temporary problem, where additional funding is considered likely to be effective, or where the relative payoff to come from additional investment is considered to be large.

2. *Psychological determinants.* Escalation can result from self-justification biases in which having been personally responsible for a decision can lead to continued commitment to try to avoid being associated with losses.
3. *Social determinants.* Escalation may occur as those most closely identified with a project throw more resources at it in an attempt to revive it and thereby save face by not being associated with a failed project. This response is encouraged by the 'hero effect' – the special praise and adoration for managers who stick to their guns in the face of opposition and seemingly bleak odds.
4. *Organizational determinants.* Organizational units are likely to resist abandoning a change that is seen as central to the organization's identity. Staw and Ross (1987b) cite the example of Lockheed's L1011 Tri-Star Jet programme, noting that Lockheed persisted with the project for more than a decade, despite huge losses and predictions that it was unlikely to earn a profit, because to abandon it would have meant admitting that they were simply a defence contractor and not, as they preferred to believe, a pioneer in commercial aircraft.

Sustaining change is helped if actions are taken to reduce the prospect of escalation occurring. Keil and Montealegre (2000) identify seven practices that can help to reduce escalation:

1. Do not ignore negative feedback or external pressure.
2. Hire an external assessor to provide an independent view on progress.
3. Do not be afraid to withhold further resources. As well as limiting losses, doing this has a symbolic value as an emphatic signal that there is concern with progress.
4. Look for opportunities to redefine the problem and generate ideas for courses of action other than the one being abandoned.
5. Manage impressions. Frame the 'de-escalation' in a way that saves face.
6. Prepare your stakeholders because, if they shared the initial belief in the rationale for the change, their reaction to an announcement of the abandonment of the change may be to resist it.
7. Look for opportunities to de-institutionalize the project, making clear that the project is not a central defining feature of the organization, so that stepping back from the change, should it occur, does not imply any weakening of commitment to the central mission of the organization.

Additional practices that can help to reduce escalation are suggested by Ghosh (1997):

1. Unambiguous feedback on progress reduces escalation: where feedback is ambiguous, the tendency of people to filter ambiguous information selectively will lead to escalation by those already committed to the change.
2. Regular progress reports reduce escalation: where they are not required, they will not necessarily be sought prior to further commitment to resources.
3. Information on the future benefits of incremental investment reduces escalation: without this specific information, decision-making is too heavily influenced by historical costs.

Being aware of the implications of the existence of the escalation of commitment is important. However, even when there is awareness, it is still challenging to manage.

Keil and Montealegre (2000) point out that the line between an optimistic 'can-do' attitude and over-commitment is very thin and difficult to discern.

What to do when change starts to fail

At an intellectual level, change can appear to be easy to create, plan and even to produce templates and checklists for. But what happens when problems start to occur, as they inevitably will? How can one mistake be prevented from turning into a major failure of the whole change effort? Sustaining a change programme requires courage – sometimes the courage to admit that it was the wrong plan or that there should be a change of direction. At other times it is a question of perseverance, of keeping going even when the going is tough.

Attention needs to be given to sustain change for as long as it is beneficial to do so; this caveat is important because there may be circumstances where it may not be beneficial to continue to maintain a change. The change may not have been success-ful or it may have produced unanticipated consequences. Buchanan and colleagues (2005) say that sustaining change can be counterproductive when:

- Changes in the wider environment render recently implemented working prac-tices, outcomes and lines of development obsolete
- Maintaining recently implemented practices impedes further and more significant developments

When transformation starts to fail there are a number of strategies managers can consider for turning the situation around, including the following:

1. *Ensure that there is clarity about the aim and outcome of the change initiative.* Some change initiatives start with a vague intention of improving something about the organization's performance or functioning. Consider the following:

    o   Is there a link between the planned change and the organization's vision for the future, purpose, core values and strategic plan? (See Chapter 3 for more information on core leadership practices.)
    o   Is there a clear picture of the organization's strengths, weaknesses, opportunities and threats and how the change effort will influence them? (See Chapter 6 for diagnostic tools.)
    o   Can the outcomes and benefits be measured?
    o   Which changes will have the greatest impact with the least risk?
    o   Is too much trying to be changed at once?
    o   Are there unrealistic timescales?

2. *Ensure that there is sufficient support and readiness for the change.* There is a network of stakeholders in and around the organization, including shareholders, customers, employees and suppliers, whose commitment needs to be gained to ensure that the change effort does not fail. Each of these stakeholder groups has an important role to play in ensuring the success of the change. Stakeholders will have their own, sometimes conflicting, agendas and needs that require delicate balancing. Some will be unconvinced about the benefits of change and others may

feel threatened by it. A project manager or sponsor who possesses sufficient credibility, experience and capability to manage the complexities of these challenges will be needed to ensure stakeholder support (see Chapter 12 for a stakeholder analysis tool).

3. *Ensure that key players are performing.* Ensure that there is clarity about the key roles and responsibilities of everyone involved in the change. Poorly defined roles mean that individuals will be unclear about their tasks, how their roles interlink with others, or about the authority they have to resolve problems within the scope of their roles. This can lead to confusion and frustration. It may also be that the wrong individuals have been selected for these roles. Sometimes, an individual is chosen because of his or her specialist knowledge without due attention being paid to the whole range of skills required (the capabilities required for change are discussed in Chapter 13).

4. *Review the implementation plan.* The rules of effective project planning apply here. There is bound to be pressure to take swift action and cut corners to save time and resources, but careful planning and monitoring are essential. Milestones need to be defined clearly and problems anticipated and acted upon swiftly. There may be opposition to changes in pace or direction, and therefore the manager will need the on-going support of leaders to secure stakeholders' commitment and additional resources (see Chapter 7 on planning and implementing change).

5. *Focus on emotional commitment to the change.* People need to be able to engage with the change effort on an emotional level. Their rational mind may understand the business benefits and what that means to them personally but their 'heart' plays an even greater role in accepting change (see Chapter 11 for a discussion of how people react to change). All key players in change have to take feelings into consideration throughout the change process. Every opportunity to communicate with employees and other stakeholders should reflect this need. The power of the unofficial network in organizations should not be underestimated, because a whispering campaign against change can seriously undermine its success.

6. *Review the communication strategy.* Communication planning and implementation are key to turning around a failing change (see Chapter 10 for a discussion on communications and their impact). Leaders and managers need to be consistent and transparent even when the news is bad because it is better for employee motivation to be honest. Bad news should be balanced, of course, with some hope: 'Here is the problem, and here is how we are going to fix it.' Otherwise there is a risk that people will be left with the impression that the change is bound to fail.

7. *Identify and address the mistakes and avoid blaming others.* Although ultimate accountability for the sustainability of change resides at the top of an organization, the responsibility for it should be part of the role of all key stakeholders. It is too easy for one team or function to blame another for the failure of a change. Managers need to ensure that there is coordination of effort and that everyone shares successes and challenges (see Chapter 4 on managing change).

8. *Recognize productive failure.* The failure of an intended change may be due to its inappropriateness. In this situation, it is important to learn from the experience (Chapter 8 discusses learning from failure).

Organizational change may vary in complexity: from the basic form of incremental change to improve on what has been done already to the highest levels of transformational change when the organization undergoes a true metamorphosis. However, sustaining it needs to be a key part of every type of change if the benefits are to be realized. If change does fail and is irretrievable then it is important to take time to learn from the failure and apply the lessons learnt to future change(s).

Implications for leaders and managers of the need to sustain change

Successful change initiatives can be undermined because too little attention is paid to holding on to the gains once the change objectives appear to be achieved (Hayes, 2014). Change may therefore fail to be sustained. When this happens the benefits from it evaporate and the organization will be left to suffer the costs. Knowing what influences and determines the sustainability of change is a starting point. However, these influences and determinants will vary depending on the nature, pace, sequence and timing of the change as well as the way in which the organization is operating. Building into the initial planning ways of sustaining the change rather than leaving it as an afterthought is vital. This should include the measuring, monitoring and reviewing of key objectives, benefits and risks.

Measuring the change

Setting clear, measurable targets or objectives at the start of a change initiative will help an organization head in the right direction, use resources efficiently, make corrections along the way and assess whether the change has achieved what it set out to do. Change measures rely on the identification of clear measurable objectives at the outset and the tracking of progress towards these objectives. Key performance indicators, objectives and reward systems that are aligned with changes and help to track the progress of change initiatives ensure that managers' attention remains focused on the change at each level and in each area of responsibility.

Performance management

Managing performance and rewarding individuals for their performance in change initiatives are important requirements for sustaining change. Reward systems should include public recognition of those whose behaviour is consistent with the desired change. This will reinforce the behaviour of individuals concerned and send signals to others about what is expected. Reward systems aligned with change remind individuals that their daily work activities have direct implications for them and that they are responsible for what they initiate or improve. The performance management process, including the setting of objectives, serves a similar function (Sackmann et al., 2009).

When change initiatives became part of individuals' personal objectives, they remain in their centre of attention rather than getting lost in their daily operational business. The appropriate use of performance objectives and a performance-based reward system can be effective instruments for reviewing and evaluating the progress of the implementation and how the change will be sustained.

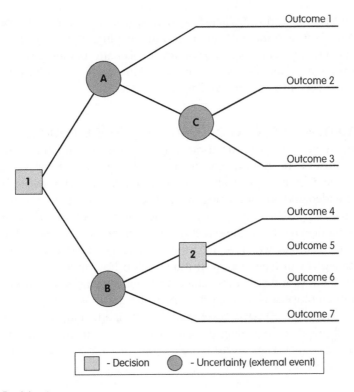

Figure 13.1   Decision tree map

Contingency planning

Along with identifying and managing benefits and risks managers also need to think through possible contingencies should events not go as planned. Two tools that aid in contingency planning are **decision tree analysis** and **scenario planning**.

Decision tree analysis

Decision tree analysis (see Figure 13.1) asks managers to consider the major choices and the possible consequences of those alternatives. They are then asked to plan for the possible actions and consider what the consequences of these actions might be. Such alternating action–consequence sequences can be extended as far as reasonable. Probabilities can also be assigned to the likelihood of each consequence. For many applications, a simple scale (very likely, likely, possible, unlikely, or very unlikely) is sufficient. This approach helps model the possible consequences to change decisions and assess the benefits and risks associated with different pathways.

Scenario planning

A second tool that helps managers with contingency planning is scenario planning (Gill, 2011: 220–1). Here a change strategy is formed by first developing a limited number of scenarios or stories about how the future may unfold and then assessing what the importance and implications of each of these would be to the organization.

By raising and testing various 'what-if' scenarios, managers can brainstorm together and challenge their assumptions in a non-threatening, hypothetical environment before they decide on a certain course of action. Scenario planning starts by painting a picture of the future and works backwards, asking what would have to happen to make this future scenario a reality and what could be done.

Measuring how people are responding to the change

Over the long term, managers can use measures such as customer satisfaction, customer retention and the bottom line to assess the validity of the change. Over a shorter timescale, they may focus attention on whether interventions are being implemented as intended and are producing the immediate outcomes that were anticipated. Another source of feedback is employees' collective perceptions of the way that the change is being managed and the effect this has on their experience of and attitudes towards the change. As we have mentioned in earlier chapters the way that the change is managed can have a powerful impact on how individuals experience the change, their attitudes towards the change and their readiness to support it. Gaining feedback from employees is an important part of measuring change.

Hayes and Hyde (2008) have developed the change management indicator (CMI) as a structured means of receiving this feedback. It is available as an online survey (www.peterhyde.co.uk). Hayes (2014) points out that the survey can be used in a number of ways, including the following:

- As a one-off diagnostic instrument to identify major areas of concern for remedial action
- As a barometer of opinion at a series of points of time, indicating whether the trend is in the desired direction
- To compare the situation in different departments, functions, locations and teams and thereby identify local issues
- As an intervention to get people thinking about the issues and to promote dialogue
- To benchmark against other organizations going through similar changes

Failure to measure and review the way a change is being implemented and managed can affect the achievement of the objectives and timescale for implementing the change. It can also undermine staff commitment to the organization, cause reputational damage and tie up resources managing unintended consequences. As a result it can ultimately adversely affect the sustainability of the change.

Further reading

Bateman, N. (2005) 'Sustainability: the elusive element of process improvement', *International Journal of Operations and Production Management*, 25(3): 261–76.
Crane, A. and Matten, D. (2007) *Business Ethics: Managing Corporate Citizenship and Sustainability in the Age of Globalization*, 2nd edn. Oxford: Oxford University Press.

Dunphy, D., Griffiths, A. and Benn, S. (2007) *Organizational Change for Corporate Sustainability: A Guide for Corporate Sustainability.* Abingdon and New York: Routledge.

Haynes, B. and Price, I. (2004) 'Quantifying the complex adaptive workplace', *Facilities*, 22(1/2): 8–18.

Lawler III, E.E. and Worley, C.G. (2011) *Built to Change: How to Achieve Sustained Organizational Effectiveness.* San Francisco, CA: Jossey-Bass.

Woodman, R.W., Bingham, J.B. and Yuan, F. (2008) 'Assessing organization development and change interventions', in T.G. Cummings (ed.), *Handbook of Organization Development*. Thousand Oaks, CA: Sage, pp. 187–215.

Contemporary Issues in Change and Transformation

14

Overview

- This chapter highlights the global trends affecting the business world and the need for capacity and capability to deal with the changes they are driving in organizations.
- Various megatrends are transforming the world, including globalization, climate change, demographic shifts and accelerated technological innovation. They are creating conditions under which the nature of change itself is changing.
- Business leaders increasingly refer to sustainability as one of the lynchpins of competition within their sector and a significant source of both opportunity for, and risk to, long-term competitive advantage. Many executives now acknowledge that the way they respond to the challenge of sustainability will affect the competitiveness of their business and the future of their company (Lubin and Esty, 2010).
- This chapter highlights the importance of promoting the ethical dimension of change – as a means of ensuring that leaders and their followers act in the interests of the many rather than just the few. This dimension of change can only be achieved, however, if organizational stakeholders are able and prepared to ensure that leaders pursue ethical rather than unethical behaviour. And this can be achieved only if the difference between ethical and unethical approaches to change is identified and clear.
- Organizations need to develop the capability and capacity to cope with the constant and rapid change they will continue to face.

We are living in an age of transformation in which the breadth and scope of possible changes are equal to, if not greater than, the aftermath of the political and economic revolutions of the late eighteenth century due to megatrends. The aim of this chapter is to discuss the major trends that are creating this global transformation and how they will impact on organizational change in future decades. Evidence is provided on the megatrends from two publications – *Global Strategic Trends – Out to 2040* and *Global Trends 2030*. The chapter discusses the implications of these trends for organizations, in particular it considers the importance of sustainability and business ethics. The chapter also considers the future capability and capacity for change in organizations, in order to cope with global changes and create sustainable change.

Learning objectives

By the end of this chapter you will be able to:

- Identify contemporary issues relating to organizational change
- Discuss the implications of the global trends for organizational change
- Identify future approaches for leaders and managers for addressing the change driven by the global trends

The impact of megatrends

We are living in a time of transformation. The world is facing the reality of a changing climate, rapid population growth, resource scarcity, resurgence in ideology, rapid technological development and innovation, and shifts in global power from West to East. Two reports provide an insight into the trends that are shaping and will continue to shape global changes in coming years: one is *Global Strategic Trends – Out to 2040*, written by a research team at the Development, Concepts and Doctrine Centre (DCDC) at the Ministry of Defence in the UK (2010); the second is *Global Trends 2030: Alternative Worlds*, based on research carried out by the National Intelligence Council (2012) in the USA. Both reports identify various megatrends that are transforming the world, including individual empowerment, the diffusion of power to multi-faceted networks from West to East and North to South, demographic patterns highlighted by ageing populations and exploding middle classes, and natural resource challenges. These trends exist today, but during the next 15–20 years they will grow and become more intertwined, producing a qualitatively different world.

The DCDC report (2013) outlines that from now until 2040 will be a time likely to be characterized by instability, both in relations between states and in relations between groups within states. Globalization, global inequality, climate change and technological innovation will affect the lives of everyone on the planet. No state, group or individual will be able to meet these challenges in isolation; only collective responses will be sufficient. The DCDC report points out that the struggle to establish an effective system of global governance, capable of responding to these challenges, will be a central theme of the era. There will be constant tension between greater interdependence between states, groups and individuals and intensifying competition between them.

The distribution of global power will change. Up to 2040, the DCDC (2010) points out that the locus of global power will move away from the USA and Europe towards Asia as the global system shifts from a uni-polar towards a multi-polar distribution of power. This shift, coupled with the global challenges of climate change, resource scarcity and population growth, is likely to result in a period of instability in international relations, accompanied by the possibility of intense competition between major powers. The hegemonic dominance of the USA will fade. It is likely to remain the pre-eminent military power, although, in political, economic and military terms, the USA is likely to be increasingly constrained as others grow in influence and confidence. However, the DCDC cautions that the rise of individual states such as China should not be considered a certainty given the nature and magnitude of the challenges they face. Nor should their eventual influence be over-estimated. Instead there will be several states and institutions competing for regional and global influence, cooperating and competing within the international community.

Underpinning these megatrends are critical changes to the global environment that will affect how the world works. The United States' National Intelligence Council (2012) defines these as **game-changers** that will determine what kind of transformed world we will inhabit in the future. These game-changers include the global economy, national and global governance, the nature of conflict, regional spillover, advancing technologies and the United States' role in the international arena. They are the raw elements that could sow the seeds of global disruption or huge advances.

Megatrends and organizational change

The social, environmental and economic consequences of the megatrends are as much a concern for businesses as they are for countries and governments. Whether organizations will be able to adapt fast enough to harness change instead of being overwhelmed by these developments is a vital question.

Companies that have managed to engineer change repeatedly are IKEA and SAS. IKEA is the privately held international home-products company founded in 1943 in Sweden, which has made many changes in the way it operates. For example, after being rocked by scandals about its use of formaldehyde in the early 1980s, the company took a proactive stance on environmental issues. In 1990 it adopted 'The Natural Step' framework as the basis for its environmental plan. Today IKEA is heavily focused on sustainability, something its employees take pride in and work to enhance. Another such company is SAS, the world's largest privately held software company and a global leader in business intelligence software. The company, headquartered in Cary, North Carolina, was founded in 1976 and has experienced decades of continuous revenue growth, which many attribute not only to the value of its products and the execution of its business but also to its knowledge of good business practices. It has been estimated that SAS saves between $60 million and $80 million a year by not having to replace people. SAS and IKEA are good examples of how leaders and managers can create a workforce that continuously looks for ways to improve the company and so remain competitive.

Activity

Think of an organization known personally to you. In what way has it reacted to megatrends? Identify any change initiatives that have been or should have been introduced to address the trends.

This activity may be carried out by you alone or by a group who can share their conclusions and identify what these have in common.

Change and sustainability

Sustainability is now on the agenda of leaders across the globe. Bonini and colleagues (2010) cite sustainability as one of the major factors that will shape and define our world in the coming era. This is echoed by Matthew Gwyther, editor of *Management Today*, who says:

> It's a mark of how far the subject of sustainability in business has advanced that it means so many different things to different bosses. What began more than a decade ago as a revivified conversation about corporate social responsibility (CSR) has now morphed into an urgent discussion. In biology – where the term originates – sustainability is about the ability to endure, so those who are not sustainable are staring at oblivion.
>
> Sustainability has come to signify the school of thought that considers how business operates in social, cultural and economic environments. Increasingly it's become a story about enlightened self-interest or 'doing the right thing' … What is important in business is to listen, to learn and to adapt behaviour. This becomes even more important when the global economy is in bad shape, as sustainability encompasses the process of surviving in a hostile environment. (2012: 1)

Although business leaders have been challenging one another to be 'good citizens' since the 1950s, the concept of 'sustainable' business is relatively new. In 1987 the Brundtland Commission coined the phrase 'sustainable development', defining it as development that meets the needs of the present without compromising the ability of future generations to meet their own needs. This concept was highlighted during the 1992 United Nations Conference on Environment and Development in Rio de Janeiro.

Since this summit, organizations worldwide have adopted practices for sustainable development, economies and societies (Gladwin et al., 1995). These practices converge around a concern for the environment, economic growth and the development of the world's poor (Stern, 2006). As such, sustainability is said to comprise the three pillars of *people, planet* and *profit* (White and Lee, 2009) – the Triple Bottom Line. Companies must become more sophisticated to survive in this environmental and social context. For example, Starbucks has established a traditional competitive advantage and has been profitable. Yet, as the case of their tax avoidance issue in the UK shows, the company is still struggling to sustain this advantage in its social context.

Increasingly, organizations are beginning to adopt sustainability as a strategic imperative. There is, however, little convergence within the literature on the process organizations go through to embrace sustainability. Some researchers argue that organizations require a paradigm shift to filter in more sustainable ways of thinking and behaving (Linnenluecke and Griffiths, 2010). Others contend that sustainability requires only moderate behavioural changes catalysed by incremental adjustments to processes, procedures and reward systems (Dunphy et al., 2007; Epstein et al., 2010; Harris and Crane, 2002).

Researchers have identified different methods to operationalize sustainability within organizations (Linnenluecke and Griffiths, 2010). Mirvis and Manga (2010) have identified two models used to integrate citizenship into organizations: the top-down approach and the catalytic approach. The top-down approach is a comprehensive, long-term approach in which leaders 'build momentum for change and promote coordinated movement on multiple fronts' (2010: 36). Through this approach, leadership creates a clear definition of organizational sustainability values that is consistently communicated and reinforced throughout the organization. In the catalytic approach, sustainability initiatives are introduced and implemented by middle-level managers (Mirvis and Manga, 2010). Which is the most appropriate model depends on the context in which the organization operates, although, like any change initiative, sustainability is more likely to stick if people at various levels are involved rather than the top of the hierarchy 'doing it' to them.

An example of a small company that is attempting to build a sustainable business model is TransferWise. The company was founded by Estonians in London and offers peer-to-peer money transfers, using the internet to match buyers and sellers in different countries and to eliminate much of the spread between bid and offer exchange rates. TransferWise is a company with a philosophy based on how little it can charge for its services, while building a global sustainable business. The company was set up in 2010 and aims to become the Skype of money transfers. It has attracted funding from Peter Thiel, the founder of PayPal and an early investor in Facebook. Their key challenge is changing behaviours – how do they get people to see that there are better things than banks.

The notion of 'sustainable development' is increasingly being adopted by organizations and, according to management consultants McKinsey and others, will be a defining force in the future. Implicitly this includes organizational change. However, Carla Miller (2012) and colleagues point out that much more clarity is needed on how organizations must change to meet the sustainability challenge and how the necessary changes may be achieved. Implementation and organizational change are the key issues on which the sustainability agenda is demanding action. This requires a change of thinking – a change of attitude that usually needs to start with leadership. Miller and colleagues go on to say they believe that leaders who lead sustainable companies will be those who explicitly drive sustainability into their business practices and strategies. The best leaders will not only transform their own businesses but also have the vision to change attitudes and mindsets in their industries. True sustainability is a product of a company's culture and evolves from it as well as developing the culture in new directions. Olivia Sprinkel (2012), a sustainability consultant at Salterbaxter, develops this further view and notes that successful change strategies for sustainability need to take into account an organization's identity.

Organizational identity is defined by Alexandra Stubbings and Nicolas Ceasar (2012) as being about 'who we are' and the image we want to portray of our values, culture and strategic intent. Stubbings and Ceasar propose a model of change for the era of sustainability which comprises of four 'E's, which we have expanded in relation to engaging and enacting:

- *Expressing* – articulating the external value-proposition through products, physical artefacts or services
- *Engaging* – with stakeholders' feedback on their impressions of the organization's activities in relation to its vision, purpose, values, strategy and employee and management competency, relationships and loyalty
- *Encoding* – through redesigning systems and processes
- *Enacting* – aligning cultural practices through creating new meaning and discourse on vision, purpose, values, strategy and identity

The four Es need to be taken into account when sustaining change, for effective leadership and management are crucial to infusing a culture of sustainable change. At the organizational level, senior leadership defines sustainability and establishes an integrated culture by aligning sustainability with business purposes and driving sustainability priorities through the organization. At the functional level, managers assume a differentiated perspective and translate organizational sustainability goals into tools and programmes for facilities, suppliers and employees. At the individual level, based upon different cultural influences, independent actors assume a fragmented perspective. Each of these perspectives influences the others and is essential to the long-term success of a commitment to sustainability (Stoughton and Ludema, 2012).

Implementation is the key issue on which the sustainability agenda is demanding action.

Various studies have attempted to address how sustainability should be implemented. For example, Rigby and Tager (2008) provide some generic pointers for what is needed to implement sustainability in organizations, which include: a vision for the company; assessment of the existing operations of the company; maximization of growth opportunities; and measurement of outcomes to determine the company's level of success. While Dunphy and colleagues (2007) and Epstein and colleagues (2010) suggest that sustainability can be implemented through awareness and reward systems. Daily and Huang (2001) assert that sustainability requires environmental training, employee empowerment and rewards. These are examples of little more than transactional leadership – necessary but not sufficient. Doppelt (2003) has suggested that for an organization to make the kind of transformation to become truly sustainable, power and authority must be skilfully distributed among employees and stakeholders through effective information-sharing, decision-making and resource allocation mechanisms. Bertels and colleagues (2011) add to this by advising that recruiting people to champion projects and creating systems for sustainability is helpful in embedding sustainability in organizations. But what is missing from these assertions is the support and role of leaders.

Responsible global leaders – who have the vision, sense of mission and the values to do this; who are aware of the pressing problems in the world; who care for the needs of others; who aspire to make this world a better place and who think and act, in word and deed, as global and responsible citizens; and who lead sustainable companies – will be those who explicitly emphasize sustainability in their business vision, mission, values, strategies and management practices. Stubbings and Ceasar (2012) outline some of the effective change practices that organizations with the right leadership are already adopting to respond strategically to the developing trends and introduce new frameworks. This goes far beyond donating to good causes. It involves transforming businesses and having the intelligence and vision to change attitudes and behaviours.

In an article in *Guardian Professional* online,[1] Jo Confino identifies what she terms as the global sustainability leaders. The names and the reason why they are on the list are as follows:

---

1 Guardian Professional, Tuesday 28 January 2014, 07:00 GMT.

- Marc Boland, chief executive of Marks & Spencer. Boland has stuck with a focus on sustainability even when he has been under intense pressure from the markets to focus only on its financial performance, and for seeking to leverage his company's influence to drive change in the company's supply chain as well as amongst other corporates.
- Paul Polman, CEO of Unilever. Polman has intense energy and a fierce commitment to a focus on the world's poor. He also has an ability to integrate the many aspects of sustainability, from climate change and deforestation to nutrition and agriculture, and therefore has a truly holistic worldview.
- Sir Ian Cheshire, CEO of Kingfisher. Cheshire recognizes that a radical change of mindset is essential in order to drive systemic change.
- Christiana Figueres, executive secretary of the UN Framework Convention on Climate Change. Figueres has called for a rapid transition of the coal industry in order to meet the challenge of an already-changing climate.
- Feike Sijbesma, CEO of DSM. Sijbesma recognizes that new business approaches are essential if companies are going to drive transformational change. Sijbesma is prepared to stand up in public and voice this at a time when many other CEOs are focusing on the short term and are too scared to put their heads above the parapet.
- Bea Perez, chief sustainability officer of Coca-Cola. Perez is seeking to follow Unilever's example by pushing for an integration of the company's marketing function with sustainability, in order that the company starts confronting the duality of trying to do good one day and creating harm the next.

Discussion Questions

1 Consider the list of leaders mentioned above. Who else would you add to the list and why?

At the beginning of the twenty-first century, CEOs tended to argue that following the principles of sustainability added nothing but cost to their business (Bevan and Gitsham, 2009). Now the situation is radically different. Business leaders increasingly refer to sustainability as one of the lynchpins of competition within their sector and a significant source of both opportunity for, and risk to, long-term competitive advantage. Many executives now acknowledge that the way they respond to the challenge of sustainability will affect the competitiveness of their business and the future of their company (Lubin and Esty, 2010).

Business ethics

The challenges of megatrends require organizations to be able to react to the diverse demands of multiple-stakeholder groups and provide an ethical orientation in dealing with heterogeneous cultural backgrounds and complex moral dilemmas. They need to be able to make ethical decisions, taking into account the different interests of a wide variety of stakeholders across the globe. We have provided an analysis of the ethical aspects of change in various chapters in this book. Here we take this further in considering the contemporary ethical challenges.

Young (2004) defines ethical challenges are a consequence of the extension of responsibility due to the globalization process. Leaders and managers have to consider the extensive social consequences of business conduct, such as environmental pollution and global warming, safety at work and workforce standards, in order to engage and respond to the growing demands of external constituencies. Additionally, organizations are faced with the diversity challenge of culturally heterogeneous contexts and how to motivate and coordinate the activities of employees from diverse backgrounds. They have to cope with increasingly challenging ethical dilemmas.

The world's most ethical companies listed in 2014 by the Ethisphere® Institute[2] include 144 companies. The list is based on the following categories.

Reputation, leadership and innovation (20%)

This category measures a company's legal compliance, litigation and ethical track record, along with the strength of the company's reputation in the marketplace. It includes concrete examples of corporate leadership in local, national, industry and/ or global initiatives that promote business ethics, responsible and sustainable business practices, environmental stewardship, good governance, transparency and social responsibility. Standard-setting and thought leadership is important, but ultimately what matters most is the quality and innovation of company's engagement with various stakeholders considered within the context of the company size, industry and performance in comparison to industry peers.

Governance (10%)

This category looks at the availability and quality of systems designed to ensure strong corporate governance (as defined by the US Sentencing Commission, Securities and Exchange Commission and other regulatory bodies), including oversight, governance principles and risk management. Actual performance of the governing authorities, as measured by governance rating agencies, is also taken into account.

Corporate citizenship and responsibility (25%)

This category reviews a wide range of a company's performance indicators associated with sustainability, citizenship and social responsibility, specifically including such areas as environmental stewardship, community involvement, corporate philanthropy, workplace impact and well-being, and supply chain engagement and oversight. The quality and effectiveness of the initiatives are considered, in addition to stated and measureable goals, accountability and transparency.

---

2 See more at: http://ethisphere.com.

Culture of ethics (20%)

This category looks at the culture of ethics in the organization, concerning widely accepted or unaccepted norms as they pertain to ethical conduct. This category looks at the culture of ethics within the organization. Focusing on the adoption of a values-based culture and how the workforce buy into the culture and know and live it.

Companies that appear on the list from outside the USA include several from Japan, including the Kao corporation, Sompo Japan Insurance and Shiseido. Shiseido was selected as an ethical company in 2014 for the third consecutive year. The following case study outlines the ethical approach of the company.

CASE STUDY

Shiseido

For approximately 140 years since it was founded in 1872, Shiseido – the cosmetic company – has been engendering the spirit of 'serving our customers through beauty and wellness' as a fundamental principle of its corporate activities. Its mission is to realize a sustainable society through dialogue and cooperation with stakeholders while also promoting management that contributes to the creation of people's beauty and health by developing activities that address social issues and meet expectations.

Background

Shiseido was founded by Yushin Fukuhara as Japan's first Western-style pharmacy in 1872, and has shifted its focus back and forth between cosmetics and pharmaceuticals since 1915. It introduced Japan to its first toothpaste in 1888 and in 1902 the company introduced Japan's first soda fountain/drugstore. Three years later, it established the chain store system, which became the backbone of the firm and the standard distribution system for the industry. In 1957 Shiseido began international expansion and is currently represented by 17 subsidiaries and more than 8,700 outlets in 69 countries. In 2014 Masahiko Uotani was named as the new president. This marked the first time in the company's history that it had adopted an outsider as president.

Corporate philosophy

Shiseido's management policies for the twenty-first century are embodied in its 'Global No. 1' long-term vision. The company's social responsibility (CSR) activities follow the concept of 'Our Way', which denotes action standards that each and every employee should take toward stakeholders, based on the Shiseido Group corporate philosophy of 'Our Mission, Values and Way.'

Shiseido's mission as a company is to accelerate and reinforce its efforts to provide customer benefits. The Shiseido Way is a charter of principles guiding the company activities. This charter incorporates its ideas and determination to work together with its customers, business partners, shareholders, employees and society. Its determination to work with shareholders is clearly defined in its stated desire to strive to earn the understanding and responsiveness of all shareholders and other investors, by achieving appropriate and sound business performances, based on high-quality growth and by pursuing transparent corporate policies.

Environmental protection

In 1990, Shiseido was the pioneer in the Japanese cosmetics industry in eliminating chlorofluorocarbons from its aerosol lines. Two years later it formulated the Shiseido Ecopolicy, a set of action plans covering the environmental protection efforts of all its divisions. By 2001, it had eliminated the use of polyvinyl chloride in its product containers and packaging and raised the level of industrial waste recycling to 60%. This resulted in a 50% reduction in unusable waste. By 2011 it had cut carbon dioxide emissions by 15% from 1991 levels.

The Shiseido Earth Care Project is an environmental project promoted by all Shiseido Group employees worldwide in every aspect of their business activities. The mission of the Shiseido Earth Care Project is to create a society in which people and the Earth coexist beautifully, based on the Shiseido Eco Policy. The Shiseido Earth Care Project symbol is visible on products that use more than 20% of plant-derived plastic, such as sugarcane-derived polyethylene, in their container. In September 2011, Shiseido adopted containers made from sugarcane-derived polyethylene. This was the first time this material was used for cosmetics in Japan.

Shiseido has also launched a replaceable refill product for its skin brightening serum. The amount of plastics used to make this refill container was reduced by approximately 60% compared with the amount used for the original product container. Adopting a refill container reduced the amount of plastics used by roughly 19 tons per year. In addition to the environmental consideration of saving resources, another main objective of introducing this refill product was closely tied to Shiseido's desire to respond to consumers' feedback, including: 'It's such a waste to throw out a wonderful package' or 'Please make a container so that we can check how much remains in the container.' Additionally, in terms of the development of the refill container, the company has put a lot of ingenuity into creating a structure so that consumers can replace the container as easily as possible.

Another environmental measure the company has implemented is that they have replaced the exterior plastic packaging with packaging made from bagasse paper (non-wood paper made from fibre after extracting the sugar content from sugarcane).

Case written by Julie Hodges and based on www.home-shiseido.co.uk/.

Discussion Questions

1 How effective is the ethical policy of Shiseido?
2 What else could the company do to become more ethical?
3 What else might they do to address the challenges raised by their customers?

Approaches to change need to be underpinned by a set of ethical values that influence the actions of individuals in organizations and the outcomes and consequences of change initiatives. The argument that change needs an ethical foundation is far from new. Such arguments can be found in the work of Barnard (1938) on leadership in the 1930s and in the work of Lewin on change in the 1940s. Even before the 2008 global financial crisis, there were increasing calls for organizations to act in a more ethical fashion. Prominent in this respect was the promotion of corporate social responsibility (CSR) and linked to employee social responsibility. However, this did not necessarily lead to a diminution of unethical behaviour. As Joseph Stiglitz (2010), the Nobel Prize-winning economist, observed in his book on the 2008 global financial crisis, the reverse seems to have been the case. Unethical and criminal behaviour appears to have escalated out of control in many organizations as society seems to have encouraged the individualistic motto of 'Every man for himself' in place of 'One for all and all for one'. We are still living in an era when organizational leaders are allowed to, and even rewarded for, putting their own egos and self-interests ahead of the interests of the many, often with disastrous results and consequences (Hodges, 2011). As Stiglitz (2010) observed, the short-term performance incentives of mortgage salesmen, of the investors and purveyors of complex and ill-understood financial instruments, and of the corporate leaders who were supposed to supervise them, were not aligned with the long-run interests of the institutions for which they work. The long-term, sustainable interests of the many are sacrificed to the short-term greed and arrogance of the few.

To avoid this in the future, the importance of promoting the ethical dimension of change – as a means of ensuring that leaders and their followers act in the interests of the many rather than the few – needs to be highlighted. If followers and other stakeholders are not to be so dazzled by the attraction of charismatic leaders that see any change as being good change, they need to ensure that the leadership of change is underpinned by a clear and transparent system of ethics and accountability. That is to say, leaders must be instilled with a moral compass fitting the organizations of which they are in charge. Leaders of tomorrow must indeed be expected to make decisions in the interest of the many rather than the few and to refrain from abusing the faith that is placed in them and the unique freedoms they enjoy. This is a point made forcibly by Barker (2001) when he asserts that leadership is 'a process of trans-formative change where the ethics of individuals are integrated into the mores of a community as a means of evolutionary social development' (p. 491). Therefore, a key question – and one of considerable contemporary importance – is: *how we can lead and manage change more ethically?*

The danger of not just allowing but even encouraging unethical change can be reduced when there is openness about and alignment of values and objectives, trans-parency in decision-making and independent external scrutiny. By and Burnes (2013) believe the fundamental flaws in some approaches to change are that they are not explicit about values and they give the impression that it is somehow unworldly or naive even to mention ethical considerations. Organizations have to move beyond general statements of ethics, such as those found in CSR statements and policies, and actually evaluate the ethical values of leaders and their intentions and actions and determine whether these are compatible with the wider interests of the organization and its stakeholders in a global context. This requires an understanding of ethics in terms of both policy and practice, and clarity about the ethical basis of different approaches to change (By and Burnes, 2013).

A critical issue in the involvement of different groups of stakeholders is the extent to which it is possible for them to recognize what is ethical and unethical. Most stakehold-ers would agree that child labour is clearly unethical, but would they recognize which change practices are unethical? If stakeholders are to be able to monitor behaviour during change, they must have a yardstick for judging whether it is potentially unethical or not. To do this, those who develop and promote particular approaches to change have to be clear about their ethical implications. Currently there is often a damaging lack of clarity regarding the ethical values underpinning approaches to change and its management (By and Burnes, 2013).

By and Burnes (2013) point out that a prime example is the famous quotation attributed to Charlie Wilson, who was president of General Motors in the early 1950s: 'What's good for General Motors is good for the country.' Many leaders appear to interpret this to mean: 'What's good for me is good for the organization.' But as By and Burnes rightly remind us, what Wilson actually said was: 'For years I thought that what was good for our country was good for General Motors, and vice versa.' Perhaps a better proposition is 'What's good for the organization is good for me', which is an entirely different matter.

As Franklin D. Roosevelt (1937) commented on the causes of the Great Depression of the 1930s:

> We have always known that heedless self-interest was bad morals; we know now that it is bad economics. Out of the collapse of prosperity whose builders boasted their practicality has come the conviction that in the long run economic morality pays.

This 'economic morality' will prevail, however, only if all organizational stakeholders are able and prepared to ensure that ethical rather than unethical behaviour during change. And this can be achieved only if the difference between ethical and unethical approaches to change is identified and clear (By and Burnes, 2013).

Impact of trends on organizational change

Organizational capacity for change

Organizational capacity for change can be conceptualized as the overall capability of an organization to either effectively prepare or respond to an increasingly unpredictable and volatile environmental context. This overall capability is multidimensional, and according to Judge (2011) it comprises three ingredients: (a) human skill sets and resources; (b) formal systems and procedures; and (c) organizational culture, values and norms. As such, Judge describes the organizational capacity for change as:

> A dynamic, multidimensional capability that enables an organization to upgrade or revise existing organizational competencies, while cultivating new competencies that enable the organization to survive and prosper. (2011:14)

It appears that a lack of capacity is a serious issue for organizations. A 2012 survey by Moorhouse Consulting in the UK's financial services sector found that staff did not have the capacity and capability to deliver change and that front-line staff could not cope with the volume of change. Ron Ashkenas (2013) supports this view that there is a problem with the under-development of capacity to implement change. As he outlines it, such capacity entails:

- A common framework, language, definitions, approaches and set of tools for managing change
- Plans for change that are integrated with other project plans as part and parcel of overall business strategy
- Clear accountability in the organization for change

Judge (2011) has taken these guidelines a step further and distilled the concept of organizational capacity for change down to eight separate and distinct dimensions.

1. *Trustworthy leaders.* No lasting change within an organization ever happens without trust between its members. As a consequence, the first essential dimension of organizational capacity for change is the extent to which an organization is perceived to be led by trustworthy leaders. A trustworthy leader is someone who is not only perceived to be competent in leading the organization but also perceived as someone who has the best interests of the organization as their priority.
2. *Trusting followers.* The second dimension is the overall level of trust held by the employees of the organization.
3. *Capable champions.* A capable champion is a manager who is able to influence others in the organization to adopt a proposed change without the formal authority to do so. Judge (2011) refers to them as 'corporate entrepreneurs' who are experts in building formal and informal coalitions to make changes and get things done. They know how to directly and indirectly handle political opposition. They are often sponsored by senior management to lead change initiatives.
4. *Involved middle management.* Judge (2011) points out that middle managers are pivotal figures in shaping an organization's response to potential change initiatives, so their involvement is crucial to organizational capacity for change.
5. *Systems thinking.* An organizational infrastructure that promotes system thinking is another key dimension. Rather than focusing on the individuals or organizational units within an organization, system thinking looks at the larger number of interactions within the organization and in between organizations as a whole.
6. *Communication systems.* Effectively designed and delivered communication up, down and across the organization (as we discussed in Chapter 10) is essential to building organizational capacity for change.
7. *Accountable culture.* According to Judge (2011), accountable cultures are results-based cultures that help to carefully monitor the outcomes of results produced. As a result, accountable cultures seek to discern what helped or hindered successful change.
8. *Innovative culture.* This dimension is about creating a culture that explores new ideas and develops the best ideas into innovative new ventures.

Judge (2011) proposes two ways that an organization's capacity for change can be assessed. First, it can be done qualitatively by interviewing individuals at different levels of the organization and attempting to characterize it along the eight dimensions above in narrative format, using anecdotes and stories to illustrate where the organization needs to be. Second, it can be done quantitatively by administering a survey such as the OCC to organizational members. The OCC survey instrument, developed by Judge (2011) is based on the eight dimensions and enables organizations to identify strengths and areas for development.

While building organizational capacity for change is not fast or easy, it is essential for ensuring that change is sustained in an organization. One company that has shown it has the capacity for change is Pesa – a Polish company that makes and repairs railway rolling stock. Pesa is different from many Polish companies in that it has built up a formidable research and development capacity.

CASE STUDY

Pesa

The Polish train and tram makers Pesa has shown the ability to out-think and out-compete with western rivals and expand far beyond its traditional borders. Since 2010 the company has won the biggest contract in its history, to replace 40% of Warsaw's trams, and has also won a 1.2 billion Euro contract from Germany's Deutsche Bahn. Pesa has risen rapidly from the brink of bankruptcy by developing its own technology and aggressively expanding into foreign markets. For 2014 its revenues were estimated to be 1.9bn zlotys ($625m) and were forecast to rise to 3bn zlotys within two years.

Pesa, located in Bydgoszcz in northern Poland, was one of 26 repair yards servicing Poland's inefficient communist-era state railways. After market reforms in 1989, the railways slashed their orders, leaving Pesa with almost no work. The company began to hunt for new business to replace the state railway work. The company noticed that a lot of grain was being shipped in old coal cars, leading to high rates of spoilage. The yard came up with the idea of revamping disused military tank transporters – the wagons had shipped Soviet tanks around the region for army exercises – and turning them into grain cars at a third of the cost of new special transporters. While this work, including repairing rail cars in Russia and Ukraine, staved off the immediate threat of collapse, the rail yard still had no clear business model and was in a very tenuous position.

Tomasz Zaboklicki, who took over as chief executive in 1998, teamed up with six other managers and in 2001 they bought the company from the government. But with banks reluctant to finance the purchase of a failing company, they were forced to clean out their personal bank accounts and take out bank loans to scrape together the money for the buyout. However, Zaboklicki and his fellow managers knew what they were doing. Pesa had been working for a few years on a project to build a simple rail bus – a diesel-powered train that could be used for short urban commutes – that was ready to roll by 2002. Zaboklicki also gambled that Poland's imminent entry into the EU in 2004 would open up a flow of cash from Brussels that towns and cities would use to upgrade their ramshackle bus and tram systems. But to take advantage of the money that would soon be pouring into Poland, Pesa had to survive. Doing so would entail some very unpleasant decisions for a union man.

The new owners began by instituting some fierce cuts. The workforce was trimmed by more than half to only 770. Frills such as the company brass band and company holiday resorts – a standard asset for state-owned companies in communist times – were chopped.

Pesa's turnaround began with locomotive sales to Italy, where the company supplied the southern city of Bari with rail buses. Pesa also broadened its product range. After repairing one tram car, the company's engineers realized they were perfectly capable of building such

(Continued)

(Continued)

vehicles themselves and so Pesa launched its own line of trams. As Pesa has grown it has won contracts in Poland, the former Soviet Union and the EU, and is aiming to move into markets in Asia and Latin America.

One of the largest successes was the 2012 German contract. Pesa was already familiar with the market, having adopted all the quality and licensing standards used by German rail manufacturers to give the company international credibility. When German unions started to protest about the prospect of such a lucrative contract going to a relatively unknown foreign company, Pesa made sure to include German brakes and engines in his bid. That worked to mollify the opposition.

Zaboklicki ploughs most of the profits back into the company – noting with pride that Pesa has only once paid its owners a dividend. He also has no interest in taking Pesa public, worrying that pressure from investors would make it difficult to plan for the long term. 'We're from here; from this company,' he says. 'That means we have a different obligation. For one thing, we want to be proud of what we do. Second, we have moral and ethical obligations to the workers. We have a different life philosophy. We don't want to astound with our riches or gain wealth at any price. Rather, we want to leave a legacy.'

Pesa is different from many Polish companies in that it has built up a formidable research and development capacity. Pumping so much money into R&D has allowed Pesa to grow from being a relatively low-tech repair facility to one that makes locomotives based almost entirely on its own technology.

Adapted by Julie Hodges from Boldness in Business, *Financial Times*, supplement, 24 March 2014 and www.pesa.pl/en/.

Discussion Questions

1   Evaluate the capacity Pesa has for change using the three ingredients identified by Judge (2011).
2   What would you suggest the company should do to continue to develop its capacity for change?

Organizational capability for change

Along with capacity, organizations also need to ensure that they have the capability to manage future change effectively. Capabilities such as agility and innovation are critical.

Organizations that are responsive to the need for change and adapt to it more rapidly and reliably display agility. **Agility** – sometimes called 'dynamic capability' – is the ability to respond to changing circumstances in a timely, effective and sustainable way. Thomas Williams and colleagues (2013) describe it as a way to turn as quickly as speedboats when necessary. They quote the case of ExxonMobil, which was one of the most admired companies in the 1980s but fell from grace in 1989 through the *Valdez* tanker oil spill and subsequent government and media scrutiny and 'the perceived arrogance and indifference' of its management. Under a new chairman the company applied lessons it had learned from that period and, through effective new strategies, vigorously pursued technical excellence and greater capital efficiency, achieved formidable profitability, purchased Mobil and regained its reputation. Exxon demonstrated a rare and distinctive ability to continually and successfully adapt to changing circumstances, namely agility.

Williams and colleagues (2013) propose four characteristics of agile companies:

- Dynamic strategizing – a sense of shared purpose, a 'change-friendly' identity and a robust strategic intent
- Ability to perceive environmental change – sensing, communicating and interpreting environmental information
- Response testing – maintaining slack in resources (people, money, time and tools), risk management and learning
- Implementing change – management delegation and autonomy, capability for change (in collective habits, practices and perspectives) embedded in line management, and performance management

In contrast, a lack of agility is when there is a failure of change programmes or suboptimal achievement of their goals. Derrick Neal and Trevor Taylor (2006) investigated major changes in the Ministry of Defence (MoD) – a UK government department – where they found that the complexities of the MoD were working against the effective delivery of change and that these failures would result in important shortcomings in military operations. Specific problems included the following:

- A lack of understanding of change management among civil servants and military staff
- A lack of a sense of urgency for change
- Failure to distinguish between incremental and transformational change, leading to unrealistic expectations of the time needed to deliver change

To avoid such situations, change capabilities need to exist at all levels in an organization. Many of the change programmes of the past few decades have been carried out by only a few people in the organization. For instance, organizations created Business Process Re-engineering (BPR) teams or task forces during the 1990s. These teams evaluated operations, documented 'as-is' processes and 'designed to-be' processes. However, much of the work associated with BPR resided in a few trained or even untrained individuals or external consultants. Moving change forward needs to be a capability of all leaders and managers. In this way, 'leading my people through change' becomes an individual capability that leaders can learn and foster. It takes all parts of the organization to effectively lead and manage change.

Innovation is another important capability that organizations will need to sustain change now and in the future. With skilled and insightful leaders and managers and the capability at all levels in the organization to adapt to changes in the environment and sustain changes internally, an organization will be positioned to drive innovation for today and tomorrow and create new opportunities to tackle the challenge of change from many angles. Innovation is not just the preserve of new start-up companies, some long-established companies can reinvent and revolutionize themselves. One such company is Germany's Bosch – which is a dominant player in the fast-growing world of consumer electronics. It supplies sensors for more than half of the world's smart-phones. Meanwhile it has built up an ebike business and is at the forefront of electronic car battery technology – while sustaining its traditional business.

CASE STUDY

Bosch

Best known for manufacturing car parts, including technology for self-driving cars, Bosch has quietly established itself as the leading manufacturer of MEMS, micro-electronic sensors. In short, MEMS make a mobile phone 'smart'. They are also the building blocks of other consumer electronic devices such as tablets and computer games controllers. This has burnished Bosch's reputation for innovation – the company invented anti-lock brakes, among a string of firsts. Furthermore, it has demonstrated that by working in novel ways a private company that is more than 125 years old can be as agile as any in Silicon Valley. Bosch produced more than 1 billion MEMS, up from 600 million in 2012. Until recently the main customer for MEMS was the car industry, which uses them for all manner of safety-critical functions, from airbag sensors to vehicle anti-skid systems. Bosch used its automotive sensor experience to pivot into consumer electronics and founded Sensortec in 2005. The shift was not without risk: in the automotive industry, Bosch must be able to guarantee 100% reliability for its sensors because of the potential for a malfunction to cause a lethal accident. While Bosch's automotive experience helped it get into the consumer electronics sector, now the latter is setting the pace of innovation.

The sensor business is as an example of how the company is learning to work in new ways. In future, the company will be on one of two speeds: the old Bosch in areas where absolute safety and reliability is required, and the new one where flexibility and agility are needed, particularly in relation to the internet.

Bosch also has a start-up culture within the company. An example of that is Bosch's eBike Systems unit. In just a short time, Bosch has become the market leader in Europe for power-assisted cycling, generating more than 100m Euros in sales last year.

Ebikes, once considered clunky and only for the lazy or unfit, are catching on among commuters who want to save energy on long uphill climbs and not arrive at work in a sweaty shirt. Two young Bosch engineers came up with the idea in 2008 of combining existing Bosch expertise in lithium ion batteries(from its power tools business) and sensor controls and electrical drives (from its automotive side) to build an ebike system. Bosch, incidentally, does not build the bicycles but rather sells the electronic system to bicycle manufacturers.

Although bankers tend to criticize conglomerates as inefficient, it appears that in innovation terms Bosch's multi-division structure has advantages. If they have an issue they can bring in experts from different areas. The company continues to invest heavily in hybrid and electric motor vehicle systems. It is likely to take years for these to make a return, because at the moment sales volumes for electric vehicles remain low. But Bosch's strategy of embracing other kinds of emobility has paid dividends. Ebikes are an opportunity to build volume more quickly and Bosch has been able to exploit its respected automotive brand to approach bicycle manufacturers.

Bosch has built up an ebike business and is at the forefront of electronic car battery technology – while sustaining its traditional business.

Adapted by Julie Hodges from Boldness in Business, *Financial Times*, supplement, 24 March 2014 and www.bosch.co.uk/.

Discussion Questions

1 What 'dynamic capabilities' does Bosch have?
2 What characteristics of an 'agile company' does Bosch display?
3 What challenges might Bosch face in the future with continuing its traditional business as well as continuing to be innovative?

Key enablers to building capability

When one of the authors of this book asked a group of Executive MBA students from across the globe what capabilities they thought were necessary to lead and manage change, their responses were both considered and practical, as shown in Table 14.1. There were a number of capabilities that were identified for both leaders and managers, which are outlined in the right-hand column in the table.

In the following financial services case study Lindsey Agness writes about her experience of designing a change-management framework and toolkit to build the capability of staff in a financial services global insurance business.

Table 14.1 Capabilities required for leading and managing change

Capabilities required to lead change	Capabilities required to manage change	Capabilities required to lead and manage
Strategic management and vision • Creation and articulation of a vision • Setting of objectives • Choice of measurement tools	Coaching of others through change	Communication to different audiences using different media.
Business knowledge • Knowing the competitive landscape • Delegation to the right people • Alignment of politics and competing interests	Project management	Emotional intelligence
Ability to influence and persuade	Listening	Flexibility and adaptability
Translation of the change vision into clear performance expectations	Empathy	Credibility
Behaving in a way that causes others to trust you	Providing feedback	Reflection and learning
	Focusing on outcomes with a 'big-picture' view	Celebration of success
	Anticipation and surfacing of conflicts	

Financial services

The company is a financial services global insurance business with a region covering Central Europe. In 2009 the company announced its plans to separate its insurance business from its main bank operations. This case study takes place in the insurance business after separation.

Although the project-management skills in the business were strong there was a lack of change-management skills. Change management in this context is defined as the 'people side' of change. The new insurance business was relatively immature and was required to prepare for either an IPO or a sale. There were many projects introduced to deliver this change as well as gearing up for the introduction of Solvency II from 1 January 2013. One of the key projects was the centralization and modernization of paper-based processes and systems. The lack of change-management capability and capacity in the organization was seen as a high risk for the portfolio of project delivery.

A change team was established to add change-management capacity to all projects. The decision to establish the team was made by the HR Director in conjunction with the Programme Director. Interestingly, this proved to be a key risk for this initiative because the HR Director left the organization and a new CEO was appointed.

The project

The project involved the following steps:

1   Assessment of current capability in the organization
2   Design of a change-management framework
3   Design of a series of change-management learning interventions
4   Delivery of the change-management interventions
5   Implementation of the framework in the form of key change projects

Assessment of current capability
A new Head of Change was appointed to the organization who rapidly began to establish the change team. There were also some external change consultants in place plus some internal team members. The level of capability was extremely low among the internal staff, and the external consultants were also somewhat inexperienced. This meant that the required capabilities needed to be defined quickly and developed within the team.

Design of a change management framework and toolkit
A change-management methodology and toolkit were developed. This provided a broad, all-encompassing framework that included the following core capabilities:

- Envision and plan the change
- Build commitment
- Build capability
- Align culture
- Re-design the organization
- Develop leaders
- Deliver benefits

Once the toolkit was created, a curriculum to develop change capability in staff as quickly as possible was designed.

Design of a series of change-management learning interventions

The curriculum had to take into consideration the need to build awareness of the potential of change management inside an immature organization. Most of the challenge at this stage was getting trained change-management practitioners into project teams because internal project managers were inexperienced.

The curriculum included:

- A six-day change management course for practitioners
- A four-day change course for the business, for example for operational managers
- A three-day 'Train the Trainer' course for practitioners to train others
- A one-day awareness course for programme and project managers
- A half-day session on personal change for those experiencing change in the workplace
- A half-day session to build change awareness for change leaders

Delivery of the change management interventions

A community of change management practitioners has so far been built throughout Central Europe, and several programmes have been run successfully within the business. Senior operational people have been convinced of the potential of change management to improve their project delivery. A change-management work stream has now been established as part of the Solvency II delivery team – the first time change management has been allocated a discrete work stream. This project has also come to the attention of senior leaders at the Group level within the business with a view to rolling out the learning interventions throughout Central Europe, Benelux and Asia.

Lessons learnt

At the time of writing, it is still early days in this project. However, a growing band of practitioners is being created who understand how to build a compelling vision, how to assess the readiness for change at the start of a project, how to build staff commitment through excellent engagement strategies and how to build capability and improve performance.

The main challenges have been the loss of the core stakeholder – the Human Resource Director – who left the company at the start of the project and the investment of time needed to convince the new CEO of the value of change management. It is therefore a testament to the project that it has been noticed at Group level and is now more likely to be managed centrally across the whole of the region. The greatest learning has been the need to start earlier to build the awareness of the senior management team in order to get their support at the start of this project. The assumption was that this was in place, but in reality it still needed to be won.

© 2015 Lindsey Agness, Managing Director The Change Corporation.

Discussion Questions

1 Based on the change management framework outlined in this case study identify the key activities you would need to carry out to lead and manage change effectively.
2 How might you address the issue of the Human Resources Director leaving the company?

While sustaining change is an achievement in itself, for those organizations operating in a very fast-changing, turbulent environment, it is likely to be just one of many changes that they will have to make as they seek to maintain their competitiveness. In this context, it will become increasingly important that organizations develop and embed a change capability and, by doing so, produce an organization that Lawler and Worley (2011) describe as being 'built to change'.

But knowing and feeling what change needs to be made and what needs to be done to effect it are still not enough, witness Barack Obama's mantra in his 2008 American presidential campaign – 'Yes we can. We can change. Yes, we can' – that has proved to be so difficult to carry out. As we have discussed in this book, organizations need the capacity and capability not just for what to change but also how to change.

Implications of contemporary issues for leaders and managers

As outlined in this chapter, current and future change and transformation in organizations will be influenced by megatrends in the global business environment. These trends will continue to increase the need for sustained change. The issues discussed in this chapter have a number of practical implications for managers and leaders.

Leadership and the megatrends

Global megatrends and developments have implications for organizations and therefore for their leaders. The reality of these megatrends means that institutions and communities need a new kind of leadership capability – a capability to deal with uncertainty, inspire others to transcend old habits and mindsets, orchestrate adaptive and creative problem solving, manage the stresses and losses associated with change, and produce results with others that go beyond what is currently imagined or foreseen. The next generation of leaders will have to be flexible, internationally mobile and adaptable. But most crucial of all, they must be highly ethical, collaborative and have especially strong conceptual and strategic thinking skills as well as emotional intelligence to lead change in their companies.

Building sustainability

Sustainability depends on the personal and corporate commitment of leaders and managers to the environment, enacted in proactive strategy choices and the pursuit of environmental innovation (Branzei et al., 2000). This commitment has implications for an organization's vision, purpose, core values, culture, strategy, core competencies and brand as well as how it will empower its people and engage them in this quest for sustainability. Leaders and managers therefore need to examine their organization closely by asking:

- What is our organization for? What is our purpose or mission?
- What or where do we want our organization to be? What is our vision of the future for our organization?

- How do we add value, and how will this change?
- What do we stand for in the eyes of our customers, our employees, the wider public and other key stakeholders?
- What are we good at? Are there new ways to leverage this? Or will it need to change?
- Do we have the right capabilities, values and culture to keep pace with and take advantage of this changing context?
- What are the most effective approaches to organizational learning and change that will keep us fit for and able to lead in the age of sustainability?
- How will the need for change of the sustainability agenda change our organizations?
- How can we, and will we, change our organizations? What strategies will we need to implement?
- How can we empower and engage our people in the necessary changes or transformation?

Developing ethical leadership

Ethical change leadership (ECL) is defined by Rebecca Newton (2013) as the demonstration of decision-making and ethical implementation of organizational change. Newton points out the importance of fostering and developing ECL characteristics and capabilities in an organization. Many factors influence the extent to which an organization develops leaders who behave ethically when faced with the many challenges and uncertainties of change. Newton highlights the following factors as being key to developing ECL:

- Being aware of, modelling and promoting a code of conduct for the change, outlining what is and what is not acceptable in the organizational context
- Seeking to gain others' input into changes
- Understanding the consequences of decisions taken and the impact of one's actions on others involved in the change
- Making the moral (as well as right) change decisions in the context of the organization and within the boundaries of government regulations and the law
- Facilitating others to engage in the above activities during organizational change

Dexter Dunphy and Suzanne Benn (2013: 209) go further and point out the skills that are required both to be ethical and to develop sustainable futures for their organizations. These skills are in three major areas: (i) skills associated with managing one's own personal change (self-change skills); (ii) skills associated with leading change in interpersonal relationships; and (iii) skills of change project leadership including skills for leading organizational change interventions. Dunphy and Benn describe each of these as follows:

- *Self-change skills.* Effective change leaders need to be able to manage the process of personal change within themselves. Effective transformational leaders show the intimate connection between self-transformation, the ability to transform others and, as a result, the ability to transform organizations.
- *Interpersonal change skills:* Effective change leaders need to have a broad repertoire of interpersonal skills which they draw upon to influence others. They are

aware of and accurately assess their personal impact on others and on the organization – a characteristic that has been labelled 'reflexivity' (Benn et al., 2009).

- *Change project leadership skills.* Effective change leaders also need to have the skills necessary to manage change projects. Modern organizations are less and less hierarchical structures and more and more moving to networks of interrelated change projects. They are characterized less by repetitive standardized operations that continue for lengthy periods largely unchanged and more by changing initiatives with differing timeframes.

Leaders and managers will need to consider how to address the ethical aspects of change as the frequency of change accelerates. Leaders should consider what ethical leadership means to them. Brown and colleagues (2005) propose a leadership concept that they explicitly refer to as ethical leadership. Ethical leadership is defined by Brown and colleagues (2005) as the demonstration of normatively appropriate conduct through personal actions and interpersonal relationships, and the promotion of such conduct to followers through two-way communication, reinforcement and decision-making. They define two underlying dimensions of ethical leadership. The first dimension is the leader as a moral person who embraces positive characteristics and values, such as being honest and trustworthy, a fair decision-maker and someone who cares about people. The second dimension of ethical leadership is characterized by the leader as a moral manager. This dimension emphasizes the role of an ethical leader as a positive role model who fosters ethical conduct among followers and disciplines unethical behaviour. With the growing interest and importance of ethical leadership, in parallel with rapid and continuous organizational change, questions around how to lead change ethically are of paramount importance. Organizations are faced with how to develop leaders who behave ethically when faced with the many challenges and uncertainties of change.

Building capability

To sustain change, organizations need to deliberately develop the capability for change. It can be expensive to rely on external consultants or interim managers. Therefore organizations should seek to build and embed leading and managing change as core organizational activities and capabilities. Organizations can then derive the greatest benefit from change by having their own capabilities to lead and manage it successfully.

Building capability is about maximizing the contribution of people for the benefit of the organization and individuals within the organization in a planned and managed way. The two main elements to building capability are:

1. Learning and development: this involves acquiring and applying the desired behavioural capabilities (skills, knowledge and attitudes) to enable the organization to achieve its vision and objectives.
2. Managing people performance: this is about ensuring that people performance strategies and HR policies and practices are aligned with and support the strategic business objectives.

Table 14.2   Building capability

Elements	Plan	Do	Review
Learning and development	Identify and agree skills, knowledge and attitudes that will be required. Identify learning and development needs. Agree the learning and development strategy and plan. Agree objectives in learning contract and/or personal development plan.	Implement actions in learning contracts and/or personal development plans.	Evaluate learning and development interventions. Apply and test learning.
Managing people performance	Agree business performance measures. Review and align HR policies, procedures and practices.	Communicate and implement new performance management system and HR policies.	Observe, coach and feedback to individuals. Assess business impact and ROI. Monitor, review, evaluate and improve performance management systems and policies.

Table 14.2 illustrates how to build capability, focusing on these two elements.

Building capability is important because it helps people to understand what needs to change and why. It also helps to motivate people to make the required behavioural changes that are necessary to achieve objectives and successfully implement and sustain change. It ensures people receive consistent messages about what is important in the organization and that people are accountable for what they do and that their contribution is recognized.

Further reading

Curran, S.R. and Saguy, A.C. (2013) 'Migration and cultural change: A role for gender and social networks?', *Journal of International Women's Studies*, 2(3): 54–77.

Ferrell, O.C., Fraedrich, J. and Ferrell, L. (2012) *Business Ethics: Ethical Decision-making and Cases*. CengageBrain.com.

Hamel, G. (2012) *What Matters Now: How to Win in a World of Relentless Change, Ferocious Competition, and Unstoppable Innovation*. San Francisco, CA: Jossey-Bass.

McMillan, M.S. and Rodrik, D. (2011) *Globalization, Structural Change and Productivity Growth* (No. w17143). Cambridge, MA: National Bureau of Economic Research.

Wei, Y.D. (2013) *Regional Development in China: States, Globalization and Inequality*. London: Routledge.

Conclusion

15

Business success requires a strong commitment to sustainability and, in particular, sustainable change. As Jeremy Darroch, CEO of Sky, said: 'In recent years, sustainability has moved right to the top of the business agenda' (cited in Gwyther, 2012). The sustainability revolution is creating a deep and enduring shift in people's consciousness. Timothy Galpin and Lee Whittington (2012) point out that sustainability now appears to be the strategic imperative of the twenty-first century. They do, however, go on to say that sustainability efforts have often not been as productive as they should be and that this is a leadership issue. These remarks are pertinent to our concern in this book with sustainable change and its leadership and management. Indeed, they are fundamental to it.

The sustainability of organizational change is crucial to the development, growth, success and survival of any organization operating within an ever-changing environment (Buchanan et al., 2005; Farjoun, 2010). Yet sustaining change is more fragile than we think – or even wish to think. All parents have walked into a room full of chaotic, noisy children, stopped the noise and restored order only to discover that the order disappeared soon after the children were alone again. According to Kotter (2002), this is the sustainability of change problem in a basic form.

Sustaining change can be difficult at any stage of life. If this challenge is not addressed in an organization, enormous resources will be wasted. This is evident from the consensus among researchers and practitioners alike that a majority of organizational change initiatives fail (see, for example, Beer and Nohria, 2000; Burnes, 2009a; By et al., 2011). The constant reference made to the somewhat dubious figure of a 70% failure rate is arguably less important than the apparent consensus that too much organizational change does in fact fail.

There is no one right way to manage and sustain change because the success of any approach is to a great extent dependent on its context. What may work in one organization is likely to fail in another and vice versa. When change efforts fail or fade over time, people tend to drift back to their old ways of working and behaving. Doyle and colleagues (2000) refer to this move backwards as 'initiative decay' or 'improvement evaporation effect'. To prevent the gains from change being lost and new practices and behaviours being abandoned, change must cease being something separate from normal business practices and become the norm. It needs to become, to use Nadler's (1988) term, 'baked in the organization'. That is, it must become an integral part of 'business as usual'. To be sustained means that it is no longer labelled as 'change'. Unless this happens, and the change seeps into the 'bloodstream' of corporate life, the change may prove to be just a passing fad or fashion that reaps no benefits.

In this final chapter we summarize our discussion of sustaining change in organizations, together with our conclusions. We focus on the key influences for sustaining change under the headings of leadership, management and individual influences. We begin by reviewing the need to institutionalize change.

Institutionalizing change

To be sustainable, change needs to be in the lifeblood of an organization: it needs to be institutionalized. Jacobs (2002) defines institutionalization as change that has relative endurance and staying power over a period of time or has become part of the ongoing, everyday activities of the organization. Kotter (1995) cites two factors that are critical to the institutionalization of change:

1. Showing employees how the new ways of working, behaviour and attitudes have helped improve performance; and
2. Ensuring that the next generation of managers personifies the new approach.

To sustain any change there needs to be an understanding of the challenges that can impede change so that leaders and managers can deal with them. Researchers have provided lists of what these challenges can be. For example, Senge and colleagues (1999) identified the following four processes that can limit or constrain the sustaining of change:

1. Reaching the tough or real problems, having first addressed the easy ones typified by comments like, 'We've picked all the quick wins ...'
2. Reaching the limit of managers' commitment to change
3. Reaching serious issues that are difficult to discuss and might lead to conflict
4. Lack of systematic thinking, such as tackling symptoms rather than problems

Senge and Kaeufer (2000) build on this list and specified the following factors: fear and anxiety about the change; a lack of concern with performance measurement; and the dangers of innovations acquiring cult status and becoming isolated from the organization. In a survey of fellow consultants at KPMG, Brown and colleagues (2009) found that 65% of the reasons cited for why change failed focused on the following three barriers to sustaining change: the organization's approach to change; the quality of leadership; and employees' level of understanding about what was expected of them following the change.

A far more complex picture was reported by Buchanan and colleagues (2005). On the basis of a review of the literature, they identified ten factors that interact in different ways to affect the sustainability of change:

1. Those who initiated the change move on elsewhere.
2. Accountability for development becomes diffused.
3. Knowledge and experience of new practices is lost through turnover.
4. Old habits are imported with recruits from less dynamic organizations.
5. The issues and pressures that triggered the change initiative are no longer visible.
6. New managers want to drive their own agenda.
7. Powerful stakeholders are using counter-implementation tactics to block progress.
8. Funds run out.
9. Other priorities come on stream, diverting attention and resources.
10. Staff at all levels suffer 'initiative fatigue', and enthusiasm for change falters.

The relative importance of these factors is determined by context. For example, a management style that elicits enthusiastic commitment in one setting may trigger cynicism, resentment and a lack of support for change in another. Consequently, Buchanan and colleagues (2005) felt that more work would have to be done before they could offer managers any simple prescription for sustaining change. They did, however, point to three issues that appear to affect the extent of initiative decay: (i) how the change is perceived; (ii) how the change is implemented; and (iii) the timing, sequence and pacing of the change process. There are a number of opinions provided in the literature for how to make change stick in organizations but the question still remains about how to influence the sustainability of change. From the topics we have covered in this book and our experience with organizational change we identify the following influences on sustaining change: leadership, management and individual. Within each influence it is important to remember that there will be content and process issues (remember the 'what' and 'how' of change). We consider each influence in turn.

Leadership influences on sustaining change

Sustaining change starts with the intentions and actions of leaders (see the discussion of leadership in Chapter 3). Recognizing why to change as well as when, what and how to change are key imperatives for leaders.

Need to change

Addressing the question of 'why change' is a precondition to being able to define the desired future state or the vision of an organization (see Chapter 5). If the question 'why change?' is never addressed, no one should expect the emergence of any sense of a shared vision. The answer to 'why' is a prerequisite to the 'what' and 'how' of change. Diagnosing where an organization is currently is a prerequisite for identifying its future direction. Diagnosis should not, however, be a one-off activity but on-going (as discussed in Chapter 6). It can begin with a review of the total organization and then a review of its different functions, departments and teams. The choice of which model to use for diagnosis is often one of personal preference.

However, it is important to develop a healthy scepticism towards the utility of different models used for diagnosis and constantly reassess which is most appropriate for the intended purpose. All models are simplifications of the real world, and the utility of any particular model in the context of change needs to be judged in terms of whether or not it provides a helpful conceptual framework for the context in which it is being applied.

Diagnosis can also help in identifying the readiness for change within a team or across a whole organization. Creating readiness for change can influence individuals' commitment to the proposed change. Commitment to change is the glue that brings people and change goals together, helping them understand the purpose of change and, as a consequence, increasing employees' individual efforts to change their work behaviours.

Vision for change

Leaders need to ensure that the organization's vision and goals for the change are clear, as outlined in Chapter 3. People crave clarity about what is going to change and often demand the security of policies and processes that are not subject to change. Change is challenging because there is no shortage of uncertainties. In turn, there is no shortage of people who actively oppose changes. Some disagree with the reason for change; others are simply comfortable with the status quo.

The way that leaders present proposed change to people can have a significant effect on whether individuals engage with the change or not. When Julio Linares was CEO of Spain's telecom operator, Telefonica de Espana, he used three approaches to engage people in change projects. The first was clear communication so people understood how the change contributed to the overall company targets and visions and to individual targets. Second, Linares ensured that a large proportion of the company's employees felt a meaningful ownership of the changes by involving people at different levels in designing and tweaking them. Finally, Linares made sure employees were making real progress and that goals were still relevant by holding regular progress evaluations, the results of which were widely communicated.

Many people may not want to change but, if the rationale for the change and its benefits are clear to them, as was evident in the approach used by Linares, this can help. Efforts must be made to educate and inform people of changes (see the discussion of communications in Chapter 10). This means that leaders must make transparent both what is being changed and how the change will be achieved. Even when opinions, attitudes and values are transformed on account of knowledge and wisdom gained, changes in behaviour may lag behind. So leaders need to be aware of this and ensure that they understand how and why people react to change in the way that they do (see Chapter 11).

Changing structures

When contemplating changes to organizational structures leaders need to consider what they have learnt from previous restructures, for a structure cannot be changed without careful consideration. As Mullins points out:

> Organizations cannot, without difficulty, change their formal structure at too frequent an interval. (2007: 648)

It is often when a significant change such as a merger or acquisition occurs that a fundamental rethink of an organization's structure is carried out. The motivation for most mergers and acquisitions is some form of value creation for key stakeholders, such as financial synergies, market penetration, access to resources, operational synergies, economies of scale, and an enhanced reputation. Mergers and acquisitions are, however, high-risk options that do not always deliver anticipated or expected strategic synergies. They also involve significant transformation efforts, such as restructuring (see Chapter 9).

When the need to change an existing structure does occur, there are a range of factors that need to be taken into account. A critical one is how people will react to it. Employees who are comfortable with the status quo may resent and resist any imposed changes. Equally, processes, systems and policies may need to be redesigned to accommodate the proposed changes. Adapting an organizational structure to changed circumstances is a complex process and the impact on, and the reactions of, the people in the organization need to be considered and addressed. Any attempts at changing the structure as well as other types of change are, however, fraught with power, politics and conflict.

Power, politics and conflict

Power is an important social process that transforms individual interests into coordinated activities that in turn accomplish valuable ends (see Chapter 12 for a discussion on power, politics and conflict). Politics is the practical domain of power (Buchanan and Badham, 1999, 2009). It is about creating legitimacy for certain ideas to influence the acceptance of change. Ambitious leaders (and managers) can be very power conscious, which Mast et al. (2010: 460) call 'power motivation'. Such individuals know that organizational developments can bring crucial changes, particularly to their areas of responsibility. At the same time, change initiatives, whether it is their formulation, communication or implementation, provide excellent opportunities for leaders to gain, keep or increase their influence, power and control – or to lose it. For when change happens there are strong personal and group interests at stake (Clegg and Walsh, 2004; Diefenbach, 2013). This is well argued by Kets de Vries (1993: 22), who says that 'Leadership is the exercise of power, and the quality of leadership – good, ineffective or destructive – depends on an individual's ability to exercise power.'

Leading (and managing) with power means recognizing that, in almost every organization, there are varying interests. This suggests that one of the first things leaders need to do is to diagnose the political landscape and ascertain the relevant interests and the important political subdivisions that characterize the organization. It is essential that leaders do not assume that everyone is going to agree to the change. Leading with power means understanding that, to get things done, leaders need power and that it is therefore imperative to understand where power comes from and how these sources of power can be developed. Leaders are sometimes reluctant to think very purposefully or strategically about acquiring and using power, owing to its negative connotations. Leading with power means understanding the strategies and tactics through which power is developed and used in organizations. Leaders responsible for initiating change and taking it forward also need to be powerful enough to maintain the momentum and address any conflict that arises.

Conflict is a means to solve problems and bring about change. It can, if used in a positive way, be an effective device by which leaders can drastically change the existing power structure and entrenched attitudes. If there is no conflict, it invariably means that the real problems are not being addressed. Change devoid of conflict is likely to suffer from apathy, stagnation and other debilitating diseases. Conflict can remove complacency, though it is not often liked in organizations and therefore is sidestepped or ignored. Leaders do, however, have to manage conflict in a way that is constructive rather than destructive.

Leading change – six core themes

Leaders of change need to understand and accept that aversion to change is part of the human condition, but it can be reduced, minimized or even avoided through effective leadership. This means understanding that leadership is showing the way and inducing or helping people in a variety of ways to pursue it.

As we discuss in Chapter 3, the leadership literature suggests six core themes in leadership: vision, purpose or mission, values, strategy, empowerment and engagement. Effective leadership therefore comprises six associated core practices. In the context of organizational change, effective leadership entails focusing on having a vision and a purpose for change, ensuring the change effort are underpinned by the organization's core values, having a strategy for change, and empowering and engaging those involved or affected by change so that they are able and willing to contribute to the change effort.

In more detail, effective leaders of change:

- Define and communicate a valid and appealing vision of the future that is intended as a result of a change and how the vision for the change is to be developed and implemented.
- Define and communicate a valid and appealing purpose for a change and its linkage to the organization's vision, values and strategy.
- Identify and personally display, promote and reinforce shared values that inform and support the organization's vision, purpose and strategies. In identifying the shared values, leaders need to consider the principles or standards that are considered to be important or beneficial in leading change efforts and, in particular, those that are deemed to be 'good' or 'bad' or 'right' as opposed to 'wrong'.
- Develop, communicate and implement rational strategies for change or transformation that are informed by shared values.

- Empower people to be *able to do* what needs to be done by giving them the knowledge, skills, self-confidence, opportunity, freedom, authority and resources to manage themselves in a change programme and thereby ethically be accountable for their performance.
- Engage people in the change effort by influencing, motivating and inspiring them to *want to do* what needs to be done, to devote discretionary effort to it willingly, even eagerly. Leaders need to consider how they will use their position and personal power, including the use of inspirational speech and language.

Declaring victory too soon

The embedding of change may take years in some cases. It is therefore advisable for leaders not to declare victory too soon. A survey by Kotter (1995) found that the gains achieved in 10 out of 12 re-engineering change programmes evaporated because victory was declared too soon. Within two years, the initial gains had slowly disappeared. And in 2 out of 10 cases it was soon hard to find any trace of re-engineering. Based on this research, Kotter (1995: 66) advises that: 'While celebrating a win is fine, declaring the war won can be catastrophic.' The reason is that, until a change is firmly embedded in an organization's culture, there remains the possibility of regression to pre-change practices. There may still be people who are hoping that the change will fail and that things will return to normal. However, the existence of people who feel this way may not always be obvious. Such people may nod and agree with everything that is being proposed but remain silent and deeply resentful of the change and be simply waiting to return to their old ways of working to which they are committed. Declaring victory too soon can also encourage leaders to switch their attention and resources to other change opportunities without sustaining the current change they are focusing on. So it is vital that leaders do not declare the change a success too early.

Leading change ethically

Ethical principles, moral values and moral integrity displayed by leaders are key influences on the success or failure of organizational change (see Chapter 14 for a discussion on ethics). Mendonca says, 'It is the leader's moral principles and integrity that give legitimacy and credibility to the vision and sustain it' (2001: 266). Thomas Diefenbach supports this and says that 'many managers and leaders need to have a thorough look at how they behave, how they treat others, and how they conduct their office' (2013: 166). The fairness with which leaders treat their followers is a core dimension of ethical leadership (Den Hartog and De Hoogh, 2009; Gill, 2011), which exerts an influence on the success, acceptance and sustainability of organizational change (Van Dijke and De Cremer, 2008). The point is, as Carl Rhodes (2013) says, that the perception of justice and fairness among employees is something that can be manipulated by leaders in order to implement transformations.

Organizational change is a process that is characterized by multiple and complex ethical challenges for organizations and their leaders. This reflects Trevino and Brown's (2004: 77) argument that 'the environment has become quite complex and is rapidly changing, providing all sorts of ethical challenges and opportunities to express greed'. Rebecca Newton observes that:

Practitioners must encourage leaders to be mindful of common organizational change pitfalls which can prevent the development of ethical change leadership. Such pitfalls include secrecy around the change and subsequent lack of trust and sense of collaboration and a change in the degree to which organizational members and stakeholders are informed and involved. Any decrease in information and involvement surrounding the change may be perceived as unethical behaviour, as it breaks from their expectation of organization/team/unit norms and what is considered 'acceptable' based on past experience' (2013: 50).

Leaders themselves need to act ethically in order to address these challenges and create an ethical culture. As Tyler and De Cremer (2005: 529) explain: 'Leaders motivate their followers to accept change by exercising their authority via fair procedure.' Employees are more likely to accept organizational change if they perceive the process by which it is implemented is fair (see Chapter 7 on the planning and implementing of change).

Sustainable change can be achieved only through ethical and socially responsible leadership. Key issues for leaders to consider, therefore, are the well-being, satisfaction and commitment of employees during and after a change process; the clarity and intention of a vision for change; integrity with respect to organizational core values; allowing, indeed encouraging, employee voice; and providing and ensuring meaning and value in employee work. An understanding and acceptance of corporate social responsibility and ethical principles, including the organization's espoused core values, in managing change is important too. And it is particularly important for each individual leader involved in the change process to accept such responsibility in his or her own actions, methods, intentions and their consequences.

Leading change means leaders changing themselves, what they do and how they do it, as well as changing others. Leaders of change therefore need humility and receptiveness as well as resilience and persistence. Effective leaders of change understand that change brings with it risk of errors, mistakes or failure. They also understand that these bring with them something positive, namely the opportunity for both themselves and their staff to learn, improve and develop. Willingness to take risks and experiment, and to learn and apply the lessons from success and especially from failure, starts with them as a role model and then helping others to do the same. Failure is the greatest teacher if one is willing to learn. Contributing in this way to a healthy and positive learning culture is part and parcel of being an effective and virtuous corporate 'citizen'.

Learning, development and reflection

Several studies have shown that, for change to be sustained, leaders need to create an organization that is capable of continuous self-reflection and learning (Garvin, 1993; Probst and Raisch, 2005; Senge, 1990). Learning is important for providing individuals with the capabilities to sustain change, as we discuss in Chapter 8. Massey and Williams (2006) call for a learning and development support structure to help embed change, especially for those involved in change agent roles. The structure, they say, should offer support such as coaching, mentoring, learning and development, and on the job development opportunities for individuals to gain the new skills, knowledge and behaviour required to sustain the change (see Chapter 9 for how to restructure organizations).

Learning and development are about developing the ability to get something done rather than developing the ability to talk about getting something done. They are about moving from diagnosis and analysis to experimentation, action and implementation and learning from them. To learn from experience it is necessary to make the time to reflect on that experience, as we tend to get more learning from the experience when we reflect on it. There is much that can be learnt about change from other people. This is where action research and action learning – as well as the dialogic forms of organizational development (OD) – can be of benefit. People are more likely to succeed with change actions if they have discussed the actions with others and have the support of others during the implementation process.

It is important that the value of learning is recognized as a continuous collective process. Organizations that engage in learning enable staff at all levels to learn collaboratively and continuously and to put this learning to use in sustaining changes in their organization. The influence of learning and development on sustaining change is highlighted in the following case example of Amey.

CASE EXAMPLE

Training and development for sustainable change in Amey

Government cuts had a dramatic impact on the UK public services supplier Amey. As a result of the cuts the company had to change quickly and drastically, to become leaner, more effective and performance-driven. Amey set itself the task of increasing its revenues by 7.2%. In order to identify ways to achieve this it carried out employee research with a sample of staff. The findings concluded that processes could be reduced to save time and money, overheads were not proportionate and, with up to 11 levels of management between the CEO and the front line, it had too many managers.

To implement the changes the first step was to engage staff with the need for change. Amey launched a staff workshop on how to make their working practices leaner. Managers were briefed in order to cascade change communications down to their reports. The company also launched a collection of DVD communications, with messages from the Group HR Director and from the Chief Executive, and these were put on the staff website. Staff hits online increased from 4,000 to 11,000. Amey also appointed 'change champions' across its business to lead their colleagues through the change process. And an Employee Assistance Programme (EAP) was implemented to support staff who were confused by the proposed changes in the company.

Only seven months on, the company had changed for the better. HR costs had been cut by 20% per employee through changes to the department's own systems, while management approval levels were reduced from 11 to 4. The decision to involve staff feedback in changes also proved a success for Amey, with one employee saving £2,500 every year by having a cheaper soap in washrooms and another devising a way to recycle tar onsite – saving a massive £1.3m. In total, the company saved £20m and, while such a transformation can disillusion and disengage employees, Amey's staff satisfaction jumped from 56% to 68% – not least because of the employer's ongoing training, communication and development programmes.

Adapted by Julie Hodges from www.hrmagazine.co.uk/hro/news/1019673/hr-excellence-awards-2011-most successful-change-management-programme-amey#sthash.DaRltMct.dpuf.

The influence of learning and development to sustain change is also illustrated in a study of the impact of change over a 30-year period carried out by Boss and colleagues (2010). The study found evidence that learning and development interventions can generate positive, lasting change in an organization. Interventions such as team-building sessions and management and leadership development programmes were found to have a positive impact on sustaining change. Porras and Robertson (1992), however, warn that sustained organization change is not likely to occur unless development interventions span the various sub-systems of the organization. Multi-dimensional learning and development interventions that are tailored to alleviate problems in each organizational function are often necessary to produce sustained change. This has been recognized by leaders in companies such as Bombardier and ANZ Bank.

When Pierre Beaudois took over the aerospace division at Bombardier, with a mandate for change, he and his team understood that boosting factory performance would require building lean capabilities through learning and development. Lean capabilities were something the company sorely lacked despite its engineering experience. Crucially, they took time to work out that ensuring those capabilities were put to full use would mean changing workers' mindsets from a focus on what engineering could make possible to valuing individuals, enhancing the role of teamwork and understanding the needs of customers. And at ANZ Bank, as part of a transformation programme, the company trained more than 6,000 leaders in areas such as self-awareness, resilience and the ability to energize themselves and others in order to sustain transformation. Such programmes that produce behavioural change both inform and empower employees. To this end, learning and development also fosters a sense of responsibility and commitment – employee engagement. In turn, it stimulates investigative and problem-solving skills and ultimately individual and collective agency. Having the capability to effect meaningful change, both as change agents and as members of a team, helps to enable people to reflect on what they have learnt and take appropriate action to sustain change.

Reflection is a key tool for learning, with the aim of increasing the ability to improve performance. It is the opportunity to look back at experiences and question them in greater depth to make sense of them in order to repeat what worked well and to learn from mistakes. Reflection can take different forms, with people sharing what they have experienced, what it really meant, what worked, what did not, what needs answering and what needs changing. Without purposeful and focused reflection and dialogue, valuable knowledge and learning can remain untapped and therefore unprofitable. People need to be helped with reflection to know that it is acceptable to share their thoughts and feelings. They need to be encouraged to listen actively to others' perspectives on the same experiences and agree what it is right to take forward. Although intended benefits that were not realized or delivered as promised are expensive, what adds to the perpetual bill, of change in organizations, is the consequences of not learning and applying the lessons. Questions for leaders (and managers) to consider when reflecting on a change process include:

- What did we achieve, and what did we set out to achieve?
- Are our projects delivering our intended benefits?
- How are we partnering with other departments, disciplines, suppliers and customers?

- What is our communication strategy?
- How are we helping stakeholders to change effectively?
- How do we keep our eye on the big picture, yet get to the details and administration?
- Do we have strong sponsorship of our change projects and programmes?
- Are we doing too much? Is it all delivering benefit?
- Are we aligned with other changes that are happening elsewhere in the organization?
- What is going well and what could we do differently?

Asking such questions (and others you may want to add to the list) as part of the reflection process can provide valuable feedback about how to improve performance and support the progression of the implementation of change. Thus learning requires both the experience of action and reflection to enable change to be sustained.

Activity

Reflect on your experience of change and identify some of the occasions when new ways of working were not maintained.

List some of the factors that you think undermine the sustaining of change and contribute to its decay.

Management influences on sustaining change

Managers play a key influence in sustaining change, as we discuss in Chapter 4. If not managed carefully change, can lead to uncertainty and, even worse, increase the stress levels of individuals.

Why does change, which can be so exciting and lead to so many great opportunities, stress so many people? The short answer is: change initiatives are too often unfocused, uninspiring and unsuccessful. Often managers (and leaders) approach change as a shift from 'Point A' to 'Point B'. Along the way, there may be changes in the external environment which trigger the need to move to Point C instead, then Point D, and so on. In such situations employees could be asked or even told to constantly alter their behaviours and to take on additional responsibilities without receiving extra resources, recognition or relief from any of their other responsibilities. They do not have a clear sense of where their organization is heading, what their role in that transition might be, or which elements of change should be their top priorities. To make things worse, organizations often tend to launch multiple change initiatives, even when existing projects are still being implemented, without considering the impact on individuals.

Managing people through change

The rich and extraordinary variation in individuals' attitudes cannot be ignored by managers. Employees are not waiting passively to be managed as a single entity through a process of change. They each have their own personal agenda and challenges that are deeply rooted in their personalities. This embodies their sensitivities and their reactions to uncertainty and risk. Any organizational change has to navigate this reality successfully to maximize achievement of its objectives. Managers need to foster support, participation and trust among employees by encouraging open communication and involving employees in decision-making about the change (see Chapters 10 and 11).

Change in organizations may actually create new opportunities for management to enhance commitment among the workforce. Change, in other words, may not necessarily be just a source of problems. It may also be a source of opportunities too. Ensuring that employees are actively involved in the process of change and that their interests are adequately taken into account, rather than undermining and eroding commitment among the workforce, is a vital part of the management of change. If effectively managed, change can actually help to enhance and reinforce employees' sense of commitment to the organization. As Johann Wolfgang von Goethe (1749–1832), the German dramatist, novelist, poet and scientist, said:

> If you treat an individual as he is, he will remain how he is. But if you treat him as if he were what he ought to be and could be he will become what he ought to be and could be. (Anster, 1888)

Change may be appropriate and necessary in the opinion of leaders and managers. But until everyone understands the what, why, when, who, where and how of the change, there is potential for negative reactions to the change.

Managers need to be prepared to tackle the difficult or high-risk problems, to accept change in their own behaviour and to address systematically the underlying causes of problems. They need to role model the new behaviour they wish to see in others and continue to do so even after change is implemented.

Managers need to understand where adverse reactions to change are coming from and why. Building supportive work relationships and communicating effectively all contribute to creating positive attitudes to change and, therefore, to the success of implementing and sustaining change.

Building trust

Managers need to build trust between themselves and employees as trust is a key enabler for sustaining change. Employees' trust in their supervisor has been found to play an important role, not only in preventing cynicism about change (Albrecht, 2002; Wanous et al., 2000) but also in encouraging employees to support change and to be emotionally committed to the organization during times of change (Albrecht, 2002; Gómez and Rosen, 2001; Neves and Caetano, 2006; Stanley et al., 2005). In turn, organizational commitment is connected to several aspects of organizational change, such as how fair (Colquitt et al., 2001; Lines et al., 2005) and favourable the change is perceived to be, employees' readiness for change (Fedor et al., 2006; Madsen et al., 2005), and the extent to which they are allowed to participate in a change initiative.

Employees' trust in their manager plays an important role too in achieving change and organizational commitment. Trusting relationships help to create open dialogue between employees and managers and address problems and difficult issues when they occur rather than waiting until they escalate (Sackmann et al., 2009). Trust helps managers and their staff work through difficult issues in times of uncertainty and to deal with any negative aspects of change. As such, the ability of managers to build trust is a key influence on sustaining change in an organization.

Managing the benefits and costs of change

Managers must manage change – in terms of its benefits and costs (see Chapter 14). Studies have found that the benefits and costs of change can influence its sustainability (or lack of). For example, Reisner carried out a study in the US Postal Service, which attempted to transform itself from 'the butt of sitcom jokes into a profitable and efficient enterprise' (2002: 218). However, the study found that the attempts to change the Service were not sustained. One of the 'momentum busters' was the inability to steer funding through a budget process that favoured traditional initiatives over innovations. As a result, the changes lacked the funds to sustain them. Rimmer and colleagues point out that the costs of implementation can increase in a number of ways:

> through consultants fees, benchmarking, travel, new equipment, downtime during installation, customer and competitor surveys, redundancies and management time. There are 'twin peaks' in the typical revenue curve. The first peak comes during the first two years, associated with 'two transient phenomena', concerning cost reductions from obvious economies, and the 'novelty effect', as those involved become more interested and excited. However, after the easy gains of the first peak, the rate of performance improvement can slow down. (1996: 218)

Monitoring costs as well as benefits is therefore important since costs can fluctuate at different times during the implementation of change.

Managing the timing, sequence and pace of change

Sustaining change entails managing the timing, sequencing and pacing of events, as we discuss in Chapter 2. On the one hand, delayed change can increase costs and not deliver benefits. On the other hand, change that is rushed might not allow enough time for individuals to adapt to it, and it could, as Buchanan and colleagues (2005) say, create fatigue and as a result encourage initiative decay. Time has to be allowed for change to become part of the business as usual – hence the warning early in this chapter about not declaring victory too soon. There also has to be enough time given for the change to demonstrate benefits beyond the initial easy gains. As Rimmer and colleagues say:

> The critical problem for sustainability is winning the time, especially during periods when it is perceived that costs exceed benefits – a period of uncertain duration, when best practice may be discontinued as not cost-effective. (1996: 219)

The perceived benefits of the change over time need to be greater than the perceived costs in order for change to be sustainable. So managing the time, sequence and pace of change is important to its sustainability.

Skills for managing change

Leadership and management are complementary processes in pursuing sustainable organizational change. Without managing change effectively, change initiatives and efforts will fail or disappoint, however 'good' leadership is. So managers of change first need to make sure they understand and support the organization's vision, purpose and strategies for change and also the underlying values that will inform it. Managers also need to understand and practise effective management of the change process. This comprises several sets of skills: planning, organizing, directing, implementing, monitoring and controlling the various aspects of change. Moreover, managers need to understand the meaning of tasks, actions, outputs and their consequences, and to understand and formulate accountabilities, objectives and key performance measures. They also need to provide quality communications.

Quality communication during change is associated with several positive reactions: greater acceptance of change and support for it, lower levels of anxiety and uncertainty, increased trust in management, and decreased turnover intentions (Bordia et al., 2004a). It is important to provide staff with information that will help them to understand the rationale for the change, when and how changes will occur, how the changes will affect their jobs, and their level of autonomy regarding these changes. However, it is not merely the amount of information that determines reactions to change but also its content. Employees who understand the circumstances surrounding a proposed change will be more likely to engage with it and commit themselves to the organization. They will have more information about the future direction of the organization and realize the personal benefits of ensuring the success of the change.

So management influences are key to sustaining change and transformation in organizations. For as Burnes observes:

> Managing and changing organizations appears to be getting more rather than less difficult, and more rather than less important. Given the rapidly changing environment in which organizations operate, there is little doubt that the ability to manage change successfully needs to be a core competence for organizations. (2005: 85)

Individual influences on sustaining change

Sustaining change is dependent on the capability and commitment of individuals to ensuring that the change is embedded. Individuals will, however, have their own perceptions about the change. For instance, they may perceive it as threatening their status or adding extra work to their already overloaded work schedule. Individuals may then appear to oppose the change and as a result be viewed in negative terms, as 'resistors'.

The reality, however, is that many people will react positively to change. People will embrace rather than resist change if the outcome is important to them and they have been convinced that they will be better rather than worse off. People pay attention to the process and will want to have a warning of the need for the change and know how the change is being managed, the vision of where the organization is going, the reasons for the change and what training and development will be provided to help them make the transition.

Individual involvement in change

Employee involvement in change initiatives is central to increasing the likelihood of sustaining change. Oreg and colleagues (2011) emphasize that active involvement in change allows employees to select changes they feel they can accomplish and boosts their self-efficacy. In addition, the increased participation of individuals in change initiatives creates a sense of individual control over the change and leads to greater readiness and support for the change, as outlined in Chapter 6. Active involvement also allows employees to take a role in dealing with difficult change issues related to their jobs and can increase perceptions that they can benefit from the change. As Robert Doppelt says:

> For an organization to make the kind of transformation to become truly sustainable, power and authority must be skilfully distributed amongst employees and stakeholders through effective information sharing, decision-making and resource allocation mechanisms. (2003: 2)

Indeed, employees who are involved in the change, rather than just having it imposed on them, respond more positively to organizational change. Hornung and Rousseau (2007) found that employees report greater benefits from change and are more likely to be committed to the change if they participate in it.

Capability and capacity for change

Along with building commitment to change, leaders and managers also need to build capabilities among individuals to sustain change (see Chapter 14 for a discussion on the need for capabilities). Change agents, as we discuss in Chapter 12, need the skills, resilience and agility to create dialogue that convinces people about the change. They also need to have knowledge of the prevailing political and power influences and be familiar with the connections and social practices that affect and alter decision-making.

Along with the capability for change, individuals also need to have clarity about their roles and responsibilities during change. The redesign of organizational roles is a common outcome of many organizational changes. However, role changes can be a critical element of the process of change, not just a product of change. Beer, Eisenstat and Spector (1990) argue that most change programmes do not work because they are guided by a theory of change that is fundamentally flawed. They argue that too much emphasis is placed on attempting to change people's behaviour by changing their attitudes and beliefs through exposing them to new perspectives. It is an approach that treats change like a conversion experience in which, once people 'get religion', changes in their behaviour will surely follow. However, they argue that the more significant direction of causality is that both behaviour and attitudes are most influenced by the roles, relationships and responsibilities in which people find themselves. It is important, therefore, that there is clarity about roles and responsibilities as well as ensuring individuals have the required capabilities for change.

Individual recognition and reward

Individuals involved in the change process must also be recognized and rewarded appropriately, not only to ensure their commitment to change but also to show that they are valued members of staff. Too many organizations emphasize the technical aspects of change and neglect many of the related people-issues. Involving people at an early stage can help win their hearts and minds. As Kotter (1995) says, change sticks when it is rooted in the social norms and shared values of an organization. Until this is achieved, change will be subject to degradation as soon as the pressures to maintain it are removed.

Individual, as well as leadership and management influences, are therefore key factors in sustaining change in organizations.

Summary

Future change and transformation in organizations will be influenced by current meg-atrends in the global business environment, as we described in Chapter 14. These trends will continue to increase the need to develop change as a core capability and institutionalize an organizational capacity for change, giving organizations a competitive edge in a rapidly changing market.

Organizations can no longer cling to what they think is true about their customers and markets since those facts are changing before their very eyes. Leaders within organizations need to create environments that foster co-creation and non-hierarchical networks and equip employees to manage ambiguity, complexity and uncertainty. Organizations that continue to believe that what made them successful in the past will make them successful in the future will soon become dinosaurs (or end up in the death spiral that we discussed in Chapter 5). The past decade has witnessed the rise and fall of many once-innovative companies, including the General Electric Company (GEC), International Computers Limited (ICL), Dell, Blockbuster, Motorola and Sony, who all failed to adapt to their business environment and evolve their products or practices.

Organizations have to be mindful to the fact that the nature of change itself is changing. As Ron Ashkenas asks:

> Is it possible that everything we know about change management is wrong and that we need to go back to the drawing board? Should we abandon Kotter's eight success factors ... and everything else we know about engagement, communication, small wins ... and all of the other elements of the change management framework? (2013: 1)

According to Kennedy Consulting Research and Advisory in the USA:

> the Change Management movement is becoming a global trend and [change] is no longer deemed to [have the] 'nice to have' status [of a project]. Change Management is finally getting its due diligence, enabling a new level of executive commitment to a culture of change and organizational agility ... (2013: 2)

So the world of change is changing – and organizations with it.

Sustaining change is like practising a musical instrument: there are new pieces of music to learn and always room for improvement. That is why sustaining change successfully is grounded in learning as well as the context in which an organization operates. The humourist Will Rogers once remarked that, even if you are on the right track, you will eventually get run over by a train if you just sit there (Thiele, 2013). To ensure change is sustained, organizations have to learn and to adapt.

In a complex and dynamic global business world, change and transformation are vital for the survival of an organization. The challenge for organizations is to build a cadre of leaders, managers and individuals with the capability and capacity to collectively accomplish what is needed to survive, thrive and sustain change, in an ethical way.

Glossary

Action learning. The purpose of action learning is that a group of peers, each seeking to bring about change, meet regularly to discuss where they are each experiencing difficulty and then test in action the ideas that arise from the discussion. In organizations today action learning is usually practised through action learning groups.

Action research. Action research (conceived by Kurt Lewin) is a way of using research in an interventionist way so that the person carrying out the research is both a discoverer of problems and solutions, and is involved in decisions about what is to be done and why. Action research sees organizational change as a cyclical process where theory guides practice and practice in turn informs theory.

Agility. Sometimes called dynamic capability, agility is the ability to respond to changing circumstances in a timely, effective and sustainable way.

Appreciative inquiry. This is a method for exploring ideas that people have about what is valuable in what they do and then to work out ways in which they can be built on the good practice. The emphasis is on appreciating the activities and responses of people rather than concentrating on their problems.

Acquisition. An acquisition is the purchase of an asset such as a factory, a division or an entire company.

Balanced Scorecard. An integrated set of measures built around the mission, vision and strategy. Measures address the financial perspective, customer perspective, internal business process perspective, and learning and growth perspective. They provide a balanced view on what is required to enact the strategy.

Benefits realization. Benefits realization is the process of organizing and managing, so that potential benefits, arising from investment in change, are actually achieved. It should be the core process of any change initiative. The key activities for realizing benefits include: engaging stakeholders, developing a business case, identifying risks, developing tracking mechanisms, continually tracking benefits, communicating achievement of benefits, monitoring and reviewing progress against the benefits.

Burke–Litwin model. This model seeks to address the complexity and interdependence of the internal and external factors affecting change. It illustrates how the external environment affects the performance of the organization and how organizational performance affects the external environment. The model is predictive rather than prescriptive in that it specifies the nature of causal relationships and predicts the likely effect of changing certain elements rather than others. It also differentiates between two types of change: transformational change and transactional/incremental change.

Capability/ies. Structural, cultural and contextual attributes necessary, for example, for leading and managing change effectively. Include human competencies (both individual and collective knowledge, skills and attitudes).

Capacity. In the context of organizational change, capacity can be defined as the organization's total workload for running current operations and conducting change activities.

Catalyst for change. This is the trigger for a change to be initiated. The catalyst can be internal or external to the organization.

Change. Change is the introduction or experience of something that is different. Change comes in many guises including: modification, development, metamorphosis, transmutation, evolution, regeneration and revolution. Change is something that happens to people, even if they do not agree with it. Organizational change is triggered by a proactive or reactive response to something in the external environment or internally in the organization. Organizational change can be planned or emergent alterations to the whole or parts of an organization to improve the effectiveness and efficiency of the organization.

Change agents. Change agents are the individuals or groups of individuals whose task it is to effect change. They can be any members of an organization involved in facilitating, initiating, influencing or implementing change, whether or not they have an official title, which recognizes or formalizes that responsibility.

Change agency. Change agency is emergent and fluid and it is typically driven by a number of people. The change agent is a member of that cast, formally appointed or self-appointed, seeking to drive a change agenda. Those who take on the role of change agents will themselves change over time, as an initiative develops and matures, as other projects and individuals come into play and as responsibility changes.

Change leadership. Showing the way with change and inducing or helping people to pursue it.

Change management. Translating the vision for change, its purpose and the organization's underpinning core values into strategies, action plans, accountabilities, objectives, key performance measures, tasks, action and outputs.

Communications plan. The key quadrants of a communications plan are: message, methods, audience and feedback. These are the four aspects of communication where managers and leaders must make active decisions about the best approach to adopt. The four elements need to be considered holistically.

Competency. Individual or collective knowledge, skills and attitudes that provide the ability to perform a particular task or activity.

Conflict. Conflict is an inevitable feature of human interaction, especially during times of change. The consequences of conflict may be *destructive* or *constructive* depending on the situation. If managed constructively, conflict can offer positive value in enhancing creativity and ensuring change is sustained.

Contingent reward. The practice of promising and delivering rewards in exchange for achieving desired or expected performance. An aspect of transactional leadership that motivates people to do what is desired by the leader or manager.

COPS. This framework can be used for scanning an organization internally to establish how healthy the organization is and whether the different elements are aligned with one another. Four separate aspects of the organization are considered and the relative strengths and weaknesses of each are assessed: Culture, Operations, People, and Systems.

Corporate social responsibility (CSR). An organization's concern for the environment, employee (and supplier) working conditions and human rights based on its core values and ethical standards.

Creativity. The ability to generate new and original ideas, associations, methods, approaches and solutions – a process known as 'ideation' – in relation to a given problem or topic. A process of invention.

Crowdsourcing. The practice of obtaining needed services, ideas or content by soliciting contributions from a large group of people, and especially an online community, rather than traditional employees or suppliers.

Culture. Culture is like an iceberg – only one-tenth of it is visible – which makes it difficult to see all the elements of it, and hence to identify and define them. Edgar Schein defined culture as the artefacts (above the waterline and are tangible for everyone to see); espoused beliefs/values and basic assumptions (below the water line and invisible). This is what makes culture so hard to define because much of it is intangible and invisible to people inside and outside an organization.

Cynicism. Cynicism about change involves an individual's negative attitude towards the purpose or potential success of change efforts.

Decision tree analysis. Decision tree analysis asks managers to consider the major choices and the possible consequences of those alternatives. They are then asked to plan for the possible actions and consider what the consequences of these actions might be.

Diagnosis. The analysis of the organization in its environment, understanding its strengths and limitations, examining the various parts of the organization at each level and how they affect and are affected by one another and by the whole, and analysing the implications of anticipated changes.

DICE. An acronym for four 'hard' (management) factors that need to be addressed in a change programme: its Duration, Integrity of the project team, Commitment of all involved and Effort/workload implications.

Distributed leadership. This is the (hierarchically) vertical dispersal of leadership and associated authority and responsibility.

Downsizing. This refers to interventions aimed at reducing the size of the organization. This typically is accomplished by decreasing the number of employees through redundancies, attrition, redeployment or early retirement, or by reducing the number of organizational units or management layers through divestiture or outsourcing.

Driver. A driver is a factor that directly influences or causes change.

Due diligence. Due diligence aims to explore every facet of the company that is to be acquired or merged with (i.e. target company) in as much detail as possible prior to the final agreement. An over-riding question for due diligence is: will this merger or acquisition work?

Dynamic capabilities. The ability of the firm to purposefully create, extend or modify its resource base to address a rapidly changing environment. Dynamic capabilities are antecedents to functional competencies (e.g. marketing and technological) that in turn have a significant effect on performance. Dynamic capabilities are important in managing both external environmental change and internal change. (See **Agility**)

Emergent change. This is the continuous, open-ended, cumulative and unpredictable process of aligning and re-aligning an organization to its changing environment.

Emotional intelligence. The ability to perceive and understand the feelings and needs of oneself and other people, to display self-control and self-confidence, and to respond to others' needs and feelings in appropriate ways. Often referred to as EQ.

Employee social responsibility (ESR). Employees' concern for the environment, working conditions and human rights, reflecting their espoused values and ethical standards and their everyday decisions and actions at work.

Empowerment. The essence of empowerment is giving people power. Empowerment is giving people the knowledge, skills, self-confidence, opportunity, freedom, authority and resources to manage themselves and be accountable for their performance.

Engagement. The intellectual, emotional and spiritual commitment to what one is doing, shown by discretionary attention and effort devoted to it. Results from being influenced, motivated or inspired to *want to do* what needs to be done.

Ethical change leadership (ECL). This is the demonstration of decision-making and ethical implementation of organizational change.

Ethics. A code of conduct or behaviour that reflects a set of moral values to be applied in given circumstances.

Field theory. Field theory is an approach to understanding group behaviour by identifying and mapping the totality and complexity of the field in which the behaviour takes place.

Fishbone (Ishikawa) diagram. The Ishikawa diagram can be used to help understand the root causes of problems or opportunities. It was devised in the 1960s by Kaoru Ishikawa, who pioneered quality management processes in the Kawasaki shipyards in Japan. The diagram is also known as the fishbone diagram because of its resemblance to the skeleton of a fish. It can be used to help think through all of the possible causes of a problem and what needs to change. The model provides a cause-and-effect analysis. The purpose of a cause-and-effect analysis is to identify the causes, factors, or sources of variation that lead to a specific event, result, or defect in a product or process.

Fionnphort model. This model identifies three areas: direction, leadership and energy for implementing change.

Force field analysis. A process of identifying and analysing the force field (restrainers and drivers) in an organization and then strengthening the drivers and addressing the restrainers to accomplish change.

Framing. A term used in relation to inspirational language to refer to connecting one's message with the needs and interests of those whose commitment is needed (e.g. in a change effort).

Full-range leadership (FRL) model. A comprehensive model of leadership developed originally by Bernard M. Bass that describes aspects of leadership ranging from highly effective transformational leadership (q.v.) to ineffective laissez-faire leadership (q.v., actually non-leadership) and including transactional leadership (q.v.).

Future–present model. A basic framework that focuses on identifying what the current situation is and what the future situation should be.

Game-changers. Game-changers determine what kind of transformed world we will inhabit in the future. These game-changers include the global economy, national and global governance, the nature of conflict, advancing technologies and the role of the major economic powers in the international arena.

Group dynamics. Kurt Lewin was the first psychologist to write about 'group dynamics' and the importance of the group in shaping the behaviour of its members. Dynamics stress that group behaviour, rather than of the individuals, should be the main focus of change.

Hilltops. How individuals perceive the impact of change depends on their own personal view of it, from their own perspective – their 'hilltop'. A leader or manager will be looking at the change from their hilltop in the organization, and what they see below may be different from what a member of their staff may see who is elsewhere in the organization – on their hilltop – and looking down. To appreciate how staff view the change, a leader or manager needs to move from their own hilltop across to the hilltop that their employees are standing on.

Implementation Compass. This provides a structure for an implementation strategy. The Implementation Compass helps to assess the current status in preparing to implement a change and to maintain momentum throughout implementation. Each of the eight points on the compass has a number of prompts to help guide leaders and mangers through effective implementation.

Innovation. Changing something that is already established by introducing new and original ideas, associations, methods, approaches and solutions. Implementation of the outputs of creativity, also requiring organizational agility and flexibility.

Laissez-faire leadership. A passive, inert form of leadership, in reality non-leadership, characterized by avoiding taking a stand, ignoring problems, not following up and refraining from intervening in problematic situations, usually resulting in conflict among others and poor performance.

Leadership. Showing the way and inducing or helping people to pursue it.

Learning communities. These are networks of people who share a common interest in a specific area of knowledge or capability and are willing to work and learn together over a period of time and share that knowledge. They are based on the premise that learning is largely a social activity in which people learn best in groups.

Learning contract. A learning contract is a formal written agreement between an employee and his or her manager that specifies: what the individual needs to learn; the resources needed and strategies available to assist in learning it; what will be produced as evidence of the learning having occurred; and how the outcome will be assessed – what will the individual be doing or saying that is different. A learning contract can provide a means of monitoring the learning progress. It can be amended to suit individuals and their particular circumstances. Learning contracts can also be agreed with colleagues in an action learning group and with managers during performance management reviews.

Learning disabled. This occurs when an organization becomes incapable of looking outside, reflecting on success and failure, accepting new ideas and developing new insights, it decreases its customer focus, and costs increase.

Learning organization. An organization can proactively sustain change by making continuous learning part of its culture, by becoming an organization that learns – a learning organization. A learning organization is an organization that has developed the continuous capacity to adapt and change. It is an organization that is skilled at creating, acquiring and transferring knowledge, modifying its behaviour to reflect new knowledge and insights and adjusting itself to adapt to internal and external environmental changes, thereby achieving sustainability and development.

Linear models of change. Linear models of change consider change as a step-by-step process.

Management. Producing orderly results that keep something working efficiently. This entails translating the group's or organization's vision for the future, its purpose and its core values into strategies, action plans, accountabilities, objectives, key performance measures, tasks, action and outputs through planning, organizing resources, communication, monitoring performance and progress, and control, which are guided by policies, operational procedures and best practice.

Management by exception. An aspect of transactional leadership that entails focusing on performance or behavioural deviations from expectations as way of motivating and influencing people to do what needs to be done.

Merger. A merger involves the mutual decision of two relatively equal companies to combine to become one legal entity with the goal of producing a company that is worth more than the sum of its parts.

Moral intelligence. The ability to differentiate right from wrong according to universal moral principles. Universal moral principles include empathy, responsibility, reciprocity respect for others and caring for others.

Moral values. Values (q.v.) that reflect what is right versus what is wrong and what is good versus what is bad.

Network structure. Also known as spider webs, starbursts or cluster organizations – aims to manage the diverse, complex and dynamic relationships among multiple organizations and units, each specializing in a particular business function or task.

Organization. An organization can be defined as 'a social arrangement for achieving controlled performance in pursuit of collective goals' (Buchanan and Huczynski, 2010: 8). This definition emphasizes that it is the preoccupation with performance and the need for control which distinguishes organizations from other social arrangements.

Organizational development (OD). OD is a process for instigating, implementing and sustaining change. It involves activities individual, group/team and organizational interventions.

Organizational silence. Organizational silence is described by Morrison and Milliken (2000) as the withholding of opinions and concerns about organizational problems by employees. This highlights a challenge for change, in that employees may choose not to change, yet remain silent.

Open-Space Technology (OST). This is a scalable and adaptive method devised by Harrison Owen (2008). It can be used in meetings of anything from five to 2,000 people. OST is most distinctive for its initial lack of an agenda. Participants create the agenda for themselves, within a self-organizing process called 'open space.'

Organizational structures. An organization's formal structure is defined by how tasks are formally divided, grouped or coordinated, in essence the social structuring of people and processes. *Functional structures* tend to have centralized control and separate functional departments, such as marketing, production, human resources, IT and customer service. A *divisional structure* groups all relevant organizational functions into individual divisions. Each division contains all the necessary resources and functions within it. In a *matrix structure* employees have two and sometimes more reporting relationships. One line of authority, often the functional area, manages the formal side of the employment contract, such as performance management and salary negotiations. The other lines of authority are used to involve employees in projects and other change initiatives. A *flat structure* has relatively few levels of hierarchy. Its aim is to: improve the focus on customer needs and the speed of response; to reduce the levels of bureaucracy in the organization; to facilitate greater empowerment and to reduce dysfunctional status differences. The *shamrock* (a small three-leaved plant), a structure developed by Charles Handy (1989), has three distinct parts: the *core workforce, contractual fringe* and *flex workers.*

Outcomes. The consequences of producing something (as a result of a change programme).

Outputs. What is produced (as a result of a change programme).

PESTELI. A framework that covers external factors. Traditionally known by the acronym PEST, which stands for Political, Economic, Society, Technology, it has been expanded to include Environment, Legislation and Industry.

Planned change. An intentional intervention for bringing about change to an organization and is best characterized as deliberate, purposeful and systematic.

Political behaviour. Political behaviour happens whenever people get together in groups and where an individual or group seeks to influence the thoughts, attitudes or behaviour of another individual or group.

Power. Power is a dynamic variable that changes as conditions change. Power can be far more positive and subtle when it shapes and forms what others want to do of their own volition. In this way power can be seen as the capacity or capability of an individual to influence the behaviour or attitude of one or more people at a given time. 'Hard' power is associated with authority or position power and the use of 'carrots and sticks'. 'Soft' power is the power of personality and interpersonal skills, such as charisma, use of language and bestowed respect, associated with influence, motivation and inspiration.

Power bases. Power stems from an individual's position in an organization, along a set of dimensions known as power bases. In the 1950s, Raven and French (1958) developed a classic model that identified sources of power and, in so doing, replaced the traditional view that power primarily derived from formal authority. Raven and French's sources of power are: Coercive, Reward, Legitimate, Expert, Information and Referent.

Power tactics. Power tactics are used to translate power bases into specific actions.

Project management. Project management provides an approach for the planning and implementation of sustainable change. It comprises the activities of planning, communication, setting clear, measurable objectives for the change, and evaluating their achievement by using clearly defined success measures, as well as monitoring and control to keep the project focused and on track through to completion so that all intended potential benefits are delivered.

Psychological contract. The psychological contract consists of organizational obligations (to be fulfilled by the organization) and employee obligations (to be fulfilled by employees), based on promises made by the employer and employee, respectively. The contract tends to be based on trust and defines the perceptions of the terms of an individual's relationship with their employer, and the organizational obligations to them.

Punctuated equilibrium. This occurs when change oscillates between long periods of stability and short bursts of transformational change that fundamentally alter an organization's strategies, systems and structures.

Purpose. The reason for which something is done or for which something (the organization, the change initiative) exists; its intentions for action. Sometimes termed 'mission'.

Purposeful conversations. Purposeful conversations allow the sharing of meaning and ideas, are driven by the vision, deepen mutual understanding and create purposeful action. They can be facilitated in meetings, workshops and online discussion forums.

Readiness for change. This refers to organizational members' beliefs, attitudes and intentions regarding the extent to which changes are needed and the organization's capacity to successfully make those changes.

Recognizing the need to change involves complex processes of perception, interpretation and decision-making that, if not managed carefully, can lead to inappropriate outcomes. Recognizing the potential need for change can be done through conducting an analysis of the external environment and an internal assessment of the organization.

Resilience. Resilience is the capability that enables one person to respond well and thrive during the change process, while a colleague with apparently similar skills and experiences struggles to cope. Resilience helps people gain control much more quickly during times of change. It helps them maintain higher performance levels and improves their sense of wellbeing. Resilience also helps people make sense of change more quickly, so that they understand the impact on them and other people.

Resistance to change. Resistance to change is defined as an individual's tendency to resist and avoid making changes, to devalue change generally and to find change aversive across diverse contexts and types of change. Employee resistance to change is often not a result of negative attitudes toward change but comes from a well-grounded understanding of the implications of change that are different from the understanding of leaders and managers. People will often resist change out of genuine self-interest, knowing that the change will have adverse effects on them and others in the organization. They may have well-informed grounds for considering them ill advised and have alternatives that they think are better.

Rhetorical crafting. The art of impressive or persuasive speech, using examples, citing quotations, reciting slogans, varying one's speaking rhythm, using familiar images, metaphors and analogies to make the message vivid.

Ring road issue. A driver that is so pervasive in nature and influence that it will affect the life of everyone on the planet over the next 30 years.

Risk. The probability of an event or issue being realized that may lead to an undesirable effect on the organization or on people within it.

Risk management. The activities involved in the planning, monitoring and controlling of actions that will address the threats and problems identified, so as to improve the likelihood of the risks not occurring. In general, risk management is based on four steps: risk identification, risk analysis/assessment, risk treatment and the monitoring of risks.

Scenario planning. Scenario planning involves developing a limited number of scenarios or stories about how the future may unfold and then assessing what the implications of each of these would be to the organization. By raising and testing various 'what-if' scenarios, managers can brainstorm together and challenge their assumptions in a non-threatening, hypothetical environment before they decide on a certain course of action.

Servant leadership. Leadership that reflects the desire to serve the needs and interests of followers and others.

Seven-S framework. A framework that focuses on the interaction of different parts of an organization. The premise of the model is that successful change is based on the interdependence between seven variables: strategy, structure, systems, staff, style, skills and shared values.

Shared leadership. This is the (hierarchically) horizontal sharing of leadership and associated authority and responsibility, usually concerning two people and some division of labour.

Spiritual intelligence. The ability to understand that human beings have an animating need for meaning and a sense of worth or value in what they seek and do (to varying extents and in varying ways, as with all human needs) and responding appropriately to this need.

Stakeholders. Those who have a vested interest in the success of an organization or group (or a change effort), such as investors, employees, managers, customers, suppliers, government and society at large. Stakeholders may affect a change initiative or may be affected by it.

Stakeholder analysis. The identification and assessment of those who can affect the change or who are affected by the change. Included in this is the analysis of the power, influence and motivations of key stakeholders.

Strategic change. A major change in the way an organization responds to its environment or stakeholders.

Strategy. Strategy is about how to get from where we are now to where we want to be. It is a journey plan for fulfilling the organization's vision and purpose or for a change initiative and provides a route map for travelling to the 'destination' (represented the a vision). Producing a strategy entails identifying and exploiting opportunities, anticipating and responding to threats, and not only responding positively to the need for change but also creating change.

Sustainable. 'Sustainable' derives from the Latin *sustinere*, which literally means 'to hold up'. Something is sustainable if it endures, persists or holds up over time. Change is sustained when it becomes an integrated or mainstream way of working and behaving rather than something added on.

SWOT. This is an acronym for examining an organization's strengths, weaknesses, opportunities and threats, and using the results to identify priorities for action. The main principle underlying SWOT is that internal and external factors must be considered simultaneously when identifying aspects of an organization that need to be changed.

Transactional leadership. Conducting a transactional relationship with other people, i.e. an arrangement based on managing them by exception and the promise and delivery of rewards for achieving agreed expectations (known as contingent reward).

Transformation. This is the marked change in nature, form or appearance of something. Transformation involves massive programmes of change to turn around or renew an organization.

Transformational leadership. Transforming the way people feel about themselves and what they believe it is possible to achieve, particularly in respect of the common good, and likely to achieve performance beyond previous expectations. According to Bernard M. Bass's model, transformational leadership comprises the elements of individualized consideration, intellectual stimulation, inspirational motivation and idealized influence.

Transition. This is the process or period of adapting to the change. Transition is different from change and it is very often the transition that people resist – not the change itself. Transition involves shifting from the current state or phase to another, for example, an individual changing from one role to another, a group changing from one decision process to another, or an organization going from one structural arrangement to another. Transition is what happens as people go through change. Change can happen very quickly, while transition usually occurs more slowly.

Triple bottom line. The triple bottom line adds to the traditional idea of organizational effectiveness – economic success – to include 'people' and 'planet' as well as 'profit'. A term originally ratified for use by the United Nations in public sector accounting but subsequently applied more broadly.

Trust. Trust is defined as the degree of confidence that individuals have in the goodwill of their leaders, specifically the extent to which they believe that their managers and leaders are honest, sincere and unbiased in taking their positions into account. Employees' trust in leaders and managers, as well as in the organization is an expression of confidence in their reliability and honesty in times of change and transformation.

Values. Principles or standards of behaviour that are felt to be important or have worth or merit. (Also see Moral values)

Virtual structures. Virtual structures are a set of economically independent organizations operating together to meet the needs of customers or other stakeholders. Such an organization structure is a culmination of an information-based and constantly evolving enterprise. In this way, virtual structures are essentially like a network of connections into individuals, groups, teams and parts of formal organizations. They are suited to rapid exchanges of information for solving problems or locating resources. Virtual structures can be short-lived and because of the loose structure, dissolving one can occur rapidly.

Vision. A mental image of what the future will or could be like, involving the ability to think about or plan the future with imagination and wisdom. Vision defines what or where the organization wants or needs to be. A vision for change defines the outcome of the intended change.

World Cafe. A 'World Cafe' or 'Knowledge Cafe' is a type of meeting or workshop that aims to provide an open and creative conversation on a topic of common interest to identify collective knowledge, share ideas and insights, and gain a deeper understanding of the subject and the issues involved.

References

Abrahamson, E. (2004) *Change Without Pain*. Cambridge, MA: Harvard Business Press.

Ackerman, L. (1986) 'Development, transition or transformation: The question of change in organizations', *OD Practitioner*, December, 1–8.

Adler, N.J. (1997) *International Dimensions of Organizational Behaviour*, 3rd edn. Cincinnati, OH: South-Western College Publishing.

Albrecht, S.L. (2002) 'Perceptions of integrity, competence and trust in senior management as determinants of cynicism toward change', *Public Administration and Management: An Interactive Journal*, 7(4): 320–43.

Allen, J., Jimmieson, N.L., Bordia, P. and Irmer, B.E. (2007) 'Uncertainty during organizational change: Managing perceptions through communication', *Journal of Change Management*, 7(2): 187–210.

Amble, B. (2010) 'CEOs misunderstand employee engagement', *Management-Issues*, 7 December. Downloaded from www.management-issues.com/2010/12/7/research/ceos-misunderstand-employee-engagement.asp?section=research&id=6102&specifi er=&mode=print&is_authenticated=0&reference= on 4 January 2011.

American Management Association (1994) *Survey on Change Management*. New York, NY: AMA.

Amis, J., Slack, T. and Hinings, C.R. (2004) 'The pace, sequence, and linearity of radical change', *Academy of Management Journal*, 47(1): 15–30.

Anderson, D.L. (2012) *Organization Development: The Process of Leading Organizational Change*, 2nd edn. London: Sage.

Anderson, D. and Anderson, L.A. (2010a) *Beyond Change Management: How to Achieve Breakthrough Results through Conscious Change Leadership*, 2nd edn. San Francisco, CA: Pfeiffer.

Anderson, D. and Anderson, L.A. (2010b) *The Change Leader's Roadmap: How to Navigate Your Organization's Transformation*, 2nd edn. Hoboken, NJ: Pfeiffer.

Anster, J. (1888) 'Prelude at the theatre' (trans. from the German), *Faust*, Johann Wolfgang von Goethe (1749–1832). London: White and Allen, pp. 214–30.

Argyris, C. (1970) *Intervention Theory and Method: A Behavioural Science View*. Reading, MA: Addison-Wesley.

Argyris, C. (2000) *Flawed Advice and the Management Trap*. Oxford: Oxford University Press.

Argyris, C. and Schon, D. (1978) *Organizational Learning: A Theory of Action Approach*. Reading, MA: Addision Wesley.

Armenakis, A.A. and Bedeian, A.G. (1999) 'Organizational change: A review of theory and research in the 1990s', *Journal of Management*, 25(3): 293–315.

Armenakis, A.A. and Harris, S.G. (2002) 'Crafting a change message to create transformational readiness', *Journal of Organizational Change Management*, 15(2): 169–83.

Armenakis, A.A. and Harris, S.G. (2009) 'Reflections: Our journey in organizational change research and practice', *Journal of Change Management*, 9(2): 127–42.

Armenakis, A., Bernerth, J., Pitts., J. and Walker, H. (2007) 'Organizational change recipients' beliefs scale: Development of an assessment instrument', *Journal of Applied Behavioural Science*, 43(4): 481–505.

Armenakis, A.A., Harris, S.G., Cole, M.S., Lawrence Fillmer, J. and Self, D.R. (2007) 'A top management team's reactions to organizational transformation: The diagnostic benefits of five key change sentiments', *Journal of Change Management*, 7(3–4): 273–90.

Armenakis, A.A., Harris, S.G. and Feild, H.S. (1999) 'Making change permanent: A model for institutionalising change interventions', in W. Pasmore and R. Woodman (eds), *Research in Organizational Change and Development*. Stamford, CT: JAI Press, pp. 97–128.

Armenakis, A.A., Harris, S.G. and Mossholder, K.W. (1993) 'Creating readiness for organizational change', *Human Relations*, 46(6): 681–703.

Ashford, S.J. (1988) 'Individual strategies for coping with stress during organizational transitions', *Journal of Applied Behavioral Science*, 24(1): 19–36.

Ashforth, B. (1994) 'Petty tyranny in organizations', *Human Relations*, 47(7): 755–78.

Ashkenas, R. (2013) 'Change management needs to change', HBR Blog Nework, *Harvard Business Review*, April. Downloaded from http://blogs.hbr.org/2013/04/change-management-needs-to-change on 27 September 2013.

ASTD (2013) *The ASTD Competency Model*. Alexandria, VA: American Society for Training & Development.

Atkinson, J.M. (1984) *Our Masters' Voices: The Language and Body Language of Politics*. London: Methuen.

Atkinson, P. (2003) 'Shaping a vision – living the values', *Management Services*, 47(2): 8–11.

Auguste, G. and Gusatz, M. (2013) *Luxury Talent Management: Leading and Managing a Luxury Brand*. London: Palgrave.

Auster, E.R. and Ruebottom, T. (2013) 'Navigating the politics and emotions of change', *MIT Sloan Management Review*, 18 June.

Bacharach, S.B. and Lawler, E.J. (1998) 'Political alignments in organizations: Contextualization, mobilization, and coordination', *Power and Influence in Organizations*, 67–88.

Bacher, E. and Walker, S. (2013) 'The relationship between transformational leadership and followers' perceptions of fairness', *Journal of Business Ethics*, 116(3): 667–80.

Bachrach, P. and Baratz, M.S. (1970) *Power and Poverty: Theory and Practice*. New York, NY: Oxford University Press.

Balogun, J. (2006) 'Managing change: Steering a course between intended strategies and unanticipated outcomes', *Long Range Planning*, 39(1): 29–49.

Balogun, J. and Hope Hailey, V. (2004) *Exploring Strategic Change*, 2nd edn. Hemel Hempstead: Prentice Hall.

Balogun, J. and Hope Hailey, V. (2008) *Exploring Strategic Change*, 3rd edn. Hemel Hempstead: Prentice Hall.

Balogun, J. and Johnson, G. (2004) 'Organizational restructuring and middle management sense-making', *Academy of Management Journal*, 47: 523–49.

Balogun, J. and Johnson, G. (2005) 'From intended strategies to unintended outcomes: The impact of change recipient sensemaking', *Organization Studies*, 26(11): 1573–601.

Baltes, B.B., Zhdanova, L.S. and Parker, C.P. (2009) 'Psychological climate: A comparison of organizational and individual level referents', *Human Relations*, 62(5): 669–700.

Bamford, D. and Forrester, P. (2003) 'Managing planned and emergent change within an operations management environment', *International Journal of Operations and Production Management*, 23(5): 546–64.

Bandura, A. (1986) *Social Foundations of Thought and Action: A Social Cognitive Theory*. Englewood Cliffs, NJ: Prentice Hall.

Bargal, D. and Bar, H. (1992) 'A Lewinian approach to intergroup workshops for Arab-Palestinian and Jewish youth', *Journal of Social Issues*, 48(2): 139–54.

Barker, R.A. (2001) 'The nature of leadership', *Human Relations*, 54(4): 469–94.

Barnard, C. (1938) *The Functions of the Executive*. Cambridge, MA: Harvard University Press.

Barnett, W. and Carroll, G. (1995) 'Modeling internal organizational change', *Annual Review of Sociology*, 21: 217–36.

Barney, J. (2002) 'Strategic management: From informed conversation to academic discipline', *Academy of Management Executive*, 16(2): 53–8.

Barrales-Molina, V., Bustinza, Ó.F. and Gutiérrez-Gutiérrez, L.J. (2013) 'Explaining the causes and effects of dynamic capabilities generation: A multiple-indicator multiple-cause modelling approach', *British Journal of Management*, 24: 571–91.

Barrett, D.J. (2002) 'Change communication: Using strategic employee communication to facilitate major change', *Corporate Communications: An International Journal*, 7(4): 219–31.

Barrett, F.J. (1995) 'Creating appreciative learning cultures', *Organizational Dynamics*, 24(2): 36–49.

Barsh, B., Capozzi, M.M. and Davidson, J. (2008) 'Leadership and innovation', *The McKinsey Quarterly*, January.

Barsoux, J-L. and Narasimham, A. (2013) 'Insular Takeda adopts a global outlook', *Financial Times*, 28 October.

Bartol, K.M. and Martin, D.C. (1994) *Management*. New York, NY: McGraw-Hill.

Bartunek, J. (1984) 'Changing interpretive schemes and organizational restructuring: The example of a religious order', *Administrative Science Quarterly*, 22: 410–25.

Bartunek, J.M., Rousseau, D.M., Rudolph, J.W. and DePalma, J.A. (2006) 'On the receiving end: Sensemaking, emotion, and assessments of an organizational change initiated by others', *Journal of Applied Behavioral Science*, 42(2): 182–206.

Bass, B.M. (1985) *Leadership and Performance Beyond Expectations*. New York, NY: The Free Press.

Bass, B.M. (1988) 'The inspirational processes of leadership', *Journal of Management Development*, 7(5): 21–31.

Bass, B.M. (1990) *Handbook of Leadership*. New York, NY: Free Press.

Bass, B.M. (1992) 'Assessing the charismatic leader', in M. Syrett and C. Hogg (eds), *Frontiers of Leadership*, 414-418. Oxford: Blackwell. [pp ?]

Bass, B.M. and Avolio, B.J. (1994) 'Introduction', in B.M. Bass and B.J. Avolio (eds), *Improving Organizational Effectiveness through Transformational Leadership*. Thousand Oaks, CA: Sage.

*Bass, B.M. and Riggio, R.E. (2006) *Transformational Leadership*, 2nd edn. Mahwah, NJ: Erlbaum.

Bass, B.M. and Bass, R. (2008) *The Bass Handbook of Leadership: Theory, Research, & Managerial Applications*, 4th edn. New York: Free Press.

*Bate, P. (1990) 'Using culture concept in an organization development setting', *Journal of Applied Behavioural Science*, 26(1): 83–106.

Bateman, N. (2005) 'Sustainability: the elusive element of process improvement', *International Journal of Operations and Production Management*, 25(3): 261–276.

Battistelli, A., Montani, F., Odoardi, C., Vandenberghe, C. and Picci, P. (2013) 'Employees' concerns about change and commitment to change among Italian organizations: The moderating role of innovative work behavior', *International Journal of Human Resource Management*, June: 1–28.

Beckhard, R. (1969) *Organization Development: Strategies and Models*. Reading, MA: Addison-Wesley.

Beckhard, R. and Harris, R. (1987) *Organizational Transitions: Managing Complex Change*, 2nd edn. Reading, MA: Addison-Wesley.

Beckhard, R. and Pritchard, W. (1992) *Changing the Essence – The Art of Creating and Leading Fundamental Change in Organizations*. San Francisco, CA: Wiley.

Beer, M. (1980) *Organization Change and Development: A Systems View*. Santa Monica, CA: Goodyear.

Beer, M. (1988) 'Leading change', *Harvard Business School Teaching Note*.

Beer, M. (1990) *Leading Change*. Cambridge, MA: Harvard Business School Publishing.

Beer, M. (2000) 'Research that will break the code of change: The role of useful normal science and usable action science, a commentary on Van de Ven and Argyris', in M. Beer and N. Nohria (eds), *Breaking the Code of Change*. Boston, MA: Harvard Business Review Press, pp. 243–67.

Beer, M. (2001) 'How to develop an organization capable of sustained high performance: Embrace the drive for results-capability development paradox', *Organizational Dynamics*, 29(4): 233–47.

Beer, M. and Eisenstat, R.A. (1996) 'Developing an organization capable of implementing strategy and learning', *Human Relations*, 49(5): 597–619.

Beer, M. and Nohria, N. (2000) 'Cracking the code of change', *Harvard Business Review*, 78(3): 133–41.

Beer, M., Eisenstat, R.A. and Spector, B. (1990) *The Critical Path to Corporate Renewal*. Cambridge, MA: Harvard Business School Press.

Begley, T.M. and Czajka, J.M. (1993) 'Panel analysis of the moderating effects of commitment on job satisfaction, intention to quit and health following organizational change', *Journal of Applied Psychology*, 78(4): 552–6.

Behling, O. and McFillen, J.M. (1996) 'A syncretical model of charismatic/transformational leadership', *Group and Organizational Management*, 21(2): 163–85.

Bell, D. and Shelman, M. (2011) 'KFC's radical approach to China', *Harvard Business Review*, 89 (11): 137–42.

Benn, S., Dunphy, D. and Martin, A. (2009) 'Governance of environmental risk: New approaches to managing stakeholder involvement', *Journal of Environmental Management*, 90(4): 1567–75.

Bennebroek Gravenhorst, K.M., Werkman, R.A. and Boonstra, J.J. (2003) 'The change capacity of organisations: general assessment and five configurations', *Applied Psychology*, 52(1): 83–105.

Bennett, J.A. (2000) 'Mediator and moderator variables in nursing research: Conceptual and statistical differences', *Research in Nursing & Health*, 23: 415–20.

Bennis, W. (1998) 'The leadership challenge: Generating intellectual capital', Keynote Address, The Brathay Conference: 'The Leadership Odyssey', Windermere, Cumbria, 14–15 May.

Bennis, W. (2010) 'Leadership competencies', *Leadership Excellence*, February, 20.

Bennis, W. and Nanus, B. (1985) *Leaders: The Strategy for Taking Charge*. London: Harper & Row.

Berger, C.R. and Bradac, J.J. (1982) *Language and Social Knowledge: Uncertainty in Interpersonal Relations*. London: Hodder Arnold.

Berger, C. and Calabrese, J. (1982) 'Some explorations in initial interaction and beyond: Toward a developmental theory of interpersonal communication', *Human Communication Research*, 1(2): 99–112.

Berntsen, D. and Bohn, A. (2010) 'Remembering and forecasting: The relation between autobiographical memory and episodic future thinking', *Memory & Cognition*, 38: 265–78.

Berry, J.W. (2005) 'Acculturation: Living successfully in two cultures', *International Journal of Intercultural Relations*, 29(6): 697–712.

Bertels, S., Papanin, L. and Papania, D. (2011) 'Sustainability, employment and organisational outcomes'. Paper presented at the Academy of Management Annual Meeting – West Meets East: Enlightening, Balancing and Transcending.

Bevan, D. and Gitsham, M. (2009) 'Context, complexity and connectedness: Dimensions of globalization revealed', *Corporate Governance*, 9(4): 435–47.

Birkinshaw, J. and Duke, J. (2013) 'Employee led innovation', *Business Strategy Review*. http://bsr.london.edu/lbs-article/772/index.html (accessed June 2014).

Blake, R.R. and Mouton, J. (1964) *The Managerial Grid*. Houston, TX: Gulf.

Blanchard, H. (2012) 'How do you get leaders to change?', *Chief Learning Officer*, October, 26–9.

Boddy, D. (2002) *Managing Projects: Building and Leading the Team*. Harlow: FT/Prentice Hall.

Bonini, S., Göner, S. and Jones, A. (2010) 'How companies manage sustainability', *McKinsey Global Survey Results*. (www.mckinsey.com/insights/sustainability/how_companies_manage_sustainability_mckinsey_global_survey_results).

Bordia, P., DiFonzo, N. and Schulz, C.A. (2000) 'Source characteristics in denying rumors of organizational closure: Honesty is the best policy', *Journal of Applied Social Psychology*, 11: 2309–2321.

Bordia, P., Hobman, E., Jones, E., Gallois, C. and Callan, V.J. (2004a) 'Uncertainty during organizational change: Types, consequences, and management strategies', *Journal of Business and Psychology*, 18(4): 507–32.

Bordia, P., Hunt, E., Paulsen, N., Tourish, D. and DiFonzo, N. (2004b) 'Uncertainty during organizational change: Is it all about control?', *European Journal of Work and Organizational Psychology*, 13(3): 345–65.

Bordia, P., Restubog, S.L.D., Jimmieson, N.L. and Irmer, B.E. (2011) 'Haunted by the past – effects of poor change management history on employee attitudes and turnover', *Group & Organization Management*, 36(2): 191–222.

Boss, R., Dunford, B., Boss, A. and McConkie, M. (2010) 'Sustainable change in the public sector: The longitudinal benefits of organizational development', *Journal of Applied Behavioural Science*, 46(4): 436–72.

Bourgeois, L.J. (1984) 'Strategic management and determinism', *Academy of Management Review*, 9(4): 586–96.

Bovey, W.H. and Hede, A. (2001) 'Resistance to organisational change: The role of defence mechanisms', *Journal of Managerial Psychology*, 16(7): 534–48.

Bowers, D.G., Franklin, J.L. and Pecorella, P.A. (1975) 'Matching problems, precursors, and interventions in OD: A systemic approach', *Journal of Applied Behavioral Science*, 11(4): 391–409.

Bradford, D.L. and Burke, W.W. (eds) (2005) *Reinventing Organization Development*. San Francisco, CA: Pfeiffer.

Branzei, O., Vertinsky, I. and Zietsma, C. (2000) 'From green-blindness to the pursuit of eco-sustainability: An empirical investigation of leader cognitions and corporate environmental strategy choices', *Academy of Management Proceedings*, 2000(1): C1–C6.

Bridges, W. (1980) *Transitions*. Reading, MA: Addison-Wesley.

Bridges, W. (1992) *Managing Transitions: Making the Most of Change*. Reading, MA: Addison-Wesley.

Brinkley, I. (2006) *Defining the Knowledge Economy*. London: The Work Foundation.

Brinkley, I. (2010) *Knowledge Economy Strategy 2020*. London: The Work Foundation.

Briscoe, D. (2004) *International Human Resource Management*, Vol. 5. London: Routledge.

Brislin, R., Worthley, R. and MacNab, B. (2006) 'Cultural intelligence: Understanding behaviors that serve people's goals', *Group & Organization Management*, 31(1): 40–55.

Brooks, I. (2009) *Organisational Behaviour: Individuals, Groups and Organisation*. London: Pearson Education.

Brown, D.L., Guidry, R.P. and Patten, D.M. (2009) 'Sustainability reporting and perceptions of corporate reputation: An analysis using fortune', *Advances in Environmental Accounting and Management*, 4: 83–104.

Brown, J.S. and Duguid, P. (1991) 'Organizational learning and communities-of-practice: Toward a unified view of working, learning, and innovation', *Organization Science*, 2(1): 40–57.

Brown, M. and Cregan, C. (2008) 'Organizational change cynicism: The role of employee involvement', *Human Resource Management*, 47(4): 667–86.

Brown, M.E., Treviño, L.K. and Harrison, D.A. (2005) 'Ethical leadership: A social learning perspective for construct development and testing', *Organizational Behavior and Human Decision Processes*, 97(2): 117–34.

Brown, S. and Eisenhardt, K. (1997) 'The art of continuous change: Linking complexity theory and time-paced evolution in relentlessly shifting organizations', *Administrative Science Quarterly*, 42: 1–34.

Brown, T.E. (2004) 'Skunk works: A sign of failure, a sign of hope?', in T.E. Brown and J. Ulijn (eds), *Innovation, Entrepreneurship and Culture*, Cheltenham: Edward Elgar, pp. 130–46.

Brugha, R. and Varvasovszky, Z. (2000) 'Stakeholder analysis: A review', *Health Policy and Planning*, 15(3): 239–46.

Bruhn, J. (2004) 'Leaders who create change and those who manage it: How leaders limit success', *The Health Care Manager*, 23(2): 132–40.

Bryant, M. and Cox, J.W. (2003) 'The telling of violence: Organizational change and atrocity tales', *Journal of Change Management*, 16(5): 567–83.

Buchanan, D.A. (1999) 'The logic of political action: An experiment with the epistemology of the particular', *British Journal of Management*, 10(s1): 73–88.

Buchanan, D. (2003) 'Getting the story straight: Illusions and delusions in the organizational change process', *Tamara: Journal of Critical Postmodern Organizational Science*, 2(4): 7–21.

Buchanan, D. and Badham, R.J. (1999) 'Politics and organizational change: The lived experience', *Human Relations*, 52(5): 609–29.

Buchanan, D.A. and Badham, R.J. (2009) *Power, Politics and Organizational Change*, 2nd edn. London: Sage.

Buchanan, D. and Fitzgerald (2007) 'Improvement evaporation: why do successful changes decay', in D. Buchanan., L. Fitzgerald and D. Ketley (eds) *The Sustainability and Spread of Organizational Changes: Modernizing healthcare*. London: Routledge, p22–40

Buchanan, D.A. and Huczynski, A.A. (2010) *Organizational Behaviour*, 7th edn. Harlow: Pearson.

Buchanan, D. and Storey, J. (1997) 'Role-taking and role-switching in organizational change: The four pluralities', *Innovation, Organizational Change and Technology*, 127–45.

Buchanan, D., Fitzgerald, L., Ketley, D., Gollop, R., Jones, J., Lamont, S., Neath, A. and Whitby, E. (2005) 'No going back: A review of the literature on sustaining organizational change', *International Journal of Management Reviews*, 7(3): 189–205.

Bunker, B.B. and Alban, B.T. (1992) 'Large group method: Development and trends', in B.B. Jones and M. Brazzel (eds), *The NTL Handbook of Organization Development and Change*. San Francisco, CA: Pfeiffer, pp. 287–301.

Buono, A.F. and Bowditch, J.L. (1989) *The Human Side of Mergers and Acquisitions*. San Francisco, CA: Beard Books.

Burke, W.W. (1994) *Organization Development: A Process of Learning and Changing*. Reading, MA: Addison-Wesley.

Burke, W.W. (2002) *Organization Change: Theory and Practice*, Thousand Oaks, CA: Sage.

Burke, W.W. (2008) *Organization Change: Theory and Practice*, 2nd edn. Thousand Oaks, CA: Sage.

Burke, W.W. and Litwin, G. (1992) 'A causal model of organizational performance and change', *Journal of Management*, 18(3): 523–45.

Burnes, B. (1996) 'No such thing as ... a "one best way" to manage organizational change', *Management Decision*, 34/10: 11–18.

Burnes, B. (2003) Series Editor's Preface, to Patrick Dawson, *Reshaping Change: A Processual Perspective*. Abingdon: Routledge, pp. xi–xii.

Burnes, B. (2005) 'Complexity theories and organizational change', *International Journal of Management Reviews*, 7(2): 73–90.

Burnes, B. (2009a) *Managing Change*, 5th edn. Harlow: FT/Prentice Hall.

Burnes, B. (2009b) 'Reflections: Ethics and organizational change–time for a return to Lewinian values', *Journal of Change Management*, 9(4): 359–81.

Burnes, B. (2013) 'Looking back to forward', in R.T. By and B. Burnes (eds), *Organizational Change, Leadership and Ethics*. London: Routledge, pp. 243–58.

Burnes, B. and Jackson, P. (2011) 'Success and failure in organizational change: An exploration of the role of values', *Journal of Change Management*, 11(2): 133–62.

Burns, L.R. and Wholey, D.R. (1993) 'Adoption and abandonment of matrix management programs: Effects of organizational characteristics and interorganizational networks', *Academy of Management Journal*, 36(1): 106–38.

Burns, T. and Stalker, G.M. (1961) *The Management of Innovation*. London: Tavistock.

Bushe, G.R. and Marshak, R.J. (2008) 'The post modern turn in OD to meaning making: From diagnosis to meaning making', *OD Practitioner*, 40(4): 10–12.

By, R.T. (2005) 'Organisational change management: A critical review', *Journal of Change Management*, 5(4): 369–80.

By, R.T. and Burnes, B. (eds) (2013) *Organizational Change, Leadership and Ethics*. London: Routledge.

By, R.T., Burnes, B. and Oswick, C. (2011) 'Change management: The road ahead', *Journal of Change Management*, 11(1): 1–6.

Byham, W.C. (1988) *Zapp! The Lightning of Empowerment*. Pittsburgh, PA: Development Dimensions International Press.

Caldwell, R. (2003) 'Change leaders and change managers: Different or complementary?', *Leadership & Organization Development Journal*, 24(5): 285–93.

Cameron, K.S. (1994) 'Strategies for successful organizational downsizing', *Human Resource Management*, 33(2): 189–211.

Cammann, C., Fichman, M., Jenkins, D. and Klesh, J. (1983) 'Assessing the attitudes and perceptions of organizational members', in S. Seashore, E. Lawler, P. Mirvis and C. Cammann (eds), *Assessing Organizational Change: A Guide to Methods, Measures, and Practices*. New York, NY: John Wiley & Sons, pp. 71–138.

Carbonell-López, J.I. (2013) 'Leading change through passion, vision, and humility', *Leadership Advance Online*, XXIV. www.regent.edu/acad/global/publications/lao/issue_24/2lao-carbonell-lopez.pdf (accessed June 2014).

Carnall, C. (2007) *Managing Change in Organizations*, 5th edn. Harlow: Pearson Education.

Cartwright, S. and Cooper, C.L. (1993) 'The role of culture compatibility in successful organization', *Academy of Management Executive*, 7(2): 57–69.

Cartwright, S. and Cooper, C.L. (1995) 'Organizational marriage: Hard versus soft issues?', *Personnel Review*, 24(3): 32–42.

Cawsey, T., Deszca, G. and Ingols, C. (2007) *Toolkit for Organizational Change*. London: Sage.

CBI and IPA (2011) *Transformation through Employee Engagement: Meeting the Public Services Challenge*. London: Confederation of British Industry.

CCL (Centre for Creative Leadership) (2012) 'Let's talk some more about change', *CCL's Leading Effectively Blog*, 19 November.

CCL (Centre for Creative Leadership) (2012) *Leading Effectively e-Newsletter*, December. Greensboro, NC: Center for Creative Leadership.

CCL (Centre for Creative Leadership) (2013) *Adapting to Organizational Change*. Greensboro, NC: Center for Creative Leadership.

Chambers, L., Drysdale, J. and Hughes, J. (2010) 'The future of leadership: A practitioner view', *European Management Journal*, 28(4): 260–8.

Champy, J.A. (1997) 'Preparing for organizational change', in Frances Hesselbein, Marshall Goldsmith and Richard Beckhard (eds), *The Organization of the Future*. San Francisco, CA: Jossey-Bass, pp. 9–24.

Chanlat, J.F. (1997) 'Conflict and politics', *Handbook of Organizational Behaviour*, 472–80.

Chatman, J.A. (1991) 'Matching people and organizations: Selection and socialization in public accounting firms', *Administrative Science Quarterly*, 36: 459–84.

Chen, G. (2005) 'An organizational learning model based on western and Chinese management thoughts and practices', *Management Decision*, 43(4): 479–500.

Cherim, S. (2002) 'Influencing organizational identification during major change: A communication based perspective', *Human Relations*, 55: 1117–37.

Chilkoti, A. (2013) 'India plc goes shopping', *Financial Times*, 25 June, p. 19.

Choi, M. (2011) 'Employees' attitudes toward organizational change: A literature review', *Human Resource Management*, 50(4): 479–500.

Chou, L-F., Wang, A-C., Wang, T-Y., Huang, M-P. and Cheng, B-S. (2008) 'Shared work values and team member effectiveness: The mediation of trustfulness and trustworthiness', *Human Relations*, 61(12): 1713–42.

Chynoweth, C. (2010a) 'Win their hearts if you want success', *The Sunday Times*, Appointments, 17 October, p. 4.

Chynoweth, C. (2010b) 'Win over staff and profit will follow', *The Sunday Times*, Appointments, 24 October, p. 4.

Chynoweth, C. (2012) 'Middle way to win power', *The Sunday Times*, Appointments, 22 July, p. 2.

Cinite, I., Duxbury, L. and Higgins, C. (2009) 'Measurement of perceived organizational readiness for change in the public sector', *British Journal of Management*, 265–77.

CIPD (2009a) *Shared Purpose and Sustainable Organisation Performance*, Research Insight. London: Chartered Institute of Personnel and Development.

CIPD (2009b) *Employee Engagement*, Factsheet. London: Chartered Institute of Personnel and Development.

CIPD (2010) *Quarterly Survey Report: Employee Outlook. Emerging from the Downturn?* London: Chartered Institute of Personnel and Development.

CIPD (2011) *Sustainable Organisation Performance: What Really Makes the Difference?* Final Report. London: Chartered Institute of Personnel and Development.

CIPD (2012) 'Change programmes undermined by skills and leadership errors', *People Management*, Chartered Institute of Personnel and Development, 12 April.

Clampitt, P., DeKoch, R. and Cashman, T. (2000) 'A strategy for communicating about uncertainty', *Academy of Management Executive*, 14(4): 41–57.

Clarkson, M.B. (1995) 'A stakeholder framework for analysing and evaluating corporate social performance', *Academy of Management Review*, 4(4): 497–505.

Clases, C., Bachmann, R. and Wehner, T. (2003) 'Studying trust in virtual organizations', *International Studies of Management and Organization*, 33(3): 7–27.

Claver, E., Llopis, J., Gonzalez, M.R. and Gascó, J.L. (2001) 'The performance of information systems through organizational culture', *Information Technology and People*, 14(3): 247–60.

Clegg, C. and Walsh, S. (2004) 'Change management: Time for a change!', *European Journal of Work and Organizational Psychology*, 13(2): 217–39.

Clegg, S.R. and Palmer, G. (1996) *The Politics of Management Knowledge*. London: Sage.

Clegg, S.R., Courpasson, D. and Phillips, N. (2006) *Power and Organisations*. London: Sage.

Coch, L. and French, J.R.P. (1948) 'Overcoming resistance to change', *Human Relations*, 1(4): 512–32.

Coetsee, L. (1999) 'From resistance to commitment', *Public Administration Quarterly*, 23: 204–222.

Cohen, A.R. (2003) 'Transformational change at Babson College', *Academy of Management Learning and Education*, 2(2): 155–80.

Cohen, S. and Wills, T.A. (1985) 'Stress, social support, and the buffering hypothesis', *Psychological Bulletin*, 98(2): 310.

Cole, S. (2013) 'Imagining our future … and changing it', *The Psychologist*, 26(11): 840–1.

Collins, P.M. and Hopson, R.K. (2007) 'Building leadership development, social justice, and social change in evaluation through a pipeline programme', in K.M. Hannum, J.W. Martineau and C. Reinelt (eds), *The Handbook of Leadership Development Evaluation*. San Francisco, CA: Wiley, pp. 173–98.

Colquitt, J.A., Conlon, D.E., Wesson, M.J., Porter, C.O. and Ng, K.Y. (2001) 'Justice at the millennium: A meta-analytic review of 25 years of organizational justice research', *Journal of Applied Psychology*, 86(3): 425.

Colvin, J.G. and Slevin, D.P. (1988) 'The influence of organizational structure', *Journal of Management Studies*, 25: 217–34.

Conger, J. (1999) 'The new age of persuasion', *Leader to Leader*, Spring, pp. 37–44.

Conway, E. and Monks, K. (2011) 'Change from below: The role of middle managers in mediating paradoxical change', *Human Resource Management Journal*, 21(2): 190–203.

Covey, S.R. (1989) *The Seven Habits of Highly Effective People*. New York, NY: Fireside.

Covey, S.R. (1992) *Principle-Centered Leadership*. London: Simon & Schuster.

Covin, T.J. and Kilmann, R.H. (1990) 'Participant perceptions of positive and negative influences on large-scale change', *Group and Organization Management*, 15(2): 233–48.

Crampton, S.M., Hodge, J.W. and Mishra, J. (1998) 'The informal communication network: Factors influencing grapevine activity', *Public Personnel Management*, 1(22): 569.

Crane, A. and Matten, D. (2007) *Business Ethics: Managing Corporate Citizenship and Sustainability in the Age of Globalization*. Oxford: Oxford University Press.

Creelman, D. (2003) 'Interview: Rob Lebow on accountability, freedom and responsibility', www.HR.com, 17 November.

Cripe, E.J. (1993) 'How to get top-notch change agents', *Training and Development*, 47(12): 52–8.

Cross, R. and Prusak, L. (2002) 'The people who make organizations go – or stop', *Harvard Business Review*, 80(6): 104–12.

Cummings, T.G. and Feyerherm, A.E. (1995) *Interventions in large systems*. San Francisco: Wiley.

Cummings, T. and Worley, C. (2009) *Organization Development and Change*, 9th edn. Mason, OH: South-Western Cengage Learning.

Daft, R.L. (1995) *Organization Theory and Design*. Minneapolis, MN: West Publishing.

Dahl, R.A. (1957) 'The concept of power', *Behavioral Science*, 2(3): 201–15.

Daily, B.F. and Huang, S.C. (2001) 'Achieving sustainability through attention to human resource factors in environmental management', *International Journal of Operations and Production Management*, 21(12): 1539–52.

Dalberg-Acton, J.E.E. (1887), 'Letter to Bishop Mandell Creighton', April 5, 1887, published in *Historical Essays and Studies*, J.N. Figgis and R.V. Laurence (eds), (1907). London: Macmillan.

Dale, B.G. (1996) 'Sustaining a process of continuous improvement: Definition and key factors', *The TQM Magazine*, 8(2): 49–51.

Damodaran, A. (2001) *Corporate Finance: Theory and Practice*, 2nd edn. Chichester: Wiley International.

David, S. and Congleton, C. (2013) 'Emotional agility', *Harvard Business Review*, November. Downloaded from http://hbr.org/2013/11/emotional-agility/ar/pr on 22 October 2013.

Dawson, P. (1994) *Organizational Change: A Processual Approach*. London: Paul Chapman.

Dawson, P. (2003a) *Understanding Organizational Change: The Contemporary Experience of People at Work*. London: Sage.

Dawson, P. (2003b) *Reshaping Change: A Processual Perspective*. Abingdon: Routledge.

Dawson, P. (2005) 'Changing manufacturing practices: An appraisal of the processual approach', *Human Factors and Ergonomics in Manufacturing & Service Industries*, 15(4): 385–402.

Dawson, P. and McLean, P. (2013) 'Miners' tales: Stories and the storytelling process for understanding the collective sensemaking of employees during contested change', *Group and Organization Management*, 38(2): 198–229.

deKlerk, M. (2007) 'Healing emotional trauma in organizations: An O.D. framework and case study', *Organizational Development Journal*, 25(2): 49–56.

De Smet, A., Lavoie, J. and Hioe, E.S. (2012) 'Developing better change leaders', *McKinsey Quarterly*, April.

De Vries, D.K. (1993) *Leaders, Fools and Imposters. Essays on the Psychology of Leadership*. San Francisco, CA: Jossey-Bass.

De Wit, B. and Meyer, R. (2004) *Strategy: Process, Content and Context*. London: Thomson Learning.

Dea, W. (2013) 'Change management fails for three reasons', *Huffington Post*, New York, NY, 18 July.

Dean, J.W., Brandes, P. and Dharwadkar, R. (1998) 'Organizational cynicism', *Academy of Management Review*, 23(2): 341–52.

DeLuca, J.R. (1984) 'Managing the socio-political context in planned change efforts', in A. Kakabadse and C. Parker (eds), *Power, Politics and Organizations: A Behavioiral Science View*. New York, NY: Wiley, pp. 127–47.

Den Hartog, D.N. and De Hoogh, A.H. (2009) 'Empowering behaviour and leader fairness and integrity: Studying perceptions of ethical leader behaviour from a levels-of-analysis perspective', *European Journal of Work and Organizational Psychology*, 18(2): 199–230.

Denis, J.L., Lamothe, L. and Langley, A. (2001) 'The dynamics of collective leadership and strategic change in pluralistic organizations', *Academy of Management Journal*, 809–37.

Denning, S. (2008) 'Stones in the workplace', *HR Magazine*, September: 130–131.

Denning, S. (2010) *The Leader's Guide to Radical Management: Reinventing the Workplace for the 21st Century*. London: Wiley.

Dervitsiotis, K.N. (2002) 'The importance of conversations-for-action for effective strategic management', *Total Quality Management*, 13(8): 1087–98.

Desanctis, G. and Monge, P. (1998) 'Communication processes for virtual organizations', *Journal of Computer-Mediated Communication*, 3(4): 693–793.

Development, Concepts and Doctrine Centre (DCDC) (2010) *Global Strategic Trends*, 4th edn. London: Ministry of Defence.

DeWitt, R.L. (1998) 'Firm, industry, and strategy influences on choice of downsizing approach', *Strategic Management Journal*, 19(1): 59–79.

Diefenbach, T. (2013) 'Incompetent or immoral leadership?: Why many managers and change leaders get it wrong', in R.T. By and B. Burnes (eds), *Organizational Change, Leadership and Ethics*. London: Routledge, pp. 149–70.

Dike, D. (2012) 'Why change? Why not?', *Management Issues*, 26 March. Downloaded from www.management-issues.com/2012/3/26/opinion/why-change-why-not.asp on 4 April 2012.

Dirks, K.T. and Ferrin, D.L. (2002) 'Trust in leadership: Meta-analytic findings and implications for research and practice', *Journal of Applied Psychology*, 87(4): 611–28.

Doppelt, R. (2003) 'The seven sustainability blunders', *The Systems Thinker*, 14(5): 1–7.

Doyle, M., Claydon, T. and Buchanan, D. (2000) 'Mixed results, lousy process: The management experience of organizational change', *British Journal of Management*, 11(s1): S59–S80.

Drakulich, A. (2012) 'Change management: How to deal', *PharmTech.com*, 14 August.

Drucker, P. (1980) *Managing in Turbulent Times*. New York, NY: Harper Paperbacks.

Drucker, P.F. (1999a) *Management Challenges for the 21st Century*. New York, NY: HarperCollins.

Drucker, P.F. (1999b) 'Managing oneself', *Harvard Business Review*, March–April, 65–74.

Dryburgh, A. (2013) 'Change is hard, so the saying goes. But is it?', *Management Today*, April, 16. www.managementtoday.co.uk/news/1175126/change-hard-so-saying-goes-it/ (accessed June 2014).

DuBrin, A.J. (2012) *Principles of Leadership*, 7th edn. London: Cengage.

[C11Q11]Duck, J.D. (2001) *The Change Monster: The Human Forces That Fuel or Foil Corporate Transformation and Change*. New York, NY: Crown Business.

Duke Corporate Education (2011) *Learning and Development in 2011: A Focus on the Future*. Accessed at dukece.com/papers-reports/documents/FocusFuture.pdf.

Dunphy, D. and Benn, S. (2013) 'Leadership for sustainable futures', in R.T. By and B. Burnes (eds), *Organizational Change, Leadership and Ethics*. London: Routledge, pp. 195–215.

Dunphy, D., Griffiths, A. and Benn, S. (2007) *Organizational Change for Corporate Sustainability: A guide for leaders and change agents of the future* (2nd edn). London: Routledge.

Dunphy, D. and Stace, D. (1993) 'The strategic management of corporate change', *Human Relations*, 46(8): 905–18.

Dutton, J.E., Ashford, S.J., O'Neill, R.M. and Lawrence, K.A. (2001) 'Moves that matter: Issue selling and organizational change', *Academy of Management Journal*, 44: 716–36.

Dyke, G. (2004) *Inside Story*. London: HarperCollins.

Easterby-Smith, M., Crossan, M. and Nicolini, D. (2000) 'Organizational learning: Debates past, present and future', *Journal of Management Studies*, 37(6): 783–96.

Eden, C. (1993) 'Strategy development and implementation: Cognitive mapping for group support', in J. Hendry, G. Johnson and J. Newton (eds), *Strategic Thinking: Leadership and the Management of Change*. Chichester: John Wiley & Sons, pp. 115–122.

Eden, C. and Huxham, C. (1996) 'Action research for management research', *British Journal of Management*, 7(1): 75–86.

Edmondson, A.C. (2011) 'Strategies of learning from failure', *Harvard Business Review*, 89(4): 48.

Edwards, G. and Turnbull, S. (2013) 'A cultural approach to evaluating leadership development', *Advances in Developing Human Resources*, 15(1): 46–60.

Edwards, R. and Usher, R. (2001) 'Lifelong learning: A postmodern condition of education?', *Adult Education Quarterly*, 51(4): 273–87.

Egan, G. (1994) *Working the Shadow Side: A Guide to Positive Behind-the-Scenes Management*. San Francisco, CA: Jossey-Bass.

Elias, S.M. (2009) 'Employees' commitment in times of change: Assessing the importance of attitudes toward organizational change', *Journal of Management*, 35(1): 37–55.

Ellis, P. (2013) 'Corporate ethics education yields rewards', *National Defense Magazine*, USA, 8 August.

Elrod, P.D., II and Tippett, D.D. (2002) 'The death valley of change', *Journal of Organizational Change Management*, 15: 273–92.

Epstein, M.J., Buhovac, A.R. and Yuthas, K. (2010) 'Implementing sustainability: The role of leadership and organizational culture', *Strategic Finance*, 91(10): 41–7.

Evans, J.D. (2012) 'Facilitating organizational change with a network of change champions', *Training & Development*, ASTD, 8 June.

Fahy, J. (2000) 'The resource-based view of the firm: Some stumbling-blocks on the road to understanding sustainable competitive advantage', *Journal of European Industrial Training*, 24(2–4): 94–104.

Fairhurst, G. and Sarr, R. (1996) *The Art of Framing*. San Francisco, CA: Jossey-Bass.

Farjoun, M. (2002) 'Towards an organic perspective on strategy', *Strategic Management Journal*, 23: 561–94.

Farjoun, M. (2010) 'Beyond dualism: Stability and change as a duality', *Academy of Management Review*, 35(2): 202–225.

Fedor, D.B., Caldwell, S. and Herold, D.M. (2006) 'The effects of organizational changes on employee commitment: A multilevel investigation', *Personnel Psychology*, 59(1): 1–29.

Feldman, M.L. and Spratt, M.F. (1999) *Five Frogs on the Log: A CEO's Field Guide to Accelerating the Transition in Mergers, Acquisitions and Gut Wrenching Change*. New York, NY: HarperBusiness.

Ferris, G.R. and Kacmar, K.M. (1992) 'Perceptions of organizational politics', *Journal of Management*, 18(1): 93–116.

Ferris, G.R. and King, T.R. (1991) 'Politics in human resources decisions: A walk on the dark side', *Organizational Dynamics*, 20(2): 59–71.

Ferris, G.R., Hochwarter, W.A., Douglas, C., Blass, R., Kolodinsky, R.W. and Treadway, D.C. (2002) 'Social influence processes in human resources systems', in G.R. Ferris and J.J. Martocchio (eds), *Research in Personnel and Human Resources Management*, Vol. 21. Oxford: JAI Press/Elsevier Science, pp. 65–127.

Ferris, G.L., Perrewé, P.L., Anthony, W.P. and Gilmore, D.C. (2003) 'Political skill at work', in L.W. Porter (ed.), *Organizational Influence Processes*. New York, NY: ME Sharpe, pp. 395–406.

Field, K.F. (2001) 'Working outside the box', *Design News*. www.designnews.com, 24 February.

Finkelstein, S., Harvey, C. and Lawton, T. (2007) *Breakout Strategy: Meeting the Challenge of Double-Digit Growth*. New York, NY: McGraw-Hill.

Fiol, C.M. and O'Connor, E.J. (2002) 'Future planning + present mindfulness = strategic foresight'. Paper presented at the International Conference on 'Probing the Future: Developing Organizational Foresight in the Knowledge Economy', University of Strathclyde Graduate School of Business, Glasgow, 11–13 July.

Fishbein, M. and Ajzen, I. (1975) *Belief, Attitude, Intention and Behavior: An Introduction to Theory and Research*. Reading, MA: Addison-Wesley.

Flamholtz, E. and Randle, R. (2011) *Corporate Culture: The Ultimate Strategic Asset*. Stanford, CA: Stanford Business Books.

Flanagan, R. (2000) 'Leadership during cultural and institutional change'. Paper presented at the National Leadership Conference, MCI-METO, The Royal Military Academy, Sandhurst, 24 May.

Fleisher, C.S. and Bensoussan, B.E. (2003) *Strategic and Competitive Analysis: Methods and Techniques for Analysing Business Competition*. Upper Saddle River, NJ: Prentice Hall.

Folger, R. and Skarlicki, D.P. (1999) 'Unfairness and resistance to change: Hardship as mistreatment', *Journal of Organizational Change Management*, 12: 35–50.

Ford, J.D., Ford, L.W. and D'Amelio, A. (2008) 'Resistance to change: The rest of the story', *Academy of Management Review*, 33: 362–77.

Fox, D., Ellison, R. and Keith, K. (1988) 'Human resource management: An index and its relationship to readiness for change', *Public Personnel Management*, 17(3): 297–302.

Fox, S. and Amichai-Hamburger, Y. (2001) 'The power of emotional appeals in promoting organizational change programs', *Academy of Management Executive*, 15: 84–93.

Frahm, J. and Brown, K. (2007) 'First steps: Linking change communication to change receptivity', *Journal of Organizational Change Management*, 20(3): 370–87.

Frame, J.D. (2003) *Managing Risk in Organizations: A Guide for Managers*, San Francisco, CA: Jossey-Bass.

Franco, M. and Almeida, J. (2011) 'Organisational learning and leadership styles in healthcare organisations: An exploratory case study', *Leadership and Organization Development Journal*, 32(8): 782–806.

Freeman, R.E. (1984) *Strategic Management: A Stakeholder Approach*. Boston, MA: HarperCollins.

French, W.L. and Bell, C.H. (1973) *Organization Development*. Englewood Cliffs, NJ: Prentice Hall.

French, W.L. and Bell, C.H. (1999) *Organization Development: Behaviour Science Interventions for Organization Improvement*, 6th edn. Upper Saddle River, NJ: Prentice Hall.

French Jr., J.R.P., Raven, B. (1959) 'Bases of social power', in D. Cartwright (ed.), *Studies in Social Power*. Oxford: University of Michigan Press, pp. 150–67.

Fried, Y., Tiegs, R., Naughton, T. and Ashforth, B. (1996) 'Managers' reactions to corporate acquisition: A test of an integrative model', *Journal of Organizational Behavior*, 17: 401–27.

Frost, P.J. and Egri, C.P. (1991) 'The political process of innovation', *Research in Organizational Behavior*, 13(229): 95.

Fugate, M., Kinicki, A.J. and Prussia, G.E. (2008) 'Employee coping with organizational change: An examination of alternative theoretical perspectives and models', *Personnel Psychology*, 61: 1–36.

Furnham, A. (2010) 'You don't need to be married to your job – just engaged', *The Sunday Times*, Appointments, 16 May, p. 2.

Furrer, O., Thomas, H. and Goussevskaia, A. (2008) 'The structure and evolution of the strategic management field: A content analysis of 26 years of strategic management research', *International Journal of Management Reviews*, 10(1): 1–23.

Gagnon, M.A., Jansen, K.J. and Michael, J. H. (2008) 'Employee alignment with strategic change: A study of strategy-supportive behavior among blue-collar employees', *Journal of Managerial Issues*, 425–443.

Galbraith, M.W. and Zelemark, B.S. (1991) 'Adult learning methods and techniques', in M.W. Galbraith (ed.), *Facilitating Adult Learning*. Malabar, FL: Krieger Publishing, pp. 105–110.

Gallagher, K., Rose, E., McClelland, B., Reynolds, J . and Tombs, S. (1997) *People in Organisations: An Active Learning Approach*. Oxford: Blackwell Business.

Galpin, T.J. and Herndon, M. (2000) *The Complete Guide to Mergers and Acquisitions: Process Tools to Support M&A Integration at Every Level*. San Francisco, CA: Jossey-Bass.

Galpin, T.J. and Whittington, J.L. (2012) 'Sustainable leadership: From strategy to results', *Journal of Business Strategy*, 33(4): 40–8.

Gardini, M., Giuliani, G. and Marricchi, M. (2011) 'Finding the right place to start change', *McKinsey Quarterly*, November.

Garten, J.E. (2001) *The Mind of the CEO*. New York, NY: Basic Books.

Garvin, D.A. (1993) 'Building a learning organization', *Harvard Business Review*, 71(4): 78–91.

Garvin, D.A. (2000) *Learning in Action: A Guide to Putting the Learning Organization to Work*. Cambridge, MA: Harvard Business Press.

Gaughan, P.A. (2002) *Mergers, Acquisitions, and Corporate Restructurings*, 3rd edn. New York, NY: John Wiley & Sons.

Gentry, W.A., Eckert, R.H., Munusamy, V.P., Stawiski, S.A. and Martin, J.L. (2013) 'The needs of participants in leadership development programmes: A qualitative and quantitative cross-country investigation', *Journal of Leadership & Organizational Studies*, pre-published April 2, 2013, DOI: 10.1177/1548051813483832.

Georgiades, N. and Macdonnell, R. (1998) *Leadership for Competitive Advantage*. Chichester: John Wiley & Sons.

Gersick, C. (1991) 'Revolutionary change theories: A multilevel exploration of the punctuated equilibrium paradigm', *Academy of Management Review*, 16: 10–36.

Ghosh, D. (1997) 'De-escalation strategies: Some experimental evidence', *Behavioral Research in Accounting*, 9: 88–112.

Ghoshal, S. and Bartlett, C.A. (1977) *The Individualized Corporation*. London: Heinemann.

Ghosn, C. (2002) 'Nissan motor company', *Fast Company*, June: 80.

Giangreco, A. and Peccei, R. (2005) 'The nature and antecedents of middle managers' resistance to change: Evidence from an Italian context', *International Journal of Human Resources Management*, 16(10): 1812–29.

Giddens, A. (1981) *A Contemporary Critique of Historical Materialism*. London: Macmillan.

Gilbert, C., Eyring, M. and Foster, R. (2012) 'Two routes to resilience', *Harvard Business Review*, 90(12): 65–73.

Gill, R. (2003) 'Change management – or change leadership?', *Journal of Change Management*, 3(4): 307–18.

Gill, R. (2006) *Theory and Practice of Leadership*. London: Sage.

Gill, R. (2008) 'Sustaining creativity and innovation: The role of leadership', *LT Focus*, The Leadership Trust, Summer.

Gill, R. (2011) *Theory and Practice of Leadership*, 2nd edn. London: Sage.

Gill, R. (2012) 'Agree to agree', Letter to The Editor, *The Times*, London, 17 July, p. 21.

Gioia, D.A., Nag, R. and Corley, K.G. (2012) 'Visionary ambiguity and strategic change: The virtue of vagueness in launching major organizational change', *Journal of Management Inquiry*, 21(4): 364–75.

Gladwell, M. (2002) *The Tipping Point: How Little Things Can Make a Big Difference*. Boston, MA: Little, Brown.

Gladwin, T.N., Kennelly, J.J. and Krause, T.S. (1995) 'Shifting paradigms for sustainable development: Implications for management theory and research', *Academy of Management Review*, 20(4): 874–907.

Glover, L. (2001) 'Communication and consultation in a greenfield site company', *Personnel Review*, 30(3): 297–316.

Goh, S., Cousins, J. and Elliott, C. (2006) 'Organizational learning capacity, evaluative inquiry and readiness for change in schools: Views and perceptions of educators', *Journal of Educational Change*, 7: 286–318.

Gold, J., Thorpe, R. and Mumford, A. (2010) *Leadership and Management Development*, 5th edn. London: CIPD.

Goldsmith, J. (2010) 'British Gas in dispute over employee disengagement', newsletters @bnet.online.com, http://blogs.bnet.co.uk/sterling-performance/2010/03/11/british-gas-in-dispute-over-employee-disengagement.

Goldsmith, M. (2008) 'Mission control: Align purpose and goals', *Leadership Excellence*, June: 13–14.

Gómez, C. and Rosen, B. (2001) 'The leader–member exchange as a link between managerial trust and employee empowerment', *Group and Organization Management*, 26(1): 53–69.

Goodstein, L.D. (2010) 'Strategic planning: A leadership imperative', Chapter 4 in *The ASTD Leadership Handbook* (ed. Elaine Biech). Alexandria, VA: ASTD Press and San Francisco, CA: Berrett-Koehler, pp. 43–54.

Goold, M. and Campbell, A. (2002) 'Structured networks: Towards the well-designed matrix', *Long Range Planning*, 36(5): 427–39.

Gordon, G.G. and DiTomaso, N. (1992) 'Predicting corporate performance from organizational culture', *Journal of Management Studies*, 29: 783–98.

Gould, S.J. (1978) *Ever Since Darwin: Reflections in Natural History*. London: Burnett Books.

Government of Nigeria (2008) *Concept for Nigeria's Vision 2020*. The Presidency, Government of Nigeria, NV2020/NSC (2008) 02.

Grady, V. (2013) 'Change management vs. change leadership: What's the difference?', *Government Executive*, April 23.

Graetz, F. (2000) 'Strategic change leadership', *Management Decision*, 38(8): 550–62.

Gray, J. (2010) *How Leaders Speak*. Toronto: Dundurn Press.

Greasly, K., Watson, P. and Patel, S. (2009) 'The impact of organisational change on public sector employees implementing the UK government's back to work programme', *Employee Relations*, 31(4): 382–97.

Greenleaf, R. (1977), *Servant Leadership*. New York, NY: Paulist Press.

Greenwood, R. and Hinnings, C.R. (1996) 'Understanding radical organizational change: Bringing together the old and the new institutionalism', *Academy of Management Review*, 21: 1022–54.

Greer, L.L., Caruso, H.M. and Jehn, K.A. (2011) 'The bigger they are, the harder they fall: Linking team power, team conflict, and performance', *Organizational Behavior and Human Decision Processes*, 116(1): 116–28.

Greiner, L.E. (1972) 'Evolution and revolution as organizations grow', *Harvard Business Review*, 50(4): 37–46.

Greiner, L.E. and Schein, V.E. (1989) *Power and Organization Development: Mobolizing Power to Implement Change*. Reading, MA: Addison-Wesley.

Grey, C. (2003) 'The fetish of change', *Tamara, Journal of Critical Postmodern Organizational Science*, 2(2): 1–19.

Grieves, J. (2010) *Organizational Change: Themes and Issues*. Oxford: Oxford University Press.

Gronn, P. (2002) 'Distributed leadership', in *Second International Handbook of Educational Leadership and Administration*. Amsterdam: Springer, pp. 653–96.

Gupta, R. and Wendler, J. (2005) 'Leading change: An interview with the CEO of Proctor and Gamble', *McKinsey Quarterly*, July.

Gwynne, P. (1997) 'Skunk works, 1990s style', *Research-Technology Management*, 40(4): 18–23.

Gwyther, M. (2012) 'The rising stars of sustainability: Winners of the MT sky futures leaders awards 2012', *Management Today*, October. Downloaded from www.managementtoday.co.uk/news/1155930/the-rising-stars-sustainability-winners-mt-sky-futures-leaders-awards-2012/ on 4 January 2014.

Hameed, I., Roques, O. and Arain, G.A. (2013) 'Nonlinear moderating effect of tenure on organizational identifications (OID) and the subsequent role of OID in fostering readiness for change', *Group and Organization Management*, 38(1): 101–27.

Hamel, G. (2007) *The Future of Management*. Cambridge, MA: Harvard Business School Press.

Hammer, M. and Champy, J. (1993) *Re-engineering the Corporation*. London: Nicolas Brealey.

Hammond, M. and Collins, R. (1991) *Self-Directed Learning: Critical Practice*. London: Kogan Page.

Hammond, S.A. (1998) *Thin Book of Appreciative Inquiry*, 2nd edn. Bend, OR: Thin Book Publishing Company.

Handy, C. (1989) *Age of Unreason*. London: Random House.

Hannan, M.T. and Freeman, J. (1988) *Organizational Ecology*. Cambridge, MA: Harvard University Press.

Hansen, M.T. (2012) 'Ten ways to get people to change', HBR Blog Network, *Harvard Business Review*, 21 September. Downloaded from http://blogs.hbr.org/cs/2012/09/ten_ways_to_get_people_to_chan.html on 26 September 2012.

Hanson, P.G. and Lubin, B. (1995) *Answers to Questions Most Frequently Asked About Organization Development*. Thousand Oaks, CA: Sage.

Hardy, C. and Clegg, S.R. (1996) 'Some dare call it power', in *Handbook of Organization Studies*. London: Sage, pp. 622–41.

Hardy, C. and O'Sullivan, L. (1988) 'The power behind empowerment: Implications for research and practice', *Human Relations*, 51(4): 451–83.

Hargie, O. and Tourish, D. (2000) *Handbook of Communication Audits for Organization*. London: Routledge.

Harris, J. (2006) 'A coaching and mentoring framework to facilitate change within a public sector organisation'. Unpublished MBA dissertation, University of Strathclyde.

Harris, L.C. and Crane, A. (2002) 'The greening of organizational culture: Management views on the depth, degree and diffusion of change', *Journal of Organizational Change Management*, 15(3): 214–34.

Harrison, R. (1970) 'Choosing the depth of organizational intervention', *Journal of Applied Behavioral Science*, 6(2): 181–202.

Harshak, A., Aguirre, D. and Brown, A. (2010) *Making Change Happen, and Making It Stick: Delivering Sustainable Organizational Change*. New York, NY: Booz & Company.

Hax, C.A. and Majluf, N.S. (1982) *The Strategy Concept and Process*, 2nd edn. Upper Saddle River, NJ: Prentice Hall.

Hayes, J. (2010) *The Theory and Practice of Change Management*, 3rd edn. Basingstoke: Palgrave Macmillan.

Hayes, J. (2014) *The Theory and Practice of Change Management*, 4th edn. Basingstoke: Palgrave Macmillan.

Hayes, J. and Hyde, P. (2008) 'The change management indicator'. www.peterhyde.co.uk/documents/TheChangeManagementIndicator.pdf (accessed June 2012).

Helfat, C.E., Finkelstein, S., Mitchell, W., Peteraf, M., Singh, H., Teece, D. and Winter, S.G. (2007) *Dynamic Capabilities: Understanding Strategic Change in Organizations*. Malden, MA: Wiley-Blackwell.

Heller, R. (1997) *In Search of European Excellence*. London: HarperCollins Business.

Hendry, C. (1996) 'Understanding and creating whole organizational change through learning theory', *Human Relations*, 48(5): 621–641.

Herold, D.M., Fedor, D.B., Caldwell, S. and Liu, Y. (2008) 'The effects of transformational and change leadership on employees' commitment to a change: A multilevel study', *Journal of Applied Psychology*, 93(2): 346.

Herscovitch, L. and Meyer, J.P. (2002) 'Commitment to organizational change: Extension of a three-component model', *Journal of Applied Psychology*, 87: 474–87.

Higgins, M.C., Weiner, J. and Young, L. (2012) 'Implementation teams: A new lever for organizational change', *Journal of Organizational Behavior*, 33(3): 366–88.

Higgs, M.J. (2013) 'Leadership narcissism, ethics and strategic change: Is it time to revisit our thinking about the nature of effective leadership?', in R.T. By and B. Burnes (eds), *Organizational Change, Leadership and Ethics*. London: Routledge, pp. 171–91.

Hill, T. and Westbrook, R. (1997) 'SWOT analysis. It's time for a product recall', *Long Range Planning*, 30(1): 46–53.

Hinings, C.R. and Greenwood, R. (1988) *The Dynamics of Strategic Change*. Oxford: Blackwell.

Hirschhorn, L. (2002) 'Campaigning for change', *Harvard Business Review*, 80(7): 93–104.

Hodges, J. (2011) 'The role of the CEO and leadership branding: Credibility not celebrity', in R. Burke, G. Martin and C. Cooper (eds), *Corporate Reputation*. Aldershot: Gower, pp. 181–98.

Hofstede, G. (2001) *Culture's Consequences: Comparing Values, Behaviors, Institutions, and Organizations Across Nations*. Thousand Oaks, CA: Sage.

Holt, D.T., Armenakis, A.A., Field, H.S. and Harris, S.G. (2007) 'Readiness for organizational change: The systematic development of a scale', *Journal of Applied Behavioural Science*, 43: 232–55.

Hornung, S. and Rousseau, D.M. (2007) 'Active on the job – proactive in change: How autonomy at work contributes to employee support for organizational change', *Journal of Applied Behavioral Science*, 43(4): 401–26.

Horth, D.M. and Vehar, J. (2012) *Becoming a Leader Who Fosters Innovation*. Greensboro, NC: Centre for Creative Leadership.

House, J.S. (1981) *Work Stress and Social Support*. Sydney: Addison-Wesley.

House, R.J. and Aditja, R.N. (1997) 'The social scientific study of leadership: Quo vadis?', *Journal of Management*, 23(3): 409–73.

Howieson, B. and Hodges, J. (2014) *Public and Third Sector Leadership: Experience Speaks*. London: Emerald.

Hoy, H (2013) 'Auto industry: Hybrid carmakers', *Financial Times*, December 11.

Huff, A.S. (2000) 'Changes in organizational knowledge production', *Academy of Management Review*, 25: 288–93.

Hughes, M. (2006) *Change Management: A Critical Perspective*. London: CIPD.

Hughes, M. (2011) 'Do 70 per cent of all organizational change initiatives really fail?', *Journal of Change Management*, 11(4): 451–64.

Hurley, R. (2012) 'How Mattel regained trust', Financial Times, January 2, 2012. Accessed on January 10, 2012 at http://www.ft.com/cms/s/0/61baac6e-2a84-11e1-9bdb-00144feabdc0.html#axzz38UMdY91j

Hurley, R.F., Church, A., Burke, W.W. and Van Eynde, D.F. (1992) 'Tension, change and values in OD', *OD Practitioner*, 29: 1–5.

Hutchison, S. (2001) 'Communicating in times of change: Contributing to the success of business transformation', *Strategic Communication Management*, 5(2): 28–31.

Hutton, D.W. (1994) *The Change Agents' Handbook: A Survival Guide for Quality Improvement Champions*. Milwaukee, WI: ASQC Quality Press.

Hutton, W. (1995) *The State We're In*. London: Jonathan Cape.

Huy, Q. (2002) 'Emotional balancing of organizational continuity and radical change: The contribution of middle managers', *Administrative Science Quarterly*, 47(1): 31–69.

Iles, V. and Sutherland, K. (2001) *Organisational change: A review for health care managers, professionals and researchers*. London: NCCSDO.

Institute for Corporate Productivity (2013) *Critical Human Capital Issues 2013*. Seattle, WA: ICP. Available at http://.go.i4cp.com/critical-issues-2013-report.

Isabella, L.A. (1990) 'Evolving interpretations as a change unfolds: How managers construe key organizational events', *Academy of Management Journal*, 33(1): 7–41.

Ishikawa, K. (1985) *What is Total Quality Control?* Englewood Cliffs, NJ: Prentice Hall.

Itami, H. and Roehl, T.W. (1987) *Mobilizing Invisible Assets*. Cambridge, MA: Harvard University Press.

Iverson, R.D. (1996) 'Employee acceptance of organizational change: The role of organizational commitment', *International Journal of Human Resources Management*, 7(1): 122–49.

Jackson, S., Schuler, R.S. and Vredenburgh, D.J. (1987) 'Managing stress in turbulent times', in A.W. Riley, S.J. Zaccoro and C. Rosen (eds), *Occupational Stress and Organizational Effectiveness*. London: Greenwood Press, pp. 141–66.

Jacobs, R.L. (2002) 'Institutionalizing organizational change through cascade training', *Journal of European Industrial Training*, 26(2/3/4): 177–82.

James, W. (1890) *The Principles of Psychology*. New York, NY: Holt.

Janis, I. (1982) *Victims of Groupthink: A Psychological Study of Foreign Policy Decisions and Fiasco*, 2nd edn. Boston, MA: Houghton Mifflin.

Jayne, V. (2010) 'Paul Aitken: On leading change', *Management*, February, 36–7.

Jehn, K.A., Chadwick, C. and Thatcher, S.M.B. (1997) 'To agree or not to agree: The effects of value congruence, individual demographic dissimilarity, and conflict on workgroup outcomes', *International Journal of Conflict*, 8: 287–305.

Jick, T.D. and Peiperl, M.A. (2003) *Managing Change: Cases and Concepts*. New York, NY: McGraw-Hill/Irwin.

Jones, T. (2010) 'What's your vision', *Leadership Excellence*, 27(3): 6–7.

Johnson, I. (2005) 'Strategic conversation: Defining, measuring and applying the construct in organisations'. Unpublished PhD thesis, Griffith University, Australia.

Judge, W. (2011) *Building Organizational Capacity for Change: The Strategic Leader's New Mandate*. New York, NY: Business Expert Press.

Judge, W. and Douglas, T. (2009) 'Organizational change capacity: The systematic development of a change', *Journal of Organizational Change Management*, 22(6): 635–49.

Jung, D.I. and Avolio, B.J. (2000) 'Opening the black box: An empirical investigation of the mediating effects of trust and value congruence on transformational and transactional leadership', *Journal of Organizational Behaviour*, 21: 949–64.

Kanaga, K. and Prestridge, S. (2002) 'The right start: A team's first meeting is key', *Leadership in Action*, 22(2): 14–17.

Kanter, R.M. (1979) 'Power failure in management circuits', *Harvard Business Review*, 57(4): 65.

Kanter, R.M. (1983) *The Change Masters*. New York, NY: Simon & Schuster.

Kanter, R.M. (1989) 'The new managerial work', *Harvard Business Review*, 67(6): 85.

Kanter, R.M. (1997) *Rosabeth Moss Kanter on the Frontiers of Management*. Cambridge, MA: Harvard Business Press.

Kanter, R., Stein, B. and Jick, T. (1992) *The Challenge of Organizational Change: How Companies Experience It and Leaders Guide It*. New York, NY: Free Press.

Kaplan and Norton, D. (1996) *The Balanced Scorecard*. Cambridge, MA: Harvard Business School Press.

Karr, J-B.A. (1849) *Les Guêpes (The Wasps)*, January.

Katzenbach, J.R., Steffen, I. and Kronley, C. (2012) 'Culture change that sticks: Start with what's already working', *Harvard Business Review*, 90(7/8): 110–17.

Keil, M. and Montealegre, R. (2000) 'Cutting your losses: Extricating your organization when a big project goes awry', *Sloan Management Review*, 41(3): 55–68.

Keller, S. and Price, C. (2011) 'Organizational health: The ultimate competitive advantage', *McKinsey Quarterly*, 2: 94–107.

Kellerman, B. (2004) *Bad Leadership*. Cambridge, MA: Harvard Business Press.

Kelly, J. (1993) *Facts against Fictions of Executive Behavior: A Critical Analysis of What Managers Do*. Westport, CT: Quorum Books.

Kenexa (2010) *Exploring Leadership and Managerial Effectiveness*, 2010 WorkTrends Research Report. Wayne, PA: Kenexa Research Institute.

Kennedy, J.A. and Kray, L.J. (2014) 'Who is willing to sacrifice ethical values for money and social status? Gender differences in reactions to ethical compromises', *Social Psychological and Personality Science*, 5(1): 52–9.

Kennedy Consulting Research and Advisory (2013) *Change Management Consulting Market*. Keene, NH: Kennedy Consulting Research and Advisory. Available at http://www.kennedyinfo.com/consulting/research/change-management-consulting 2012

Keohane, N.O. (2010) *Thinking About Leadership*. Princeton, NJ: Princeton University Press.

Kiefer, T. (2005) 'Understanding the emotional experience of organizational change: Evidence from a merger', *Advances in Developing Human Resources*, 4: 39–61.

Kitchen, P.J. and Daly, F. (2002) 'Internal communication during change management', *Corporate Communications: An International Journal*, 7(1): 46–53.

Klein, N. (2001) *No Logo*. London: Flamingo.

Klein, S.M. (1996) 'A management communication strategy for change', *Journal of Organisational Change Management*, 9(2): 32–46.

Knowles, M. (1975) *Self-Directed Learning: A Guide for Learners and Teachers*. Chicago, IL: Follett.

Knowles, M. (1986) *Using Learning Contracts*. San Francisco, CA: Jossey-Bass.

Kohles, J.K. (2012) 'A follower-centric approach to the vision integration process', *Leadership Quarterly*, 23(3): 476–87.

Kool, M. and van Dierendonck, D. (2012) 'Servant leadership and commitment to change, the mediating role of justice and optimism', *Journal of Organizational Change Management*, 25(3): 422–33.

Kotter, J.P. (1985) *Power and Influence*. New York, NY: Free Press.

Kotter, J.P. (1990a) 'What leaders really do', *Harvard Business Review*, May–June: 156–67.

Kotter, J.P. (1990b) *A Force for Change: How Leadership Differs from Management*. New York, NY: Free Press.

Kotter, J.P. (1995) 'Leading change: Why transformation efforts fail', *Harvard Business Review*, May–June: 11–16.

Kotter, J.P. (1996) *Leading Change*. Boston, MA: Harvard Business School Press.

Kotter, J.P. (1997) 'Leading by vision and strategy', *Executive Excellence*. October, 15–16.

Kotter, J.P. (2002) *The Heart of Change*. Boston, MA: Harvard Business Press.

Kotter, J.P. (2012a) 'Accelerate!', *Harvard Business Review*, 90(11): 44–58.

Kotter, J.P. (2012b) *Leading Change*. Boston, MA: Harvard Business Review Press.

Kotter, J.P. and Schlesinger, L.A. (1979) 'Choosing strategies for change', *Harvard Business Review*, 57(2): 106–14.

Kotter, J.P. and Whitehead, L. (2010) *Buy-In: Saving Your Good Idea from Getting Shot Down*. Boston, MA: Harvard Business School Press.

Kouzes, J.M. and Posner, B.Z. (1991) *The Leadership Challenge*. San Francisco, CA: Jossey-Bass.

Kouzes, J.M. and Posner, B.Z. (2011) *Credibility: How Leaders Gain and Lose It, Why People Demand It*, 2nd edn. San Francisco, CA: Jossey-Bass.

Kubler-Ross, E. (1973) *On Death and Dying*. London: Tavistock.

Kubr, M. (2002) *Management Consulting: A Guide to the Profession*, 4th edn. Geneva: International Labour Office.

Kumar, K. and Thibodeaux, M.S. (1990) 'Organizational politics and planned organization change a pragmatic approach', *Group and Organization Management*, 15(4): 357–65.

Kuprenas, J.A. (2003) 'Implementation and performance of a matrix organization structure', *International Journal of Project Management*, 21(1): 51–62.

Kurtzman, J. (2010) *Common Purpose: How Great Leaders Get Organizations to Achieve the Extraordinary*. San Francisco, CA: Jossey-Bass.

Kuyatt, A. (2011) 'Managing for innovation: Reducing the fear of failure', *Journal of Strategic Leadership*, 3(2): 31–40.

Lamm, E. and Gordon, J.R. (2010) 'Empowerment, predisposition to resist change, and support for organizational change', *Journal of Leadership & Organizational Studies*, 17(4): 426–37.

Landsberg, M. (1996) *Tao of Coaching: Boost Your Effectiveness at Work by Inspiring and Developing Those Around You*. London: HarperCollins.

Lane, O. (1988) 'Using learning contracts: Pitfalls and benefits for adult learners', *Training and Development in Australia*, 15(1): 7–9.

Larkin, T.J. and Larkin, S. (1996) 'Reaching and changing frontline employees', *Harvard Business Review*, May–June: 95–104.

Lavelle, L. (2005) 'In brief', *BusinessWeek*, 28 February.

Laver, M. (1997) *Private Desires, Political Action: An Invitation to the Politics of Rational Choice*. London: Sage.

Lawler, E.E. (1986) *High Involvement Management: Participative Strategies for Improving Organizational Effectiveness*. San Francisco, CA: Jossey-Bass.

Lawler III, E.E. and Worley, C.G. (2011). *Built to Change: How to Achieve Sustained Organizational Effectiveness*. London: Wiley.

Lawrence, P.R. and Lorsch, J.W. (1967) 'Differentiation and integration in complex organizations', *Administrative Science Quarterly*, 12(1): 1–47.

Lawrence, P.R. and Lorsch, J.W. (1986) *Organisation and Environment: Managing Differentiation and Integration*. Boston, MA: Harvard Business Press.

Lawrence, S.A. and Callan, V.J. (2011) 'The role of social support in coping during the anticipatory stage of organizational change: A test of an integrative model', *British Journal of Management*, 22: 567–85.

Leadbeater, C. (2000) *Living on Thin Air*. Harmondsworth: Penguin.

Leavitt, H.J. (1964) 'Applied organizational change in industry: Structural, technological and humanistic approaches', in J.G. March (ed.), *Handbook of Organizations*. Chicago, IL: Rand McNally, pp. 1144–51.

Leitch, C., Harrison, R., Burgoyne, J. and Blantern, C. (1996) 'Learning organizations: The measurement of company performance', *Journal of European Industrial Training*, 20(1): 31–44.

Lencioni, P.M. (2002) 'Make your values mean something', *Harvard Business Review*, 80(7): 113–17.

Lennick, D. and Kiel, F. (2008) *Moral Intelligence*, Upper Saddle River, NJ: Pearson Education.

Levin, L. (2000) 'Transforming our business through people'. Paper presented at the Third Annual Leadership Conference, 'The Head and Heart of Leadership', The Leadership Trust Foundation, Ross-on-Wye, 6–7 September..

Levy, C., Sissons, A. and Holloway, C. (2011) *A Plan for Growth in the Knowledge Economy. A Knowledge Economy Programme Paper*. London: The Work Foundation.

Lewin, K. (1947) 'Frontiers in group dynamics: Concept, method and reality in social science; social equilibria and social change', *Human Relations*, 1(2): 143–53.

Lewis, A.C. and Grosser, M. (2012) 'The change game: An experiential exercise demonstrating barriers to change', *Journal of Management Education*, 36(5): 669–97.

Lewis, L.K. and Seibold, D.R. (1998) 'Reconceptualizing organizational change implementation as a communication problem: A review of literature and research agenda', in M.E. Roloff (ed.), *Communication Yearbook 21*. Thousand Oaks, CA: Sage, pp. 93–152.

Lewis, L.K., Hamel, S.A. and Richardson, B.K. (2001) 'Communicating change to non-profit stakeholders: Models and predictors of implementers' approaches', *Management Communication Quarterly*, 15(1): 5–41.

Liguori, M. (2012) 'The supremacy of the sequence: Key elements and dimensions in the process of change', *Organization Studies*, 33(4): 507–39.

Lines, R. (2004) 'Influence of participation in strategic change: Resistance, organizational commitment and change goal achievement', *Journal of Management Studies*, 40(3): 193–215.

Lines, R. (2007) 'Using power to install strategy: The relationships between expert power, position power, influence tactics and implementation success', *Journal of Change Management*, 7(2): 143–70.

Lines, R., Selart, M., Espedal, B. and Johansen, S.T. (2005) 'The production of trust during organizational change', *Journal of Change Management*, 5(2): 221–45.

Linkow, P. (1999) 'What gifted strategic thinkers do', *Training & Development*, 53(7): 34–7.

Linnenluecke, M.K. and Griffiths, A. (2010) 'Corporate sustainability and organizational culture', *Journal of World Business*, 45(4): 357–66.

Lippitt, M. (1997) 'Say what you mean, mean what you say (creating effective corporate communication)', *Journal of Business Strategy*, 18(4): 18–20.

Lippitt, R., Brown, J. and Westley, B. (1958) *Planned Change: A Comparative Study of Principles and Techniques*. New York, NY: Harcourt, Brace and World.

Lloyd, M. and Maguire, S. (2002) 'The possibility horizon', *Journal of Change Management*, 3(2): 149–57.

Longbotham, G.J. and Longbotham, C.R. (2006) 'A scientific approach to implementing change', *Journal of Practical Consulting*, 1(1): 19–24.

Longenecker, C., Papp, G. and Stansfield, T.C. (2006) 'Characteristics of successful improvement initiatives', *Industrial Management*, 48(5): 25–31.

Lubin, D.A. and Esty, D.C. (2010) 'The sustainability imperative', *Harvard Business Review*, 88(5): 42–50.

Luecke, R. (2003) *Managing Change and Transition*. Boston, MA: Harvard Business School Press.

Lukes, S. (2005) *Power: A Radical View*. Basingstoke: Palgrave Macmillan.

Lundberg, C.C. (1990) 'Towards mapping the communication targets of organisational change', *Journal of Organizational Change Management*, 3(3): 6–13.

Maccoby, M. (2000) 'Narcissistic leaders', *Harvard Business Review*, 78(1): 69–77.

Maccoby, M. (2005) 'Creating moral organizations', *Research Technology Management*, 48(1): 59–60.

Madsen, S.R., Miller, D. and John, C.R. (2005) 'Readiness for organizational change: Do organizational commitment and social relationships in the workplace make a difference?', *Human Resource Development Quarterly*, 16(2): 213–34.

Magni, M. and Maruping, L. (2013) 'Sink or swim: Empowering leadership and overload in teams' ability to deal with the unexpected', *Human Resource Management*, 52(5): 715–39.

Mahoney, J. (2000) 'Path dependence in historical sociology', *Theory and Society*, 29(40): 507–48.

Maitlis, S. (2005) 'The social process of organizational sensemaking', *Academy of Management Journal*, 48: 21–49.

Malekzadeh, A.R. and Nahavandi, A. (1988) 'Acculturation in mergers and acquisitions', *Academy of Management Review*, 13(1): 79–90.

Marshak, R. (1993) 'Lewin meets Confucius: A re-review of the OD model of change', *Journal of Applied Behavioural Science*, 24(4): 393–415.

Martin, I. and Cheung, Y. (2002) 'Change management at Mobile Oil Australia', *Business Processes Management Journal*, 8(5): 447–62.

Martin, J. (2005) *Organizational Behaviour and Management*. London: Cengage Learning EMEA.

Martin, R. L. (2011). *Fixing the Game: Bubbles. Crashes and What Capitalism Can Learn*. Cambridge, MA: Harvard Business Press.

Massey, L. and Williams, S. (2006) 'Implementing change: The perspective of NHS change agents', *Leadership and Organization Development Journal*, 27(8): 667–81.

Mast, M.S., Hall, J.A. and Schmid, P.C. (2010) 'Wanting to be boss and wanting to be subordinate: Effects on performance motivation', *Journal of Applied Social Psychology*, 40(2): 458–72.

Maurer, R. (1996) *Beyond the Walls of Resistance*. Austin, TX: Bard Books.

Mayer, R.C., Davis, J.H. and Schoorman, F.D. (1995) 'An integrative model of organizational trust', *Academy of Management Review*, 20: 709–34.

Mayo, A. (2002) 'Forever change', *Training Journal*, June: 40.

McCall, M.W. (1979) 'Power, authority, and influence', *Organizational Behavior*, 185–206.

McClelland, D.C. (1975) *Power: The Inner Experience*. Oxford: Irvington.

McClelland, D.C. and Burnham, D.H. (1976) 'Power is the great motivator', *Harvard Business Review*, 73(1): 126–39.

McDonald, K.S. and Mansour-Cole, D. (2000) 'Change requires extensive care: An experiential exercise for learners in university and corporate settings', *Journal of Management Education*, 24: 127–48.

McFee, A. (2011) 'What every CEO needs to know about the Cloud', *Harvard Business Review*, November: pp 3–10.

McKendall, M. (1993) 'The tyranny of change: Organizational development revisited', *Journal of Business Ethics*, 12(2): 93–104.

McKinsey & Company (2010) 'What successful transformations share: McKinsey Global Survey results', *McKinsey Quarterly*, March.

McKinsey & Company (2011) 'Creating more value with corporate strategy', McKinsey Global Survey results. *McKinsey Quarterly*, downloaded at http://e.mckinseyquarterly.com/11497b51blayfousubkh3iqaaaaaaatxj54ucgpj2syyaaaaa on 25 January 2012.

McKinsey & Company (2012) *Debt and Deleveraging: Uneven Progress on the Path to Growth*. Washington, DC: McKinsey Global Institute.

McLagan, P. (2002) 'Change leadership today', *Training & Development*, 56(11): 26–31.

Meaney, M. and Pung, C. (2008) 'McKinsey global survey results: Creating organizational transformations', *The McKinsey Quarterly*, August, pp. 1–7.

Meglino, B.M. and Ravlin, E.C. (1998) 'Individual values in organizations: Concepts, controversies, and research', *Journal of Management*, 24: 351–89.

Mendonca, M. (2001) 'Preparing for ethical leadership in organizations', *Canadian Journal of Administrative Sciences*, 40(2): 458–72.

Menon, S.T. (2001) 'Employee empowerment: An integrative psychological approach', *Applied Psychology: An International Review*, 50(1): 153–80.

Meyer, J. (2012) *Welcome to Entrepreneur County*. London: Constable.

Miller, C., Hind, P. and Magala, S. (2012) 'Sustainability and the need for change: Organisational change and transformational vision', *Journal of Organizational Change Management*, 25(4): 489–500.

Milliken, F.J. (1987) 'Three types of perceived uncertainty about the environment: State, effect, and response uncertainty', *Academy of Management Review*, 133–43.

Mintzberg, H. (1973) *The Nature of Managerial Work*. New York, NY: Harper & Row.

Mintzberg, H. (1979) *The Structuring of Organizations: A Synthesis of the Research*. Englewood Cliffs, NJ: Prentice Hall.

Mintzberg, H., Ahlstrand, B. and Lampel, J. (1998) *Strategy Safari*. Harlow: FT/Prentice Hall.

Mirvis, P.H. and Manga, J. (2010) 'Integrating corporate citizenship: Leading from the middle', *Global Challenges in Responsible Business*, 78–106.

Mishra, A. and Spreitzer, G. (1998) 'Explaining how survivors respond to downsizing: The roles of trust, empowerment, justice and work redesign', *Academy of Management Review*, 23(3): 567–88.

Molineux, J. (2013) 'Enabling organizational cultural change using systematic strategic human resource management – a longitudinal case study', *Journal of Human Resource Management*, 24(8): 1588–613.

Moorhouse Consulting (2008) *Turning a Vision into Reality*. London: Moorhouse, January.

Moorhouse Consulting (2009) *The Benefits of Organisational Change*. London: Moorhouse, September.

Moorhouse Consulting (2012a) *Too Much Change? Financial Services Survey 2012: The Results*. London: Moorhouse, October, 3.

Moorhouse Consulting (2012b) *Start With the End in Mind and You'll Head in the Right Direction: The Benefits of Organisational Change*. London: Moorhouse, September.

Moorhouse Consulting (2013) *Barometer on Change 2013: If a Change Is Worth Doing, Focus on Doing It Well*. London: Moorhouse, May, 12. Downloaded at http://moorhouseconsulting.com/news-and-views/publications-and-articles/baro... on 3 September 2013.

Moran, J.W. and Brightman, B.K. (2001) 'Leading organizational change', *Career Development International*, 6(2): 111–18.

Morgan, D.E. and Zeffane, R. (2003) 'Employee involvement, organizational change and trust in management', *International Journal of Human Resource Management*, 14: 55–75.

Morgan, G. (2006) *Images of Organization*. London: Sage.

Morrison, E.W. and Milliken, F.J. (2000) 'Organizational silence: A barrier to change and development in a pluralistic world', *Academy of Management Review*, 25: 706–25.

Mourkogiannis, N. (2006) *Purpose: The Starting Point of Great Companies*. New York, NY: Palgrave Macmillan.

Mowday, R.T., Steers, R.M. and Porter, L.W. (1979) 'The measure of organizational commitment', *Journal of Vocational Behavior*, 14: 224–47.

Mueller, U. and Etzold, V. (2012) 'Minimal change can be best' Financial Times, April 30, 2012. Accessed April 2012 at http://www.ft.com/cms/s/0/eda4a8ec-92b7-11e1-b6e2-00144feab49a.html#axzz38UMdY91j

Mullins, L.J. (2007) *Management and Organisational Behaviour*. Harlow: FT/Prentice Hall.

Mullins, L.J. (2010), *Management & Organisational Behaviour*, 9th edn. Harlow: Pearson Education.

Nadler, D.A. (1988) 'Concepts for the management of organisational change', in M.L. Tushman and W.L. Moore (eds), *Readings in the Management of Innovation*, 7th edn. New York, NY: Ballinger, pp. 718–32.

Nadler, D.A. (1993) *Feedback and Organizational Development: Using Data Based Methods*. Reading, MA: Addison-Wesley.

Nadler, D.A. and Shaw, R.B. (1995) *Discontinuous Change: Leading Organizational Transformation*. San Francisco, CA: Jossey-Bass.

Nadler, D. and Tushman, M. (1980) 'A model for diagnosing organizational behavior', *Organizational Dynamics*, 9(2): 35–51.

Nadler, D.A. and Tushman, M.L. (1989) 'Organizational frame bending: Principles for managing reorientation', *Academy of Management Executive*, 3(3): 194–204.

Nadler, D. and Tushman, M. (1995) 'Types of organizational change: From incremental improvements to discontinuous transformation', in D. Nadler, R. Shaw and A. Walton (eds), *Discontinuous Change: Leading Organizational Transformation*. San Francisco, CA: Jossey-Bass, pp. 15–34.

Nanus, B. (1992) *Visionary Leadership*. San Francisco, CA: Jossey-Bass.

National Intelligence Council (NIC) (2012) *Global Trends 2030:Alternative Worlds*. London: National Intelligence Council (www.dni.gov/nic/globaltrends).

Naylor, J. (2004) *Management*. Harlow: Pearson Education.

Neal, D. and Taylor, T. (2006) 'Spinning on dimes: The challenges of introducing transformational change into the UK Ministry of Defence', *Strategic Change*,15: 15–22.

Nelissen, P. and van Selm, M. (2008) 'Surviving organizational change: How management communication helps balance mixed feelings', *Corporate Communications: An International Journal*, 13(3): 306–18.

Neves, P. and Caetano, A. (2006) 'Social exchange processes in organizational change: The roles of trust and control', *Journal of Change Management*, 6(4): 351–64.

Neville, S. (2013) 'Shared vision is key to changing a system', *Financial Times*, 11 December, 2.

Newton, R. (2013) 'Perceptions and development of ethical change leadership', in R.T. By and B. Burnes (eds), *Organizational Change, Leadership and Ethics*. London: Routledge, pp. 35–54.

NHS Modernisation Agency (2002) *Improvement Leaders' Guide to Sustainability and Spread*. Ipswich: Ancient House Printing Group.

Nicotera, A. and Cushman, D. (1992) 'Organizational ethics: A within-organization view', *Journal of Applied Communication Research*, 20: 437–63.

Nolan, T.M., Goodstein, L.D. and Goodstein, J. (2008) *Applied Strategic Planning: An Introduction*, 2nd edn. San Francisco, CA: Pfeiffer/Wiley.

Oakland, J. (2014) *Total Quality Management and Operational Excellent: Text and Cases*, 4th edn. Oxford: Routledge.

Oakland, J.S. and Tanner, S.J. (2006) 'Quality management in the 21st century – implementing successful change', *International Journal of Productivity and Quality Management*, 1(1–2): 69–87.

O'Connor, N. and Kotze, B. (2008) 'Learning organizations: A clinician's primer', *Australasian Psychiatry*, 16(3): 173–8.

Ogbonna, E. and Harris, L. (1998) 'Organizational culture: It's not what you think ...', *Journal of General Management*, 23(3): 35–48.

Ogbonna, E. and Harris, L.C. (2002) 'Organizational Culture: A Ten Year, Two-Phase Study of Change in the UK Food Retailing Sector', *Journal of Management Studies*, 39(5): 673–706.

Ogburn Jr., C. (1957) 'Merrill's marauders: the truth about an incredible adventure', *Harper's Magazine*, January.

Olivier, R. (2001) *Inspirational Leadership: Henry V and the Muse of Fire*. London: The Industrial Society [now The Work Foundation].

Ordanini, A. and Rubera, G. (2008) 'Strategic capabilities and internet resources in procurement: A resource-based view of B-to-B buying process', *International Journal of Operations and Production Management*, 28(1): 27–52.

Oreg, S. (2003) 'Resistance to change: Developing an individual differences measure', *Journal of Applied Psychology*, 88(4): 680.

Oreg, S., Vakola, M. and Armenakis, A. (2011) 'Change recipients' reactions to organizational change: A 60-year review of quantitative studies', *Journal of Applied Behavioural Science*, 47(4): 461–524.

O'Regan, N. and Ghobadian, A. (2012) 'John Lewis Partnership lessons in logical incrementalism and organic growth: A case study and interview with the Chairman, Mr Charlie Mayfield', *Journal of Strategy and Management*, 5(1): 103–12.

Orlikowski, W. (1996) 'Improvising organisational transformation over time: A situated change perspective', *Information Systems Research*, 7(1): 63–92.

Orlikowski, W. and Hofman, J. (1997) 'An improvisational model for change management: The case of groupware technologies', *Sloan Management Review*, 38(2): 11–21.

Owen, H. (2008) *Open Space Technology*. San Francisco, CA: Berrett–Koehler.

Palmer, C. and Fenner, J. (1999) *Getting the Message Across: A Review of Research and Theory About Disseminating Information in the NHS*. London: Gaskell.

Pankakoski, M. (1998) 'Change agent 007 – licence to simulate', *Games in Operations Management*, 3–14.

Pascale, R. and Athos, A. (1981) 'The art of Japanese management', *Strategic Management Journal*, 3(4): 381–3.

Pate, J., Martin, G. and Staines, H. (2000) 'Exploring the relationship between psychological contracts and organizational change: A process model and case study evidence', *Strategic Change*, 9(8): 481–93.

Paton, R. and McCalman, J. (2008) *Change Management: A Guide to Effective Implementation*, 3rd edn. London: Sage.

Patterson, K. and Winston, B. (2006) 'An integrative definition of leadership', *International Journal of Leadership Studies*, 1(2): 6–66.

Peccei, R., Giangreco, A. and Sebastiano, A. (2011) 'The role of organisational commitment in the analysis of resistance to change: Co-predictor and moderator effects', *Personnel Review*, 40(2), 185–204.

Perkins, B. (2012) 'Change management is not optional', *Computerworld*, 5 November.

Peters, T.J. and Waterman, R.H. (1982) *In Search of Excellence: Lessons from America's Best Run Companies*. New York, NY: Harper & Row.

Pettigrew, A. (1985) *The Awakening Giant: Continuity and Change in ICI*. Oxford: Blackwell.

Pettigrew, A. (1987) 'Context and action in the transformation of the firm', *Journal of Management Studies*, 24(6): 649–69.

Pettigrew, A. (1990) 'Longitudinal field research on change theory and practice', *Organizational Science*, 1(3): 267–92.

Pettigrew, A. (2000) 'Linking change processes to outcomes: A commentary on Ghoshal, Bartlett and Weick', in M. Beer and D. Nohria (eds), *Breaking the Code of Change*. Boston, MA: Harvard Business Review Press, pp. 243–67.

Pettigrew, A., Ewan F. and McKee, L. (1992) 'Shaping strategic change – The case of the NHS in the 1980s', *Public Money & Management*, 12(3): 27–31.

Pettigrew, A. and Whipp, R. (1991) *Managing Change for Competitive Success*. Oxford: Blackwell.

Pettigrew, A. and Whipp, R. (1993) *Managing Change for Competitive Success*. London: Wiley.

Pettigrew, A., Woodman, R. and Cameron, K. (2001) 'Studying organizational change and development: Challenges for future research', *Academy of Management Journal*, 44: 697–713.

Pettinger, R. (2010) *Organizational Behaviour: Performance Management in Practice*. London: Routledge.

Pfeffer, J. (1977) 'The ambiguity of leadership', *Academy of Management Review*, 104–12.

Pfeffer, J. (1992) 'Understanding power in organizations', *California Management Review*, 34(2): 29–50.

Pfeffer, J. (1998) *The Human Equation*. Cambridge, MA: Harvard Business School Press.

Pfeffer, J. (2010) *Power: Why Some People Have It – and Others Don't*. New York, NY: HarperCollins.

Pfeffer, J. and Salancik, G.R. (1978) *The External Control of Organizations*. New York, NY: Harper & Row.

Piderit, S.K. (2000) 'Rethinking resistance and recognizing ambivalence: A multidimensional view of attitudes toward and organizational change', *Academy of Management Review*, 25(4): 783–94.

Pierson, P. (2000) 'Increasing returns, path dependence, and the study of politics', *American Political Science Review*, 94(2): 51–267.

Pilbeam, S. and Corbridge, M. (2006) *People Resourcing: Contemporary HRM in Practice*. Harlow: Pearson Education.

Pitt, M.R., McAulay, L. and Sims, D. (2002) 'Promoting strategic change: "Playmaker" roles in organizational agenda formulation', *Strategic Change*, 11: 155–72.

Podsakoff, P.M. and Schriesheim, C.A. (1985) 'Field studies of French and Raven's bases of power: Critique, reanalysis, and suggestions for future research', *Psychological Bulletin*, 97(3): 387–411.

Poole, M.S. (1997) 'Communication', in N. Nicholson (ed.), *The Blackwell Encyclopaedic Dictionary of Organizational Behaviour*. Oxford: Blackwell, pp. 77–80.

Porras, J.I. and Robertson, P.J. (1992) 'Organizational development: Theory, practice, research', in M.D. Dunnette and L.M. Hough (eds), *Handbook of Organizational Psychology*, 2nd edn. Palo Alto, CA: Consult. Psychology Press, pp. 719–822.

Porter, M.E. (1991) 'Towards a dynamic theory of strategy', *Strategic Management Journal*, Winter Special Issue, 12: 95–117.

Porter, M.P. (1996) 'What is strategy?', *Harvard Business Review*, November/December: 61–71.

Postma, T. and Kok, R. (1999) 'Organizational diagnosis in practice: a cross-classification analysis using the DEL-technique', *European Management Journal*, 17(6): 584–597.

Prevett, H. (2013) 'Culture wasn't built in a day', *The Sunday Times*, 24 February.

Price, D. (2009) 'The context of change', in D. Price (ed.), *The Principles and Practice of Change*. Basingstoke: Palgrave Macmillan, pp. 3–23.

Priem, R.L. and Butler, J.E. (2001) 'Is the resource-based view a useful perspective for strategic management research?', *Academy of Management Review*, 26(1): 22–40.

Priem, R.L. and Rosenstein, J. (2000) 'Is organization theory obvious to practitioners? A test of one established theory', *Organization Science*, 11(5): 509–24.

Probst, G. and Raisch, S. (2005) 'Organizational crisis: The logic of failure', *Academy of Management Executive*, 19(1): 90–105.

Prochaska, J. (2002) 'A new view of creativity and innovation', Letter to the Editor. *Leadership in Action*, 22(2): 24.

Prochaska, J.O., DiClemente, C.C., Velicer, W.F. and Rossi, J.S. (1993) 'Standardized, individualized, interactive, and personalized self-help programs for smoking cessation', *Health Psychology*, 12: 399–405.

Protogerou, A., Caloghirou, Y. and Lioukas, S. (2008) *Dynamic Capabilities and Their Indirect Impact on Firm Performance*. Working Paper 08–11, Danish Research Unit for Industrial Dynamics. www.druid.dk.

Provis, C. (2004) 'Negotiation, persuasion and argument', *Argumentation*, 18(1): 95–112.

Pugh, D. (1993) 'Understanding and managing organizational change', in C. Mabey and B. Mayon-White (eds), *Managing Change*. London: Paul Chapman/Open University.

Putnam, L.L. and Sorenson, R.L. (1982) 'Equivocal messages in organizations', *Human Communication Research*, 8(2): 114–32.

Quinn, J.B. (1980) *Strategies for Change: Logical Incrementalism*. Homewood, IL: Richard D. Irwin.

Quinn, J.B. (1993) 'Managing strategic change', in C. Mabey and B. Mayon-White (eds), *Managing Change*. London: Paul Chapman/Open University.

Quinn, R.E. and Spreitzer, G.M. (1997) 'The road to empowerment: Seven questions every leader should consider', *Organizational Dynamics*, 26(2): 37–49.

Quirke, B. (1996) *Communicating Corporate Change: A Practical Guide to Communication and Corporate Strategy*. London: McGraw-Hill.

Rafferty, A.E., Jimmieson, N.L. and Armenakis, A.A. (2012) 'Change readiness: A multilevel review', *Journal of Management*, 39(1): 110–35.

Rajan, A. (2000a) *How Can Leaders Achieve Successful Culture Change?* Tonbridge, Kent: Centre for Research in Employment & Technology in Europe.

Rajan, A. (2000b) *Does Management Development Fail to Produce Leaders?* Tonbridge, Kent: Centre for Research in Employment & Technology in Europe.

Randolph, W.A. and Kemery, E.R. (2011) 'Managerial use of power bases in a model of managerial empowerment practices and employee psychological empowerment', *Journal of Leadership & Organizational Studies*, 18(1): 95–106.

Raven, B.H. and French, J.R., Jr (1958) 'Legitimate power, coercive power, and observability in social influence', *Sociometry*, 83–97.

Ravenscraft, D.J. and Scherer, F.M. (1987) *Mergers, Sell-Offs, and Economic Efficiency*. Washington, DC: Brookings Institution Press.

Reed, J. (2007) *Appreciative Inquiry*. Thousand Oaks, CA: Sage.

Reichers, A.E., Wanous, J.P. and Austin, J.T. (1997) 'Understanding and managing cynicism about organizational change', *Academy of Management Executive*, 11: 48–59.

Reisner, R.A. (2002) 'When a turnaround stalls', *Harvard Business Review*, 80(2): 45–52.

Revans, R.W. (1982) 'What is action learning?', *Journal of Management Development*, 1(3): 64–75.

Rhodes, C. (2013) 'Justice and the ethical quality of leadership', in R.T. By and B. Burnes (eds), *Organizational Change, Leadership and Ethics*. London: Routledge, pp. 55–72.

Richardson, P. and Denton, D.K. (1996) 'Communicating change', *Human Resource Management*, 35(2): 203–16.

Rigby, D. and Tager, S. (2008) 'Learning the advantages of sustainable growth', *Strategy and Leadership*, 36(4): 24–8.

Rijal, S. (2010) 'Leadership style and organizational culture in learning organizations: A comparative study', *International Journal of Management and Information Systems*, 14(5): 119–28.

Rimmer, M., Macneil, J., Chenhall, R., Langfield-Smith, K. and Watts, L. (1996) *Reinventing Competitiveness: Best Practice in Australian Enterprises*. Melbourne: Pitman.

Roath, R. (2013) 'Will the girl scouts earn a badge for change leadership?', www.kotterinternational.com/news-and-insights/2013/06/28/will-the-girl-scouts-earn-a-badge-for-change-leadership (accessed June 2014).

Robbins, S.P. (2005) *Organizational Behaviour*, 11th edn. Englewood Cliffs, NJ: Prentice Hall.

Robbins, S.P., Judge, T.A. and Campbell, T.T. (2010) *Organizational Behaviour.* Harlow: FT/Prentice Hall.

Roberto, M.A. and Levesque, L.C. (2005) 'The art of making change initiatives stick', *MIT Sloan Management Review*, 46(4): 53–60.

Robinson, S.L. (1996) 'Trust and breach of psychological contract', *Administrative Science Quarterly*, 41: 574–99.

Roche, D. (2013) 'Explorers showed me the way to go', Leading Edge, Appointments Supplement, *The Sunday Times*, 27 January, p. 4.

Roe, R. and Ester, P. (1999) 'Values and work: Empirical findings and theoretical perspectives', *Applied Psychology: An International Review*, 48: 1–21.

Rogers, E.M. (1962) *Diffusion of Innovations*. New York, NY: The Free Press.

Rogers, E.M. (1983) *Diffusion of Innovations*. London: Simon & Schuster.

Rollag, K. and Parise, S. (2005) 'The bikestuff simulation: Experiencing the challenge of organizational change', *Journal of Management Education*, 29: 769–87.

Roosevelt, F.D. (1937) 'Second Inaugural Address', January 20, 1937. Accessed at http://www.bartleby.com/124/pres50.html

Rousseau, D.M. (1990) 'New hire perceptions of their own and their employer's obligations: A study of psychological contracts', *Journal of Organizational Behavior*, 11(5): 389–400.

Rousseau, D.M. (1998) 'Why workers still identify with organizations', *Journal of Organizational Behaviour*, 19: 217–33.

Rousseau, D.M. and Tijoriwala, S.A. (1999) 'Assessing psychological contracts: Issues, alternatives and measures', *Journal of Organizational Behavior*, 19(S1): 679–95.

Rowden, R.W. (2001) 'The learning organization and strategic change', *SAM Advanced Management Journal*, 66(3): 11–16.

Rowson, J. (2012) *The Power of Curiosity: How Linking Inquisitiveness to Innovation Could Help to Address Our Energy Challenges*. RSA Social Brain Centre, London: Royal Society of Arts, p. 3.

Rubin, H. (1997) *The Princessa: Machiavelli for Women*. New York, NY: Doubleday.

Rubin, R.S., Dierdorff, E.C., Bommer, W.H. and Baldwin, T.T. (2009) 'Do leaders reap what they sow? Leader and employee outcomes of leader organizational cynicism about change', *The Leadership Quarterly*, 20: 680–8.

Ruigrok, W., Pettigrew, A., Peck, S. and Whittington, R. (1999) 'Corporate restructuring and new forms of organizing: Evidence from Europe', *Management International Review*, 39: 41–64.

Rumelt, R. (2012) *Good Strategy, Bad Strategy: The Difference and Why It Matters*. New York, NY: Crown Business.

Ryan, L. and Macky, K.A. (1998) 'Downsizing organizations: Uses, outcomes and strategies', *Asia Pacific Journal of Human Resources*, 36(2): 29–45.

Sackmann, S.A., Eggenhofer, P. and Friesl, M. (2009): 'Sustainable change: Long-term efforts toward developing a learning organization', *Journal of Applied Behavioral Science*, 45(4): 521–49.

Sagiv, L. and Schwartz, S.H. (2007) 'Cultural values in organisations: Insights for Europe', *European Journal of International Management*, 1(3): 176–90.

Salaman, G. and Asch, D. (2003) *Strategy and Capability: Sustaining Organizational Change*. Oxford: Blackwell.

Salancik, G.R. and Pfeffer, J. (1977) 'Who gets power – and how they hold on to it: A strategic-contingency model of power', *Organizational Dynamics*, 5(3): 3–21.

Scherer, A., Palazzo, G. and Matten, D. (2009) 'Introduction to the special issue', *Business Ethics Quarterly*, 19(3): 327–47.

Schein, E. (1997) *Organizational Culture and Leadership*, 3rd edn. San Francisco, CA: Jossey-Bass.

Schein, V. (1977) 'Political strategies for implementing organizational change', *Group & Organization Management*, 2(1): 42–8.

Schön, D.A. (1963) 'Champions for radical new inventions', *Harvard Business Review*, 41(2): 77–86.

Schrage, M. (2012) 'Are you driving too much change, too fast?', HBR Blog Network, *Harvard Business Review*, 14 November. Accessed December 2012 at http://blogs.hbr.org/2012/11/are-you-driving-too-much-change/

Schumpeter, J. (2011) 'Fail often, fail well', *The Economist*, 16 April, p.75.

Schwartz, S.H. (1992) 'Universals in the content and structure of values: Theoretical advances and empirical tests in 20 countries', in M.P. Zanna (ed.), *Advances in Experimental Social Psychology*, Volume 25. San Diego, CA: Academic Press, pp. 1–65.

Schweiger, D.M. and DeNisi, A.S. (1991): 'Communication with employees following a merger: A longitudinal field experiment', *Academy of Management Journal*, 34: 110–35.

Seabright, M.A. and Moberg, D.J. (1998) 'Interpersonal manipulation: Its nature and moral limits', in M, Schminke (ed.), *Managerial Ethics: Morally Managing People and Processes*. Mahwah, NJ: Lawrence Erlbaum Associates, pp. 153–75.

Seel, R. (2000) 'New insights on organisational change', *Organisations & People*, 7(2): 2–9.

Seijts, G.H. and Latham, G.P. (2012) 'Knowing when to set learning goals versus performance goals', *Organizational Dynamics*, 41(1): 1–6.

Selznick, P. (1957) *Leadership in Administration: A Sociological Interpretation*. Evanston, IL: Row Peterson.

Senge, P.M. (1990) *The Fifth Discipline: The Art and Practice of the Learning Organisation*. London, Random House Business Books.

Senge, P.M. and Kaeufer, K.H. (2000) 'Creating change', *Executive Excellence*, 10: 4–5.

Senge, P.M., Kleiner, A., Roberts, C., Ross, R., Roth, G. and Smith, B. (1999) *The Dance of Change: A Fifth Discipline Resource.* London: Nicholas Brealey.

Senior, B. (2002) *Organizational Change*, 2nd edn. London: Prentice Hall.

Senior, B. and Fleming, J. (2006) *Organizational Change,* 3rd edn. London: Prentice Hall/FT.

Sennet, R. (2001) 'Failure', in G. Salaman (ed.), *Understanding Business Organisations.* London: Routledge in association with the Open University, pp. 203–12.

Sennet, R. (2006) *The Culture of the New Capatalism.* New Haven, CT: Yale University Press.

Seo, M-G, Taylor, M.S., Hill, N.S., Zhang, X., Tesluk, P.E. and Lorinkova, N.M. (2012) 'The role of affect and leadership during organizational change', *Personnel Psychology*, 65: 121–65.

Shamir, B. (1995) 'Social distance and charisma: Theoretical notes and an exploratory study', *Leadership Quarterly*, 6: 19–47.

Shapiro, D.L. and Kirkman, B.L. (1999) 'Employees' reaction to the change to work teams: The influence of "anticipatory" injustice', *Journal of Organizational Change Management*, 12: 51–67.

Shaw, P. (2002) *Changing Conversations in Organizations: A Complexity Approach to Change.* London: Routledge.

Shea, G.P. and Solomon, C.A. (2013a) *Leading Successful Change: 8 Keys to Making Change Work.* Philadelphia, PA: Wharton Digital Press.

Shea, G.P. and Solomon, C.A. (2013b) 'Change management is bigger than leadership', HBR Blog Network, *Harvard Business Review*, 29 March. Accessed on 24 July 2014 at http://blogs.hbr.org/2013/03/change-management-is-bigger-th/

Shepherd, D.A., Patzelt, H. and Baron, R.A. (2013) '"I care about nature, but ...", disengaging values in assessing opportunities that cause harm', *Academy of Management Journal*, 56(5): 1251–73.

Sherman, A.J. and Hart, M.A. (2006) *Mergers and Acquisitions from A to Z*, 2nd edn. New York, NY: AMACOM.

Silvester, J. (2010) 'What makes a good politician?', *The Psychologist*, 23(5): 394–7.

Sims, P. (2012) *Placing Little Bets.* London: Free Press.

Single, A.W. and Spurgeon, W.M. (1996) 'Creating and commercializing innovation inside a skunk works', *Journal of Product Innovation Management*, 13(5): 459–60.

Sirkin, H.L., Keenan, P. and Jackson, A. (2005) 'The hard side of change management', *Harvard Business Review*, 83 (10): 108-18.

Smeltzer, L.R. (1991) 'An analysis of strategies for announcing organization-wide change', *Group and Organization Management*, 16(1): 5–24.

Smeltzer, L.R. and Zener, M.E. (1992) 'Development of a model for announcing major layoffs', *Group and Organization Management*, 17(4): 446–72.

Snow, C.C. and Miles, R.E. (1992) 'Causes for failure in network organizations', *California Management Review*, 34(1): 53–7.

Snow, C., Miles, R.E. and Coleman, H.J., Jr (1992) 'Managing 21st century network organizations', *Organizational Dynamics*, 19: 5–20.

Soanes, C. and Stevenson, A. (eds) (2004) *The Concise Oxford English Dictionary*, 11th edn. Oxford: Oxford University Press.

Sockell, D. (2013) 'Empowering employees to integrate ethics and social good into their work', *The Guardian*, 15 August.

Sorensen, P.E., Yaeger, T.F. and Bengtsson, U. (2003) 'The promise of appreciative inquiry: A 20 year review', *OD Practitioner*, 35(4): 15–21.

Sorge, A. and Van Witteloostuijn, A. (2004) 'The (non)sense of organizational change: An essay about universal management hypes, sick consultancy metaphors and healthy organizational thoeries', *Organizational Studies*, 25(7): 1205–31.

Spector, B. (2007) *Implementing Organizational Change: Theory and Practice*. Upper Saddle River, NJ: Pearson.

Spencer, S. (1999) *Who Moved My Cheese?* Reading, MA: Random House.

Spreitzer, G. and Porath, C. (2012) 'Creating sustainable performance', *Harvard Business Review*, 90(1): 92–9.

Spreitzer, G.M. and Quinn, R.E. (1996) 'Empowering middle managers to be transformational leaders', *Journal of Applied Behavioral Science*, 32(3): 237–61.

Sprinkel, O. (2012) 'Introduction to Sustainability forever? Embedding sustainability in your brand and culture', *Directions*, February, p. 1. SalterBaxter/Ashridge Business School.

Stace, D. (1996) 'Dominant ideologies, strategic change and sustained performance', *Human Relations*, 49: 553–70.

Stacey, R.D. (2001) *Complex Responsive Processes in Organizations*. London: Routledge.

Stacey, R.D. (2007) *Strategic Management and Organisational Dynamics: The Challenge of Complexity to Ways of Thinking About Organisations*. Hemel Hempstead: Prentice Hall.

Stacey, R.D. and Griffin, D. (2005) 'Leading in a complex world', in D. Griffin and R. Stacey (eds), *Complexity and the Experience of Leading Organizations*. Abingdon: Routledge, pp. 3–13.

Stanley, D.J., Meyer, J.P. and Topolnytsky, L. (2005) 'Employee cynicism and resistance to organizational change', *Journal of Business and Psychology*, 19(4): 429–59.

Staw, B.M. and Ross, J. (1987a) 'Behavior in escalation situations: Antecedents, prototypes, and solutions', *Research in Organizational Behavior*, 9: 39–78.

Staw, B.M. and Ross, J. (1987b) 'Knowing when to pull the plug', *Harvard Business Review*, 65(2), 68–74.

Steinem, G. (1984) *Outrageous Acts and Everyday Rebellions*. New York, NY: Henry Holt & Co.

Steiner, G.A. (1965) 'Introduction', in Gary A. Steiner (ed.), *The Creative Organization*. Chicago, IL: University of Chicago Press, pp. 1–30.

Stern, N. (2006) *Review on the Economics of Climate Change*. London: HM Treasury.

Stern, S. (2008) 'Messages lost in translation', *FT.com*, 15 December.

Stevens, G.W. (2013) 'Toward a process-based approach to conceptualizing change readiness', *Journal of Applied Behavioural Science*, 49(3): 333–60.

Stewart, T.A. (2010) 'Putting strategy into practice', *Strategy+Business*, 19 April.

Stickland, F. (1998) *The Dynamics of Change*. London: Routledge.

Stiglitz, J.E. (2010) *Freefall: Free Market and the Sinking of the Global Economy*. London: Allen Lane.

Stoughton, A.M. and Ludema, J. (2012) 'The driving forces of sustainability', *Journal of Organizational Change Management*, 25(4): 501–17.

Strange, J.M. and Mumford, M.D. (2002) 'The origins of vision: Charismatic versus ideological leadership', *The Leadership Quarterly*, 13: 343–77.

Strebel, P. (1996) 'Breakpoint: How to stay in the game', *Financial Times, Mastering Management*, Part 17: 13–14.

Stubbings, A. and Ceasar, N. (2012) 'Sustainability as usual' in 'Sustainability forever? Embedding sustainability in your brand and culture', *Directions*, February, 1–4. SalterBaxter/Ashridge Business School.

Sudarsanam, P.S. (1995) *The Essence of Mergers and Acquisitions*. Hemel Hempstead: Prentice Hall.

Sudarsanam, P.S. (2003) *Creating Value from Mergers and Acquisitions [Electronic Resource]: The Challenges: An Integrated and International Perspective*. Harlow: Pearson Education.

Sutherland, R. (2010) 'Employee engagement: Are more firms listening to their staff, or are they just paying lip service?', *The Observer*, 22 August.

Sutton, R.I. and Kahn, R.l. (eds) (1986) *Prediction, Understanding and Control as Antidotes to Organizational Stress*. Englewood Cliffs, NJ: Prentice Hall.

Svara, J.H. (2006) 'The search for meaning in political-administrative relations in local government', *International Journal of Public Administration*, 29(12): 1065–90.

Taffinder, P. (1998) *Big Change: A Route-Map for Corporate Transformation*. Chichester: John Wiley & Sons.

Tannenbaum, M.A. (2003) 'Organizational values and leadership', *The Public Manager*, 32(2): 19–20.

Tenkasi, R.V. and Chesmore, M.C. (2003) 'Social networks and planned organizational change: The impact of strong network ties on effective change implementation and use', *Journal of Applied Behavioural Science*, 39: 567–82.

Thaler, R.H. and Sunstein, C.R. (2009) *Nudge: Improving Decisions About Health, Wealth, and Happiness*. Harmondsworth: Penguin.

Thames, B. and Webster, D.W. (2009) *Chasing Change: Building Organizational Capacity in a Turbulent Environment*. Hoboken, NJ: Wiley.

Thiele, L.P. (2013) *Sustainability*, Cambridge, UK/Malden, MA: Polity Press.

Thomas, K.W. (1992) 'Conflict and negotiation processes in organizations', in M.D. Dunnette and L.M. Hough (eds), *Handbook of Industrial and Organizational Psychology*. Palo Alto, CA: Consulting Psychologists Press, pp. 651–717.

Thomas, K.W. and Kilmann, R.H. (1974) *Thomas–Kilmann Conflict Mode Instrument*. Tuxedo, NY: Xicom, Inc.

Thompson, D. (2012) *Oracles: How Prediction Markets Turn Employees into Visionaries*. Boston, MA: Harvard Business School Press.

Thorne, M. (2000) 'Interpreting corporate transformation through failure', *Management Decision*, 38(5): 305–14.

Timmins, N. (2007) 'When all else fails, reorganize. But do the sums first', *Financial Times*, 18 April, p. 15.

Todnem, G. and Warner, M.P. (1994) 'Demonstrating the benefits of staff development: An interview with Thomas R. Guskey', *Journal of Staff Development*, 15(3): 63–4.

Tompkins, C. and McGraw, M-J. (1988) 'The negotiated learning contract', in D. Boud (ed.), *Developing Student Autonomy in Learning*, 2nd edn. London: Kogan Page, pp. 172–91.

Tony, A. (2007) 'The effect of leadership on change in organizations'. Unpublished MBA dissertation, University of Strathclyde, p. 47.

Top-Consultant (2010) 'Kenexa Research Institute: UK leaders lag behind in the first global ranking of leadership effectiveness', www.consultant-news.com/printArticle. aspx?id=7280, 14 October (accessed June 2014).

Tosi, H.L., Rizzo, J.R. and Carroll, S.J. (1994) *Managing Organizational Behavior*. Malden, MA/Oxford: Blackwell.

Toterhi, T. and Recardo, R.J. (2012) 'Managing change: Nine common blunders – and how to avoid them', *Global Business and Organizational Excellence*, 31(5): 54–69.

Transformation Alliance, The (2012) 'Transforming the European organisation – starting from the right foundations', Roundtable Discussion, Nice, 8 June.

Trevino, L.K. and Brown, M.E. (2004) 'Managing to be ethical: Debunking five business ethics myths', *Academy of Management Executive*, 18(2): 69–81.

Turnbull, S. (2001) 'Corporate ideology – meanings and contradictions for middle managers', *British Journal of Management*, 12: 231–42.

Tushman, M.L. (1977) 'Special boundary roles in the innovation process', *Administrative Science Quarterly*, 22(4): 587–605.

Tushman, M.L. and O'Reilly, C.A. (2002) *Winning Through Innovation: A Practical Guide to Leading Organizational Change and Renewal*. Cambridge, MA: Harvard Business Press.

Tushman, M. and Romanelli, E. (1985) 'Organizational evolution: A metamorphosis model of convergence and reorientation', in B. Staw and I. Cummings (eds), *Research in Organization Behaviour*, Vol. 7. Greenwich, CT: JAI Press, pp. 171–222.

Tushman, M., Newman, W. and Romanelli, E. (1986) 'Convergence and upheaval: Managing the unsteady pace of organization evolution', *California Management Review*, 29(1): 29–44.

Tyler, T.R. and De Cremer, D. (2005) 'Process-based leadership: Fair procedures and reactions to organizational change', *The Leadership Quarterly*, 16(4): 529–45.

Ulrich, D. and Smallwood, N. (2013) 'Leadership sustainability: What's next for leadership improvement efforts', *Leader to Leader*, Fall: 32–8.

Van Dam, K., Oreg, S. and Schyns, B. (2008) 'Daily work contexts and resistance to organisational change: The role of leader–member exchange, development climate, and change process characteristics', *Applied Psychology*, 57(2): 313–34.

Van der Heijden, K. (1993) 'Strategic vision at work: Discussing strategic vision in management teams', in J. Hendry, G. Johnson and J. Newton (eds), *Strategic Thinking: Leadership and the Management of Change*. Chichester: John Wiley & Sons, pp. 137–150.

Van der Heijden, K. (1996) *Scenarios: The Art of Strategic Conversation*. Chichester: Wiley.

van Dijke, M. and De Cremer, D. (2008) 'How leader prototypicality affects followers' status: The role of procedural fairness', *European Journal of Work and Organizational Psychology*, 17(2): 226–50.

Van Maurik, J. (2001) *Writers on Leadership*. London: Penguin.

Vansina, L.S. (1988) 'The general manager and organisational leadership', in M. Lambrechts (ed.), *Corporate Revival: Managing Into the Nineties*. Leuven, Belgium: University Press.

Vansina, L.S. (1999) 'Leadership in strategic business unit management', *European Journal of Work and Organizational Psychology*, 8(1): 87–108.

Vardiman, P.D., Houghton, J.D. and Jinkerson, D.L. (2006) 'Environmental leadership development: Toward a contextual model of leader selection and effectiveness', *Leadership and Organization Development Journal*, 27(2): 93–105.

Vince, R. and Broussine, M. (1996) 'Paradox, defense and attachment: Accessing and working with emotions and relations underlying organizational change', *Organization Studies*, 17(1): 1–21.

Wacker, J., Heldmann, M. and Stemmler, G. (2003) 'Separating emotion and motivational direction in fear and anger: Effects on frontal asymmetry', *Emotion*, 3(2): 167.

Wagner, J.A., III and Hollenbeck, J.R. (2010) *Organizational Behavior: Securing Competitive Advantage*. New York, NY/Abingdon: Routledge.

Walker, H.J., Armenakis, A. and Bernerth, J.B. (2007) 'Factors influencing organizational change efforts: An integrative investigation of change content, context, processes and individual differences', *Journal of Organizational Change Management*, 20(6): 761–73.

Wanberg, C.R. and Banas, J.T. (2000) 'Predictors and outcomes of openness to changes in a reorganizing workplace', *Journal of Applied Psychology*, 85(1): 132.

Wanous, J.P., Reichers, A.E. and Austin, J.T. (2000) 'Cynicism about organizational change measurement, antecedents, and correlates', *Group and Organization Management*, 25(2): 132–53.

Ward, M. (1994) *Why Your Corporate Culture Change Isn't Working*. Aldershot: Gower.

Wardrop-White, D. (2001) *The Crystal Bridge: A Practical Manual for Internal Consultants*. Edinburgh: PricewaterhouseCoopers.

Weber, M. (1946) *From Max Weber: Essays in Sociology*. Translation by H. Gerth and C.W. Mills (eds). London: Routledge.

Webley, S. (1999) 'Sources of corporate values', *Long Range Planning*, 32(2): 173–8.

Weick, K. (2000) 'Emergent change as a universal in organisations', in M. Beer and N. Nohria (eds), *Breaking the Code of Change*. Boston, MA: Harvard Business Review Press, pp. 223–42.

Weick, K. and Quinn, R. (1999) 'Organizational change and development', *Annual Review of Psychology*, 50: 361–86.

Weisbord, M. (2012) 'The organization development contract', in John Vogelsang et al. (eds), *Handbook for Strategic HR: Best Practice from the OD Network*. New York: AMACOM/OD Network.

Wernerfelt, B. (1995) 'The resource-based view of the firm: Ten years after', *Strategic Management Journal*, 16(3): 171–174.

White, L. and Lee, G.J. (2009) 'Operational research and sustainable development: Tackling the social dimension', *European Journal of Operational Research*, 193(3): 683–692.

White, L.P. and Wooten, K.C. (1983) 'Ethical dilemmas in various stages of organizational development', *Academy of Management Review*, 8(4): 690–7.

Whitson, D.H. and Clark, D.K. (2002) 'Management audits: Passé, or a useful quality improvement tool?', *Public Management*, 84(4): 6.

Whittington, R., Pettigrew, A., Peck, S., Fenton, E. and Conyon, M. (1999) 'Change and complementarities in the new competitive landscape: A European panel study, 1992–1996', *Organization Science*, 10(5): 583–600.

Williams, T., Worsley, C.G. and Lawler, E.E., III (2013) 'The agility factor', *Strategy and Business*, 15 April.

Wilson, D.C. and Rosenfeld, R.H. (1990) *Managing Organizations: Text, Readings and Cases*. London: McGraw-Hill.

Woodall, J. (1996) 'Managing culture change: Can it ever be ethical?', *Personnel Review*, 25(6): 26–40.

Woodman, R.W. (1995) 'Understanding organizational change: A schematic perspective', *Academy of Management Journal*, 38(2): 537–54.

Woodman, R.W., Bingham, J.B. and Yuan, F. (2008) 'Assessing organization development and change interventions', in T.G. Cummings (ed.), *Handbook of Organization Development*. Thousand Oaks, CA: Sage, pp. 187–215.

Woodward, S. and Hendry, C. (2004) 'Leading and coping with change', *Journal of Change Management*, 4(3): 155–83.

Worthing, I. (2003) 'Business organisations: The external environment', in I. Worthing and C. Britton (eds), *The Business Environment*. Harlow: FT/Prentice Hall, pp.1–3.

Young, I.M. (2004) 'Responsibility and global labor justice', *Journal of Political Philosophy*, 12(4): 365–88.

Young, M. (2009) 'A meta model of change', *Journal of Organizational Change Management*, 22(5): 524–48.

Young, M. and Post, J.E. (1993) 'Managing to communicate, communicating to manage: How leading companies communicate with employees', *Organizational Dynamics*, 22(1): 31–43.

Yousef, D.A. (2000) 'Organizational commitment: A mediator of the relationships of leadership behavior with job satisfaction and performance in a non-western country', *Journal of Managerial Psychology*, 15(1): 6–24.

Yukl, G. (2006) *Leadership in Organizations*. London: Simon & Schuster Trade.

Yukl, G. and Tracey, J.B. (1992) 'Consequences of influence tactics used with subordinates, peers, and the boss', *Journal of Applied Psychology*, 77(4): 525.

Zaccaro, S.J. and Banks, D.J. (2001) 'Leadership, vision, and organizational effectiveness', in Stephen J. Zaccaro and Richard J. Klimoski (eds), *The Nature of Organizational Leadership: Understanding the Performance Imperatives Confronting Today's Leaders*. San Francisco, CA: Jossey-Bass, pp. 181–218.

Zaltman, G. and Duncan, R. (1977) *Strategies for Planned Change*. Chichester: John Wiley & Sons.

Zeffane, R. and Connell, J. (2003) 'Trust and HRM in the new millennium', *International Journal of Human Resource Management*, 14: 3–11.

Zimmermann, P., Wit, A. and Gill, R. (2008) 'The relative importance of leadership behaviours in virtual and face-to-face communication settings', *Leadership*, 4(3): 321–37.

Index

Entries in Figures and Tables are indicated by page numbers in bold.